Editor-in-Chief
Asa S. Knowles

Chancellor, Northeastern University

THE INTERNATIONAL ENCYCLOPEDIA OF HIGHER EDUCATION

Volume 7

N-Q

Jossey-Bass Publishers

San Francisco • Washington • London • 1978

THE INTERNATIONAL ENCYCLOPEDIA OF HIGHER EDUCATION
Volume 7
Asa S. Knowles, Editor-in-Chief

Copyright © 1977 by: Jossey-Bass, Inc., Publishers
433 California Street
San Francisco, California 94104
&
Jossey-Bass Limited
28 Banner Street
London EC1Y 8QE

Library of Congress Cataloging in Publication Data

Main entry under title:

The international encyclopedia of higher education.

    Includes index.
    1. Education, Higher—Dictionaries. I. Knowles,
Asa Smallidge, 1909–
LB15.157   378'.003   77-73647
ISBN 0-87589-323-6 (set)
ISBN 0-87589-330-9 (v. 7)

Manufactured in the United States of America
Composition by Chapman's Phototypesetting
Printing by Hamilton Printing Company
Binding by Payne Edition Bindery

COVER DESIGN BY WILLI BAUM
FIRST EDITION
First printing: December 1977
Second printing: November 1978

Code 7729

THE
INTERNATIONAL
ENCYCLOPEDIA
OF HIGHER
EDUCATION

NAMIBIA, TERRITORY OF

Population: whites 99,000; blacks 852,000 (1974). School enrollment: whites—all levels: 23,185 (1973); blacks—primary: 129,927 (1975); postprimary: 4584 (1975); higher education—in South Africa: 35. Language of instruction: Afrikaans, English, and mother tongues. [Source: Population figures: South Africa 1975 Official Yearbook; *black enrollments:* Bantu Education Journal.]

Namibia, also known as South-West Africa, is the only colonial territory in Africa south of the Sahara. As a colony, its educational system reflects the policy of the occupying power, the Republic of South Africa. Namibian education is organized in accordance with the apartheid policy of South Africa. (Apartheid theory divides the nonwhite Namibian population into twelve mutually incompatible "nations.") Thus, education for whites and nonwhites is separately administered, and students are physically separated by race and, in the case of nonwhites, further separated by "nations." Depending on "nationality," there are different curricula, different teacher training and salary scales, different teacher/pupil ratios and amounts spent per pupil on education, different attendance rates, different laws, and different administering authorities.

Although the nonwhite population groups are separated by "nation," enough similarities exist so that the system can be divided into two groups for descriptive purposes: whites and nonwhites.

Education for Whites

Education for whites is divided into twelve grades, called substandards A and B followed by standards I-X. A junior certificate is obtained on satisfactory completion of standard VIII (grade 10), and the matriculation (secondary school certificate) is obtained after standard X (grade 12). In 1973 there were eighty-five white schools of all types, with 1232 teachers and 23,185 pupils; in 1960 there were sixty-three schools, with 666 teachers and 16,257 pupils (*South-West Africa Survey,* 1975, p. 62). The 1973 teacher/pupil ratio was 1:18.8.

Preuniversity education for white children is administered by territorial officials in accordance with the territory's Education Ordinance 27 of 1962 as amended. This ordinance makes such education free, and it is compulsory to age sixteen or until attainment of the junior certificate.

Despite the formidable difficulties posed by the great distances and scattered population of rural Namibia, virtually all educable white children are enrolled in either local day or boarding schools. In the latter case the territorial administration provides financial assistance to families not able to afford hostel fees or who have several children in hostels at the same time.

Afrikaans and English are official languages in the territory, as they are in South Africa. Chapter VI of the ordinance requires pupils to be educated in the language in which they are most proficient; the other official language must be taught as a subject in every grade. Instruction in German may be authorized where that language is widely used. In fact, Afrikaans and German predominate in the territory; English is less used.

Since Namibia has no university, students must pursue postsecondary education outside the territory. Many German-speaking students go to Germany. Loans and scholarships are available to all qualified white students to attend universities, teacher training colleges, or technical institutions.

Education for Blacks

Preuniversity education for blacks runs one year longer than white education. An extra grade, standard VIIA, is inserted after standard VII (grade 9). Consequently, the junior certificate requires three years' study beyond the upper primary level. The matriculation requires two additional years. The extra year was added to assist blacks in overcoming deficiencies in early education. The government plans to discontinue the extra year and to restructure black education so that upper primary school will consist of two years instead of the present four. There will be three years between the junior certificate and matriculation instead of two years (*South-West Africa Survey*, 1975, p. 63, n. 2).

Education for most blacks is governed by the Bantu Education Act, Act 47 of 1953 as amended, and is not compulsory. It is controlled by the South African Department of Bantu Administration and Development, except in cases where that department has relinquished authority to certain homeland governments. The education of three of the "national" groups—coloureds, Namas, and Rehoboth Basters—is governed by three separate but virtually identical laws and administered by the South African Department of Coloured, Rehoboth and Nama Relations.

The mother tongue is encouraged as the medium of instruction. In the lower grades it is required, and the upper level for such instruction is constantly being raised (*South-West Africa Survey*, 1975, p. 63). The two official languages are taught as subjects of instruction in the early years, after which one language—usually Afrikaans—becomes the language of instruction. A survey of Namibian refugees in Zambia who had attended school in the territory showed that few are able to function adequately in English without extensive remedial work (Lewis-Jones, 1974, p. 7).

The curriculum for black students, which is substantially identical with that for blacks in the Republic of South Africa (*South-West Africa Survey*, 1975, p. 63), emphasizes crafts and manual training rather than academic subjects. Instruction in the mother tongue is at the expense of competence in the two official languages, in which secondary and advanced education and examinations are given.

Education is free for all nonwhite students in Namibia. Books, stationery, and board and lodging at hostels are also provided without charge (*South-West Africa Survey*, 1975, p. 64). In 1973–74 the government spent R75.75 (1 rand = US $1.45) on the education of each African student in Namibia. Of this amount approximately R50 apparently represented the cost of books, stationery, and hostel while the remainder covered teachers' salaries, school buildings and equipment, and administration (*South African House of Assembly Debates,* September 20, 1974, column 506, Q and A). This expenditure for Africans should be compared with the amounts spent per white child per year in South Africa in 1973–74, which ranged from R387 in the Transvaal to R557 in Natal (*South African House of Assembly Debates,* September 6,

1974, columns 359–360, Q and A). It is assumed that the amount spent on white children in the territory falls somewhere in or near this range (Horrell, 1968, p. 73)—that is, four to seven times the amount spent on African pupils.

Government statistics indicate that the number of nonwhite children and young adults (many Africans start school long after the normal age of six or seven) enrolled in school tripled between 1960 and 1973, from 43,624 to 138,890 (*South-West Africa Survey,* 1975, p. 62). During that period the nonwhite population increased by 60–100 percent, depending on the population figures accepted. Assuming a black population of some 900,000, approximately 15.5 percent of the total black population is enrolled, as compared with 25.8 percent of all whites. The significance of the increased enrollment, however, is diminished by further data. In particular, the number of teachers increased during the same period by a factor of only 2.64, from 1310 to 3453. Thus, either the enrollment figures are inflated or the already high pupil/teacher ratio rose from 33.2:1 to 39.9:1. The number of schools increased during the same period from 313 to only 592 (*South-West Africa Survey,* 1975, p. 62).

Most black students do not remain in school long enough to become functionally literate. *The South-West Africa Survey* (1975) shows that only 2664 (1.92 percent) of the 138,890 blacks enrolled are in the upper five grades, teacher training and vocational training included. The deputy minister of Bantu Administration and Education stated in parliament that, as of March 1974, 31.3 percent of all enrolled African pupils in Namibia were in the first grade and 18.5 percent in the second grade; the percentage of children in each grade dropped steadily thereafter, with only 2.1 percent in the upper five grades (forms 1–5), of whom only .06 percent were in the final year (*South African House of Assembly Debates,* March 14, 1975, columns 497–498, Q and A).

Namibia has seven centralized, compre-

hensive boarding schools offering secondary education, teacher training, and vocational training for blacks (*South-West Africa Survey,* 1975, p. 64). There is also an agricultural school in Owambo with eighteen students (*South African House of Assembly Debates,* August 23, 1974, columns 172–173, Q and A), as well as St. Mary's mission school at Odibo, Owambo, which in 1974 the authorities threatened to close. Students may enter teacher training at these institutes at the end of standard VI (grade 8) or after completing the junior certificate or the matriculation. Students who seek to learn a trade, such as tailoring, are supposed to enter after standard VI, but reports indicate that many have no more than a lower primary education.

Black students who pass the matriculation are eligible for scholarships or loans for university studies, teacher training, or technical training in one of South Africa's university colleges or other institutions for nonwhites.

ELIZABETH S. LANDIS

Bibliography

Horrell, M. *South-West Africa.* Johannesburg: South African Institute of Race Relations, 1968.

Lewis-Jones, H. *Report on the Survey of the Educational Situation and Needs of Namibians in Independent Countries.* Geneva: International University Exchange Fund, 1974.

Official Records of the General Assembly, Thirtieth Session. Supplement 24, A/10024. Vol. 1. New York: United Nations, 1975.

Report of the United Nations Council for Namibia. Supplement 24, A/9624. Vol. 1. New York: United Nations, 1974.

Report of the United Nations Council for Namibia. A/10024. Vol. 1. New York: United Nations General Assembly, 1975.

South Africa 1975 Official Yearbook. Johannesburg: South African Department of Information, 1975.

South-West Africa Survey, 1974. Pretoria: South African Department of Foreign Affairs, 1975.

UNESCO: *Apartheid: Its Effects on Education, Information and Culture.* Notes and Documents 40/75. New York: United Nations, 1975.

See also: Africa, Southern: Regional Analysis.

NATIONAL ACADEMY OF EDUCATION, United States

Founded in 1965 to promote scholarly research and discussion in the field of education, the National Academy of Education represents a wide variety of disciplines, institutions, and educational viewpoints. The constitution of the academy provides for a regular membership of fifty persons, whose scholarly and scientific writing have been judged as outstanding. The members are arranged in four sections of ten members each: (1) history and philosophy of education; (2) politics, economics, sociology, and anthropology of education; (3) psychology of education; and (4) study of educational practice. In addition, a maximum of ten outstanding persons may be elected as members-at-large. A small number of members *emeriti* and foreign associates participate in the academy's activities in addition to distinguished educators who are nonmembers.

The academy was initially supported by the Carnegie Corporation of New York. In addition, its study and advisory committees have been aided by grants from the Carnegie Corporation, the Ford Foundation, and the United States Office of Education, while its programs for the encouragement of younger scholars have been assisted by the Spencer Foundation.

The academy holds semiannual meetings for the presentation of reports on research in progress and the discussion of educational policy issues; arranges postdoctoral programs for young scholars to work for specified periods of time with academy members; sponsors fellowship programs to assist young scholars in their research work on educational theory and practice; and arranges for study and advisory committees dealing with the critical issues of educational theory and policy. In addition, the academy is in the process of organizing a new series of task forces and commissioning critical reviews of research in order to inform the public better in matters relating to educational thought and scholarship.

The work of the many committees of the academy has resulted in three principal publications: *Policy Making for American Public Schools* (Syracuse: National Academy of Education, 1969); *Research for Tomorrow's Schools,* edited by Lee J. Cronbach and Patrick Suppes (New York: Macmillan, 1969); and *Toward a Literate Society,* edited by John B. Carroll and Jeanne Chall (New York: McGraw-Hill).

Stanford University
Ventura Hall
Stanford, California 94305 USA

NATIONAL ACADEMY OF LETTERS (Sahitya akademi), India

The *Sahitya akademi* (National Academy of Letters) was established to work for the development of Indian letters, to set high literary standards, to foster and coordinate literary activities in all the Indian languages, and to promote the cultural unity of the country. Although set up by the government, the academy, registered as a society under Indian law, functions as an autonomous organization.

The supreme authority of the academy is vested in the general council, which consists of eighty-two members: the president; the financial adviser; five members nominated by the government of India; twenty-one representatives of the states of India; twenty representatives of the twenty languages recognized by the *Sahitya akademi;* twenty representatives of the universities of India; eight persons elected by the general council for their eminence in the field of letters; and two representatives each from the two sister academies, the *Sangeet natak* and the *Lalit kala* (the National Academy of Music, Dance, and Drama and the National Academy of Art), and the Indian Council for Cultural Relations. The tenure of the general council is five years.

The general policy of the *Sahitya akademi* and the basic principles of its programs are laid down by the general council and are implemented by the secretary under the direct supervision of the executive board.

An advisory board composed of eminent writers and scholars helps to formulate specific programs in each language.

The academy is fully financed by the government of India. It is also free to receive donations for the furtherance of its aims and objects. At its head office in New Delhi, the academy maintains a library containing books in all the Indian languages, besides a few foreign languages. Regional offices are located at Bombay, Calcutta, and Madras.

Every year since its inception, the *Sahitya akademi* has awarded prizes, along with a copper insignia, to the outstanding books of literary merit published in any of the Indian languages recognized by the academy. The academy also elects distinguished men of letters, both Indian and foreign, as its fellows and honorary fellows.

The *Sahitya akademi*'s program is designed primarily to meet the challenge posed by a multilingual society; that is, the anomaly that writers and readers in one language know very little of what is being written in a neighboring language of the same country. The academy works to devise means whereby Indian writers may come to know each other and whereby readers may appreciate the immense variety and complexity of their country's literary heritage. The academy's program seeks to meet this need in two ways: by publishing informative material regarding literary activities in all the Indian languages; and by translating literary classics, both old and modern, from one Indian language into the others. There is, besides, a program for translating foreign classics into all the major Indian languages, so that the great literary masterpieces of the world may be made available to all Indian readers. The academy exchanges literary information and material with various foreign literary and cultural societies, and it cooperates with UNESCO on appropriate projects.

Publications of the academy include a comprehensive *Bibliography of Indian Literature,* covering books published in all the Indian languages from 1900 through 1953;

a *Who's Who of Indian Writers,* containing factual informative material about the writers in all the Indian languages; *Contemporary Indian Literature,* projecting the relative importance of the sixteen major languages of India. It also plans to bring out anthologies and selections, dictionaries, and critical editions of the works of the fifth-century Hindu dramatist and poet Kalidasa. It publishes *Indian Literature,* a quarterly journal in English, to acquaint readers in India and abroad with current literary activities in all the Indian languages. The academy has so far brought out more than 750 publications in English and Indian languages.

Rabindra Bhavan
New Delhi, India

R. S. KELKAR

NATIONAL ACADEMY OF SCIENCE, LETTERS, AND ARTS
(Accademia nazionale di scienze lettere e arti), Italy

From the year of its founding in 1683 until 1752, the *Accademia nazionale di scienze lettere e arti* (National Academy of Science, Letters, and Arts) was called *Accademia dei dissonanti* (Academy of the Disagreeing); from 1752 to 1860 it was called *Accademia ducale dei dissonanti* (Ducal Academy of the Disagreeing); and from 1860 to 1959, *Reale accademia di scienze lettere e arti* (Royal Academy of Science, Letters, and Arts). The goal of the academy is to contribute to the progress of scientific research through the organization of study groups and publications of its members.

Members of the academy are divided into three categories: forty active members, sixteen corresponding members, and thirty honorary members. The academy is financed by the government, which makes a modest annual fixed contribution and a more substantial contribution for special projects presented to the ministry. Grants are also received from banks and local public agencies.

The history of the academy can be found

in the pamphlet *Statuto;* the academic role of the academy until 1958 is described in the pamphlet entitled *Breve storia dell' accademia.*

Palazzo Coccapani
Corso Vittorio Emanuele II, N. 59
41100 Modena, Italy

GINO GOLDONI

NATIONAL AIR AND SPACE MUSEUM
See Smithsonian Institution.

NATIONAL ASSOCIATION FOR FOREIGN STUDENT AFFAIRS, United States

Founded in 1948 as the National Association for Foreign Student Advisers, the National Association for Foreign Student Affairs (NAFSA) is a professional association for persons engaged in the field of international educational exchange of students and scholars. Its basic purpose is to develop the knowledge and competence of personnel concerned with international education and the welfare of foreign students. It sets standards and acts as a spokesman for international educational exchange.

Among NAFSA's 2500 members are approximately 1000 representatives of academic institutions, as well as representatives of the business community, local citizens' groups active in foreign student affairs, and courtesy associates from the embassies and legations in Washington, D.C.

The five professional interest groups of NAFSA represent special areas of concern in international education. The admissions section deals with the interests of persons involved in admission of foreign students to United States institutions. The Association of Teachers of English as a Second Language focuses on the concerns of teachers of English to foreign students in the United States. Through the Council of Advisers to Foreign Students and Scholars, information on specific concerns and needs

of foreign student advisers at United States colleges and universities is exchanged. NAFSA's community section, composed of community groups across the country, conducts programs for foreign students. As the newest interest group in the membership, the section on United States students abroad provides for exchange of information among counselors of United States students who wish to work, study, or travel abroad. Through the student caucus, United States and foreign students interested in international education participate in the association. In an effort to ensure the participation of the membership and to meet local needs, NAFSA is divided into twelve geographical regions. Each region is administered by a team composed of representatives of each of the special-interest groups.

To meet the professional development needs of its membership, NAFSA conducts regional and national meetings and workshops. The association has provided over 575 professional grants for individual educational projects, workshops, and seminars in the United States and abroad.

Through the NAFSA Field Service Program, funded by a grant from the Bureau of Educational and Cultural Affairs of the Department of State, professional development assistance is available to all institutions enrolling foreign students, regardless of membership in NAFSA. Through this program, newcomers to the field are funded to visit other institutions or programs for in-service training grants. In addition, experienced and knowledgeable professionals are provided to institutions requesting free consultations in specific areas such as foreign student admissions, English as a second language, community services, and United States–foreign student relations. Over 1400 institutions interested in establishing new programs or changing existing programs have utilized this free consultation service.

Through other contracts and grants with the Agency for International Development and the Bureau of Educational and Cultural Affairs, NAFSA offers grants to individuals and organizations. The grants have supported programs to enhance the experience of foreign students studying at United States colleges and universities; the grants also have supported pilot projects and community activities that can be replicated in other communities or institutions.

The association issues numerous professional papers, manuals, guidelines, reports, and studies in foreign student education and international educational exchange. Publications include *NAFSA Newsletter,* ten issues annually, and *NAFSA Directory,* biennial listing of NAFSA members and all institutions of higher education reporting enrollment of foreign students.

1860 19th Street NW
Washington, D.C. 20009 USA

NATIONAL ASSOCIATION FOR PUBLIC CONTINUING AND ADULT EDUCATION, United States

The National Association for Public Continuing and Adult Education (NAPCAE) is a professional organization representing adult educators and providing services for adult education programs in public schools, community colleges, universities, government agencies, and business and industry. The association's purpose is to provide leadership for the development and implementation of public continuing and adult education. Membership is open to anyone who supports this purpose. The association is financed by membership dues, publication sales, and special projects.

Working closely with state and federal officials, NAPCAE seeks active support for legislation that will extend and enrich adult education offerings in the public sector in the country. The association offers a consultant network service that functions at the state and local levels. This service provides program evaluations, develops short- and long-range program plans, and conducts training seminars and an annual conference.

The NAPCAE publications include *Pulse of Public Continuing and Adult Education,* eight times a year; *Techniques for Teachers of Adults,* eight times a year; *Swap Shop,* six times a year; and *Public Continuing and Adult Education Almanac and Membership Directory,* annually.

1201 16th Street NW
Washington, D.C. 20036 USA

NATIONAL ASSOCIATION FOR WOMEN DEANS, ADMINISTRATORS, AND COUNSELORS, United States

The National Association for Women Deans, Administrators, and Counselors (NAWDAC), an affiliate of the Federation of Organizations for Professional Women, is an independent organization for women educators. Founded in 1916 as the National Association of Deans of Women, NAWDAC is the third-oldest professional association originally dedicated to serving student personnel workers and the only national professional association for women administrators and counselors from all levels of education. The organization provides information, assistance, and support for women educators who serve students through guidance, counseling, advising, administration, research, or teaching in an educational institution or agency.

The NAWDAC membership of over 2300 includes women from the fifty United States and several foreign countries. NAWDAC is one of the very few professional organizations to grant full membership privileges to graduate student members, including the right to vote, to hold office, and to be represented on the executive board.

The NAWDAC headquarters, established in Washington, D.C., in 1931, informs members about national legislation affecting women and education and activities of other educational women's groups.

The annual conference each spring focuses on current issues and concerns of members. A placement service at the conference is provided for candidates and employers. NAWDAC offers the Ruth Strang Award annually for an oustanding manuscript by a woman. NAWDAC also has been an active supporter of passage and ratification of the United States Equal Rights Amendment. It joined with a group of associations in writing the "Joint Statement on Women in Higher Education," concerning the status of women students, faculty, and staff in institutions of higher education in the United States.

Funding for the association is derived from membership dues, publication sales, conference registration fees, placement service fees, foundations, grants, and gifts from members and friends.

NAWDAC publishes *Journal of NAWDAC; Bulletin,* quarterly newsletter; *Pre-Conference Exchange;* and *Post-Conference Exchange.*

1028 Connecticut Avenue NW
Washington, D.C. 20036 USA

NATIONAL ASSOCIATION OF COLLEGE ADMISSIONS COUNSELORS, United States

The National Association of College Admissions Counselors (NACAC) is a non-profit educational association that provides admissions officers and secondary school counselors with a forum for sharing information, talking over common problems, and maintaining high professional standards. The association was founded in 1937 by eighteen colleges in the central United States as the Association of College Representatives. It was renamed the Association of College Admissions Counselors in 1939 and received its present name in 1968. NACAC comprises 1850 member institutions, including 975 colleges and universities and 875 secondary schools, 18 associations, and 13 school districts in the United States. Members are grouped in eleven state and seven regional associations representing all states and the District of Columbia.

The executive director conducts the association's business and administers the national office. NACAC is governed by an assembly and an executive board composed of elected representatives from member schools, colleges, and universities. The organization is financed by membership dues.

NACAC sponsors several national college fairs in major population centers each year for students and their parents, as well as veterans and others interested in continuing their education. Representatives of colleges, professional and graduate schools, and trade and vocational schools as well as representatives of local, state, and national testing, scholarship, and financial aid agencies are available for consultation.

Another student service offered by NACAC is Ask Us, a clearinghouse for high school juniors and seniors, college transfer students, veterans, and two-year-college graduates. The college-search service presents the credentials of registered students to over 150 member colleges and universities. The employment assistance service initiates contact between employers and candidates seeking positions in admissions, financial aid, guidance, and counseling. Annual conferences are held on admissions and related problems.

Publications include *NACAC Journal,* quarterly; *NACAC Newsletter; NACAC Membership Directory,* biennial; a map of four-year colleges and universities in the United States; and special reports.

9933 Lawler Avenue
Skokie, Illinois 60076 USA

NATIONAL ASSOCIATION OF COLLEGE AND UNIVERSITY ATTORNEYS, United States

Membership in the National Association of College and University Attorneys (NACUA) is open to any nonprofit, accredited institution of postsecondary education. Member institutions include community colleges, traditional liberal arts colleges, urban and research universities, and professional schools. Facilitating the exchange of legal information among the institutions, the association works through the attorney representatives of the member institutions. Each member institution may designate one primary representative and as many additional representatives as desired. These representatives, who must be licensed attorneys, may be full-time members of the institution's legal staff; retained attorneys maintaining private law practice; legal representatives of a state, city, or county; or law school faculty. Since more than half of the member institutions rely on counsel who are not part of the permanent staff, the services of the association are designed to fulfill the large needs of the institutions for assistance in understanding and coping with developments in the law. The association serves 700 higher education institutions and 1500 attorneys. The dues for member institutions are based on enrollment.

NACUA convenes an annual three-day conference for representatives of member institutions and special guests. Conference topics, chosen for their current impact and applicability to the problems and needs of postsecondary education, are designed to present both in-depth reviews on matters of particular interest and overviews of current and continuing areas of interest to the practitioner in the field of college and university law.

Under the supervision of an executive director, a national office in Washington, D.C., collects, reviews, and disseminates information relating to all aspects of law concerning postsecondary education, including governmental developments having significant legal implications. The office also manages the Exchange of Legal Information Program, a service through which the attorneys who represent NACUA member institutions can learn of the work of other attorneys or matters relevant to their own. The collection of information is organized under about 250 topic headings.

NACUA has established sections covering areas of substantive law. In addition, the executive director maintains close liaison with national associations representing the interests of the education community.

Between 1966 and 1972 NACUA published the *College Counsel,* featuring papers presented at annual conferences. In 1973 this publication was replaced by a quarterly law review, the *Journal of College and University Law,* which summarizes recent cases and other developments affecting colleges and universities. The *College Law Manual,* originally published in 1968, was succeeded by the bimonthly *College Law Digest.* NACUA also publishes a president's newsletter, an annual membership directory, and occasional special reports.

One Dupont Circle
Washington, D.C. 20036 USA

NATIONAL ASSOCIATION OF COLLEGE AND UNIVERSITY BUSINESS OFFICERS, United States

Founded in 1950, the National Association of College and University Business Officers (NACUBO) is a professional organization serving higher education in the field of business and financial management.

Regular membership includes nonprofit public and private institutions of higher education that grant associate or higher degrees. Nonprofit organizations such as libraries, foundations, state commissions, or other associations interested in higher education or the field of business management in education may become associate members. Provisional members are nonprofit institutions not yet accredited but moving actively toward accreditation.

The association encourages excellence and creative leadership in business and financial management in higher education. It makes the judgment and experience of the business office professional available to higher education at the national level and opens channels of communication on problems in business management that are important to higher education. It also gives the business officer continuing opportunity for professional contact, expression, and growth and cultivates professional attitudes, ideals, and standards.

Approximately 1450 colleges and universities, including more than 5500 individual representatives, are members of NACUBO. Associate members number 30.

Four independently organized regional groups—the Central, Eastern, Southern, and Western Associations of College and University Business Officers—maintain their individual identities within the national organization. Many NACUBO activities are sponsored jointly by the national office and the regional associations.

Affairs at the national level are conducted by a board of directors whose members include three representatives from each regional association: immediate past president, president, and vice-president. The national officers, who serve as directors-at-large, are elected from and by the board. A national office was established in Washington, D.C., in 1967.

National committees conduct continuing studies in such areas as taxation, investments, and insurance; develop plans and recommendations in areas such as accounting principles, professional development, and programs for small colleges; and serve the association itself in managing workshops or acting as liaisons with professional groups and activities. Some two hundred volunteers serve the professional each year in such capacities. The Committee on Governmental Relations is voluntarily supported by a number of member institutions having substantial programs of federally sponsored research and instruction. The committee's office, located within the association's national headquarters, provides a point of contact and communication on technical administrative questions of concern to the colleges, universities, and federal agencies.

Workshops, often cosponsored by regional associations, cover such fields as budgeting, student loans, and investments. Accounting workshops are held at three levels: Introduction to Fund Accounting, Intermediate Fund Accounting, and Senior Accounting Officers. The association cooperates in sponsorship of the American Council on Education Institute for Chief Business and Academic Officers.

The Higher Education Administration Referral Service (HEARS), a cooperative program supported by fourteen associations with interests in the management field, was established in 1972 under the auspices of NACUBO. The HEARS program is administered independently from the NACUBO Washington office.

The association's Information Exchange Service is designed to assist member institutions, promptly and effectively, when questions or problems arise in the field of college and university management. The Circulating Library, a system for loaning resource materials to member institutions, is a part of the service.

The association publishes *Business Officer,* monthly report; *Special Reports* and *Memorandums,* published irregularly; *Professional Calendar,* quarterly; and two series, Professional File and Studies in Management. Manuals and guidelines are available in fields such as accounting, planning and budgeting, student records, copyrights, patents, physical plant, and insurance.

College and University Business Administration was published by the Administrative Service of the association. The service provides continuing and up-to-date revisions and supplements of the reference work.

The association, in cooperation with eight other higher education associations, publishes *Federal Regulations and the Employment Practices of College and Universities,* up-to-date information on many areas of federal law which affect institutional employment practices.

One Dupont Circle
Washington, D.C. 20036 USA

NATIONAL ASSOCIATION OF LOCAL GOVERNMENT JUNIOR COLLEGES
(Zenkoku koritsu tanki daigaku kyokai), Japan

Seventeen junior colleges founded the *Zenkoku koritsu tanki daigaku kyokai* (National Association of Local Government Junior Colleges) in August 1950. In 1975 the association numbered forty-eight junior colleges, including twenty-one women's junior colleges. The association is governed by ten directors, two inspectors, and one secretary general.

Kokuritsu kyoiku kaikan
3-2-3 Kasumigaseki, Chiyoda-ku
Tokyo 100, Japan

FUJIO ANDO

NATIONAL ASSOCIATION OF STATE UNIVERSITIES AND LAND-GRANT COLLEGES, United States

The National Association of State Universities and Land-Grant Colleges (NASULGC) was formed by a merger in 1963 of three educational associations in the United States: Association of American Agricultural Colleges and Experiment Stations, founded in 1887 as the first higher education association in the United States; National Association of State Universities, founded in 1895; and State Universities Association.

NASULGC has a membership of 130, including 71 land-grant institutions, 32 state universities, 26 major campuses of multicampus universities, and an urban university. Owing their origins to federal legislative acts designed to develop higher education in the United States, these institutions were the first to try to provide universal educational opportunities. They grant 38 percent of all degrees awarded in the United States, including 64 percent of all doctoral degrees.

The association seeks to focus public attention on the contributions that state universities and land-grant colleges have made to higher education in the United States. It serves as a communication link among member institutions and other organizations, institutions, and agencies. Work of the association is financed through dues paid by member institutions.

The association's business is conducted by a professional staff under the direction of an executive director in Washington, D.C. The Office of Governmental Relations serves as the coordinating and information arm of the association regarding all federal activities of interest to higher education.

The Office of Research and Information, a fact-gathering and dissemination agency, carries on programs related to the needs, contributions, and general philosophy of state and land-grant universities. The office seeks to inform the public of accomplishments and innovative programs in the member institutions. About twenty times a year the office publishes *For Your Information*, a report on significant developments in public higher education.

Officials in member institutions who are concerned with international activities work closely with the International Programs Office to improve the relationship between universities and developing countries in international education and training. Liaison is maintained between the universities and government agencies, other educational associations, and private organizations. The office publishes *International Letter*, a monthly report on significant legislation in the international field and on international program activities of member institutions.

The Office for the Advancement of Public Negro Colleges, based in Atlanta, Georgia, was established in 1968 to seek ways to increase private voluntary support for thirty-four public colleges and universities. The services are available to public institutions in NASULGC and the American Association of State Colleges and Universities. *Advancement Newsletter*, published monthly by the office, provides information on the accomplishments of public Negro colleges, especially in the field of development.

The Office of the Executive Director publishes *Circular Letter* about thirty times a year for member institutions. Special reports and publications are also issued by the NASULGC offices or as a combined activity with other associations of higher education.

One Dupont Circle
Washington, D.C. 20036 USA

NATIONAL ASSOCIATION OF SUMMER SESSIONS, United States

The National Association of Summer Sessions (NASS)—organized in April 1964 in Washington, D.C., as the National Association of College and University Summer Sessions—seeks to develop quality summer session standards and programs. The association offers opportunities for summer session deans and directors to share common experiences and problems.

Institutional voting membership is open to colleges and universities in the United States that have summer programs and maintain accreditation by one of the regional accrediting associations. Colleges and universities located outside the United States may become institutional members by a majority vote of the membership at the association's annual meeting. Individual nonvoting membership is open to individuals who are not affiliated with a member institution but who have a professional interest in the purpose of the association. NASS has 413 members, 401 institutions and 12 individuals.

An executive council conducts the business of the organization between annual meetings. NASS is divided into eight regional associations, each headed by a vice-president. Committees focus on problems of large summer programs and smaller sessions. The annual national meeting, attended by administrators of summer programs and liaison representatives of national and regional educational associations, provides an opportunity to exchange information on government- and foundation-supported activities affecting the programs, personnel, and potential of summer sessions.

NASS serves as a clearinghouse for information and research on college or university summer session operations. Research activities are not limited to summer sessions but may be based on studies in other areas—for instance, higher education, continuing higher education, or adult education—when the findings are applicable to summer sessions.

NASS publishes a newsletter and proceedings of the annual meeting.
Secretary
University of Connecticut U-56
Storrs, Connecticut 06268 USA

NATIONAL ASSOCIATION OF TEACHERS IN FURTHER AND HIGHER EDUCATION, United Kingdom

The National Association of Teachers in Further and Higher Education (NATFHE) was founded in January 1976 through the amalgamation of the Association of Teachers in Colleges and Departments of Education (ATCDE), formed in 1943, and the Association of Teachers in Technical Institutions (ATTI), formed in 1904. NATFHE's organization was a logical development of the reorganization of the British teacher education system, its integration into the public sector of further and higher education, and the consequent establishment of common negotiating machinery for teachers throughout the sector.

The principal purposes of NATFHE are to protect and promote the professional interests of members, individually and collectively; to regulate conditions of their employment and the relations between them and their employers; to advance further and higher education generally and professional and vocational training in particular; to promote research into educational development and the exchange of ideas concerning education; to place the views of members before various educational authorities and other bodies and before the general public; to render legal advice and assistance in professional matters to members; and to promote and maintain standards of professional conduct.

NATFHE's 65,000 members work in polytechnics, colleges of education, institutes of higher education, colleges of technology, colleges of further education, colleges of art, colleges of agriculture, and in adult education. NATFHE is financed by membership subscriptions; student membership is free.

The association is involved in all levels of policymaking and negotiation. Nationally NATFHE is recognized by the various local associations and the government as the voice of further and higher education teachers (except universities) in negotiations on salaries, superannuation, conditions of service, and educational matters. Regular negotiations take place with local authorities, college governing bodies, and college principals on all the concerns of the association. Members are entitled to insurance at preferential rates, discount trading facilities, and assistance with home buying.

As an influential voice in educational policymaking, NATFHE is the major pressure group for promoting further and higher education interests from college level up to the Department of Education and Science. NATFHE has direct access to the Secretary of State for Education and Science and is regularly consulted by the Department of Education and Science on major policy matters. Members of Parliament holding NATFHE membership form a sizable group in the House of Commons.

Represented on many official bodies, such as the Advisory Committee for the Supply and Training of Teachers and the National Advisory Council for Industry and Commerce, NATFHE members sit on over five hundred national educational bodies, ranging from examining and validating bodies to professional and advisory institutions.

Having firm links with other teacher unions both nationally and internationally and with the trade union movement generally, NATFHE is affiliated to the Council for Educational Advance and the National Federation of Professional Workers and is a member of the World Confederation of Organizations of the Teaching Profession. Reciprocal and joint membership arrangements exist between NATFHE and a number of other teacher unions.

NATFHE publications include the *NATFHE Journal* and *Education for Teaching,* newsletters covering further and higher education, and major statements of policy.

Hamilton House, Marbledon Place
London WC1H 9BH, England

PAULA LANNING

NATIONAL ASSOCIATION OF UNIVERSITIES AND INSTITUTES OF HIGHER EDUCATION
(Asociación nacional de universidades e institutos de enseñanza superior), Mexico

The *Asociación nacional de universidades e institutos de enseñanza superior* (ANUIES: National Association of Universities and Institutes of Higher Education) grew out of informal meetings of a small group of Mexican rectors held in 1940, 1941, and 1943 in Mexico City, Guadalajara, and Monterrey, Mexico, to exchange information and examine the problems common to Mexican universities. In 1944 the rectors held an *asambleas nacionales de rectors* (national assembly of rectors) in San Luis Potosi, Mexico; and, in 1948, in Oaxaca, Mexico, they appointed a commission to draw up the statutes of ANUIES. The constitutive assembly met in Hermosillo, Mexico, in March 1950 to approve the statutes; in 1961 the statutes were amended. By 1974 seventy universities and institutes of higher education in Mexico were members of ANUIES. The association is governed by a general assembly, a national council, regional councils, and an executive secretary general.

Representing Mexican institutions of higher education both inside Mexico and abroad, ANUIES coordinates activities among the educational institutions and acts as a liaison between the universities and federal and state educational authorities. ANUIES studies specific academic and administrative questions of each member institution as well as economic problems of higher education in general. The association encourages the exchange of personnel, information, and services among member institutions and promotes research and cultural studies that respect regional characteristics while contributing to the overall national education plan.

ANUIES publishes *Revista de la educación superior,* trimestrially, and an annual statistical report.

Ciudad universitaria
Mexico 20, D.F., Mexico

ALFONSO RANGEL GUERRA

NATIONAL ASSOCIATION OF UNIVERSITY ASSISTANT PROFESSORS
(Asociación nacional de profesores adjuntos de universidad), Spain

The *Asociación nacional de profesores adjuntos de universidad* (National Association of University Assistant Professors), a voluntary association of assistant professors in Spanish universities, was founded to safeguard the interests of its members; to supervise the training and selection of assistant professors; to encourage respect of its members' rights and duties; and to enhance the prestige and social influence of assistant professors. The association is a strictly professional organization, with no political overtones.

Each university association is governed by a permanent commission made up of a president, vice-president, secretary, vice-secretary, treasurer, and vice-treasurer. The permanent commissions of the asso-

ciations make up the national governing body, which elects the national president.

The association derives its funding primarily from its members' annual dues.

31-7° Calle Alcalá
Madrid 14, Spain

RAMÓN FERNÁNDEZ ESPINAR

NATIONAL ASSOCIATION OF UNIVERSITY PROFESSORS
(Associazione nazionale professori universitari di ruolo), Italy

The *Associazione nazionale professori universitari di ruolo* (ANPUR: National Association of University Professors) was founded in Italy just after World War II by a majority of Italian university professors. Represented by a section in each Italian university, ANPUR is directed by a board consisting of a president, two vice-presidents, and four counselors.

Participating in the debate on university reform in Italy, ANPUR defends the economic and legal interests of its members and encourages members to be conscious of their changing roles and duties in the growing Italian universities. In July 1975, at the initiative of ANPUR, the Italian Constitutional Court gave university professors the highest status possible in a state career.

Istituto de Glottologia
via Santa Maria 36
Università di Pisa
Pisa, Italy

ROMANO LAZZERONI

NATIONAL CATHOLIC EDUCATIONAL ASSOCIATION, United States

The National Catholic Educational Association, established in 1904 as a Catholic higher education organization, groups 8500 Catholic schools, from kindergarten through graduate level, and 4000 individual members.

Eight associations, with separate officers,

bylaws, and staff, operate within the national organization, focusing on seminaries, secondary schools, elementary schools, administrators of Catholic education, religious education, boards of education, special education, and colleges and universities.

The College and University Department is a voluntary association of 225 regionally accredited colleges and universities that seek to strengthen the contribution of the Catholic community to American education. The business of the department is managed by an executive committee of fifteen members and four officers. The members and officers are elected at the annual meeting by the membership. An executive secretary, who serves as the staff officer for the department, is chosen by the executive committee. The department depends on dues to finance its operations. Projects beyond the normal activities are funded from outside sources.

The College and University Department has regional units corresponding to the regions of the United States college and university accrediting associations. Each region—except the Northwest, which is inactive—holds at least one annual meeting. The department's section on teacher education meets in conjunction with the American Association of Colleges for Teacher Education.

The College and University Department works closely with the Lutheran Education Conference of North America and other associations of church-related colleges. The department is a member of the International Federation of Catholic Universities.

Four standing commissions work within the College and University Department. The Commission on Purpose and Identity focuses on the objectives of a value-committed institution. The Commission on College Relations attempts to promote a greater understanding between the college and its sponsoring religious body, a religious community or diocese. The Commission on Campus Ministry, which publishes *Guidelines for Campus Ministry at Catholic Colleges and Universities*, assists administrators, faculty, and campus min-

isters to understand and promote an active campus ministry at institutions of higher education. Workshop and consulting services are provided by the Commission on Management and Planning.

The College and University Department of the National Catholic Educational Association publishes periodic reports and the quarterly *College Newsletter*.

One Dupont Circle
Washington, D.C. 20036 USA

NATIONAL CENTER FOR HIGHER EDUCATION MANAGEMENT SYSTEMS, United States

The National Center for Higher Education Management Systems (NCHEMS), which was established in 1971 at Boulder, Colorado, conducts research, development, dissemination, and evaluation activities designed to improve planning and management in postsecondary education. The center, funded primarily by the National Institute of Education, extends its services to institutions and systems, state and federal agencies, and organizations in all sectors and at all levels of postsecondary education.

Good planning and management decisions cannot be made by purely mechanical processes or routinized procedures. Therefore, the NCHEMS mission of improving planning and management in postsecondary education translates directly into improving the capabilities of the individuals who carry out planning and management functions. In consequence, NCHEMS formulates programs of research and development whose objectives are to strengthen the capabilities of planners and managers with respect to all the functions for which they bear responsibility.

NCHEMS programs also take into account the fact that the postsecondary education enterprise embraces many thousands of institutions and systems of all sizes and levels of sophistication, serving myriad individual needs. The tasks and responsibilities of planners and managers vary according to the nature and goals of their particular institutions. Research and development programing at NCHEMS undertakes to differentiate among the kinds of planning and management capabilities needed at various levels and settings, or required to develop and administer specific kinds of programs.

The dominant element in the framework for NCHEMS program design is planning and management *functions,* comprising five categories that apply almost universally to postsecondary education institutions and systems: needs assessment, program planning and goal setting, resource allocation, resource utilization, and evaluation.

Four basic kinds of planning and management capabilities have been identified, any one of which may address one or more of the five functions: information, concepts and analytic tools, organization analyses, and personnel development.

Many different kinds of constituents, with distinct needs, proliferate in postsecondary education. To address all these demands, numerous kinds of institutions and systems, providing a huge diversity of programs, are required. Some NCHEMS activities, therefore, approach research and development tasks from the differentiated perspectives of planners and managers: *in various settings,* such as a state coordinating agency, a major research university, a community college, or a proprietary vocational school; *at different levels,* such as academic vice-president, director of institutional research, dean, or department or unit chairman, in the various settings; and *with different program responsibilities,* such as research and instruction, plus a host of drastically different support programs—health care, student housing, public broadcasting, athletics, and so on. While planners and managers in all these settings and circumstances perform the same generic functions, such as needs assessment or resource allocation, their needs often are so particularized that tailor-made products must be developed to meet them.

The NCHEMS program framework may be seen, then, as having three dimensions: *functions, capabilities,* and *audiences.* The five planning and management functions form the backbone of the framework. Research and development in any of the capability areas may cut across more than one of the functions, in much the same way that a central library or computer center will simultaneously support instruction, research, and public service within an institution of higher education. But the ultimate purpose of all efforts to enhance the four basic capabilities obviously is to better equip planners and managers to execute one or more of their five basic functions. Similarly, tailoring a product to the needs of decision makers in terms of their setting, level, or program responsibility also is intended to improve their performance with respect to one or more of the planning and management functions. To fully understand the NCHEMS approach to program planning, and the way it achieves interrelation and integration of specific projects, one should begin by examining the particular characteristics of those functions:

Needs assessment. The needs and desires of individuals and groups for the kinds of services that postsecondary education can provide must be adequately assessed as a first step in accommodating them. Such assessment also is essential in determining whether resources are being wasted on activities irrelevant to the mission of specific postsecondary education, systems, institutions, or programs.

Program planning and goal setting. Having assessed constituency requirements, planners and managers must determine appropriate policies and objectives and develop and mount programs responsive to the needs of those to be served.

Resource allocation. Because resources available to postsecondary education are limited and likely to remain so, planners and managers must allocate resources in ways that will best achieve institutional and program goals.

Resource utilization. Once resources are

allocated, it is important to ensure that space, energy, and supplies are not used inefficiently and that personnel are not underutilized or their efforts misdirected.

Evaluation. Planners and managers should assess the extent to which constituent expectations are being met and take corrective action as required. This means that they must constantly evaluate programs to determine whether they are yielding intended results.

Categorizing planning and management functions so broadly and defining them in such general terms give little indication of the complexity of the typical decision maker's tasks. That complexity becomes more apparent when one makes even a general analysis of the kind of capabilities needed to carry out those functions. Generally speaking, those needs fall into the categories already named.

Information for planning and management. Almost all decisions about postsecondary education are made on the basis of imperfect information and consequently involve some degree of uncertainty. Typically, less than total knowledge is available about current and past conditions, the full range of decision alternatives is not spelled out, and the consequences of various possible decisions are not adequately projected. Better decisions will result in proportion as the decision maker has more facts and therefore has to make fewer guesses to fill out the decision puzzle.

Efforts to improve planning and management information involve several components. First, there is the removal of uncertainty from the information itself—definitional work to specify and standardize the meaning of particular items of information. (Consider the uncertainty surrounding the specific meaning of so widely used a term as *full-time equivalent student,* for example.) Second, there is the obvious need to make data accessible to decision makers in usable form; raw information in huge amounts is stored in file drawers, on punch cards, and on computer tapes here and there on the typical college campus, but it is without utility to the plan-

ner or manager because no system exists for its collection and analysis. Moreover, a large need for information from sources outside postsecondary education—census data, employment statistics, and such— goes unsatisfied because the campus decision maker does not have the means to acquire or analyze it. Finally, there is the need to improve the flow of information among the various groups and individuals involved in decision making. Because the decision process in postsecondary education is so multifaceted and involves so many interrelations, sound decisions depend heavily on the maintenance of constant communication among the interested parties—and particularly across the institutional, state, and national levels of involvement and concern.

Concepts and analytical tools. In postsecondary education as elsewhere, good decision making in real-world situations depends in large part on whether those involved have a good grasp of relevant basic concepts. The range of issues and problems is far too wide to allow each to be addressed specifically and individually: a set of decision concepts that can be reliably applied to many problems is requisite. Success in retailing is served by a knowledge of basic economic concepts about the forces governing supply and demand. So also must postsecondary education planners and managers have a conceptual understanding of the multiple forces at work in their domain and be able to reach knowledgeable decisions and govern their actions accordingly. To this end, NCHEMS has undertaken to assemble and test a set of concepts—a frame of decision references that can be applied to the general range of planning and management functions. The center also develops analytic tools with which to investigate some of the forces operating in postsecondary education—and to analyze the ramifications of alternative courses of action.

Organizational analyses. Because of the pluralistic nature of postsecondary education and the divergent perspectives and values of involved interest groups, organization and decision processes tend to be more complex than and different from those in private industry. The participative nature of postsecondary decision making frequently results in the active involvement of administrators, faculty, students, alumni, community groups, and external funders. (Consider, for example, how many constituent groups may be involved in decisions related to tuition charges.) But there has been little systematic study of these processes in postsecondary education. Therefore, NCHEMS seeks to identify the decision-making and organizational processes that appear most conducive to improved planning and management.

Personnel development. Improved planning and management ultimately depend on increasing the skills and capabilities of those who can use new concepts, analytic tools, and information in resolving specific problems. NCHEMS therefore promotes the professional development of planners and managers in a variety of ways, such as training sessions and sponsorship of national meetings.

The governing and advisory structure of NCHEMS is extensive, embracing all types of institutions—public, private, and proprietary; two-year, four-year, and graduate-level; liberal arts colleges, comprehensive colleges, major research-oriented universities, and vocational/technical schools. Representation also extends to all types of state agencies—governing boards, budget offices, coordinating councils, legislative agencies, executive offices, national organizations, and federal agencies. A self-perpetuating board of directors, broadly representative of the planning and management component of postsecondary education, appoints the director of NCHEMS and exerts final authority over center policies, programs, operations, and planning.

The NCHEMS National Advisory Council is appointed by the director of the center with the advice and consent of the board. The council channels advice to the board of directors from national and regional educational associations and governmental

agencies and keeps the board aware of the perspectives of the major interest groups in postsecondary education. The council comprises representatives of higher education associations, national professional organizations that have an interest in or concern for postsecondary education planning and management systems, national compacts for education, and state legislative and executive offices.

The NCHEMS Participants Advisory Assembly consists of liaison representatives designated by the heads of more than six hundred institutions and agencies that participate in the NCHEMS program. The assembly members constitute the primary basis for maintaining liaison between the staff and the various segments of postsecondary education. The Participants Advisory Assembly conducts national reviews of the center's products and provides a forum for discussion of the status and development of management systems in postsecondary education.

Task forces and advisory committees are established for limited periods to provide consultation for specific NCHEMS projects and activities. Their main responsibility is to provide advice to the staff relative to the feasibility and utility of NCHEMS products and to recommend changes and developmental directions that will enhance the usefulness and quality of products or undertakings. The structure and operation of task forces and committees may differ from project to project to provide the most effective method of obtaining advice, assistance, and evaluative feedback for each project. Generally, members are either technical experts or knowledgeable potential users.

Dissemination efforts by NCHEMS include training, implementation assistance, wide distribution of research and development reports and users' manuals, and general-information publications. In addition, NCHEMS has a highly developed network of established relationships with institutions, state and federal agencies, and consultants and task forces knowledgeable in areas related to the center's projects. Cooperative research and development undertakings often grow out of these relationships.

On request, NCHEMS has worked closely with various federal agencies in developing reporting standards and providing consultation, on projects ranging from development of planning models to analysis of the impact of legislation. The center has worked both with the National Center for Education Statistics and the National Science Foundation in developing data definitions and reporting formats for collecting information about postsecondary education. NCHEMS has developed a national planning model for use by the Office of Education and also has developed a financing scheme which has had some influence on legislation affecting federal support of postsecondary education.

The center frequently works with consortia of institutions and state agencies in joint problem-solving ventures. For example, NCHEMS worked closely with the Center for Evaluation at the University of California at Los Angeles in developing outcomes measures, and has collaborated in various research, development, and dissemination efforts carried out by such organizations as the Center for Research and Development in Higher Education at Berkeley, California, and the Education Commission of the States, Denver, Colorado.

NCHEMS has cosponsored a number of major national conferences and seminars. In addition, NCHEMS holds national assemblies at which institutional, agency, and association leaders address issues of importance to planners and managers in postsecondary education.

The long-range program plans and specific research and development projects that implement those plans in furtherance of the NCHEMS mission derive from policy and priority decisions made by the NCHEMS board. These were representative undertakings in 1976: (1) A manual was developed to help departmental chairmen and the heads of divisions, schools, and colleges within an institution systemat-ically examine such questions as the functions of various academic units, program demand, resource requirements in terms of faculty, facilities, and finances, and outcomes. (2) At a number of colleges and universities, information exchange procedures were implemented; these procedures enable institutions to collect and share a large assortment of standardized planning and management information—useful not only for external comparison and reporting but also for internal management and planning. (3) Information exchange procedures were adapted to the special needs of major research-oriented universities. (4) A set of measures of educational outcomes was developed. (5) Standard data definitions and collection procedures were developed for use in providing information to state agencies responsible for postsecondary education coordination and planning.

A number of NCHEMS publications and other products are in wide use in postsecondary education. They include *Higher Education Finance Manual:* describes in lay terms the way in which financial accounting is handled in institutions and suggests means by which financial information may be made more useful in the planning and management process; *Cost Analysis Manual:* provides a standard way to look at the costs of postsecondary education; *Faculty Activity Analysis:* provides procedures for determining how faculty use their time and for making use of time-utilization information obtained from faculty; and *Statewide Measures Inventory:* provides measures of various kinds of information useful in the statewide planning and management of postsecondary education. Other publications of interest are *NCHEMS Costing and Data Management System:* a computer software system designed to simplify the structuring of data for information exchange but useful also to institutions for organizing institutional data for internal use; *Resource Requirements Prediction Model 1.6:* a computer software model for examining the implications of various resource allocations in institutions; and *Student Flow Model:* another computer model, devised to aid in analyzing the flow of students into and out of the institution, as well as among departments in the institution.

Western Interstate Commission for
    Higher Education
P.O. Drawer P
Boulder, Colorado 80302 USA
                    WILLIAM JOHNSTON

NATIONAL COLLECTION OF FINE ARTS

See Smithsonian Institution.

NATIONAL COMMISSION FOR COOPERATIVE EDUCATION, United States

The National Commission for Cooperative Education was founded in 1962 with the help of funds provided by the Kettering Foundation. Its purpose has been to forward the expansion of cooperative education by encouraging institutions of higher education to adopt cooperative education programs; by convening conferences to inform industrial, labor, and governmental leaders about cooperative education; by providing consultants to institutions of higher education that need advice in developing and organizing programs; by offering a continuing public information program on behalf of cooperative education; by encouraging the development of new programs; and by assisting in the formulation of national policy in support of cooperative education.

The commission is composed of members having long experience with cooperative education in colleges, universities, and community colleges and with its operation in business, industry, and public employment. Recognizing that educational and economic benefits can result from the adoption of a cooperative program, these national leaders joined in establishing the commission as a means of increasing understanding and information about cooperative education.

Since its inception, the commission has worked diligently to expand cooperative education and to bring it to national attention. In addition to providing specific counsel and consulting services to more than six hundred institutions of higher education, it has created and participated in television and radio programs, published papers and monographs, and sponsored statewide conferences on cooperative education.

The efforts of the commission have led the federal government to enact legislation on behalf of cooperative education. In 1964 the commission was asked to advise on possible legislation to encourage and establish programs of cooperative education. As a result of this advice, Congress included under Title III of the Higher Education Act of 1965 the establishment and development of cooperative education programs as one of the fundable goals for developing institutions. A specific provision for cooperative education was made in Title IV-D in the 1968 amendments to the Higher Education Act and again in the 1972 amendments. Through testimony to the Congress of the United States and sponsorship of statewide conferences, the commission continues to play a significant role in furnishing the information utilized in developing these various items of legislation.

The challenge that the commission now faces is no longer one of trying to interest colleges, universities, and community colleges in cooperative education, but of informing business, industry, and public-sector employers of the desirability of increasing the number of job opportunities for students. In order to achieve this goal, the commission has held one-day employer institutes throughout the United States.

360 Huntington Avenue
Boston, Massachusetts 02115 USA

See also: Cooperative Education and Off-Campus Experience: Cooperative Education in the United States.

NATIONAL COUNCIL OF INDEPENDENT COLLEGES AND UNIVERSITIES, United States

The National Council of Independent Colleges and Universities (NCICU)—formed in January 1971 from its predecessor, the Federation of State Associations of Independent Colleges and Universities—is the voice of the independent sector in United States higher education. Comprised of thirty-five state associations of independent colleges and universities, NCICU was organized to interpret and strengthen the role of the independent sector through the development of public policy. Approximately one thousand institutions of higher education are served by the council.

The council promotes and advances the interest of higher education, including both publicly supported and independent colleges and universities, with special concern for the dual and pluralistic nature of the United States system. The council helps member institutions and associations to interpret—to public and private agencies, legislative bodies, and the public—the role, contribution, and needs of independent colleges and universities and facilitates the exchange of information and ideas among member institutions and associations. Representing the interest and protecting the general welfare of nonprofit, tax-exempt independent colleges and universities, NCICU speaks for member institutions and associations where a united voice is needed.

NCICU is affiliated with the Association of American Colleges (AAC), which provides central office and staff services. The president of AAC serves as executive vice-chairperson and coordinates staff activities. Each state association pays an annual fee determined by the membership at the annual meeting. A contribution to the support of the council and its activities is made by each institutional member through dues to state associations or regular dues payment to AAC.

In addition to promoting a constant exchange of information among members, the council sponsors two to three meetings a year for the professional staffs and officers of state associations and presidents of member institutions. The programs for these meetings include reports on significant developments in legislation at state and federal levels; workshops on the organization, development, and promotion of state associations and their programs; orientation sessions for new association officers and directors; and the dissemination of information of special relevance to independent higher education.

The council provides information concerning legislation, federal assistance programs, and court cases affecting independent higher education in the various states. The professional staff, officers, and directors of the council are available for consultation with the state associations and member colleges; they also assist and advise in the organization of new associations. Staff members speak to various groups on independent higher education, the state association movement, the council and its role, and related topics.

AAC bulletins and reports, dealing with federal and state legislative concerns, are routinely sent to members of the council. In addition, occasional newsletters reporting developments at the state level, changes in personnel, new ideas for the advancement of independent colleges and universities, and council news and activities are sent to the membership.

1818 R Street NW
Washington, D.C. 20009 USA

NATIONAL COUNCIL OF PERUVIAN UNIVERSITIES (Consejo nacional de la universidad peruana)

Founded by the Peruvian government in 1969, the *Consejo nacional de la universidad peruana* (National Council of Peruvian Universities) is the highest governing body of the Peruvian university system—composed of twenty-two state universities and eleven private universities. The main functions of the council are to plan the development of the university system in accordance with the national educational policy and the planning of national development; to control and evaluate academic, financial, and research aspects of the university system; to formulate the budget of the university system according to development plans; to coordinate the activities of the universities within the system and with other institutions.

Organizationally, the council is composed of rectors of the six oldest universities in Peru: *Universidad nacional mayor de San Marcos,* Lima; *Universidad nacional de ingeniería,* Lima; *Universidad nacional agraria "La Molina,"* Lima; *Universidad nacional de Trujillo; Universidad nacional de San Agustín de Arequipa;* and *Universidad nacional de la Amazonia peruana,* Lima and Iquitos. Two rectors are also elected from the private universities: *Pontificia universidad católica del Perú,* Lima; and *Universidad particular peruana "Cayetano Heredia,"* Lima. The council is headed by an elected president, who represents the council officially and legally, and an executive director, who directs the administrative functions of the council. The funds of the university system and of the council are provided by the government, mainly by a budget transference from the Ministry of Education.

The council provides financial and legal advice concerning the functioning of the universities; a specialized library on higher education matters; a program of technical and financial cooperation with other countries and institutions (involving scholarships and visits of professors); a university bookstore and a center for repairing and manufacturing laboratory instruments.

Council publications are *Cuadernos,* a bimonthly magazine published since 1970, containing articles and news about higher education and research; and *Memoria,* a yearly publication that contains a summary of the year's activities.

Petit Thouars 115
Lima 1, Peru

MARIO SAMAME BOGGIO

NATIONAL COUNCIL OF UNIVERSITY RESEARCH ADMINISTRATORS, United States

The National Council of University Research Administrators (NCURA) was founded in 1959 by a group of individuals with professional interest in problems and policies relating to the administration of research, education, and training activities at colleges and universities. Through national and regional meetings, the council provides a forum for the discussion and exchange of information and experience and thereby fosters the development of college and university research administration and the personal and professional growth of members.

Regular membership is open to individuals engaged in the administration of sponsored programs in a college or university, a university or nonprofit hospital, an organization wholly owned or administered by a college or university, a consortium of colleges and universities, or an association with members predominantly from colleges and universities. Associate membership is open to individuals who are interested in the administration of sponsored research, training, and educational programs and are employees of a public agency or nonprofit organization. There are no institutional memberships.

NCURA is organized into seven regions, which elect their own chairpersons and plan their own activities. Regional representatives join with the national president, vice-president, and secretary-treasurer to form the executive committee, the governing body of the council.

The council maintains a national office

to assist in carrying on its operations and to facilitate communications among members. Council committees focus on problems of small institutions, planning and research, federal information systems, and administration of nonfederal support. Regional meetings are held throughout the year at the discretion of the regional officers and membership. The annual meeting is held in Washington, D.C., each fall.

A newsletter is mailed to council members at least four times a year. A directory of members is published annually.

4416 Edmunds Street NW
Washington, D.C. 20007 USA

NATIONAL COUNCIL OF UNIVERSITY STUDENTS OF INDIA

The National Council of University Students of India (NCUSI) was established in September 1958 because of the need for organizing Indian students at the national level for the welfare of the student community. Vast distances and transportation and communication difficulties, coupled with the financial limitations of some student unions, had made it difficult for student unions to communicate with one another. Through NCUSI students became able to take a unified stand on questions such as national defense and the role of students in national reconstruction.

NCUSI seeks to advance and safeguard student interests; to uphold academic freedom; to preserve and develop the student unions; to improve educational standards, facilities, and teaching methods; to create interuniversity student activities for the social, cultural, and educational advancement of the student community; and to work for the good of the country.

The membership of NCUSI consists of the democratically elected student unions from any institution of higher education. The general council consists of two representatives elected by the executive committee of each university union. If a university union does not exist, representatives of the coordinating committee of the college unions in the university concerned may be provisionally seated in the general council until such time that a representative university union is formed. The annual national students' congress and general council meetings are responsible for drafting the policies and programs of NCUSI. The executive committee helps the secretariat implement all programs. An advisory committee of leading educators has been established to give advice and legal assistance to NCUSI personnel.

NCUSI organizes many important national seminars, such as the leadership training seminar at Bhagalpur University in 1972; helps to investigate and ameliorate the causes of student unrest at Indian universities; and mobilizes students to protect national interest. During the invasion of India by the People's Republic of China (in 1962) and also by Pakistan (in 1965 and 1971), NCUSI called upon all students to convene and discuss the nation's defense needs and, in particular, the role of the student in alerting and defending its integrity. NCUSI also played an active role in the Bangladesh struggle (in the early 1970s). More than a thousand students responded to a circular to work for the relief of Bangladesh refugees. NCUSI also offered relief aid during the famine in Bihar and the floods in Uttar Pradesh.

NCUSI fosters international student cooperation by establishing cordial bilateral and multilateral relations with the national unions of other countries. NCUSI is a member of the International Student Conference (ISC), headquartered in London. It hosted the Third Asian Student Conference in Bombay and has a working relationship with the International University Exchange Fund in Geneva, which provides scholarships to South African refugee students. Nearly twenty students at different medical colleges in the country have benefited from these scholarships. It also maintains a working relationship with other international educational and student organizations, such as the International Institute for Education Studies in Belgium, the World University Service in Geneva, the International Student Movement for the United Nations, and the Commonwealth Youth Exchange Council in Britain. NCUSI is an active member of the Indian Assembly of Youth.

Since NCUSI is the representative organization of Indian students, it has been working very closely with the Ministry of Education, the University Grants Commission, and the Ministry of External Affairs and is also a member of several governmental and nongovernmental committees. NCUSI collaborates with the Youth Hostels Association and All Indian Catholic University Federation for the development of the democratic student movement. NCUSI is a consultative member of the Youth and Students' Committee of the Central Citizens Council in New Delhi.

NCUSI operates a separate travel department, which makes travel arrangements for Indian students and serves as an information center for foreign students coming to India. It issues international student identity cards to students, arranges low-priced student tickets, and operates a vacation center at Mussoorie. NCUSI has a student exchange program with Australia and has hosted a French student group. It has initiated a move to coordinate the activities of several student travel groups within the universities and is also attempting to provide better facilities to traveling students.

NCUSI publishes the *Indian Student News,* which covers the activities of NCUSI and students in general. It also cooperates with the National Student Press Council of India, which is a coordinating body of student newspapers in the country, and maintains fraternal relationships with student press organizations throughout the world.

1 Scindia House, Second Floor
Jampath, New Delhi 1, India

NATIONAL DEVELOPMENT

See Planning, Development, and Coordination: National Planning of Higher Education.

NATIONAL EDUCATION ASSOCIATION, United States

Founded in 1857, the National Education Association (NEA)—a professional organization of college and university professors, elementary and secondary school teachers, administrators, principals, counselors, and others interested in American education—seeks to elevate the character and advance the interests of the profession of teaching and to promote the cause of education in the United States. Specifically, NEA strives for an independent united teaching organization, professional excellence, economic security for all educators, adequate financing for public education, human and civil rights in education, and leadership in solving social problems.

Membership in NEA is open to anyone who is actively engaged in teaching or other educational work or is interested in advancing the cause of education. Membership in the association has nine classifications: active, life, reserve, associate, educational secretary, auxiliary personnel, retired, student, and survivor. The NEA's membership numbers over 1,100,000.

The representative assembly is the legislative and policy-forming body of the association. Only active members serve as delegates. An annual meeting is held at a time and place determined by the board of directors.

A professional education association may become affiliated with NEA upon approval of the executive committee. State and local education associations and organizations in the Overseas Education Association are also eligible for affiliation with NEA.

The association publishes *Today's Education,* nine times a year; *Reporter,* eight times

a year; and *Research Bulletin,* quarterly.
1201 16th Street NW
Washington, D.C. 20036 USA

University of Sri Lanka
Faculty of Education
Colombo 3, Sri Lanka

BOGODA PREMARATNE

NATIONAL EDUCATION SOCIETY OF SRI LANKA

Established in 1951, the National Education Society (NES) of Sri Lanka aims to study the educational problems of Sri Lanka; to conduct educational research and assist individual members engaged in similar work; to publish or cooperate in the publication of papers, reports, books, and other literature related to education; and to organize or cooperate in the planning of national and regional conferences, seminars, and other meetings related to education in Sri Lanka and abroad. Other NES objectives are to further international contacts by arranging for the exchange of educators and to give advice and information on educational matters.

Membership in the society is open to teachers, educational administrators, parents, and others who are interested in its objectives. The government of Sri Lanka provides an annual financial grant; however, the society is funded mainly by individual contributions and proceeds from the sale of its publications.

The society sponsors seminars, talks, and discussion groups on educational topics of interest. Its affiliation with the World Education Fellowship (with its headquarters in London) is the main link for its international contacts.

The society publishes a journal in English, Sinhala, and Tamil. The English version is published twice a year and is currently in its twenty-fourth year of publication; the Sinhala and Tamil versions are also published twice a year and are in their ninth year of publication. These journals provide an insight into the thinking, planning, and execution of the educational activities in Sri Lanka.

NATIONAL FOUNDATION FOR EDUCATIONAL RESEARCH IN ENGLAND AND WALES

The National Foundation for Educational Research in England and Wales (NFER), an independent research institute, investigates problems of the public education system in England and Wales at the primary, secondary, higher, and vocational levels. Founded in 1946 and incorporated in 1972, the foundation also seeks to encourage national and international cooperation and dissemination in the educational research field. Research in higher education, with a national focus, is concerned with university students, curricula and instruction, and admissions. In addition to research activities, the foundation develops evaluation tools such as tests and measurements, holds conferences and seminars, and provides a documentation service.

The foundation has institutional members, including local education associations, teachers associations, universities, colleges, and polytechnics. Policy is determined by a board of management. The foundation receives funding from the government, business enterprises, publication sales, contractual research services, and membership subscriptions. The staff includes forty research professionals, seventeen research assistants, eight technicians, eleven administrative personnel, and forty-eight secretarial and clerical personnel. The foundation has a data bank on current research projects in the United Kingdom, including those in higher education.

The foundation publishes its own research through the NFER Publishing Company and Book Publishing Division,

Windsor, England. The company produces reports for NFER, research studies on behalf of other institutes, and manuscripts by individual authors in the educational field. A short history of NFER was published in 1971, *The First Twenty-Five Years: A Review of the NFER 1946–71.* Four reports on the use of aptitude tests to help universities select students for admission were published from 1972 to 1974: *After A-Level?*, *Leaving the Sixth Form, The Prediction of Academic Success*, and *A Year Between School and University.* The journal of NFER, *Educational Research*, is published three times a year.

The Mere
Upton Park
Slough, Berks SLI 2DQ, England

NATIONAL GEOGRAPHIC SOCIETY, United States

The National Geographic Society, the world's largest educational and scientific organization, was founded in 1888 in Washington, D.C., to increase and diffuse geographical knowledge. Membership in 1975 numbered over nine million. The society supports geographical exploration and basic research, especially in those disciplines contributing to the diverse science of geography, and has sponsored, wholly or in part, more than one thousand explorations and research projects. Recipients of 1500 grants, supported by an annual budget of $1,500,000, have included distinguished scientists and promising advanced students in the fields of geology, paleontology, astronomy, geophysics, oceanography, biology, anthropology, archeology, and ethnology.

While grantees are encouraged to publish results of their projects in scientific outlets of their choice, the society often undertakes this function for them. Abstracts and reviews are published in book form in the society's research report series.

Popular accounts of selected projects are issued as illustrated articles in the *National Geographic*, the society's primary instrument for the dissemination of geographical knowledge.

The world's leading colleges and universities keep the *National Geographic* and its comprehensive index on their library shelves. Scholars find that its articles, all exhaustively researched for accuracy and many written by the leading authorities in their fields, provide a reliable and readily available source of background material. The magazine's research and correspondence staff assists any serious inquirer with bibliographies and help in locating materials. Geographical maps, furnished both as supplements to the magazine and in the form of regularly updated atlases and globes, are available through the society. Geographical books supplement the magazine by exploring chosen subjects in more depth than is possible for the magazine; some are geared toward college and university courses.

In 1961 the society began presenting television documentaries, designed both for entertainment and as vehicles for the diffusion of geographical knowledge. The society also makes educational films. Although most of them are designed for classroom use by teachers from upper elementary through high school levels, some have found acceptance as curricula supplements for college-level courses. The television programs as well as a number of the society's films have won national awards.

The society provides free background geographical information to the media. Society members residing in the Washington, D.C., area may subscribe to a series of weekly lectures given in Washington's Constitution Hall each fall-winter session. The society also produces records and tapes of music from different lands.

The society houses mementos of its members' explorations and adventures for public viewing in Explorers Hall at the organization's main headquarters in Washington, D.C.

17th and M Streets NW
Washington, D.C. 20036 USA

NATIONAL HOME STUDY COUNCIL, United States

The National Home Study Council (NHSC), a voluntary association of accredited private home study schools, was founded in 1926 to promote sound educational standards and ethical business practices within the home study field. Membership in the National Home Study Council is limited to private home study schools in the United States that apply for and gain accreditation.

The accrediting commission, formed in 1955, is composed of five public members and four members from the home study field. The United States Office of Education lists the nine-member accrediting commission of NHSC as the nationally recognized accrediting agency in its field. The commission sets the academic and business standards for home study schools, evaluates schools in terms of the standards, and accredits those that meet the standards.

Though membership in NHSC is limited to private correspondence schools in the United States, the council also has ties with international organizations in the home study field. NHSC is a member of the International Council on Correspondence Education. Through its membership in the Coalition of Adult Education Organizations, NHSC participates in other adult educational activities abroad. The council cooperates with United States government agencies such as the Voice of America, the United States Information Agency, and the Department of State in disseminating information about accredited United States correspondence schools to countries throughout the world.

The NHSC schools serve more than 1,500,000 correspondence students in all fifty states and many foreign countries. They offer 500 academic, vocational, and avocational courses by mail, using texts, study guides, and workbooks, as well as recordings, slides, and kits.

The council serves as a clearinghouse for inquiries from the public and in settling student complaints. Workshops, seminars, and an annual conference are regularly sponsored by NHSC.

NHSC provides services for its members and the general public. In addition to free distribution of the *Directory of Accredited Private Home Study Schools,* the council publishes a monthly newsletter, *NHSC News,* containing information of general interest to correspondence educators. The council also publishes a number of special pamphlets, including *Home Study School Accreditation—What It Means and How It Works, The Role of Home Study Today,* and *A Counselor's Guide to Home Study.* In addition, NHSC cooperates with groups such as the Better Business Bureau in publishing *Tips on Home Study Schools.*

1601 18th Street NW
Washington, D.C. 20009 USA

NATIONAL INSTITUTE FOR EDUCATIONAL RESEARCH, Japan

The National Institute for Educational Research was founded in Tokyo in June 1949 to carry out fundamental and comprehensive research on education at all levels. A department of higher education was established in 1976, although higher education research had been conducted at the institute by a special project team since 1968. Comparative research in higher education has included cross-national studies of university administration and management; higher education systems in the United States, the United Kingdom, and the Federal Republic of Germany; graduate education in certain advanced countries; and problems of instruction in universities, especially on the undergraduate level. Other higher education research is concerned with university faculty, reform in higher education, educational psychology, and science education.

A government agency, the institute is financed through government funds. There is a staff of five and a library.

6-5-22 Shimomeguro
Meguro-ku, Tokyo, Japan

NATIONAL INSTITUTE OF EDUCATIONAL SCIENCES
(Instituto nacional de ciencias de la educación), Spain

The National Institute of Educational Sciences conducts educational, psychological, and sociological studies of the social needs, objectives, contents, methods, structure, and implications of the Spanish educational system. An autonomous unit of the Ministry of Education and Sciences, the institute was founded in 1974 to replace the *Centro nacional de investigaciones para el desarrollo de la educación* (CENIDE: National Center of Research for the Development of Education). In addition to conducting its own research, the institute coordinates and plans the activities and research of twenty-six Institutes of Educational Sciences at Spanish universities. Research topics of interest at both the central institute and the twenty-six affiliated branches include studies of university students and teachers as well as the economics of higher education.

In addition to research activities, the institute evaluates curricula, conducts postgraduate courses, organizes teacher training courses at all educational levels; holds conferences and seminars; and provides a documentation service. Funded by the government, the institute has a staff of three research professionals, forty-eight research

assistants and/or graduate students, twenty-eight technicians, ten administrative personnel, and twenty-seven secretarial and clerical personnel. The staff has access to libraries and computers.

Ciudad universitaria
Madrid 3, Spain

NATIONAL INSTITUTE OF PEDAGOGICAL RESEARCH AND DOCUMENTATION
(Institut national de recherche et de documentation pédagogiques), France

The National Institute of Pedagogical Research and Documentation traces its origin to 1879 and the founding of the *Musée pédagogique* (Pedagogical Museum), which consisted of a museum divided into several sections, including a section on the history of education, and a library. In 1903 an office of information and study was attached to the museum, and in 1936 the museum's name was changed to the *Centre national de documentation pédagogique* (CNDP: National Center of Pedagogical Documentation). In 1955 it became a public institution designed to serve as a laboratory of educational research, a center for pedagogical documentation, and a production center for educational technology. In 1956 the title was again changed to reflect these new duties: *Institut national de documentation pédagogique et de perfectionnement et distribution des moyens d'enseignement* (National Institute for Pedagogical Documentation and for the Improvement and Distribution of Educational Material). The institute at that time was more commonly known as the *Institut national pédagogique* (National Pedagogical Institute).

In 1970 the institute was divided into two distinct institutions: the *Office français des techniques modernes d'éducation* (OFRATEME: French Office of Modern Educational Techniques), established to encourage the development of educational technology through research, training, and media production; and the *Institut national de recherche et de documentation pédagogiques* (INRDP: National Institute of Pedagogical Research and Documentation), designed to conduct educational research and provide a documentation and information service.

INRDP conducts research on all educational levels, including higher education, at the request of the minister of national education or on its own initiative. It is concerned with educational structures, programs, and teaching methods. Research is also conducted at the institute's twenty-one regional centers of pedagogical research and documentation and at two centers of educational research associated with the institute: *Centre international d'études pédagogiques* (International Center of Pedagogical Studies) in Sèvres, which conducts research in secondary education, and the *Centre de recherches pédagogiques des enseignements technologiques* (Center of Pedagogical Research in Technological Teaching) in Paris. In addition to research activities, the institute, the regional centers, and thirty-seven local centers offer documentation service for national and international organizations and organize seminars, short courses, and conferences on educational questions.

The institute publishes the following periodicals, dealing with all levels of education: *Revue française de pédagogie,* quarterly; *Textes et documents pour la classe,* bimonthly; *Techniques économiques,* nine times a year; *Techniques industrielles,* monthly during the academic year; *Bulletin bibliographiques: Les livres,* monthly during the academic year; *Bulletin officiel du Ministère de l'éducation,* weekly; and *Mouvement du personnel,* ten times a year.

The institute also publishes *Recueil des lois et règlements du Ministère de l'éducation,* an ongoing collection of texts issued by the Ministry of Education. The collection is updated ten times a year through the distribution of approximately seven thousand perforated sheets that may be added to the original nineteen volumes. Another on-going publication of the institute is *Statistiques des enseignements,* a collection of statistical documents from the *Service central des statistiques et sondages* (Central Service of Statistics and Polls) of the Ministry of Education. Nineteen booklets are issued each year, covering the following subjects: the national education budget, public and private educational institutions, teaching personnel, students, and examinations and diplomas.

In addition to periodical publications, the institute publishes monographs issued in the following collections: *Recherches pédagogiques, Cahiers de documentation (Série générale, Série pédagogique,* and *Série enseignement dans le monde), Techniques de la classe et perfectionnement des enseignants, Rapports de jurys de concours, Mémoires et documents scolaires, Horaires—Programmes—Instructions, Organisation scolaire et universitaire, Equipment et constructions scolaires, Personnels de l'éducation nationale, Catalogues—Répertoires—Bibliographies, Guides pratiques, Tableaux de l'éducation nationale,* and *Thèmes divers.* A list of publications is available on request.

29 rue d'Ulm
75230 Paris, France

NATIONAL INTERFRATERNITY COUNCIL
See Fraternities.

NATIONAL LIBRARY OF FRANCE
See Libraries: National Library of France (Bibliothèque Nationale), France.

NATIONAL LIBRARY OF PEKING
See Libraries: National Library of Peking, People's Republic of China.

NATIONAL MUSEUM OF HISTORY AND TECHNOLOGY
See Smithsonian Institution.

NATIONAL MUSEUM OF NATURAL HISTORY AND MAN

See Smithsonian Institution.

NATIONAL PANHELLENIC CONFERENCE

See Fraternities.

NATIONAL PLANNING ASSOCIATION, United States

The National Planning Association, an independent, private, nonprofit, nonpolitical organization founded in 1934, conducts research and policy studies in the public interest. The association, which has two thousand individual and organizational members, brings together influential and knowledgeable leaders from business, labor, agriculture, and the professions to serve on policy committees to formulate recommendations for dealing with domestic and international developments.

The NPA's professional staff undertakes technical research designed to provide data and ideas for policymakers in government and the private sector. These activities include the preparation of economic and demographic projections for the United States and for individual regions, states, and metropolitan areas; research on national goals and priorities; planning studies for manpower training, education, medical care, environmental protection, energy needs, and other social problems; and analyses and forecasts of changing international realities and their implications for United States policies.

NPA conducts projects for the United States Office of Education and state governments, relating anticipated changes in manpower needs in the coming decades to strategies for educational planning, particularly in the vocational education area. The association's Joint Policy Committee on Vocational Education and Employment Opportunities has also dealt with this topic.

NPA's continuing work on national goals and priorities considers planning for all levels of education in relation to the attainment of other national objectives.

NPA publishes *Looking Ahead* and *Projection Highlights,* periodicals containing committee statements, summaries of current NPA research, and economic and demographic profiles and projections. NPA also publishes eight to ten policy reports yearly with more detailed committee statements, committee-sponsored analyses, research findings, and policy recommendations on national and international issues.

1606 New Hampshire Avenue NW
Washington, D.C. 20009 USA

NATIONAL POLICY AND HIGHER EDUCATION (Higher Education Report), United States

National Policy and Higher Education (Cambridge, Massachusetts: MIT Press, 1973), the report of the Task Force on Higher Education initiated by the United States secretary of health, education, and welfare, examines federal responsibilities in higher education. The report, the second of two "Newman Reports" (F. Newman was chairman of the task force), suggests means by which the federal government can effect solutions to problems in higher education. The major recommendations of the task force are described in detail in policy papers released separately. The following findings and recommendations are reported here.

The role of the federal government is to create conditions that facilitate the realization of the educational needs of American society. These conditions are largely achieved through funding, which has focused on research, access, and facilities. As funding has increased, however, so has government regulation and control of higher education, which has resulted in a decline in institutional autonomy. Consequently, the rationale supporting federal involvement in higher education needs revision. The national commitment to egalitarian goals and the changing conditions of social mobility require that increasingly limited resources be allocated in a manner encouraging a more effective system of higher education.

Federal policies should reflect three major responsibilities: (1) elimination of barriers restricting individual mobility between institutions and promotion of institutional competitiveness; (2) encouragement of new educational structures needed to serve diverse categories of students; and (3) promotion of educational effectiveness in areas of research, evaluation, and experimentation. The federal government should award a large proportion of federal higher education funds to students to encourage institutional competitiveness and discourage federal restrictions on institutional autonomy. The federal government should also implement a "G.I. Bill for Community Service," whereby students accrue benefits for social service; eliminate dependence on the accreditation process for determining institutional eligibility for federal funds; increase financial assistance to minorities and women; design techniques to measure proficiencies; and establish degree-granting examining agencies.

Effective education requires motivated learning and variety in choice of educational format. Both conditions could be enhanced by federal provisions of incentive funds to students and institutions and by federal grants awarded competitively for reform and experimentation.

NATIONAL PORTRAIT GALLERY
See Smithsonian Institution.

NATIONAL RESEARCH COUNCIL OF CANADA

Since its founding in 1916, the National Research Council of Canada (NRC) has played a major role in Canada's scientific and technological development. NRC func-

tions as a national science and engineering laboratory; a patron of Canadian scientific research; and a vital link between the scientific interests of government, industry, and universities in Canada. The council's laboratory activities are concentrated in ten major research divisions of life sciences, physical sciences, and engineering. The newest of these, the Herzberg Institute of Astrophysics, was named in honor of Gerhard Herzberg, NRC scientist and recipient of the 1971 Nobel Prize for contributions to the field of spectroscopy.

A focal point for much of the laboratory research is the 400-acre Montreal Road site on the outskirts of Ottawa, where an active research community involves some 550 scientists and engineers among its 2000 employees. Other facilities include the original Sussex Drive laboratories in Ottawa, which date from 1932, as well as regional laboratories in Saskatchewan and Nova Scotia. Atomic Energy of Canada Limited, established in 1952 as the result of a wartime nuclear energy project coordinated by NRC, is now an independent program. Another NRC undertaking—a joint undertaking between Canada, France, and Hawaii—is the construction of a large new optical telescope, scheduled for completion in 1978 atop the 14,000-foot Mauna Kea in the state of Hawaii. Viewing time and observational facilities will be shared by scientists from the three participating areas.

Applied research supported by NRC focuses on selected areas related to long-term problems of national concern, such as energy, food, building and construction, and transportation. NRC also provides research support toward social objectives such as public safety and security, protection of property, and health and environmental quality. The NRC's network of associate committees, with members drawn from universities, industry, and government laboratories, provides an efficient means for studying, coordinating, and promoting this research.

NRC is custodian of Canada's primary

physical standards, including measurements of such quantities as length, mass, heat, electricity, and time. NRC acts for Canada in international agreements concerning weights and measures.

NRC is closely allied with Canadian industry through cooperative programs of research and development and direct financial assistance. An extensive program of grants and scholarships is the main source of direct aid to engineers and scientists in Canadian universities. NRC is also the focus of a nationwide distribution network for scientific and technical information.

Montreal Road
Ottawa, Ontario, Canada K1A 0R6

NATIONAL RETIRED TEACHERS ASSOCIATION, United States

The National Retired Teachers Association (NRTA), organized in 1947, has a membership of 425,000. Supporting the welfare and service of the teaching community, NRTA fights for legislation to aid children, schools, and persons of retirement age and promotes strong local and state associations concerned with the problems of retirement.

Membership in NRTA is open to retired persons, or to persons contemplating retirement, who were involved in the field of education in public, private, parochial, or federally sponsored schools, universities, or colleges. Part-time employees and teachers who have tutored at home are also eligible. There is no age limitation. Associate membership is open to educators, administrators, spouses of NRTA members, and other persons concerned with the interests of retired teachers.

NRTA and the American Association of Retired Persons (AARP) support the NRTA/AARP Foundation to fund programs and research designed to improve the quality of life for older persons. These two associations work together in joint legislation committees to represent the best interests of retired persons.

The NRTA Consumer Information Program acts as a clearinghouse for information on community affairs; conducts consumer information programs; acquaints members with basic economic principles, budgeting, and price comparison; and assists members with consumer complaints or inquiries.

The NRTA health program, Vigor in Maturity, consists of five sessions dealing with the health and well-being of members. The association also offers crime prevention programs, a defensive driving course, and consultation on retirement tax problems. Members receive group travel opportunities, a group health insurance plan, home delivery pharmacy service, and life insurance at a reasonable cost without a physical examination.

The NRTA's Institute of Lifetime Learning offers classroom programs in Washington, D.C., and at extension centers in several major cities. Home study courses are available through Pepperdine University, Los Angeles, California.

The association provides individual members with opportunities for involvement in service at the state and local levels. The NRTA Senior Community Service Aides Project recruits disadvantaged persons, fifty-five and over, who are unemployed, and places them in employment to regain lost skills or to be trained in an entirely new occupation.

NRTA publishes *Proceedings,* annual; *NRTA Journal,* bimonthly; and *NRTA News Bulletin,* monthly.

1909 K Street NW
Washington, D.C. 20006 USA

NATIONAL STAFF COLLEGE FOR EDUCATIONAL PLANNERS AND ADMINISTRATORS, India

The National Staff College for Educational Planners and Administrators was established by the government of India in 1971 following a recommendation by the Indian Education Commission (1964–

1966) and the Working Party on Educational Planning, Administration and Evaluation in the Fourth Plan (1969–1973). The Asian Institute of Educational Planning and Administration—set up in 1962 under a ten-year agreement between the government of India and UNESCO for the training of educational planners and administrators from different Asian countries—was merged into the staff college as its international division in 1972.

The staff college undertakes, aids, promotes, and coordinates research in various aspects of education, especially planning and administration. Research includes comparative studies in planning techniques and administrative procedures in the different states of India and in other countries of the world. The staff college also provides preservice and in-service training through conferences, workshops, meetings, seminars, and briefing sessions for senior educational officers of the central and state governments and union territories and organizes orientation and training programs and refresher courses for teachers and for university and college administrators connected with educational planning.

In addition to research and teaching activities, the staff college provides, on request, consultancy services to state governments and other educational institutions; acts as a clearinghouse for information in educational planning and administration services and other programs; and provides, on request, facilities for training and research in educational planning and administration to other countries, especially in the Asian region, and collaborates with them in such programs. The staff college is an autonomous organization fully financed by the government of India.

Publications of the staff college include the following: *Report of the Study Group on the Training of District Education Officers* (1972), *Educational Innovations in India: Some Experiments* (1974), and *Administration and Financing of Education in India with Special Reference to the Fifth Five Year Plan* (1974). It has also published reports of state seminars on educational planning and administration. Copies of these documents can be supplied on request.

17-B Sri Aurobindo Marg
New Delhi 110016, India

NATIONAL THEATER OF THE OPERA

See Libraries: National Library of France (Bibliothèque Nationale), France.

NATIONAL UNION OF DANISH STUDENTS
(Danske studerendes faellesråd)

The *Danske studerendes faellesråd* (DSF: National Union of Danish Students) is a trade union organization for students at higher educational institutions in Denmark. All student councils of major higher educational institutions in Denmark, representing approximately 65,000 students, are members. Although it is not a political organization, DSF regards its work as political in the sense that the struggle of students is part of the general social struggle. DSF seeks to develop the struggle of students in solidarity with and support of the working class in Denmark and abroad. DSF takes political stands against capital and narrow academic interests.

The union promotes discussions, debates, and campaigns on such topics as the role of students in society; the function and role of educated people in society; and the effect of the general economic, social, and political situation on students. The union arranges demonstrations; analyzes the economic and social conditions of students; and negotiates with the state on questions concerning housing problems, stipends, and other financial student affairs.

DSF is highly involved in questions concerning the content, structure, and role of the educational system. The union believes that the educational system should be transformed from an elitist, hierarchical structure, where the content serves narrow economic and political interests of the ruling power, to a system for and in the interest of the masses of people. Based on these principles, DSF promotes discussions and campaigns among students and works for institutional reform.

DSF launches solidarity campaigns in favor of liberation movements, especially in the Third World, and informs and promotes discussions on general political and economic questions, especially concerning the European Economic Community.

DSF regularly publishes books and pamphlets on matters of interest to its members. Books have been published on research in Denmark, the health sector and the medical educational system, educational planning by the state, the teaching colleges in Denmark, the building sector in Denmark and problems of the housing sector, and women in the educational system.

Knabrostraede 3
1210 Copenhagen K, Denmark

NATIONAL UNION OF FINNISH STUDENTS (Suomen ylioppilaskuntien liitto/Finlands studentkårers förbund)

The *Suomen ylioppilaskuntien liitto/ Finlands studentkårers förbund* (SYL: National Union of Finnish Students), the principal student organization in Finland, was founded in 1921 to represent its member unions and students at home and to safeguard and further their common interests. The total membership of SYL is approximately 70,000 students. There are thirty member organizations, student unions from all the Finnish universities and other institutions of higher education as well as several smaller professional schools. Since 1971 SYL has been an associate member of the International Union of Students (IUS).

The chief governing body of SYL is the congress, which meets twice a year, in November and March. Each member organization is entitled to elect one representative to the congress for every thousand members, or fraction thereof. Between congressional sessions, the union is directed by the executive board, consisting of a president and six other members. The secretariat is responsible for the preparation and implementation of the decisions of the executive board.

As an active participant in the progressive youth and student movement and as an associate member of IUS, SYL supports the people's fight for independence and social progress. SYL grants scholarships to national student unions in developing countries for improvement of their educational and health facilities. Financial support has been extended to students from Vietnam, Namibia, Guinea-Bissau, Chile, Greece, Bangladesh, India, and Kenya. SYL, jointly with IUS, sponsors international events such as the International Student Forum on Cooperation in June 1975.

Actively supporting the democratization of the structure and contents of all levels of Finnish education, SYL furthers development of the child-care system, implementation of a pension system, and general and equal suffrage in university administration. SYL advocates interest-free loans and extension of the repayment period.

Since 1950 the student organizations have been responsible for erecting residences to meet the housing requirements of students. This activity is funded by foundations and controlled by the students. SYL has appointed a special council for student housing policy, to promote and coordinate the work of the student housing foundations.

Opastinsilta 10 B
SF-00520
Helsinki 52, Finland

NATIONAL UNION OF FRENCH STUDENTS (Union nationale des étudiants de France)

Created at the beginning of the twentieth century, the *Union nationale des étudiants de France* (UNEF: National Union of French Students) did not become a truly national union until 1920. According to statutes adopted in 1966, UNEF acts independently of all political parties and religions. At its 1975 congress, held at Nanterre, it announced a total membership of more than 26,000. It is financed by membership dues.

UNEF found recognition in the student movement following French liberation in 1945. Beginning in 1956, UNEF declared its opposition to sending a French expeditionary force to Algeria and its support of the Algerian people's right to self-determination. Immense student demonstrations were held to oppose the wish of the de Gaulle government to send students to fight in Algeria. UNEF played a major national role in the general strike of May–June 1968 by issuing its "Call to the Population" on May 6, 1968.

The following associations were created by UNEF or through its initiative: the Central Offices of Study, National Center of Studies, Office of University Sports, Office of University Tourism, Health Foundation, Students of France, Preventive University Medicine, University Bureau of Statistics, Student Social Security, UNEF Information, and University Club.

15 rue Soufflot
75240 Paris, France

NATIONAL UNION OF HIGHER EDUCATION (Syndicat national de l'enseignement supérieur), France

The *Syndicat national de l'enseignement supérieur* (SNESup: National Union of Higher Education) groups teaching personnel of higher education to defend their material and moral interests and support the development of public university service. Affiliated with the *Fédération de l'éducation nationale* (FEN: National Federation of Education), SNESup has more than ten thousand members from all university disciplines, higher education institutions, and academies.

The union representative for higher education, SNESup has members in the *Conseils d'université* (University Councils), *Comité consultatif des universités* (CCU: Consulting Committee of the Universities), *Comité national de la recherche scientifique* (CNRS: National Scientific Research Center), *Institut national de la santé, d'études et de recherches médicales* (INSERM: National Institute of Health, Studies, and Medical Research), and *Conseil national de l'enseignement supérieur et de la recherche* (CNESER: National Council of Higher Education and Research).

In defending the professional interests of university professors, the union seeks employment security for its members as well as better compensation and means of advancement. It supports a plan to limit university positions only to those who receive a diploma from the *instituts de préparation à l'enseignement supérieur* (IPRES: preparatory institutes for higher education). The union also seeks to maintain a close liaison between teaching and research and works to obtain an adequate budget for both.

Opposing any form of social segregation, SNESup encourages democratization of university management at all levels and believes that union activity must be accompanied by profound political change before the objectives of the group can be fully realized. Supporting the common program of the French left, the union aligns itself with the popular and democratic forces of France.

SNESup has relationships with other unions of higher education in both capitalist and socialist countries. Affiliated with the *Fédération mondiale des travailleurs scientifiques* (FMTS: World Federation of Scientific Workers), the union is also represented in the *Fédération internationale des syndicats d'enseignants* (FISE: International Federation of Teachers' Unions) in UNESCO.

The congress of SNESup meets biennially to set the goals of the union and elect an administrative commission. The commission directs the group's activities through the national office and the secretary general. SNESup is funded by membership dues, gifts, and subscriptions.

SNESup publishes the *Bulletin du Syndicat national de l'enseignement supérieur,* monthly.

78 rue du Faubourg Saint-Denis
75010 Paris, France

NATIONAL UNION OF ICELANDIC STUDENTS
(Stúdentaráð háskóla Íslands)

The *Stúdentaráð háskóla Íslands* (SHI: National Union of Icelandic Students) is an organization representing 2550 students at the University of Iceland. SHI's elected twenty-eight members meet monthly to set policy, make decisions, and pass resolutions. Occasional meetings of the entire student body are held, but the majority of decisions are made by the council. Student unions exist in every faculty, and SHI maintains relationships with them.

The council nominates representatives to the State Loan Fund, the Students' Welfare Institution, and the National Committee of Icelandic Youth. Student representatives of the university *consistorium* are elected at the same time as those for the council and have a seat on the council also. The council works on a committee with other organizations of students and scholars to improve student loans.

SHI has four committees, whose members are elected by the council: student interests (such as loans and housing), educational affairs, international affairs, and cultural affairs. Each member of the council is a member of one of the committees. The executive committee consists of a president, a vice-president, a treasurer, and representatives from the committees for student interests, educational affairs, and international affairs. Elected by the council, the executive committee directs the council headquarters and coordinates work of the committees between meetings of the student council.

A student newspaper is published monthly and mailed to each student.

University of Iceland
Reykjavík, Iceland

NATIONAL UNION OF IRAQI STUDENTS

Founded in November 1961, the National Union of Iraqi Students (NUIS) seeks to further and safeguard student interests; to develop a feeling of unity among its members; to maintain amicable relations with university authorities, with other universities, and the general public; and to work for Arabic freedom and unity. NUIS aims to strengthen existing bonds between the various ethnic groups in Iraq while protecting their cultural heritage; to eliminate illiteracy by supporting the introduction of compulsory primary school education and free education at all levels; to assist the Iraqi government in implementing the social, cultural, and economic aspects of the current five-year plan; and to maintain and establish ties with other student societies in the Arab countries as well as other parts of the world. Every student enrolled in the University of Mosul is automatically a member of NUIS.

Among the specific responsibilities of the union are the daily management of various restaurants and clubs on the campuses; administration of the residence halls; and assistance to needy students in obtaining grants and free accommodations in residence halls. Off-campus social service activities include assisting traffic police, operating blood donor programs, and building homes for resettled villagers. The union is also responsible for organizing tours, within the country and abroad; off-campus sports; and other social and cultural events.

The union advertises its work, aims, and activities through meetings and discussions presented on a weekly local television program produced by students. It also publishes a journal titled *The Socialist*.

University of Mosul
Mosul, Iraq

NATIONAL UNION OF ISRAEL STUDENTS

The National Union of Israel Students groups university students from the Hebrew University of Jerusalem, Tel Aviv University, Bar-Ilan University, Technion —Israel Institute of Technology, Haifa University, and University of Ben-Gurion, as well as from Bezalel Academy of Arts and Design, Weizmann Institute of Science, Rubin Academy of Music, and Wingate College of Physical Education. Representing 60,000 students in Israel, the union is concerned with student welfare and benefits.

The union maintains a student travel agency, a printing press, and photocopying equipment and offers low-priced books and stationery to members. The organization has a network of volunteer activities in community centers in underprivileged areas in Israel and maintains close links with overseas student unions, primarily in Asia and Europe.

3 Reyness Street
Shikun Ben Zion, Kiryat Moshe
Jerusalem, Israel

ZAKI SHALOM

NATIONAL UNION OF NORWEGIAN STUDENTS (Norsk studentunion)

The *Norsk studentunion* (NSU: National Union of Norwegian Students) is the official student organization of high schools and universities of Norway. Its principal concerns are students' welfare and university and high school matters affecting students although relationship with other national and international unions is also an important consideration.

High schools and fields of study sections of universities elect NSU delegates, who serve as links between the NSU executive organs and students. Once a year all delegates assemble for the NSU congress (*Landsting*), which draws up the working program and political resolutions of the union. The executive board, like the congress, is a political organ which implements resolutions and prepares for the next congress. The board consists of the first and second leaders, five members, and seven deputies elected by the congress. Members who work for the board are not volunteers but are remunerated in accordance with NSU policy. A small secretariat of four persons manages NSU activities. NSU fees are a part of each student's term bill.

Kontor: Lokkevn 7
Oslo 1, Norway

NATIONAL UNION OF SOUTH AFRICAN STUDENTS (Nasionale unie van suid afrikaanse studente)

The National Union of South African Students (NUSAS) was founded in 1924 as a confederation of student representative councils of South African universities. Initially, the national union was composed mainly of white students from English and Afrikaans universities. With the development of Afrikaner nationalism and opposition to white domination, strains developed within the national union, culminating in the Afrikaans students' breaking away in the late 1930s and early 1940s. At this time black colleges joined the national union, and it became an organization more clearly opposed to the South African power structure. This opposition developed and was given further impetus when the nationalist government gained power in 1948. Since that time it has been an organization consistently committed to the establishment of a free and equal society in South Africa. With the reemergence of black consciousness in the late 1960s, a further division occurred within the national union. Feeling that they could best pursue their concerns in their own organization, black students broke away to form the militant South African Students Organization. The increasing militancy of white students matched this move; and the national union, now composed primarily of English-speaking white students, remains one of the few opposition groups within South Africa. The consistent governmental opposition shown by the national union has resulted in a series of state attacks on the organization and its leadership.

NUSAS has the dual responsibility of serving the student community and South African society. Consequently, it runs an extensive seminar program covering a wide range of issues pertinent to the position of students in the university and society; it also develops media programs and organizes projects and campaigns which involve publications and research for black worker organizations, legal commissions, community development projects, and environmental action. In the 1970s it has campaigned for free and compulsory education for all South Africans, recognition of the rights of workers, and the release of all political prisoners.

The national union is attempting to include a wider range of students while maintaining a firm commitment to its principles and action. Small sections of Afrikaans universities have indicated interest in the national union, and informal working relationships are being established with black students.

In 1976 NUSAS published a national student newspaper.

11 Jamieson Street
Cape Town, South Africa

N. G. E. STENT

NATIONAL UNION OF STUDENTS IN SYRIA
(Union nationale des étudiants de Syrie)

The *Union nationale des étudiants de Syrie* (National Union of Students of Syria) is a trade union that represents Syrian Arab students who are studying in Syria and abroad. Emphasizing Arab unity, the union urges Syrian students to assume responsibility in building a united Arab socialist society. The union plays an important role in the diffusion of Arab culture inside and outside the student milieu by promoting the development of teaching programs and sending representatives to various councils and committees and to the Supreme Council of Universities (in Cairo). Students are encouraged to use their theoretical knowledge to solve society's problems and work toward this end in scientific camps for medicine, pharmacy, agriculture, and veterinary medicine. Children of working people attend the university through the union's assistance in supplying scholarships, housing, and tutors.

An international conference of students was held in Damascus in February 1975 with the help of the International Union of Students. Some sixty organizations participated in the conference.

Union publications include a magazine, a newspaper, research reports, and information bulletins.

P.O. Box 3028
Damascus, Syria

NATIONAL UNION OF STUDENTS, United Kingdom

The National Union of Students (NUS) has 660,000 members in universities; polytechnics; and colleges of education, further education, and technology—about 95 percent of the students in Great Britain and Northern Ireland. NUS therefore reasonably claims to represent the interests and views of students.

Northern Ireland students are members of two national unions. They are affiliated to NUS and also to the Union of Students in Ireland (USI). NUS works closely with USI, and both organizations are attempting to promote one united student movement in Northern Ireland.

NUS is governed by a conference of representatives of all affiliated student unions; the conference, held twice a year, makes the union's policy decisions and elects a president and executive. NUS is funded by the local college student unions, which pay between 5 and 9 percent of their income to NUS. The student unions themselves are funded by the fees of their members, which are usually part of the approved college fees.

In order to provide services for its members which they cannot get as reliably or as cheaply anywhere else, NUS runs three businesses: an insurance brokerage, a printing shop, and a student travel service. Profits are put back into the student movement. In addition, one of its most important activities every year is connected with the following year's rate of student grants. Each year, at meetings between representatives of NUS and ministers and civil servants at the Department of Education and Science, NUS presents its claim for student grants for the following year and the statistical evidence on which the claim is based. In recent years, when grants have noticeably failed to keep up with the cost of living, these meetings have been accompanied by mass demonstrations for "fair grants" in the center of London. In 1975 such demonstrations were attracting more than 30,000 students.

Other NUS issues are demands for more and cheaper student accommodations and for a change in the binary system, by which higher education is divided into prestige universities and "the rest," and a campaign against recent cuts in education budgets. When widespread opposition to the war in Vietnam developed in the late 1960s, NUS supported antiwar activities. Working in conjunction with solidarity organizations, the NUS executive and local colleges gave substantial support for the daily antiwar vigils outside the United States Embassy. Another aspect of NUS activity was in support of medical aid to Vietnam. It has also supported civil rights activities. Students in Northern Ireland have always been active in the civil rights movement, and NUS has been able to cooperate closely with Northern Ireland Civil Rights Association.

A large number of publications are produced by NUS. Only a few of them are listed here: *NUS Yearbook 1975/76, NUS Is Your Union, The Case Against Loans, NUS Executive Report on Exams, Expansion of Higher Education, Entrance to Higher Education, Student Participation in College Government, Student Grants Casework, Why We Don't Need Loans, Safety in College, Academic Freedom and the Law, Manual on Student Union Organisation, Entrance to Further and Higher Education, Vacation Grants, Grants Yesterday and Tomorrow, Drugs and the Law, Grants for Mature Women Students, Sabbatical Leave for Union Officers in Colleges of Education.*

3 Endsleigh Street
London WC1, England

FRANCIS BECKETT

NATIONAL UNIVERSITY EXTENSION ASSOCIATION, United States

The National University Extension Association (NUEA) consists of universities, colleges, and other institutions of higher education dedicated to lifelong learning and public service. Founded at the University of Wisconsin in 1915, the association includes publicly and privately supported institutions, large and small, as well as certain other organizations within and outside the United States. Through extension programs, NUEA members make their institutional and community resources available to youth and adults, individuals and groups, volunteer organizations, governmental units, and private industry. The association seeks to make continuing education available and attractive to individuals in all segments of the population.

Membership in NUEA is on an organizational as well as individual basis. NUEA has institutional, associate, affiliate, and professional memberships. Institutional members are regionally accredited, nonprofit colleges, universities, or other institutions of higher education that have ongoing continuing education programs as integral parts of their total educational package. Each institutional member has at least one staff member who devotes a major portion of his time to the direction and administration of the institution's continuing education policy.

Associate membership is a temporary status for institutions that do not fully qualify for institutional membership. These include developing institutions in the process of obtaining accreditation and institutions in the process of implementing a program in continuing education, community service, or other extension areas.

Affiliate members are institutions of higher education outside the United States that otherwise qualify for institutional membership but do not wish to exercise all the privileges of institutional membership; or nonprofit, nonacademic organizations, associations, or agencies that have a special interest in continuing higher education and extension activities. Some of the types of nonacademic organizations eligible for affiliate membership are federal, state, and local government agencies; professional and trade associations; labor unions; charitable and social organizations; and foundations.

Institutional, associate, and affiliate members are accorded similar rights and privileges, except that associate and affiliate members may not hold office in the association or vote at its business meetings. Affiliate members are eligible to participate fully in all NUEA national and regional meetings and have the right to be heard on

any subject under discussion, but they are not bound by the association's decisions or those of its working committees.

Professional membership is for the professional continuing education staff and faculty of member institutions. Such membership is a prerequisite for voting or holding office in association councils and divisions and enables individuals to receive association publications at special rates.

NUEA encourages the maintenance of the highest professional academic standards. The association serves as a clearinghouse for information on independent study, community development, educational technology, extension administration, conferences and institutes, special degree programs, the continuing education unit, and extramural classes. NUEA also provides technical assistance to member institutions and other groups. Annual professional meetings are held at national and regional levels. NUEA promotes special recognition and awards programs for distinguished achievement by persons in the field of extension and continuing education. Cooperating with related associations in adult education, NUEA seeks solutions to problems and issues pertinent to the educational interests and needs of adults. It also acts as a liaison to the legislative and executive branches of the United States government.

NUEA has several affiliate members outside the United States, including Canada, Argentina, and the Netherlands. Through the International Documents Exchange Program, NUEA publications are sent to adult education associations around the world. The association maintains membership in the International Council on Correspondence Education and the Coalition of Adult Education Organizations and participates in international adult education conferences on an ad hoc basis.

NUEA publishes *NUEA Newsletter,* biweekly; *NUEA Spectator,* quarterly professional journal for extension administrators; *Continuing Education Recruiter,* monthly listing of personnel vacancies at member institutions and personnel availabilities; and proceedings of annual meetings.

The *Guide to Independent Study Through Correspondence Instruction* provides a listing of correspondence and independent study courses offered by sixty-two institutions for credit, certificates of achievement, or personal enrichment. The courses are available to English-speaking persons throughout the world. The *Directory of U.S. College and University Degrees for Part-Time Students* lists 2848 degrees which can be completed through part-time study. All the known "special" and "external" degrees are listed, including those available to students any place in the world.

A series of continuing education publications is cosponsored by NUEA and the American College Testing Program. NUEA has also published *Family and Personal Development in Adult Basic Education: Curriculum Guide and Resource Units,* by Edmonia W. Davidson; and *Joint Report on Registrations,* with the Association for Continuing Higher Education.

One Dupont Circle
Washington, D.C. 20036 USA

NATIONAL ZOOLOGICAL PARK
See Smithsonian Institution.

NATURAL SCIENCES (Fields of Study)

The term *natural sciences* refers to those fields of study that are involved in gathering evidence, verifying conclusions, and classifying information about the natural environment. Specifically, the natural sciences, as listed by UNESCO, include astronomy, the biological sciences, chemistry, the geological sciences, meteorology, oceanography, and physics.

Astronomy, a study of the stars and planets, has moved through positional astronomy and the early Greek concern with cosmology, the theoretical study of the origins and structure of the universe, into celestial mechanics and physical as-

tronomy, which involves highly developed instrumentation for radio astronomy and astrophysics. Stellar classification and stellar evolution are related fields.

The biological sciences study living organisms at all levels. They include three main divisions: botany, the study of plants; microbiology, the study of bacteria and other microorganisms; and zoology, the study of animals. Subdivisions, within these main divisions, are anatomy (and the related comparative anatomy), the structure of organisms; biochemistry and biophysics, chemistry and physics as applied to living organisms; cytology, the study of cells; ecology, the study of interrelationships of organisms and their environment; embryology, the study of the formation and development of embryos; entomology, the study of insects; genetics, the study of the heredity and variation of organisms; histology, the study of tissues and their organization; molecular biology, the study of molecules involved with living organisms and their interrelationships; pathology, the study of diseases and malfunctioning of plants and animals; physiology, the functions and processes of living things; taxonomy, the classification of plants and animals by their natural relationships; and radiobiology, the study of the effects and interactions of all forms of radiation with life processes.

Chemistry, the science dealing with the composition, structure, and properties of substances and their transformations, has these subdivisions: analytic chemistry, the identification of materials (qualitative analysis) and the determination of the percentage composition of mixtures or the constituents of a pure compound (quantitative analysis); biochemistry and biophysics, chemistry and physics applied to living organisms; inorganic chemistry, chemical compounds that do not contain carbon (with the exception of carbon dioxide) and compounds containing a carbonate radical; nuclear chemistry, changes in or transformations of the atomic nucleus; organic chemistry, substances that contain the element carbon (with the exception of carbon dioxide and various carbonates); and physical chemistry, applications of the concepts and laws of physics to chemical phenomena.

The geological sciences, dealing with the earth and its rocks and minerals, has these subdivisions: geomorphology, the form of the earth, the general configuration of its surface, and the changes that take place in the evolution of landforms; geophysics, the earth's structure, composition, and development; historical geology, changes that have occurred on the earth since its beginning; paleontology, animal and plant fossil remains; physical geography, comparisons and generalizations of geographical facts, particularly of the present situation; mineralogy, the study of minerals; stratigraphy, the formation, composition, sequence, and correlation of the stratified rocks as parts of the earth's crust; and structural geology, the study of the causes of structural features of rocks and their geographic distribution.

The science dealing with the earth's atmosphere and its phenomena, especially its weather, is meteorology. Its branches are atmospheric thermodynamics; physics of weather forecasting; and synoptic meteorology, which is concerned with atmospheric conditions existing at a given time over an extended region. Instrumentation plays a major role in all these areas.

Oceanography encompasses all the studies that relate to the sea. It brings together knowledge from the marine sciences, including ocean boundaries and the topography of the ocean's bottom. Chemical oceanography involves the chemistry of sea water, while physical geography studies the physics of sea water, tides, and currents. The organisms that live in the oceans are studied in biological oceanography.

Physics studies all types of energy and its interactions with matter. Within this field are acoustics; atomic structure; cryogenics; crystallography; electricity and magnetism; mechanics (including quantum and statistical); molecular, particle, plasma, and solid-state physics; nuclear phenomena; optics;

relativity; and thermodynamics. Considered the most basic of the natural sciences, physics establishes mathematical laws to explain and predict the behavior of mass and energy.

Mathematics has frequently been called the "mother of the sciences" and even "the basic science." In many scientific societies around the world scientists and mathematicians are organized together under the simple word *science*, as is done in the American Association for the Advancement of Science, the oldest such national scientific organization. Mathematics has been an important tool for scientists from their very earliest use of simple arithmetic in record keeping, to statistics, and now to computers.

All facets of mathematics are intertwined in the various sciences: the physics of moving bodies involves applications of geometry and calculus; simple and complex graphing involves algebra and geometry; probability and statistics enter into the work of almost all scientists; and trigonometry is employed regularly in making measurements.

A major development in modern science is the interdisciplinary and multidisciplinary approach to scientifc problems. Just as biochemistry and biophysics have spanned living and nonliving boundaries, environmental problems of population, pollution, and poverty are attacked by teams of natural and social scientists: sociologists, economists, anthropologists, historians, philosophers, and psychologists.

Two areas outside the narrower definitions of natural sciences that interact well with modern sciences are medicine and industry. Medical chemistry, pharmacology, and industrial microbiology are important to the world's health. Bioengineering and biogeochemistry, which deal with the interactions between living organisms and their mineral environment, are rapidly developing fields. Such studies may involve the effects plants have on the weathering of rocks or the chemical transformations that produce petroleum and coal.

The rudiments of the natural sciences

must have begun with observations made by prehistoric man; the paintings of Stone Age man reveal something of the quality of his observations of the form and habits of the animals he hunted for survival. Later, with the development of agriculture, came the development of tools and a recognition of the need for mathematics in surveying. As tools became more sophisticated, they became scientific instruments; and modern technology flourished. Energy sources, studied and used, moved from fire and water to electricity and magnetism and on to modern-day fission and fusion. Conservation of human energy was better achieved as science suggested means of using simple, and later complex, machines. With the wedge and the wheel, technology rolled forward.

Persons from all parts of the globe have made important contributions to the history of science, and now teams of individuals from various countries work together cooperatively. Problems of feeding the world's people are being attacked by plant physiologists, geneticists, agronomists, chemists, plant pathologists, entomologists, and engineers. The "green revolution" to produce new and better food crop strains is dependent on such cooperation. Moreover, physicists and chemists work to harness the energy of the atom and, at the same time, look for other combinations to make new elements. Teams of chemists, physicists, geologists, astronomers, and biologists search for life on other planets, while others try to duplicate life on earth.

The unraveling of DNA and modern genetics continue as genetic engineers use "super enzymes" to cut DNA into smaller segments and recombine them into new molecules. Studies to bring about mass production of plants through tissue culturing are now limited to ornamentals, but they will shortly be used on food crops. Work progresses to establish nitrogen fixation in nonleguminous plants such as corn.

While a number of countries put spaceships into orbit, others assist in training and necessary communications systems. While one country has an abundance of an important natural resource, another has the facilities to make it into a viable product. Scientists in still other countries then modify the method for their situation.

In addition to food shortages, a major concern to the world is energy sources. While fusion and fission controlled by man is being worked on, other scientists try to tame the geothermal forces under the earth's surface as they locate other fossil energy materials. Scientists are attempting to harness the sun, using photosynthesis and nitrogen-fixing organisms to produce hydrogen gas as a future energy source.

Although highly trained scientists are produced in many universities in all parts of the world, the need for even greater numbers of skilled technicians remains. The research of every producing scientist must be supported by laboratory technicians, instrument specialists, skilled craftsmen, business managers, and those skilled in communicating knowledge to others. A secondary school degree or its equivalent is rapidly becoming a minimum background even to assist the technicians; and the two-year tertiary degree, sometimes labeled an associate degree, is being awarded in many nations. Laboratory technicians, field managers, animal and plant growers, and instrument builders, particularly in developing countries, can all begin with this basic background. However, for most persons wanting to embark on a scientific career, the four-year tertiary degree is almost crucial, because it allows an introduction to a number of sciences while giving more time to beginning a specialty and gives laboratory/technical training, as well as theoretical study. The base is laid for the pursuit, then, of graduate studies in a more specialized area.

Highly specialized graduate study in the sciences, which may terminate in a doctor of science or a doctor of philosophy degree, requires an independent science research project. Almost one-on-one tutoring usually occurs toward the end of such study. Classes before that are usually small and are shared with others of like background and interest. Intensive study and dedication to one's objectives are crucial in such programs.

J. DAVID LOCKARD

Levels and Programs of Study

Programs in the natural sciences generally require as a minimum educational prerequisite a secondary education, although mature students with relevant work experience may sometimes be admitted with lower qualifications. Programs deal with the principles and applications of one or more branches of the natural sciences and consist of classroom and laboratory study, experimental techniques, and fieldwork. Programs lead to the following awards: certificate or diploma, bachelor's degree (B.Sc.), master's degree (M.Sc.), the doctorate (Ph.D.), or their equivalents.

Programs that lead to an award not equivalent to a first university degree are designed to prepare students for careers as relatively high-level technicians in various branches of science. The practical, technical aspects of the subjects included are emphasized, with relatively little time spent on the more general, theoretical principles involved. The principal kinds of programs included are those dealing with biological sciences (for example, general biology, botany, zoology, limnology, microbiology, entomology); chemistry (for example, inorganic chemistry, organic chemistry, industrial chemistry); physics (for example, general physics, thermal physics, spectroscopy, X-ray and radiation physics); geological sciences (for example, geology, geophysics, physical geography, mineralogy, paleontology); astronomy; meteorology; oceanography; and metallurgy. Background courses, designed to supplement and assist in mastering the major subject, include related courses such as mathematics, computer science, statistical analysis, social sciences, and humanities.

Programs may be full time or part time, day or evening. Many are of relatively short duration—that is, less than one year—and

include retraining, refresher, and sandwich courses. Practical demonstrations, fieldwork, and shop work (including periods of employment) are commonly included in these programs. The programs are often conducted in technical institutes or technical colleges but many different kinds of agencies sponsor them, including professional societies, employers and employers' associations, trade unions, and research institutes (both public and private).

Programs that lead to a first university degree stress the theoretical and scientific principles of the subjects included, as well as the mastery of experimental techniques as a basis for research and investigation. Principal kinds of programs included are general programs in natural sciences; biological sciences (general biology, zoology, botany, entomology, microbiology); chemistry (inorganic chemistry, organic chemistry, general chemistry, physical chemistry); physics (general physics, mechanics, optics, thermodynamics, relativity, electricity, electronics, atomic and nuclear physics); geological sciences (mineralogy, petrography, physical geology, paleontology, stratigraphy, geomorphology); astronomy (basic astronomy, astrophysics, stellar evolution, stellar classification, radio astronomy); meteorology (synoptic meteorology, physics of weather forecasting, synoptic meteorological laboratory methods, atmospheric thermodynamics); and oceanography (elements of oceanography, biological oceanography, chemical oceanography, physical oceanography, geological oceanography). Programs in any of the natural sciences usually include background courses in other natural sciences, chosen to supplement and enhance understanding of the major specialty, and many of the programs also include courses in mathematics, statistics, computer science, social sciences, and the humanities.

Programs may be full time or part time, day or evening. At this level, however, most programs are full time, although students may undertake them on a part-time basis. Part-time programs are mainly refresher courses. Most programs are conducted by universities, colleges, or similar institutions through regular lectures, seminars, laboratory periods, and fieldwork, but some are provided through correspondence or through broadcasts (radio or television).

Programs that lead to a postgraduate university degree emphasize the theoretical principles of the subjects included in the programs; and original research work, as substantiated by the presentation and defense of a scholarly thesis, is usually an important element. The programs followed by individual students at this level are usually restricted to one specialized area within one of the physical sciences. In most cases, the research content of the program is paramount.

The principal kinds of programs included fall within such disciplines as the biological sciences, (for example, specialties in zoology, botany, or microbiology); chemistry (for example, inorganic chemistry, organic chemistry, or physical chemistry); geological sciences (for example, geology, paleontology, or mineralogy); physics (for example, mechanics, light, heat, electricity, high-energy physics, or quantum physics); astronomy, including astrophysics and radio astronomy; meteorology; oceanography; and other natural sciences such as metallurgy. Many programs in the natural sciences at this level also include background studies in related areas in the natural sciences, mathematics, statistics, and social sciences. In the main, these programs are full time, although advanced students often do part-time teaching or supervise less advanced students in laboratories or fieldwork.

[This section was based on UNESCO's *International Standard Classification of Education (ISCED)* (Paris: UNESCO, 1976).]

Major International and National Organizations

INTERNATIONAL

International Council of Scientific Unions
Conseil international des unions scientifiques
51 boulevard de Montmorency
75016 Paris, France

The major international organization in the field. Includes the following scientific unions: International Council of Scientific Unions, International Astronomical Union, International Union of Geodesy and Geophysics, International Union of Pure and Applied Chemistry, International Union of Radio Science, International Union of Pure and Applied Physics, International Union of Biological Sciences, International Geographical Union, International Union of Crystallography, International Union of Theoretical and Applied Mechanics, International Union of the History and Philosophy of Science, International Mathematical Union, International Union of Physiological Sciences, International Union of Biochemistry, International Union of Geological Sciences, International Union for Pure and Applied Biophysics, International Union of Nutritional Sciences, International Union of Pharmacology.

NATIONAL

A sampling of national science organizations worldwide includes:

Argentina:
  Asociación argentina de ciencias
    naturales
  avenida Angel Gallardo 470
  Buenos Aires

Australia:
  Australian and New Zealand Association
    for the Advancement of Science
  Science House
  157 Gloucester Street
  Sydney, New South Wales 2000

Austria:
  Naturwissenschaftlicher Verein für
    Kärnten
  Museumgasse 2
  A-9020 Klagenfurt

Belgium:
  Fédération belge des sociétés scientifiques
  31 rue Vautier
  1040 Brussels

Canada:
  Science Council of Canada
  150 Kent Street
  Ottawa 4, Ontario

Denmark:
  Selskabet for naturaerens udbredelse
  Kemisk laboratorium III
  Universitetsparken 5
  2100 Copenhagen

Federal Republic of Germany:
  Wissenschaftstrat
  Marienburgerstrasse 8
  Cologne-Marienburg

France:
Association française pour l'avancement
des sciences
250 rue Saint-Jacques
75 Paris 5e

Israel:
Association for the Advancement of
Science in Israel
P. O. Box 7266
Jerusalem

Italy:
Società italiana di scienze naturali
Corso Venezia 55
Milan 20121

Società italiana per il progresso delle
scienze
viale di Porta Tiburtina 36
00185 Rome

Japan:
Nihon gakujutsu shinko-kai
Japan Society for the Promotion of
Science
2-1-2 Hitotsubashi
Chiyoda-ku, Tokyo

Spain:
Asociación española para el progreso de
las ciencias
Calle de Valverde 24
Madrid

United Kingdom:
British Association for the Advancement
of Science
Fortress House, Saville Row
London W1, England

United States:
American Association for the
Advancement of Science
1515 Massachusetts Avenue NW
Washington, D. C. 20005

Consult the following for more complete
organizational listings:

*Guide to World Science: A New Reference Guide
to Sources of World Scientific Information.*
(2nd ed., 25 vols.) Guernsey, Channel
Islands: Francis Hodgson, 1974–1975.

Minerva, Wissenschaftliche Gesellschaften. Berlin,
Federal Republic of Germany: de Gruyter,
1972.

World Guide to Scientific Associations. Pullach/
Munich, Federal Republic of Germany:
Verlag Dokumentation; New York: Bowker,
1973.

The World of Learning. London: Europa,
1947–. Published annually.

Yearbook of International Organizations. Brussels:
Union of International Associations,
1948–. Published biennially.

Principal Information Sources

GENERAL

Guides to the literature include:

Deason, H. J. (Comp.) *The AAAS Science Book
List.* (3rd ed.) Washington, D. C.: American
Society for the Advancement of Science,
1970. Subtitled "A Selection and Annotated
List of Science and Mathematics Books for
Secondary School Students, College Under-
graduates, and Nonspecialists."

Grogan, D. *Science and Technology: An Introduction to the Literature.* (2nd ed.) Hamden,
Connecticut: Linnet Books, 1973.

Jenkins, F. B. *Science Reference Sources.* (5th ed.)
Cambridge, Massachusetts: MIT Press,
1969.

Lasworth, E. J. *Reference Sources in Science and
Technology.* Metuchen, New Jersey: Scarecrow Press, 1972.

Maichel, K. *Guide to Russian Reference Books.*
Vol. 2: *Science, Technology and Medicine.*
Stanford, California: Hoover Institution
Press, 1967.

Malclès, L. N. *Les sources du travail bibliographique.* (4 vols.) Vol. 3: *Bibliographies spécial-
isées (Sciences exactes et techniques).* Geneva:
Droz, 1950–1958.

Malinowsky, H. R. *Science and Engineering
Reference Sources: A Guide for Students and
Librarians.* Littleton, Colorado: Libraries
Unlimited, 1967.

Parker, C. C., and Turley, R. V. *Information
Sources in Science and Technology.* London:
Butterworth, 1975.

Walford, A. J. *Guide to Reference Material* (3rd
ed.) Vol. 1: *Science and Technology.* London:
Library Association, 1973. An introductory
guide to selected information sources and
guides in the field.

Histories and introductions to the field
include:

Barber, B., and Hirsch, W. (Eds.) *The Sociology
of Science.* New York: Free Press, 1962.
Collection of professional writings concerning the relationship between science and
social organizations and institutions of
modern times.

Boas, M. *The Scientific Renaissance 1450–1630.*
New York: Harper & Row, 1966.

Colborn, R. (Ed.) *Modern Science and Technology.*
New York: Van Nostrand, 1965. Collection of
eighty-one articles.

Crombie, A. C. *Augustus to Galileo: A History of
Science, A. D. 400–1650.* Cambridge, Massachusetts: Harvard University Press, 1953.

Gray, D. E., and Coutts, J. W. *Man and His
Physical World.* (3rd ed.) New York: Van Nostrand, 1958. Comprehensive survey text cov-

ering astronomy, chemistry, physics, and geology.

Hoyt, E. P. *A Short History of Science.* Vol. 1: *Ancient Science.* Vol. 2: *Modern Science.* New York: John Day, 1965, 1966. General background reading; bibliography and index included.

Isaacs, A. *Introducing Science.* New York: Basic Books, 1963.

Sarton, G. *A History of Science.* Cambridge, Massachusetts: Harvard University Press, 1952–1959. Deals with history of science in pre-Christian civilization.

Taton, R. (Ed.) *History of Science.* (4 vols.) New York: Basic Books, 1963–1966. A useful reference source; includes bibliographies and indexes.

Comparative education information sources include:

Comber, L. C., and Keever, J. P. (Eds.) *Science Education in Nineteen Countries.* New York: Halsted Press, 1973.

La enseñanza de la ciencias y de la ingeniería en la América latina. Washington, D. C.: Pan American Union, 1964–. National reports on the teaching of science and engineering in several Latin American countries. Included are Bolivia, Ecuador, Chile, Costa Rica, El Salvador, Guatemala, Honduras, Mexico, and Nicaragua.

Exell, R. B. H. (Ed.) *Basic Sciences in Southeast Asian Universities: A Seminar Report.* Bangkok, Thailand: Association of Southeast Asian Institutions of Higher Education, 1969.

Korol, A. G. *Soviet Education for Science and Technology.* Westport, Connecticut: Greenwood Press, 1974. Reprint of 1957 edition.

Lockhard, J. D. (Ed.) *Tenth Report of the International Clearinghouse on Science and Mathematics Curriculum Developments.* College Park: University of Maryland Science Teaching Center, 1977. New reports are published biennially.

Quibain, F. I. *Education and Science in the Arab World.* Baltimore: Johns Hopkins University Press, 1966. Part 2 deals with higher education in Iraq, Jordan, Lebanon, Libya, Syria, and Egypt.

The Teaching of Sciences in African Universities. Paris: UNESCO, 1964.

CURRENT BIBLIOGRAPHIES

Applied Science and Technical Index. New York: Wilson, 1958–.

Bulletin signalétique. Paris: Centre national de la recherche scientifique, 1940–. Various sections deal with the natural sciences.

CC-LS (Current Contents, Life Sciences). Philadelphia: Institute for Scientific Information, 1958–.

CC-PCS (Current Contents, Physical and Chemical Sciences). Philadelphia: Institute for Scientific Information, 1961–.

Dissertation Abstracts International. Section B: *The Sciences and Engineering.* Ann Arbor: University of Michigan Microfilms, 1938–.

Government Reports Announcements. Washington, D.C.: U.S. Department of Commerce, National Technical Information Service, 1946–.

Referativnyĭ zhurnal. Moscow: Akademiia nauk, SSSR, Institut nauchnoĭ informatsii, 1953–. Various sections deal with the natural sciences.

Science Citation Index. Philadelphia: Institute for Scientific Information, 1961–.

Technical Book Review Index. London: Special Libraries Association, 1935–.

Further listings may be found in:

Owens, D. B., and Hanchey, M. M. *Abstracts and Indexes in Science and Technology: A Descriptive Guide.* Metuchen, New Jersey: Scarecrow Press, 1974.

PERIODICALS

A sampling of the many periodicals devoted to science includes *Académie des sciences. Comptes rendus hebdomadaires des sciences* (France), *Advancement of Science* (UK), *Akademiia nauk SSSR doklady* (USSR), *American Philosophical Society Proceedings, Endeavor* (UK), *Experientia* (Switzerland), *Franklin Institute Journal* (US and UK), *Journal of College Science Teaching* (US), *Journal of Research in Science Teaching* (US), *Minerva* (UK), *Mosaic* (US), *National Academy of Science Proceedings* (US), *Nature* (UK), *Naturwissenschaften* (FRG), *New Scientist* (UK), *New York Academy of Sciences. Transactions, Ricerca scientifica* (Italy), *Royal Society of Canada. Transactions, Science* (US), *Science Education* (US), *Scientia* (Italy), *Scientific American* (US).

For extensive listings of journals in the field see:

Harvard University Library. *Current Journals in the Sciences.* Cambridge, Massachusetts: Harvard University Press, 1975.

Himmelsbach, C. J., and Brochiner, G. F. *A Guide to Scientific and Technical Journals in Translation.* New York: Special Libraries Association, 1973.

Ulrich's International Periodicals Directory. New York: Bowker, biennial.

World List of Scientific Periodicals Published in the Years 1900–1960. (4th ed.) London: Butterworth, 1963–1965.

ENCYCLOPEDIAS, DICTIONARIES, HANDBOOKS

Brockhaus der Naturwissenschaft and Technik. (8th ed.) Leipzig, German Democratic Republic:

Brockhaus, 1962. Compact encyclopedia of science and technology.

Collocott, T. C. (Ed.) *Chambers Dictionary of Science and Technology.* New York: Barnes & Noble, 1971.

DeVries, L. *German-English Science Dictionary for Students in Chemistry, Physics, Biology, Agriculture and Related Sciences.* (3rd ed.) New York: McGraw-Hill, 1959.

Dictionar technic poliglot: Romînă, rusă, engliză, germană, franceză, maghiară. Bucharest: Editura Technică, 1963. Polyglot dictionary of scientific and technical terms in six languages; includes approximately 30,000 terms.

Enciclopedia della scienza e della tecnica. (12 vols.) Milan: Mondadori, 1971.

Ghaleb, E. *Dictionnaire des sciences de la nature/ Dictionary of the Natural Sciences. Arabic-Latin-French-English-German-Italian.* (3 vols.) New York: International Publications Service, 1973.

Handbook of Chemistry and Physics. Cleveland, Ohio: Chemical Rubber Co., 1913–. Published annually.

Handwörterbuch der Naturwissenschaft (2nd ed., 10 vols.) Jena, German Democratic Republic: Fischer, 1931–1935. Lengthy documented articles, alphabetically arranged; bibliographies included.

Harper Encyclopedia of Science. (Rev. ed.) New York: Harper & Row, 1967.

McGraw-Hill Encyclopedia of Science and Technology: An International Reference Work. (3rd ed., 15 vols.) New York: McGraw-Hill, 1971. Updated by the *McGraw-Hill Yearbook of Science and Technology.*

Uvarov, E. B., and Chapman, D. R. *The Penguin Dictionary of Science.* New York: Schocken Books, 1972.

Van Nostrand's Scientific Encyclopedia. (4th ed.) New York: Van Nostrand, 1968.

Guides to polyglot and bilingual dictionaries include:

Bibliography of Interlingual Scientific and Technical Dictionaries. (5th ed.) Paris: UNESCO, 1969. Lists approximately 2500 dictionaries in seventy-five languages.

Rechenbach, C. W., and Garnett, E. R. *A Bibliography of Scientific, Technical and Specialized Dictionaries: Polyglot, Bilingual, Unilingual.* Washington, D.C.: Catholic University of America Press, 1969.

DIRECTORIES

Directories to educational facilities and scientific establishments include:

American Universities and Colleges. Washington D. C.: American Council on Education, 1928–. Published quadrennially.

Cass, J., and Birnbaum, M. *Comparative Guide to Science and Engineering Programs.* New York: Harper & Row, 1971. Lists schools and programs in the United States.

Commonwealth Universities Yearbook. London: Association of Commonwealth Universities, 1914–. Published annually.

Guide to World Science: A New Reference Guide to Sources of World Scientific Information. (2nd ed., 25 vols.) Guernsey, Channel Islands: Francis Hodgson, 1974–1975. Includes descriptions of science policies and structures in various countries as well as a directory of scientific establishments worldwide.

Harvey, A. (Comp.) *Directory of Scientific Directories.* (2nd ed.) New York: International Publications Service, 1972. International directory to approximately 1800 directories in mathematics, astronomy, physics, chemistry, geology, anthropology, biology, medicine, engineering, and agriculture. Includes institutes, learned societies, universities, and individuals.

Peterson's Annual Guides to Graduate Study, 1976. Book 3: *Biological and Health Sciences.* Book 4: *Physical Sciences.* Princeton, New Jersey: Peterson's Guides, 1975.

The World of Learning. London: Europa, 1947–. Published annually. Includes universities, colleges, learned societies, and research institutes worldwide.

World List of Universities. Paris: International Association of Universities, 1971–. Published biennially.

RESEARCH CENTERS, INSTITUTES, INFORMATION CENTERS

Directories to research institutes include:

Battelle Memorial Institute. *Directory of Selected Scientific Institutions in the USSR.* Columbus, Ohio: Merrill, 1963.

Directory of Research Institutions and Laboratories in Japan. Tokyo: Society for the Promotion of Science, 1964.

Directory of Selected Research Institutes in Eastern Europe. Prepared by Arthur D. Little, Inc. New York: Columbia University Press, 1967. A comprehensive guide to the scientific research institutes in Bulgaria, Czechoslovakia, Hungary, Poland, Romania, and Yugoslavia.

Hilton, R. *Scientific Institutions of Latin America with Special Reference to Their Organization and Information Facilities.* Stanford: California Institute of International Studies, 1970. Lists international, United States, and European organizations promoting science and science information in Latin America.

Minerva, Forschungsinstitute. Berlin, Federal Republic of Germany: de Gruyter, 1972. Lists research institutes throughout the world.

Research Centers Directory. (5th ed.) Detroit: Gale Research, 1975.

Directories to information and documentation centers are:

Aslib Directory: A Guide to Sources of Information in Great Britain and Ireland. London: Association of Special Libraries and Information Bureaus, 1922–.

Directory of Special Libraries and Information Centers. Detroit: Gale Research, 1961–.

U. S. Library of Congress. *International Scientific Organizations: A Guide to Their Libraries, Documentation and Information Services.* Washington, D.C.: U.S. Government Printing Office, 1962.

U. S. National Referral Center. *A Directory of Information Sources in the United States: Physical Sciences, Biological Sciences and Engineering.* Washington, D.C.: U.S. Government Printing Office, 1965.

World Guide to Scientific Information and Documentation Services. Paris: UNESCO, 1965.

World Guide to Technical Information and Documentation Services. Paris: UNESCO, 1969. Companion volume to *World Guide to Scientific Information and Documentation Services.* Lists principal centers offering scientific and technical information and documentation services.

[Bibliography prepared by Nancy Cottrill.]

See also: Astronomy; Biological Sciences; Chemistry; Geological Sciences; Meteorology; Oceanography; Physics.

NAURU, REPUBLIC OF

Population: 7500 (mid 1975 estimate). Student enrollment in primary school: 1648 (49 percent female); secondary school: 477 (49 percent female); university (abroad): 6; other postsecondary: 10. Expenditure on education as percentage of the national budget: 5%. [Secondary school enrollment figure does not include teacher training. Figures are for 1975.]

The Republic of Nauru, which became independent in 1968, is a small island in the Central Pacific. Education is compulsory for ages six to sixteen. Primary education is conducted in nine schools; secondary education in two. There is one trade school.

The Republic of Nauru is part of the official region of the University of the South Pacific, in Suva, Fiji. As of June 30, 1975, six full-time students from Nauru

were enrolled in the university. In addition, some fourteen students were enrolled as external students.

In 1975, 101 Nauruans studied abroad at various levels. Principal countries of study in addition to Fiji were Australia, New Zealand, and Papua New Guinea.

Education in Nauru is free. The great majority of students overseas are being educated at government expense.

[Information supplied by Secretary for Health and Education, Nauru.]

See also: Oceania: Regional Analysis.

NAUTICAL SCIENCE (Field of Study)

Nautical science is the science of the management and operation of waterborne transportation and support systems and encompasses a wide variety of individual disciplines. It is dedicated to the support and enhancement of domestic and foreign commerce and associated activities and is in the midst of a conceptual change without precedent throughout its history and development.

Nautical science is rooted in the transport of commodities in increasingly larger and faster vessels. However, since the mid 1960s what has been described as a revolution in cargo-handling techniques and ocean transport management has taken place, with the widespread use of large reusable freight containers on some of the major trade routes. Although designed primarily to reduce the time a ship spends in port by automating cargo operations and to allow the movement of cargo inland without repeated handling of cargo into and out of road and rail vehicles, "containerization" has also led to an integrated approach to ocean transport management.

Many ship operators are now more aptly described as transport companies. They can offer a shipper a through-transport service by either carrying out or arranging for inland transport, a function previously left to the freight forwarder. They have also formed large consortia in order to better allocate the tremendous cargo-carrying capacity of large and fast container vessels and to rationalize the considerable capital investment which the ships and their containers represent. Thus, the container ship of today, sailing rapidly between a few major container terminals, contrasts sharply with the traditional general cargo ship of yesterday, sailing from port to port collecting relatively small loads of cargo.

Although these expensive technological developments open new horizons to the nautical scientist, they may make it more difficult for him to cope with traditional ocean transport problems. In the future he will have to apply sophisticated solutions to increasingly sophisticated problems (that is, container stowage, movement, and control) while retaining his ability to find simple solutions to less sophisticated but equally pressing problems.

The field of nautical science may be broken down roughly into (1) ship design, (2) ship operations, (3) shoreside support, and (4) business and financial management.

Traditionally, ships have been designed to satisfy the unique requirements of diverse cargoes and shippers: the fast clipper ship for the Far East trade in the nineteenth century, the whaler, the whaleback ore carrier on the Great Lakes, and the tanker. Never in the past, however, has there been anything to match the demand for specialized carriers to carry the highly specialized cargoes that are common in the 1970s. There are container ships, barge-carrying ships, tankers capable of carrying nearly a half million tons of oil, ships designed to transport liquefied natural gas, self-unloading ore ships, roll-on–roll-off ships, drill ships, research ships, ocean-mining ships, and combination ships, with others still on the drawing boards. Although there are still many ordinary break-bulk ships, the trend is toward vessels that do not resemble the traditional ships and are utilized in highly specialized ways. This trend will continue to make the task of the port planner and terminal designer, the naval architect, and the marine engineer more complex.

A second branch of the field, ship operations, has traditionally been the main thrust in nautical science, but the field has expanded rapidly since the end of World War II, with the greatest acceleration occurring since 1960. The increasing speeds and sizes of ships have been matched with an increase in sophistication of navigational equipment and aids. As a result, the shipmaster, like the airline pilot, must know something about a large array of automated equipment, ranging from radar and computerized collision avoidance systems, through Loran, Omega, and satellite communications systems. In addition, he must be expert in the old skills of fixing his vessel's position by the sun, moon, stars, and planets.

Getting the ship from port to port is only a small part of ship operations, however. The ships are operated for the sole purpose of transporting cargoes and to earn money for their owners; cargo handling is second in importance only to the safety of the vessel and her crew. Not only must the cargo be kept moving, but it must be stowed on the ships in such a manner as to preserve the stability of the ship as well as her trim for safety and economy of operation. This stowage and the protection of the ship and her cargo are important aspects of nautical science.

A third branch of nautical science, shoreside support, involves bunkering (fuel), provisioning, crewing, booking of cargo, repair, customs, and dozens of items of ship's business that enable the ship to keep moving without delays.

Finally, the advent of containerization and an integrated approach to transport has pushed the shipping industry into the area of high finance. Thus, the business of running ships and shipping companies is a science in itself. In addition to the study of business and marketing practices common to all businesses, nautical science must include chartering, brokerage, marine underwriting, and marine labor relations.

There are many fields related to nautical science. In addition to the usual support subjects—mathematics, physics, chemistry, humanities—nautical science is also closely involved with oceanography, ocean engineering, meteorology, law, and propulsion engineering systems. Oceanography (specifically, the physics of the oceans) and ocean engineering (specifically, marine structure) can be included in a limited sense as part of nautical science. These fields are important in their own right as allied fields dealing with off-shore drilling and the exploitation of marine mineral resources. Weather forecasting and weather mapping are important tools for the nautical scientist, since long-range prediction of weather and sea conditions is necessary to effect the best routes for avoiding bad weather.

A complete understanding of international regulations for the prevention of collisions at sea is essential to all mariners, but the multiplicity of regulations and laws not directly related to navigation makes familiarity with the law, especially admiralty, necessary. Finally, although propulsion systems have long been the responsibility of the marine engineer, the development of bridge–engine room control systems has brought the field within the province of nautical science.

Like the law and medicine, nautical science as an academic discipline is rooted in an apprentice system, in which the would-be shipmaster would "read" for the profession by shipping at an early age as cadet, midshipman, or cabin boy. Eventually shipping company cadet programs and school-ships were developed; and finally, as technology advanced, accredited academies and colleges began to grant degrees in nautical science. Formal education in the field dates back to the early nineteenth century with the advent of the schoolships, where a student's time was divided between shipboard routine and formal studies.

New developments in the field include the specialization of cargo ships, containerization and an integrated approach to transport, and the technological explosion in electronics and computerization. Combinations of traditional college studies, nautical science business management, and

shipboard experience on the latest and most modern ships keep the science current. In all maritime nations some sort of licensing of ships' officers is required. Applicants for a marine license are required to pass a comprehensive examination at least once, and often as many as four times; in the United States, for example, an applicant must pass four examinations before he can be licensed to sail as master.

Interested nations are attempting—through the Inter-Governmental Maritime Consultative Organization (IMCO), a United Nations specialized agency—to unify laws, rules, and regulations; set internationally applicable standards for safety; and reduce or eliminate the pollution of the sea by ships. These efforts are reflected in the nautical science curricula.

The field of nautical science is in no way restricted to any one country, although the traditional seafaring nations are in the fore in developing the discipline. Most maritime-oriented nations have had for many years varying types of schools where nautical science is the primary discipline. In the United States there are five state academies (California, Maine, Massachusetts, New York, and Texas) and the United States Merchant Marine Academy at Kings Point, New York. In addition, most of the maritime unions operate training and up-grading schools for the benefit of their members. Although they are not all research oriented, these schools train seamen to operate and manage merchant ships. The United Kingdom has a number of schools, but most are operated by shipping companies. Denmark, Norway, Portugal, and Spain, among others, have schoolship programs, some of which are still using sailing ships. Japan has a nautical science and fisheries program at the University of Tokyo. National academies have been established in the Republic of Korea and Indonesia. The newest national academy is in Egypt and is designed to serve Middle Eastern countries.

There is, in addition, a limited amount of student exchange; students from nations without formal programs may attend other nations' academies. In few other fields is internationalization so complete. Nautical science is flourishing internationally, and the trend is toward expansion. Ships from all maritime countries are competing in waterborne commerce, and the problems and needs in training personnel are basically similar in all.

LELAND PEARSON

Levels and Programs of Study

Programs in nautical science usually require as a prerequisite a secondary education, preferably in the field of science, although mature students with related work experience may be admitted with lower educational qualifications. The usual award is a bachelor's degree (B.Sc.) or the equivalent. Programs deal with the essentials of the nautical sciences and consist primarily of classroom sessions, laboratory exercises, and in-ship training. Principal course content usually includes shipbuilding, naval architecture, stability, seamanship, spherical trigonometry, nautical astronomy, navigation, navigational aids, meteorology, oceanography, hydrography, marine biology, and marine law.

This section was based on UNESCO's *International Standard Classification of Education (ISCED): Three Stage Classification System, 1974* (Paris: UNESCO, 1974).

Major International and National Organizations

INTERNATIONAL

Association of Western European Shipbuilders
1 Frederiksgade
1265 Copenhagen K, Denmark

Baltic and International Maritime Conference (BIMCO)
19 Kristianiagade
2100 Copenhagen, Denmark
   (Members in 82 countries.)

Federation of National Association of Ship Brokers and Agents
% Institute of Chartered Shipbrokers
Baltic Exchange Chambers
25 Bury Street
London EC3A 5BA, England

Inter-Governmental Maritime Consultative Organization (IMCO)
Organisation intergovernmentale consultative de la navigation maritime (OMCI)
101–104 Piccadilly
London W1V 0AE, England
   A specialized agency of the United Nations, responsible for international cooperation on technical and certain legal matters affecting international shipping as well as prevention of pollution of the maritime environment by ships.

International Association for Rhine Ship Register
89 Schiedamsevest
Rotterdam 2, Netherlands

International Association of Classification Societies (IACS)
% Registro italiano navali
Casella Postale 1195
via Corsica
12–16128 Genoa, Italy

International Association of Dredging Companies (IADC)
21 Duinweg
The Hague 2011, Netherlands

International Association of Independent Tanker Owners (INTERTANKO)
P.O. Box 1452 Vika
Radhusgaten 25
Oslo 1, Norway

International Association of Lighthouse Authorities (IALA)
Association internationale de signalisation maritime (AISM)
43 avenue du Président Wilson
75116 Paris, France

International Association of Ports and Harbours
Kotohira-Kaikan Building
1 Kotohira-cho, Minato-ku
Tokyo 105, Japan
   Develops and promotes waterborne commerce; about 300 member port authorities and affiliated organizations in fifty nations.

International Cargo Handling Co-ordination Association (ICHCA)
Abford House
15 Wilton Road
London SW1V 1LX, England

International Chamber of Commerce
International Headquarters
38 cours Albert 1er
75008 Paris, France

International Chamber of Shipping
30–32 St. Mary Axe
London EC3A 8ET, England
   National association of private shipowners in twenty-two countries.

International Christian Maritime Association
150 route de Ferney
1211 Geneva 20, Switzerland

International Container Bureau
Bureau international des containers
38 cours Albert 1er
75008 Paris, France

International Council of Marine Industry
   Associations
31 Great Queen Street
London WC2B 5AD, England

International Hydrographic Organization
avenue Président J. F. Kennedy
Monte Carlo, Principality of Monaco

International Labour Organisation
CH 1211 Geneva 22, Switzerland

Internationale Maritime Committee (IMC)
Comité maritime international (CMI)
17 Borzestraat
B.2000 Antwerp, Belgium
   National associations in thirty-three countries.

International Maritime Pilots' Association
20 Peel Street
London W8, England

International Passenger Ship Association
   (IPSA)
Suite 631
17 Battery Place
New York, New York 10004 USA

International Shipowners' Association (INSA)
Sieroszewskiego Street 7
Gdynia, Poland

International Shipping Federation Limited
146–150 Minories
London EC3N 1ND, England
   National shipowners' associations in nineteen countries.

International Tanker Owners Pollution
   Federation Limited
41–43 Mincing Lane
London EC3R 7AE, England

International Transport Workers' Federation
Maritime House
Old Town, Clapham
London SW4 0JR, England

International Union for Inland Navigation
19 rue de la Presse
Brussels, Belgium

International Union of Marine Insurance
Stadthausquai 5
8001 Zurich, Switzerland

Latin American Shipowners' Association
   (LASA)
Asociación latino-americana de armadores
   (ALAMAR)
Casilla de Correos 767
Montevideo, Uruguay
   Promotes the development of the merchant marine in ten countries of Latin America.

Northern Shipowners' Defence Club
Radhusgaten 25
Oslo, Norway

Oil Companies International Marine Forum
12th Floor, Portland House
London SW1E 5BH, England

Organisation for Economic Co-operation and
   Development (OECD) Maritime Transport
   Committee
2 rue André Pascal
75775 Paris, France

Permanent International Association of
   Navigation Congresses (PIANC)
Association internationale permanente des
   congrès de navigation (AIPCN)
Résidence Palace, Quartier Jordaens
155 rue de la Loi
B-1040 Brussels, Belgium

Union internationale de la navigation fluviale
   (UINF)
International Union for Inland Navigators
19 rue de la Presse
Brussels 1, Belgium

NATIONAL

Australia:
   Australasian Steamship Owners'
      Federation
   Box 365 F, G.P.O.
   Melbourne, Victoria 3001
Belgium:
   Union des armateurs belges
   Belgian Shipowners' Association
   Lijnwaadmarkt 9
   B-2000 Antwerp
Canada:
   Canadian Shipowners' Association
   (National Organization of Canadian
      Ocean Shipping Operators)
   Suite 600
   620 St. James Street West
   Montreal, Quebec H3C 1C7

Dominion Marine Association
Suite 710
Blackburn Building
85 Sparks Street
Ottawa, Ontario K1P 5A7

Chile:
Liga marítima de Chile
avenida Errázuiz 471
Valparaiso

Denmark:
Danmarks rederiforening
Amaliegade 33
1256 Copenhagen K

Federal Republic of Germany:
Deutscher nautischer Verein von 1868
Palmaille 120
D-2000
Hamburg-Altona

Verband deutscher Reeder e.V.
P.O. Box 325
6 Esplanade
2 Hamburg 36

Finland:
Suomen laivanvarustajain yhdistys r. y.
Finlands redareförening
S. Kajen 10A
Helsinki 13

France:
Académie de marine
3 avenue Octave Gréard
F-75006 Paris

Comité central des armateurs de France
73 boulevard Haussmann
Paris 8e

Greece:
Union of Greek Shipowners
42 Mitropoleos Street
Athens

India:
Indian National Shipowners' Association
Scindia House, Ballard Estate
Bombay

Israel:
Chamber of Shipping of Israel
P.O. Box 1220
Haifa 31000

Italy:
Academia nazionale de marina
mercantile
via Garibaldi 4
I-16124 Genoa

Associazione armatori liberi
via Garibaldi 12, Genoa
viale Asia 3–9, 00144 Rome

Confederazione nazionale degli armatori
liberi
via dei Sabini 7
00187 Rome

Japan:
Japanese Shipowners' Association
Kaiun Building
6-4-2-chome
Hirakawa-cho, Chiyoda-ku
Tokyo

Nihon kokai gakkai
% Tokyo shosen daigaku
2-1-6 Etchujimamachi, Koto-ku
Tokyo 135

Netherlands:
Koninklijke Nederlandse
redersvereniging
Stationsweg 137
The Hague 2006

New Zealand:
New Zealand Shipowners' Federation
Incorporated
P.O. Box 1022
Wellington

Norway:
Norges rederforbund'
Radhusgaten 25
Oslo 1

Skibfartens arbeidsgiverforening
Radhusgaten 25
Oslo 1

Pakistan:
Pakistan Shipowners' Association
Ralli Brothers' Building
Talpur Road
Karachi 2

Portugal:
Grêmio dos armadores de marinha
mercante
Rua da Boa Vista No. 81–1 D
Lisbon 2

South Africa:
South African Shipowners' Association
P.O. Box 27
Cape Town

Soviet Union:
Scientific and Engineering Society of
Water Transport
Staropansky per. 3
Moscow

Spain:
Oficina central maritima (OFICEMA)
Ruiz de Alarcón 25
Madrid (14)

Sweden:
Sveriges redareförening
Avenyen 1
411 36 Göteborg

Turkey:
Türk armatörler deneği
Inonu Caddesi No. 31
Park Palas Apt. Daire 5, Taksim
Istanbul

United Kingdom:
Officers Merchant Navy Federation
133–137 Whitechapel High Street
London E1, England

Chamber of Shipping of the United
Kingdom
30–32 St. Mary Axe
London EC3A 8ET, England

United States:
American Institute of Merchant Shipping
(AIMS)
1625 K Street NW
Suite 1000
Washington, D.C. 20006

An extensive list of national associations having to do with nautical and naval science (including classification societies) may be found in:

Directory of Shipowners, Shipbuilders, and Marine Engineers. London: IPC Business Press, annual.

Principal Information Sources

GENERAL

Guides to the literature include:

Albion, R. G. H. *Naval and Maritime History: An Annotated Bibliography.* (4th ed.) Mystic, Connecticut: Muson Institute of American Maritime History and Maritime Historical Association, 1972.

Mariners' Museum, Newport News, Virginia. *Dictionary Catalog of the Library.* (9 vols.) Boston: Hall, 1964.

Metcalf, N. *Transportation Information Sources.* Detroit: Gale Research, 1968.

Schultz, C. R. (Comp.) *Bibliography of Maritime and Naval History Periodical Articles Published 1972–73.* Mystic, Connecticut: Maritime Historical Association, 1975. An annual publication supplementing the Albion work listed above.

Sources of Information in Transportation. Evanston, Illinois: Northwestern University Press, 1964.

Transportation Documentation Services. Evanston, Illinois: Transportation Center Library, Northwestern University, 1971.

General texts in the field of nautical science include:

Bross, S. R. *Ocean Shipping.* Cambridge, Maryland: Cornell Maritime Press, 1956.

Frankel, E. G., and Marcus, H. S. *Ocean Transportation.* Cambridge, Massachusetts: MIT Press, 1973.

McDowell, C. E., and Gibbs, H. M. *Ocean Transportation.* New York: McGraw-Hill, 1954.

Metcalfe, J. V. *Principles of Ocean Transportation.* New York: Simmons-Boardman, 1959.

Comparative education sources in the field include:

Borkar, S. R. "Employment and Training of Seamen in India: A Perspective Study." *Indian Shipping,* September 1974, pp. 17–21.

Borkar, S. R. "Training of Personnel for the Soviet Merchant Marine." *Motor Ship,* December 1974, p. 1421.

Current Literature in Traffic and Transportation. Evanston, Illinois: Northwestern University Transportation Center, twice monthly. Includes a section on merchant seamen, which lists periodical articles on training and education.

"Education for Maritime Needs." In *Research and Education for Maritime Research.* Washington, D.C.: Panel on Support for Maritime Research and Education, Maritime Transportation Research Board, Division of Engineering, National Research Council, 1973.

Grey, M. "Training Officers for a Fast-Changing Shipping Industry." *Fairplay,* January 16, 1975, p. 9.

Lewarn, B. "Australian Seafarers: Trained, Educated or ?" *Australian Transport,* September–October 1974, pp. 43–52.

Maritime Research Information Service. *M.R.I.S. Abstracts* (listed below, in section on current bibliographies). See section on maritime labor, education, and training.

Palmer, J. "All of One Company: British and Commonwealth Brings In All Aspects of Officer Training." *Fairplay,* January 4, 1973, pp. 31–32.

Randeri, J. D. "Training of Merchant Navy Officers." *Indian Shipping,* July 1974, pp. 15–17.

United States Congress, House Committee on Merchant Marine and Fisheries. *Maritime Education and Training.* Washington, D.C.: U.S. Government Printing Office, 1975.

Historical perspectives on the field include:

Barker, J. R., and Brandwein, R. *United States Merchant Marine in National Perspective.* Lexington, Massachusetts: Heath, 1970.

Hornell, J. *Water Transport: Origins and Early Evolution.* North Pomfret, Vermont: David & Charles, 1970. Reprint of 1946 edition.

May, W. E. *A History of Marine Navigation.* New York: Norton, 1973.

CURRENT BIBLIOGRAPHIES

British Ship Research Association. Journal of Abstracts. Wallsend, Northumberland, England: British Ship Research Association, 1946–. Abstracts naval engineering literature.

Hansa. Hamburg, Federal Republic of Germany: C. Schrödter, 1864–. Every other issue contains references to ship technology and operation literature.

Journal of Maritime Law and Commerce. Silver Spring, Maryland: Jefferson Law Book Company, 1969–. Includes a current annotated bibliography in each issue.

Marine Engineering/Shipbuilding Abstracts. London: Institute of Marine Engineers, 1938–. Abstracts literature on ship technology, design, and construction; references primarily from European papers and periodicals.

Maritime Research Information Service. *M.R.I.S. Abstracts.* Washington, D.C.: Maritime Administration, National Research Council, National Academy of Sciences, and National Academy of Engineering, 1970–. Semiannual abstracting service, with monthly issues beginning January 1975, listing research on shipping and ship design, construction, and operation.

Referativnyĭ zhurnal: Vodnyi transport. Moscow: Akademiia nauk, SSSR, Institut nauchnoĭ informatsii, 1962–. Abstracts literature relating to shipbuilding, shipping, waterways, and ports.

Ship Abstracts. Oslo: Ship Research Institute of Norway, 1973–. Scandinavian abstracting service on ship technology, ship operation, and ocean engineering; covers approximately 400 periodicals, report series, and technical papers from all over the world.

PERIODICALS

Journals important to the field of nautical science include *American Neptune, Canadian Shipping and Marine Engineering, Cargo Handling and Shipbuilding Quarterly* (Australia), *Cargo Systems International (ICHCA)* (UK), *Courrier des messageries maritime* (France), *Fairplay: International Shipping Weekly* (UK), *Hamburg Kurier* (FRG), *Hansa* (FRG), *Harbour and Shipping* (Canada), *Holland Shipbuilding, IMCO Bulletin* (UK), *Institute of Marine Engineers Transactions* (UK), *Institute of Navigation Journal* (UK), *International Shipbuilding Progress* (Netherlands), *Japan Shipbuilding and Marine Engineering, Journal de la marine marchande* (France), *Journal of Commerce* (UK), *Journal of Marine Research* (US), *Journal of Ship Research* (US), *Mar* (Chile), *Marina mercantile* (Italy), *Marine d'aujourd'hui* (France), *Marine Engineering/Log* (US), *Marine Engineers Review* (UK), *Marine Observer* (UK), *Marine Pollution Bulletin* (UK), *Mariner's Mirror* (UK), *Marine Technology* (US), *Maritime History* (UK), *Maritime Reporter and Engineering News* (US), *Maritime Studies and Management* (UK), *Morskoy flot* (USSR), *Motor Ship* (UK), *Nautica* (Netherlands), *Nautical Magazine* (UK), *Nautisk tidskrift* (Sweden), *Naval Architect* (UK), *Naval Engineers Journal* (US), *Navigation* (France), *Navigator* (Denmark), *Norwegian Shipping News, Polish Maritime News, Propulsor* (Poland), *Review of Maritime Transport* (UN), *Safety at Sea International* (UK), *Schiffbauforschung* (GDR), *Schiffstechnik* (FRG), *Schiff und Hafen* (FRG), *Sea Breezes* (UK), *Seewirtschaft* (GDR), *Ship and Boat International* (UK), *Ship Building and Transport Review International* (Netherlands), *Shipbuilding Marine Engineering International* (UK), *Seafarer's Log* (US), *Seaway Review* (US), *Shipping* (UK), *Shipping Digest* (US), *Shipping World and Shipbuilder* (UK), *Tanker and Bulk Carrier* (UK), *Work Boat* (US), *World Ports* (US).

More extensive listings of periodicals dealing with nautical science and naval architecture may be found in:

British Ship Research Association. Journal of Abstracts. Wallsend, Northumberland, England: British Ship Research Association, 1946–.

Ship Abstracts. Oslo: Ship Research Institute of Norway, 1973–.

ENCYCLOPEDIAS, DICTIONARIES, HANDBOOKS

De Kerchove, R. *International Maritime Dictionary.* (2nd ed.) New York: Van Nostrand Reinhold, 1961. A comprehensive dictionary in English with French and German equivalents.

Glosario de terminológica maritima interamericana. Washington, D.C.: Pan American Union, 1964. In Spanish, English, Portuguese, and French.

Glossary of Maritime Technical Terms. London: Intergovernmental Maritime Consultative Organization, 1963. In English, French, Spanish, and Russian.

McEwen, W. A., and Lewis, A. H. *Encyclopedia of Nautical Knowledge.* Cambridge, Maryland:

Cornell Maritime Press, 1953. Dictionary treatment of nautical science subjects in one volume.

Noel, J. V., and Buch, T. J. *Naval Terms Dictionary.* (2nd rev. ed.) Annapolis, Maryland: United States Naval Academy, 1966.

Segditsas, P. E. *Elsevier's Nautical Dictionary.* Amsterdam: Elsevier, 1965–66. In English, French, Italian, Spanish, and German.

United States Naval Oceanographic Office. *Naval Dictionary.* (2nd ed.) Washington, D.C.: U.S. Government Printing Office, 1969.

DIRECTORIES

Directories to study in the nautical sciences include:

United States Department of the Navy. *University Curricula in the Marine Sciences and Related Fields.* Washington, D.C.: U.S. Government Printing Office, 1971. Lists curricula from 134 United States academic institutions offering courses in marine-related fields.

World Guide to Universities. New York: Bowker; Pullach/Munich, Federal Republic of Germany: Verlag Dokumentation, 1972. Lists universities throughout the world having programs in naval science.

The World of Learning. London: Europa, annual. Provides comprehensive details on colleges and universities throughout the world.

Among the numerous general directories in the field are:

Directory of Shipowners, Shipbuilders and Marine Engineers. London: IPC Business Press, annual. Lists shipping companies and other marine services as well as international and national nautical associations.

International Shipping and Ship-Building Directory. (87th ed.) London: Benn Brothers, 1975. A trade directory listing shipping lines, shipbuilders, and other marine services internationally.

Jane's Fighting Ships. London: Macdonald, annual. The recognized authority on the navies of the world.

Jane's Freight Containers. London: Sampson Low, Marston, annual. Includes information on national port facilities, on ship operators, and on all aspects of containerization.

Jane's Ocean Technology. London: Jane's Yearbook; New York: Franklin Watts, annual.

Jane's Surface Skimmers, Hovercraft, and Hydrofoils. London: Sampson Low, Marston, annual. Worldwide survey of surface vehicles.

RESEARCH CENTERS, INSTITUTES, INFORMATION CENTERS

The National Maritime Research Center is at the U.S. Merchant Marine Academy at Kings Point, New York.

A list of naval architects, experiment tanks, and research centers in nineteen countries is found in the above-mentioned *Directory of Shipowners, Shipbuilders and Marine Engineers.*

NEGRO STUDENTS

See Access of Minorities: Blacks in the United States.

NEPAL, KINGDOM OF

Population: 11,555,000 (1973 midyear estimate). Student enrollment in primary school: 392,229; secondary school (academic, vocational, technical): 216,309; higher education: 20,637 (1975). Student enrollment in higher education as percentage of age group (18–22): 1.9%. Language of instruction: Nepali and English. Academic calendar: July to May, two semesters. Percentage of gross national product (GNP) expended on all education: 1.02%; higher education: .35%. [Except where otherwise indicated, figures are for 1973–74. Sources: Central Bureau of Statistics; Ministry of Education; Planning Division, Tribhuvan University.]

Education in Nepal in the period before 1768 was conducted within the teachings of two major religions of the country, Hinduism and Buddhism. Priests and other religious leaders were trained to propagate the faiths in established systems of institutions. During the Shah Dynasty (1768–1846), however, educational efforts deteriorated as the internal political condition became unstable. Although this period eventually saw the unification of the country, growing nationalism, and the introduction of a national language, the Buddhist educational structure especially suffered.

Nepalese education was not a government priority under the Ranas, a clan of despotic rulers who assumed the position of prime minister, which was inherited within the clan for more than one hundred years (1846 to 1951), while the powers of the legitimate king were held in abeyance. The educational system, which included Tri-Chandra College (1918), was similar to the education introduced by Britain into India in the nineteenth century. However, government policy limited facilities so that by 1951 there were only two colleges in the country, Tri-Chandra College and the Sanskrit College.

After the introduction of democracy in 1951, higher education flourished. The number of colleges increased to thirty-three in 1961 and forty-nine by 1970. In 1959 Tribhuvan University started functioning; and all colleges previously affiliated with Indian universities such as Patna University became its constituent colleges. In 1969 the government, the univeristy, and the Ford Foundation in the United States established the Center for Economic Development and Administration (CEDA). The center provides in-service training and career development for the public and private sectors and conducts applied research.

Before 1970 there were no well-defined national policies and objectives for education. The new colleges were established without consideration for regional needs and potentials, and the limited financial resources were therefore misused. Moreover, because almost all books for higher education were written by foreigners, there were very few books dealing with the problems of the country. As a result, educated youth had more knowledge of other nations than Nepal and were ignorant of the problems of their own country. The government had been aware of these negative trends in higher education for some time and had felt the need for change. Suggestions for improvement were sought from the Nepal National Educational Planning Commission in 1954, from a UNESCO team in 1962, from the Nepal All-Round National Education Committee in 1966, from the National Education Advisory Council in 1968, and from a number of other experts in education. The political change of 1960, a change which created the "partyless *Panchayat* Democracy" (a five-tier administrative pyramid with the king at its head and *panchayats* at village, district, and national levels), also gave urgency to the need for change in the system. Thus, the National Education System Plan was introduced in 1970. It covers the development of the higher education system through 1976 under the direction of the national university.

National Educational Policy and Legal Basis of Educational System

The National Education System Plan is "primarily aimed at counteracting the elitist bias of the inherited system of education by linking it more effectively to productive enterprises and egalitarian principles" (*National Education System Plan*, 1971, p. i). The plan calls for unifying education in one productive system that serves the country's needs and aspirations. The concept of education as a means to attaining white-collar employment is being replaced by a concept that regards education as an investment in human resources for the development of the country.

Priorities under the policy include special emphasis on vocational instruction, balancing quantitative growth with qualitative improvement, and increasing facilities in remote areas. A significant change in higher education is manifest in the curricula, which have been visibly altered to reflect an applied and practical bias and thus meet the manpower needs of the country. Private postsecondary institutions have been amalgamated into the university; yet all private teaching staff have retained positions in their institutions. Technical training institutes under the direction of different ministries are integrated into the university, but the ministries retain responsibility for in-service training. In higher education one goal is to decrease enrollments in general disciplines from 80 percent to 40 percent and to increase enrollments in technical studies from 20 percent to 60 percent. Under the plan, the target for enrollments in third-level programs is 19 percent of all students with secondary education.

Tribhuvan University was established under the Tribhuvan University Act of 1959. New legislation encompassing the major changes in higher education is contained in the Tribhuvan University Act of 1971.

Types of Institutions

Higher education is undergoing reorganization to meet the manpower requirements of the country; its aim has been to maintain a high standard of teaching. No agency other than the institutes set up for each major discipline under the university is allowed to impart higher education. In 1974–75 there were seventy-seven campuses affiliated to twelve institutes. These institutes were formed by amalgamation of private colleges and government training institutes; each may have a central campus at the main university location or in any other part of the country. As the manpower demand of the nation changes, institutes can be created or deactivated. Efforts are made to locate them close to active national development work.

Education is offered at four levels: certificate, diploma, degree, and doctoral research. Four institutes have courses leading to the certificate level: the Institute of Forestry, the Institute of Engineering, the Institute of Medicine, and the Institute of Applied Science and Technology. Two offer courses at the certificate and diploma levels: the Institute of Law and the Institute of Agriculture and Animal Science. The Institute of Education and the Institute of Business Administration, Commerce and Public Administration have programs leading to the degree level. Three institutes give instruction at the research level: the Institute of Humanities and Social Sciences, the Institute of General Science, and the Institute of Sanskrit. The Institute of Nepal and Asian Studies accepts students at the research level only.

Relationship with Secondary Education

Secondary education is of seven years' duration and is divided into lower secondary schooling of four years and secondary schooling of three years. The lower secondary level is designed to build character by cultivating loyalty to the king and the country and to provide prevocational education. The secondary level is intended to create useful citizens by emphasizing vocational education. This instruction is conducted in three types of schools: general high schools, vocational high schools, and Sanskrit high schools. All of the schools provide some vocational training, but more emphasis is placed on vocational education in the vocational high schools than in the Sanskrit high schools. Students fifteen years of age and above may sit for the school-leaving examination. Successful completion of the examination leads to the award of the School Leaving Certificate (SLC).

Primary education, designed only to create literacy, is of three years' duration. Although there is a movement to make primary education compulsory, it has not yet been accomplished. Beginning with the fiscal year 1975–76, primary education was free throughout the kingdom.

Admission Requirements

Under the National Education System Plan, the Ministry of Education authorizes the number of students to be admitted to the institutes on the basis of manpower needs. Entrance into certificate-level instruction is based on possession of the SLC and successful completion of an entrance examination. Admission to diploma-level study is based on possession of a certificate and successful completion of an entrance examination, while study at the degree level requires possession of a diploma and successful completion of an entrance examination. A degree is required to conduct doctoral research.

Administration and Control

The National Education Committee co-ordinates the functions of Tribhuvan University and the Ministry of Education; it also provides policy guidelines under the National Education System Plan. The committee is guided by the king or a person nominated by the king. The minister of education holds the position of chairman of the National Education Committee (NEC). The vice-chancellor of the university is a member of the committee. National manpower needs are communicated to the university by the National Planning Commission and the Ministry of Education.

The university is an autonomous body which functions within the guidelines, rules, and policies of the National Education Committee. It has a decentralized administrative structure under which each institute is vested with adequate administrative and financial powers.

The king is chancellor of the university, while the minister of education is pro-chancellor ex officio. The executive head of the university is the vice-chancellor, who is assisted by the rector in academic matters, and in the coordination of the institutes, and by the registrar in fiscal and administrative matters.

The university council, composed of not more than fifty members, has the power to consider and make recommendations on the entire program of the university. The council approves the annual university research program and academic programs, makes academic awards, inspects the institutes, and acts on reports received. Among the members of the council are all chief administrative officers ex officio, as well as five representatives of graduates and two teacher representatives. The chancellor may nominate twenty members, among whom are members of the National *Panchayat*, government employees, representatives of the business community, journalists, students, donors, and distinguished persons.

A technical committee (*prabidhik samiti*) is charged with overseeing academic and policy-related administrative matters. It is comprised of the vice-chancellor as chairman; the rector as vice-chairman; the registrar as secretary; the deans; the secretary of education, who is directly responsible to the minister of education; and a few nominated members.

Each of the twelve institutes is headed by a dean, who is appointed for a period of three years by the chancellor on the recommendation of the vice-chancellor. Each institute has a faculty board, which prepares the curriculum and sets requirements for admission and examinations. There are also subject committees for the different subjects of each institute. These committees are responsible for advising and suggesting changes and developing, reviewing, and amending curricula, subject to approval by the faculty board.

Programs and Degrees

The central administration, which is headed by the vice-chancellor at the university level and by the dean at the institute level, is responsible for the establishment and maintenance of academic standards. Fields of study correspond to the disciplines taught at each institute. The university offers programs at four levels, each lower level being a prerequisite for entrance into the next level. The certificate granted requires two years of study with satisfactory progress and successful completion of final examinations at the end of each semester; the diploma generally requires an additional two years of study with satisfactory internal assessment and successful final examinations. The degree is conferred after an additional three years of study, success in the semester examinations, and completion of the National Development Service (a one-year period of compulsory social service in rural areas); the doctoral degree is awarded after completion of a research program.

Not all institutes administer programs at all four award levels, nor is the duration of time required to receive an award for a particular level completely uniform. It may differ from institute to institute, depending on the nature of training.

Two new aspects of the curriculum, introduced by the plan, are internal assessment and semester examinations. Internal assessment, which counts for 20 to 50 percent of the program grade at all award levels, is a series of short tests given during the semester. The semester examinations replace the final examination which was previously given at the end of two years of study and which registered failure rates as high as 90 percent. Another new aspect is the compulsory National Development Service. Under this scheme, students who have completed the first year of the degree program spend one year working in rural areas (in an education service or a health, agriculture, or construction corps) for national development. According to the plan, this service will also be made compulsory for the second year of diploma programs.

Financing and Student Financial Aid

Beginning with the fiscal year 1975–76, full responsibility for the financing of higher education was taken over by the government.

Fifty percent of the students studying in institutes that offer technical programs are given scholarships. There is provision for outstanding students in all institutes to receive merit scholarships. Students from remote areas are given encouragement for higher education through special aid, and free tuition and fees are provided to the poor. Financial aid also is available from private donors.

Requests to foreign governments for scholarships are handled by the Foreign Aid Division of the Ministry of Finance on the basis of estimates determined by the Manpower Division of the National Planning Commission. Efforts are made to secure scholarships in disciplines for which the country lacks educational facilities. The selection of students for foreign scholarships is the responsibility of the Ministry of Education; individuals who complete study under foreign scholarship are required to work five years for the government.

Student Social Background and Access to Education

Any school graduate who fulfills the admission requirements has access to higher education. Although there is provision for scholarships and for free tuition and fees to students, students in remote areas do not yet have the same opportunity for higher education as those in urban areas. Of the total number of graduates of the university, 10,887 (or over 50 percent) came from the Katmandu Valley; 791 were from an economically well-off area, the eastern Terai; and only 17 were from the mountainous areas covering the entire west.

Equality of opportunity is extended to women and minorities. Coeducation is encouraged, although there is one campus exclusively for girls. Of the 3582 female students enrolled in higher education in 1974–75, 1444 were at the campus for women.

Teaching Staff

There are four teaching ranks in the university system for those with academic qualifications: professor, reader, lecturer, and assistant lecturer. Three other positions—instructor, deputy instructor, and assistant instructor—are staffed by those who do not have the academic qualifications suitable for the post of assistant lecturer but who have a vocational background.

All appointments are made by the University Service Commission, whose chairman and one other member are nominated by the chancellor; one member is from the Public Service Commission; and the rector, the registrar, and the appropriate dean are members ex officio. The registrar acts as secretary of the commission.

Research Activities

The Research Division, which is under the direct authority of the rector's office, coordinates the research activities of the institutes, foreign scholars, and government agencies. Research financed by Tribhuvan University is being conducted on such current educational problems as the semester examinations, the impact of the introduction of the semester system on higher education, the trends in examination results and their impact on enrollment, and the physical and educational facilities of the campuses.

At the institute level, there are research committees to promote research on the campuses. Research is being conducted in the fields of botany, zoology, and chemistry in the Institute of Science; political science, economics, history, culture, Hindi, geography, *panchayat* (national ideology), and Nepali in the Institute of Humanities and Social Sciences; and sociology, anthropology, and Nepal studies in the Institute of Nepal and Asian Studies.

The National Planning Commission may also finance research projects.

Current Problems and Trends

The National Education System Plan for 1971–1976 delineates in detail the problems of Nepalese education at the beginning of this decade. In the middle 1970s some of the basic problems of education are the trend toward high enrollments in general disciplines and the lack of textbooks and physical facilities, well-trained and properly oriented teachers, and sufficient financing.

Although the National Education System Plan is an attempt at extending education to the majority of citizens in the country, education will not reach all eligible children. The enrollment targets envisioned by the plan are as follows: primary education, 64 percent of all eligible children of the age group six to nine; lower secondary education, 40 percent of all children with primary education; secondary education, 50 percent of all children with lower secondary education; higher education, 19 percent of students with second-

ary education. This means an enrollment in higher education of some 3 percent of the relevant age group.

Against the background of an age-old educational system in Nepal, the current national system can be considered an innovation in itself. It has brought radical change to the technical, financial, and administrative aspects of learning. The new system contains the provision that degree-level students work in rural areas for one year under the National Development Service. This provision, which gives a student the opportunity to acquire first-hand information on conditions in the country, makes education more practical and attuned to the needs of the nation. Another noteworthy aspect of the system is enlargement of the teacher-training program. This is effected by the opening of new campuses, the introduction of short-term training for full-time teachers, and the encouragement of a new role for teachers as participants in the learning process rather than as deliverers of *ex cathedra* lectures (Bhatt and Mohsin, 1975, p. 98).

By January 1975 seventeen districts of seventy-five in the country had come under the implementation of the plan. It is envisioned that by December 1976 the plan will be in effect throughout the country.

Relationship with Industry

Under the new system, each faculty board contains representatives from employing organizations, including those in the industrial sector. The central campus of the Institute of Applied Science and Technology is in Dharan, adjacent to the industrial town of Biratnagar. There has been an effort to establish a closer relationship with industry by organizing campuses in industrial towns.

International Cooperation

Nepal has received cooperation in education from various governments and international agencies, notably India, the United Kingdom, the United States of

America, and the United Nations Development Programme (UNDP). Nepal is a member of the Colombo Plan for Cooperative Economic Development in South and Southeast Asia. Under the plan, Nepalese may study abroad in higher technology programs; equipment also is provided for domestic technical training and research.

[Research Division, Tribhuvanan University.]

Educational Associations

Nepal College and University
 Teachers' Association
Saraswati Sadan
Katmandu, Nepal

Nepal National Federation of Students
10/250 Pyukha Tole
P.O. Box 379
Katmandu, Nepal

Bibliography

Agrawal, G. R. "Higher Education for Business in Developing Nations: A Proposed Model for Nepal." Unpublished doctoral dissertation, Texas Tech University, Lubbock, Texas, 1973.

Aryal, K. R. Education for the Development of Nepal. Katmandu: Shanti Prakashan, 1970.

Bhatt, D. D., and Mohsin, M. "Restructuring the Educational System in Nepal." Prospects, 1975, 5(1), 96–100.

The National Education System Plan for 1971–1976. Katmandu: Ministry of Education, 1971.

Reed, B., and Reed, M. J. Nepal in Transition. Pittsburgh: University of Pittsburgh Press, 1968.

Sharma, C. L. "Education in Nepal—Its Problems and Prospects." Journal of Abstracts in International Education, Fall/Winter 1972–73, 3(1), 22–27.

Wood, H. B. The Development of Education in Nepal. Washington, D.C.: U.S. Government Printing Office, 1965.

See also: Archives: Africa and Asia, National Archives of; South Asia: Regional Analysis.

NEPAL NATIONAL
FEDERATION OF STUDENTS

The Nepal National Federation of Students (NNFS), the oldest student organization in Nepal, aims to rid the country of illiteracy by encouraging a system of universal, free, and compulsory education and to promote social justice by eliminating national unemployment and social inequalities. It also attempts to obtain better health care and living facilities for all Nepalese students; promotes international solidarity in struggles against imperialism, colonialism, and neo-colonialism; encourages unity in the interest of national liberation; and seeks friendship and cooperation with other students through membership in the International Union of Students and the World Federation of Democratic Youth. Active membership, open to all students fifteen years of age or older, numbered 15,370 as of 1976.

The organizational structure of NNFS consists of a central executive and a national council as well as district committees and units throughout the country. Funding for NNFS is derived primarily from membership dues and donations from the business community.

NNFS conducts tours within Nepal and abroad and sponsors sports and cultural events. It offers public programs on the problems and needs of students in all levels of education. In addition, it organizes seminars, symposia, meetings, and rallies on social issues such as illiteracy and unemployment. NNFS actively participates in social service programs, procures scholarships for needy students, and vigorously works for the improvement of medical and transportation facilities within the country.

NNFS limits its publishing to occasional bulletins.

10/250 Pyukha Tole
P.B. No. 379
Kathmandu, Nepal

NETHERLANDS ANTILLES

Population: 240,700 (1976 estimate). Student enrollment in primary school: 39,900

(19,600 females); secondary school: 20,300 (10,800 females); higher education: 105 (36 females); nonuniversity education: approximately 800; university education abroad: approximately 1000. Language of instruction: Dutch. Percentage of national budget expended, on education: approximately 30%. [Figures are for 1976.]

The Netherlands Antilles, an autonomous part of the Netherlands, consist of two groups of islands: Aruba, Curaçao, and Bonaire, located close to the South American mainland; and Saba, Saint Eustatius, and Saint Martin, located in the Leeward Islands, some 500 miles to the north. The Netherlands Antilles have been exposed to many cultures. Although Dutch is the official language, Spanish and English are widely spoken. There is also a local dialect, which incorporates traces of Dutch, French, English, Portuguese, Spanish, and various African languages.

Education is not compulsory, but the educational system is well developed and there is little illiteracy. There are 31 government and 114 private primary schools with an enrollment of 39,900 students. The 17 government and 50 private—but generally government-subsidized—secondary schools enroll 21,300 students. Graduates from secondary school receive a secondary school diploma.

There are limited facilities for university-level higher education on the islands of Curaçao and Aruba. Nonuniversity higher education, which consists of teacher training and vocational training, is available in programs of varying length. Three-year teacher training programs lead to teacher qualifications for teachers in infant or other schools; head teachers for infant schools are trained in an additional one-year program. Training for teachers in general and technical schools lasts four years. A business administration program of three and a half years' duration leads to a certificate equivalent to a Bachelor of Arts degree. The School for Secondary Administrative Education offers a three-

year program of secretarial and accounting training, while the School for Personnel, Social and Educational Work awards a secondary vocational certificate after three years.

Students generally attend higher education institutions abroad, in Canada, Colombia, the Netherlands, and the United States. In 1976, approximately 740 government and 260 private scholarships were awarded to students from the Netherlands Antilles for study abroad.

[Information supplied by R. W. A. Naaldijk, Acting Director, Department of Education, Curaçao, Netherlands Antilles.]

NETHERLANDS, CENTRAL ARCHIVES OF

See Archives: Northern Europe, National Archives of.

NETHERLANDS, KINGDOM OF THE

Population: 13,491,000. Student enrollment in primary school: 1,535,000; secondary school: 1,167,000 full time and 102,000 part time; higher education—university: 113,000 full time; higher education—nonuniversity: 90,000 full time and 54,000 part time. Student enrollment in higher education as percentage of age group (20–24): 21.2%. Language of instruction: Dutch. Academic calendar: September to July. Percentage of gross national product (GNP) expended on education: 8.2%; university education: 1.8%. [Figures are for 1973.]

Higher education in the Netherlands began in 1575, when the prince of Orange rewarded the town of Leiden for its heroism during the Spanish siege of the city in 1573–74 by establishing the first Dutch university at Leiden. In 1614 a second university had its inception as an academy in the city of Groningen, and a third was established in Utrecht in 1636. All three achieved state university status in the nineteenth century. Also founded during the seventeenth century was the *Athenaeum il-*

lustre (1632), which became the municipal university, the University of Amsterdam, in 1877.

In the years between the founding of the first universities in the sixteenth and seventeenth centuries and the last quarter of the nineteenth century, no new universities were established; however, the period was marked by increasing concern for education, and a number of institutions offering professional education at different levels were established. The constitution of 1848 included a provision for free education; that is, any group—regardless of political or religious predilection—could found a school without governmental approval. The provision gave rise to a struggle for financial equality, which was finally resolved in 1917, when a constitutional amendment led to equal government financial support for public and private nonuniversity institutions. The private universities received the same support in 1968.

The last quarter of the nineteenth century and first quarter of the twentieth were marked by an unprecedented growth in higher education. In 1880 the Free University, Amsterdam was founded on Calvinist principles; in 1905 the first state technological university, the Delft University of Technology, combining several smaller professional schools, was established. In 1913 the Netherlands School of Economics, a private, nondenominational institution, was established at Rotterdam, and in 1918 the State Agricultural University, originally founded in 1876 as a national college, achieved university status. In 1923 the private Catholic University of Nijmegen was opened; and in 1927 the second university-level school of economics and second Catholic institution of higher education opened in Tilburg; it became the *Katholieke hogeschool Tilburg* (Tilburg University) in 1963.

In the years directly preceding and following World War II, there was a hiatus in the expansion of education, but since the mid 1950s there has been a consider-

able increase in institutions as well as in efforts to make education more responsive to the manpower needs of the country. Two new state technological universities— the Technological University of Eindhoven (1956) and Twente University of Technology at Enschede (1961)—were established. In 1973 the Rotterdam School of Economics and the State Medical School Rotterdam (1966) merged into Erasmus University of Rotterdam. In 1975 the State Medical School of Maastricht was established as the first component of a new state university. In addition, many new technical and other specialized colleges have opened to provide degree programs at the postsecondary level.

A series of student revolts in 1968 and 1969 resulted in the passing in 1970 of a new law, *Wet universitaire bestuurshervorming,* to democratize decision making at the university level. The effect of the law has been to accord students, junior staff members, and technical and clerical personnel influence on the various councils and committees and to give them a voice in shaping higher education policy.

National Educational Policy

In a report entitled *Government Tertiary Education Policy* (*Het overheidsbeleid inzake het tertiair onderwijs,* 1971), the Commission on the Development of Higher Education, a governmental commission charged with reviewing the long-range growth of higher education in the Netherlands, outlined four goals that should serve as the basis of national education policies: (1) providing citizens with the ability to exercise their civil duties in addition to the responsibilities of their professional lives, (2) advancing personal development, (3) providing the educated and skilled manpower necessary for the welfare of the nation, and (4) providing a source of innovation for society. The commission is preparing recommendations for policies and programs that will help meet all of these goals.

Legal Basis of Educational System

Governmental authority over education in general emanates from Article 208 of the constitution of 1917. Among specific laws concerning higher education are (1) the University Education Act (*Wet op het wetenschappelijk onderwijs,* 1960), which establishes the general provisions governing universities, including their organizational structure, admission requirements, faculty ranks, budget procedures, and operation of the academic council; (2) the Academic Statute (*Academisch statuut,* 1963), which stipulates the fields of study to be offered by universities and establishes the general requirements for obtaining degrees; (3) the Further Education Act (*Wet op het voortgezet onderwijs,* 1963), which governs higher vocational education; (4) the University Administration Reform Act (*Wet universitaire bestuurshervorming,* 1970), which democratizes the decision-making process in universities; and (5) the Act on Reform of University Education (*Wet herstructurering wetenschappelijk onderwijs,* 1975), which for the first time legally limits the duration of university programs and the number of years that students may be matriculated.

Types of Institutions

Higher education is provided in public and private universities and higher vocational institutions. Public higher education is provided by the state or the municipalities. Private educational institutions (a large number of them are denominational) enjoy financial equality with public institutions and have to comply with the general rules laid down in the University Education Act of 1960 and the Further Education Act of 1963. A number of institutions which do not fall within the competence of either of these acts are aided by grants under a separate regulation. Although public universities do not possess as much autonomy as private universities, they are independent in university administration and management and in promoting university education and research.

University institutions are legally distinguished as *universiteiten* (universities) and *hogescholen* (university-level institutions). The main difference between them is that a university must have at least three faculties, including a faculty of medicine or a faculty of mathematics and natural sciences. In this article both kinds of institutions are referred to as universities. Their administrative structures, courses, examinations, and degrees have been established in the University Education Act (1960) and in the Academic Statute (1963).

There are eight state universities. Four are general: the State University of Leiden (1575), the State University of Groningen (1614), the State University of Utrecht (1636), and Erasmus University of Rotterdam (1973). Three are technological: Delft University of Technology (1905), the Technological University of Eindhoven (1956), and Twente University of Technology (1961) at Enschede. And one is agricultural: the State Agricultural University at Wageningen (1918). There are three private universities: the Free University, Amsterdam (1880); the Catholic University of Nijmegen (1923); and Tilburg University (1927). In addition, there is one municipal university: the University of Amsterdam (1877).

Approximately 350 higher vocational institutions have their legal basis in the Further Education Act of 1963. Most are small, with an enrollment of 500 students or less; and most are private, often denominational. Higher vocational schools include sociopedagogical and teacher training institutions, technical colleges, and schools of agriculture, business, and arts.

Relationship with Secondary Education

Education is compulsory from the age of six to fifteen, although students generally complete secondary education between the ages of sixteen and nineteen.

Primary schools offer six years of general education (ages six to twelve). Full-time secondary education (ages twelve to eighteen) consists of three types of schools:

six-year university preparatory schools, schools offering four- or five-year programs of general education, and vocational schools offering four-year programs on a lower or a higher level. These schools come under the Further Education Act (1963), which promotes the merger of the schools into a single institution (*Scholengemeenschap*) as well as the creation of a common curriculum for the first three years of study, called orientation years (*brugjaren*).

The university preparatory schools are subdivided into two types, the *gymnasium* and the *atheneum*. The *gymnasium* has a mathematics and science track, with Latin and Greek as obligatory subjects. The second track offers a classical education. The *atheneum* also has a mathematics and science track but does not require Greek and Latin. The second track in the *atheneum* emphasizes modern languages and subjects such as economics. Certificates from all these programs qualify students for university admission.

The five-year programs of general education and the four-year higher-level vocational schools give access to nonuniversity higher education institutions. Vocational education on the secondary level is provided at agricultural, commercial, nautical, sociopedagogic, and technical schools and at schools for domestic science and kindergarten teachers. For the great majority of graduates the secondary vocational school is the last stage in full-time education. Only a small number of students continue their education in higher vocational institutions.

Admission Requirements

Admission to the universities has generally been open to all who have a secondary school-leaving certificate from a preuniversity school and who have the prerequisite courses for their intended fields of study. Graduates of higher vocational schools are also eligible for admission to universities, as are persons aged twenty-five or over who do not necessarily have the requisite secondary education but who can demonstrate through an examination that they have the general knowledge and ability to handle and benefit from a university education. In 1972, when student demands for university places increased beyond the institutions' capacity to accommodate them, admission to certain faculties was restricted by the provisions of the Registration of Student Authorization Act. According to this act, which will be in force until 1977, places in overcrowded faculties will be assigned by a lottery system allocating some influence to grades on the school-leaving certificate. Applicants who are not selected may appeal to the university admissions clearinghouse, which will administer the lottery.

Admission to higher vocational institutions requires a diploma from a five- or six-year program or from a four-year higher vocational course. The university and other postsecondary institutions have specific requirements regarding programs of study at the secondary level; however, the universities must enroll all qualified students, while the nonuniversity institutions may restrict their admissions.

Administration and Control

Most of the universities are public, while most of the higher vocational schools are private. Both public education and private education, however, are state supported and to this extent fall under the jurisdiction of the minister of education and science. The agricultural institutions, however, come under the authority of the minister of agriculture and fisheries. The relevant ministry is responsible for authorizing all new institutions, creating new faculties within existing institutions, approving budgets, and ensuring that the institutions adhere to their specific statutes.

A Netherlands Universities Council functions on the national level to form a link both between the individual universities and the *hogescholen* and between them and the community. The council also functions as a coordinating and advisory agency to the minister of education and science. Either on request or on its own initiative, the council may make recommendations to the crown or the ministers on behalf of the university institutions represented on the council.

Each institution is represented on the council by three members, although they have only one vote. One of the members is the *rector magnificus* (head of the university); the two others are elected by the university council (the highest administrative body within the university). The remainder of the members of the council are the chairman, the vice-chairman, and ten others appointed by the crown.

In 1975 the minister of education and science created a new Higher Education Council to perform similar functions for the higher vocational schools. The council consists of one representative from each of the approximately 350 institutions. It is viewed as part of the ministry's effort to merge all sectors of higher education into a single administrative structure.

Responsibility for internal operation and administration of the universities is established by the 1970 Act on the Reform of University Governance, which decentralized and democratized decision-making authority. In accordance with the 1970 act, universities are governed by a university council and the council's board of governors, which has the responsibility for the application of government laws. Membership of the university council cannot exceed forty. A minimum of five sixths of the council membership must represent the university community in the following proportions: one third must be selected from the academic staff for at least two-year terms, one third from the student body for at least one-year terms, and one third from the technical and clerical personnel for at least two-year terms. Nonuniversity members constitute the remaining one sixth of the council's membership. In public universities these members are appointed by the minister of education and science after receiving recommendations from the council, while in private universities appointments are made by the founding organization.

The university council (1) prepares budget recommendations for ministerial approval, (2) draws up institutional development plans, (3) establishes administrative regulations, and (4) establishes guidelines for the organization and coordination of teaching and research activities. The board of governors is responsible for the daily operation of the university. Its members are partly elected by the university council from the academic staff and partly appointed by the crown or, in the case of private universities, by the founding association.

At middle-management level, administration is in the hands of the faculty council and the faculty executive committee. (In technological institutions the faculties are referred to as departments. The term *faculty* here includes both designations.) The duties of the faculty council include organizing and coordinating teaching and research, determining the curriculum, arranging for examinations, setting up teaching and research units, and submitting to the university council a list of candidates recommended for appointment as professors and assistant professors (readers). The council recommends the appointment to the minister, or, in private universities, to the foundation.

At least half of the members of the faculty council itself are representatives of the academic staff. The remaining members are elected by students and members of the nonacademic staff. The faculty council elects from among its numbers a faculty executive committee of, at most, five members. The committee conducts the day-to-day affairs, prepares board meetings, and implements the decisions. The chairman of the faculty executive committee (the dean) is also chairman of the faculty council and is elected from among professors and assistant professors. All the deans form the committee of deans, which draws up a list of nominations for the appointment of the *rector magnificus* for submission to the crown and advises on matters of teaching and research.

The smallest organizational unit in the university is the teaching and research unit embracing all personnel and students contributing to teaching and research. The executive committee of the unit establishes the duties of the members of the teaching and research unit and outlines an annual research program, which requires the approval of the faculty council. The committee consists of the unit's tenured academic staff and of representatives of the nontenured faculty and the technical and clerical staff and students. The number of representatives is determined by the faculty council.

In higher vocational education, the responsibility for the institution rests entirely with the minister in state institutions or—in the case of private institutions—with the board of the foundation or association that runs the institution. There are as yet no statutory provisions for the formal right of codetermination of principals, teachers, students, and technical staff.

Programs and Degrees

The universities may be distinguished on the basis of their fields of study. Technological universities provide programs in architecture, engineering, general sciences, and various branches of technology. Arts and sciences universities offer programs in the humanities, economics, law, medicine (sometimes including dentistry), mathematics and sciences, social sciences, theology, and veterinary medicine. The agricultural university offers programs in agriculture, forestry, dairy and food science, horticulture, plant pathology, rural economy and sociology, and soil science.

The first university degree nominally requires five or six years of study, during which (generally at the end of three years) a student must pass a *kandidaatsexamen* to continue studies; this examination does not result in receipt of a degree. University work culminates in receipt of a *doctorandus* degree (Drs.) after passage of the *doctoraal examen;* students of law, however, receive instead a *Meester in de rechten* (Mr.), while

students in agricultural and engineering sciences receive the title *Ingenieur* (Ir.).

In order to practice, students in medicine, dentistry, pharmacy, and veterinary medicine must pass an additional professional examination after one or two years of further training. There are no formal doctoral programs provided at Dutch universities. Students who receive the *doctorandus* or equivalent may submit a research project to a department. On acceptance of the project, the student is assigned a supervisor. After a thesis has been accepted and defended, the doctoral degree is awarded.

The Act on Reform of University Education (1975) is expected to bring about important changes in the duration of study. The objectives of the act are (1) to reduce the length of first-degree programs, (2) to establish a maximum duration of enrollment, and (3) to create better conditions for university research.

Thus, university degree programs will consist of an orientation year (which students may attend for two years). Three additional years (sometimes four years) lead to the *doctoraal examen.* The act also introduces a year of research after the *doctoraal examen* for graduates who qualify. Very able graduates may be appointed as research assistants for a maximum period of four years.

The length of higher vocational training courses is subject to a statutory maximum for each sector, varying from two to five years. The length of the course and the subjects for each sector are determined by the minister, who is usually advised by committees composed of representatives of teachers and of nonacademic groups (particularly industrial groups).

Technical colleges provide programs in the same fields as those offered at technological universities. Such programs last four years, with the final year devoted to practical work, and lead to the title *ingenieur* (ing.). Other technical colleges provide programs of two to three years' duration. For example, a student may become qualified as a laboratory analyst in two years or as a laboratory assistant in three years. Sociopedagogic institutions offer four-year full-time and part-time programs for community workers. Teacher training institutions include forty-five training schools for nursery school teachers and ninety-three colleges for primary school teachers. Both have programs lasting three years. Seven new independent institutions, in cooperation with one or more universities, offer training for secondary school teachers in programs lasting four to four and a half years. There are also business schools, art schools, nautical schools, and agricultural schools offering programs of varying duration.

Financing

The central government provides the financial support necessary to operate both the universities and the higher vocational schools, whether public or private. The University Education Act provides for annual budgets to be submitted by the universities. The budgets must be supported by financial schedules—also submitted annually—which contain a forecast of financial developments during the subsequent four years. On the basis of these, the ministers prepare a general financial schedule. In addition, the universities are now required to submit development plans once every four years, containing a statement on research and teaching policy.

The planning procedure for higher vocational education has been in existence since 1968. Each year the minister approves a plan containing the names of institutions eligible for financial support in the subsequent three calendar years.

Student Financial Aid

Students and their parents receive various forms of financial assistance to enable them to meet their expenses for higher education. Assistance includes family allowances, tax relief, and—where the parental income is below a certain level—student grants. Although in 1975 only about 10 percent of the students qualified

for maximum grants, and about 60 percent did not qualify for any grants, beginning in 1977 all students will receive a minimum annual grant applicable to both university and higher vocational studies.

Student Social Background and Access to Education

Prior to the Further Education Act of 1963, access to the universities was limited largely to students from the *gymnasium* and the science programs of the *atheneum,* but since the implementation of the act in 1968, all students from preuniversity schools have equal access. As the act also stimulated the individualizing of curricula and as admission to the university has also been opened to those holding diplomas from higher vocational schools, incoming university students now represent a more heterogeneous educational background.

There has also been an increase in part-time students, particularly in sociopedagogic schools, technical colleges, and secondary teacher training institutions. The universities, however, have not developed many part-time programs because Dutch universities do not have the right to oblige students to attend lectures as a prerequisite to examinations, although they have the right to demand evidence of practical work.

In humanities and social sciences such practical work is of minor importance. In these departments part-time students, with employers' cooperation, may prepare themselves for the examinations without particular facilities of the university. This situation is far from satisfactory from an educational point of view. Therefore, some departments have special evening courses for part-time students.

Teaching Staff

The ranks of university teaching staff, in descending order, are *professoren* (professors), *lectoren* (assistant professors), *wetenschappelyke hoofdmedewekers* (senior lecturers), *wetenschappelijke medewerkers I^e klas* (lecturers first class), and *wetenschappelijke medewerkers* (lecturers). In public universities professors and assistant professors are appointed by the crown and in private universities by the board of the appropriate association or foundation. Appointments are made after consideration of recommendations by the board of governors of the university, following a recommendation submitted to the board by the relevant faculty council and a special selection committee. There are no formal selection procedures for appointments to the rank of senior lecturer, lecturer first class, and lecturer; appointments are made by the university's board of governors.

Salary scales applicable to both public and private universities are determined by the government. Tenure, as a rule, is granted to a lecturer after four years of teaching. Promotion is almost automatic up to the rank of senior lecturer.

Teachers at state higher vocational schools are appointed by the minister of education, while those at private institutions are appointed by the board of the foundation or association that operates the school.

Research Activities and Relationship with Industry

The central government provides the funding for university research through the normal university budget. In addition, the *Organisatie voor zuiver-wetenschappelijk onderzoek* (Organization for Pure Scientific Research), an independent but government-financed organization, allocates funds to individual scholars, research teams, and institutes. For the technological universities the *Organisatie voor toegepast natuurwetenschappelijk onderzoek* (Organization for Applied Research in the Sciences) is also important. This organization, also financed by the central government, has many institutes and laboratories and cooperates with university researchers. Although the amount of contract research is small, the relations between universities and industry are good—partly because a considerable amount of fundamental research is undertaken by industry in the Netherlands. Many

university professors and other academic staff became advisers to industry; a considerable number of them have actually started their careers in industrial research.

International Cooperation

The international exchange of students and teachers is fostered by cultural agreements with other countries. The organization responsible for coordinating such activities is the Netherlands Universities Foundation for International Cooperation (NUFFIC). Within the Netherlands the universities have played a minor role in developing and providing educational programs for foreign students, especially those from developing countries.

[Information received from the Ministry of Education and Science and from Professor R. A. de Moor, Katholieke Hogeschool Tilburg.]

Bibliography

Bevers, J. A. A. M., and Wiegersma, S. *De invoering van een studiepuntenstelsel in het hoger onderwijs.* Publication 5 of the Commissie ontwikkeling hoger onderwijs. The Hague: Staatsuitgeverij, 1975.

Commissie ontwikkeling hoger onderwijs. *Het overheidsbeleid inzake het tertiair onderwijs. Begrippen en uitgangspunten.* Publication 2. The Hague: Staatsuitgeverij, 1971.

Commissie ontwikkeling hoger onderwijs. *Ontwikkeling hoger onderwijs.* Publication 4. The Hague: Staatsuitgeverij, 1974.

Commissie ontwikkeling hoger onderwijs. *Algemene opleidingen in het hoger onderwijs.* Publication 6. The Hague: Staatsuitgeverij, 1975.

de Groot, A. D. *Selectie voor en in het hoger onderwijs. Een probleemanalyse.* Publication 3 of the Commissie ontwikkeling hoger onderwijs. The Hague: Staatsuitgeverij, 1972.

Maris, A. G. "The Progress of Higher Education in the Netherlands." *Higher Education and Research in the Netherlands,* 1967, 2(1), 9–13.

de Moor, R. A. "Diversification of Dutch Tertiary Education." *Paedagogica Europaea,* 1975, 10(1), 73–86.

Posthumus, K. *De universiteit: Doelstellingen, functies, structuren.* The Hague: Staatsuitgeverij, 1968.

Posthumus, K. *Universitair onderwijs: Doelstellingen, functies, structuren.* The Hague: Staatsuitgeverij, 1970.

Posthumus, K. *Universitair onderwijs. Structuren.* The Hague: Staatsuitgeverij, 1970.

Thoolen, B. A., and Ruiter, R. "The Long-Term Development of Education in the Netherlands." In K. Eide (Ed.), *Long Range Policy Planning in Education.* Paris: Organisation for Economic Co-operation and Development, 1973.

See also: Academic Dress and Insignia; Agriculture in Higher Education: History of Agricultural Education; Aid to Other Nations: Bilateral Participation in Higher Education; Archives: Northern Europe, National Archives of; Cooperative Education and Off-Campus Experience: Cooperative Education Worldwide; Health Services, Worldwide University; Internationalization of Higher Education; Manpower Planning: Role of Government; Science Policies: Highly Industrialized Nations: Western Europe; Western Europe and the United Kingdom: Regional Analysis.

NETHERLANDS UNIVERSITIES' COUNCIL (Academische raad)

The *Academische raad* (Netherlands Universities' Council), established in 1961, is the consultative, coordinating, and advisory body of the Dutch universities. Its major aims are to promote cooperation between the universities and to adapt university teaching to the development of science and learning and to the needs of society. The total membership of the council, including its committees and working parties, numbers 1300. A bureau composed of fifty-five people is directed by the general secretary of the council, who is appointed by the crown for an indefinite period on the nomination of the council. The council is financed through the Ministry of Education and Science.

The University Administration (Reform) Act of 1970 emphasized the role of the council as the policy-setting organization in all matters concerning interuniversity cooperation. Each university is represented by its *rector magnificus* and two other members on the plenary council of the Netherlands Universities' Council; each university also selects a deputy for each of the three members. In addition, the crown appoints a maximum of ten members to the plenary council. The chairman and the vice-chairman of the plenary council are appointed by the crown for a four-year period from three nominees submitted by the council.

The decisions and recommendations of the plenary council are prepared by an executive council, which may also act on behalf of the plenary council in urgent cases and on matters authorized by the plenary council. Each university designates one of its three members on the plenary council to sit on the executive council, which also includes three of the ten plenary council members appointed by the crown. The chairman and the vice-chairman of the plenary council serve in the same capacity on the executive council.

The council, either by request or on its own initiative, makes recommendations on behalf of the universities to the minister of education and science; the minister of agriculture, who is responsible for higher education in agriculture; and the minister of science policy. These ministers seek the advice of the council on all legislative proposals concerning university education and science. The council also makes recommendations to the universities.

The council has established several permanent advisory committees of experts in fields such as research, planning, review of curricula, libraries, and relations between secondary and tertiary education. Recommendations on particular problems are often prepared by ad hoc committees or working parties. There are forty-five permanent committees for the specific fields of university teaching and research, for regular interuniversity consultation, and for cooperation between faculties or subfaculties.

Recommendations and reports of the council and its committees are published in Dutch. Information about the activities of the council and its committees is also published in Dutch at regular intervals in the bulletin of the council, *A. R. Bulletin.*

36 Javastraat
The Hague, Netherlands

NEW CALEDONIA

Population: 126,000 (estimate). Student enrollment in primary and secondary school: 38,500. Language of instruction: French. [Figures are for 1974.]

New Caledonia is a French overseas territory located in the South Pacific to the east of Australia. The educational programs, examinations, and diplomas are identical to those in France. There are presently no faculties in New Caledonia; however, higher programs in law and economics are available under the auspices of the University of Bordeaux I in France. An extension of the *Conservatoire national des arts et métiers* in Paris trains engineers.

The programs offered in law and economics are the below degree-level *capacité en droit,* which requires two years of study, and the degree programs *licence en droit* and *licence ès sciences économiques,* which require four years of study. Admission requirements for the degree programs are the *baccalauréat* or equivalent. Students with a stipulated grade in the examination for the *capacité en droit* also are admitted, while students over twenty with two years of work experience and students over twenty-four may be admitted after an entrance examination.

The programs of study at the *Conservatoire national des arts et métiers* are divided into three cycles and comprise both practical and theoretical study. The first cycle lasts three or four years and leads to the *diplôme du premier cycle technique* (DPCT) or *diplôme du premier cycle économique* (DPCE). The second cycle lasts two or three years and leads to the *diplôme d'études supérieures techniques* (DEST) or the *diplôme d'études supérieures économiques* (DESE). Applicants over twenty-five with sufficient work experience are admitted to the third cycle, which requires an oral examination, submission of a study of original research, and a set program of courses. The third cycle leads to the *diplôme d'ingénieur CNAM* or *diplôme économiste CNAM.*

The programs of study in law are fi-nanced by the territory. The French government finances only the travel from France of the jury that conducts the examinations. The programs at the *Conservatoire national des arts et métiers* are financed by the French Ministry of Education.

Students who wish to pursue programs of study not available on the islands, such as medicine, pharmacy, and foreign languages, may attend institutions in France and are assisted by scholarships from the territory or the French government.

[Information submitted by C. Bondarenko, Vice-Rectorat, L'inspecteur d'académie, Noumea, New Caledonia.]

NEW HEBRIDES

Population: 95,000 (1974). British system: Student enrollment in primary school: 11,315 (5034 females); secondary school: 738 (274 females); higher education: 56 (24 females), plus 118 (21 females) abroad. French system: Student enrollment in primary and secondary school: approximately 8000. [Unless otherwise noted, figures are for 1975. Source for British statistics: British Education Service, Vila, New Hebrides.]

New Hebrides is an Anglo-French condominium located in the South Pacific between New Caledonia and Fiji. The islands are administered by two high commissioners, one British and one French.

The British and French education administrators oversee the separate but parallel educational systems. The British Education Service administers six primary schools and one secondary school and assists a number of schools run by district committees or voluntary agencies. It also runs an institution for primary teacher training, Kawenu College. The college offers a three-year program leading to the New Hebrides Teachers Certificate.

The French Education Service is in charge of forty-seven primary schools and assists a number of French mission schools. There are two government *lycées* and four private secondary schools.

Except for the teacher training college, there is no higher education. The British Education Service awards about one hundred scholarships for higher education overseas. Most students generally attend regional institutions in the South Pacific area, although some also attend higher education institutions in the United Kingdom. Principal countries of study are Australia, Fiji, New Zealand, Papua New Guinea, and the Solomon Islands.

French students seeking higher education generally go to France.

[Information received from J. M. Morris, Chief Education Officer, British Education Service, Vila, New Hebrides.]

NEW STRUCTURES OF POST-SECONDARY EDUCATION, TOWARDS

See Organisation for Economic Co-operation and Development.

NEW STUDENTS AND NEW PLACES (Higher Education Report), United States

In its report *New Students and New Places: Policies for the Future Growth and Development of American Higher Education* (New York: McGraw-Hill, October 1971), the Carnegie Commission on Higher Education presents its projections to the year 2000 for enrollment in higher education in the United States and examines ways in which these projections would be affected if recommendations in the commission's various reports were adopted. The report presents two enrollment projections, one based on past and current trends, the other on prospective trends reflecting the implementation of the commission's recommendations.

According to the report, the commission's proposals to ensure greater equality of opportunity and to expand adult education will increase student numbers. However, enrollment will be reduced by proposals to reduce time per degree, shift enrollments to two-year colleges, and reduce graduate enrollments. The net result of the commission's recommendations will be about one million fewer students in higher education in 1980 than current trends indicate. Educational costs will also be reduced, and by 1980–81 the savings should be in the area of $2,000,000,000 to $4,000,000,000 per year.

No matter which projection is used, the commission believes that the enrollment growth of the 1970s will level off in the 1980s and resume somewhat in the 1990s. It anticipates reduced growth rates in the long run and predicts that the percentage of college-age population actually in college will level off at about 50 percent by the year 2000. Predictions of future enrollments, however, are becoming more uncertain because of financial uncertainties, birthrate fluctuations, labor market conditions, and cultural influences.

Most of the additional new students could be absorbed by existing institutions; however, not all campuses are ideally located for this purpose. The report proposes the creation of 175 to 235 new community colleges and 80 to 105 comprehensive colleges by 1980; 60 to 70 of the new comprehensive colleges and 80 to 125 of the new community colleges should be located in large metropolitan areas with populations of about 5,000,000 or more. No new doctoral-granting universities are needed. Efforts to maintain private liberal arts colleges should be continued.

Increased attention should be given to the size, structure, and growth rate of individual campuses. The commission suggests the following minimum and maximum enrollments for each type of institution: from 1000 to 2500 students for liberal arts colleges, from 2000 to 5000 for community colleges, from 5000 to 10,000 for comprehensive colleges, and from 5000 to 20,000 for university campuses. Structure options such as decentralized campuses or "cluster colleges" and consortia should be encouraged, and growth rates of 3 to 5 percent a year should probably not be exceeded by any single campus.

An increasing number of students are seeking higher education on a part-time basis as adults; therefore, existing weaknesses in the organization and structure of adult higher education must be eliminated. The commission favors more flexible patterns of participation in higher education and urges state and federal government agencies and private foundations to increase support for the development of external degree programs and open universities.

NEW YORK PUBLIC LIBRARY

See Libraries: New York Public Library, United States.

NEW ZEALAND

Population: 3,042,800 (1974). Student enrollment in primary school: 521,000; secondary school: 304,000; higher education—university (full and part time): 39,000; higher education—nonuniversity (teacher and technical training, full and part time): 109,000; higher education—total: 148,000. Language of instruction: English. Academic calendar: February/March to October/November. Percentage of gross national product (GNP) expended on all education: 5.3%; higher education: 2.5%. Percentage of national budget expended on education: 17%. [Source: New Zealand Official Yearbook 1975. Except where otherwise noted, figures are for 1973.]

University education in New Zealand dates back to 1869, when the University of Otago was established by an ordinance of the Provincial Council of Otago. Five years later the university merged with Canterbury College at Christchurch, founded 1873, to become the basis for a University of New Zealand. Before the end of the century these two original constituent colleges were joined by three others: Lincoln College, also in the South Island; Auckland University College in the North Island; and Victoria College, Wellington. The constituent colleges did the teaching, and the University of New Zealand granted the degrees; examination scripts and theses submitted by candidates were usually assessed by external examiners in the United Kingdom.

In 1961 the University of New Zealand was dissolved. Lincoln became a substantially self-governing and independent constituent college of the University of Canterbury; and the University of Canterbury, the University of Otago, the University of Auckland, and Victoria University of Wellington became fully autonomous degree-granting universities. Two other institutions, Massey University and the University of Waikato, achieved similar status in 1964.

Coordination among these institutions was ensured by the establishment of the University Grants Committee and, with it, an Entrance Board Committee, a Research Committee, a Curriculum Committee, a Scholarship Committee, and a Council of Legal Education. These committees make recommendations to the Grants Committee, which implements them for New Zealand.

Types of Institutions

New Zealand's six universities are autonomous degree-granting institutions established by act of parliament and funded from the country's internal revenues. Two areas of higher education, teacher training and technical education, are outside the university system. Eight teachers colleges train selected students, who are paid by the New Zealand Department of Education, which also registers teachers. Fourteen technical institutes, including the New Zealand Technical Correspondence Institute, provide vocational training for technicians and skilled tradesmen. The institutes are controlled by the New Zealand Department of Education; and the assessment of their students is largely in the hands of national external examining bodies, such as the Technicians Certification Authority. Staff in the institutes teach subjects according to nationally determined standards.

With the exception of a Roman Catholic

college for training teachers, and places for denominational training of ministers of religion, all higher education in New Zealand is provided by public institutions.

An additional source of higher education on the university level is provided through a program of extension courses which the government has required the universities to sponsor. Students in these courses pay a small fee to attend classes which the University Grants Committee finances. The main function of the program is to provide refresher courses for college graduates and to keep the public abreast of recent developments in a given field. In some universities extension departments are being renamed Centres of Continuing Education. Among the responsibilities envisaged for university centers of continuing education are training students for work (paid and unpaid) within the community, developing community leadership, providing technical assistance for the solution of community problems, and training students to become adult educators.

Relationship with Secondary Education and Admission Requirements

The Education Act of 1964 provides free education in state primary and secondary schools, and compulsory education for all children between six and fifteen. Primary and secondary education are administered by the Department of Education in conjunction with education boards and school committees. The course of study prior to entrance to higher education is eight years of primary school and four or five years of secondary study.

Universities in New Zealand are bound by uniform entrance standards, and as of 1975 virtually any qualified applicant was able to enroll at the university of his choice. Entrance standards are established by the Universities Entrance Board, which consists of the chairman of the University Grants Committee and representatives of the universities, private and public secondary schools, and the New Zealand Department of Education. Candidates must

be sixteen years of age or be enrolled full time in a secondary school at the form-6 level, where students are prepared for university entrance. Candidates take the entrance examination in four or five subjects, English being a compulsory subject.

If the principal of a school believes that a student is capable of undertaking university studies, the school may, according to rights vested in it by the Universities Entrance Board, accredit that student, who then does not have to take the entrance examination. Although the University Entrance Examination qualifies a student for the university without his having to undergo further examinations, many (about 50 percent in 1975) are now choosing to participate in an extra year of schooling (form 7) to prepare more adequately for university studies. At the end of that year they acquire a Higher School Certificate; they may also take the Universities Bursaries or Entrance Scholarships examinations. Additional financial assistance may then be awarded to those with a high pass.

Although no restrictions limit university entry to those with the basic entrance qualifications, in some faculties, such as medicine and veterinary medicine, an overload of applications has resulted in the establishment of priorities. Students who at the end of their first year (intermediate year) earn the highest examination results are given preference, or preference is given on the basis of results in the University Bursaries Examination.

Entrance requirements for other schools of higher education are contingent on the particular studies to be followed. Students who wish to become primary school teachers and seek admission to a teachers college must have a sixth-form certificate and must take a three-year course at the college. Those who wish to become secondary school teachers must have completed at least the University Entrance Examination and must take three years of study concurrently at the teachers college and university. A student who has a university degree needs only one year of study at the teachers college to qualify for placement on the secondary level. In all cases, the student, having completed the course of training, must work for a year as an assistant teacher to demonstrate competence. Only then will the Trained Teachers Certificate, which is the basic qualification for a teacher in New Zealand, be awarded. Two or three years of secondary education suffices for admission to some trade courses offered by the technical institutes. There are no minimum entry requirements for technician courses, which take five years and lead to the New Zealand Certificate. However, entering students who have earned a School Certificate or who have sat for the University Entrance Examination are exempted from some subjects.

Administration and Control

Each university in New Zealand is governed by a council chaired by the chancellor, who is the ceremonial head of the university. The council generally has about twenty members and is made up of nominees of the government, representatives of the body of graduates, the students' association, local authorities, teaching staff, the professorial board, and the vice-chancellor (ex officio), who, as the academic and administrative head of the university, acts as the main link between the council and the professorial board or senate. The council confers all degrees and awards, makes statutes and regulations, manages the property of the university, and otherwise administers the university by instituting academic offices and appointing and removing staff. The council is advised by the professorial board or senate on all academic matters, including those that relate to student discipline. This board also approves the courses of study proposed by individual students.

Each university appoints a registrar to be responsible for the general administration of the institution: enrollment of students, organization of examinations, keeping of academic records of students, preparation of official publications, organization of academic ceremonies such as graduation, col-

lection of fees and payment of scholarships and bursary allowances, and planning and upkeep of buildings.

Both students and staff have representation on their university's governing body and the right to vote. Usually it is the president of the students' association who represents students on the council. In some university councils the students are merely coopted members, but in most universities the students' association is represented by statute. Sometimes students have two seats on the council. Graduates and the professorial board have the right to several seats on a university council, and usually the subprofessorial staff also appoints one or more representatives. Thus, students and staff can share in making institutional policy and in the control of their university. At the national level, they can influence policy either through the New Zealand Association of University Teachers or through the New Zealand University Students' Association.

The New Zealand universities do not deal directly with the government but deal instead with the University Grants Committee, whose function is to coordinate the planning and financing of the universities and serve as a buffer between the universities and the government. This arrangement insulates the universities from direct political control, and it also allows the greatest possible autonomy to the individual university, which must plan access and revise its own development within the limits of its government grant received through the University Grants Committee. The government, however, can reject proposals made by the University Grants Committee.

Programs and Degrees

Among the powers granted each university by act of parliament is the power to confer degrees and award other academic qualifications. These degrees and qualifications, however, must be approved by the University Grants Committee and recommended by the professorial board. A university council also has power to award honorary degrees or academic distinction.

The individual universities in New Zealand define and establish programs of study and curriculum content. Their autonomy is limited, however, since they cannot offer a new degree or diploma program without the prior approval of the University Grants Committee's Curriculum Committee. The Curriculum Committee is directed by the chairman of the University Grants Committee and includes representatives of the New Zealand universities and of the New Zealand Department of Education. Thus, curriculum changes in one university can be studied in relation to the offerings at other universities, the technical institutes, and the teachers colleges.

The first degree offered by the university is the bachelor's degree. In some faculties, such as arts, commerce, and science, courses are divided into units, which are the equivalent of a year's work in a subject. These subjects are taught in three "stages" of increasing sophistication. At least three of the eight or nine units required for a bachelor's degree must be taken on a higher level than stage one, and at least one unit must be taken at stage three. Because the unit system is relatively rigid, some faculties are now discarding it in favor of programs that can be more flexibly organized. On the average, whether or not the unit system is used, the bachelor's degree requires three years of study in the faculties of agriculture and commerce, agricultural science, arts, horticulture, horticultural science, and science. Five years are required for architecture, dentistry, and law, while medicine requires six. A bachelor's (honors) degree usually needs an additional year of study.

The master's degree generally requires one or two years of study after the bachelor's degree. It may be earned through course work or by completion of a thesis or by a combination of both. In some instances the master's degree may be awarded with honors or distinction.

The Doctor of Philosophy (Ph.D.) generally takes a minimum of two years of advanced study, research, and the presentation and acceptance of a thesis. A Doctor of Literature (D.Litt.), a Doctor of Science (D.Sc.), or a Doctor of Law (LL.D.) usually involves eight years beyond the bachelor's degree while a Doctor of Music (Mus.D.) takes five.

Financing

Although the universities are virtually independent of government, they are financed, up to 85 percent, by government grants; other monies come from tuition (12 percent) and miscellaneous income (3 percent). A University Grants Committee disburses the government funds in the form of quinquennial grants for current expenditure and specific grants for major capital works.

The committee, an independent statutory body, functions thus as a buffer between universities and government to ensure a balanced development of university education. In addition to disbursing the funds between the universities, it advises the government on what funds are needed. The universities then deploy the monies as they see fit.

The system of quinquennial grants has some disadvantages; it is adversely affected both by changing patterns in enrollment and by the rate of inflation, and there have been adjustments during quinquennia to cover rising costs such as staff salaries. A five-year planning period, however, seems to lessen the risk of political interference and has been an acceptable system of financing and control for a decade of expansion. To operate effectively the plan depends on efficient administration in each university, since each university is responsible for its budget decisions on staffing, equipment, library, and general upkeep.

Student Financial Aid

When a New Zealand resident qualifies for university entrance, he or she gains the right to receive free tuition the first year at the university. If the student makes satisfactory academic progress, he or she will receive free tuition for the minimum number of years required to qualify for the degree of his choice. A substantial boarding allowance is also paid to help those students who must live away from home in order to study at a university. Since 1976 the New Zealand government has provided a standard tertiary bursary for all full-time students at universities and technical institutes; students at teachers colleges have a choice of a tertiary bursary without bonding or a more substantial payment with bonding. The bursary support available (without any form of bonding) to full-time university students—together with their earnings from the long vacation, which lasts about twelve weeks—means that university education is within reach of all who meet the required academic entrance standard and wish to undertake university study.

Student Social Background and Access to Education

Most first-year students who study full time at the universities have come directly from secondary school, but a sprinkling have been out in the work force and, as a consequence of their experience, have determined to undertake university study. Since the 1970s a number of women with grown children have enrolled for university study, usually as part-time students.

As a result of social processes at work in New Zealand, fewer students come from manual workers' families than from professional or other higher-income families. Nevertheless, since the mid 1960s there has been a high proportion of students at the universities whose parents did not experience university education. There are special provisions for admission of adults who lack normal entrance qualifications, and there are opportunities for part-time and extramural study, so that some university education is possible for all who want it.

Students entering the universities automatically become members of the students' association of that university. The students' associations of all New Zealand universities are members of the New Zealand University Students' Association. This body negotiates directly with the New Zealand government's Ministry of Education, with the University Grants Committee, and with the government Departments of Labor and of Immigration, about problems faced by the individual universities. The New Zealand University Students' Association concerns itself with political issues within and beyond New Zealand. It makes detailed submissions on social questions to the government and has its own Research Office for the Study of Higher Education. It interests itself in university building programs, assessment and teaching in universities, student representation on university councils and academic boards, and students' bursary allowances. The association has organized national students' arts festivals and has published a number of handbooks. It operates its own insurance scheme and its own travel bureau. The association aims at encouraging a concerted effort by New Zealand students to achieve reforms in the country's university system and communicates and cooperates with universities in other countries, particularly with the University of the South Pacific in Fiji.

Teaching Staff

Full-time university teachers in New Zealand usually hold a continuing appointment. Retirement is required at the end of the year they reach the age of sixty-five. In faculties of law and commerce, some part-time appointments are commonly made in order that practicing members of these professions may provide some of the teaching. The lowest in rank, the junior lecturer, may have tenure from one to five years, by which time he will have been promoted to a position as a lecturer or will have left the university. The chairman of each department makes recommendations for needed staff to the council; the council, in turn, on the advice of the professorial board, determines which positions it will set up and at what salary level. These academic vacancies are usually advertised and applications called for from suitably qualified persons; advertisements are placed in national newspapers and in overseas publications. Each university council makes its own appointments to the teaching staff, decides on promotion of its staff, and sets its conditions of employment. Salary scales, however, are determined by the University Grants Committee.

Since 1923 university teachers in New Zealand have had their own association, the Association of University Teachers of New Zealand. Membership is voluntary, but the association attracts about 90 percent of university teachers. The association is concerned primarily with improving the conditions of service of university teachers, protecting members from injustice, and promoting the welfare of higher education. AUT, an incorporated society with a national office and paid secretariat, makes submissions direct to the University Grants Committee concerning university salary scales, which are reviewed triennially. Since 1969 AUT has conducted regular surveys of the staffing structure of New Zealand universities and surveys of staff recruitment and losses. Academic freedom has always been of prime concern to the association, and it has formulated policies on such important matters as entrance to the universities, graduate employment, the training of university teachers, and the optimum use of university facilities.

Research Activities

The University Grants Committee provides for the general research needs (both basic and applied) of the New Zealand universities within the quinquennial block grants. Grants are made for travel and field expenses, microfilm, books, and other material. The amounts allocated to a university's internal research committee appear to vary significantly among the universities, although all are affected by the shortage in general funds caused by inflation. Staff in New Zealand universities also may apply for funds from the University Grants Committee's Research Committee. This committee usually allocates its money for the purchase of large pieces of equipment, but it is prepared to examine projects involving items of expense other than equipment, especially when these projects are recommended by a university's internal research committee.

A New Zealand Council for Educational Research was established in 1933 and funded for its first five years by grants from the Carnegie Corporation of New York. Since 1944 it has received considerable financial support from the New Zealand government, but the organization has remained under independent control.

Current Problems and Trends

In a report to the minister of education, the 1973–74 Educational Development Conference's Working Party on Organisation and Administration of Education examined the relationship between the New Zealand university system and the rest of the educational system, especially the other tertiary institutions (that is, the teachers colleges and the technical institutes). The working party looked at the factors influencing the individual student's choice of a particular type of tertiary education and at the possibilities for moving more freely from one type of education to another. It noted the value of the careers advisory service, which the University Grants Committee has supported in all the universities, and implied that should the government ever direct students into courses, rather than leaving the student unequivocally free to choose for himself, the government would then be morally responsible for solving a student's subsequent employment problems. In New Zealand there is concern about the number of arts graduates who have employment problems when they enter the work force. New Zealand has faced shortages of university-trained specialists.

The training and supply of teachers are regulated by the Department of Education according to its estimates of the numbers and kinds of teachers likely to be needed.

A vocational training council exists to inform the technical institutes of changing vocational training needs of industry and commerce.

The universities in the 1960s experienced a rapid expansion of enrollments, but in the mid 1970s New Zealand seems to face a more static situation. The universities may, therefore, have to cooperate to ensure the most efficient national use of the resources available.

Relationship with Industry

Cooperation between industry and the universities has been largely restricted to the provision of prizes, scholarships, and bursaries, made available to individual students selected by industrial firms. Some awards require students to accept some kind of obligation to the donor firms while others do not. Some degree and diploma courses require students to undertake approved work in industry during vacations.

At the University of Otago chairs of departments have been endowed in economics, English, chemistry, music, physics, physiology, medicine, and surgery. A cancer research department has also been endowed. At the University of Canterbury the chair for wood science is endowed, as is the chair of management. Victoria University of Wellington has an endowed chair in economics. Victoria University has established an industrial relations center and an industrial development staff to serve the interests of applied electronics, applied fisheries, pedology and transportation. Massey University has an endowed chair in food technology. At the University of Auckland the leading New Zealand forestry firm endowed a chair in plant pathology.

An interesting new development in cooperation between industry and university has been the institution at the University of Waikato of a B.Sc. (Tech.), which requires a student to spend two six-month periods in paid employment in industry or at a research establishment outside the university; during that time the student is under the direction of his employer but is also supervised by a member of the academic staff of the university.

ELLIE M. BOYD

Educational Associations

Association of University Teachers of New Zealand
P.O. Box 28-017
Kelburn, Wellington, New Zealand

New Zealand Federation of University Women
P.O. Box 7065
Hamilton, New Zealand

New Zealand University Students' Association
P.O. Box 6368
Te Aro
Wellington C1, New Zealand

Bibliography

New Zealand Official Yearbook 1975. Wellington: Department of Statistics, 1975.

Parkyn, G. W. *Success and Failure at the University*. (2 vols.) Wellington: New Zealand Council for Educational Research, 1969.

Seminar on Aspects of Tertiary Education. Trends and issues in higher education; seven papers presented at a seminar organized by the Association of University Teachers of New Zealand. Wellington: New Zealand Council for Educational Research, 1970.

See also: College Entrance Examination Board; Courts and Higher Education; Financing of Higher Education: University Grants Committee; Health Services, Worldwide University; Library Administration Outside the United States; Oceania: Regional Analysis; Science Policies: Highly Industrialized Nations: Australia and New Zealand.

NEW ZEALAND TEACHERS COLLEGES ASSOCIATION

The New Zealand Teachers Colleges Association (NZTCA) had its beginnings in the early 1940s but entered a more serious stage of growth and organization about 1962, following a national review of most aspects of education. NZTCA's major purposes are to promote and advance education in general and teacher training in particular and to uphold and maintain the interests of its members.

New Zealand teacher training (both elementary and secondary) is undertaken in teachers training colleges under the control of college councils and a degree of control by the Department of Education. There are eight colleges, including one for secondary teacher training and one combining primary and secondary teacher training. NZTCA has rights of negotiation for the college staffs recognized by the Department of Education and supplies legal assistance to individual members, on request. About 85 percent of the 600 full-time staff are members. Membership fees are set at the annual meeting.

NZTCA negotiates salary increases and conditions of service, sometimes jointly with the interested teachers association. Members (including principals) in each college organize a branch, which has a member on the executive. Each branch undertakes some subcommittee responsibility for studying and reporting on a special topic such as study leaves or in-service training. The organizational patterns are eminently democratic, and the elected president represents executive views regularly to the Department of Education's superintendent of teacher training and to the minister of education.

Without the NZTCA publications, the student inside or outside New Zealand would have only a limited picture of the teacher training sector in the country and of the special features of the different colleges. A journal has been published since 1963, the first such New Zealand publication in the field. Some key reports or articles are published as special papers distributed widely to inform those outside the membership. The freedom of NZTCA to hold and to publish dissenting views is highly valued by members.

P.O. Box 3044
Wellington 1, New Zealand
I. J. WHYLE

NEW ZEALAND UNIVERSITY STUDENTS' ASSOCIATION

Formed in 1929, the New Zealand University Students' Association (NZUSA) has 37,000 members comprising student associations at New Zealand's six universities and one agricultural college: University of Auckland; Massey University, Palmerston North; University of Otago, Dunedin; University of Canterbury, Christchurch; Victoria University of Wellington; University of Waikato, Hamilton; and Lincoln College, Christchurch. Under its constitution, NZUSA's objectives are to represent the view of students of New Zealand nationally and internationally and to function as a major, informed, and principled pressure group, with education (as a first priority), student welfare, and social reform (including international matters) among its areas of concern. NZUSA functions principally as a trade union, seeking the best possible working conditions for its members, and has a larger membership and full-time staff than most of the country's industrial unions of workers.

NZUSA owns a travel company, the Student Travel Bureau Ltd (STBLtd), which operates extensive student charter flights to Australia, Asia, and Europe; group flights to North America; and special flights within Asia and Europe. STBLtd also administers a student discount scheme on New Zealand's major domestic airline. It has sales offices on six university campuses. NZUSA's major sources of finance are dues paid by its members and surpluses from the operations of its travel company. It does not receive any outside funding.

During 1975 NZUSA campaigned for the introduction of the standard tertiary bursary—a reformed system of government support for students at the universities, technical institutes, and teacher training colleges; this support had been promised by the labor government in its

1972 election policy. The NZUSA campaign, conducted in cooperation with the national associations of technical institute students and student teachers, included nationwide demonstrations by some 10,000 students in March 1975 and culminated in the introduction of the new tertiary bursary by the government in its May 1975 budget. Throughout the remainder of the year, NZUSA representatives were deeply involved in discussions with government agencies on the introduction of the new policy.

NZUSA also participated in major campaigns for social reforms in New Zealand. In the late 1960s and early 1970s, it played an important part in campaigns against New Zealand's sporting contacts with South Africa and New Zealand's military involvement in the Vietnam war. Contemporary issues include working with other organizations in pressing for abortion and homosexual law reform and for changes in the tenancy laws. Other priorities are fighting racism in New Zealand and foreign control of the New Zealand economy.

The New Zealand Students' Arts Council, which includes some teacher training colleges and technical institutes as well as universities, is another NZUSA service. The council operates a varied cultural program for students, including film programs, tours of musical groups, arts festivals, fine arts exhibitions, dance workshops, and theater productions.

P.O. Box 6368
Te Aro
Wellington, New Zealand

NEW ZEALAND VICE-CHANCELLORS' COMMITTEE

The New Zealand Vice-Chancellors' Committee membership consists of vice-chancellors of Lincoln College, Christchurch, and the following universities: University of Auckland; University of Waikato, Hamilton; Massey University, Palmerston North; Victoria University of Wellington; University of Canterbury, Christchurch; and University of Otago, Dunedin. The committee's purpose is to discuss problems of common concern to the universities, such as parliamentary legislation, salaries, superannuation, computers, library resources, overseas aid, university relationships with other tertiary educational institutions, and liaison with the University Grants Committee.

The committee meets six times annually, usually in Wellington, the capital city and home of its secretariat. In addition to ad hoc committees on library resources and on computers, two standing committees, on library resources and computers, report directly to the Vice-Chancellors' Committee. The committee is represented on the New Zealand Historic Places Trust and the Technicians Certification Authority and other committees and boards. The expenses of the committee are shared by the constituent universities.

The committee makes recommendations and decisions on appointments, scholarships, fellowships, and conferences. More recently, emphasis has been given to the committee's role as a coordinator and disseminator of information and as a guard against undue overlapping in curricular developments.

The committee has initiated continuing research projects on students' academic performance and on graduate employment. The committee recently sponsored a survey of New Zealand university library resources.

Victoria University of Wellington
Private Bag
Wellington, New Zealand

L. S. TAIAROA

NEWMAN REPORT (FIRST)
See Report on Higher Education (Higher Education Report), United States.

NEWMAN REPORT (SECOND)
See National Policy and Higher Education
(Higher Education Report), United States.

NEWSPAPERS, STUDENT
See Student Publications.

NICARAGUA, REPUBLIC OF

*Population: 2,188,600. Student enrollment
in primary school: 317,683; secondary school
(academic, vocational, technical): 65,656; university: 16,000 (1975). Language of instruction: Spanish. Academic calendar: May to
March, two semesters. Percentage of national
budget expended on all education: 11% (1975);
higher education: 2.1%. [Except where otherwise noted, figures are for 1974–75.]*

The first institution of higher education
in Nicaragua was the *Seminario conciliar de
San Ramón,* founded in the city of León on
December 15, 1670, as a measure of the
Council of Trent. By a decree of the Court
of Cádiz on January 10, 1812, the seminary
attained university status as the University
of León. It remained the only university in
the nation for almost one hundred and fifty
years. In 1947 it was renamed the National
University; and on March 25, 1958, its present judicial organization and autonomy
were authorized by an executive decree. In
accordance with the amendment of May 5,
1966, to Article 105 of the constitution of
the republic, the university's official name
was changed to *Universidad nacional autónoma de Nicaragua* (UNAN: National Autonomous University of Nicaragua). The
main campus of the university has remained
in León, although branches have been established in other cities since 1947.

Nicaragua's second university, the private *Universidad centroamericana* (UCA:
Central American University), was founded
in 1960. The university, located in Managua, is a private partnership, based upon
Christian ideology and administered by the
Society of Jesus. Maximum authority for
the university is vested in a board of directors, which consists of members from private business, the professoriate, and the
Society of Jesus.

In the fifteen years between 1960 and
1975 higher education expanded rapidly.
The three institutions that existed in early
1960—*Universidad nacional autónoma de
Nicaragua; Escuela nacional de agricultura
y ganadería* (ENAG: National School of
Agriculture and Animal Husbandry), in
Managua; and *Escuela nacional de enfermería*
(ENE: National School of Nursing), in
Managua—had a combined enrollment of
1535 students. By 1975 more than 16,000
students were attending institutions of
higher education in Nicaragua, and two
more institutions had been founded: the
Central American University and the *Instituto politécnico de Nicaragua* (POLI: Polytechnic Institute of Nicaragua), also in
Managua. The greatest increases took place
at the National Autonomous University of
Nicaragua, which in 1975 enrolled more
than 13,000 students.

Enrollments in the other institutions
have stabilized because of financial factors
and the destruction of many of the physical
facilities of these institutions during the
1972 earthquake in Managua, the site of
most of the institutions of higher education
in the nation.

Since half of the population in 1975 was
under fifteen years of age, enrollments are
expected to continue to grow; by 1980 an
enrollment figure of 26,000 students is
projected for UNAN.

Legal Basis of Educational System

The state regulates the institutions of
higher education through legal disposi-
tions that guarantee their academic, financial, and administrative authority. The
structure and organization of UNAN are
delineated in Articles 105 and 336 of the
constitution of the country and in the statutes of the university approved by the
board of directors on April 2, 1963.

UCA achieved its legal status and autonomy under Article 518 of July 23, 1960. The National School of Agriculture and Animal Husbandry was created by Decree 25 of October 16, 1951. The other institutions of higher education function under statutes, which, by law, must be approved by the Ministry of Education.

Types of Institutions

The system of higher education in Nicaragua is composed of all institutions that require a secondary school diploma for entry. There are some schools of accounting and business that offer postsecondary education; however, since their entrance requirements are more flexible than those of the institutions at university level, they are not included among the higher education institutions in this description. The higher education sector thus consists of the two universities, the National School of Agriculture and Animal Husbandry, the National School of Nursing, and the Polytechnic Institute of Nicaragua. The Central American University, which is run by the Society of Jesus, and the Polytechnic Institute, which is administered by the Baptist Church, are private institutions; the other three institutions are maintained by the state.

Another important component of the higher education system is a privately founded regional institution, the *Instituto centroamericano de administración de empresas* (INCAE: Central American Institute for Business Administration), which offers postgraduate programs in business administration and management to participants from all the Central American states.

Relationship with Secondary Education

The Ministry of Education is responsible for the planning, administration, and coordination of national education and also for vocational and teacher training. Private institutions function subject to approval of the ministry as to standards of teaching staff and examinations. The private institutions are largely financed and administered by religious bodies. Their enrollment is generally drawn from the upper socioeconomic classes.

According to government regulations, the system of education in Nicaragua consists of (1) preprimary schools for children under six, privately administered; (2) six years of primary school, divided into two cycles of four and two years, respectively; (3) basic secondary education, lasting three years; (4) two years of specialized secondary education, divided into preuniversity study, agricultural *lycées*, and commercial, normal, and technical-vocational schools. With the exception of the programs in the technical-vocational schools, specialized programs lead to the diploma of *bachillerato* in sciences and letters, which enables the graduate to enter higher education. Graduates of the normal schools receive the title of teacher, *maestro normalista*, while graduates of the agricultural *lycées* and the commercial schools receive the diploma of *bachillerato* in agricultural sciences or business, respectively.

Admission Requirements

The principal requirement for admission to higher education institutions is the secondary school diploma, *bachillerato*, or equivalent qualifications. All specialized secondary schools except the vocational-technical schools award this diploma. Although in principle there are no restrictions on access to the university, the increasing numbers of students and the scarcity of job opportunities in some fields have forced the adoption of certain admission restrictions. Students usually enter a general studies program for two semesters. Successful completion of this program gives free access to all fields of study except architecture, medicine, medical technology, and odontology, which have admission quotas.

Administration and Control

The state, through the Ministry of Education, maintains relations with, and coordinates the activities of, the institutions of higher education. The government has a representative on the governing boards of UNAN and POLI. UNAN is responsible to the state in financial matters. The National School of Agriculture and Animal Husbandry, which trains personnel for the development of the nation's agricultural resources, is under the authority of the Ministry of Agriculture, while the National School of Nursing is under the Ministry of Public Health.

Although the names of the governing bodies of the institutions of higher education differ, similarities exist in their organizational structure. At UNAN, the governing body is the university council *(junta universitaria);* at UCA, the board of directors *(junta de directores);* at POLI, the directive council *(consejo directivo).* Each of these bodies is composed of twelve to fifteen members, who are empowered to formulate general policy of the institution, approve the rules and regulations of the faculties, approve or change plans and programs of study for the different fields of study, and ratify the appointment of high administrators and professors.

At the universities the highest authority is the rector; in the other institutions, the director general. The rector is the legal representative of the university and in charge of its administration. Both the rector *(director)* and the vice-rector *(sub-director)* are elected: in UNAN, by a special assembly consisting of the faculty councils *(juntas directivas de facultades)* for a period of four years; in UCA, by the board of directors for three years; in POLI, by the board of trustees; and at ENAG and ENE, by their respective governing minister.

Each faculty has a directive council *(junta directiva),* consisting of the dean, a vice-dean, a secretary, and representatives of the teaching staff and the students. The council recommends nominees for teaching positions and curriculum plans to the governing body.

The secretary general authorizes the

official documents, decrees, and agreements of the university and, in some of the other institutions, works in close cooperation with the chief executive. In addition to these bodies, there are also others with advisory powers—for instance, a high council *(consejo superior),* a general university assembly *(asamblea general universitaria),* and organizations such as a planning board *(junta de planificación)*—which cooperate directly in the administration of the institution. All these bodies have representation of both students and faculty in accordance with their respective statutes.

Programs and Degrees

Students entering the universities attend two semesters of interdisciplinary study in the general studies program. With certain restrictions (fields with quotas), the successful student then enters the professional faculty of his choice. The faculties are relatively independent of each other, although the existence of various departments (which is not a common feature) makes possible a certain interchange. The universities follow the semester and credit hour system of the United States.

The institutions of higher education offer programs at two levels: professional and intermediate. Professional study leading to the title *licenciado* or titles such as architect, engineer, and medical doctor is offered at the universities in a course of study lasting from four years (social work, teaching) to five years (accounting, architecture, dentistry, engineering, law) to six years (medicine).

The National Autonomous University also offers a number of programs at the intermediate level leading to careers as technicians. These generally last from two years (industrial supervision, journalism, marketing, topography) to three years (sales techniques).

Although POLI awards the *licenciado* in a four-year program of marketing techniques or finance, most of its programs last two to three years and lead to careers as technicians (administrative technician, electromechanical technician, professional nurse). The School of Nursing offers the title *enfermera graduada* (graduate nurse) after a three-year program; the National School of Agriculture and Animal Husbandry awards the title *ingeniero agrónomo* (agricultural engineer) after a five-year program.

The regional business institute, INCAE, offers a program leading to the master's degree in business management and also arranges courses and seminars of value to the socioeconomic development of the Central American region.

Financing

The income of the National Autonomous University, the National School of Agriculture and Animal Husbandry, and the National School of Nursing is derived principally through government contributions. The Central American University raises 49 percent of its income through tuition, the rest through contributions; the Polytechnic Institute also relies on tuition and contributions for its income.

In accordance with the constitution of the republic, the contribution of the state toward financing the National Autonomous University should be no less than 2 percent of the national budget. The state also makes additional contributions toward the university's endowment. The contribution from the state represents about 80 percent of the university's budget.

Although the private institutions receive relatively little government support, government contributions have been of crucial importance in some cases. For instance, UCA reconstructed the major portion of the university after the 1972 earthquake with support from the government and AID (Agency for International Development) in the United States. Loans from the Inter-American Development Bank, secured by the government, have also assisted UCA as well as the development of UNAN's medical campus in León and the new project, *Recinto universitario "Rubén Darío"* in Managua.

Student Financial Aid

In addition to the programs of financial aid available to each institution of higher education through the Office of Student Welfare (which, for example, in 1972–73 benefited 1541 students at UNAN), there is also a program of financial aid, called *Educrédito,* which supplies loans to needy students. Once the student has graduated, the loans are to be repaid with a small interest, in payments proportionate to the student's receipts. During the academic year 1975–76, *Educrédito* loaned 355.360 córdobas (7 córdobas = US$1) to students at undergraduate and intermediate levels and 1,500,000 at the postgraduate level. In 1974 a total of 258 students received loans through the program.

Student Social Background and Access to Education

Nicaragua is a country of great social contrasts. Despite the rapid increases in student enrollments, access to higher education has not been equalized and the great majority of students belong to the middle classes. By custom, affluent families tend to send their children abroad for study to the United States, Mexico, Spain, or Brazil. The growth of the government's loan program, *Educrédito,* might assist students of more limited means to attend higher education, although the numbers of such loans granted are still low.

There has been a marked increase of female enrollment, which in the decade 1962 to 1972 increased from 21.5 percent to 34.4 percent of total enrollment.

Each university has a central association consisting of students elected by their peers: CUUN *(Centro universitario de la Universidad nacional)* and CEUUCA *(Centro estudiantil universitario de la Universidad centroamericana).* The student representation on the governing bodies of the institutions of higher education is considerable. For instance, UNAN's university council has one student representative while each faculty council has two student members. The higher university council at UCA has five student representatives, the faculty councils have two student representatives, and the planning council has one student member.

Teaching Staff

Among the institutions of higher education, UNAN has best defined the categories of teaching staff, although a teaching career as such—with clearly defined norms for salary, promotion, and tenure—does not exist. Article 27 of UNAN's organic law sets forth four classes of teaching staff: full professor, assistant professor, associate professor, free professor. According to Article 61 of the statutes, a full or assistant professor must hold a university degree and be a recognized authority in the subject area. In accordance with Article 14, clause (p) of the organic law, appointment is made by the university council on the recommendation of the faculty council. Article 4 of the *Reglamento de derechos y obligaciones de los profesores de tiempo completo y medio tiempo* (teachers' rights and duties) states the period of contract: "The initial contract for full- and part-time teachers will be for a period of one year, renewable for an additional two years on mutual agreement. The second contract may be made for four years, renewable for the same period on mutual agreement. The third contract is for an indefinite period of time."

Research Activities

The principal task of the higher education institutions in Nicaragua has been the teaching and training of future professionals. As a result of the lack of extensive programs of postgraduate study and the part-time nature of the appointment of a large percentage of the teaching staff, research has not been an essential part of university activities. Article 3 of UNAN's organic law states that the university is "to collaborate with the state institutions in the study of cultural, social, and economic problems without losing its character as an autonomous center." Thus, the general policy of the university has been directed toward research of problems in areas of public health, education, law, and development. Studies undertaken to date have dealt with such areas as municipal administration, urban transportation systems, and a number of agricultural problems.

Current Problems and Trends

The system of higher education in Nicaragua is plagued by a number of major problems: (1) There is no national development plan to guide the output of graduates into areas of national need; coupled with the great increases in student numbers, this lack of planning might result in serious employment distortions. (2) Despite increases in enrollments at the secondary level and a virtually free access to higher education, the country has only limited financial means for university expansion. (3) There is a lack of unity and coordination of higher education; although the Ministry of Education has a representative on the governing boards of UNAN and POLI, there is no official representation in the governing board of UCA. (4) Academic standards are low, and research activities are negligible. (5) Students lack incentives for a teaching career; since there is no definite policy regulating the teaching profession, well-qualified persons often prefer other careers, for which security and benefits are guaranteed by the state.

These problems have been recognized by the state. New offices such as the Direction of National Planning have been created and are expected to give support to new higher education programs. Government financial support has also increased: from nine million córdobas in 1969–70 to twenty-seven million in 1975–76. The institutions at the university level, with the exception of the National School of Nursing, have joined together as the Nicaraguan

Association of Institutions of Higher Education (ANIES) with the goal of coordinating their educational efforts in order to avoid costly duplication and to promote relations between the different sectors of the educational system in the country.

International Cooperation

With the exception of the master's degree programs in business administration at INCAE, there are no postgraduate programs in Nicaragua. The students must thus go abroad for graduate study, generally to the United States. Many organizations have been of assistance to Nicaragua in this regard: the Latin American Scholarship Program for American Universities (LASPAU), the Ford Foundation, USAID, and others. In 1973–74, nearly five hundred Nicaraguan students attended universities in the United States. The universities also maintain bilateral contacts with universities abroad; for instance, UNAN participates in a cooperative program of engineering education, research, and training with Louisiana State University of the United States.

In addition to cooperation in the joint regional business institute, INCAE, Nicaraguan universities work in close conjunction with other Central American universities. UNAN is a member of the *Confederación universitaria centroamericana* (Central American University Confederation), which encourages mutual assistance and development among its member institutions. The confederation also encourages the establishment of regional higher education institutions. UCA and POLI are members of the *Federación de universidades privadas de América central y Panamá* (FUPAC: Federation of Private Universities of Central America and Panama). Nicaraguan universities also belong to international associations such as the International Association of Universities and the *Unión de universidades de América latina* (UDUAL: Union of Universities of Latin America).

JUAN B. ARRIEN

Educational Associations

Asociación nicaragüense de mujeres universitaria
(Nicaraguan Association of University Women)
Apartado Postal 2501
Managua, Nicaragua

Centro universitario de la Universidad nacional (CUUN)
(University Center of the National University)
Universidad nacional autónoma de Nicaragua
León, Nicaragua

Centro estudiantil universitario de la Universidad centroamericana (CEUUCA)
(University Student Center of the Central American University)
Universidad centroamericana
Managua, Nicaragua

Bibliography

Arellano, J. E. *Historia de la Universidad de León.* (2 vols.) León: Editorial universitaria, 1973, 1974.

Consejo superior universitario centroamericano (CSUCA). *Oferta y demanda de recursos humanos en Centroamérica.* San José: Universidad de Costa Rica, Departamento de publicaciones, 1966.

Fundis, R. J. *Población estudiantil 1960–67.* Managua: Universidad nacional autónoma de Nicaragua, 1967.

Informe anual de INDE y sus programas de FUNDE y EDUCRÉDITO. Managua: Instituto nicaragüense de desarrollo (INDE), 1974.

Presupuesto general de ingresos y egresos de la república. Managua: Ministerio de hacienda y presupuesto. Dirección general del presupuesto, 1975.

Tünnermann Bernheim, C. *Reseña histórica de la conquista de la autonomía universitaria.* León: Editorial universitaria, 1958.

Universidad centroamericana. *Informe estadístico curso 1973–74.* Managua: Librería UCA, 1975.

Universidad nacional autónoma de Nicaragua. Departamento de registro. *La UNAN en cifras 1972–73.* León: Editorial universitaria, 1973.

Yeaza, M. E. "Access to the Autonomous National University of Nicaragua and Employment of Graduates." In *Planning the Development of Universities—III.* Paris: UNESCO, 1974.

See also: Archives: Mediterranean, the Vatican, and Latin America, National Archives of; Central America: Regional Analysis.

NICARAGUAN ASSOCIATION OF INSTITUTIONS OF HIGHER EDUCATION
(Asociación nicaragüense de instituciones de educación superior)

The *Asociación nicaragüense de instituciones de educación superior* (ANIES: Nicaraguan Association of Institutions of Higher Education) was founded in November 1968 to coordinate work among member institutions and encourage cooperation with national and international public and private organizations. Four institutions of higher education in Nicaragua are members: *Universidad nacional autónoma de Nicaragua, Universidad centroamericana, Escuela nacional de agricultura y ganadería,* and *Instituto politécnico de Nicaragua.*

The association studies the academic and administrative problems of Nicaraguan higher education within the context of the whole national education plan and makes recommendations to the institutions and educational authorities concerning the improvement of education at all levels. ANIES encourages exchange of personnel, information, and services among member institutions; promotes the development of teaching activities and research in the institutions while respecting individual characteristics of each; and negotiates in the name of the association and its members for financial and technical assistance for the advancement of Nicaraguan higher education in all respects. By special agreements, members grant equivalencies to students for work completed at other member institutions.

The association is directed by an executive council composed of rectors or general directors of institution members. A president is elected on a rotating basis each year from among these representatives. Under Nicaraguan law, the association may acquire property and it may receive donations.

Instituto politécnico
Apartado 3595
Managua, Nicaragua

NIGER, REPUBLIC OF

Population: 4,600,000 (1975). Student enrollment in primary school: 120,984; secondary school: 12,298; higher education: 937 (university: 521; nonuniversity: 416); higher education abroad: 605. Language of instruction: French. Academic calendar: October to June. Percentage of national budget expended on higher education: 3.2%. [Figures are for 1975 unless otherwise indicated. Source: Service central de la statistique.]

The first institution of higher education in Niger, the *Centre d'enseignement supérieur,* was founded in 1971 and developed into the University of Niamey in 1973. Prior to 1971, students desiring higher education had attended institutions in France or in neighboring countries such as the Ivory Coast, Senegal, or Togo.

The slow development of higher education in Niger can be understood in terms of the historical development of the republic. Niger came within the sphere of interest of France in the late 1800s. In 1904 French military conquest of the area was completed; the military territory of the Niger was set up, and final borders were agreed upon between France and the United Kingdom. From 1904 to 1922 Niger was administered from the Sudan (present-day Mali). In 1922 it was joined as a colony to the federation of French West Africa under a civilian government. Niger achieved autonomy in 1957 and became independent on August 3, 1960.

The first comprehensive law on education for French West Africa was passed in 1896 and augmented by further ordinances in 1903, which established a dual system: one track for Europeans and a few assimilated Africans, another for the rest of the Africans. The system comprised preparatory, elementary, and regional schools as well as one advanced primary school in each territory. Higher education was available in Senegal. Further reorganization of the system took place in 1912 and 1924, but the basic structure changed little during the rest of the colonial period.

Before the arrival of the French, the only education in Niger had been instruction in the Koran, conducted in koranic schools in the Muslim areas. Throughout the French colonial rule, Niger remained one of the educationally least developed French territories; its school system was restricted to the training of personnel to assist the French administrators, and educational facilities were limited in accordance with the need for subordinate administrators. In 1945, when the population numbered more than two million, the nation had only 60 primary schools with an enrollment of 4500 students.

Since independence educational growth has been substantial, although it has been confined mainly to the two lower levels of education. In 1960, 21,000 students were enrolled in primary education. This figure represented 3.6 percent of the age group; by 1974 enrollments had increased to more than 110,000 students, representing 12.3 percent of the age group. Correspondingly, enrollments in secondary education increased from 1400 in general and technical education in 1961 to more than 11,000 in 1974. Since 1971 enrollments in higher education have also shown a steady increase, from 120 students in 1971–72 to 1250 students in 1975; however, 605 students were studying abroad in the latter year. Since independence the government has devoted almost 20 percent of the annual national budget to education. In the middle 1970s higher education is being given considerable emphasis by the government, which guides enrollment increases by awarding scholarships only in studies that have national priority.

Legal Basis of Educational System

The right of every citizen to an education is protected in the constitution of 1959. Each institution of higher education is established by law. The National School of Administration was founded as a public autonomous institution by Law 70-4 of January 22, 1970. The Center of Higher Education was created by Law 71.31 of September 6, 1971, and developed into the University of Niamey by Law 73.23 of September 20, 1973; subsequent decrees established or incorporated the schools within the university. Additional structural and administrative changes are made by decree.

Types of Institutions

Higher education is available at the University of Niamey, which consists of five schools: the school of sciences, the school of letters, the school of health sciences, the higher school of agronomy, and the school of pedagogy. There are also two institutes at the university: the Institute of Human Sciences Research and the Institute for Research into the Teaching of Mathematics.

Nonuniversity higher education is offered at the *Ecole nationale d'administration* (National School of Administration) and in certain courses at the *Ecole nationale de police* (National Police School). All other vocational training is at the secondary level.

Relationship with Secondary Education and Admission Requirements

Most primary and secondary schools in Niger are public, although government-assisted private schools provide education for some 9 percent of the student enrollment. Primary school lasts six years and leads to the *certificat d'études primaires élémentaires* (CEPE). Entry to secondary education requires possession of the CEPE and success in an entrance examination. Secondary education is divided into two cycles; the first cycle lasts one to four years, and the second cycle lasts two to four years, depending on specialization.

The first cycle can be general or specialized education. General education lasts four years and is offered in the *collèges d'enseignement général* or in some *lycées*. The program of study concludes with the examination for the *brevet d'études du premier cycle* (BEPC). The specialized cycle lasts one to three years. One year of study is required for titles such as certified nurse at the National School of Public Health; *gardien de la paix* (peace officer) at the National Police School; and surveyor at the National School of Animal Husbandry. Two years are required for the title *agent d'administration* at the National School of Administration, which also offers a three-year program for the diploma of *agent techniques.*

The second cycle of secondary education is also conducted in general or specialized programs. The three-year general program offered at the *lycées,* which admit holders of the BEPC after a competitive entrance examination, leads to the *baccalauréat.* A technical *baccalauréat* is offered at the technical *lycée* in Maradi. The *baccalauréat* (or equivalent qualifications) or success in an entrance examination determines entry to the university.

Specialized, or vocational, education is available in the second cycle in programs lasting two to four years. Programs at this level are offered by the School of Public Health, the National School of Administration, the National Police School, the Institute of Practical Rural Development, the School of Animal Husbandry, the National School of Posts and Telecommunications, and the normal schools.

Administration and Control

The Ministry of Education is the central authority for education in Niger. The vocational institutions are administered by their respective ministries. The Ministry of Education—headed by the minister, who is assisted by a secretary general—consists of five departments: literacy and adult education, youth and sports, primary education, secondary and technical education, and higher education and scientific research. The National Commission for Educational Reform and Literacy Planning and a technical adviser are also responsible to the minister. The directors of the departments are nominated by the minister. The ministry sets standards and awards degrees, except for those certificates and diplomas that fall within the jurisdiction of other ministries.

The rector, who is the chief executive of the university, is appointed by the president of the republic. Each school and research institute at the university is headed by a director, who is appointed by the rector on the recommendation of the university council.

Administrative and academic affairs are the responsibility of the university council, consisting of the rector, the directors, the professors, representatives of the Ministries of Finance, Health, and Rural Development, and one or two student representatives of each school.

The National School of Administration was created as a public autonomous institution; however, all administrative and other changes are made by decree. The director is assisted by an administrative council, which is broadly based with members drawn from among the administrators of the school, from ministerial departments, and from business and industry. The president also appoints members to the council. In addition, the council has three teacher representatives.

Programs and Degrees

Although the university has existed only since 1973, it incorporated the former *Centre d'enseignement supérieur* in Niamey and thus had the advantage of well-established programs in certain fields. The school of sciences offers programs at three levels: two-year programs for the *diplôme universitaire d'études scientifiques* (DUES), three-year programs leading to the *licence* (the first degree), and four-year programs for the *maîtrise* in the fields of mathematics-physics, physics-chemistry, chemistry-biology, and biology-geology. The school also offers a preparatory year for agronomy students and science courses in conjunction with the school of health sciences. The school of letters has a two-year program leading to the *diplôme universitaire d'études littéraires* (DUEL) in French, English, history, and geography. The school is planning to expand and will award the *licence* in three-year programs and the *maîtrise* in four-year programs in the same fields. The school of pedagogy trains science teachers for the *collèges d'enseignement général* in a two-year program, educational counselors in two years, and primary school inspectors in one year. The school plans to offer one-year programs in educational counseling and two-year programs to train teachers for *lycées*. The higher school of agronomy has five sections: agronomy, animal husbandry, rural engineering, agro-sociology, and soil science; it trains agricultural engineers in a four-year program, the first two years of which are given jointly with the school of sciences. The school of health sciences has a paramedical program lasting four years and also offers a six-year medical program for physicians. The first year of study in this program was offered in 1974–75.

The National School of Administration, which offers education at three levels (lower, middle, and higher), trains department chiefs (*chefs de division*) in a four-year program. The third level of study at the National Police School leads to the title police commissioner after a program of eighteen months.

Financing and Student Financial Aid

Higher education is financed by the state, aided by French subsidies. All foreign scholarships are channeled through the government, which awards them according to national manpower needs. Once selected, students cannot change their fields of study except by agreement of the Ministry of Planning without having to pay back all of the financial aid received.

Student Social Background and Access to Education

Because of financial and other restrictions, only about 12 percent of the age group have access to primary education. Student wastage is high: about 11 percent of students continue from primary into secondary and technical education, and about 1200 students attend higher education. Thus, only an elite group of students reach higher education. In addition to financial restrictions, several other factors militate against a rapid expansion of the system. The language of instruction is French, and the educational process includes several major examinations (undertaken after grades 6, 10, and 12) which are given in French in accordance with French standards. Thus, failure rates are high. Most of the schools, especially at the secondary level, are located in the southern areas of the country, making access to education less available to the nomadic peoples of the north. Access to education has also been affected by the financial strains of the Sahelian drought; by the lack of facilities and qualified teachers; and by resistance to education on the part of village leaders and parents, especially among the nomadic peoples.

The percentage of women enrolled at all levels of education has grown steadily from some 20 percent in 1958 to about 34 percent in 1974. Female enrollment in higher education, however, is still only about 12 percent of the total. The number of female teachers at the primary level increased five percent, from 28 to 33 percent, between 1973 and 1974.

Teaching Staff

The ranks of teaching staff at the university are *professeur* (professor), *maître de conférences* (senior lecturer), *maître-assistant* (lecturer), and *assistant*.

The staff provided under technical assistance from France are appointed by the rector (in agreement with the French Ministry of Cooperation) for a period of two years; their salaries are paid by the French government. National and locally appointed staff are compensated from the national budget; their appointments are made by the rector on the recommendation of the department. Qualifications for appointment are university degrees such as *doctorat de spécialité* or Ph.D. Promotion requires an examination by the *Comité consultatif universitaire* (Consultative University Committee). The teaching staff at the school of agronomy and the nonuniversity institutions hold part-time appointments at the university and are also employed in government service, research, or industry.

Research Activities

The Institute of Human Sciences Research at the university coordinates all human sciences research in the country and undertakes basic research on the large ethnic groups and on the human problems connected with national development. It also cooperates with institutions and associations in other nations and undertakes publication, alone or in cooperation with other organizations. The Institute for Research into the Teaching of Mathematics is concerned with promoting the teaching of mathematics and also conducts research into methods of instruction and the need for adoption and revision of programs. Other research institutes generally deal with projects in the field of agriculture and are not attached to the university.

Current Problems and Trends and Cooperation with Industry

The task of increasing literacy in a nation where the formal school system reaches only 12 percent of the population is one of the major problems in Niger. The low output of graduates of higher education, and the attendant lack of qualified personnel for teaching positions and for government and business, hinders expansion of the educational system and national development. An attempt is being made to alleviate personnel shortages by directed study—that is, the granting of scholarships in accordance with stated manpower needs. The mandatory government service upon graduation is seen as one way to provide needed personnel in fields where the need is greatest. Financial restrictions, along with the problem of absorbing graduates in an economy which is 90 percent rural, continue to limit the output of graduates of higher education and thus force Niger to rely on foreign personnel, mainly French.

In 1973 an educational reform for the ruralization of the lower levels of the educational system was initiated. The ruralization program is expected to integrate the formal school system with the government's adult literacy programs. The creation of a separate department of literacy and adult education within the Ministry of National Education is evidence of the government's concern with literacy training. All expansion of educational programs is taking place within strict national manpower plans.

There is little industry in Niger, but in order to ensure full employment of the graduates of higher education a Manpower Department is charged with maintaining records of available positions, both in government and in private enterprise.

International Cooperation

Like most of the other former French territories, Niger has maintained close ties with France in educational matters; programs and examinations are closely attuned to those in France. Niger also is a recipient of French assistance, which is given in the form of capital and technical assistance and in the form of scholarships. In 1974 *Fonds d'aide et de coopération*, the French technical assistance agency, granted 104 scholarships to students from Niger. Scholarships were also granted by a number of other nations and organizations, among them the European Economic Community, several Arab states, Belgium, Canada, Switzerland, and the Soviet Union. The greatest number of students studied in France, Senegal, Togo, and the Soviet Union. Niger has also been a recipient of assistance from the United Nations, which participated in the establishment of the National School of Administration and other projects.

[Assistance received from B. Ba, Rector, University of Niamey.]

Bibliography

Annuaire des statistiques scolaires, 1973–74. Niamey: Ministère de l'éducation nationale, de la jeunesse et des sports, 1974.

Bolibaugh, J. B. *Educational Development in Guinea, Mali, Senegal, and Ivory Coast.* Washington, D.C.: U.S. Department of Health, Education and Welfare, 1972.

Bolibaugh, J. B., and Hanna, P. R. *French Edu-*

cational Strategies for Sub-Saharan Africa: Their Intent, Derivation and Development. Stanford, California: Stanford University, Comparative Education Center, 1974.

Hinkmann, U. *Niger.* Munich, Federal Republic of Germany: R. Oldenburg Verlag, 1968.

Labrousse, A. *La France et l'aide à l'éducation dans 14 états africains et Malgache.* Paris: International Institute of Educational Planning, April 1971.

Moumouni, A. *Education in Africa.* New York: Praeger, 1968.

Obichere, B. *West African States and European Expansion: The Dahomey-Niger Hinterland 1885–1898.* New Haven, Connecticut: Yale University Press, 1971.

Rapport annuel 1970–71. Niamey: Ecole nationale d'administration, 1971.

Scanlon, D. E. (Ed.) *Traditions of African Education.* New York: Teachers College Press, Columbia University, 1964.

Séré de Rivières, E. *Histoire du Niger.* Paris: Berger-Levrault, 1965.

Université du Niger: Année 1974–75. Niamey: University of Niamey, 1974.

See also: Archives: Africa and Asia, National Archives of.

NIGERIA, FEDERAL REPUBLIC OF

Population: 80,000,000 (estimated 1973). Student enrollment in primary school: 4,450,000; secondary school (academic, vocational, technical): 649,900; higher education: 40,000 (1976). Language of instruction: English. Academic calendar: September to June. Percentage of gross national product (GNP) expended on all education: 2.6% (1971; 3.4% estimated for 1980); higher education: .02% (1971; .05% estimated for 1980). [Enrollment figures are for 1973.]

Since attaining independence from Great Britain in 1960, Nigeria has been steadily building on the educational foundations established during the previous hundred years by Western missionaries and the British colonial administration.

Prior to the 1840s, when the first missionary schools were established in the south, only northern Islamic training for a small number of Muslim boys. When British rule began in 1861, the traditional Koranic schools and the missionary schools were, for the most part, allowed to function

independently, although occasionally financial support was provided by the British. Most missionary schools were designed to propagate Christianity and offered little training beyond the primary level.

In the early 1920s the Phelps-Stokes Fund of New York, a private American foundation, conducted a survey of British East, Central, and West Africa, delineating the weaknesses of the educational system. Soon afterward, the British colonial administration began to take a more active role in providing education for Nigerians. The survey had exposed "the British government's neglect of African education and the gap between what the few existing schools were teaching and the actual needs of the people" (Fafunwa, 1971, p. 22). The British responded by establishing schools designed primarily to prepare nationals for low-level clerical positions within the colonial administration. The majority of these schools offered only primary education; however, several secondary schools had been established by this time as well.

In 1932 Yaba Higher College, the first institution to provide higher education in Nigeria, was established by the British in response to demands of local leaders. However, the institution did little more than provide training for intermediate personnel for the civil service. In 1948 the college became the nucleus of another higher education institution, the University College, Ibadan, which was established on the recommendation of the Commission on Higher Education in West Africa, generally known as the Elliot Commission. The Elliot Commission was formed in 1943 to carry out a study of higher education in British West Africa, and its report was published in 1945. The University College was closely monitored by the University of London and the Inter-University Council for the Colonies (Fafunwa, 1974). Like its predecessor, University College failed to satisfy the demands for a full Nigerian University controlled by Nigerians.

A turning point in the development of education occurred in 1954, when Nigeria became a federation and attained self-government over internal affairs, including education. Numerous primary and secondary schools were established, and more students were enrolled at the two levels between 1954 and 1959 than during the whole period of British rule.

The expansion of facilities at the primary and secondary levels led to increased demands for comparable expansion at the higher education level. In the mid 1950s plans were made for a University of Nigeria to be located in Nsukka. Due to the initiative of Nnamdi Azikiwe, then premier of the Eastern Region, the university structure was to follow the model of the American land-grant college.

In 1959 the federal minister of education appointed a commission to determine Nigeria's needs in the area of postsecondary and higher education through 1980. The commission, commonly known as the Ashby Commission, recommended that the government give support to the embryonic University of Nigeria, that the University College be developed into a full university, and that two additional universities be formed. A fifth university was recommended in a minority report. The government accepted both the majority and minority reports; and by 1962, just two years after attaining independence from Great Britain, Nigeria had established five full universities. By late 1975 this figure had doubled: In 1972 the University of Benin was formally established; and the additional four universities called for in the Third Five-Year Development Plan had been established. In addition, the federal government had established three university colleges.

In August of 1975 the federal government assumed full control of higher education, formerly the responsibility of either the federal or state governments. The federal government's decision to assume control over higher education was made largely to prevent individual states or organizations from establishing new universities without first seeking the approval of the federal government, which is obliged to

give financial assistance to the universities for current and capital expenditure.

Perhaps the most far-reaching decision in the history of education in Nigeria was made by the federal government in 1974, when former head of state General Yakubu Gowon announced plans for the introduction of free universal primary education in 1976. A massive preparation program was undertaken in an effort to provide the facilities and the staff necessary to implement the program.

Legal Basis of Educational System

Prior to August 1975 the universities of Nigeria were established under state or federal law with the approval of the federal government. In 1955 the government of the Eastern Region enacted the University of Nigeria Law, which called for the establishment of the University of Nigeria. After the 1960 opening of the university, it began to operate under the University of Nigeria Law, 1961, to which minor amendments were later added.

The University of Lagos began operation under the University of Lagos Act, 1962, superseded by the University of Lagos Decree 3 of 1967. The University of Ife first operated under the Provisional Law of 1961, which provided for its establishment. In 1970 the government of the Western State replaced the provisional law with the University of Ife Edict 14 of 1970.

The University of Benin, formerly the Institute of Technology, was raised to university status by the government of the Mid-Western State with the Institute of Technology Edict, 1972. In 1974 the federal government assumed control of the university. The University of Ibadan was established by a University Act, 1962, from the former University College, Ibadan; and Ahmadu Bello University was established by a law of June 1962. In September 1975 two new universities, at Calabar and Jos (based on the existing university colleges), were established by the federal military government as were universities at Maiduguri and Sokoto and the university colleges in Ilorin, Port Harcourt, and Kano.

Types of Institutions

Higher education is available at the ten universities and at polytechnics, teacher training institutions, and private institutions.

The University of Nigeria, Nsukka is the country's oldest university; it was established in 1960, two years before the University College, Ibadan was raised to full university status. Patterned after the American land-grant college, the university has the distinction of being the first institution in former British-controlled Africa to develop outside the British academic sphere of influence. In 1974 the university consisted of twelve faculties: agricultural sciences, arts, biological sciences, business administration, education, engineering, law, medicine, physical sciences, social sciences, and two faculties of environmental studies. In addition to the main campus at Nsukka, the university had campuses in Enugu and Calabar. In 1975 the Calabar campus became one of the four new universities called for under the Third Five-Year Development Plan (1975–1980). Institutes of economic development, African studies, and education are also attached to the university.

Ahmadu Bello University opened in 1962, absorbing the Zaria branch of the Nigerian College of Arts, Science and Technology; the Research and Special Services Division of the Ministry of Agriculture (Northern Nigeria) at Samaru; and the School for Arabic Studies in Kano. The university consists of eleven faculties: administration, agriculture, arts and Islamic studies, arts and social sciences, education, engineering, environmental design, law, medicine, science, and veterinary medicine. The university also operates institutes of administration, agricultural research and special services, education, health, and child development research. Formerly attached to the university was the Abdullahi

Bayero College, which became an autonomous university college in 1975. Also part of the university are the division of agricultural and livestock services training, the adult education and general extension services unit, and a school of basic studies.

The University of Ibadan gained its present status in 1962 after operating since 1948 as University College, Ibadan. The university has faculties of arts, science, medicine, social sciences, education, agriculture, forestry, and veterinary science. In addition, the university operates institutes of African studies, applied science and technology, education, child health, and social and economic research. A branch campus, six hundred miles away in Jos, became a university in 1975.

The University of Ife opened in 1962 with faculties of agriculture, arts, economics and social studies, law, and science. Five faculties have since been added: education, pharmacy, technology, health science, and administration. The university also operates institutes of administration, African studies, agricultural research and training, education, physical education, and population and manpower studies. A branch campus of the university operates in Ibadan.

The University of Lagos was established in 1962 as an urban university with an emphasis on education in the fields of commerce and business administration, economics, and other social sciences. The university consists of a college of education, a college of medicine, and faculties of social sciences, law, engineering, arts, sciences, and business administration. In addition, the university operates a comparative education study and adaptation center, a continuing education center, and an institute of child health.

The University of Benin, which achieved university status in 1972, consists of faculties of engineering, medicine and pharmacy, science, education, and arts and social sciences.

Aside from the universities, higher education is available in a number of institutions. Advanced teacher training is provided in six teacher training colleges, most of which are affiliated to the universities. The polytechnics and the technical colleges provide mainly technical or commercial training. Other postsecondary training is available in private religious colleges, trade centers, and government training institutions such as police colleges, the air force school, and the navy training school.

Adult education is a function of the universities as well as the state governments and other public or private agencies. Literacy training is the main responsibility of the Adult Education Division of the state governments. At the University of Ife, adult education takes the form of short-term training courses designed for personnel such as teachers, clerks, and typists. The Continuing Education Center at the University of Lagos coordinates adult education programs with professional bodies and with commercial and employer associations, trade unions, cooperative societies, and similar organizations throughout the country (*Directory of Adult Education Centres in Africa,* 1974). The programs include postprofessional short courses, seminars, workshops, and conferences designed for groups such as banking executives, architects, town planners, and estate surveyors and valuers.

The Division of Extra-Mural Studies at the University of Nigeria offers both long-term and short-term intensive courses on and off campus, in the form of seminars, conferences, workshops, refresher courses, in-service training, and extramural tutorial classes (*Directory of Adult Education Centres in Africa,* 1974). Ahmadu Bello University provides adult education courses through its Adult Education and General Extension Services Unit. In addition to the normal classroom approach, courses such as trade unionism, health, and Nigerian culture are presented via television and radio.

Relationship with Secondary Education

The general system of education in Nigeria consists of six or seven years of primary education and five years of secondary education. For some students second-

ary education is followed by two years of higher school in preparation for university admission.

In order to gain admission to secondary school, students must pass the first school-leaving examination. Access to secondary school has been limited, since expansion at the secondary level has not kept pace with that at the primary level. Approximately 12 percent of all primary school students gain access to secondary school. Fees are charged at the secondary level, but, according to terms of the current five-year development plan, secondary fees will be eliminated; in the meantime, fees are being lowered and made uniform throughout the federation.

At the end of the secondary school program, students sit for either the West African Certificate Examination; the General Certificate of Education Examination, ordinary level; or the examinations of overseas professional bodies such as the Royal Society of Arts. Some students enter the university on the basis of these examinations, while others enter a two-year higher school program leading to the Higher School Certificate or the General Certificate of Education, advanced level.

Admission Requirements

Although admission requirements vary among certain faculties or departments, admission to the universities is generally determined by the results of one of several examinations. Upon completion of the secondary school program, students who achieve a certain number of passes or credits on the West African Certificate Examination or the General Certificate of Education Examination, ordinary level, may be accepted for a one-year preliminary course at the university after passing a concessional entrance examination. Approximately three fifths of those admitted to the university enter in this manner. The remaining two fifths are admitted directly to the degree programs after earning the Higher School Certificate of Education, advanced level.

Admissions to a university are determined by individual admissions committees. The minimum age limit at most of the universities is seventeen.

Administration and Control

Universities in Nigeria have considerable autonomy; each higher education institution is autonomous in administrative, financial, and academic affairs and in the appointment of faculty and staff. However, since the universities are recipients of government grants, the government exercises certain control. The National Universities Commission, an independent body set up by the federal government, serves as an intermediary between the government and the universities. The commission is responsible for disbursing federal funds to the universities and advising the federal government on the financial needs of the universities and on other related matters. Members of the commission include eminent laymen, senior academicians, and a few government representatives. A 1974 decree gave the commission greater powers and control than in the past over the financial and physical organization of the universities. The decree provided for an executive secretary and a full-time chairman for the commission.

The universities are connected to their respective governments through the visitor, who at the Universities of Ibadan and Lagos is the head of state and at the other universities is the governor of the state. The visitor appoints the chancellor, a ceremonial officer. Under a new 1975 edict, the visitor at the University of Ife has the additional power of removing the chancellor for good cause after consultation with the university council. The visitor also has the authority to confirm, alter, or overrule decisions of the council.

The chief executive officer of the university is the vice-chancellor, who works in consultation with the pro-chancellor. Other administrative officers include the deputy vice-chancellor, the registrar, the bursar, and the librarian.

The governing board of the university is the university council, which is respon-sible for general policy and finance. The council is composed of 80 percent laymen and 20 percent academic staff, including the vice-chancellor and his deputy. The chairman of the council is the pro-chancellor.

The university senate is the ultimate academic authority. It defines and establishes courses of study and curriculum content and sets academic standards, including degree requirements and levels of achievement. The senate works through its academic committees, such as the committee of deans.

For each faculty at the university there is a faculty board, which is responsible for details of syllabi and examinations and may also deal with matters referred to it by the senate. The graduate and teaching members of the staff form the congregation. At the University of Benin the congregation also includes the vice-chancellor, the deputy vice-chancellor, deans, and other officers as determined by the senate.

Several of the universities operate colleges or institutes with varying administrative structures. At Ahmadu Bello University the institutes of administration, education, health, and agricultural research are semiautonomous within the university. The institutes generally are under the authority of the university council. Each institute has a board of governors, which includes representatives of the government and the university. At the University of Lagos the colleges of education and medicine are governed by separate courts of governors.

Programs and Degrees

Traditionally, curricula in Nigerian universities have been patterned after the British system; however, there now is a trend to replace the former single honors degree courses with more broadly based courses. Several of the universities have followed the pattern first established by the University of Nigeria, Nsukka and have introduced a general studies program based on the American university system.

The first degree awarded at the university is the bachelor's degree, which requires three years of study beyond higher school or four, including a preliminary year of study at the university. The first degree in medicine, veterinary medicine, dental surgery, and engineering generally requires five years of study. The next degree offered at the university is the master's degree, which is awarded after one to three years of study beyond the bachelor's degree. Candidates may enroll in the master's program on a full-time or, at the universities of Ibadan and Ife, a part-time basis.

The doctoral degree requires at least one full year or two years of part-time study after the Master of Philosophy degree at the University of Ife, while at the University of Ibadan the doctoral degree program requires three full years of study or four years of part-time study beyond the bachelor's degree. The doctoral program at the University of Lagos involves two years of study beyond the master's degree.

The universities offer numerous diploma and certificate programs below degree level and at the postgraduate level. Most of these courses extend for a period of one or two years.

Certificates and diplomas below degree level are awarded in areas such as animal health and husbandry, electrical engineering, music education, public administration, international affairs, education, law, mass communication, forestry, and Arabic and Islamic studies. At the postgraduate level, diploma or certificate courses include education, drama, meteorology, public health, agriculture, librarianship, tropical medicine, and journalism.

Financing

The Nigerian National Universities Commission disburses grants from the federal government to institutions of higher education for capital and recurrent expenditures. In addition, all Nigerian universities charge fees, which cover tuition, room and board, and examinations. About 90 percent of all undergraduates live on campus. Student fees, however, account for only a small percentage of the income received by the universities, and in 1975 the universities in addition cut tuition fees by about 50 percent.

Student Financial Aid

Numerous scholarships are available for university study, and approximately 40 percent of all undergraduates benefit from a scholarship program. Many agencies award scholarships to students. The largest contributors are the federal and state governments, followed by statutory corporations (such as the marketing boards), foundations, and foreign governments. During the 1973–74 academic year the Federal Scholarships Board granted 1700 graduate bursaries, 127 postgraduate bursaries, and 542 technical bursaries. The government also grants loans to needy students; in 1973 the Students' Loan Board granted nearly five thousand loans.

Student Social Background and Access to Education

Enrollments at the higher education level reflect the imbalance that exists between educational opportunities in the north and south at the lower levels of education. Some northern states—such as Kano, North-Eastern, and North-Western—have little more than 10 percent of their school-age population enrolled in primary school; in contrast, some southern states, such as Lagos, have nearly reached universal enrollment. With the introduction of universal primary education in 1976, the imbalance at the primary school level should be gradually eliminated.

In addition to the north-south imbalance, there is a rural-urban imbalance. Students from the better secondary schools in urban areas generally have easier access to the university than do those from rural secondary schools. The universities also have a larger male than female enrollment and a larger enrollment of students who identify themselves as being Christians than students who are Muslims. Students from all financial levels in society are represented at the universities; a large number are from relatively poor families, where education is viewed as a means of social mobility.

Teaching Staff

The types and ranks of teaching staff are professor, reader, associate professor, senior lecturer, lecturer grades I and II, assistant lecturer, and graduate assistant. There is a hierarchy of tutors—comprising tutor, senior tutor, and principal tutor—in colleges involved in programs below degree level, particularly in affiliated teacher training colleges and agricultural colleges.

Faculty selection, appointment, and promotion are competitive and are based on academic excellence, research activities, and teaching ability. Salary rates are determined by each university council in concert with other university councils. In 1972 the federal government set up a salary review commission, whose report created a uniform salary rate for faculty and staff in all public institutions of higher learning.

Research Activities

Some basic and applied research is undertaken in the universities by the academic staff. The control of research activities is vested in each university, and the heads of academic departments supervise the research of faculty members. Although the universities provide modest financial assistance for research, staff are encouraged to seek outside assistance. Those who receive grants from the university are expected to submit regular progress reports.

Current Problems and Trends

The present educational system, patterned after the British system, has come under heavy criticism as being unsuited to the needs of the state. Discussions have centered on developing a viable substitute more responsive to local needs. The Sixth Form, or higher school—which leads to the Higher School Certificate or the General Certificate of Education, advanced level— has come under special criticism; and the University of Ife and Ibadan Polytechnic are phasing out their Higher School Certificate courses and are instead expanding their teacher training colleges in preparation for universal primary education.

Like many other developing countries, Nigeria faces the problem of a shortage of facilities at the higher education level as the universities are finding it increasingly difficult to cope with the growing number of students who possess the qualifications necessary for university entrance. The four new universities and three university colleges will help alleviate this problem, and the aim is to increase university enrollment from the 1975 level of more than 20,000 to 53,000 by 1980.

Among other problems is the shortage of staff in the engineering, technology, and medical departments, which serves to limit enrollments at a time when national manpower need in these areas is great. At the same time, the number of applicants in the arts continues to grow, creating a surplus of arts graduates each year. Another area of concern is the shortage of trained intermediate-level manpower, a problem that will likely continue until the lower-level but equally vital positions can be made more attractive in comparison with the prestigious positions that require a university degree.

In an effort to make higher education more responsive to the needs of society, the medical faculties are now making clinical courses available in peripheral hospitals, as opposed to the usual practice of offering clinical courses only in one central hospital.

As of 1973 all university graduates have been involved in a program, the National Youth Service Corps, designed to build national unity and at the same time provide a pool of skilled manpower able to be deployed where most needed. Members of the National Youth Service Corps serve their country after graduation for a one-year period as teachers, farmers, hospital workers, and road construction workers. Members of the corps are paid during their period of service, and many are employed by the Federal Public Service Commission at the end of their service. The program is being expanded to include graduates of technical colleges, polytechnics, and other postsecondary institutions.

Relationship with Industry

Several areas of study, such as engineering, geology, and related studies, have agreements with industry to provide students with work experience before graduation. Such practical experience is being demanded by the professional associations. The practical training required is of varying lengths, from summer vacations to six months, in different fields. Some industries also have established scholarships for undergraduate and postgraduate students in the universities. Others have erected buildings for academic departments, and some have supplied equipment. On the whole, the participation of industrial concerns in the universities represents approximately 5 percent of total university finances. Also, there is some collaboration between industry and academic departments in specialized research, particularly electronics, mining, building trades, and highway designs.

International Cooperation

Nigeria has been a recipient of a substantial amount of international assistance. Since independence the major international contributors to the development of Nigeria's first five universities were the governments of the Federal Republic of Germany, Great Britain, the Netherlands, and the United States; the Ford, Carnegie, and Rockefeller Foundations in the United States; and the Nuffield Foundation in the United Kingdom. The aid has been used for construction, research, staff development, scholarships, and equipment.

Several Nigerian universities operate exchange programs with universities around the world. As an example, students enrolled at the University of Ibadan for the study of French attend the University of Dakar in Senegal for six weeks during their vacation following the end of the first year of study; at the end of their second year, they enroll in the same university or the University of Paris (Sorbonne) for a one-year period.

[Questionnaire answered by Alexander O. Ajayi, Registrar, University of Ife, Ile-Ife, Nigeria.]

Educational Associations

Nigerian Union of Teachers
29 Commercial Avenue
P.M.B. 1044
Yaba, Lagos, Nigeria

Nigerian Association of University Women
P.O. Box 1440
Lagos, Nigeria

National Union of Nigerian Students (NUNS)
University of Nigeria
Nsukka, Nigeria

Bibliography

The Admission and Academic Placement of Students from Selected Sub-Saharan African Countries. A Workshop Report. Washington, D.C.: National Association for Foreign Students Affairs and American Association of Collegiate Registrars and Admissions Officers, 1973.

African Colleges and Universities. A Digest of Information. New York: African American Institute, 1970.

Ayida, A. A., and Onitiri, H. M. (Eds.) *Reconstruction and Development in Nigeria.* Proceedings of a National Conference. Ibadan: Oxford University Press, 1971.

Directory of Adult Education Centres in Africa. Dakar, Senegal: Regional Office for Education in Africa Documentation Section, 1974.

Directory of African Universities. Accra-North, Ghana: Association of African Universities, July 1974.

Fafunwa, A. B. *A History of Nigerian Higher Education.* Lagos: Macmillan, 1971.

Fafunwa, A. B. *The Growth and Development of Nigerian Universities.* OLC Paper No. 4. Washington, D.C.: Overseas Liaison Committee, American Council of Education, April, 1974.

Fafunwa, A. B., and Hanson, J. W. "The Post Independence of Nigerian Universities." In P. Altbach (Ed.), *University Reform.* Cambridge, Massachusetts: Schenkman, 1974. Pp. 95–115.

Investment in Education: The Report of the Commission on Post-School Certificate and Higher Edu-

cation in Nigeria. Lagos: Federal Ministry of Education, 1960.

Nduka, O. "Toward a National Policy on Education in Nigeria." *Prospects,* Winter 1973, *3,* 438–450.

Nelson, H. D., and others. *Area Handbook for Nigeria.* Washington, D.C.: U.S. Government Printing Office, 1972.

Nigeria Handbook. Lagos: Federal Ministry of Information, 1973.

Nigerian Human Resource Development and Utilization. A final report prepared for the United States Agency for International Development. New York: Education and World Affairs, Committee on Education and Human Resource Development, Nigeria Project Taskforce. December 1967.

Ogunlade, F. O. "Education and Politics in Colonial Nigeria: The Case of King's College, Lagos (1906–1911)." *Journal of the Historical Society of Nigeria,* June 1974, *7,* 325–346.

Okafor, N. *The Development of Universities in Nigeria.* Essex, England: Longman Group, 1971.

Okedara, F. T. "Adult Education in Nigeria." *West African Journal of Education,* February 1972, *16,* 55–68.

Oyemakinde, W. "Manpower Training and the Nigerian Labour Market" *Pan-African Journal,* Winter 1974, *7,* 323–330.

Taiwo, C. O. "The Administration and Control of Education in Nigeria." *West African Journal of Education,"* 1972, *16* (1), 5–10.

Taiwo, C. O. "The Education Edicts of Nigeria." *West African Journal of Education,* June 1974, *18,* 183–187.

Tims, W. *Nigeria: Options for Long-Term Development.* Report of a mission sent to Nigeria by the World Bank. Baltimore: Johns Hopkins University Press, 1974.

Yesufu, T. M. (Ed.) *Creating the African University.* Ibadan: Oxford University Press, 1973.

See also: Africa, Sub-Saharan: Regional Analysis; Archives: Africa and Asia, National Archives of; Cooperative Education and Off-Campus Experience: Cooperative Education Worldwide; Health Services, Worldwide University; Planning, Development and Coordination: Regional Planning of Higher Education.

NIGERIA UNION OF TEACHERS

The Nigeria Union of Teachers (NUT) was founded in 1931 to promote the association of teachers in all the states of Nigeria; to provide means for the cooperation of teachers and the expression of their collective opinions upon matters affecting the interests of education and the teaching profession; to cooperate with governments, ministries of education, universities, and all recognized agencies in Nigeria for the improvement of education and the teaching profession; to endeavor to secure the removal of difficulties, abuses, and obsolete regulations detrimental to progress; and to offer advice and assistance of teachers to governments, ministries of education, boards of education, universities, and other organizations—public or private—that are involved with educational affairs. In 1974 the Nigerian military government invited NUT to participate in forming a new national policy on education.

NUT has an important involvement with higher education through its representation on boards of delegates and professional committees (responsible for designing major policies affecting undergraduate, postgraduate, diploma, and certificate courses) in institutes of education at the following universities: University of Ibadan, University of Lagos, University of Ife, and University of Nigeria, Nsukka.

The *Nigerian School Master,* published three times a year, is the official journal of NUT.

29 Commercial Avenue
P.M.B. 1044
Yaba, Lagos, Nigeria

S. K. BABALOLA

NONACADEMIC PERSONNEL ADMINISTRATION

Universities exist for the teaching of students and the carrying out of research. Therefore, it is understandable that attention is most often concentrated on the role of the academic staff, whose function is to carry out these activities, and on the student, whose role is that of consumer. But there is another significant group in the university—the nonacademic staff—

that is far greater in number than academic staff.

Increasing Awareness of Nonacademic Staff

Although the position of nonacademic personnel has previously been subordinate to that of the rest of the university community, there is evidence from many countries of a new awareness of their role and significance. In the United Kingdom there is now a comprehensive national negotiating structure; there are moves to coordinate salaries among Australian universities; the personnel function is beginning to emerge in India; Canadian nonacademic staff are increasingly being considered as an integral and vital part of the university; and universities in the Republic of South Africa are directing a great deal of attention to the problems of nonacademic staff employment.

There appear to be three main reasons for this growing awareness. First, all countries have experienced a rapid expansion of higher education, and this has emphasized the problem of organization. Clearly, nonacademic manpower is an important element in the organization as well as a large consumer of recurrent finance. In many countries the problems of inflation have replaced the problems of earlier decades; the business function has become a very important partner to the academic function.

Second, there has been an undoubted growth in personnel management and labor relations, as specialties and universities, like other employers, are having to respond to this change. In some countries this process has developed for both academic and nonacademic staff. In others, however, there is still a reluctance to regard academic staff as employees in the same way as nonacademic staff—particularly where academic staff play a principal part in university government.

Third, government legislation and intervention have influenced the universities in various ways. There have been legislation on employment and labor relations policies and inquiries into salary systems and levels. Governmental social policies have had their effect, as have governmental reforms of universities. All these different forces have helped, to a greater or lesser extent, to stimulate the growing awareness of nonacademic staff employment.

Categories and Organization of Nonacademic Staff

Nonacademic staff have generally been defined as those whose function is either to assist academic staff or to provide general services for the university community. However, there are some staff positions that are variously defined. For example, in the United Kingdom and Australia, senior administrative staff and senior library staff are traditionally regarded as having academic status. On the other hand, such positions are clearly of nonacademic status in other countries, such as South Africa, Poland, and the Netherlands. In Canada different universities vary in their treatment of senior library staff, but senior administrators are regarded as nonacademic. In Nigeria senior library staff have recently been given academic status.

It may be as difficult to generalize with other categories. In the United States, for example, senior computer and all research staff may be regarded as nonacademic, whereas in the United Kingdom many staff in both categories are clearly academic in status. In the Netherlands certain computer staff are regarded as academic, but there is no distinct category of research staff.

Apart from personnel in these gray areas, it is easy to identify the three main groups of nonacademic staff in all universities. First there are the laboratory technical staff, who work very closely with academics in teaching and research and who bring to universities as great a range of technical skills as may be found in many outside industries. Technicians work in a great variety of situations, including teaching in laboratories, workshops, and research centers. The second group is that of clerical and related staff, which can be subdivided into those with typing and secretarial skills, those involved with clerical duties, and those with supervisory or junior managerial responsibilities. Such personnel work in either academic or administrative departments. The third major group consists of manual workers and related staff. These staff members usually work in the service areas of the university—in cleaning, portering, security, catering, and maintenance—but a few may work in various capacities in academic departments. In all countries there are various other small groups that do not fit easily into the three main categories. These include workers in health centers, student facilities, museums, library binderies, and television services.

Most universities are organized into academic departments, academic services, and administrative departments. Academic departments are concerned with teaching and research in specific fields of study. Academic services provide some kind of direct assistance with teaching and research, such as libraries, computer centers, and audiovisual aids units. Administrative departments are concerned with the business function of the university rather than with its academic function. All three subdivisions employ nonacademic staff; technical staff are found in academic and academic service departments, clerical staff in all three areas, and manual staff principally in administrative departments.

The methods by which staff levels are determined vary greatly and are difficult to describe without full information on the systems of organization and financing in individual countries. To give one example of organization, in the University of Hong Kong the nonacademic staff needs of academic departments are calculated on the basis of a ratio with academic staff, while the nonacademic staff needs of administrative departments are adjusted as and when the demands on their services make adjustment necessary. Once the general level of staffing has been determined, it may be maintained either by use of a departmental establishment, which gives the maximum number of each type or grade of employee that may be appointed until the university decides to change the staffing level of the department, or by use of a financial limitation. The latter technique is often employed with manual staff, where it may be necessary to have the flexibility to fill vacant posts in different ways to meet the fluctuating demands of the work.

In the United Kingdom, the Federal Republic of Germany, Canada, and South Africa, among others, the system of controlling and filling vacant posts is being affected by the current economic climate. Many universities in different countries are having to abolish vacant posts or to lay off some nonessential staff.

Personnel and Labor Relations Administration

It is difficult to generalize about the way in which personnel management has developed in universities. In the United Kingdom many of the first personnel administrators were people who had been carrying out personnel duties as part of a more general administrative role. In the United States personnel administration often arose out of the employment of nonacademic staff and was originally associated with that category only.

Personnel administration may be the ultimate responsibility of the chief administrator of the university, although he may delegate the actual detailed work involved to a specialist administrator. In some countries it is that personnel administrator who acts on behalf of the university in the appointment of staff; in others it is the chief administrator; and in some, such as Poland and South Africa, it is the head of the university. The relationship of the personnel department to other parts of the administration is governed very much by the method of organization of the individual university. The personnel department must be in close contact with the finance department, in relation to such activities as the paying of salaries and pension administration, and for policy matters, such as the authorization for filling new or vacant posts. Most other internal relationships involve the personnel department in its role as an advisory department to line management; in this respect, it is unique in having working contacts with all other departments in the university.

Practice varies concerning the personnel department's responsibility for both academic and nonacademic staff. In the United Kingdom there are a number of universities where academic staff are still appointed by the officer responsible for academic and student affairs. In the United States academic staff are beginning to be handled by central personnel offices, whereas in the Netherlands and South Africa personnel departments deal with both categories.

However, whether or not the personnel department handles academic staff, the actual range of activities undertaken by the department is governed by the organization of the university and the stage of development that the university, or even the country, has reached in terms of personnel management policies. It would be hard to find a personnel department not responsible for staff recruitment, conditions of employment, and labor relations, but there are many that do not handle the payment of salaries and wages, pension schemes, health and safety regulations, and staff communications. In Canada and the United States, where universities have kept up with the general level of social development, personnel departments generally handle all these matters.

Personnel departments base many of their actions on the information contained in personal and other records systems. Therefore, it is essential that records are kept accurately and are readily accessible. There are many systems in operation. For example, the *Institut teknoloji kebangsaan* in Malaysia allocates a record of service book to each employee in which every as-

pect of his employment is recorded. In other countries there are a vast number of different manual systems involving personal files and record cards. The computer is used extensively in the calculation of salaries and wages and is being used to an increasing extent in the maintenance of personnel records systems.

Safeguarding the confidentiality of personnel records from unauthorized persons is a universally accepted principle of personnel management. However, the question of how much access employees should have to their own personal files is a more controversial matter. The University of Alberta in Canada, for example, allows nonacademic staff members complete access to their own files on request, and this is written into the personnel manual of procedures. Similar policies are now being adopted in the United States.

Classification of Nonacademic Staff

The extent to which the three groups of nonacademic staff can be analyzed into definite job structures varies considerably. The *Handbook of College and University Administration* (Knowles, 1970) calls on universities to introduce a systematic classification of each new job and a regular review of existing jobs, and, in the United States, personnel classification is well developed.

However, such classification is possible only when a basic structure has been established. The structure may be just a series of rates of pay loosely related to general levels of responsibility, or it may be a range of rates that are very closely linked to a hierarchy of detailed job descriptions. In both cases personnel may be recruited into the system on the basis of experience, qualifications, and potential, but the methods of review of grading level are bound to be different. Where the system is informal and ill defined, changes in grading are difficult to control because they tend to be made on grounds of personal merit. When the system is closely defined, changes in grading must be related to the criteria of the system alone.

Clearly, there may be some relation between the formality or informality of the system and the type of staff involved. For example, it is possible to construct a very detailed system of job definitions for laboratory technical staff but more difficult to do so for secretarial staff or maintenance workers. It is also very difficult to classify positions in small institutions, where jobs may contain several separate elements.

A formal and detailed system of grading can only be constructed and maintained by job evaluation techniques. In the United Kingdom there has been a very comprehensive grade restructuring of laboratory technical staff, using approximately fifty standard job descriptions and a points-rated factor plan. In Sweden, where university nonacademic staff are part of the government sector, a national exercise of job classification is to be introduced. Other countries have not yet advanced into this area, although there is a clear trend in that direction in South Africa and in the West Indies.

Recruitment

The principles of recruitment are universal, but there are variations in the degree of involvement of the personnel department and in the methods used to attract applicants. The two main sources of applicants are press advertisements and employment agencies. The particular newspaper or journal used depends on the type of vacancy and the location of the university. For clerical and unskilled manual posts, it may be necessary to advertise only in the immediate vicinity of the university, but for more senior and skilled posts, advertisements may have to be placed in national or regional newspapers or in specialist publications. In the United States affirmative action procedures require that jobs be advertised in minority publications. It is unlikely that many nonacademic posts will be advertised between countries, but this may happen when countries have close relations (as do, for example, Australia and New Zealand). Advertisements may be placed directly with the newspaper or through an intermediate advertising agency.

Employment agencies exist in many countries either as private organizations that charge fees for their services or as part of the state or national administration. In the United States each state operates its own employment service under the Federal Employment Security Commission, and in the United Kingdom the government Department of Employment operates local employment exchanges.

The university personnel department notifies the agency of the requirements of the post and the salary to be offered, sometimes by means of a regular bulletin of vacancies. Internal advertising of vacancies can also be useful, and existing employees can do much to attract suitable applicants into the service of the university. For most salaried posts it will be necessary for the applicant to submit details of his qualifications and experience, but such a procedure is not always necessary for unskilled manual posts.

Several countries report the introduction of measures to curb expenditure by the abolition or freezing of vacant posts. Such a step requires the personnel department to ensure that authorization has been given to fill a vacancy before any steps are taken to recruit.

Selection procedures vary among countries and among the three groups of nonacademic staff. For example, at the University of Alberta, the Office of Personnel Services conducts all preliminary interviewing and testing, but the employing department makes the final selection. At the University of Malaya, the Recruitment Unit also carries out the procedure of narrowing down the choice of candidates to a short list, but a senior officer has to confirm the short list. In South Africa there is a greater use of selection committees, and the role of the personnel department is to advise the committee. Nigerian universities also use appointments and promotions committees for interviewing permanent staff. These procedures may well not apply for manual staff, where the employing department may carry out the entire appointment procedure alone.

In most countries the appointment can be made once selection has taken place, but at the University of Natal in South Africa a committee of the senate has to approve all salaried appointments before offers are made. At the University of Malaya, it is the vice-chancellor who gives final approval. Temporary staff are usually engaged by less formal procedures, but in Nigeria a formal procedure does have to be used before a temporary appointment can be made permanent.

The extent to which universities manage to attract the right type of employees will depend on factors such as the competitiveness of university rates of pay; the employment prospects in the town, region, or country concerned; the job requirements of the university; and its image as an employer. Nigeria, for example, reports difficulties in staffing universities because of the rapid expansion of universities in a restricted labor market. In South Africa there are no difficulties, and the universities are regarded as excellent employers. In the United States problems may be caused by the government policy of affirmative action, whereby universities, like other employers who receive federal funds, must provide employment opportunities for minority groups. Problems arise when universities are forced to lay off employees according to customary procedures that may conflict with affirmative action policies.

Salaries and Wages

Universities may find it difficult to recruit or retain staff when university employee salaries do not match salaries paid for similar work outside the university or are inconsistent with those paid to other employees within the university. In the past universities were sometimes able to attract nonacademic staff by factors other than pay, because a university was widely regarded as an interesting and secure place in which to work. However, as society developed, other employers were able to offer the same degree of security as well as higher salaries and good fringe benefits.

In many countries university salary structures had been informal and ill defined, but as universities grew, it became obvious that the salary relationships between employees had to be rationally defined. In order to solve these problems— often as a result of union pressure—many countries have formalized their university salary systems. Where the government is the employer, as in the Netherlands and Sweden, such rationalization can be carried out as part of a larger exercise. However, where universities are autonomous employers, as in the United Kingdom and Australia, any rationalization is made more complicated by the universities' having to reach a common view among themselves, as well as an agreement with unions.

As an alternative approach, some universities relate their levels of pay to those paid in a specific sector outside the university. For example, the University of Singapore keeps its salaries in line with those paid by the Singapore government; United Kingdom universities generally pay their skilled maintenance craftsmen the same rates as are paid craftsmen in the industry concerned. These links are convenient, but they have the disadvantage of not being controlled by universities. There is also the risk of inequities when only some staff are subject to such links. Where the government or state is not the employer but is the financier, the government can affect the level of salary settlements. In the United Kingdom, for example, technical staff salaries are determined nationally, clerical scales on a seminational basis, and manual rates locally. Thus, the pattern of determination of salary levels is extremely complex, particularly where different categories of staff are treated differently.

Rationalization of salary structures may

mean that there is less room for maneuver in determining the rate of pay of each employee. Apart from manual staff, where fixed hourly rates of pay may be applied, most countries seem to operate salary scales whereby employees are appointed at or near the bottom of the scale and advance by annual increments to the top of the scale. Some flexibility is possible at the time of appointment but only within certain limits.

Once the employee has been appointed, there may be an opportunity to vary the salary paid by the use of an additional increment that may be given for personal merit or for an abnormally heavy workload. For example, bonuses are paid in Nigeria for special responsibility; long-service increments are paid by the University of Alberta; and in Sweden a nonmonetary long-service award is made. The University of Singapore pays its staff an additional month's salary at the end of each year, while the University of Natal pays a vacation bonus. In the United Kingdom all nonacademic staff in London are paid an additional allowance in recognition of the higher costs of travel and living in the city.

Methods of payment also vary. In some countries permanent or salaried staff are paid monthly, but at some American universities, all staff are paid weekly. Payment may be made by cash or check or by direct transfer to a bank, but some universities, such as Northeastern University in Boston, Massachusetts, will forward salary checks to employees' residences rather than distribute them at the university.

Conditions of Employment and Retirement

Hours of work and paid leaves. The hours of work will be in accordance with normal university practice if the appointment is to be full time but will be by mutual agreement if the appointment is part time. The definition of full-time employment varies, but most appointments will be within the range of thirty-five to forty hours per week. In Sweden clerical employees work shorter hours during the summer; in Nigeria university staff members work on Saturday mornings.

There will also be agreement on the number of weeks of paid leave to which the employee is entitled. It is difficult to generalize, but leave usually includes an annual vacation period plus a certain number of national holidays. With some exceptions, such as Sweden, where entitlements seem higher, there appears to be a range of two to four weeks' annual vacation. Some universities that recruit staff from abroad provide for long leave after a certain period of service, whereas others, such as the University of Alberta, increase the period of basic leave with length of service.

The number of national holidays varies among countries, but, in every case, university holidays follow the particular arrangements of the country concerned. Some universities also close for short periods at certain times of the year, in addition to national holidays.

Universities may also have arrangements to enable employees to undertake public service, such as jury service. Most universities have clear regulations and periods of entitlement for compassionate leave and for paid leave for medically certified sickness. Sick leave often is related to length of service and may provide for periods of half pay as well as full pay. The existence of a national sick pay scheme, as in the United Kingdom, or private sickness insurance schemes, will affect university regulations and practices. Universities in some countries provide maternity leave for female employees, and in Sweden this leave is also extended to prospective fathers. Overtime, often worked during the absence of other staff on vacation or sick leave, may be compensated by two methods—additional payment at an enhanced rate (governed by the day or time that the hours were worked) or the awarding of time off in lieu of payment. Where time off is given, the period concerned may be calculated by overtime enhancements.

Retirement. In most countries nonacademic staff are required to retire from their posts between the ages of sixty and sixty-five, although in Nigeria the government has suggested a retirement age of fifty-five years. Superannuation schemes, which provide retirement pensions and death benefits, vary greatly between and within countries. In Sweden, Poland, the Netherlands, and Nigeria, nonacademic staff are subject to the government superannuation scheme, whereas Australia has a variety of schemes. In some cases both the employer and the employee make regular contributions to retirement funds, while in others the employee is not required to contribute.

In other cases of termination of employment, a set period of notice of termination is agreed to on both sides, to enable the employer to find a replacement and the employee to find alternative employment. The notice period may vary in length from two weeks to six months and may depend on the employee's age or length of service. In many countries hourly staff may be on shorter periods of notice, and in most countries there is provision for instant dismissal for misconduct.

Welfare and Services

As well as the formal conditions of employment, many universities now offer a range of other benefits that may be available to both staff and students as members of the university community or to staff only. The University of the West Indies pays the full contribution to a sickness insurance scheme for all its staff and their dependents; the University of Cape Town in South Africa pays half the contributions to such a scheme; free medical care is given in Poland, Nigeria, Sweden, and at the University of the South Pacific. Practices vary in the United States and the United Kingdom, while universities in the Netherlands do not provide medical care. In Poland and some British universities, day nursery facilities are provided for the children of staff; in Nigeria there are university staff schools, which include

nurseries and which are open to children from the community at large. Most universities provide catering facilities on campus for staff, and in many countries such services are subsidized.

There are various ways in which universities provide financial assistance to staff. Some Australian universities contribute toward the cost of moving for newly appointed nonacademic staff from overseas. Nigerian universities offer loans for the purchase of houses and automobiles, and universities in South Africa also give loans for house purchase. In Poland staff may obtain rented accommodation through a cooperative building society, while senior staff in Nigerian universities may either obtain partly furnished rented accommodation or receive a housing allowance.

Training and development. The range of training facilities available to nonacademic staff generally depends on the stage of managerial development of the university concerned and on local recruitment prospects. It is often difficult to justify the establishment of a training program, and, by a curious irony, this appears to be as much a problem among universities as among other employers. Therefore, in many countries, there is little staff training in universities. In Poland and South Africa, universities use outside agencies and carry out little training themselves; Nigerian universities seem to concentrate on administrative training. There is a more systematic approach in countries like the United States, Canada, and the United Kingdom, but even so there are great variations.

In an ideal situation, universities would carry out several different types of training. There is a need for some kind of induction to help all staff understand and appreciate the organization which they have joined. For certain categories, such as technicians, accountants, cooks, and electricians, the university may recruit young secondary school graduates in trainee positions and then subject them to a period of on-the-job training and classroom study, the latter often being undertaken at another institution. There is also a need to ensure that staff are able to keep up with developments in their own field and that they can gain instruction in specialized techniques. Staff also need encouragement to develop their own work capacity to enable them to obtain promotion within the university or in other organizations. Universities are in the unique position of being able to offer higher education, that is not necessarily work-related to all staff. Often the fees for such studies are waived or reduced.

Staffing procedures. The two main operating procedures relating to nonacademic staff in universities are those for promotion and discipline. Many countries have comprehensive systems for review of the grading and salary position of individual staff members. In accordance with normal university practice, most promotion procedures involve the use of the committee structure, except where the promotion is to fill a vacancy in a higher grade. The Chinese University of Hong Kong uses a periodic review of staff to build up a record of individual performance. South Africa is in the process of introducing annual reviews, and such reviews are already in existence in the Netherlands. In India there is some feeling that universities have given too much attention to academic staff promotion and not enough to non-academics.

Discipline is a more difficult problem, and labor unions may be involved in the determination and operation of the procedure. Disciplinary action can vary from the withholding of annual increments or the issuing of a formal warning to dismissal. In the Netherlands dismissal procedures are complicated and rarely invoked. At the University of Natal only the council can dismiss nonmanual staff, while in Nigeria there is a detailed system of warning and appeal before notice of termination can be given. Permanent employees in South Africa can appeal to the minister of education against dismissal.

Dismissal may also be made on grounds of redundancy: in such circumstances, a secondary procedure may exist, as at the University of Alberta, where the conditions of employment for nonacademic staff contain a clause about layoff. Staff may be subject to a probationary procedure on first appointment; in South Africa, the Netherlands, and Nigeria, all permanent appointments are made for two years in the first instance. In the United Kingdom most appointments are also made subject to probation of varying lengths. However, the validity of this procedure is being brought into question by new government legislation on labor relations.

Labor Relations

The degree of union pressure on universities varies considerably from country to country. The percentage of unionization is low in the Netherlands but very high in Sweden. Universities in South Africa have staff associations rather than labor unions, and similar associations are also developing in India. In Poland each university has one union for all categories of staff, whereas in the West Indies nonacademic staff belong to one local union of workers. In Nigeria there is a University Workers' Union in each university, and these unions have formed a national federation. In the United States there are nine major unions in operation among nonacademic staff, while in the United Kingdom there are three. In both the United States and the United Kingdom, the majority of the members of these unions work outside universities; thus, there is a tendency for them to import outside labor relations practices into the university community. Australian universities are experiencing similar problems that are compelling them to work together on salary structures.

Bargaining. This complex pattern of types of union and extent of involvement makes it difficult to generalize about the level and type of bargaining machinery. Where there are staff associations or workers' unions, all bargaining takes place locally. In countries where universities are not part of a national structure, bargaining can be done without difficulty. However, where universities are advised or obliged to follow governmental policy then much may be determined at the regional or national level. National determination of salaries and other conditions occurs in countries such as Sweden, Poland, and Nigeria, while in other countries bargaining occurs at several levels or entirely at the local level.

When a union has established a base within the university, it will ask for recognition (perhaps by the use of a ballot among the staff), for facilities to conduct its business, and for a grievance procedure. In the United States it may also ask for an agreement on seniority rights among staff for promotion, transfer, and layoff. There is little evidence of nonacademic staff being involved in the management of universities with the one clear exception of Sweden where, under the terms of an experiment started in 1968, staff are involved in the decision-making processes.

Grievance procedures. One important aspect of the work of unions is the pursuit of individual grievances; here the procedures evolving in universities are probably similar to those in other sectors. Clearly, much can be solved informally between the local union official and personnel officer; but, in the United Kingdom, for example, agreements are being signed with all nonacademic labor unions that provide for a complex local, regional, and national structure for resolving grievances, including individual cases. Industrial action among nonacademic staff has taken place in the United Kingdom and Nigeria, but in some countries, such as the Netherlands, university nonacademic staff, as civil servants, are not permitted to strike.

Role of Government

There are many aspects to government's role in the development and execution of nonacademic personnel policies. In countries such as Sweden and the Netherlands, the government itself is the employer and thus directly shapes the personnel function. This is particularly true in Sweden, where universities are a part of the national negotiating structure between the government and its employees. In both Nigeria and Malaysia, government inquiries into public service salaries have resulted in the establishment of common scales and rates. In Malaysia as of 1975, it was expected that all conditions soon would be determined by a Statutory Authorities Service Commission. Where universities rely on the government for the majority of their finances, as in the United Kingdom, government may influence salary settlements indirectly.

Government can also affect nonacademic personnel administration through its general social policies. In the United States the affirmative action and unemployment insurance programs are recent examples of this type of external pressure, while South African apartheid policies offer an extreme example of the way in which a government can dictate the terms under which universities employ particular categories of staff.

Some governments have provided legislation that is directly aimed at employment and labor relations. The Nigerian government, for example, has a labor code that employers are expected to observe. In the United Kingdom there has been a steady flow of legislation since the early 1960s covering such topics as conditions of employment, redundancy, training, health and safety, labor relations, and employment protection. Thus, in the United Kingdom a new aspect of the role of the university personnel department is the examination and interpretation of government legislation. In that respect the pressures on the personnel administrator, particularly in regard to nonacademic staff, are quite different from those on most of his administrative colleagues.

Bibliography

Commonwealth Conference of Registrars of Universities of the Southeast Asian and Pacific Area. *Workshop on Personnel Administration*. Hong Kong: Commonwealth Conference, 1974.

Knowles, A. S. (Ed.) *Handbook of College and University Administration*. New York: Mc-Graw-Hill, 1970.

Löwbeer, H. *University Democracy in Sweden: A Report for OECD*. Stockholm: Office of the Chancellor of the Swedish Universities, 1972.

Subramaniam, M. K. *Management-Staff Association Relations: Some Observations*. Hyderabad, India: Seminar of the Registrars and Administrative Officers, Administrative Staff College of India, 1975.

ROGER J. MAYHEW

See also: General Administration, Organization for; Remuneration: Faculty, Staff, and Chief Executive Officers.

NORDIC COUNCIL

The Nordic Council, an intergovernmental advisory body created in 1953 (with Finland joining in 1956), considers economic, social, cultural, environmental, communications, and legal questions according to the Helsinki Treaty of 1962. Member countries are Denmark, Iceland, Finland, Norway, and Sweden.

The organizational structure consists of the presidium (the president and four vice-presidents), the council, standing committees, the council of ministers, and the secretariat. The council meets annually, in one of the Nordic capitals, to elect the presidium, which takes care of the council's work between sessions. Each delegation elects its own president, but the council president is from the host country; the other four serve as vice-presidents.

The seventy-eight delegates to the council are elected annually from each country's parliament (six from Iceland and eighteen from each of the other countries: Norway, Sweden, Denmark, and Finland). The council sends recommendations to the council of ministers, which in turn sends progress reports to the council annually. Council members serve on the following standing committees: economic, cultural, legal, social, environmental, and communications.

The Nordic Council has a national secretariat in each country. A collegium, made up of the heads of these secretariats, prepares the Nordic Council's work. The presidium secretariat has responsibility for joint Nordic activities and deals particularly with the council of ministers, which is responsible for a broad range of Nordic cooperation. The council of ministers requires the support of the member governments before making decisions, usually unanimous ones.

The standing committee that probably has the most direct relationship to higher education is the cultural committee, created in 1972 by the ministers of culture and education. The committee aims to encourage common planning for a Nordic cultural community and works for a single educational system for Scandinavia. Since many university qualifications are valid in the entire region, the council encourages the harmonization of school curricula and the teaching of all Nordic languages in the schools of the Nordic countries.

Academic institutions created on the recommendation of the Nordic Council are the Nordic Institute of Theoretical Physics, Copenhagen; Institute of Maritime Law, Oslo; Institute of African Studies, Uppsala; Institute of Asiatic Studies, Copenhagen; Institute for Social Planning, Stockholm; Scandinavian Institute of Public Health, Göteborg; Nordic Institute of Folklore, Turku (Åbo); Nordic College for Training of Journalists, Århus; Institute of Vulcanology, Reykjavík; and Nordic Samic Institute, Kautokeino, Norway.

The Nordic Cultural Fund, which is administered by a common authority under the secretariat for cultural cooperation, awards a literature prize annually to a Scandinavian author and a prize for music to a Scandinavian composer every two years.

NORDVISION is an activity of the council that links national television and radio corporations.

Publications of the council consist of *Nordisk kontakt,* an outline of the parliamentary work in Nordic countries. The *Nordic Statistical Yearbook* reports on joint research projects and conferences.

Gamla riksdagshuset
8-103 10 Stockholm 2, Sweden

NORTH AFRICAN STUDIES

See Area Studies (field of study).

NORTH AMERICA:
REGIONAL ANALYSIS

The three countries on the North American continent are Canada, the United States, and Mexico. In the 1970s the basic characteristics of their educational systems, particularly those that differentiate them from each other, remain consistent with basic patterns established in their colonial pasts and developed by particular sociopolitical events in their individual histories.

Educational Aims and
Programs of Instruction

In general, the three countries of the North American continent share the same concept of the function of higher education institutions: instruction, research, and service to the community. However, how these terms are understood, the degree of emphasis allotted to each, and the means by which these aims are achieved indicate significant distinctions among the three systems.

Mexico. The idea of general education, which is an important aspect of the English-language system, plays almost no part in Mexican higher education. The Mexican university, modeled on the sixteenth-century continental European university

and the nineteenth-century Napoleonic university, conceives of higher education as an instrument to prepare students for a particular profession. This concept applies as well to the technological institutions and normal schools. The transmission of broad cultural ideas is considered to be the province of the secondary school, and admission to the university presupposes graduation from the preparatory or higher level of the secondary school, where such subjects as history, mathematics, geography, and literature are part of the curriculum.

In 1973 eighty-seven different professional courses were available at the 134 different institutions—universities, technical schools, higher normal schools, and specialized schools (Rangel Guerra, 1974). The programs, which generally last four to five years, lead to the licentiate or other professional title. In general, the curriculum is fairly rigid, with few opportunities for electives. Instruction is largely by lecture, and qualification depends heavily on terminal examinations. Promotion, as it is understood in the United States, does not usually exist. Final certification is normally based on the accumulation of passes in courses required for final professional accreditation.

The second main function of higher education—research and the preparation of research workers—is undertaken at research institutes, although advanced degrees, offered through the faculties of the universities, also require research. In 1929 several scientific institutes became affiliated with the National Autonomous University of Mexico. As of 1975 there were thirty-two such institutes divided among the various universities.

Until the 1960s service was largely seen as a secondary function of the university. As early as the 1940s candidates for the first degree were required to show some proof of paid employment in socially useful jobs undertaken during their school career, but it was not until the 1960s, when the universities began to respond to increasing social and economic pressures, that service became an important aspect of higher education. Since that time there has been a steady growth in university-industry programs and extension programs. The establishment of open schools and continuing education courses have also served to broaden the base of education and meet the real needs of the people.

United States. In contrast to the concept of education as professional training that prevails in Mexico, the idea of higher education as the transmission of general knowledge is central to the United States system. Although the early colonial colleges were sponsored by specific religious groups, they were never considered as mere training grounds for clergymen. From the beginning their aim was to transmit cultural concepts—admittedly Protestant—necessary for the formation of well-informed men. This idea of general education persists today.

In almost all institutions in the United States, the work of the first two years of a four-year program is distributed among courses in English, history, modern foreign languages, science, and mathematics. Occupational training does not begin until the third year, when a student chooses major and minor fields. It is true that many majors require prerequisites, and to that extent, of course, the first years might be considered as preprofessional training. However, full professional training, such as that in law, medicine, and business administration, is usually the function of graduate schools; in undergraduate schools general education remains the primary objective. Even in the case of explicitly professional undergraduate institutions— colleges of nursing, engineering schools, agricultural schools—some general education courses are customarily required.

Undergraduate programs usually last four or five years and lead to a Bachelor of Arts or Bachelor of Science degree. Junior colleges and community colleges provide an associate degree after completion of a two-year program. In 1975 there

were over three hundred fields of specialization leading to the bachelor's degree or to advanced degrees. In contrast to the Mexican university, where program requirements are fairly rigid, most institutions in the United States allow the student a wide choice of electives, even in the final years. The idea that a student should be free to study what he wishes derives principally from the mid-nineteenth-century German university. In the United States the system of a broad curriculum and much freedom of choice for the student was pioneered by Charles Eliot of Harvard, Andrew White of Cornell, and William Rainey Harper of Chicago. Most institutions in the United States have adopted this system. Faculty advisers guide the student in the choice of required and elective courses leading to specialization.

Instruction is often by lecture, particularly in the first two years, supplemented by group discussion. In the final years, seminars, small classes, and sometimes independent studies constitute the main teaching methods. Although examinations are an important part of determining qualifications, papers, term work, and class participation are taken equally into account.

Research activities are extensive in all universities, and here again the German university system had an important formative influence. The idea that the professor should be allowed to pursue his own research and be free to publish and teach the results was practiced at the universities of Berlin, Leipzig, Heidelberg, Bonn, and Munich. In the United States Johns Hopkins was the first institution modeled after those in Germany. Offering only graduate work, it opened in 1876 with eight professors and forty-four students for the express purpose of providing a new kind of education, which would allow the greatest intellectual freedom in attainment of the advanced degree. Other universities— Harvard, Yale, Columbia, Princeton, Wisconsin, Michigan, Clark, Stanford, and Chicago—soon after opened or remodeled graduate schools on the principles expounded at Johns Hopkins. Today research activities are considered, as they were in Germany, a means of expanding existing knowledge and of providing opportunities for students to acquire professional skills. Research projects are variously funded by the institutions, the federal government, industry, and nonprofit organizations. Since World War II such projects, particularly in scientific and technological fields, have grown rapidly, causing many institutions to develop academic positions on the level of vice-president or dean to coordinate their activities. Other institutions have established separate foundations or centers, staffed largely by professors and graduate students, to pursue research.

The third function of the university—service—is an integral part of United States institutions. Extension courses were pioneered early in the twentieth century. Adult education courses, community college programs, and industry-university related programs can all be seen as attempts by higher education to meet the needs of the community. In the 1960s these programs received special attention and expansion. In order to reach students from different ethnic groups—those, that is, who had strong racial, linguistic, and cultural ties with a nation other than the United States—"ethnic" courses were introduced into curricula. In many cases these served to attract students who had previously considered education to be irrelevant. Many institutions also made a deliberate attempt to recruit students from minority groups whose members have been discriminated against on the basis of language, race, religion, or nationality. This was a further example of higher education's desire to serve its constituency.

Canada. In the nineteenth century many of the English-language universities in Canada came under the influence of the United States liberal arts college; thus, it is not surprising that general education should also play an important part in Canada. That this is so is evidenced by the traditional dominance of arts and science faculties, which offer instruction in the humanities and in the social, physical, and biological sciences. Indeed, it is significant that schools that offer only professional programs did not attain faculty status until 1973, and therefore could not award degrees; prior to that date such schools were considered as subordinate to a faculty and on the level of a department. Admission to arts and science programs in the maritime provinces required eleven to twelve years of preuniversity training, and in the western provinces, thirteen years of preuniversity training. Programs leading to the bachelor's degree generally require three years—four years for a bachelor's degree with honors. Admission to professional faculties, such as law, medicine, dentistry, business administration, and theology, often requires a student to complete two years of arts and science before application; the requirement underlines the stress Canadian universities give to general education.

On the other hand, French-language institutions—which followed more closely the continental European university model and originally offered instruction in only four faculties (law, medicine, theology, and letters, with philosophy and social sciences added later)—were more professionally oriented. Liberal arts programs were provided by the highly prestigious classical colleges, which offered eight-year programs, the final four at the university level. Although these institutions were affiliated with the universities, they maintained separate facilities and were considered the training ground for Quebec's intellectual elite. In 1967 this system was changed. Classical colleges disappeared. The Bachelor of Arts and Bachelor of Science degrees were awarded at the university in a three-year program for students who held a *diplôme d'études collegiales,* which signifies completion of a two-year higher secondary program at a college of general and professional training.

Instruction in Canadian universities has traditionally been by lecture. As in Mexico, examinations were, in the past, the chief means of determining a student's progress. Since the 1960s, however, there has been increasing emphasis on seminars and individual study, and term work has assumed an importance equal to examinations as a means of evaluation. In the professional faculties requirements are still fairly rigid, largely because professional certification is determined by professional examinations rather than by the university.

The role of research as a university function was not fully realized until World War II, when it became apparent that the universities could provide trained researchers for the national war effort. Since that time the federal government has contributed extensively to research conducted by the academic community on projects of national interest.

The concept of service to the community as a function of the university has also been relatively late in developing. Until the 1960s, when the provincial governments began to reassess the role of the universities and to integrate them into the entire postsecondary educational system, the universities had remained relatively aloof. Community needs were more closely served by the non-degree-granting institutions, which were less demanding in admission requirements and provided education in such community-oriented professions as nursing, teaching, and agriculture. With the reorganization of the 1960s, many of these functions were absorbed by the universities. At the same time there was an expansion of adult education and extension programs. An open university, designed on the British model, for those who could not be accommodated in traditional institutions, was initiated; and work-study programs, in which the student alternates supervised regular employment with classroom study, were adopted by some faculties.

Internal Structure

The relationship between higher education institutions and the government as well as the aims these institutions emphasize necessarily affect their internal structure.

Mexico. In Mexico lines of communication are kept open between the Secretariat of Public Education, which is responsible for higher technical education, and the National Polytechnic Institute through the office of the director general. The director general, who is the executive head of the institute, is assisted by a technical council made up of representatives of the teachers and students of each school of the institute.

In the universities the chief administrative authority is either a board of governors *(junta de gobierno)*, essentially an arbitrating body, or—more commonly— a university council that acts as a senate. The council is composed of the directors of the faculties, schools, and institutes of the institution; of representatives of the teaching and administrative staff; and of representatives of the students. It is presided over by the rector, who is the executive head of the university and its legal representative. The rector, whose term is generally limited, carries out the recommendations of the council. His major power is a veto by which he can suspend action on resolutions (Gonzáles Avelar and Lara Sáenz, 1969, p. 34). A director coordinates the work of each faculty, school, or institute, assisted by a technical council composed of representatives of teachers, students, and members of the appropriate profession.

United States. In the United States the governing board of public or private institutions is usually called the board of regents or board of trustees. Such a board differs fundamentally from the ruling body in the Mexican university in that the members, usually determined by popular election or appointed by state governments, did not until the late 1960s include representatives from the teaching staff or student body. The precedent for this lay board was established in the colonial colleges and has been maintained as a way of ensuring a dispassionate and unbiased control and of giving the general public a voice in the conduct of their higher education institutions.

The governing boards are responsible

for all institutional goals and policies, which are then put into effect by the chief executive officer, the president—or, in some instances, the provost, chancellor, or rector. In most United States universities this chief executive officer has far greater power than his counterpart in Mexico. He is generally appointed for an indefinite term. He is responsible for the administrative and academic functioning of the university and often plays an important role in the formulation of policy. Many universities also have an academic senate composed of faculty members and student representatives. The senate functions as a consultative and deliberative body, considering recommendations made to it on admissions, courses, and examination requirements. Since the 1960s the power of the senate has increased in many universities, thus bringing the United States system closer to the two-tier system that prevails in Canada.

Individual units within the university are referred to as colleges or schools, as opposed to the Mexican designation of faculties. Each unit is headed by a dean selected from the teaching staff. Fields of study are referred to as departments and come under the direction of a department chairman, appointed from the faculty and responsible to the dean.

Canada. The Canadian university is characterized by the two-tier structure put into effect through the University of Toronto Act of 1906 and thereafter copied by most institutions. One tier consists of a board of governors composed primarily of laymen, although, since faculty and student demands for representation in the 1960s, it has come to include these members as well. The board represents the corporate power of the institution and makes final decisions on all matters of policy. It appoints the president, exercises financial control, and approves recommendations from the academic senate.

The senate, whose membership is drawn from the academic and administrative staff, is responsible for academic policy

as the second tier. Theoretically responsible to the board, in actuality the senate reserved to itself, by provisions of the Toronto act, the final say on all matters of admission requirements, courses of study, examinations, and recommendations for degrees. The chancellor, who is the honorary or ceremonial head of the university; the president, the executive head of the university appointed by the board after consultation with the senate; and the chairman of the board hold joint membership on both the senate and the board. Otherwise the membership of the two bodies is entirely separate. Because the president alone is responsible for the appointment or dismissal of academic staff, and because the senate controls academic policy, interference in academic freedom or tenure is impossible. At the same time, the existence of the board of governors prevents direct government interference in university matters.

Increasing pressure in the 1960s for teachers and students to be represented on the board of governors has resulted in most universities allowing their participation. This change has led some officials to recommend a unicameral system, such as that which has existed at Laval University since it was founded in 1852. Others suggest a redefining of the responsibilities of the two bodies.

In essence, the organizational structure of the Canadian university is very similar to that of United States universities. Unfortunately, however, the nomenclature overlaps, which makes any comparison difficult. Thus, the major organizational unit in United States institutions is the college or school—college of liberal arts, school of agriculture. In Canada such a unit is referred to as a faculty; as in the United States, this unit is headed by a dean appointed by the board and responsible for the coordination of activities within his unit. The faculty is further subdivided into departments, which have their own directors. In the past there have also been schools responsible for professional courses, but until the 1970s most of these were non-degree granting and had only the status of a department; in the 1970s these schools became faculties in their own right.

What distinguishes the Canadian system from that in the United States is the existence of a college structure that is the consequence of the Canadian move to federate and affiliate colleges under the umbrella of one central university. The colleges and universities that enter into federation or are affiliated retain their own identity and their own faculties but are represented on the senate, faculty councils, and committees of the parent university in those areas of study with which they are concerned. Thus, for example, a student might identify first with Scarborough College, rather than with the University of Toronto, with which it is federated. However, the faculty of liberal arts within Scarborough would be considered as part of the faculty of liberal arts at the University of Toronto.

Other variations also exist. In some instances departments are organized as colleges or schools. At the University of Quebec the faculty structure has been entirely abandoned and a modular pattern adopted. The student identifies with a module, which offers a program of study that may cut across departmental lines. On the graduate level, centers and institutes have been established for interdisciplinary study; as of the mid 1970s some of these centers are beginning to enroll undergraduates.

The organizational patterns of the Canadian universities are thus more complex and varied than those of its neighbors to the south. In Mexico the tendency is toward centralization and uniformity, with the National Autonomous University and the National Polytechnic Institute providing the basic model. In the United States there are a large number of individual institutions, all with similar basic patterns. In Canada federation and affiliation have resulted in the paradoxical situation of diversity within uniformity.

One other point remains to be noted here. One of the chief distinctions among the three systems is the role of the student. The Mexican university, which derives ultimately from that in Bologna (a corporation of students), has a history of student participation. The Canadian and United States universities, which derive from the Northern European University of Paris (a corporation of masters), have, until the 1960s, largely relegated the student to a secondary position (Benjamin, 1965, p. 47).

Staff

In the English-speaking liberal arts faculties and in the classical colleges of Quebec, where instruction is seen as the discovery and transmission of general knowledge necessary for the formation of a good citizen, the higher education academic staff tends to be a fully committed body of scholars. They see their primary function as teaching, their primary loyalties as to their institution. In Mexico, where the main aim of instruction is conceived as professional training, identification is often with the profession rather than with the teaching institution. These distinctions are most clearly manifest in the amount of time the professor devotes to the institution, in the conditions of service, and in the kinds of associations to which the teaching staff belong.

All three systems have a roughly comparable system of ranks comprising four positions ranging from instructor (United States), lecturer (Canada), or assistant (Mexico), to full professor. The title varies in the three systems and may indeed vary within each system. In each system the rank is directly related to qualification, experience, and seniority.

One of the distinguishing features among the three systems is the amount of time that those staff members in the three higher ranks are expected to give in teaching and service to the institution. In both the United States and Canada full participation is expected, with special leaves granted for research and scholarly pursuits that will contribute to the institution's status. In Mexico the vast majority of the teaching staff is part or half time, and many derive a large part of their income from professional positions outside the university.

Conditions of appointment also vary among the three systems. In the United States positions are publicly advertised and appointments are made by the president on the recommendation of a faculty dean, advised by a department chairman, who has usually interviewed the applicants and weighed their qualifications. The basic requirement is normally the doctoral degree, with publications, research, and experience also taken into consideration. In Canada the system is roughly the same. In Mexico, where qualification for appointment often rests on public competitive examinations, the above system may seem disconcertingly personal. Mexican faculties are also inclined to give far more consideration than their northern counterparts to professional efficiency as demonstrated outside the university.

In keeping with the divided allegiance of the Mexican teaching staff, a candidate is considered eligible for retirement after thirty years of service in a government-related position, which need not necessarily mean thirty years at the university. In the United States and Canada retirement is usually automatic at sixty-five years of age.

As might be expected, teaching associations in Mexico have a much more explicitly trade union character than those that have traditionally existed in the United States and Canada. In Mexico professors at institutions under the Secretariat of Public Education belong to the National Union of Educational Workers. Those in nonpublic institutions belong to the Association of University Professors. In addition, those whose profession requires a government-granted license also belong to related professional associations.

In the United States and Canada, where institutional loyalty has played a large part in staff relationships and where faculty members have more often thought of themselves as a community of scholars rather than as "job holders," organizations

have been more concerned with the condition of services than with salaries. Since the 1960s this situation has changed. Dissatisfaction with salaries in an inflationary economy, with the faculty role in institutional governance, and with promotion procedures, as well as worries over job security, have increased the pressure for representative bodies that will have collective bargaining power. In the United States efforts have been made to unionize faculty under the National Education Association (NEA), a professional organization of educators and all persons concerned with education; the American Federation of Teachers (AFT), a teachers union representing all levels of teaching; and the American Association of University Professors (AAUP), an interdisciplinary association of teaching and research personnel at institutions of higher education. In Canada staff associations exist in most institutions. These associations make up the entire membership of the Canadian Association of University Teachers (CAUP), and several of these associations are certified as bargaining agents.

Student Body

Higher education in all three countries has traditionally been the province of a socioeconomic and intellectual elite. Although there is no tuition in Mexican public institutions, and although it is minimal in most public institutions in the United States and Canada, only those who could afford to live away from home and in the urban centers where most universities were founded could afford to participate. In the 1970s, however, the student body in all three countries is far more heterogeneous than before. The reasons can be found in new social and economic legislation, changing cultural patterns, and a reexamination of the role of higher education in relation to late-twentieth-century national needs. What these specific changes have been and how they have affected the constitution of the varying student bodies constitutes a basis for comparison.

Mexico. Although every Mexican has

the constitutional right to education, a study conducted in 1969 indicated that the expenses of education were inequitably distributed. Forty percent of the poorest Mexicans received only 25 percent of the official education offered. In the three lowest strata, which represented 51 percent of the population, only 6.7 percent participated in high school training and 3.6 percent in higher education. The economic situation was probably the single most important factor in determining who would get a university education (Puente Leyva, 1969).

The statistics are grim; yet they represent an improvement on the past. In 1971 only 1.5 percent of the eligible eighteen to twenty-two age group were in higher education. In 1975 the figure was 8.9 percent (*Estadística básica del sistema educativo nacional, 1974–75,* 1975). These figures represent Mexico's concerted effort to broaden the base of educational opportunity. A systematic use of open schools; continuing education programs; and innovative educational methods, particularly in the rural areas, have made education increasingly available. At the same time, the National Council of Science and Technology has carried out a controlled national scholarship program for the development of human resources at the higher levels. A National Fund created in 1966 by the Bank of Mexico has further provided scholarships that supplement those traditionally awarded by public and private institutions. Changing cultural values, as well as a broadening of professional offerings, have also meant an increase in the number of women students. Although the proportion of women students still lags behind that of the United States, where women's colleges have existed since the mid-nineteenth century, the proportion of increase has been substantial. Between 1962 and 1968, for example, the female population at the National Autonomous University of Mexico grew by 66 percent (Ramírez and Chapoy, 1970).

United States. In the 1975–76 academic year the average freshman in the United States was unmarried, Caucasian, middle class, and male ("The American Freshman," 1976). This statement may be informative, but it is misleading in that it cannot convey the very dramatic changes that have taken place in the student body of United States institutions since the 1960s. In that period the national concern with the development of human resources manifested itself in higher education by an all-out attempt to reach a population, which, to a large extent, had been previously ignored or slighted. For the first time in United States history minority groups were actively recruited by many universities; ethnic programs were introduced to attract students who felt traditional programs were irrelevant; and the Civil Rights Act of 1964 enforced laws against racial and ethnic discrimination. As of 1976, as a consequence, members of minority groups make up 13.5 percent of the student body of United States institutions ("The American Freshman," 1976).

Women have had a place in American higher education since the mid-nineteenth century; that place, however, has been relatively small. In the 1960s, as the forces of the women's liberation movement began to raise their voices, female enrollment began to increase. In 1972 Title IX of the Education Amendments Act forbade discrimination on the basis of sex in most United States higher education institutions. In 1975 women made up an estimated 44 percent of total enrollment, in contrast to 29.1 percent in 1947 (Grant and Lind, 1976).

In the 1960s new open-admissions programs were introduced in many universities. This caused an influx of students who, because of their racial or economic background, or both, had had a preuniversity education that did not sufficiently prepare them for university courses. In many universities special tutorial programs were set up to aid these students. The community college program was expanded, and more federal funding than ever was poured into grants and scholarships. The effect of these programs was to provide opportunities for education to almost all students who would be capable of profiting from postsecondary education.

In 1870 less than one tenth of 1 percent of the total population attended higher education institutions in the United States (Benjamin, 1965, p. 169). In 1975 more than 5 percent of the population was enrolled in higher education, representing 35.3 percent of the eighteen to twenty-four age group. This increase in enrollment speaks for itself. It has not been drawn from one segment of the population but from all segments. Although the average freshman may retain his statistical identity, the average student body in the 1970s is far more representative of the national constituency than it has ever been.

Canada. In Canada the integration of the university system with the provincial postsecondary institution and the elevation of schools to faculty status have probably had the greatest effects on changing the composition of the traditional university student body. No longer are degrees the exclusive province of the elite. At the same time, new programs introduced in the 1960s, which allowed students to combine study with self-supporting jobs, increased opportunities for poor students. In 1960, 3.3 percent of students were part time; by 1970 the figure had risen to almost 10 percent. In 1970 women represented 25 percent of full-time enrollments in Canadian higher education; in 1975 they represented 35 percent.

The introduction of alternative education institutions—the Northern College of Applied Arts and Technology in Ontario and the colleges of general and vocational education in Quebec—and the expansion of community colleges from which students may transfer to four-year institutions have been further contributing factors to the growing change in the Canadian student body.

Facing the Future

As the higher education institutions in these three countries of the North Amer-

ican continent move into the final quarter of the twentieth century, they are in many ways much closer to each other than they have ever been in their histories. Expanding enrollments, increasing financial pressures, and growing social demands have not been exclusive to any one system. Although the specific means by which each country has attempted to deal with these pressures are rooted in the precedents of their own particular pasts, the outcome has been surprisingly similar. If certain words can be understood to bind the three systems together, they would be democratization, expansion, and self-conscious reassessment in light of the demands posed by a changing world.

[Facts and statistical data pertaining to the nations cited herein are based on research of contributing authors and other research conducted under the auspices of *The International Encyclopedia of Higher Education.* These materials are now on file at the Center for International Higher Education Documentation at Northeastern University, Boston, Massachusetts.]

Bibliography

Adell, B. L., and Carter, D. C. *Collective Bargaining for University Faculty in Canada.* Kingston, Ontario: Industrial Relations Centre, Queen's University, 1972.

"The American Freshman: National Norms for Fall 1975." *Chronicle of Higher Education,* 1976, *11*(16), 4.

Arizmendi Rodríguez, R. "Sistema centralizado de información: Un modelo operacional para instituciones de educación superior." *México,* 1974, *3*(4), 36–63.

Benjamin, H. R. *Higher Education in the American Republics.* New York: McGraw-Hill, 1965.

Carnegie Council on Policy Studies in Higher Education. *The Federal Role in Postsecondary Education. Unfinished Business 1975–1980.* San Francisco: Jossey-Bass, 1975.

Carr, R. K., and VanDyck, D. K. *Collective Bargaining Comes to the Campus.* Washington, D.C.: American Council on Education, 1973.

Classification of Institutions of Higher Education. Berkeley, California: Carnegie Commission on Higher Education, 1973.

Estadística básica del sistema educativo nacional, 1974–75. Mexico City: Secretaría de educación pública, 1975.

Flexner, A. *Medical Education in the United States and Canada.* New York: Arno Press, 1972. (Originally published 1910.)

Gonzáles Avelar, M., and Lara Sáenz, L. *Legislación mexicana de la enseñanza superior.* Mexico City: Instituto de investigaciones jurídicas, Universidad nacional autónoma de México, 1969.

Grant, W. V., and Lind, C. G. *Digest of Education Statistics.* Washington, D.C.: U.S. Government Printing Office, 1976.

Harvey, E. B., and Lennards, J. L. *Key Issues in Higher Education.* Toronto, Ontario: Ontario Institute for Studies in Education, 1973.

Houwing, J. F., and Michaud, L. F. *Changes in the Composition of Governing Bodies of Canadian Universities and Colleges 1965–70.* Ottawa, Ontario: Association of Universities and Colleges of Canada, Research Division, 1972.

Knowles, A. S. "Faculty Personnel Policies and Regulations." In A. S. Knowles (Ed.), *Handbook of College and University Administration.* New York: McGraw-Hill, 1970.

National Commission on the Financing of Postsecondary Education. *Financing Postsecondary Education in the United States.* Washington, D.C.: U.S. Government Printing Office, 1973.

Newman, F. *Report on Higher Education.* Washington, D.C.: U.S. Government Printing Office, 1971.

Newman, F. *National Policy and Higher Education.* Cambridge, Massachusetts: MIT Press, 1973.

Puente Leyva, J. *Distribución del ingreso en un area: El caso de Monterrey.* Mexico City: Siglo XXI Editores, 1969.

Ramírez R., and Chapoy, A. *Estructura de la UNAM.* Mexico City: Fondo cultura popular, 1970.

Rangel Guerra, A. "Situación actual de la educación superior en los estados: Sus proyecciones a 1980." *Revista de la educación superior,* 1974, *2*(3), 3–20.

Siegrist Clamont, J. *En defense de la autonomía universitaria.* Mexico City: Editores Jus, 1955.

Statistics of Higher Education—1975. Mexico City: National Association of Universities and Institutes of Higher Education, 1975.

United States Department of Commerce. *Social and Economic Status of the Black Population in the United States, 1974.* Current Population Reports, Special Studies Series No. 54. Washington, D.C.: U.S. Government Printing Office, 1975.

University Education Growth 1960–61 to 1971–72. Ottawa, Ontario: Information Canada, 1974.

ANTOINETTE FREDERICK

See also: Canada, Dominion of; Mexico, United States of; United States of America.

NORTH AMERICAN INDIANS
See Access of Minorities: The North American Indian.

NORTH AMERICAN STUDIES
See Area Studies (field of study).

NORTHEAST ASIA: REGIONAL ANALYSIS

The countries of Northeast Asia afford a variety of social and cultural contrasts in addition to their differing political, economic, and educational configurations. Pertinent educational generalizations about the region, therefore, are difficult to present, and those that are offered here must be tempered by the understanding that ideological diversity and contrast are more common than pedagogical uniformity and similarity. It must also be noted that analysis of the educational systems in some countries of Northeast Asia, such as the People's Republic of Mongolia, the People's Republic of China (P.R.C.), and the Democratic People's Republic of Korea (D.P.R.K.), are based on population and higher education enrollment figures that are, in some cases, only approximations. More precise information is available, however, for Japan, the Republic of Korea (R.O.K.), and the Republic of China (Taiwan) because of more careful statistics taking and generally open academic discussion in those countries.

(The data in this article are based on the *1975 World Population Data Sheet* as well as on research by contributing authors and the staff of the *International Encyclopedia of Higher Education.* Information compiled by the latter is on file at the Center for International Higher Education Documentation of Northeastern University, Boston, Massachusetts.)

Comparative Enrollments in Higher Education

Differences between the percentage of each country's total population receiving higher education and its economic development, as recorded in national income statistics or gross national product estimates, immediately reveal some discrepancies in the educational systems of this region. Clearly, some of the "poorer" nations make an inordinate sacrifice and place a high priority on providing their citizens opportunities for tertiary education. For example, Mongolia, which has one of the sparsest populations in Asia, records 1 percent of its total population enrolled in some form of higher education. On the other hand, the People's Republic of China—the largest nation in the world with the most numerically extensive educational system— has only five hundred thousand students in higher education, according to its Ministry of Education, and thus has one of the area's lowest percentages in terms of either total population (barely .05 percent) or of those who attended the subordinate primary and secondary schools (only .2 percent). The Republic of China (Taiwan), with 1.5 percent of its population receiving higher education, is sustained on a per capita gross national product (GNP) only one-sixth that of Japan, yet Japan is barely equal educationally, with a similar 1.5 percent of its population enrolled in higher education institutions.

The relative population profiles of the countries in the area also account for some of the educational differences among them. In Japan, 24 percent of the population is under age fifteen and the median age is thirty (*World Population Data Sheet*, 1975). This configuration provides the more evenly balanced of populations in Northeast Asia and, coupled with the highest GNP in Asia, explains in part Japan's abil-

ity to enroll one third of its eighteen- to twenty-two-year-olds in tertiary education. The People's Republic of China, in contrast, with one third of its population under age fifteen and a median age of barely twenty-four, enrolls not quite .05 percent of its population in universities and maintains one of the lowest GNPs in Asia—less than one third of Taiwan's and only one fifteenth of Japan's (*World Population Data Sheet*, 1975).

Important demographic and political factors must, of course, be taken into account when analyzing the Chinese situation, and the sparse, uncertain statistics on education in that country necessitate caution when comparing China to its neighbors. It should also be noted that the statistics on university enrollments in China (at five hundred thousand, they are at last comparable to the pre-1966 Cultural Revolution levels) fail to include a nearly equal number enrolled in so-called peasants' and workers' colleges and cadre schools, which may be more properly considered as ideological or adult education rather than university-level training.

Differing Value Systems

The values of Northeast Asia also vary greatly from country to country. Japan, for example, reflects one of the most competitive and rigorous value systems with a series of hierarchical examination hurdles dominating the life of its students from the earliest school age throughout their academic career. Japanese tertiary institutions are diverse, catering to a wide variety of intellectual levels, professional aspirations, and secular and sectarian tastes. They are also spread somewhat inequitably throughout the island nation, with excessive concentrations in the principal cities. Although some of these same features characterized higher education in the People's Republic of China prior to 1966, any such similarities have long since disappeared. Japanese university students, like those in the Republic of Korea and the Republic of China, have risen through competitive primary and secondary schools by their own intellectual merit, scholarship, perseverance, and ability to pass severe examinations. They have had virtually no labor experience and are not likely to be significantly involved in any practical productive tasks during their studies. Upon graduation Japanese students are less likely to undertake any period of physical labor in the course of their professional employment than students of the PRC.

In contrast, university students of the post–Cultural Revolution period in the People's Republic of China differ from their counterparts in Japan in that they come from particular political castes with peasant, worker, and military backgrounds principally represented; they are selected for advanced study by their former fellow factory workers, and they must have been engaged in productive labor for at least three years after leaving high school before they can even consider the privilege of application for university entrance.

The basic differences in the educational systems of Northeast Asia stem largely, in fact, from the political and ideological distinctions of their countries. Higher education in the P.R.C., the D.P.R.K., and Mongolia is based on a communistic and tightly articulated underlying structure. The criteria for admission to higher education in these countries are based first on ideological grounds, second on academic ability. Similarly, the uses of higher education are defined in terms of political compatibility and a continuing understanding of the need to serve the state, that is, the "people." These political needs are seen as paramount, taking precedence over individual, personal, or professional goals.

In contrast, the higher education in the three noncommunist areas—Japan, the R.O.K., and the Republic of China—can be characterized as a tightly articulated competitive academic system extending down from the universities and colleges into the secondary systems and rooted even in the quality of education obtained at the primary level. In this approach, examina-

tions and curricula are based on information input and knowledge output. Admission to prestige institutions depends heavily on the student's socioeconomic standing, on his financial ability to invest in preparatory education adequate to help him pass the crucial entrance examination. Because of the hierarchical, intellectually based ordering of institutions, this articulated network even continues past graduation. A degree from a prestige institution goes far in guaranteeing entry to the best positions in government, business, academic life, and the professions, whereas graduates from the less prestigious universities are directed into positions roughly according to the rank of the schools from which they graduated.

Examples of the Two Koreas

The two Koreas perhaps reflect best the divergent systems of higher education available in a politically divided Asia. Some statistical background may be helpful in examining the contrasts. The Republic of Korea, with a population of 33,000,000, has approximately 260,000 students, or roughly .8 percent of its population, enrolled in colleges and universities. The Democratic People's Republic of Korea, with a population of 15,000,000, has 220,000 students, or 1.4 percent of its citizens, in higher education. Per capita GNP in the two countries is estimated to be almost equal, but the annual rate of population growth of 2.6 percent in the D.P.R.K., with its somewhat pronatalist policies, is considerably higher than that of 2.0 percent in the R.O.K., where one of Asia's most successful population control programs has been in effect for nearly two decades (*World Population Data Sheet*, 1975). In the R.O.K. only 37 percent of the population is under age fifteen, with a median age of 20.4, whereas in the D.P.R.K. 42 percent of the population is under age fifteen, with a median age of 18.6 (*World Population Data Sheet*, 1975). The Korean War resulted in an older population moving South, and the high casualties in the

North produced a somewhat more youthful population, one that necessitates differing educational demands and manpower needs. Assuming the continuation of present trends, the R.O.K. will have a population of 52,000,000 by the year 2000 and will double its numbers in thirty-five years, but the D.P.R.K. has the capacity to double its population in twenty-seven years and is expected to reach approximately 28,000,000 by the year 2000 *(World Population Data Sheet,* 1975).

There is some justification to the claim that during the thirty years since the founding of the Korean Workers Party in 1946, the underdeveloped, backward, colonial, and agrarian society of the D.P.R.K. has been transformed into a modernized, socialist, agricultural state, underpinned by a gradually extending system of light and heavy industry. If the D.P.R.K. continues to increase the proportion of its college-age population receiving higher education, it may exceed the Japanese percentage within a decade. Thus, by the mid 1980s the D.P.R.K. could be maintaining one of the largest systems of higher education in proportion to age cohorts and total population of any country in Asia.

Professional and qualitative standards are difficult to estimate on a comparative basis, but according to available evidence, a rigorous, expanding, polytechnically oriented higher education structure is in the process of being established in the D.P.R.K. In the R.O.K. the intensively competitive, factional, and hierarchical qualities of certain aspects of its higher education are barely balanced by its reputation for generally high standards. The R.O.K. makes rather fewer provisions than the D.P.R.K. for the intellectual development of poor children, whose parents have little hope of providing them with the high school background so necessary to enter universities. Excellent public and private universities in the R.O.K. exist side by side with a few proprietary, profit-motivated, and somewhat chauvinistic tertiary institutions. This higher education

mosaic of coexisting excellence and dysfunctionality contrasts sharply with the efficient, highly planned, and perhaps less uneven system of colleges and universities in the D.P.R.K.

Control of Student Activities

The Northeast quadrant includes the most populous and the smallest of Asian nations, the most technically advanced and the more simplistic of societies. Yet in spite of the divergence of geographical circumstances and political constraints, all the countries recognize education, scientific instruction, and the fulfillment of manpower training needs as paramount considerations in planning for national development. However, each country has encouraged higher education for somewhat differing reasons and in somewhat differing ways. In the People's Republic of China, for example, the Cultural Revolution closed the universities for almost four years and has since kept in ferment the debate as to the role that higher education should play in a revolutionary society. In the D.P.R.K., on the other hand, debate has been muted, and educational growth a more orderly development. There has been no radical ferment in Pyongyang, where students have been more responsive to direction. The same is true for both Mongolia and the Republic of China, where educational authorities carefully monitor the activities of students. The situation in these three countries stands in violent contrast to Japan, and to a lesser degree the R.O.K., where confrontation, conflict, student disturbances, strikes, and lockouts have been serious during the last two decades.

Future Developments in Higher Education in Northeast Asia

The years since the Cultural Revolution have seen in the P.R.C. a continuance of educational reforms aimed at the integration of work and study. Workers' and peasants' colleges operated by industrial units and communes have been held up for emulation as models of "further" rather than "higher" education. In the decade ahead, the development of a greater variety of continuing education institutions serving different manpower needs will undoubtedly be one of the major tasks for educational planners in the People's Republic of China. But these institutions will not be universities of the same order as those so designated in Japan, for example. However, the workers' college may well have greater relevance for a developing revolutionary society such as the People's Republic of China than the Japanese-model university, which has experienced some difficulty in obtaining jobs for all its graduates in a depressed labor market.

The educational goals of the socialist systems vary in most major respects from those of the noncommunist nations in Asia. In the former, emphasis is placed on the individual's direct contribution to his fellow workers and to the state in nation building. The focus in the noncommunist nations is on individual, familial, and personal-professional goals—the indirect contribution to the nation through use of specialized personal skills is recognized, but is not paramount. Personal development, perhaps at the detriment of community development, is accepted in one system; it is not in the others. The continuing social alienation of intellectual youth may be a great factor in one society, but not in another, where the continual constraints of the state are ever present. In general, although the diffferences in goals between the two ideologically different groups of nations in Northeast Asia are important, it is clear that educational generalizations about them, however useful as intellectual exercises, are subject in practice to severe caveats, whether contrasting the P.R.C. and Japan, Mongolia, and the Republic of China, or the two Korean republics.

Bibliography

Burn, B. *Higher Education in Nine Countries: A Comparative Study of Colleges and Universities Abroad.* New York: McGraw-Hill, 1971.

Cummings, W. K., and Amano, I. "Japanese Higher Education." In Philip G. Altbach (Ed.), *Comparative Higher Education Abroad: Bibliography and Analyses.* New York: Praeger, 1976, pp. 222–274.

Education in Korea. Seoul, Republic of Korea: Ministry of Education, 1972.

Education in Taiwan Province, Republic of China. Taipei: Taiwan Provincial Government Department of Education, 1974.

Educational Innovation in the Republic of Korea. Paris: UNESCO, 1974.

Educational Statistics, 1974. Tokyo: Japan Ministry of Education, 1974.

Fraser, S. E., and Hsu, K. L. *Chinese Education: The Cultural Revolution and Its Aftermath: A Bibliographical Guide.* New York: International Arts and Science Press, 1972.

Fraser, S. E., Kim, Hyung-chan, and Kim, Sun Ho. *North Korean Education and Society: A Select and Partially Annotated Bibliography Pertaining to the Democratic People's Republic of Korea.* London: University of London, Institute of Education, 1972.

Hawkins, J. N. *Mao Tse-tung and Education: His Thoughts and Teachings.* Hamden, Connecticut: Shoe String Press, 1974.

1975 World Population Data Sheet. Washington, D.C.: Population Reference Bureau, 1975.

Price, R. F. *Education in Communist China.* (Rev. ed.) London: Routledge & Kegan Paul, 1975.

STEWART E. FRASER

See also: China, People's Republic of; Japan; Korea, Democratic People's Republic of; Mongolian People's Republic.

NORTHERN EUROPE, NATIONAL ARCHIVES OF

See Archives: Northern Europe, National Archives of.

NORTHERN EUROPE: REGIONAL ANALYSIS

See Western Europe and the United Kingdom: Regional Analysis.

NORWAY, KINGDOM OF

Population: 4,007,378 (1975 estimate). Student enrollment in primary school: 584,978; secondary school (academic, vocational, technical): 139,495; higher education: 64,582 (university: 39,268; nonuniversity: 25,314). Language of instruction: Norwegian. Aca-

demic calendar: September to June, two semesters. Percentage of national budget expended on church and education: 12% (1975). [Except where otherwise indicated, figures are for 1974–75.]

Innovation, experimentation, and reform characterize Norway's educational system during the post–World War II period. In response to social pressure to provide equal educational opportunities for all, the Norwegian government implemented a series of reforms. In 1959 it extended compulsory education from seven to nine years; in the late 1960s it introduced a comprehensive program in upper secondary academic and vocational schools; and in the 1960s and 1970s it expanded higher education to include a network of regional colleges.

The development of higher education in Norway is relatively new. In 1811 *Kongelige Frederiks universitet* (renamed *Universitetet i Oslo* in 1939), the first institution of higher learning, was founded in Oslo by a royal decree of Frederik VI, then king of Denmark and Norway. The king established the university in response to the increasing demand of the Norwegian citizens for national and cultural independence from the long union with Denmark (1397–1814).

The university commenced operations in 1813, shortly before King Frederik was forced to relinquish control of Norway. Once free of Danish rule, Norway formed a representative assembly on May 17, 1814, and established a national constitution based on ideas drawn from France, Spain, and the United States. Another union, this time with Sweden, followed almost immediately. Under the new arrangement, Norway remained independent with its own parliament and retained its constitution; this was a personal union with the Swedish king, similar to that of Finland with the Russian czar during the same period.

More than 130 years passed before another university, the University of Bergen, was established in 1948. However, several other institutions of higher learning had been founded in the interim: the Agricul-

tural College of Norway in 1859 (which became the Agricultural University of Norway in 1919), the Free Faculty of Theology (1907), the Norwegian Institute of Technology (1910), the Norwegian School of Economics and Business Administration (1936), and the Veterinary College of Norway (1936).

In 1968 two additional universities were established, the University of Tromsø and the University of Trondheim. According to the latest government-approved development plan for higher education, no additional universities are planned until 1980 or 1985; however, expansion within the existing universities is expected to continue. The emphasis in higher education will be on the decentralization of study, which will be accomplished by expanding the system of regional colleges and relaxing admission requirements to allow persons over twenty-five years old with five years of work experience access to the higher education institutions.

Legal Basis of Educational System

Higher education institutions in Norway are established by royal decree or by parliamentary resolution. The University of Oslo was established by the Royal Decree of 1811, while the Norwegian School of Economics and Business Administration and the University of Bergen were organized according to parliamentary resolutions of 1936 and 1946. The first three regional colleges were established by a parliamentary resolution of June 1969.

Types of Institutions

University education is available at the University of Oslo, the University of Bergen, the University of Trondheim, the University of Tromsø, and six schools of university status.

The University of Oslo, the oldest and largest of the higher education institutions in Norway, has faculties of theology, law, medicine, liberal arts, dentistry, social sciences, mathematics and natural sciences.

The University of Bergen, inaugurated

in 1948, incorporated the former Bergen Museum, established in 1825. The university has faculties of liberal arts, mathematics and natural sciences, medicine, social sciences, and dentistry, and operates a biological station open to research workers from Scandinavian and non-Scandinavian countries.

The University of Trondheim was established by integrating the Royal Norwegian Society of Sciences and Letters; the Museum *(Kongelige norske videnskabers selskab, Museet)*, founded in 1790; the College of Arts and Science, founded in 1922 as an advanced teachers college; and the Norwegian Institute of Technology, established in 1910. The two latter institutions offer separate programs. The Museum is a research center for the fields of botany, zoology, archeology, and anthropology; it provides no regular instruction. The College of Arts and Science offers courses in liberal arts, mathematics and natural sciences, and social sciences. The Institute of Technology provides the only program available in Norway for civil engineers and also has courses for the training of architects.

The University of Tromsø was founded in 1968 (and opened in 1972) to meet the educational and research needs of northern Norway. The university's research programs emphasize medicine, wildlife and marine biology, and fisheries; the educational program, designed primarily for training teachers and doctors, includes courses in medicine, liberal arts, social sciences, mathematics and natural sciences, and fisheries. The university is based in scientific institutions and hospitals in Tromsø; construction of a permanent campus began in 1975.

Other higher education institutions with university status include the Oslo School of Architecture, the Free Faculty of Theology, the Norwegian School of Economics and Business Administration, the Norwegian College of Physical Education and Sport, the Veterinary College of Norway, and the Agricultural College of Norway.

Nonuniversity higher education is available in a number of specialized schools that offer nondegree programs leading to employment. Included in this category are the schools of arts and crafts, nursing, social work, teachers colleges, technical schools, conservatories of music, and the regional colleges. The State Academy of Art for painters and sculptors and the newly established Advanced School of Music, both of which offer the highest education in their fields, are also in this category.

The regional colleges provide a two-year postsecondary program in economics, administration, social sciences, humanities, technology, natural sciences, environmental study, and tourism. The colleges are also experimenting with interdisciplinary courses designed to develop the student's relationship to his environment, his future profession, and his place in Norwegian society. The Norwegian parliament has endorsed a proposal that 25 percent of the monies allocated to the colleges be used to develop this concept (called *allmennfag*) and to meet the needs of higher adult education.

An institution common to Scandinavian countries is the folk high school, established in the second half of the nineteenth century to provide spiritual, cultural, and practical subjects for students over seventeen years of age. The folk high schools are private, self-governing institutions and offer courses which usually last six to eight months; however, a few schools provide a two-year program.

Relationship with Secondary Education and Admission Requirements

The general Norway education system consists of nine years of compulsory school, which includes six years of primary and three years of intermediate education. The student may then enroll in one of a wide variety of academic and vocational schools at the upper secondary level.

After completing the basic school program, students who plan to attend the university usually enroll in the *gymnasium*, which offers a three-year general secondary program leading to the university matriculation examination, the *examen artium*. The *examen artium* is also a prerequisite for admission to most other higher education institutions. Exceptions are the four-year program at the teachers colleges and the three-year program offered at the technical colleges.

Students can earn a certificate equivalent to the *examen artium* through part-time study and practical experience and thereby gain admission to a higher education institution. The *examen artium*, or its equivalent, does not guarantee entry into the field of the applicant's choice; in most faculties a strict *numerus clausus* (restriction on numbers) is maintained due to lack of facilities and instructors.

Administration and Control

Higher education institutions in Norway are autonomous within the budget limitations established by parliament and the Ministry of Church and Education. The institutions also must adhere to parliamentary laws concerning administration, examinations, the granting of degrees, and other activities.

The chief executive officer at the universities is a rector, who is elected by the faculty governing bodies. He is assisted by a director, who is responsible for the management of the nonacademic aspects of the institution. The rectors and directors of the universities and institutions of university status cooperate closely through the Conference of Rectors of Universities and Colleges, which meets twice a year to discuss matters pertaining to higher education.

The supreme governing body at the university is the university parliament or senate. Members of this body include the rector and representatives from the teaching staff, the nonacademic staff, and the student body. Methods of selection for the university parliament or senate differ among institutions. At the University of Oslo members of the teaching staff of each faculty elect a faculty leader, who serves on the senate for a two- or three-year term. The nonacademic staff and the students also elect representatives. The universities are divided into faculties or institutes, headed by a dean, director, or chairman. Each faculty or institute is governed by a board consisting of teachers, nonacademic staff, and students.

The regional colleges are experimenting with student and faculty involvement in governance and administration. The college at Kristiansand, for instance, is governed mainly by a senate steering committee; half of its members are students. The committee handles most of the tasks normally associated with the chief executive officer, and many of its decisions are final.

The director of a regional college is the formal executive officer. He represents the institution in the local community and serves as secretary to the regional board, but his authority on campus is limited. Each college has a regional board consisting of two members appointed by the Ministry of Church and Education; other members are selected by the college faculty and students or are representatives of the county. There also is a central board for all regional colleges.

By law, Norwegian students participate in the administration of higher education institutions and are free to form their own associations. The student council or parliament represents the student body at each institution and elects a member to serve on the university parliament or senate.

Programs and Degrees

The degree programs offered at Norwegian universities differ among faculties. In most faculties students must pass a preliminary examination in philosophy, the *examen philosophicum*, at the end of the first or second semester in order to continue their studies for a first degree. The *candidatus magisterii (cand. mag.)* is the first degree awarded in faculties of liberal arts, mathematics and natural sciences, social sciences, and fisheries. The average length of study for the *cand. mag.* degree is four to five years. Students who hold the *cand. mag.* degree may work toward the higher degree of *candidatus* within a field of designated study. These degrees include *candidatus philosophiae, candidatus philologiae* (humanities), *candidatus realium* (mathematics and natural sciences), and *candidatus sociologiae* or *paedagogiae*. Candidates are required to take several written and oral examinations and present a thesis. The *candidatus* degree programs require another two to three years of study beyond the *cand. mag.* degree.

In the fields of political science and languages, students may earn the *magister artium* degree as an alternative to the *cand. mag.* and the *candidatus* degrees. Students in this program are required to pass examinations in two minor subjects and to complete examinations and a thesis in a major field of study. Seven years of study are required for the *magister artium* degree.

The first degree in the faculties of theology, law, medicine, dentistry, and agriculture is the *candidatus,* awarded after five to six years of study. The next degree awarded by the faculties is the *licentiatus.* Students must hold the *candidatus* degree before enrolling in the three- to four-year *licentiatus* program. Degree candidates are required to pass examinations in several subjects and to present a thesis.

The highest degree awarded by Norwegian universities is the doctor's degree, which is based on many years of study and research, culminating in the submission of a doctoral thesis to a committee of specialists. Doctoral candidates are required to present two trial lectures before publicly defending their theses, which must meet stringent requirements for scientific originality and merit. There is no time limit in the doctor's degree program.

Financing and Student Financial Aid

Higher education is financed by the Norwegian government. The major portion of funds is supplied by the national government; however, regions and communities make small contributions to local institutions. The universities, colleges, and other institutions receive an annual budget from the Norwegian parliament. Higher education institutions manage their own budgets within a framework established by the Ministry of Church and Education.

No tuition fees are charged at higher education institutions; however, students must pay for their own living expenses and are required to pay small matriculation and semester fees to the student welfare organization. The Norwegian State Loan Fund for Education provides loans and scholarships to needy students to help meet these expenses. Students have up to fifteen years to repay their educational loans. Students living away from home during their study period do not have to repay scholarships.

Student Social Background and Access to Education

Since World War II the Norwegian government has made an effort to provide equal educational opportunities for all. Access to higher education has been limited in parts of the kingdom by the lack of institutions in isolated areas. The growth in the university-age population and the implementation of a *numerus clausus* in many faculties has also contributed to limit access. The University of Trondheim and the University of Tromsø, established in 1968, and the development of the regional college system have helped to alleviate these two problems.

All students who hold a valid student card are compulsory members of a student welfare organization. Each of the five welfare organizations is governed by a board consisting of representatives from the higher education institutions in a region.

These organizations administer student social services, including housing, meals, bookstores, travel, and health services. They receive operating funds from matriculation and semester fees and government grants, and they operate on a nonprofit basis.

Teaching Staff

Members of the university teaching staff are classified as professors, assistant professors, and lecturers. The government must approve the appointment of professors and assistant professors upon the recommendation of the faculty and senate. All other teaching staff are appointed by the senate. Most appointments are for life.

A professor is appointed to a chair after his qualifications are approved by a special committee appointed by the faculty. The committee includes one member of the faculty and members of the staff of other Norwegian and foreign higher education institutions.

All salaries are determined by a uniform scale set by the government.

Research Activities

University staff are encouraged to carry out research and are expected to spend 50 percent of their time on research. Research appointments are based on the scientific qualifications of the candidate. Research workers are generally allowed to select their own subjects.

The scientific research councils allocate funds for university research. The Research Council for Science and the Humanities awards the major portion of its grants to the universities and colleges, while the Council for Scientific and Industrial Research gives only small support to university research. The Norwegian Agricultural Research Council awards most of its grants to the Agricultural College of Norway.

Research is an integral part of all degree programs at the universities, and as the student progresses from the licentiate to the doctoral level, increasingly sophisticated research is required.

Current Problems and Trends

The need for additional facilities at the higher education level led to the development of the regional college system in the late 1960s and early 1970s. The first three colleges were opened in 1969 and an additional three in 1971. The colleges emphasize professional and vocational education leading to employment in the community; however, they also provide programs designed to enable students to transfer to the universities or to other higher education institutions.

The regional colleges offer new interdisciplinary programs, which often present problems in transfer, since no similar programs exist in the universities. A university committee has been appointed to develop new procedures for evaluating students who transfer from the regional colleges as well as the teachers colleges and other postsecondary institutions.

Only limited expansion at the higher education level is planned for the next several years in Norway. Most expansion will probably occur in the regional college system.

Relationship with Industry

Practical training is required in several fields of study at higher education institutions. Students in fields such as engineering, architecture, and agriculture may be required to gain practical experience prior to admission or may do practical work during the course of study. Graduates from the teachers colleges undergo a period of supervised practical training before they are certified.

International Cooperation

The program of study at Norwegian higher education institutions is designed to prepare students for careers in Norway; however, a small number of foreign students are admitted to Norwegian institutions each year. Because of limited facilities, foreign students are not usually admitted to the faculties of medicine, dentistry, engineering, business administration, agriculture, or veterinary medicine. Many Norwegian students in these fields study abroad, usually in other Scandinavian or European countries or in the United States.

The University of Tromsø has agreements with the University of Umeå (Sweden), the University of Oulu (Finland), and the Technical College of Luleå (Sweden) for joint research in areas such as archeology, Lappish studies, geology, and arctic medicine.

The University of Bergen and the Norwegian School of Economics and Business Administration participate in an exchange program with the University of California whereby about twenty students from the University of California attend Bergen for a year of study.

[Information supplied by Willy Haugli, Director, and Helge M. Sønneland, Information Officer, University of Tromsø, Norway.]

Educational Association

Norsk studentunion (NSU: National Union of Norwegian Students)
Lokkeveien 7
Oslo 1, Norway

Bibliography

Dahlin, Å. (Ed.) *Etterutdanningspolitikk.* Oslo: Universitetsforlaget, 1970.

Dittman, R. *Norway: A Study of the Educational System of the Kingdom of Norway and a Guide to to the Academic Placement of Students from Norway in United States Educational Institutions.* World Education Series. Washington, D.C.: American Association of. Collegiate Registrars and Admissions Officer (AACRAO), 1971

Hamdal, G. (Ed.) *Universitetsstudier under debatt.* Oslo: Universitetsforlaget, 1970.

Hove, O. *The System of Education in Norway.* Oslo: Royal Norwegian Ministry of Church and Education, 1968.

Imatrikuleringskomiteen 1971. *Year til universiteter og høyskoler.* Oslo: Universitetsforlaget, 1971.

Kintzer, F. C. "Norway's Regional Colleges." *Higher Education,* 1974, *3,* 303–314.

Mosby, H. *Que Vadis Universitas.* Oslo: Universitetsforlaget, 1971.

Nordahl-Olsen, G. (Ed). *University Studies in Norway.* Oslo: Universitetsforlaget, 1975.

Sjogren, C. (Ed.) *The Admission and Academic Placement of Students from Nordic Countries: A Workshop Report.* Washington, D.C.: National Association for Foreign Student Affairs and the American Association of Collegiate Registrars and Admissions Officers, n.d.

Tranøy, K. E. *Universitetet i Norge.* Oslo: Universitetsforlaget, 1967.

See also: Academic Dress and Insignia; Adult Education: Role of Labor and Industry; Aid to Other Nations: Bilateral Participation in Higher Education; Archives: Northern Europe, National Archives of; Cooperative Education and Off-Campus Experience: Cooperative Education Worldwide; Planning, Development, and Coordination: Regional Planning of Higher Education; Research: Financing and Control of Research; Science Policies: Highly Industrialized Nations: Western Europe; Short-Cycle Education; Western Europe and the United Kingdom: Regional Analysis; Women and Higher Education: Equal Rights and Affirmative Action.

NORWAY, NATIONAL ARCHIVES OF
See Archives: Northern Europe, National Archives of.

NUCLEAR ENGINEERING
(Field of Study)

Nuclear engineering is a branch of engineering devoted to the exploitation of the energy potential of nuclear reactions for peaceful purposes. The principal foci of the field are the fission reaction, in which atoms are split into lighter elements, and the fusion process, whereby two light elements are fused into one heavy element. In each reaction an excess of energy is produced, and the excess energy may be used to provide the world with large amounts of energy. For that purpose, fission power reactors are in widespread use throughout the world. Controlled fusion power has not yet been demonstrated but is believed feasible within the twentieth century.

The fission technology branch of the discipline is now well developed. The basic nuclear reactions, the probabilities for various types of nuclear events, and laws of neutron migration have evolved since the 1940s. The area of reactor physics uses these basic natural phenomena to provide the methods and techniques to design reactors for power production, ship propulsion, isotope production, and other special purposes. Reactor engineering is an area of fission technology whereby conventional areas of heat transfer, fluid flow, and structural analysis are applied to the design of reactors to guarantee safe, environmentally harmless, and economical use of the energy released in the fission process. Radiations are produced as a by-product of the fission process within nuclear reactors, and materials in the reactor are subject to intense radiation levels. Nuclear materials is the area of the field concerned with the effects of radiation upon the physical properties of materials. Part of the area of radiation physics overlaps the field of nuclear engineering, because an understanding of radiation effects upon materials necessitates an understanding of the interactions of radiation with matter. Similarly, that part of biomedical engineering concerned with the measurement, detection, and biological effects of radiation is usually considered part of nuclear engineering.

The fusion branch of nuclear engineering is composed of the area of plasma physics and the emerging area of fusion technology. Plasma physics is the study of ionized states of matter. The fusion process requires enormous temperatures for the constituent atoms to fuse together. The required temperatures are so high that the atoms are ionized in the fusion device. Uncontrolled fusion reactions in the form of thermonuclear weapons have been produced, but a controlled fusion process has not yet been demonstrated. Scientific opinion is now very optimistic about fusion feasibility, and much research in the field is beginning to focus upon the technical problems of fusion reactor design (such as cooling to remove heat), radiation effects upon the confinement and shielding materials, and economics. These areas are now lumped under the term *fusion technology* but undoubtedly will mature into smaller, more specialized areas of fusion engineering, fusion materials, and fusion physics.

Because of the scale and complexity of nuclear power plants, almost all areas of science and engineering are related to nuclear engineering. The design, construction, and operation of a power plant involve the conventional skills of civil, mechanical, and electrical engineering. The processing of spent fuel to recover useful by-products of nuclear reactions, as well as radioactive wastes, involves the methods and talents of chemical engineers. Finally, since both nuclear power plants and reprocessing plants use radioactive materials, the health physics area is also closely related to nuclear engineering.

The nuclear engineering profession is very new, beginning shortly after World War II and the development of the atomic bomb. Evolution of the discipline was hampered by the restrictions of security until the early 1950s, when the Atoms for Peace Program was announced at the United Nations. This program was followed by the First International Conference on the Peaceful Uses of Atomic Energy, sponsored by the United Nations in 1955. Since that time international cooperation, with a worldwide sharing of information, has characterized the profession.

Academic programs began to appear as soon as information was made publicly available. The first degree programs in nuclear engineering were offered at North Carolina State University in Raleigh, North Carolina, in 1950. Graduate programs developed in many United States and Western European countries in the middle-to-late 1950s. Undergraduate programs evolved out of most of these graduate programs. By the mid 1970s there were forty-nine graduate degree programs and forty-one undergraduate degree programs in the United States alone.

The realization that oil supplies are dwindling has had a large, favorable impact on the nuclear engineering profession. The worldwide growth of nuclear power has been accelerating, particularly since the formation of the international oil cartel. In the United States nuclear power is now the cheapest means of producing electricity and the least environmentally harmful. Nuclear economics are even more favorable in countries with less fossil resources than the United States. It is estimated that by the end of the twentieth century 50 percent of the electric generation in the world will be by nuclear means.

The search for future energy sources has concentrated upon short-term alternatives to oil and long-term alternatives with essentially inexhaustible supplies. For short-term alternatives, only fission reactors and coal are available. For the long-term needs, research is focusing on solar power and two aspects of the nuclear engineering profession: breeder fission reactors and fusion power. Thus, the growth of the nuclear industry appears inevitable through the remainder of the twentieth century.

Education in the nuclear engineering field is well developed in the United States, Canada, and Western Europe. Programs of instruction for both undergraduate and graduate degrees have existed for almost twenty years. These academic programs are strongly coupled to national programs in nuclear technology. In countries for which nuclear power is not important, there has been little in the way of academic programs. Thus, in Latin America, Africa, and the Middle East there are few degree programs. In Asia there are programs in India, Japan, the Republic of China, and the Republic of Korea. However, the oil crisis of the 1970s has influenced the development of nuclear engineering programs in various countries throughout the world, including Brazil, Argentina, and other Latin American countries. Further, even in the oil-rich Middle East, Iran is leading in the development of a program in nuclear engineering.

KENT HANSEN

Levels and Programs of Study

Programs in nuclear engineering generally require as a minimum prerequisite a secondary education and lead to the following awards: certificate or diploma, Bachelor of Science or Engineering, Master of Science or Engineering, Doctor of Engineering, or their equivalents. Programs deal with the principles and practices of nuclear engineering and consist of classroom and laboratory instruction and, on advanced levels, seminars, discussions, and research in specialized areas of nuclear engineering.

Programs that lead to awards not equivalent to a first university degree deal with the practical aspects of nuclear engineering technology and emphasize the application of mathematics, physics, and engineering principles and practices to the operation of nuclear power plants. Programs usually last two years, full time. Principal course content for such programs usually includes mathematics, physics (including nuclear physics), radioisotopes, chemistry, electronics, instrumentation, and reactor principles.

Programs that lead to a first university degree deal with both the principles and practices of nuclear engineering and are concerned largely with the application of fission and fusion processes to the production of electricity, steam, and energy for propulsion. Principal course content usually includes basic courses in chemistry; physics through modern quantum physics; mathematics through partial differential equations; and engineering fundamentals, including materials, structures, thermodynamics, and heat transfer. Also included are courses in introductory reactor physics, reactor engineering, and nuclear physics.

Programs that lead to a postgraduate

university degree concentrate on a specialized area of nuclear engineering. Emphasis is placed on research work as substantiated by the presentation of a scholarly thesis or dissertation. Principal subject matter areas within which courses and research projects tend to fall include advanced nuclear physics, advanced reactor physics, advanced reactor engineering, reactor materials, applied radiation physics, bioengineering, plasma physics, and fusion technology.

[This section was based on UNESCO's *International Standard Classification of Education (ISCED): Three Stage Classification System, 1974* (Paris: UNESCO, 1974).]

Major International and National Organizations

INTERNATIONAL

European Atomic Energy Community (EURATOM)
51–53 rue Belliard
1040 Brussels, Belgium

European Atomic Energy Society
Société européenne d'énergie atomique
% Centre d'étude de l'énergie nucléaire
avenue E. Plasky 144
1040 Brussels, Belgium

European Organization for Nuclear Research
Organisation européenne pour la recherche nucléaire
Meyrin
1211 Geneva 23, Switzerland

Inter-American Nuclear Energy Commission
Commission interamericaine de l'énergie nucléaire
% General Secretariat of the OAS
Washington, D.C. 20006 USA

International Atomic Energy Agency (IAEA)
11 Karntnerring
P.O. Box 590
1011 Vienna, Austria
    The most significant international organization in the field and the only organization with membership from all parts of the world. The IAEA publishes extensively and produces a number of important series covering many different aspects of the nuclear sciences, including Bibliographic Series, Proceedings Series, and Technical Report Series.

Joint Institute for Nuclear Research
P.O. Box 79
Moscow, Soviet Union

OECD Nuclear Energy Agency (NEA)
(formerly European Nuclear Energy Agency)
Agence de l'OCDE pour l'énergie nucléaire
38 blvd. Suchet
75016 Paris, France

    For additional organizations see:

Directory of International Agencies. New York: Simon & Schuster, 1970.
Haslett, A. W. (Ed.) *World Nuclear Directory: An International Reference Book.* (4th ed.) London: Harrap, 1970. Includes both national and international organizations.
Yearbook of International Organizations. Paris: Union of International Associations, 1974.

NATIONAL

Canada:
    Canadian Nuclear Association
    65 Queen Street, West
    Toronto, Quebec

United Kingdom:
    British Nuclear Energy Society
    1–7 Great George Street
    London SW 1P 3AA, England

    Institution of Nuclear Engineers
    Holwood House
    24 Holwood Road
    Bromley, Kent, England

United States:
    American Nuclear Society
    244 E. Ogden Avenue
    Hillsdale, Illinois 60521

    For a fuller listing of national organizations, including governmental agencies and commissions, see:

Anthony, L. J. *Sources of Information on Atomic Energy.* Elmsford, New York: Pergamon Press, 1966.
Haslett, A. W. (Ed.) *World Nuclear Directory: An International Reference Book.* (4th ed.) London: Harrap, 1970. An extensive listing of national organizations covering over seventy-five countries.

Principal Information Sources

GENERAL

Guides to the literature in the field include:

Anthony, L. J. *Sources of Information on Atomic Energy.* Elmsford, New York: Pergamon Press, 1966. A guide to organizational and documentary information in the nuclear energy field.
International Atomic Energy Agency Publications. Catalogue. Vienna: IAEA, 1972.
Jacobs, J. M., and others. *Bibliographies of Inter-*

est to the Atomic Energy Program. (2nd ed.) Oak Ridge, Tennessee: U.S. Atomic Energy Commission, Division of Technical Information, 1962.

Winton, H. N. M. *Man and the Environment: A Bibliography of Selected Publications of the United Nations System 1946–1971.* New York: UNIPUB/Bowker, 1972. Provides a few pertinent sources dealing with nuclear engineering and the environment.

Wiren, H. N. *Guide to Literature on Nuclear Engineering.* Washington, D.C.: American Society for Engineering Education, 1972.

Introductions to the field of nuclear engineering are provided by:

Foster, A. R., and Wright, R. L., Jr. *Basic Nuclear Engineering.* (2nd ed.) Boston: Allyn & Bacon, 1973.

Murphy, G. *Elements of Nuclear Engineering.* New York: Wiley, 1961. A general survey of the field of nuclear engineering, including radiation, fission, fusion, and other nuclear transformations.

Simon, A. L. *Energy Resources.* Elmsford, New York: Pergamon Press, 1974. Offers a general discussion of energy and its resources, with a chapter on atomic energy.

Weinstein, R. *Nuclear Engineering Fundamentals.* New York: McGraw-Hill, 1964.

Another important source of information is provided by:

International Atomic Energy Agency. *Peaceful Uses of Atomic Energy: Proceedings of the 4th International Conference on the Peaceful Uses of Atomic Energy (Geneva, 6–16 September 1971).* (15 vols.) Vienna: IAEA, 1972. These proceedings were jointly sponsored by the United Nations and IAEA. The broad topics covered in the fifteen volumes are nuclear power; nuclear fuels and materials; health, safety, and legal aspects; isotope and irradiation; international administrative aspects; and selected subjects of particular interest to developing countries.

The following important early works in the field are part of the McGraw-Hill Series in Nuclear Engineering (New York: McGraw-Hill):

Benedict, M., and Pigford, T. H. *Nuclear Chemical Engineering.* 1957.

Bonilla, C. F. (Ed.) *Nuclear Engineering.* 1957.

Ellis, R. H. *Nuclear Technology for Engineers.* 1959.

El-Wakil, M. M. *Nuclear Power Engineering.* 1962.

Glower, D. D. *Experimental Reactor Analysis and Radiation Measurement.* 1965.

Hosington, D. B. *Nucleonics Fundamentals.* 1959.

Meghreblian, R. V., and Holmes, D. K. *Reactor Analysis.* 1960.

Price, W. J. *Nuclear Radiation Detection.* (2nd ed.) 1964.

Schultz, M. A. *Control of Nuclear Reactors and Power Plants.* (2nd ed.) 1961.

Stephenson, R. *Introduction to Nuclear Engineering.* (2nd ed.) 1958.

A historical account of nuclear fission is provided by:

Graetzer, H. G., and Anderson, D. L. *The Discovery of Nuclear Fission: A Documentary History.* New York: Van Nostrand Reinhold, 1971.

For a general discussion of nuclear engineering education see:

Seaborg, G. T. *Education and the Atom: An Evaluation of Government's Role in Science Education and Information, Especially as Applied to Nuclear Engineering.* New York: McGraw-Hill, 1964. Includes a section on graduate and undergraduate education in nuclear engineering in the United States, as well as on the international nuclear community and cooperation in international education.

Nuclear Science Teaching III. Vienna: IAEA, 1975. Examines the teaching of nuclear science and related fields at the secondary and early university levels.

Weaver, L. E. (Ed.) *Education for Peaceful Uses of Nuclear Explosives.* Tucson: University of Arizona Press, 1970. Provides a discussion of nuclear explosives engineering education in the United States; covers educational development, university research, legal problems and educational programs, and the status of nuclear engineering.

CURRENT BIBLIOGRAPHIES

Bibliographies and abstracts are significant sources of current information in nuclear engineering. The most important abstracting service in its field is:

Nuclear Science Abstracts. Oak Ridge, Tennessee: U.S. Atomic Energy Commission, Technical Information Series, 1948–.

Other important abstracting and bibliographical services are provided by:

Bulletin signalétique. Part 150: *Physique, chimie, et technologie nucléaires.* Paris: Centre national de la recherche scientifique, 1940–.

The Energy Index. New York: Energy Reference Department, Environment Information Center, 1973–.

International Nuclear Information System (INIS) Atomindex. Vienna: IAEA, 1970–. Provides a data base for identifying publications dealing with nuclear science.

List of Bibliographies on Nuclear Energy. Vienna: IAEA, 1960–. Information on bibliographies published in English, French, German, and Russian.

Physics Abstracts. Science Abstracts Section A. London: Institution of Electrical Engineers, 1898–.

Referativnyĭ zhurnal: Yadernyye reaktory. Moscow: Akademiia nauk, SSSR, Institut nauchnoĭ informatsii, 1953–.

Zentralblatt für Kernforschung und Kerntechnik. Berlin, Federal Republic of Germany: Institut für Dokumentation der deutschen Akademie der Wissenschaften zu Berlin, 1961–. Particularly useful for German and Eastern European literature on nuclear physics and engineering.

Progress reports also include useful current information and developments:

Advances in Nuclear Science and Technology. New York: Academic Press, 1962–. Offers critical reviews covering all aspects of atomic energy, with particular attention to nuclear engineering.

Annual Review of Nuclear Science. Palo Alto, California: Annual Reviews, 1952–.

PERIODICALS

Among the significant international journals in nuclear engineering are *Annals of Physics* (US), *Atomic Energy Review* (Austria), *Atomwirtschaft/Journal of Nuclear Engineering* (FRG), *Canadian Research and Development, Energie nucléaire* (France), *Euronuclear* (UK), *Euro-Spectra* (US), *Journal of Nuclear Energy/Atomnaya energiya* (UK, USSR), *Journal of Nuclear Science and Technology* (Japan), *Journal of Physics B: Atomic and Molecular Physics* (US), *Nuclear Engineering and Design* (Netherlands), *Nuclear Engineering International* (UK), *Nuclear Fusion* (Austria), *Nuclear India, Nuclear Physics* (Netherlands), *Nuclear Science and Engineering* (UK), *Nuclear Technology* (US), *Nuklearna energija* (Yugoslavia), *Nukleonika* (Poland), *Rivista di ingegneria nucleare* (Italy), *Schweizerische Vereinigung für Atomenergie* (Switzerland), *Soviet Journal of Nuclear Physics/Yadernaya fizika, Zeitschrift für Physik* (Series A) (FRG).

For a more complete listing of journals in the field see:

Anthony, L. J. *Sources of Information on Atomic Energy.* Elmsford, New York: Pergamon Press, 1966. See Index to Periodicals, pp. 243–245.

Haslett, A. W. (Ed.) *World Nuclear Directory: An*

International Reference Book. (4th ed.) London: Harrap, 1970. Pp. 695–714.

List of Periodicals in the Field of Nuclear Energy. Vienna: IAEA, 1963. Contains information on nuclear energy literature from thirty-six countries.

Ulrich's International Periodicals Directory. New York: Bowker, biennial.

ENCYCLOPEDIAS, DICTIONARIES, HANDBOOKS

Atomic Energy: Glossary of Technical Terms. (4th ed.) New York: United Nations Terminology Section, 1958. A polyglot dictionary in English, French, Spanish, and Russian.

Clason, W. E. (Ed.) *Elsevier's Dictionary of Nuclear Science and Technology; In Six Languages: English/American, French, Spanish, Italian, Dutch, and German.* (2nd ed.) Amsterdam: Elsevier, 1970.

Concise Encyclopedia of Nuclear Energy. New York: Wiley-Interscience, 1962.

Etherington, H. *Nuclear Engineering Handbook.* New York: McGraw-Hill, 1958. A standard in the field.

Flugge, S. (Ed.) *Handbuch der Physik.* (54 vols.) Berlin, Federal Republic of Germany: Springer-Verlag, 1955–1973. Many of the volumes are concerned with atomic energy.

Glossary of Terms Used in Nuclear Science. London: British Standards Institution, 1962. An English dictionary.

Karpovich, E. A. *Russian-English Atomic Dictionary.* (2nd ed.) New York: Technical Dictionaries, 1959.

Newnes Concise Encyclopedia of Nuclear Engineering. London: Newnes, 1962.

U.S. Atomic Energy Commission. *Reactor Handbook.* (2nd ed.) New York: Wiley-Interscience, 1960–1964. A four-volume work dealing specifically with engineering.

DIRECTORIES

Atomic Handbook. London: Morgan, 1965–. An international directory which includes names of international organizations, nuclear energy facilities, journals, nuclear yearbooks, and reference books.

Directory of Nuclear Reactors. (9 vols.) Vienna: IAEA, 1959–1971.

Haslett, A. W. (Ed.) *World Nuclear Directory: An International Reference Book.* (4th ed.) London: Harrap, 1970. The most comprehensive guide to atomic energy organizations (national and international), government departments and agencies, universities and institutes; covers seventy-six countries; appendix lists major journals in the field in each country.

Meetings on Atomic Energy: A Quarterly World-

Wide List of Conferences, Exhibitions and Training Courses in Atomic Energy, Together with a Selective List of Meetings on Space Science. Vienna: IAEA, 1969–.

Power and Research Reactors in Member States. Vienna: IAEA, 1974.

World Survey on Major Facilities in Controlled Nuclear Fusion. Vienna: IAEA, 1973. Primarily a technical listing of major experiments in fusion and plasma physics conducted in various centers throughout the world.

RESEARCH CENTERS, INSTITUTES, INFORMATION CENTERS

Anthony, L. J. *Sources of Information on Atomic Energy.* Elmsford, New York: Pergamon Press, 1966. Includes the names of important research centers, laboratories, and institutes throughout the world. See Part 2.

Some of the important laboratories include:

Atomic Energy Research Establishment
Harwell, Berkshire, England

Australian Institute of Nuclear Science and Engineering
Lucas Heights, Australia

Brookhaven National Laboratory
Upton, Long Island, New York USA

European Organization for Nuclear Research
Organisation européenne pour la recherche nucléaire
Meyrin
1211 Geneva 23, Switzerland

Japan Atomic Energy Research Institute
Tokyo, Japan

Joint Institute for Nuclear Research
Dubra, Moscow, Soviet Union

Also see:

Minerva, Forschungsinstitute. Berlin, Federal Republic of Germany: de Gruyter, 1972.

World Survey of Major Facilities in Controlled Nuclear Fusion. Vienna: IAEA, 1973. Provides information on important centers of research for major experiments.

NURSING (Field of Study)

Nursing, a health-related profession, is concerned with meeting the health care needs of the individual and society. The basic functions of nursing are the prevention of illness, the promotion of health, the maintenance of health, and rehabilitation. Members of the profession provide patient care by assessing patient needs, formulating a plan of nursing care, implementing the plan, evaluating the plan's effectiveness, and modifying the plan according to the patient's response and changing needs. Nursing functions interdependently with the other health care disciplines by coordinating health services for the well-being of the individual and his family. Nursing service and nursing education are the two main components of the nursing profession.

Nursing service is concerned primarily with the care of the patient and his family through coordination of medical, social, and specialized services; reporting and recording patient response or lack of response to therapy; maintaining an environment in which the patient's physical, emotional, spiritual, social, and economic needs can be met; and collaborating with the various members of the health care team to ensure the patient's optimal recovery or a tranquil death. Nurses may practice in a variety of settings: hospitals (specialized or general); long-term health care institutions; military, civil, or federal health care agencies; industry; public and private institutions; community agencies; religious institutions; and physicians' offices. Within these settings, one may find general-duty or first-level nurses; practitioners in areas such as pediatrics, adult health care, and maternal child care; and clinical specialists in ambulatory or acute care settings like intensive care, coronary care, or oncologic care.

Nursing education is concerned with the preparation of practitioners to administer effective and efficient nursing care through a planned program of didactic and clinical instruction. The faculty and members of the health team and colleagues in academic settings provide educational programs in accordance with the philosophy, purposes, and objectives of the educational unit (hospital, college, or university) that sponsors them. An ongoing program of evaluation and faculty development is important in ensuring effective and up-to-date education for students.

Medicine is the oldest health care discipline with which nursing has collaborated. The nurse implements the physician's prescriptions for care by observing, collecting, assessing, interpreting, and reporting to the physician the patient's response to the prescribed plan of care. With the advances in medicine and scientific technologies, a number of allied health disciplines have emerged to meet specific health care needs of the sick. Among these disciplines are physical, respiratory, occupational, rehabilitation, speech and hearing therapies, and laboratory and X-ray technologies. The nurse provides physical and emotional support for the patient and ensures that the planned program of therapy recommended by the therapist is implemented. For example, the nurse may collaborate with a respiratory therapist by preparing the patient both physically and emotionally for treatment; assist an occupational therapist by discussing the patient's interests, needs, and limitations; and assist a speech and hearing therapist by noting the problems, needs, and progress of the patient and discussing them with the therapist and other health team members.

In the United States nurses are required to take a licensure examination for registration. The examination for the registered nurse is a standardized test used in all United States jurisdictions, thus facilitating licensure by endorsement in another state. The examination for the practical nurse is also standardized and used in all the states but California. (California's examination is not accepted in many states.) Nurses from other countries are required to write the licensure examination for United States registration.

Similar laws or health care practice acts have been enacted in other countries and are regulated by ministries of health and education and general nursing councils. South Africa passed the first bill (1891) to regulate nursing practice. In Canada, Nova Scotia was the first province to pass a bill requiring nurses to be registered. The title of licensed professional nurse varies from country to country, but in 1975 there was no provision for international licensure.

Nursing has its roots in antiquity, when women provided simple care for the sick and suffering. During the early Christian era, a group of women called deaconesses, the predecessors of public health nurses, visited the sick and poor in the slum areas of the Roman empire. Gradually, the deaconesses were replaced by members of the religious orders, and nursing care was no longer considered important. During the Crusades of the eleventh century, two hospitals were established in Jerusalem and one in England under the control of the Knight Hospitallers of St. John. The standard of care in these hospitals was high, but between the sixteenth and eighteenth centuries nurses were untrained and illiterate, and the quality of care deteriorated.

In 1860 Florence Nightingale, founder of modern nursing, established a school of nursing at St. Thomas Hospital in London, which became a prototype for nursing programs throughout the world. Nightingale's insistence that nursing should be under the control of nurses met with vigorous opposition from physicians. Nevertheless, the school opened with fifteen students who met the admission requirements—completion of an elementary education, possession of good character, capacity to assimilate a program of lectures given by physicians and the sisters, and ability to write. Graduates of the program were expected to teach others how to nurse in the Nightingale tradition. Two programs were offered: one, a year in length for institutional and home nursing; the other, a two-year program for nurses qualified to become administrators and teachers.

Until the twentieth century, nursing education was largely a system of apprenticeship training. Gradually, through the determination and commitment of a number of nurse leaders, nursing education moved into institutions of higher education. A number of reports generated by the profession and members of several disciplines provided impetus for this transition. Some of the reports were the Weir Report (1932) in Canada, the Goldmark Report (1923), the Brown Report (1948), and the American Nurses' Association's First Position on Education for Nursing (1965) in the United States.

As an academic discipline, nursing has had a relatively brief history. In the United States Isabel Hampton Robb, supported by an advisory committee of nurse leaders, convinced James Russell, dean of Teachers College, Columbia University, New York, of the need to offer courses of instruction to qualified nurses at a collegiate level. Thus, in 1899 a course in hospital economics was offered, and two students enrolled in the course. Eight years later, M. Adelaide Nutting accepted the chair at Columbia University to become the world's first professor of nursing. The first nursing program to become an integral part of a university was developed by the University of Minnesota in 1909. The graduates of this program were not awarded a degree. Two five-year nursing programs leading to a bachelor's degree were established in 1916: one at Teachers College, Columbia University, and the other at the University of Cincinnati in Ohio. The curricula in both of these colleges included public health nursing and teaching. Yale University followed with a five-year nursing program in 1923.

Many countries outside the United States—for example, Canada, the United Kingdom and other Commonwealth countries, Israel, and countries in Europe, Latin America, Asia, and Africa—have developed basic and postbasic programs in colleges and universities. Some countries have hospital schools of nursing which have close affiliations with universities. In 1901 basic and postbasic nursing programs were established in institutions of higher learning in Canada. The University of British Columbia (in Vancouver) established a nursing program which offered a five-year

curriculum leading to the degree of Bachelor of Arts in Applied Science (Nursing). In 1920 one-year programs for graduate nurses were established at McGill University in Montreal and at the University of Toronto. Five years later the first program in nursing which was not under the direction of a hospital was developed at the University of Toronto.

In 1918 the Royal College of Nursing instituted courses of study at King's College, University of London. Bedford College instituted similar courses of study in 1920. Three years later the University of Leeds offered a program leading to a diploma in nursing. In 1931 Peiping Union Medical College offered a course of study for men and women who had been awarded diplomas in nursing by the Nurse Association of China.

In the United States there are three types of programs leading to licensure and registration in nursing: the associate degree, the baccalaureate degree, and the hospital program leading to a diploma in nursing. The diploma or hospital program is the predecessor of professional programs in nursing education. The curricula vary in length from two to three years; courses of instruction include theory and practice in nursing and courses in physical, biological, behavioral, and social sciences. Graduates of these programs are prepared as general-duty or first-level nurses to give skilled nursing care to patients in acute care settings (intensive care units), in hospitals, infirmaries, clinics, physicians' offices, homes, and long-term health care facilities.

The associate degree programs, the newest of the nursing programs, are located in community or junior colleges, and the graduates are prepared to function in a capacity similar to that of the diploma graduate. The curriculum is two years in length and includes courses in nursing theory and practice; in the physical, behavioral, biological, and social sciences; and in the liberal arts. Graduates of the diploma and associate degree programs function under the guidance of the baccalaureate degree graduate, assisting in the planning of patient care and supervising the technical members of the nursing care team.

The baccalaureate program in nursing is offered in the senior college or university, and the curriculum includes nursing theory and practice; physical, behavioral, biological, and social sciences; and liberal arts, including electives. The baccalaureate program prepares the nurse for practice and for participation in health planning and provides the foundation for graduate study. Graduates of this program function as generalists, assessing patient needs and implementing, evaluating, and modifying the nursing care regime. The baccalaureate graduate serves as the leader of the nursing team and collaborates with members of the health care team.

Some senior colleges and universities offer nursing programs leading to master's or doctoral degrees in nursing. Graduates of master's programs are qualified to teach or administer in the area of their specialization; for example, maternal-child nursing, psychiatric nursing, or medical-surgical nursing. They are also qualified to conduct research, contribute to the professional literature, function as nurse clinicians, or pursue advanced study at the doctoral level. Graduates of the doctoral program are prepared to assume leadership positions in nursing, conduct research, and contribute to the professional literature.

The need for a council of nurses at an international level was advocated first by Ethel Bedford Fenwick, of England, to a group of nurse leaders attending the International Council of Women in London in 1899. Enthusiasm and support for the idea were generated in the group; and members from the United Kingdom, the United States, Canada, New Zealand, the Netherlands, Denmark, the Australian states of New South Wales and Victoria, and Cape Province in South Africa formed a committee to draft a provisional constitution, which was amended and adopted in 1900. The aims of the International Council of Nurses (ICN), a federation of national

nurses' associations, include promoting the organization of national nurses' associations; assisting such associations in developing and improving standards of excellence in education, in health service for the public, and in nursing practice; ensuring autonomy for nurses in the governance of their national organizations; promoting the social and economic welfare of nurses; and promoting the full participation of nurses in policymaking and planning councils in health organizations on the local, state, regional, national, and international levels. The membership of the ICN has increased over the past seventy-five years to include nursing associations from eighty-four countries; the ICN thus functions as a means of communication between nurses throughout the world. In 1969 the ICN established the Nursing Abroad Programme, which assists nurses who desire to work or study outside their own countries. The organization also serves in a liaison and consultative capacity to world organizations such as the World Health Organization (WHO), UNESCO, UNICEF, the International Hospital Federation, and the International Labour Organisation (ILO). The official publication of the ICN is the *International Nursing Review,* which is published bimonthly at its headquarters in Geneva.

Recognizing the urgent need for nurses to continue their learning to keep abreast of advances in scientific and medical technology and nursing practice, the ICN and the member agencies have supported continuing education. Many countries award continuing education units in recognition of successful completion of these programs. Peer review is not a new practice in nursing but has been given more emphasis in recent years. Certification for nurse practitioner programs has been introduced under the egis of the American Nurses' Association and clinical specialty groups. Career mobility, at the national and international levels, has been recognized; and opportunities for advancement in nursing, with credit awarded for past learning and life experiences, allow a student to achieve career goals more easily. With the expansion of knowledge, nurses have begun to function in various practitioner roles for the improvement of health care to patients within health care agencies as well as in rural and outreach areas. Nurses have also become increasingly involved in promoting the status of women; the role of the male nurse; and the health, social, economic, and political welfare of the poor. Increased emphasis has been placed on the need for the expansion of research in nursing. The number of nurses contributing to the body of professional literature has increased steadily since Clara Weeks wrote the first nursing textbook in 1885.

JUANITA OUTLAW LONG

Levels and Programs of Study

Programs in nursing generally require as a minimum prerequisite a secondary education, although in some cases mature students, especially those with relevant work experience, are often admitted with lower educational qualifications. The usual awards for nursing programs are certificate or diploma, bachelor's degree, master's degree, the doctorate, or their equivalents.

Programs consist primarily of classroom, hospital, and laboratory instruction dealing with the principles and practices of caring for the sick. Principal course content usually includes subjects such as human anatomy and physiology, pharmaceutical chemistry, biochemistry, microbiology, social sciences, nursing techniques and procedures, psychiatric nursing, pediatric nursing, obstetrical nursing, geriatric nursing, and public health nursing. Clinical experience in subjects such as surgery, medicine, obstetrics, gynecology, and psychology usually forms an indispensable part of the program. Background courses often included are mathematics, humanities, general biology, general physics, general chemistry, biochemistry, pharmacology, microbiology, sociology, and psychology.

[This section was based on UNESCO's *International Standard Classification of Education (ISCED): Three Stage Classification System, 1974* (Paris: UNESCO, 1974).]

Major International and National Organizations

INTERNATIONAL

International Committee of Catholic Nurses
Comité international catholique des infirmières et assistantes médico-sociales (CICIAMS)
32 rue Joseph 11
B-1040 Brussels 4, Belgium

International Council of Nurses (ICN)
Conseil international des infirmières (CII)
P.O. Box 42
1211 Geneva 20, Switzerland
　Florence Nightingale International Foundation is the education and research division of ICN and grants scholarships for postbasic education in nursing.

International Red Cross: Nursing Service
17 chemin des Crets
Petit-Saconnex
1211 Geneva 19, Switzerland

Northern Nurses Federation (NNF)
Verband Krankenschwestern im Norden
Östermalmsgatan 33
11426 Stockholm 0, Sweden

West European Group of Nurses
Groupement du nursing de l'ouest européen (GNOE)
Österreichischer Krankenpflegeverband
Mollgasse 3a
A-1180 Vienna, Austria

World Health Organization (WHO)
Divison of Nursing
1211 Geneva 27, Switzerland

For a listing of other international organizations relating to nursing see:

Medical Research Index. (4th ed., 2 vols.) Guernsey, Channel Islands: Francis Hodgson, 1971.

NATIONAL

There are seventy-four national nursing associations affiliated with ICN. Some of them are:

Australia:
　Royal Australian Nursing Federation
　33 Queens Road, Suite 18
　Melbourne, Victoria 3004

Canada:
　Canadian Nurses' Association
　50 The Driveway
　Ottawa, Ontario K2P 1E2

Denmark:
>   Dansk Sygeplejeraad
>   Vimmelskaftek 38
>   1161 Copenhagen K

Finland:
>   Suomen sairaanhoitajaliitto
>   Töölöntullinkatu 8
>   00250 Helsinki 25

India:
>   Trained Nurses Association of India
>   L-16 Green Park
>   New Delhi

Japan:
>   Nihon kango kyokai
>   2–8 Ban 5-chome
>   Jingumae, Shibuya-ku
>   Tokyo

Norway:
>   Norsk sykepleierforbund
>   Sognsveien 72
>   P.O. Box 5136
>   Oslo 3

South Africa:
>   South African Nursing Association
>   P.O. Box 1280
>   Van der Stel Building, Pretorius Street
>   Pretoria

Sweden:
>   Svensk sjuksköterskeförening
>   P.O. Box 5277
>   Östermalmsgatan 19
>   S-102 46 Stockholm 5

United Kingdom:
>   Royal College of Nursing and National
>   Council of Nurses of the United
>   Kingdom
>   Henrietta Place, Cavendish Square
>   London W1M OAB, England

United States:
>   American Nurses' Association, Inc.
>   2420 Pershing Road
>   Kansas City, Missouri 64108

>   National League for Nursing
>   10 Columbus Circle
>   New York, New York 10019

For information on nursing associations affiliated with ICN see:

National Reports of Member Associations. Geneva: ICN, 1973.

Principal Information Sources

GENERAL

Guides to the literature include:

Concordia, M. *Basic Book and Periodical List: Nursing School and Small Medical Library.* (4th ed.) Peru, Illinois: St. Bede Abbey Press, 1967.

Interagency Council on Library Tools for Nursing. "Reference Sources for Nursing." *Nursing Outlook,* April 1970, *18,* 47–52; and May 1974, *22,* 331–337. Provides a list of sources that are recommended for nursing libraries.

Nursing Studies Index. Philadelphia: Lippincott, 1900–1959. Provides an annotated guide to nursing research published in English.

Stearns, N. S., Ratcliff, W. W., Betchell, M. E., and Zeller, K. "Core Nursing Library for Practitioners." *American Journal of Nursing,* April 1970, *70,* 818–823.

Thompson, A. M. C. (Ed.) *A Bibliography of Nursing Literature 1859–1960, with an Historical Introduction.* London: Library Association of the Royal College of Nursing, 1968. A bibliographical guide to nursing; includes literature on nursing in many countries.

Histories of the field include:

Bridges, D. *A History of the International Council of Nurses 1899–1964: The First Sixty-Five Years.* Philadelphia: Lippincott, 1967.

Nutting, M. A., and Dock, L. *A History of Nursing.* (4 vols.) New York: Putnam's, 1907–1912.

Seymer, L. R. *A General History of Nursing.* (4th ed.) London: Faber & Faber, 1969.

Stewart, I. M., and Austin, A. L. *A History of Nursing, from Ancient to Modern Times.* (5th ed.) New York: Putnam's, 1962.

Works dealing with nursing education include:

The Evaluation of Nursing Education: Report of a Working Group Convened by the Regional Office for Europe of the World Health Organization. Copenhagen: Working Group on the Evaluation of Nursing Education, 1969.

World Health Organization. "Planning and Programming for NURSING Services." *Public Health Papers,* 1971, *44,* 1–123.

Both ICN and WHO publish literature of interest to nurses around the world.

CURRENT BIBLIOGRAPHIES

The important research tools in nursing are:

Cumulative Index to Nursing Literature. Glendale, California: Glendale Adventist Hospital Publications Service, 1961–.

Hospital Literature Index. Chicago: American Hospital Association, 1945–.

Index Medicus. Chicago: National Library of Medicine, 1960–.

International Nursing Index. New York: American Journal of Nursing Co., 1966–.

Some of the abstract journals of interest to the field of nursing include:

Abstracts of Reports of Studies in Nursing. Published in *Nursing Research.* New York: American Journal of Nursing Co., 1952–..

Excerpta Medica. Amsterdam: Excerpta Medica Foundation, 1947–.

Hospital Abstracts. London: H. M. Stationery Office, 1961–.

PERIODICALS

Some of the important journals in nursing are *Agnes Karll-Schwester-Der Krankenpfleger* (FRG), *American Journal of Nursing, AORN Journal* (US), *Canadian Nurse, Deutsche Krankenpflege-Zeitschrift* (FRG), *Infirmière* (Belgium), *International Journal of Nursing Studies* (UK), *International Nursing Review* (Switzerland), *Irish Nurse, JOGN Nursing* (US), *Journal of Continuing Education in Nursing* (US), *Journal of Nursing Administration* (US), *Journal of Nursing Education* (US), *Journal of Practical Nursing* (US), *Journal of Psychiatric Nursing and Mental Health Services* (US), *Kango* (Japan), *New Zealand Nursing Journal, Nursing Clinics of North America* (US), *Nursing Forum* (US), *Nursing Journal of India, Nursing Mirror and Midwives Journal* (UK), *Nursing Outlook* (US), *Nursing Research* (US), *Nursing Times* (UK), *Queen's Nursing Journal* (UK), *RN* (US), *Sairaanhoitaja/Sjuksköterskan* (Finland), *South African Nursing Journal/Verplegingstydskrif, Tidskrift för Sveriges sjuksköterskor* (Sweden), *Voprosy okhrany materinstva i detstva* (USSR), *Zeitschrift für Krankenpflege/Revue suisse des infirmières* (Switzerland).

For a listing of nursing journals see:

Pings, V. M. *A Plan for Indexing the Periodical Literature of Nursing.* New York: American Nurses' Foundation, 1966. Includes a list of 182 nursing journals.

Ulrich's International Periodicals Directory. New York: Bowker, biennial.

ENCYCLOPEDIAS, DICTIONARIES

Hansen, H. *Encyclopedic Guide to Nursing.* New York: McGraw-Hill, 1957.

Miller, B. F., and Keane, C. B. *Encyclopedia and Dictionary of Medicine and Nursing.* Philadelphia: Saunders, 1972.

Olson, L. M., and Dorland, W. A. *A Reference Handbook and Dictionary of Nursing.* Philadelphia: Saunders, 1960.

Pearce, E. C. *Medical and Nursing Dictionary and Encyclopedia.* (13th ed.) London: Faber & Faber, 1966.

Petry, L. (Ed.) *The Encyclopedia of Nursing.* Philadelphia: Saunders, 1952.

DIRECTORIES

Directory of Career Mobility Programs in Nursing Education. New York: National League for Nursing, annual. State-by-state listing of programs that offer one or more types of career mobility patterns in nursing education in the United States.

Directory of Schools of Nursing in the European Region. Copenhagen: WHO, Regional Office for Europe, 1971. Lists schools for thirty-one countries.

Facts About Nursing. Kansas City, Missouri: American Nurses' Association, 1935–. An annual publication providing statistical information on American nursing and nursing education.

State-Approved Schools of Nursing—R.N. and L.P.N./L.V.N. New York: National League for Nursing, annual. Directories of all state-approved schools of nursing and schools of practical/vocational nursing in the United States that meet all the minimum requirements set by law.

World Directory of Post-Basic and Post-Graduate Schools of Nursing. Geneva: WHO, 1965. International guide to facilities for graduate nurses.

RESEARCH CENTERS, INSTITUTES, INFORMATION CENTERS

Medical Research Index: A Guide to World Medical Research. (4th ed.) Guernsey, Channel Islands: Francis Hodgson, 1971. Lists, by country, nursing research establishments.

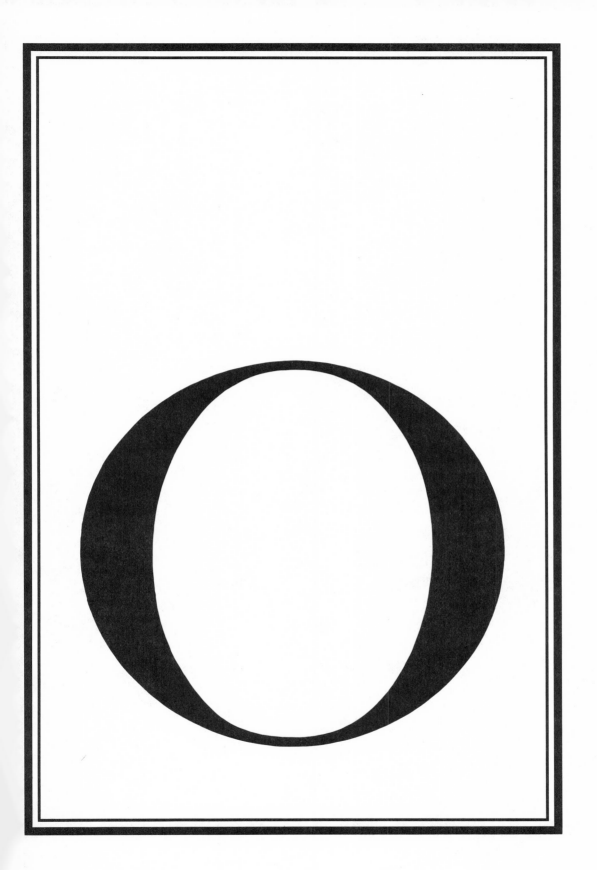

OBJECTIVES AND AIMS OF HIGHER EDUCATION

See Philosophies of Higher Education, Historical and Contemporary.

OCCUPATIONAL THERAPY
(Field of Study)

The World Federation of Occupational Therapists, in its *Recommended Minimum Standards* (1971), defines occupational therapy as a form of medical treatment concerned with people who are physically, socially, or mentally sick and are disabled either temporarily or permanently. Activities are designed to promote the restoration and maximum use of function, with the aim of helping such people meet the demands of their working, social, and domestic environment and participate in life in its fullest sense. Such treatment may include any or all of the following aspects: to assist in diagnosis; to restore particular physical, psychological, or mental function; to hasten convalescence; to restore work capacity; to promote social adjustment and integration; to test the stability of recovery; and to promote and maintain health. Thus, occupational therapy is concerned with factors that prevent or impede an individual's ability to function as well as with factors that promote, influence, or enhance the ability to function. In countries where the profession has been developed for many years and where health care programs are more traditionally established—for example, Denmark, Australia, the United States, and the United Kingdom—prevention and health maintenance are now given as much attention as the more traditional concerns—that is, the reduction of pathology and the effects of a specific disability.

Occupational therapy intervention may occur at any point in the continuum of comprehensive health care, but the specific health needs of each country determine when it can be most appropriately used. The service is rendered in a variety of settings: hospitals and institutions, day care centers, schools, the community and home, social service agencies, and industry. In any such setting the occupational therapist works in collaboration with other personnel such as doctors, nurses, physical therapists, psychologists, speech therapists, social workers, community health care workers, teachers, family members, industrialists, technicians, vocational counselors, and employment agencies.

Although occupational therapy has been a recognized profession since 1917, it gained international impetus as a direct result of World War II. By 1952 ten countries saw the need for an international professional organization and founded the World Federation of Occupational Therapists (WFOT). To qualify for membership in the WFOT, a country must have a national association and, if possible, one training school or course. Currently, there are twenty-four member countries and five associate member countries in Asia, the Middle East, Europe, Africa, Canada, Latin America, and the United States.

Minimum standards for the education of occupational therapists were developed and approved by the WFOT. These standards, revised in 1971, are used throughout the world for establishing training schools or courses for occupational therapy. International standards for education require a minimum length of study of two and a half years. In countries where occupational therapy has been established for some time, courses are three years or more in length. Some countries have university-based courses; others are attempting to shift to university settings. Though the basic course content is common to all countries, the specific therapeutic activities differ according to the social and economic structure of the country and, in larger countries, may even differ from one region to another.

The first educational programs for therapists in the United States were instituted in hospitals or art schools. In 1923 the American Occupational Therapy Association (AOTA) established minimum standards for professional education. Since 1940 new programs have been established in colleges and universities. The first college programs in occupational therapy were three-year diploma courses, followed by baccalaureate degree programs accredited jointly by the AOTA and the American Medical Association (AMA). Since about 1955 educational programs for entry-level positions in occupational therapy have been instituted both above and below the baccalaureate level. The certified occupational therapy assistant (COTA) was established as a recognized support level of occupational therapy personnel. Programs for the preparation of the COTA shifted from hospital-based, short-term training courses to certificate and associate degree programs within two- or four-year colleges and universities. At this time the WFOT does not recognize an assistant or support level of personnel. Master's degree programs were established in the United States for students with baccalaureate degrees in fields other than occupational therapy. Advanced master's programs for those with credentials as occupational therapists registered (OTR) were developed to provide an in-depth knowledge base for specialized practice, administration, teaching, and/or research.

In the United States occupational therapy education and practice are responding to two new challenges. The first is the need to increase opportunities for upward mobility within professions by devising alternate routes to professional certification without compromising professional standards. Since 1973 certified occupational therapy assistants who meet specified criteria related to the length, diversity, and quality of their practical experience have been able to take the national certification examination; if they pass this examination, they become certified as occupational therapists registered, bypassing the traditional academic route. COTAs may also more readily transfer into four-year baccalaureate programs, receiving credit for two years of undergraduate work and, in some schools, academic credit for practical experience. Concomitant with opportunities for upward mobility is the development of proficiency examinations based on evidence of competency rather than the acquisition of formal academic knowledge. The second challenge derives from research findings about the role of sensory-motor integration in the development of cognitive-perceptual-motor abilities. Professional course content in the United States has been expanded to incorporate intervention of all three levels, so that practitioners are increasingly able to provide more comprehensive services for children with developmental delays and adults with physical and/or emotional problems influenced by sensory deficits. Such application of knowledge to practice is beginning to appear throughout the world.

The profession, through organizations a

international, national, and local levels, provides continuing education programs, publications, and other resources for maintenance and improvement of competence. Studies are under way to formalize educational and other criteria for more tangible evidence of continuing professional competence.

NANCY H. TALBOT

Major International and National Organizations

INTERNATIONAL

Pan American Health Organization (PAHO)
525 23rd Street NW
Washington, D.C. 20037 USA

Rehabilitation International
122 East 23rd Street
New York, New York 10010 USA

World Federation of Occupational Therapists (WFOT)
Fédération mondiale des ergothérapeutes
P.O. Box 26445
Arcadia, Pretoria, South Africa

World Health Organization (WHO)
1211 Geneva 27, Switzerland
    WHO is very supportive of programs training rehabilitation personnel.

NATIONAL

A sample listing of organizations in the field includes:

Argentina:
    Asociación argentina de terapeutas
        ocupacionales
    avenida Belgrano 1732 4to piso
    Buenos Aires

Australia:
    Australian Association of Occupational
        Therapists
    18 Mahara St.
    Bardon, Queensland 4065

Belgium:
    Fédération nationale belge des
        ergothérapeutes
    avenue des Aubépines 64
    B1180 Brussels

Canada:
    Canadian Association of Occupational
        Therapists
    4 New Street, Suite M19
    Toronto, Ontario M5R 1P6

Denmark:
    Foreningen af aut. ergoterapeuter
    Søborg Hovedgade 1
    2860 Søborg

Federal Republic of Germany:
    Verband der Beschäftigungs-
        Therapeuten (Ergotherapeuten) der
        Bundesrepublik Deutschland, e.V.
    Stiftung Rehabilitation
    Postfach 101409
    69 Heidelberg 1

Finland:
    Suomen toimintaterapeutit/Finlands
        verksamhetsterapeuter
    Puistokatu 11C 14
    SF-00140 Helsinki 14

France:
    Association nationale française des
        ergothérapeutes
    3 rue de Stockholm
    75008 Paris

India:
    The All-India Occupational Therapists
        Association
    % B. M. Institute of Mental Health
    Ashram Road, near Nehru Bridge
    Ahmadabad 9

Ireland:
    Association of Occupational Therapists
    50 Wellington Road
    Dublin 4

Israel:
    Association of Occupational Therapists
    Arlozrof Street 93
    Tel Aviv

Japan:
    Japanese Association of Occupational
        Therapists
    1-2-7 Umenzono Kiyoseshi
    Tokyo 184

Netherlands:
    Nederlandse vereniging van arbeids
        ergotherapeuten
    Kreek 141
    Lelystad

New Zealand:
    New Zealand Association of O.T.s (Inc.)
    40 Palmerston Road
    Havelock North, Hawke Bay

Norway:
    Norsk ergoterapeutforbund
    Parkveien 57
    Oslo 2

Philippines:
    Occupational Therapy Association of the
        Philippines
    929 E. de los Santos Avenue
    Quezon City

Portugal:
    Associação portuguêsa de terapéutica

ocupacional
avenida da República 45, 2° Esq.
Alges, Lisbon 3

South Africa:
South African Association of
Occupational Therapists
P.O. Box 17289 Hillbrow
Johannesburg

Soviet Union:
All-Union Scientific Medical Society
of Therapists
ul. Petrovka 25
Moscow

Spain:
Asociación española de terapeutas
ocupacionales
Puerta del Sol 10, 4° 60E
Madrid 14

Sweden:
Föreningen sveriges arbetsterapeuter
Högalidsgatan 40A
117 30 Stockholm

Switzerland:
Verband schweizerischer
Ergotherapeuten
Institut für Ergotherapie
CH 4004 Basel

United Kingdom:
British Association of Occupational
Therapists
20 Rede Place
Bayswater, London W2, England

United States:
American Occupational Therapy
Association
6000 Executive Boulevard, Suite 200
Rockville, Maryland 20852

Venezuela:
Asociación venezolana de terapeutas
ocupacionales
Apartado 7690, Carmelitas
Caracas 101

Principal Information Sources

GENERAL

Guides to the literature include:

Bibliography on Occupational Therapy (2nd ed.)
Pretoria, South Africa: World Federation of
Occupational Therapists, Library Commit-
tee, 1974.
*Bibliography on Self-Help Devices and Orthotics,
1950–67.* Rehabilitation Monograph No. 3.
New York: New York University Medical
Center, Institute of Rehabilitation Medicine,
1968. A complete listing of articles from the

American Journal of Occupational Therapy plus
listings from other journals and books.

Overviews and texts for the field include:

Jentschura, G. *Beschäftigungstherapie.* (2nd ed.)
Stuttgart, Federal Republic of Germany:
Georg Thieme Verlag, 1974.
Jones, M. S., and Jay, W. *Approach to Occupa-
tional Therapy* (3rd ed.) London: Butter-
worth, 1976.
Meldman, M. J., Wellhausen, M., and Jacob-
son, J. *Occupational Therapy Manual.* Spring-
field, Illinois: Thomas, 1969.
Mountford, S. W. *Introduction to Occupational
Therapy: A Textbook for Students.* Baltimore:
Williams & Wilkins, 1971; Edinburgh:
Livingstone, 1971.
Willard, H. S., and Spackman, C. S. *Occupa-
tional Therapy* (4th ed.) Philadelphia: Lippin-
cott, 1971.

Sources discussing training and education
include:

Binswanger, R., and de Spindler, I. (Eds.) *Occupational Therapy Today—Tomorrow. Its Present Position and the Possibilities of Development.*
Proceedings of the Fifth International Congress of the World Federation of Occupational Therapists, Zurich, 1970. New York:
Karger, 1971.
Bodmer, H. "La formation des ergothérapeutes." *Praxis,* 1974, *63,* 462–463.
Canadian Journal of Occupational Therapy. Toronto, Ontario: Canadian Association of Occupational Therapists, 1934–. The section
"International News Letters" is a regular
feature of the journal; the letters, sent by the
national organizations, discuss the need for
and training of occupational therapists
around the world.
*Information on Exchange of Occupational Therapists
Among W.F.O.T. Countries.* Pretoria, South
Africa: International Committee of the
World Federation of Occupational Ther-
apists, 1972.
Katzenstein, U. P. "Form und Inhalt der Aus-
bildung von Arbeitstherapeuten in der
DDR." *Zeitschrift für die gesamte Hygiene
und ihre Grenzgebiete,* 1972, *18,* 58–59.
*Recommended Minimum Standards for the Educa-
tion of Occupational Therapists.* Pretoria, South
Africa: Council of the World Federation of
Occupational Therapist, 1971.
Saldias, E. G. "Paramedical Education in Re
habilitation in South America." *Archives o
Physical Medicine,* 1969, *50,* 704–708.

The World Federation of Occupationa
Therapists International Relations Committe
circulates a monthly newsletter among membe
countries which carries information on devel
opments in each country.

Histories for the field include:

American Journal of Occupational Therapy, 1971, 25, 223–246. Includes a historical perspective of occupational therapy in the United States from the 1880s to the present.

Spackman, C. S. "A History of the Practice of Occupational Therapy for Restoration of Physical Function: 1917–67." *American Journal of Occupational Therapy*, 1968, 22, 67–71.

CURRENT BIBLIOGRAPHIES

Excerpta Medica. Section 19: *Rehabilitation and Physical Medicine*. Amsterdam: Excerpta Medica Foundation, 1958–.

Hospital Literature Index. Chicago: American Hospital Association, 1945–.

Index Medicus. Bethesda, Maryland: National Library of Medicine, 1960–.

Rehabilitation Literature. Chicago: National Easter Seal Society for Crippled Children and Adults, 1940–.

PERIODICALS

Journals for the field include *American Journal of Occupational Therapy, Arbeidsterapeuten N.A.T.L.* (Norway), *Arbetsterapeuten* (Sweden), *Australia Occupational Therapy Journal, Beschäftigungstherapie und Rehabilitation* (FRG), *Boletín informativo de la Asociación española de terapeutas ocupacionales, British Journal of Occupational Therapy, Canadian Journal of Occupational Therapy, Ergoterapeuten* (Denmark), *Ergothérapie* (Switzerland), *Fédération nationale belge des ergothérapeutes. Bulletin* (Belgium), *Information Bulletin* (Venezuela), *Israeli Journal, Journal d'ergothérapie* (France), *Journal of the New Zealand Occupational Therapists Association, Inc., Journal of Rehabilitation in Asia* (India), *Nederlands tijdschrift voor arbeids-ergotherapie, Occupational Therapy Association of the Philippines. Newsletter, Occupational Therapy Bulletin and Newsletter* (India), *Occupational Therapy Ireland Journal, South African Journal of Occupational Therapy.*

For a more extensive listing of journals related to the field see:

Ulrich's International Periodicals Directory. New York: Bowker, biennial.

ENCYCLOPEDIAS, DICTIONARIES, HANDBOOKS

American Occupational Therapy Association. *Reference Handbook for Continuing Education in Occupational Therapy*. Dubuque, Iowa: Kendall Hunt, 1970.

Ethridge, D., and McSweeney, M. *Research in Occupational Therapy*. Dubuque, Iowa: Kendall Hunt, 1971.

MacDonald, E. M. (Ed.) *Occupational Therapy in Rehabilitation: A Handbook for Occupational Therapists, Students and Others Interested in This Aspect of Reablement*. (3rd ed.) Baltimore: Williams & Wilkins, 1970; London, Baillière, Tindall, 1970.

DIRECTORIES

Allied Medical Education Directory. Chicago: American Medical Association, 1974. Lists the essentials of an accredited educational program along with actual accredited programs in the United States.

Saldias, E. G. "Paramedical Education in Rehabilitation in South America." *Archives of Physical Medicine*, 1969, 50, 704–708. Lists training courses available in South America.

RESEARCH CENTERS, INSTITUTES, INFORMATION CENTERS

For a listing of information centers in the field consult:

Bibliography on Occupational Therapy. (2nd ed.) Pretoria, South Africa: World Federation of Occupational Therapists, Library Committee, 1974.

[Bibliography prepared by Marion Levine.]

OCEANIA: REGIONAL ANALYSIS

The early anthropologists recognized four racial divisions of Oceania: Australia, Micronesia (the groups of islands lying north of the equator), Melanesia (from New Guinea east to Fiji), and Polynesia (a vast triangle with Hawaii at its apex and a base line stretching eastward from New Zealand to Easter Island). In light of subsequent ethnographic and linguistic studies, the divisions remain valid only as a matter of geographical convenience. The study of higher education in the region requires a different basis of identification, derived not from anthropological but from political and constitutional factors, such as the legacies of former colonial powers, the present relationship between these powers and their erstwhile dependencies, and the progress of the island colonies toward independence—a movement in which higher education, or the lack of it, is a vital element.

Since World War II six governments have been responsible for island territories in the Pacific: Australia, New Zealand, the

United States, the United Kingdom, France, and the Netherlands. (In 1962 the Netherlands withdrew when Dutch New Guinea, under pressure from the United Nations, became a province of Indonesia.) In 1947 these six governments created the South Pacific Commission (Smith, 1972), empowered to recommend measures for the social and economic development of the peoples of the South Seas. The commission became the instrument through which the identity of the South Pacific as a region was ultimately conceived and promoted.

The early colonial days were largely dominated by economic exploitation and Christian evangelism. An essential component of the evangelical influence was widespread development of basic literacy. Elements of the British, French, and American modes of education were introduced. The British pattern, derived either directly from the United Kingdom or from variants of English and Scottish practices adapted by Australia and New Zealand, was in turn cross-fertilized by American practices, particularly in curriculum organization. In the anglophone territories there was considerable flexibility in development; in the francophone islands of French Polynesia, New Caledonia, and the French elements of the New Hebrides condominium, adherence to the French system remained inviolate. Against this background the independent states of Oceania emerged, each free to inherit and develop its own educational system and to determine, within economic and geographic constraints, the pattern of education on which its future would in large measure depend.

Omitting the scattered small Micronesian groups north of the equator (Commonwealth of the Marianas) and the state of Hawaii, Oceania contains several sovereign states in complete charge of their own educational destinies: the historically independent Commonwealth of Australia, Dominion of New Zealand, and Kingdom of Tonga, and former dependencies that recently achieved independence—Western Samoa (1962), Fiji (1970), Papua New Guinea (1975), Republic of Nauru (1968),

and the Cook Islands (1975). The new independent states of Tonga, Western Samoa, Fiji, Nauru, and the Cook Islands, together with the Polynesian and Micronesian groups that still remain dependent territories, are universally known throughout Oceania simply as *the Islands*. About ten thousand of these islands are scattered over six million square miles of ocean.

While a basic common origin and a strong sense of cooperation give some cohesion to educational development throughout Oceania, developments in the tertiary systems of the two metropolitan countries—Australia and New Zealand—and the Islands are sufficiently different to warrant separate treatment.

Developments in Australia and New Zealand

Higher education in Australia may be said to date from 1850 with the establishment of the University of Sydney. Some years later, in 1869, the foundation of the University of Otago in Dunedin, in the South Island of New Zealand, marked a similar development across the twelve hundred miles of the Tasman Sea. No proper comparison can be made between the two systems, since orders of magnitude—geophysical, demographic, ethnic, and economic—are so disparate. However development in both countries has followed the basic patterns of their British origin, proceeding along familiar lines with vast quantitative expansion since World War II and considerable diversity of opportunities for vocational education at the tertiary level in a wide variety of institutions.

The established structures of the two educational systems make it comparatively easy to identify issues that involve policy decisions at specific points in the system—for example, the relationship between teacher education and the universities—or trends perceptible throughout the system, such as the development of vocational and technical education or the liberalization of curricula.

Despite considerable administrative divergencies caused by constitutional patterns—in Australia a federation of state with a division of authority between the individual states and the federal government and in New Zealand a strongly centralized government that has assumed all the responsibilities of the original provinces—and basic differences in economic and industrial development, the common origin of the education systems of both countries has been sufficient to ensure that, faced with similar issues, their policies will reflect similar trends, though actual solutions may in some cases differ.

Both systems have encountered pressing calls for the expansion of tertiary education in response to social demand, economic necessity, and egalitarian principles, resulting in the development of a multiplicity of programs in new institutions of varying types—in particular the colleges of advanced education in Australia and the very new (1975) community colleges in New Zealand. The possibilities of off-campus education at degree level are being developed and are likely to meet with considerable success since New Zealand and Australia (in particular the state of Queensland) have earned global recognition for the success of their methods of conducting education by correspondence, a virtue enforced by geographical necessity. This expansion has been accompanied by a greatly enhanced provision of scholarships, bursaries, and grants to equalize the opportunities for profiting from the new facilities. In New Zealand the goal of equal opportunities has been assisted by a less mechanistic approach to selection for entry to university education, based on accreditation and internal assessment rather than a single qualifying examination.

The development of technical education has resulted in one issue that is common to both countries: the relationship between the universities and expanding technical institutions. Since 1966 Australia has developed a considerable number of colleges of advanced education in response to the combined demand for technical and general education at the third level. These institutions have in many cases been formed through the development of existing teachers colleges (and, in some cities, technical

institutes) emerging as polytechnics in the cities and smaller interdisciplinary institutions in rural centers. Their awards range from an associate diploma (two years) to a master's degree requiring six years of full-time study. As of 1975 the colleges were controlled by a Commission of Advanced Education, while university finance and development were subject to the overall control of the Universities Commission. A proposal under discussion in 1975 advocated the establishment of a tertiary education commission to be responsible to the Australian federal government for the balanced development of universities and colleges, the coordination of tertiary education, and the implementation of triennial programs.

Meanwhile, a more modest approach to technical education at the tertiary level has been made by New Zealand, which has been largely content to extend the resources of its technical institutes, some of which have developed into polytechnics. To cater to the smaller urban centers and their rural hinterlands, a number of community colleges started to be established in 1975, offering the more modest vocational opportunities of the technical institutes, short courses of every conceivable type, and a home for local activities, such as drama, music, and craft groups.

The relations between technical education, teacher education, and the universities in New Zealand have not developed as markedly as in Australia. Both the technical institutes and the teachers colleges are seeking greater autonomy and would appear to welcome control by a grants committee; they have their own councils but are effectively subject to the overriding control of the Department of Education. However, based on a nationwide educational development conference, the Advisory Council on Educational Planning (1974) recommended that the Vice-Chancellors' Committee and the Standing Committee on Relationships in Tertiary Education be asked to examine further possibilities for cooperation among technical institutes, teachers colleges, and universities in order to devise national guidelines for cross-crediting and to ensure reasonable national consistency.

The development of higher education in Australia and New Zealand has been consistent with their conservative approach to innovation. The Australian move toward a tertiary education commission, a proposal strengthened by the rising rolls and standards of the colleges of advanced education, will undoubtedly be accepted. In New Zealand two controversial proposals, neither of which has yet been implemented, concern components of the very new community colleges; both of them derive from the administrative problems posed by scattered small townships in rugged pastoral country. (Incidentally, the inclusion of the term *community* in the title of the new institutions is significant in view of the call for participation of the community in the educational process, which is typical of New Zealand but not of Australian development.) The first proposal is the possible development of the colleges to include the thirteenth and fourteenth school years presently provided in the small all-age rural schools—a change that would lead to more generous staffing and, therefore, a wider choice of courses for preuniversity students. Major obstacles to the proposal are logistics, conservatism, and the tenacious hold of rural school principals on their senior pupils. The second proposal is to make some first-year university courses available at the colleges. Again logistics and staffing problems intervene, but the colleges may well serve as tutorial centers for the correspondence-degree courses conducted by Massey University at Palmerston, North New Zealand, on behalf of the university system as a whole.

A final area of interest is the number of part-time students in both systems. According to the *Statesman's Yearbook 1975/76* (1975), in Australia over 50 percent of the students in colleges of advanced education and 76 percent of university students are in part-time attendance; the figures for New Zealand are 92 percent in technical institutes and 34 percent in universities—this last a most encouraging drop from previous years, since the figures relating to technical education clearly reflect the number of students already engaged in industry and commerce. The reasons relating to the high number of part-time university students are more complex. Factors would certainly include ease of access to the university coupled with the need to earn a living and the very large number of employed teachers working toward graduate status.

Common to both systems is the continued expansion of assistance to students from developing countries through such mechanisms as the Colombo Plan for Cooperative Economic Development in South and Southeast Asia; the scholarship and fellowship plan to assist postgraduate exchanges of the Commonwealth Cooperation in Education Program; bilateral or private arrangements; and, in some Australian universities, ad hoc courses in such fields as educational planning. On a regional level, as trustee for the United Nations, Australia has been instrumental in the establishment of the University of Papua New Guinea and the Papua New Guinea University of Technology. New Zealand—with a strong Polynesian element in its population and trustee responsibilities for Western Samoa, the Cook Islands, the Tokelau Islands, and Niue—had long exercised a dominating influence over education in Polynesia through its Office of Islands Education and Scheme of Cooperation with Fiji (to which it supplied secondary teacher training and some administrative staff). In addition to this work New Zealand has cooperated most effectively with the United Kingdom—which was responsible for education in Fiji, the protectorate of the Solomon Islands, the Crown Colony of the Gilbert Islands, Tuvalu (formerly the Ellice Islands), the anglophone element of the New Hebrides, and Pitcairn Island—in the establishment of the University of the South Pacific (1968), contributing the buildings and land of what had been a Royal New Zealand Air Force base. Through its Aid Programme, New Zealand also was responsible for establishing in Malaysia the Faculty of Agriculture in the University of Malaya and teacher training colleges in Sabah and Sarawak.

Developments in Papua New Guinea and the Islands

In 1975 there were three universities in the Islands: the regional University of the South Pacific at Suva, Fiji, the University of Papua New Guinea at Port Moresby, and the Papua New Guinea University of Technology at Lae.

Before the advent of the three universities in the late 1960s, provision of tertiary education other than by the award of scholarships to institutions in the two metropolitan countries—Australia and New Zealand—was minimal. In 1951, when a special commission of the Research Council of the South Pacific Commission instigated an inquiry into the possibility of establishing a regional technical institute in Fiji and drew up a detailed program, the scheme was dropped for lack of support beyond Fiji. Most small island groups maintained at least one training college for primary school teachers, generally with enrollments of under one hundred students. Fiji was the home of the Fiji School of Medicine (formerly the Central Medical School), which has trained assistant medical practitioners for the whole of the South Pacific region since 1886, and of the Derrick Technical Institute, already entering students for the technical examinations of overseas examining bodies. In addition to colleges for primary teachers, Fiji and Papua New Guinea had a number of departmental vocational training institutes in health, agriculture, communications, and similar fields. Western Samoa was planning an agricultural institute. All of these institutions had reached a standard at which association at diploma level with the new universities appeared to be a logical step, though in some cases it had not been taken by 1975.

Basic both to Papua New Guinea and to the Islands is the effect of indifferent secondary education on third-level standards. Another problem is staffing, where a sense of vocation and the opportunities for pioneer teaching and research do not always compensate for isolation from the worldwide academic community and from the amenities of a more urban and urbane mode of life. The effects of short-term contracts and comparative insecurity of tenure, as a result of which new staff are apt to seek for short-term secondment (a two-year contract with the holder's original post held open for his return at the end of the period) rather than a permanency, are damaging to the individual and the growth of the institution alike. The eternal quest for funds, both for capital and recurrent expenditure, is an occupational hazard not entirely unknown to presidents of universities in metropolitan countries, where alumni return not to coral atolls but to giant corporations. In Oceania financial assistance comes mainly from local governments, aid programs of former colonial powers, the United Nations Development Programme, and the few foundations that still have uncommitted funds. It is a stubborn field to plough.

The regional nature of the University of the South Pacific gives rise to a further series of problems not unknown, though in less intensive form, to the universities of Papua New Guinea. First come the nature and the disparities of the contributing territories—the Solomon Islands, the Cook Islands, Fiji, the Gilbert Islands and Tuvalu, the New Hebrides, Niue, the Tokelau Islands, Tonga, and Western Samoa—all with various needs, customs, and values. A multiplicity of vernaculars responds unevenly to teaching in English at the secondary level, a practice that has achieved varying success in different island groups. And there is the cost of transporting and boarding students; even their arrival on appropriate days is a matter of considerable doubt.

Innovation is of a more novel character in Papua New Guinea and the Islands than in Australia and New Zealand. Here new approaches have been demanded by environmental problems, particularly in the case of a regional university catering to three racial groups as well as Asian and Western minorities. All three universities have had to contend with a considerable number of ill-prepared students, basically the outcome of a belated onset of economic and social development. They have therefore established one- or two-year preparatory courses according to the level of attainment of candidates for admission. A more novel proposal under consideration in Papua New Guinea stretches the first-degree course into three modules of one year each, with biennial periods of work experience and self-study intervening between each module. While this scheme would greatly extend the time needed to graduate, it would also give some token of recognition to the studies completed by undergraduate dropouts and facilitate the training of middle-level cadres, more necessary in the present stage of the country's development than a large output of graduates. The University of the South Pacific has responded to ecological problems in its region by structuring its organization into three schools: natural resources, social and economic development, and education. The pattern permits considerable flexibility in interdisciplinary studies.

Again, all three universities have established close relationships with specialized postsecondary institutions, largely departmentally controlled. The University of the South Pacific provides first-year courses for the Fiji School of Medicine and the Fiji School of Agriculture and a terminal course for the Derrick Technical Institute; in 1975 it was to establish a degree course at the South Pacific Regional College for Tropical Agriculture at Alafua in Western Samoa. Another form of cooperation is in Papua New Guinea; the first two years of the University of Technology courses in agriculture and forestry are conducted at the University of Papua New Guinea.

Extramural studies are organized by all three universities, and an inquiry into university development under study in Papua New Guinea in 1975 recommended that up to 50 percent of all university recurrent expenditure be devoted to off-campus study opportunities and extensive village programs. The problems are particularly acute in the Islands, where the University of the South Pacific is faced with

the task of establishing its image in its constituent (and financially contributing) territories, when to most Islanders Suva is little more than a name. Fortified by the experience of the only other regional university, the University of the West Indies, which faced the same problem in the Caribbean, the University of the South Pacific plans to establish extension centers in the outlying island groups. Two have been started in Western Samoa and Tonga; two temporary centers are functioning in the Solomon and Gilbert Islands; and a fifth was scheduled for the Cook Islands in 1976.

The tertiary systems of the two metropolitan countries, Australia and New Zealand, are broadening and extending their facilities and, in so doing, are seeking, perhaps unconsciously, to establish identities not obviously derived from their common origin. To this process they can safely be left. What is of supreme importance in Oceania, not only to the peoples of the Islands but to the world at large, is that the tertiary education of their leaders—and they are responsive to leadership—is soundly planned and conducted to meet the specific needs of Island peoples who have suddenly become their own masters in a paradise that, through no fault of their own, has already been lost. The essence of the situation has been most movingly distilled by the chancellor of the University of the South Pacific, His Majesty King Taufa'Ahau Tupou IV of Tonga, speaking at the dedication of the Educational Television Center in Pago Pago, American Samoa, in 1964: "Our world used to end where the waters of the sea lapped at the sands of our islands. Today events from across these seas affect our daily lives minutes after they happen."

Bibliography

Advisory Council on Educational Planning. *Directions for Educational Development.* Wellington : Government Printer, 1974.

Annual Statistical Yearbook: Paris: UNESCO, 1975.

Demand for Professional Manpower in Papua New Guinea 1971–80. Port Moresby, Papua New Guinea: Department of Labour, 1971.

Directory of Educational Authorities and Summary of Education in South Pacific Territories.

Nouméa, New Caledonia: South Pacific Commission, 1970.

First Development Plan. Suva, Fiji: University of the South Pacific, 1970.

Hayden, H. "The University of the South Pacific." *New Zealand Journal of Educational Studies,* 1967, *2*(2), 93–112.

Hayden, H. "On the Quality of Education in the South Pacific." *International Review of Education,* 1971–72, *17*(2), 165–181.

Oliver, D. L. *The Pacific Islands.* (Rev. ed.) Garden City, New York: Doubleday, 1961.

Parkyn, G. W. "Success and Failure at the University": Part 1 (1959), Part 2 (1967). Wellington, New Zealand Council for Educational Research.

Report of the Working Party on the Organisation and Administration of Education. Wellington, New Zealand: Government Printer, 1974.

Report of the Higher Education Mission to the South Pacific. London: H. M. Stationery Office, 1966.

Ross, A. *New Zealand's Record in the Pacific Islands in the Twentieth Century.* Auckland, New Zealand: Longman Paul, 1969.

Smith, T. R. *South Pacific Commission.* Wellington, New Zealand: Price Milburn, 1972.

Statesman's Yearbook, 1975/76. London: Macmillan, 1975.

Tudor, J. (Ed.) *Pacific Islands Year Book.* (11th ed.) Sydney: Pacific Islands Publications, 1972.

World Survey of Education. Vol. 4: *Higher Education.* Paris: UNESCO, 1966.

HOWARD HAYDEN

See also: Australia, Commonwealth of; Fiji; Nauru, Republic of; New Zealand; Papua New Guinea; Tonga, Kingdom of; Western Samoa, Independent State of.

OCEANOGRAPHY (Field of Study)

Oceanography, the scientific study of all aspects of the world oceans, is not a single science but rather a composite of many basic sciences, such as physics, chemistry, biology, and geology. The accumulated techniques are used to study the oceans.

With water covering 71 percent of the earth's surface, the oceans have played an important role since ancient times as a source of food and recreation and as a means of transportation. The wealth of early cities rose or fell depending on their position on major trade routes. The oceans also have military value, for the outcome of international wars has frequently been decided in naval battles.

Oceanography is generally divided into four main branches: (1) physical oceanography, the study of the movement and physical properties of ocean waters and their effect on the atmosphere; (2) marine chemistry, concerned with the transport of chemical elements through the hydrosphere and chemical reactions involving the waters, dissolved substances, organisms, and sediments; (3) biological oceanography, dealing with the origin, occurrence, and distribution of life in the ocean; (4) marine geology, the study of the origin and nature of the ocean basins and the sediments and structures beneath the ocean floor. Oceanographic research does not necessarily fall totally within any one division. Besides being multidisciplinary, in that it involves many sciences, it is also interdisciplinary. Problems being studied in the ocean can and often do cut across the boundaries of numerous disciplines.

Oceanography is closely related to many other fields. Among them is meteorology, which involves the interaction of the ocean with the atmosphere. Other fields related to oceanography are the earth sciences (including geophysics, geochemistry, and geology and its branches, such as paleontology), which are all concerned with the relationship of the earth's crust to the ocean; fisheries research, which is concerned with the productivity and habitat of life in the ocean; marine engineering, concerned with the design, development, and construction of instruments and structures used in the ocean; naval architecture, concerned with the design and construction of vehicles for ocean transportation; the science of navigation, obviously of great importance to oceanography; and mathematics and computer science, important to all types of oceanography for understanding oceanographic processes and interpretation of data. Finally, due to the international interest in the development of resources of the seas, fields such as law, economics, and political science are becoming increasingly important to oceanographers.

Oceanography as a disciplined science has existed only about one hundred years, since the time of the famous *Challenger* expedition; but man has always wondered about the sea, and voyages of exploration have been made throughout recorded history. Carvings tell of the voyage of the Egyptian Queen Hatshepsut to the "Land of Punt" in 1500 B.C., and the Phoenicians claim to have made a three-year voyage from east to west around Africa about 600 B.C. But the age of exploration began in the fifteenth century A.D. Voyages by men like Bartholomeu Dias, Christopher Columbus, Vasco da Gama, and Ferdinand Magellan provided information about the oceans. Captains and navigators necessarily made observations of the seas they sailed, particularly the surface phenomena. The nature of tides, currents, temperatures—the basic data of oceanography—were recorded and gradually became better understood.

In the eighteenth century the first scientific ocean expeditions in history were made by Captain James Cook of Great Britain, starting in 1768. Although the main purpose of these voyages was not oceanographic, Cook did collect and catalog an impressive amount of data on his three voyages in the South Pacific. Soundings were made to 200 fathoms, and accurate observations were made of winds, currents, and temperatures. But it was only in the nineteenth century that oceanography began as a science distinct from exploration or maritime activities.

Due to the excitement caused by discoveries made by Wyville Thomson and W. B. Carpenter on their expeditions between 1868 and 1870, the British Admiralty organized the *Challenger* expedition, the first large-scale deep-sea expedition solely for the purpose of studying the oceans. The H.M.S. *Challenger,* a 226-foot ship, was refitted for scientific research in 1872 and spent the next three and a half years sailing around the world. She traversed all the oceans except the Arctic and logged a total of 68,890 nautical miles. Although the equipment was primitive by present-day standards, the *Challenger* collected information for fifty volumes of reports and laid the scientific foundation for every major branch of oceanography.

The last quarter of the nineteenth century was a time of rapid expansion and productivity for oceanography all over the world. There were epoch-making voyages and great improvements in instruments. The Russians made pioneer observations of temperature and density in the North Pacific when the *Vitiaz* cruised around the world from 1886 to 1889. Prince Albert of Monaco started outfitting yachts as research vessels, making improvements particularly in sampling gear. He worked mainly in the North Atlantic and Mediterranean, recording hydrographic data and collecting deep-sea animals. Alexander Agassiz, an American interested in biological oceanography who was the first to use steel cables for deep-sea dredging, traveled more than 100,000 miles on the *Blake* and later on the *Albatross,* the first ship built especially for oceanographic research. Instrumentation had advanced to the point where one haul made by the *Albatross* from 1760 fathoms brought up more deep-sea fishes than the *Challenger* had in her entire expedition.

Many great laboratories were founded during this period, particularly for marine biology and fishery research. The first one, the *Stazione zoologica* in Naples, Italy, was established in 1872 by Anton Dohrn. In 1873 the first marine biological laboratory in the United States was established on Penikese Island near Cape Cod by Louis Agassiz. It was succeeded by the United States Commission of Fish and Fisheries Laboratory and the Marine Biological Laboratory in the 1880s at Woods Hole, Massachusetts. In 1879 the distinguished Marine Biological Association Laboratory was founded at Plymouth, England.

During the first half of the twentieth century marine stations and laboratories were established in many parts of the world, including Europe, Canada, Japan, and Brazil. Several United States universities along the east and west coasts established marine facilities, usually as part of their departments of biology. These were generally small and served mainly as collecting stations.

With the advent of World War II, the larger United States laboratories—such as

Scripps Institution of Oceanography at La Jolla, California, and the Woods Hole Oceanographic Institution—were called upon for oceanographic work resulting from the complexities of modern naval warfare. For example, the precise determination of the depth of the thermocline, a horizontal layer where the temperature changes abruptly, in different parts of the world oceans was of great importance in determining the effectiveness of sonar. The oceans have been an area of intense study ever since, and this interest has been growing at an even faster rate since the early 1960s. The decade of the 1960s saw a transition from the observational regime of the explorer to the more precise realm of the formal scientist. In the 1970s theories are explored and answers sought to fundamental questions about the oceans.

Advances in modern oceanography include the use of computers at sea. Shipboard computers and their related hardware make it possible to gather much more data than was previously possible and in some cases to process the data while they are being obtained. Satellite navigation by computer makes it possible to locate a ship within a few hundred meters at any time.

Oceanography on the high seas is an expensive operation which only the largest, best-equipped laboratories can attempt. It is not surprising, therefore, that there should be cooperative efforts among laboratories within a country to make these facilities available to as many scientists as possible. International cooperation is increasing, particularly when the scope of the project is too large for any one country to undertake. Large-scale international cooperation in oceanography began in 1957–1958 with the International Geophysical Year.

Various organizations of the United Nations are active in stimulating and coordinating international oceanographic projects. The International Indian Ocean Expedition was coordinated by the Scientific Committee on Oceanic Research (SCOR), which was set up by the International Council of Scientific Unions. From 1959 to 1965 scientists from twenty-three countries took part in the study of the physical and biological properties of this previously little-known ocean.

In 1960 the Intergovernmental Oceanographic Commission (IOC) was established within UNESCO. Part of IOC's function is to develop and coordinate international programs, promote the exchange of data and publications, and make recommendations concerning education and training programs in the marine sciences.

International oceanographic research is being carried out on an unprecedented scale. In March 1968 the President of the United States proposed that the 1970s be an International Decade of Ocean Exploration and assigned the National Science Foundation the responsibility for the United States program. In December of 1968 the United Nations General Assembly Resolution 2414 endorsed "the concept of an international decade of ocean exploration to be undertaken within the framework of a long-term programme of research and exploration." The International Decade of Ocean Exploration is now a part of the long-term IOC program.

Other international programs under the IOC are the International Co-operative Investigations and the Global Investigation of Pollution in the Marine Environment. Besides these formal international agreements there are many instances where institutions and investigators make their own arrangements with other countries.

The field of oceanography is too broad for any one person to be familiar with all its facets. Oceanographers generally specialize in one discipline—biology, for example—and there may be further specialization, such as microbiology. The professional oceanographer usually has a doctorate or a master's and is capable of carrying out independent research. A person with a bachelor's degree may work as a research assistant or technician.

In the past, oceanographic programs have been conducted mainly by the highly developed countries: the United States, the Soviet Union, the United Kingdom, Canada, the Federal Republic of Germany, France, Italy, Japan, the Scandinavian countries, and South Africa. Due to the increased use of the oceans, smaller and developing countries want to have their own educational and research programs in marine science. The IOC and UNESCO Division of Marine Sciences have held workshops with educators in the marine sciences to provide guidelines and recommended curricula for these countries. A UNESCO technical paper in marine science (no. 19, entitled "Marine Science Teaching at the University Level") recommends that the undergraduate student aspiring to be a marine scientist concentrate on the fundamentals of science and mathematics and delay formal instruction in oceanography until graduate school. An elementary course in oceanography might be taken by way of introduction. Graduate instruction should include a multidisciplinary course in physical, chemical, biological, and geological oceanography as a basic knowledge of these fields. Access to a research vessel, laboratory facilities, a library of reference works, and oceanographic journals is essential.

In the United States and Canada about 20 universities and research institutions offer the doctorate in oceanography. Some 145 institutions offer courses in the marine sciences and related fields. Programs range from two-year technical courses to Ph.D. programs and include, in addition to the basic sciences and oceanography, such fields as fisheries, food science, maritime studies, naval architecture, and marine law. Although an increasing number of oceanography programs are open to the North American undergraduate student, the aspiring professional oceanographer is still advised to major in programs in the basic sciences at the undergraduate level.

In Great Britain the student in oceanography is apt to be found studying in a university's applied mathematics, physics, or geology department. Emphasis is on the basic sciences, with fewer ocean courses taught than in the United States, especially at the undergraduate level. There is less tendency to view oceanography as a separate area of study. There are a few three- or four-year programs leading to a bachelor of Science in oceanography and three- to

five-year programs in naval architecture, marine engineering, and shipbuilding. Similar programs with an emphasis on the basic sciences are found in other Western European nations, such as Germany.

In Japan the Ocean Research Institute of the University of Tokyo is engaged mainly in pure research and grants the doctorate. Tokai University in Shizuka Prefecture has bachelor's and master's degree programs in oceanography. Many institutions offer technical and engineering programs. Generally there is more emphasis on ocean engineering and fisheries and less on the basic sciences than in Europe and North America.

Nations that are just developing marine science programs tend to concentrate their resources on regional or local programs. Prior to the reopening of the Suez Canal, the Arab League Educational, Cultural, and Scientific Organization (ALECSO) held meetings of countries bordering on the Red Sea and the Gulf of Aden to set up a system for monitoring pollution in the Red Sea. Such activities tend to stimulate the development of marine stations and programs to train staff for these stations.

In South America the main research effort has been in marine biology, and there is growing interest in fisheries resources, with the aim of finding economically important species. Marine education and research programs are being developed in several countries, with the more advanced programs in Argentina, Brazil, Colombia, and Uruguay.

Africa, with the exception of South Africa, has the least oceanographic activity of any continent in the world, especially along its eastern coast. UNESCO is attempting to institute regional programs to establish a nucleus of marine scientists. Training is centered around programs of regional interest, such as coral reefs and fisheries off East Africa.

PAUL MACDONALD FYE
PHYLLIS N. LAKING

Levels and Programs of Study

Programs in oceanography generally require as a minimum prerequisite a secondary education, usually in a science program, and lead to the following degrees: bachelor's, master's, the doctorate, or their equivalents. Programs deal with fundamental and advanced principles of oceanography and consist of classroom and laboratory instruction. Principal course content for first university degree work usually includes elements of oceanography, instrumentation and methods in oceanography, survey of navigation, biological oceanography, chemical oceanography, physical oceanography, geological oceanography, and marine population dynamics. Background courses often included are general biology, general physics, general chemistry, biochemistry, statistics, mathematics, computer science, geology, humanities, social sciences, and languages.

Programs that lead to a postgraduate university degree consist of seminars, study, laboratory work, and original research work as substantiated by the presentation of a scholarly thesis or dissertation. On the advanced level the principal areas within which courses and research projects tend to fall include advanced marine geology and geophysics, advanced physical oceanography, advanced chemical oceanography, advanced biological oceanography, physiology of marine plants, fluid mechanics, ichthyology, marine population dynamics, and oceanographic techniques. Subject areas within which background studies tend to fall include appropriate specialties in botany, zoology, chemistry, physics, geology, mathematics, instrumental analysis, biochemistry, and statistics.

[This section was based on UNESCO's *International Standard Classification of Education (ISCED): Three Stage Classification System, 1974* (Paris: UNESCO, 1974).]

Major International and National Organizations

INTERNATIONAL

European Oceanic Association
Villa Richard V
rue de l'Abbaye
MC Monaco Ville, Monaco

Intergovernmental Oceanographic Commission

UNESCO Headquarters
place de Fontenoy
75007 Paris, France

International Association for Biological
   Oceanography
Universitetsparken 15
2100 Copenhagen, Denmark

International Association for the Physical
   Sciences of the Ocean
Woods Hole Oceanographic Institution
Woods Hole, Massachusetts 02543 USA

International Association of Physical
   Oceanography
Merentutkimuslaitos
Box 14166
Helsinki 14, Finland

International Commission for the Scientific
   Exploration of the Mediterranean Sea
16 blvd. de Suisse
Monaco

International Council for the Exploration
   of the Sea
Charlottenlund Slot
2920 Charlottenlund, Denmark

Mediterranean Association for Marine Biology
   and Oceanology
Fondazione A & R Dohrn
Casella Postale 383
80100 Naples, Italy

Nordic University Group on Physical
   Oceanography
Nordisk kollegium for fysisk oceanografi
Haraldsgade 6
2200 Copenhagen N.T., Denmark

For a listing of the acronyms for international oceanographic organizations see:

North, J. P. *Annotated Acronyms and Abbreviations of Marine Science Related Organizations.* Washington, D.C.: National Oceanographic Data Center, 1969.

NATIONAL

Australia:
   Commonwealth Scientific and Industrial
      Research
   Division of Fisheries and Oceanography
   Box 21
   Cronulla, Sydney, New South Wales 2230

Canada:
   Canadian Committee on Oceanography
   Sir Charles Tupper Building
   Riverside Drive
   Ottawa 8, Ontario

Federal Republic of Germany:
   Ozeanographische Forschungsanstalt der
      Bundeswehr

Lornsen-Strasse 7
23 Kiel

France:
Centre national pour l'exploitation des
océans
(Délégation à l'information)
39 avenue d'Iéna
75016 Paris

India:
Indian National Institute of
Oceanography
Panaji, Goa

Italy:
Istituto sperimentale talassografico
2 viale R. Gessi
Trieste

Japan:
Oceanographical Society of Japan
% Ocean Research Institute
University of Tokyo
Minamidai, Nakano, Tokyo

People's Republic of China:
Chinese Society of Oceanography and
Limnology
19 Lai-yang Road
Tsingtao
Shantung Province

South Africa:
Oceanographic Research Institute
P.O. Box 736
Durban

Soviet Union:
State Oceanographic Institute
Kropotkinshiy Perevlokdom 6
Moscow

United Kingdom:
Institute of Oceanographic Sciences
Wormley, Godalming
Surrey, England

United States:
National Oceanography Association
1900 L Street NW
Washington, D.C. 20036

See the following for additional information
on organizations:

*Ocean Research Index: A Guide to Ocean and Fresh-
water Research, Including Fisheries Research.*
Guernsey, Channel Islands: Francis Hodgson, 1970. An international directory of
research in ocean study; includes selected
lists of data centers, museums, and a bibliography of guides to literature and periodicals
in the field.
Undersea Technology Handbook Directory. Arlington, Virginia: Compass Publications, 1971/
72. Includes information on international
and national organizations, educational

institutes, congresses, and oceanographic
ships.
Vetter, R. C. *Oceanography Information Sources/
70.* Washington, D.C.: National Academy of
Sciences, 1970. Includes educational materials, references, directories, organizations,
and periodicals for the United States.

Principal Information Sources

GENERAL

Guides to the literature in the field include:

*Annotated Bibliography of Textbooks and Refer-
ence Materials in Marine Sciences.* (Provisional ed.) Intergovernmental Oceanographic Commission Technical Series.
Paris: UNESCO, 1975. Includes over one
hundred annotated and four hundred un-
annotated entries covering all aspects of
oceanography.
DeCarre, S. E. *A Guide to the Technical Literature of Oceanography: An Annotated Bibliography.* Washington, D.C.: U.S. Naval Oceanographic Office, 1970.
Harvey, A. P. "Oceanographic Research Literature: A Bibliography of Selected Guides
and Periodicals." In *Ocean Research Index.*
Guernsey, Channel Islands: Francis Hodgson, 1970. Pp. 411–451.
"List of Recommended Textbooks and Reference Materials in Marine Science." In *Marine
Science Teaching at the University Level.* Paris:
UNESCO, 1974. Annex 2, pp. 1–12. Contains a list of texts recommended by the
compilers of the study.
Vetter, R. C. *Oceanography Information Sources/
70.* Washington, D.C.: National Academy
of Sciences, 1970.

Introductions to the field include:

Duxbury, A. D. *The Earth and Its Oceans.* Reading, Massachusetts: Addison-Wesley, 1971.
Gross, G. *Oceanography: A View of the Earth.*
Englewood Cliffs, New Jersey: Prentice-
Hall, 1972.
Ross, D. A. *Introduction to Oceanography.* Englewood Cliffs, New Jersey: Prentice-Hall,
1976.
Weye, P. P. *Oceanography: An Introduction to
the Marine Environment.* New York: Wiley,
1970.

Other important texts are:

Defant, A. *Physical Oceanography.* Elmsford,
New York: Pergamon Press, 1961.
Dietrich, G., and Kalle, K. *Allgemeine Meeres-
kunde.* Berlin, Federal Republic of Ger-
many: Borntraeger, 1957. (English trans-
lation: Ostapoff, F. *General Oceanography.*
New York: Wiley-Interscience, 1963.)
Riley, J. P., and Skirrow, G. (Eds.) *Chemical*

Oceanography. (6 vols., 2nd ed.) London: Academic Press, 1975.

Some histories of the field are:

Deacon, M. *Scientists and the Sea, 1650–1900: A Study of Marine Science*. London: Academic Press, 1971.

Idyll, C. P. (Ed.) *Exploring the Ocean World: A History of Oceanography*. New York: Crowell, 1972.

Premier congrès international d'histoire de l'océanographie, 1st, Monaco, 1966. Monaco: Institut océanographique, 1968.

For information on education in the field see:

Marine Science Teaching at the University Level: Report of the UNESCO Workshop on University Curricula, Paris, 17–20 December 1973. Paris: UNESCO, 1974.

National Council on Marine Resources and Engineering Development. *University Curricula in the Marine Sciences and Related Fields*. Syracuse, New York: Kaufman DeDell Printing, 1975. Covers the United States only.

CURRENT BIBLIOGRAPHIES

Aquatic Sciences & Fisheries Abstracts. Rome: Food and Agriculture Organization, 1971–.

Deep Sea Research and Oceanographic Abstracts. Elmsford, New York: Pergamon Press, 1953–.

Marine Science Contents Tables. Rome: Food and Agriculture Organization, 1969–.

Meteorological and Geoastrophysical Abstracts. Boston: American Meteorological Society, 1950–.

Oceanic Abstracts. La Jolla, California: Oceanic Library and Information Center, 1966–.

Oceanic Index. La Jolla, California: Oceanic Research Institute, 1964–.

Oceanographic Abstracts and Oceanographic Bibliography. Oxford, England: Pergamon Press, 1953–.

PERIODICALS

Some of the important periodicals for the field are *Akademiia nauk SSSR izvestiia. Fizika atmosfery okeana* (USSR), *Analytical Chimica Acta* (Netherlands), *British Journal on Coastal and Estuarine Biology*, *Bulletin de l'Institut océanographique de Monaco*, *Deep Sea Research* (UK), *Deutsche hydrographische Zeitschrift* (FRG), *Earth and Planetary Science Letters* (Netherlands), *Geochimica et Cosmochimica Acta* (US and UK), *Gidrobiologicheski zhurnal SSSR* (USSR), *Internationale Revue de gesamten Hydrobiologie* (FRG), *Journal of Geochemistry* (Japan), *Journal of Geophysical Research* (US), *Journal of the Marine Biological Association of the United Kingdom*, *Journal of Marine Research* (US), *Journal of the Oceanogra-*

phic Society of Japan, *Journal of Physical Oceanography* (US), *Limnology and Oceanography* (US), *Marine Biology* (FRG), *Marine Chemistry* (Netherlands), *Marine Geology* (Netherlands), *Meteorologia si hidrologia* (Romania), *Oceanus* (US), *Okeanologiya* (USSR; also in English translation), and *Records of Oceanographic Works in Japan*.

Two sources for lists of oceanographic periodicals are:

Catalogo dei periodici. Trieste, Italy: Istituto sperimentale talassografico, 1971.

Sears, M. *Oceanographic Index: Regional Cumulation 1946–1970*. Boston: Hall, 1971.

ENCYCLOPEDIAS, DICTIONARIES, HANDBOOKS

Dictionary of Geological Terms. New York: Doubleday, 1962.

Fairbridge, R. W. (Ed.) *The Encyclopedia of Oceanography*. New York: Van Nostrand Reinhold, 1966.

Firth, F. E. (Ed.) *The Encyclopedia of Marine Resources*. New York: Van Nostrand Reinhold, 1969.

Grant, J. (Ed.) *Hackh's Chemical Dictionary*. (4th ed.) New York: McGraw-Hill, 1969.

Handbook of Oceanographic Tables. Washington, D.C.: U.S. Government Printing Office, 1967.

Hill, M. N., and Maxwell, A. E. (Eds.) *The Sea: Ideas and Observations on Progress in the Study of the Seas*. New York: Wiley-Interscience, 1962–1970.

Hunt, L. M., and Groves, D. G. (Eds.) *A Glossary of Ocean Science and Undersea Technology Terms*. Arlington, Virginia: Compass Publications, 1965.

Huxley, A. (Ed.) *Standard Encyclopedia of the World's Oceans and Islands*. London: Weidenfeld and Nicholson, 1962.

Oceanography: List of Terms Relating to Oceanography and Marine Resources. New York: United Nations, 1975. In English, French, Spanish, Russian, and Czechoslovakian.

Smith, F. G. W. *Handbook of Marine Science*. Cleveland, Ohio: CRC Press, 1974. A recent handbook for oceanographers.

Sverdrup, H. U., and others. *The Oceans, Their Physics, Chemistry and General Biology*. Englewood Cliffs. New Jersey: Prentice-Hall, 1942.

DIRECTORIES

International Directory of Marine Scientists. Rome: Food and Agriculture Organization, 1970.

Marine Science Activities of Canada and the Nations of Europe. Washington, D.C.: U.S. National Council on Marine Resources and Engineering Development, 1968. Includes descriptions of oceanographic activities and lists of organizations for various countries. Other volumes in the series cover Africa, East Asia, Latin America, and the Near East and South Asia.

Marine Science in the United Kingdom, 1967: A Directory to Scientists, Establishments and Facilities. London: Royal Society, 1967.

Oceanology International 1969 Yearbook and Directory. Beverly Shores, Indiana: Industrial Research Publishing Company, 1969.

Ocean Research Index: A Guide to Ocean and Freshwater Research, Including Fisheries Research. Guernsey, Channel Islands: Francis Hodgson, 1970.

Sea Technology Handbook Directory, 1975. Arlington, Virginia: Compass Publications, 1975. Includes information on United States educational institutions and oceanographic research vessels.

U.S. Directory of Marine Scientists. Washington, D.C.: National Academy of Sciences, 1975.

Webb, J. E. (Comp.) *Guide to the Marine Stations of the North Atlantic and European Waters.* Part I: *Northern Europe and the East Atlantic Coast.* London: Royal Society, 1974. Other volumes forthcoming.

World Directory of Marine Laboratories. New York: Van Nostrand Reinhold, 1963.

RESEARCH CENTERS, INSTITUTES, INFORMATION CENTERS

Bedford Institute
Dartmouth, Nova Scotia, Canada

Institute of Oceanographic Sciences
Surrey, England

Institute of Oceanography
University of Cape Town
Cape Town, South Africa

Institute of Oceanology
USSR Academy of Sciences
Moscow, Soviet Union

Institut für Meereskunde der Universität Kiel
Kiel, Federal Republic of Germany

Lamont-Doherty Geological Observatory
Palisades, New York 10964 USA

Ocean Research Institute
University of Tokyo
Tokyo, Japan

Scripps Institution of Oceanography
University of California, San Diego
La Jolla, California 92037 USA

Woods Hole Oceanographic Institution
Woods Hole, Massachusetts 02543 USA

OFF-CAMPUS EXPERIENCE

See Cooperative Education and Off-Campus Experience.

OFFICE AUXILIARY SERVICES

See Business and Office Technologies (field of study).

OFFICIAL CATHOLIC DIRECTORY

See Religious Influences in Higher Education: Catholicism.

OFFICIAL SEAL

See Academic Dress and Insignia; Registrar.

OMAN, SULTANATE OF

Population: 1,500,000 (1975 estimate). Student enrollment in primary school: 54,457; secondary school (academic): 1295. Language of instruction: Arabic. [Enrollment statistics are for 1975–76. Source: Ministry of Education.]

The Sultanate of Oman is located on the southeastern corner of the Arabian peninsula and is bordered by the United Arab Emirates on the north, Saudi Arabia on the northwest, and Democratic Yemen on the southwest. Oman's thousand-mile coastline extends from the Gulf of Oman in the east to the Arabian Sea in the south. Between 1932 and 1970 the sultanate, then officially known as Muscat and Oman, was ruled by Sultan Said bin Taimur, a strict conservative and isolationist. In 1970 the sultan was overthrown in a bloodless coup by his son Qabus bin Said, who initiated a development program designed to modernize the country's political, economic, and social structures.

Since 1970 the government has emphasized the expansion of modern education, which in that year consisted of three government primary schools. Education is also provided by traditional *kuttab* schools, which offer instruction based on study of the Koran. A substantial number of Omani students at all levels of education are enrolled in educational institutions abroad on either foreign or Omani government scholarships. At the higher education level scholarships have been provided by countries such as Abu Dhabi, Bahrain, Egypt, Iraq, Kuwait, Syria, and the Soviet Union.

The Omani government has given priority to the development of primary and adult education and as yet does not plan to establish a higher education institution. However, consideration is being given to the eventual development of a teacher training institution on the postsecondary level.

Bibliography

Clark, D. O., and Mertz, R. A. *The Coastal Countries of the Arabian Peninsula: A Guide to the Academic Placement of Students from Kuwait, Bahrain, Qatar, United Arab Emirates, Sultanate of Oman, People's Democratic Republic of Yemen and Yemen Arab Republic in Educational Institutions in the U.S.A.* World Education Series. Washington, D.C.: American Association of Collegiate Registrars and Admissions Officers (AACRAO), 1974.

Mertz, R. A. *Education and Manpower in the Arabian Gulf.* Washington, D.C.: American Friends of the Middle East, 1972.

Who's Who in the Arab World 1974–1975. (4th ed.) Beirut, Lebanon: Publitec Publications, 1974.

ONTARIO INSTITUTE FOR STUDIES IN EDUCATION, Canada

The Ontario Institute for Studies in Education, an independent institution within the University of Toronto, was established as a research and teaching unit in July 1965 by an act of the Ontario legislature. The institute's research program includes studies in preschool, primary, secondary, higher, and adult education. Higher education research, with a national or regional focus, is concerned with the following areas: economics of higher education, educational planning, and university students and faculty. The institute offers postgraduate courses leading to certification and graduate degrees in education. The academic departments of the institute offer concentrations in the following subjects: adult education, applied psychology, computer applications, curriculum, educational administration, educational planning, history and philosophy of education, measurement and evaluation, sociology in education, and special education. Courses at the graduate level that deal specifically with higher education are offered in the institute by the Higher Educa-

tion Group of the University of Toronto. In addition to research and teaching activities, the institute is involved in the development of college and university entrance tests.

The institute, directed by a board of governors, is funded by the Canadian government, publication sales, and contractual research services. The 161 academic staff members of the institute carry on research and development work in addition to their teaching activities. The institute's professional staff of 101 includes librarians, administrative officers, computer programmers, systems analysts, editors, writers, and video-film technicians. The general support staff—including secretaries, clerical help in the library and finance divisions, and machine operators—numbers 216. Of the ninety graduate students at the institute, approximately half receive graduate assistantships which require work on research or development projects. Others may also be involved in research activities through course work. The staffs have access to a library, microfiche equipment, and computers.

As part of the Educational Planning Occasional Papers series, the institute has published *Research into Academic Staff Manpower and Salary Issues: A Selective Bibliography* by George S. Tracz (1974). The institute also publishes a number of research reports that relate to higher education issues.

252 Bloor Street West
Toronto, Ontario, Canada M5S 1V6

OPEN-DOOR COLLEGES, THE (Higher Education Report), United States

The Open-Door Colleges: Policies for Community Colleges (New York: McGraw-Hill, June 1970), a report of the Carnegie Commission on Higher Education, reviews the role and growth of two-year colleges in the United States and assigns to them the major responsibility for providing open access to higher education. The commission urges expansion to the point where a comprehensive public community college providing general, transfer, occupational, and continuing education, as well as remedial courses and cultural programs for the local community, would be within commuting distance of every potential student. Such two-year institutions should maintain enrollments of 2000 to 5000 students, charge low (if any) tuition fees, and award either the Associate in Arts or the Associate of Applied Science degree. They should provide sound guidance and remedial programs and should adapt their occupational curricula to changing manpower needs.

While increased federal and state funding for community college expansion is recommended, the report encourages continued local support to ensure community autonomy in college government. State control of community colleges is discouraged, as are two-year academic branches of universities and specialized two-year institutions.

The report calls for a plan in every state for community college development. Such planning is urgent, since the study predicts that by 2000 community colleges will enroll over 40 percent of the undergraduate students in the United States.

OPEN UNIVERSITY

The Open University is the newest and most unusual of British universities. Designed primarily for adults who study part-time in their own homes, it requires no normal university entrance qualifications, uses a multimedia teaching system, and has enrolled over eighty thousand undergraduates since its inception in 1971. The university headquarters is at Milton Keynes, a new city being developed in North Buckinghamshire, fifty miles from London; the campus is called Walton Hall after the name of the original manor house on the site. At first sight the campus looks much like any other university, but there is a major difference: no students are in residence. Instead, many of the complex operations involved in producing the teaching materials are carried out on the campus; campus buildings house an art and photographic studio, a print

shop, a publishing and marketing department (which sells the Open University teaching materials all over the world), and large computing and mailing areas rather than classrooms. In 1975 two major additions were being planned—a broadcasting studio complex and a building for the science and technology faculties. In addition to the headquarters campus, the Open University has thirteen regional offices throughout the United Kingdom, which are responsible for the local organization of students in their respective areas.

History

The first public reference to an open university was by Sir Harold Wilson. In 1963, when he was leader of the opposition, he made a speech in Glasgow in which he talked about a University of the Air, stressing the use of the broadcasting media as an integral part of the teaching system. Subsequently, when the Labor government took power, Jennie Lee was appointed Undersecretary of State for Education, with particular responsibility for the University of the Air. A government white paper in 1966 led to the establishment of a planning committee to investigate, in detail, the idea of this university for adults.

The committee, chaired by Sir Peter Venables, Vice-Chancellor of the University of Aston and later the first Pro-Chancellor of the Open University, explored the extent to which the university was needed, designed its first organization, and appointed its initial staff. In the late 1960s the proportion of students in Britain who went on to some kind of higher education compared unfavorably with the rest of Europe, North America, the Soviet Union, and Japan; and the proportion from working class homes was no higher than it had been a generation before. These conditions were true despite a strong tradition of out-of-school education in the United Kingdom, with about half a million people taking correspondence courses and about twenty thousand (including seven thousand by correspondence) studying for external degrees with London University.

The planning committee's report, published in 1969, was immediately accepted by the government. The Open University, the new name for the University of the Air, was granted a Royal Charter the same year and admitted its first students in 1971.

Finance and Government

Unlike most United Kingdom universities, the Open University is funded directly by the government's Department of Education and Science. Most universities operate on five-year grants allocated by the University Grants Committee; the Open University receives triennial grants, so that its unusual and rapidly changing needs can be reevaluated every three years.

Government expenditure on the Open University has increased from about five million pounds in the 1969–70 academic year to fourteen million in 1974–75. The remainder of its income comes from student fees. Undergraduates pay £45 per full credit course (plus the cost of set books, which they buy themselves). In addition, some courses, including all those at foundation (first) level, require a week's residential summer school, which costs £49 per course. There is a returnable deposit of £5 for half credit and £10 for full course on the home experiment kits used in science and technology courses. Since Open University students are studying part-time, they are not automatically entitled to a grant from their local education authority, as are full-time students in the United Kingdom. Most Open University students receive a grant to meet the cost of the summer school, however, and some employers help with other fees.

The governing structure of the Open University is in many ways similar to other British universities. There are three honorary posts—chancellor, pro-chancellor, and treasurer. The other officers of the university—the vice-chancellor, who is the university's executive head; four pro-vice-chancellors (each responsible for a specific policy area), who assist the vice- chancellor; the university secretary, who is in charge of administration—are full-time salaried appointments. There are six faculties—arts, educational studies, mathematics, science, social sciences, and technology—each with a dean at its head, and an Institute of Educational Technology, headed by a director. Other directors lead the university's tutorial activities in the regions, its post-experience unit, and its operational functions.

The pro-chancellor chairs the council, which is one of the university's two governing bodies. Most of the members of the council are appointed from outside the university, but the officers of the university and elected representatives of its full-time and part-time staff and students also serve on it. The council is the body corporate that owns property, employs staff, and controls finance.

The vice-chancellor chairs the senate, which is the university's academic authority and which determines university policy in all academic matters. The senate includes all members of the full-time academic staff as well as elected representatives of the part-time tutorial staff of students and of various categories of nonacademic full-time staff. The general assembly, which brings together students and part-time tutorial staff from all of the thirteen Open University regions, is entitled to comment to the senate on any matter of general concern.

Four boards under the council and the senate formulate policy and deal with matters of detail. The academic board oversees the academic and tutorial nature of courses, the student board supervises degree structure and other matters concerning the registration of students, the planning board carries out planning at strategic and resource-allocation levels, and the staff board deals with university personnel matters.

Undergraduate Degrees

Applicants for undergraduate courses need no previous educational qualifications nor does their educational experience play any part in the admissions process. In fact, probably no more than a third of the student body has adequate qualifications for acceptance in most other United Kingdom universities. The Open University stipulates only that candidates be twenty-one years of age or over and residents of the United Kingdom. Places are offered on a first come, first served basis, qualified by a course quota (fixed by the university) and a reasonable balance among the various regions in the country. The university also has a number of schemes for special students—it enrolls blind, deaf, spastic, and other disabled students, who could not attend a residential university; it makes special arrangements for some merchant seamen and British servicemen, stationed in the Federal Republic of Germany and Cyprus, to take Open University degrees; it has groups of students in some of the United Kingdom's prisons; and in the 1974–1975 academic year, it initiated a pilot project for five hundred students between eighteen and twenty-one.

Applicants who apply, and are accepted, and pay £10 of their fee are regarded as provisionally registered. They start their courses in January and, after three months of studying, are asked to complete final registration and to pay the remainder of their fees. This trial period provides a method of self-selection, and about 25 percent of provisionally registered students do not finally register. Of those who do, about 75 percent finish the year's course successfully; consequently, it is the number of students who finally register that is used as the statistical base line for planning purposes. Once a student has finally registered, he is regarded as being within the university system until he graduates. This means that students can drop their studies—for example, to change jobs—and take them up again at a later, more convenient date.

The student gains his degree by accumulating credits. One credit is given for each course he completes successfully on the basis of continuous assessment, attendance at summer school when required, and a final examination. A full-credit course lasts thirty-four weeks and requires about twelve hours of study per week; a half-credit course lasts seventeen weeks. Students may take up to two credits a year, but the majority take only one or one and a half.

The student starts with a foundation course—a broadly based introductory course that assumes no prior knowledge of the subject areas—and then passes on to courses at the second, third, and fourth levels. Six credits, including two at the foundation level, are required for an ordinary degree; eight credits, of which at least two must be at the third or fourth level, are required for an honors degree. Exemption from up to three of the required credits may be awarded on the general basis of one exemption for each year of full-time study or its part-time equivalent completed at another institution; students who have two or three credit exemptions need only complete one of the two foundation-level credits. Students have almost total freedom of choice in courses and may elect subjects from any combination of the faculties.

Teaching System

There are seven major teaching channels in the Open University instructional system; four of these are intended to give the student new information, the others are for feedback only. New information is imparted through written course and supplementary materials, television and radio broadcasts, summer schools; feedback is effected by computer-marked and tutor-marked assignments, face-to-face tuition.

Written and supplementary materials. Each week of a course is called a unit; for each unit there is a correspondence text (a booklet specially prepared by the course team as part of a series). These texts are the core of the course, and the other elements are interrelated with them. Texts may include diagrams and self-assessment tests that provide the student with immediate feedback.

Other written materials include set books, which are prescribed reading; unlike the free correspondence texts, set books must be purchased by the student himself. In addition, a course team may produce readers containing articles collected specifically for their course. Other materials may also supplement the written texts. For example, science and technology students receive a home experiment kit and instructions for setting up a number of experiments for each course they take; students taking certain art courses receive records; those taking an educational course on the language of schoolchildren are supplied with a tape recorder and cassettes.

Broadcasts. Under a formal contract with the British Broadcasting Corporation (BBC), a number of BBC staff are assigned to the production of Open University television programs, which are guaranteed thirty hours of broadcasting per week on the national networks. Despite the original University of the Air concept, broadcasting only accounts for a maximum of one hour out of twelve of the student's study time each week. Foundation courses have one radio and one television program per week, but broadcasts for higher level courses are generally less frequent. Some courses use broadcasting to provide enrichment or background information rather than essential instruction, while others relate the programs more closely to the correspondence texts. The television programs in science, for example, provide an opportunity to observe practical work covered by the texts.

Summer schools. Summer schools are week-long residential courses held in July and August on the campuses of other universities. Teaching is by members of the Open University staff, supplemented by external tutors appointed for particular weeks. The schools provide an opportunity for students to meet others from all over the country and to take part in a week's intensive activity directed at aspects of the course most unsuited to the other media.

Assignments. Two of the remaining teaching channels—computer-marked assignments and tutor-marked assignments—provide feedback rather than instruction. Computer-marked assignments use multiple-choice objective questions; the completed assignments are sent by the student to Walton Hall, where they are marked on the computer, and an overall grade is returned to give him an idea of the extent to which he has mastered the subject being tested. This procedure allows the university to test a student's command of a far wider range of subjects than do more normal assessment procedures. By contrast, tutor-marked assignments normally use essay questions, and the tutor is encour-

aged to annotate the script to provide the student with overall comments as well as a grade. The student's final course grade is based on performance in these two kinds of assignments, attendance at summer school, and completion of a final three-hour examination at the end of the course.

Face-to-face tuition. Part-time staff, known as student tutors, provide the instruction or face-to-face tuition that constitutes the last channel of the Open University teaching system. There are about five thousand such tutors, most of whom have full-time commitments elsewhere in the educational world. Each student is assigned to a local study center, usually another educational building used for the evening, where he has the opportunity to meet other students and the tutor of his current course. Tutors' work in study centers is complemented by that of counselors, who also hold part-time appointments. A counselor will stay with a student the whole time he is in the university, helping with study problems, course choice, and, at foundation level, extra tuition.

The course team. The mechanism for coordinating the teaching elements of a course is the course team. Each course team is chaired by a senior academician and is composed of the staff who have a part to play in course development: the central academic staff, who write the texts and accompanying materials; outside consultants, when necessary; the television and radio producers, with whom the academicians make the program accompanying the course; a full-time staff tutor, who is responsible for a given subject and based in a particular area of the country, and who supervises and coordinates the part-time staff living in that area and working in his subject; a representative from the university's Institute of Educational Technology, who ensures that the course objectives are adequately defined and materials themselves are appropriately structured; a course assistant, who interfaces with the operational and administrative sides and ensures that the course stays on schedule; an editor who assists with the production of the written materials; and a faculty librarian.

The course team meets regularly over a

period of approximately two years with increasing frequency as the writing process begins. Each correspondence text goes through several drafts, is read and comcommented on by other members of the course team, and is evaluated by an external assessor. Since a course has a limited life span of four or five years, one of the team is appointed as maintenance chairman once it is completed, and his task is to organize any revisions that might be necessary as a result of feedback and to oversee the preparation of new assessment material each year.

Undergraduates

The average age of Open University students is thirty-four, and the proportion of female students (37.6 percent) is higher than the usual percentage of women students in the United Kingdom. About 30 percent of the students are teachers or members of a profession, but laboratory technicians, scientists, engineers, and housewives are also well represented. These last statistics would seem to indicate that most Open University students are middle-class; however, if students are categorized by the occupation of their parents at eighteen years of age, no fewer than 85 percent come from working-class origins.

In 1975 the Open University received 49,550 applications and provisionally registered 20,045 students. In general many more applications are received for the arts and social science courses than for mathematics, science, or technology. Although there is some concern about the success of mathematics, the results so far have been much better than with most remote teaching programs. Over nine hundred students qualified for their degree in 1972, after two years of study; in 1973 an additional three thousand graduated; and in 1974 over five thousand students graduated.

Open University students are very motivated and hard-working; their staying power and determination should be a hallmark of the Open University degree.

Postgraduate and Postexperience Students

The majority of postgraduate students work at a distance from the Open Univer-

sity. In 1975, however, about thirty full-time students were based on the campus, and about thirty members of the university's own staff were working for a higher degree. The other two hundred postgraduate students were scattered around the United Kingdom, working part time and at their own expense; these students were supervised either individually or in concert by Open University academics. As of 1975, no course work was being provided at the postgraduate levels, and the higher degrees—Bachelor of Philosophy, Master of Philosophy, and Doctor of Philosophy—were being awarded on completion of a program of research or advanced study.

The university has one other kind of student—those taking postexperience courses, which are short, self-contained, and designed to teach people a new skill or enable them to keep abreast of recent developments in their own field. These students pay a fee to cover the full cost of the course and receive a course certificate if they undertake and successfully complete the assessment requirements of the course, or a letter of course completion if they finish the course but decide not to be examined on it. Most of these courses contain all the elements of the undergraduate teaching system.

The term *postexperience* is used to cover all courses that are not part of the undergraduate program and some that are part of the undergraduate program but are taken by nondegree students. The postexperience program is still in its initial stages, and constant review may lead to changes in the type and content of courses.

Global Impact

Since its foundation in 1969 the Open University has been of considerable interest to other countries. This interest was first demonstrated by the abnormal number of visitors to the university after its opening and later by the widespread response to its newly formed consultancy service.

Basically there are two sides to the university: the part concerned with the preparation and production of course materials in a format suitable for outright purchase and use elsewhere, and the part referred to as its delivery system, which covers all ways a course is conveyed to students and supplemented by other teaching methods.

The first of these two aspects is immediately adaptable abroad, since institutions in both developed and developing countries can purchase Open University courses and use them in their own situations. The course materials have already shown themselves to be capable of considerable adaptation and translation with no ill effects. In the United States, for example, there were nineteen institutions in 1975 adapting and using Open University courses.

The delivery system is much less readily adaptable, requiring a core of part-time staff who can act as tutors and counselors, an excellent postal service and other public service facilities, a prestigious broadcasting network such as the BBC, and a reservoir of administrators experienced with computers. Without such backup resources, Open University courses are difficult to administer from a distance.

The solution may lie in using the Open University as a resource center for the production of courses to an agreed specification on behalf of institutions all over the world, which would then use them in their own circumstances and with their own delivery system. Whatever its ultimate role, the Open University has established itself as the model of a new kind of higher education that will continue to be followed throughout the world.

Bibliography

B.A. Degree Handbook. Milton Keynes, England: Open University Press, 1976.

Courses Handbook. Milton Keynes, England: Open University Press, 1976.

Mayeske, B. "Open University Experiment: University of Maryland Reports on British Transplant." *College Board Review,* Summer 1973, *88,* 2–5.

Post-Experience Courses Prospectus 1976. Milton Keynes, England: Open University Press, 1975.

Postgraduate Prospectus and Student Handbook 1976. Milton Keynes, England: Open University Press, 1975.

Truswell, H. "UNISA, South Africa's Open university." *Optima,* December 1972, *22,* 197–199.

Perry, Sir Walter. *Open University, A Personal Account by the First Vice-Chancellor.* Milton Keynes, England: Open University Press, 1976.

Perry, Sir Walter, *An Introduction to the Open University.* Milton Keynes, England: Open University Press, 1976.

WALTER PERRY

OPEN UNIVERSITY, THE (Higher Education Report), United Kingdom

In its report *The Open University* (London: H. M. Stationery Office, 1969), the Open University Planning Committee, appointed by the British secretary of state for education and science and headed by P. Venables, presents its comprehensive plan for the development of the Open University, an institution designed to provide higher education for adults who do not enter any of the existing higher education institutions in the United Kingdom. The report sets forth the objectives, the statutes, and the charter of the new university and discusses its staffing, financing, location, equipment, administrative and degree structures, and its relationship with the British Broadcasting Corporation (BBC). Specifically, the following findings and recommendations are reported.

A general undergraduate program should be offered by the university. The program, consisting of part-time study designed for students of various academic backgrounds, involves five years of correspondence work in conjunction with radio and television broadcasts, discussion groups, and short residential study. Such a program will provide students with a general knowledge of broad fields of study. Specialized full-time degree courses will continue to be the responsibility of the traditional higher education institutions.

Postgraduate study at the Open University will consist of general courses that are a continuation of the general undergraduate course; refresher courses for professionals; and courses designed to acquaint professionals with the latest developments in their field.

The Open University will require within

its administration special personnel skilled in radio and television technologies, program design, programed learning, student assessment, education by correspondence, adult education, and postgraduate education. Adequate counseling services also must be developed to assist students in selecting the course of study best suited to their abilities.

Among the problems the new university will face are the limited television services and library facilities in some areas and the difficulty of travel. In addition, special programs must be adapted to the history and culture of the different regions of the country.

OPENING CONVOCATION
See Ceremonies.

OPPENHEIMER LIBRARY
See Libraries: Bodleian Library, England.

OPPORTUNITIES FOR WOMEN IN HIGHER EDUCATION (Higher Education Report), United States

Opportunities for Women in Higher Education: Their Current Participation, Prospects for the Future, and Recommendations for Action (New York: McGraw-Hill, September 1973), a report of the Carnegie Commission on Higher Education, examines the opportunity for participation of women in higher education in the United States. The report is concerned with women as students, faculty members, administrators, and nonfaculty academic staff. The following findings and recommendations are reported.

The participation of women in education declines at each level of advancement within the educational system. At the higher education level, women are at a disadvantage with respect to admission to college, acceptance into graduate school, acceptance and promotion within faculties, and salaries received. Several reasons for the underrepresentation of women in higher education and in traditionally male-dominated fields are cited: the years devoted to child bearing and child rearing, limited geographical mobility, cultural

patterning in earlier years, the absence of female role models, and prejudice and male monopolies.

The barriers and the discrimination that women face in education must be removed. The first priority is to change policies in preprimary, primary, and secondary school programs, where women are deterred from seeking equality with men in their career goals. Other recommendations are increased mathematical training for girls, career counseling and testing free of sex bias, and greater fairness in the selection and administration of admissions criteria. The commission favors the continued existence of women's colleges but suggests that they enter into arrangements with other higher education institutions to enable their students to enroll in accounting or engineering courses. Women's courses and women's study programs offered by many colleges and universities should be continued, but only as part of existing departments.

Higher education institutions should make special efforts to attract women to advanced studies and should allow flexible study programs. Colleges and universities also should give special consideration to women in faculty selection and not discourage part-time faculty appointments; and, since women have especially benefited from continuing education, external degree and other nontraditional study programs should be developed further. In addition, colleges and universities should meet the demands of campus groups seeking to develop child care services, which will further increase opportunities for women to participate in higher education.

The commission generally favors the affirmative action objectives of the federal government and urges colleges and universities to develop affirmative action policies to eliminate sex discrimination in the employment of faculty members. However, the report acknowledges, the movement for women's equality in faculty staffing has come ten years too late. The expansion period in higher education is over, and the rate of new hires is decreasing. Consequently, it will take time to enlarge the pool of qualified women, and in some fields there is already an oversupply of doctoral degrees. However, when the inequalities have been rectified, both individuals and society will benefit. As attitudes toward sex roles continue to change, the report anticipates a trend toward full equality of opportunity for women in higher education.

OPTICAL LENS MAKING
(Field of Study)

Optical lens making as a discipline includes both formal and informal training in processing and refining optical lens products according to given specifications. In the past the optical lens product was made from glass, but technology has produced hard resin lenses, photochromic lenses, and the synthetic soft contact lens.

There are five major divisions in the lens-making field: (1) Ophthalmic products —that is, lenses manufactured and refined for use as prescription eyeglasses (glass eyewear, sunglasses, hard and soft contact lenses)—are the most universally applied products of the lens-making industry. (2) Instrumental optics include microscopes; telescopes; and metallographic, spectrophotometric, and fiber optics equipment. (3) General consumer products of lens-making processes include binoculars, readers and magnifiers, and general magnification scopes. (4) The field of photography utilizes lens products in cameras, illuminators, developers, and image projectors—virtually every phase of photography. (5) Research instruments utilizing lens systems include photomicrography, laser analyzers, enzyme analyzers, refractometers, and diffraction grating analyzers.

Fields of study related to optical lens making are most apparent in the ophthalmic lens field. The study of opticianry, for example, includes concepts of lens design, manufacture, and refinement. The study of optical systems engineering often includes actual techniques of lens surfacing and finishing. The application of lens theory, design, and processing is also used in photogrammetography; cartography; and civil, aerial, and mineralogical engineering.

Optical lens making as an art and industry originated when someone accidentally produced lenses and then tried to manufacture and refine the product in a systematic way. E. J. Fonsdyke's discovery of glass objects in Crete in 1927 suggests that crystal magnifying lenses date back at least to 1200 B.C. and very likely to 1600 B.C. Ground glass lenses at the British Museum include one processed lens from Tanis, definitely dated A.D 150.

The art and process of making optical lenses has been a closely kept secret. According to Bausch and Lomb (1970, p. 32), "The art of glass making has been, until recently, in the hands of a chosen few who learned their trade in childhood from their fathers and who have guarded most jealously their acquired knowledge." The literature also suggests that details concerning the machines used in refining the lens were kept as guarded information. According to Twyman (1955, p. 12), P. Herschel, a scientist who worked on the refinement and development of opthalmic lenses in the latter half of the nineteenth century, mentions in his collected papers of 1912 "the development of a grinding and polishing machine capable of completing the operation of ten men. He published no details of his working methods, as he evidently looked upon these as trade secrets."

Formal education in lens design, optical lens systems, and optical engineering apparently originated in European universities. Historically, Europe has maintained its superiority in optics technology, and the field has centered about the universities at Berlin and Jena and the polytechnical school in Nuremberg. Education in the techniques of optical lens making, however, has remained primarily an apprentice training program provided by manufacturers of the lens product. In 1970, according to the Bureau of Apprentice Training, United States Department of Labor, 107 optical organizations provided apprenticeship training programs.

Internationally, major optical manufacturers provide apprenticeship or on-the-job training in optical lens making. Companies providing this training include

Essilor (France), Rodenstock (Belgium), Zeiss (Federal Republic of Germany), Chance/Pilkington (Wales), Sola International (Australia), Hoya Glass (Japan), Verdos (Brazil), and Bausch and Lomb (Argentina).

In the United States a trend is emerging toward formal training programs on the postsecondary level, many of which include a cooperative work experience. One such curriculum has been established at the National Technical Institute for the Deaf, Rochester Institute of Technology, Rochester, New York, where young deaf students prepare for careers in optical finishing technology through formal course work, laboratory training, and the work-experience program. The curriculum provides multiple exit levels of certificate, diploma, or Associate of Applied Science degree in optical finishing technology. The major technical skills developed by students in the curriculum include application of optical mathematics; optical finishing terminology; prescription analysis; lens power analysis; operation and maintenance of automatic and hand finishing equipment; layout techniques; eyeglass frame techniques in metal, plastic, and combination frames; and techniques of final inspection and quality control.

[Notes: **Bausch and Lomb,** *Job Coach for Prescription Shop Operations* (Rochester, New York: Bausch and Lomb, 1970). **F. Twyman,** *Optical Glassworking* (London: Hilger and Watts, 1955).]

FREDERIC R. HAMIL

Levels and Programs of Study

Programs in optical lens making generally require a secondary education, although mature students with relevant work experience may be admitted with lower qualifications, especially into programs designed to upgrade the performance of those already employed. Usual award for successful completion of programs of one year or more, typically given in technological or similar institutes, is a certificate or diploma issued by the institution or by the examining board of a professional or technical organization. For short courses,

many of which are sponsored by employers or employers' associations, a certificate of satisfactory completion is usually given. Programs may also lead to a first university degree.

Programs deal primarily with the technology of optical lens making and consist of classroom, laboratory, and workshop study and practice. Principal course content usually includes some of the following: light dispersion, interference, polarization, refraction and diffraction; properties of materials used for lens making; geometrical optics; materials used for lens grinding; methods and equipment used for lens grinding; centering, edging, mounting, and testing of lenses; nature and function of optical equipment; lens systems; compounding lenses; elementary physics; and mathematics. Emphasis is placed on the achievement of practical competence and skill. Programs often consist of alternating periods of study and work in industrial and other enterprises (sandwich courses).

[This section was based on UNESCO's *International Standard Classification of Education: (ISCED) Three Stage Classification System, 1974* (Paris: UNESCO, 1974).]

Major International and National Organizations

INTERNATIONAL

European Association of Industries on
  Precision Mechanics and Optics
via Brisa 3
20123 Milan, Italy

International Commission for Optics
% Laboratoire physique générale et optique
Faculté des sciences et des techniques
Université de Besançon
25030 Besançon, France

NATIONAL

Austria:
    Bundesinnung der Mechaniker
    Bauernmarkt 13
    1011 Vienna

Belgium:
    Chambre syndicale des fabricants,
        grossistes et importateurs en optique
    rue Joily 148
    1000 Brussels

Federal Republic of Germany:
    Verband der deutschen

feinmechanischen und optischen
Industrie e.V.
Pipinstrasse 16
5 Cologne 1

France:
Syndicat général de l'optique et des
instruments de précision
15 rue Beaujon
75 Paris 8

Hungary:
Optikai, akusztikai és filmtechnikai
egyesület
Anker Koz 1
Budapest VI

Italy:
Associazione nazionale industriale
dell'ottica meccanica fine e di
precisione
via Brisa 3
20123 Milan

Japan:
Japan Optical and Precision Instruments
Manufacturers' Association
Kikai shinko kaikan, 1–5
Shiba Koen 21-gochi
Minato-ku, Tokyo

Netherlands:
Nederlands vereniging van leveranciers
en fabrikanten van optische producten
Herengracht 455
Amsterdam

People's Republic of China:
Institute of Optical and Precision
Instruments
Chinese Academy of Science
Changchun
Kirin

Sweden:
Svenska leverantörföreningen för
instruments och märteknik
Sveavägen 17, 6 tr.
111 37 Stockholm

United Kingdom:
Federation of Manufacturing Opticians
64 Lamb's Conduit Street
London WC1, England

United States:
Optical Manufacturers Association
1730 North Lynn Street
Arlington, Virginia 22209

Principal Information Sources

GENERAL

Some overviews and texts are:

Blaker, J. W. *Optics I: Lenses, Mirrors and Optical Instruments.* New York: Barnes & Noble, 1969.

Conrady, A. E. *Applied Optics and Optical Design.* New York: Dover, 1960.
Epting, J., and Morgret, F. *Opthalmic Mechanics and Dispensing.* Radnor, Pennsylvania: Chilton, 1974.
Fowles, G. R. *Introduction to Modern Optics.* New York: Holt, Rinehart and Winston, 1968.
Horne, D. F. *Optical Production Technique.* New York: Crane, Russak, 1972.
Jamieson, T. H. *Optimization Techniques in Lens Design.* New York: American Elsevier, 1971.
Kingslake, R. (Ed.) *Applied Optics and Optical Engineering: A Comprehensive Treatise.* (5 vols.) Vol. 3: *Optical Components;* Vols. 4–5: *Optical Instruments.* New York: Academic Press, 1969.
Klein, M. V. *Optics.* New York: Wiley, 1970.
Levi, L. *Applied Optics: A Guide to Optical System Design.* New York: Wiley, 1968.
Twyman, F. *Prism and Lens Making.* London: Hilger and Watts, 1942.
Twyman, F. *Optical Glassworking.* London: Hilger and Watts, 1955.

Two histories are:

Hoppe, E. *Geschichte der Optik.* Leipzig, German Democratic Republic: J. J. Weber, 1926.
Ronchi, V. *The Nature of Light: An Historical Survey.* Cambridge, Massachusetts: Harvard University Press, 1970.

For a discussion of career opportunities see:

Stimson, R. *Opportunities in Opticianry.* New York: Universal Publishing, 1971.

CURRENT BIBLIOGRAPHIES

Applied Science and Technology Index. New York: Wilson, 1958–.
British Technology Index. London: Library Association, 1961–.
Physics Abstracts (Science Abstracts, Set A). London: Institution of Electrical Engineers, 1898–.

See also "Revue des périodiques" in each issue of *Nouvelle revue d'optique appliquée.* Contains abstracts of articles in current international optics journals.

PERIODICALS

Some journals in the field include *Applied Optics* (US), *Nouvelle revue d'optique appliquée* (France), *Optica Acta* (UK), *Optical Engineering* (US), *Optical Society of America Journal, Optica pura y aplicada* (Spain), *Optics and Laser Technology* (UK), *Optics and Spectroscopy* (US), *Optik* (FRG), *Optika i spektroskopiya* (USSR), *Soviet Journal of Optical Technology, Svensk ur-optik tidning, Vision Research* (UK).

See also:

Ulrich's International Periodicals Directory. New

York: Bowker, biennial. See "Physics-Optics."

ENCYCLOPEDIAS, DICTIONARIES, HANDBOOKS

Bárány, N. *Finommechanika, Optika.* [*Munkatársak: Mitnyán László, Petrik Olivér és Turi Zoltán*]. Budapest: Terra, 1961. Chiefly in Hungarian; brief data in English, German, and Russian.

Noveck, S. *Russian-English Glossary of Optics and Spectroscopy.* New York: Interlanguage Dictionaries, 1959.

The Optical Industry and Systems Directory. (21st ed.) Vol. 1: *Encyclopedia and Dictionary;* Vol. 2: *Buyer's Guide and Product Tables.* Pittsfield, Massachusetts: Optical Publishing Company, 1975. Published annually; an international encyclopedia of optical, electro-optical, and laser technology and a dictionary of current terminology.

Pressley, R. D. *CRC Handbook of Lasers with Selected Data on Optical Technology.* Cleveland, Ohio: Cleveland Rubber Company, 1971.

Richter, G. (Comp.) *Dictionary of Optics, Photography, and Photogrammetry: German-English and English-German.* Amsterdam: Elsevier; New York: American Elsevier, 1966.

Schultz, E. *Wörterbuch der Optik und Feinmechanik.* Wiesbaden, Federal Republic of Germany: Brandstetter; London: Pitman, 1960–1961. Three thousand terms in optics and precision mechanics. In English, German, and French.

DIRECTORIES

Directories to postsecondary study and research in the field include:

Barron's Guide to the Two-Year Colleges. (5th ed.) Woodbury, New York: Barron's Educational Series, 1974. A United States directory.

College Blue Book. (14th ed.) New York: ECM Information Corporation, 1972. Includes programs in optical technology, optics, and optics technology in the United States.

Directory of Scientific Research Institutions in India. Delhi: Indian National Scientific Documentation Centre, 1969.

Directory: Scientific and Technical Associations and Institutes in Israel. (2nd ed.) Jerusalem: National Council for Research and Development, 1966.

Guide to German Universities. Munich, Federal Republic of Germany: Consultverlag, 1970. In volume 3, *General Index,* see "Technik: Akustik, Optik, Feinmechanik."

Industrial Research in Britain. (7th ed.) New York: International Publications Service, 1972.

Scandinavian Research Guide. (3rd rev. ed.) Stockholm: Almqvist and Wiksell, 1971.

World Guide to Universities. Pullach/Munich, Federal Republic of Germany: Verlag Dokumentation, 1972.

[Bibliography prepared by Janet Katz.]

OPTOMETRY (Field of Study)

In 1957 the International Optometric and Optical League adopted the definition of an optometrist as one "concerned with the investigation of the functions of vision, with a view to the correction or relief of visual defects due to anatomical or physiological variations, without recourse to medicine or surgery, and with the prescribing, fitting, and servicing of optical appliances for these purposes." A slightly more descriptive definition adopted by the American Optometric Association in 1963 includes reference to the optometrist's educational qualifications and licensure requirements and clarifies his role in the detection of eye diseases and abnormalities and the utilization of therapeutic measures in addition to optical appliances to "preserve, restore, and enhance the efficiency of vision." Though this fundamental concept of optometry seems not to have varied since the rudimentary origin of professional optometric service in the early seventeenth century, the technological advancements and the varying and increasing visual demands for living have shifted the emphasis from simple optical correction of visual defects to a very comprehensive concern with vision as a complex human function.

Branches or divisions within the field of optometry are not formally organized, but various types of services, all within the scope of service of the general optometric practitioner, are generally performed by optometrists with special training. Such services include contact lenses, subnormal-vision aids, visual training, orthoptics, industrial vision consulting, and ophthalmic dispensing. Nonclinical pursuits include teaching and research careers in the visual sciences and in ophthalmic-optical technology and development.

Some of the fields related to optometry include illuminating engineering, ophthalmology, and opticianry, respectively concerned with the technology and adequacy of lighting, medical and surgical treatment, and the fabrication of optical appliances. None of the many fields involved with general health and/or vision is totally unrelated to optometry.

Transparent glass and lenses were known in antiquity, and elementary optical concepts pervaded the earliest scientific writing. The invention of simple spectacles occurred in the thirteenth century, and spectacle makers' guilds originated in the fifteenth century. Formulation of guidelines for prescribing lenses for the correction and relief of categorized ocular conditions first took place in 1623 in the form of a book by Benito Daça de Valdes. Apprenticeship training patterns emerged very gradually and apparently quite haphazardly during the next 300 years.

In the early twentieth century many countries (especially the English-speaking countries) enacted registration requirements; as a result, numerous schools were created and/or chartered to qualify optometrists. Several licensing boards and organized professional societies adopted syllabi of courses to be completed by candidates, either by private instruction or at existing institutions. In the United States in this same period several university optometry curricula were established under the auspices of physics departments. A few private schools were acquiring comparable academic status under pressure of accreditation. In England the learning programs were being taken over by technical institutes, which later became universities. In Germany the programs were similarly placed in technical institutes but without the subsequent transformation into universities. In other countries with formal educational programs the patterns have varied between these three trends or as combinations. In unusual instances optometric training programs were initially established in pharmacy, psychology, general science, and ophthalmology departments. In most of the developing countries no formal programs exist. By the end of World War II most of the long-established optometric education programs had become full-scale academic

units operating within universities as schools, colleges, or departments for exclusively optometric purposes. This trend has continued.

The most dramatic new development in optometry, of both interdisciplinary and international significance, has involved contact lenses. During the period from 1950 to 1975 innovative contributions in the materials, the design, and the clinical technology of contact lenses came from every continent. Contributors included optical, ophthalmological, biochemical, pharmacological, and engineering personnel as well as optometrists. There have been numerous international and interdisciplinary conferences and meetings of newly created, almost spontaneously organized contact lens groups.

Less dramatic but unceasingly intense during the same period has been international concern with the formulation of educational standards and acquisition of legislation for the registration of optometrists and regulation of practice. Though not an interdisciplinary movement, this activity has engaged the rival concern of ophthalmology and of the commercial establishments retailing spectacles. Coupled with and reinforcing these efforts to upgrade optometric education and to professionalize optometric practice have been an increasing number and variety of ophthalmic-optical materials applicable as visual aids and the invention and improvement of clinical instruments for tonometry, biomicroscopy, ophthalmoscopy, automatic optometry, retinoscopy, fundus photography, phorometry, perimetry, visually evoked cortical responses, laser refraction, adaptometry, color perception diagnosis, eye movement recording, and stereopsis testing.

A new type of educational program, which gained strength in the United States in the 1965–1975 decade, is the optometric technicians program, typically two years in length and leading to an Associate in Arts or Sciences degree. Graduates of these curricula are employed mainly by optometrists but also by ophthalmologists, dispensing opticians, clinics, and schools.

There are thirteen schools of optometry in the United States and two in Canada. Ten of these schools are in universities. All fifteen receive federal appropriations, and eleven receive additional state or provincial tax support. The establishment of four additional schools by state and provincial governments is anticipated within the next few years. Curricular patterns are quite uniform, with minimum preoptometry college requirements of two years, including standard courses in physics, chemistry, mathematics, biology, psychology, and the liberal arts. Approximately half of the students complete baccalaureate degrees before being admitted to optometry schools. The optometry curriculum itself is four years in length and includes courses in geometric, physiological, psychological, ophthalmic, and environmental optics; ocular anatomy; pathology and pharmacology; socio-optometry; and all phases of clinical optometry, including practical clinical experience. The terminal degree is Doctor of Optometry (O.D.), following which graduates must take examinations for licensure in the state, province, or territory in which they plan to practice.

In the United Kingdom, Ireland, Australia, South Africa, and New Zealand, the curricular pattern is similar to that in the United States and Canada but with a foreshortening of the professional years to three and with fewer preoptometry course requirements. Programs usually terminate in a baccalaureate degree in optometry or ophthalmic optics, the latter reflecting a long identity of optometrists as ophthalmic opticians. A trend in terminology change from ophthalmic optician to optometrist is apparent in all these countries. Similarly, the Dr. title for optometrist does not prevail in these areas, but that may change.

In the United Kingdom a final year of practical clinical training is conducted independent of the schools in refraction hospitals or with authorized private establishments. Licensure examinations are conducted by government-appointed boards or other authorized professional agencies. The four schools in England, the school in Wales, the one in New Zealand, one of the two in South Africa, and two of the three in Australia are in universities. The school in Ireland, one in Scotland, one in South Africa, and one in Australia are in colleges of technology.

On the European continent the curricular pattern is very different, with emphasis on vocational training and technical skill rather than academic and professional competence. Three schools in the Federal Republic of Germany are classified as *Höhere Fachschule* or *Fachakademie* with professional curricula of two to two and a half years but with rather complex admission requirements of three years of apprenticeship in optical firms or the equivalent in academic accomplishment. After the formal optometric schooling two more years of internship with an authorized practitioner are required for eligibility to take the state licensing examinations. There are at least twenty additional variously chartered schools in twelve other countries of Western Europe, with typically less formalized requirements. The single exception to the traditional continental pattern is a new university school in Madrid. Licensing requirements also vary greatly from country to country.

In Eastern Europe the only recognized school is in Jena, German Democratic Republic; the program there closely resembles the program in the Federal Republic of Germany. In the Soviet Union there is no vocational or professional classification directly comparable to optometry. Except for a three-year program for advanced students in one of the national universities in Sri Lanka (Ceylon), seven two-year vocational training schools in eye clinics in India, five professional schools in private universities in the Philippines leading to the O.D. degree, and two vocationally oriented, industry-sponsored training centers in Japan, formal optometric education is virtually nonexistent in Asia and the Middle East. Except in the Philippines, licensure is not regulated. A new optometry school was created at Benin University in Nigeria in 1974, the only program in Africa outside of South Africa.

In Latin America there are two university optometry schools, one in Colombia and one in Mexico, and an independently chartered school in Venezuela. Otherwise, optometric training is limited to attendance of vocational optical courses combined with apprenticeships and individually pursued study. Except for Colombia and Panama, little or no statutory regulation exists in Latin America.

In spite of the apparent lack of organization and regulation of optometry in much of the world, there is very active communication among optometric leaders in almost every region and an obvious determination as well as dedication to upgrade the profession through appropriate educational requirements. Very rapidly continuing changes may therefore be anticipated during the next decades.

HENRY W. HOFSTETTER

Levels and Programs of Study

Programs for optometric technicians generally require as a minimum prerequisite a secondary education, but more mature students, especially those with relevant work experience, are sometimes admitted with lower educational qualifications. Such programs lead to an award not equivalent to a first university degree —usually a certificate or diploma. Programs consist primarily of classroom and laboratory instruction dealing with optical laboratory skills, office management, and the techniques of optometric services and of assisting an optometrist. Principal course content usually includes elementary ocular anatomy, physiology, and pathology; mechanical and ophthalmic optics; visual tests and measurements; eyewear selection, design, and fitting; orthoptic procedures; and office record maintenance. Background courses often included are general science, mathematics, and office management skills.

Programs in optometry that lead to a first university degree or equivalent usually grant a bachelor's degree in optometry or ophthalmic optics and, in some jurisdictions, the degree of Doctor of Optometry. Such programs generally require as a minimum prerequisite a secondary education, although some institutions additionally require successful completion of a pre-professional program in the basic sciences. Programs consist primarily of classroom, laboratory, and clinical instruction dealing with the principles and practice of optometric care. Principal course content usually includes geometric, physiological, psychological, ophthalmic, and environmental optics; ocular anatomy; pathology and pharmacology; socio-optometry; and all phases of clinical optometry, including practical clinical experience. Background or prerequisite courses usually include physics, chemistry, mathematics, biology, psychology, and the liberal arts.

Other optometry and related ophthalmic optical programs consist of organized and sustained instruction and learning dealing with the principles and practice of optometry. Because these programs require no identifiable previous education for admission, they tend to be concerned with particular topics and particular vocational or professional skills rather than with a number of related courses. Some programs provide for successive levels of accomplishment and certification, thereby permitting or warranting different levels of vocational participation or licensure in the ophthalmic field—levels ranging from laboratory technician to ophthalmic dispenser and, at the highest level, optometrist or ophthalmic optician. The programs are various combinations of part-time and full-time courses, apprenticeships, internships, assigned study, and achievement examinations. The topics variously include anatomy, physiology, and pathology of the eye; geometric, physiological, mechanical, and ophthalmic optics; visual tests and measurements; clinical optometric methodology; and practice management. Seldom do programs of this type involve any formal attempt to measure achievement, although certification of compliance with practice regulations may be customary.

[This section was based on UNESCO's *International Standard Classification of Education (ISCED): Three Stage Classification System, 1974* (Paris: UNESCO, 1974), with revisions and additions by Henry W. Hofstetter.]

Major International and National Organizations

INTERNATIONAL

American Academy of Optometry
115 West Broadway
P.O. Box 565
Owatonna, Minnesota 55060 USA

Association of Schools and Colleges of
Optometry
1730 M Street NW, Suite 411
Washington, D.C. 20036 USA

British Optical Association
65 Brook Street
London W1Y 2DT, England

International Association of Boards
of Examiners
P.O. Box 592
Wallace, North Carolina 28466 USA

International Association of Optometric
Executives
7000 Chippewa Street
St. Louis, Missouri 63119 USA

International Optometric and Optical League
65 Brook Street
London W1Y 2DT, England

International Society of Contact Lens
Specialists
35 The Square
St. Annes-on-Sea
Lancashire, England FY8 15B

National Eye Research Foundation
18 S. Michigan Avenue
Chicago, Illinois 60603 USA

Optometric Extension Program Foundation
P.O. Box 911
Duncan, Oklahoma 63119 USA

Optometric Historical Society
7000 Chippewa Street
St. Louis, Missouri 63119 USA

Sociedad americana de oftalmología y
optometría
Apartado Nacional No. 700-Chapinero
Bogotá, Colombia

Société d'optométrie d'Europe
rue aux Laines, 12
B-1000 Brussels, Belgium

The Worshipful Company of Spectacle Makers
Apothecaries' Hall
Blackfriars Lane
London EC4V 6EL, England

NATIONAL

Australia:
Australian Optometrical Association

Suite 4
609 St. Kilda Road
Melbourne, Victoria 3004

Belgium:
Association professionelle des opticiens
de Belgique
rue Capitaine Crespel 26
B-1050 Brussels

Canada:
Canadian Association of Optometrists
Suite 2001
210 Gladstone Avenue
Ottawa, Ontario K2P 076

Colombia:
Federación colombiana de optometras
graduados
Apartado Aéreo 90.422
Bogotá, D.E.

Denmark:
Danmarks Optikerforening
Skodsborgvej 234
DK 2850 Naerum

Federal Republic of Germany:
Wissenschaftliche Vereinigung für
Augenoptik und Optometrie
Adam-Karillon Strasse 32
65 Mainz

Zentralverband der Augenoptiker
Stresemannstrasse 12
4 Düsseldorf

Ireland:
Association of Ophthalmic Opticians
11 Harrington Street
Dublin

Israel:
Israel Optometric Association
P.O. Box 9490
Jerusalem

Mexico:
Sociedad mexicana de optometría A.C.
Apartado Postal 27-266
Mexico 7, D.F.

New Zealand:
New Zealand Optometrical Association
P.O. Box 1879
Wellington

Philippines:
Optometric Association of the Philippines
1235-A Fojas Bldg.
Asturias St.
Sampaloc, Manila

Scotland:
Scottish Association of Opticians
116 Blythswood Street
Glasgow C2 4JQ

South Africa:
> South African Optometric Association
> P.O. Box 3996
> Pretoria

Spain:
> Colegio nacional de ópticos
> Paseo del Prado 18–20
> Planta 12, Madrid

United Kingdom:
> Association of Optical Practitioners
> 65 Brook Street
> London W1Y 2DT, England

United States:
> American Optometric Association
> 7000 Chippewa Street
> St. Louis, Missouri 63119

> National Optometric Association
> Fulton National Bank Building,
> Suite 1935
> 55 Marietta Street NW
> Atlanta, Georgia 30303

Venezuela:
> Colegio de optometristas de Venezuela
> Apartado del Este No. 10.613—Sabana
> Grande
> Caracas

Principal Information Sources

GENERAL

Cox, M. E. *Optometry, the Profession: Its Antecedents, Birth, and Development.* Philadelphia: Chilton, 1957.

Gregg, J. R. *The Story of Optometry.* New York: Ronald Press, 1965.

Gregg, J. R. *American Optometric Association: A History.* St. Louis, Missouri: American Optometric Association, 1972.

Havighurst, R. J. *Optometry: Education for the Profession.* Washington, D.C.: National Commission on Accrediting, 1973. A report of a national study of optometric education; includes brief discussions of the history of the profession and training and curricula for the field.

Hirsch, M. F., and Wick, R. C. *The Optometry Profession.* Philadelphia: Chilton, 1968.

Hofstetter, H. W. *Optometry: Professional, Economic, and Legal Aspects.* St. Louis, Missouri: American Optometric Association, 1948. A handbook and reference source of nonclinical information about the field; includes historical, professional, legal, and educational information. Reprinted in 1964.

Lex Optometrica. St. Louis, Missouri: American Optometric Association, 1967–1975. Provides information on legal issues for the field in the United States.

Vision Literature Catalog. St. Louis, Missouri: Optometric Development Enterprises,

American Optometric Association, n.d. Provides a list of publications in the field.

CURRENT BIBLIOGRAPHIES

Current abstracting and indexing services for the field include:

Excerpta Medica. Section 12: *Ophthalmology.* Amsterdam: Excerpta Medica Foundation, 1947–.

Index Medicus. Bethesda, Maryland: National Library of Medicine, 1960–.

Low Vision Abstracts. Palo Alto, California: Loyal E. Apple, n.d.

Ophthalmic Literature. London: British Medical Association, 1947–.

Psychological Abstracts. Washington, D.C.: American Psychological Association, 1927–.

Vision Index. Berkeley, California: Visual Science Information Center, 1971. *Visual Science Information Center Thesaurus* is a supplemental tool that provides a list of terms used in the *Vision Index.*

PERIODICALS

Some of the significant journals in the field include *American Journal of Optometry and Physiological Optics, Atti della Fondazione Georgio Ronchi e contributi dell'Istituto nazionale di ottica* (Italy), *Augenoptik* (GDR), *Der Augenoptiker* (FRG), *Australian Journal of Optometry, British Journal of Physiological Optics, Canadian Journal of Optometry, Contacto: International Contact Lens Journal* (US), *Interoptics* (International Optometric and Optical League Newsletter) (UK), *Journal of the American Optometric Association, Journal of Optometric Education* (US), *Neues Optikerjournal* (FRG), *Newsletter of the Optometric Historical Society* (US), *Nordisk tidsskrift for special-optikere* (Denmark), *OAP Newsletter* (Philippines), *Ophthalmic Optician* (UK), *Optica Acta* (France), *Optical Journal and Review of Optometry* (US), *Optician* (UK), *L'opticien belge/De belgische Opticien, El óptico profesional* (Spain), *L'optique française et l'opticien lunetier, Optometric Weekly* (US), *Perception* (UK), *Photons* (Belgium), *Süddeutsche Optikerzeitung* (FRG), *Vision Research* (UK).

For additional journal listings see:

Directory of Optometric Publications. St. Louis, Missouri: American Optometric Association, 1974.

Vision Union List of Serials. (2nd ed.) Berkeley, California: Visual Science Information Center, 1970.

ENCYCLOPEDIAS, DICTIONARIES, HANDBOOKS

Autrum, H., and others. (Eds.) *Handbook of Sensory Physiology.* (8 vols.) Berlin, Federal Republic of Germany: Springer-Verlag, 1971–1975.

Borish, I. M. *Clinical Refraction.* (3rd ed.) Chicago: Professional Press, 1970.

Current Optometric Information and Terminology. St. Louis, Missouri: American Optometric Association, 1974.

Davson, H. (Ed.) *The Eye.* Vols. 1–6. New York: Academic Press, 1969–1970.

Holmes, C. *Guide to Occupational and Other Visual Needs.* Vols. 1–2. St. Cloud, Minnesota: Vision-Ease Corporation, Vol. 1, 1958; Vol. 2, n.d.

Mütze, K. *ABC der Optik.* (Rev. ed.) Hanau, Federal Republic of Germany: Werner Dausien, 1972.

The Optical Industry and Systems Directory. Pittsfield, Massachusetts: Optical Publishing, annual. Vol. 2 of the 1975 issue includes an encyclopedia with a collection of definitive, tutorial articles describing principles and applications of the optical, electro-optical, and laser technologies and a directory of current terminology of over 3000 terms.

Optometric Syllabus and Teaching Guide. London: International Optometric and Optical League, 1970.

Schapero, M., Cline, D., and Hofstetter, H. W. (Eds.) *Dictionary of Visual Science.* (2nd ed.) Philadelphia: Chilton, 1968.

Schmidt, I., and others. (Eds.) *Optometry Examination Review Book.* Vol. 1. Flushing, New York: Medical Examination Publishing, 1973.

DIRECTORIES

Blue Book of Optometrists. Chicago: Professional Press, 1974. Provides a list of schools of optometry for the United States, Canada, Virgin Islands, Puerto Rico, Mexico, Panama, and Colombia.

British and International Optical Year Book. London: IPC Business Press, annual.

Information for Applicants to Colleges of Optometry. Washington, D.C.: Association of Schools and Colleges of Optometry, annual. Provides information on schools of optometry in the United States.

International Schools and Colleges of Optometry. St. Louis, Missouri: International Library, Archives, and Museum of Optometry, American Optometric Association, 1968–.

The Opticians Register. London: General Optical Council, 1973.

RESEARCH CENTERS, INSTITUTES, INFORMATION CENTERS

American Optometric Foundation, Inc.
1730 M Street NW
Washington, D.C. 20036 USA

British Optical Association Library and Museum
65 Brook Street
London W1Y 2DT, England

General Optical Council
41 Harley Street
London W1N 2DJ, England

Gesell Institute
310 Prospect St.
New Haven, Connecticut 06511 USA

Institute for Research in Vision
Ohio State University
Columbus, Ohio 43210 USA

International Library, Archives and Museum of Optometry (ILAMO), Inc.
7000 Chippewa Street
St. Louis, Missouri 63119 USA

London Refraction Hospital
58–62 Newington Causeway
London SE1, England

Optometric Center of New York
122 East 25th Street
New York, New York 10010 USA

Volunteer Optometric Services to Humanity
Box J
Hillsboro, Kansas 67063 USA

ORGANISATION FOR ECONOMIC CO-OPERATION AND DEVELOPMENT

The Organisation for Economic Co-operation and Development (OECD) was founded in September 1961 as a successor body to the Organisation for European Economic Co-operation, created in April 1948. OECD seeks to achieve high economic growth and employment among member countries, coordinate and improve development aid, and help expand world trade. Twenty-four countries are members of OECD: Australia, Austria, Belgium, Canada, Denmark, Finland, France, Federal Republic of Germany, Greece, Iceland, Ireland, Italy, Japan, Luxembourg, Netherlands, New Zealand, Norway, Portugal, Spain, Sweden, Switzerland, Turkey, United Kingdom, and United States. Yugoslavia has a special status.

The organization began its work in the field of science and education in the late 1950s, with the creation of the Directorate for Scientific Affairs. The main projects and activities launched at that time sought to examine the contribution of education —and in particular higher education—to economic growth. During this first period, OECD had a pioneering role in clarifying the notion of educational investment and developing a methodology of educational planning designed to provide the manpower needed to meet the economic targets of member countries. Two studies specifically related to higher education, *Economic Aspects of Higher Education* (1964) and *Policy Conference on Highly Qualified Manpower* (1967), illustrate the economic orientation of early OECD work.

In the mid 1960s OECD began to orient an important part of its program to the investigation of the internal dynamics of educational systems, favoring a broader socioeconomic approach. The organization set up a higher education section within the Directorate for Scientific Affairs in 1966 and launched a number of studies on higher education within the Centre for Educational Research and Innovation (CERI), created in 1968.

The first projects of the Directorate for Scientific Affairs analyzed both quantitative and qualitative developments. Consideration of the former led to the preparation of a detailed survey of the growth of higher education systems in all OECD member countries and resulted in the publication of two reports: *Development of Higher Education 1950–1967: Statistical Survey* (1970) and *Analytical Report* (1971). Qualitative aspects were examined through a series of national case studies on innovation in higher education in France, Germany, United Kingdom, and Yugoslavia. Following a common outline prepared by the OECD secretariat, the country reports deal with institutional reforms, structure of studies and research, administration and management, recruitment and status of teachers, role of students in the academic community, the university's service function, and cost and financing.

The country reports subsequently prompted an OECD study of the problems posed by the transition from elite to mass higher education. In 1971 OECD published a report on this topic: *Towards New Structures of Post Secondary Education: A Preliminary Statement of Issues*. A special project was also launched to study the problems of the new postsecondary institutions, which were created to provide a wider range of educational opportunities. Their need to fulfill functions different from those of

traditional universities and, at the same time, their aspiration to resemble the latter in order to establish their respectability is analyzed in *Short Cycle Higher Education: A Search for Identity* (1973). A parallel project dealing with structural reforms of postgraduate studies led to *Post Graduate Education: Structures and Policies* (1972).

The OECD activities concerning new structures of postsecondary education culminated in a major intergovernmental conference, held in 1973. The proceedings —including a secretariat paper updating the 1971 report—were published in *Policies for Higher Education: General Report* (1974). The background studies appeared in two other volumes: *Structure of Studies and Place of Research in Mass Higher Education* (1974) and *Towards Mass Higher Education: Issues and Dilemmas* (1974).

The relationship between higher education and employment continued throughout the years to be an area of major concern of OECD. The various studies prepared under this special program were presented to a conference held in Venice in 1971 and were subsequently published: *Utilization of Highly Qualified Manpower* (1973). In 1974 the educational activities of the Directorate for Scientific Affairs were integrated into the newly created Directorate for Social Affairs, Manpower and Education, whose work on postsecondary education was set in a broader social perspective and more closely linked with employment and social programs.

Parallel to the work on structural reforms undertaken within the Directorate for Scientific Affairs, CERI undertook investigations in two areas concerning higher education: structure of studies and institutional management. In the early 1970s the center examined the conceptual and methodological problems involved in developing interdisciplinary studies. The results appear in the volume *Interdisciplinarity: Problems of Teaching and Research in Universities* (1972). Specific applications of this study were published in *Environmental Education at University Level: Trends and Data* (1973) and *Environmental Problems and Higher Education* (1975). A concept of regional health universities was also developed to ensure better coordination between education and the health care systems. The first results appeared in *New Directions in Education for Changing Health Care Systems* (1975). Future work will focus on the role of postsecondary institutions in socioeconomic regional development.

In 1969 CERI launched a program on institutional management in higher education to aid participating universities in the management of their own affairs and to provide for a wider dissemination of practical methods of institutional management. The initial phase, in which eight universities cooperated, emphasized research into the development of new management techniques. The findings of this research, completed at the end of 1971, appear in the series Studies in Institutional Management in Higher Education.

By 1975, with over one hundred institutions of higher education in seventeen countries participating, the activities of the institutional management program were expanded to include professional seminars for training university personnel responsible for management. Seminars held in 1973, 1974, and 1975 were devoted to program budgets for university management and planning, models and simulated decision making for institutional management in higher education, and information systems for institutions of higher education. Future seminars will deal with problems of organizing student counseling services and management of research in universities.

Information services are offered to participating institutions to improve their knowledge of methods and approaches to problem solving in the field of university management. In addition to publishing a quarterly bulletin, the program also issues special topic reports and surveys. An inquiry service provides users with information about current management practices in different countries in subject areas of interest to the user. Exchanges of specialist personnel, including North American–European exchanges, are also arranged. Finally, the program organizes international meetings, including special topic workshops and biannual general conferences.

2 rue André-Pascal
75775 Paris, France

DOROTEA FURTH

ORGANIZATION OF AFRICAN UNITY

The Organization of African Unity (OAU) was founded in May 1963 at Addis Ababa by representatives of thirty-two African governments. Previous organizations that grouped African states were the Conference of Independent African States; Union of African States; African States of the Casablanca Charter; Casablanca, African, and Malagasy Union; and Organization of Inter-African and Malagasy States. OAU was formed to defend its members' sovereign and territorial rights; eliminate colonialism; promote international cooperation; and coordinate and harmonize the economic, diplomatic, educational, health, welfare, scientific, and defense policies.

OAU membership includes forty-two countries on the African continent. The Assembly of Heads of State and Government meets annually. The Council of Ministers, composed of foreign and/or other ministers, meets twice a year. It prepares meetings of, and is responsible to, the Assembly of Heads of State and Government. Member states fund OAU in accordance with their United Nations assessment. OAU has three specialized commissions: the Economic and Social Commission; the Educational, Cultural, Scientific, and Health Commission; and the Defense Commission. Each of these commissions meets every two years to deal with African problems. The secretariat prepares studies and position papers to present to the commissions or to the Council of Ministers. The Scientific, Technical, and Research Commission is a subcommission under OAU structure. Cooperation is maintained with a number of African organizations.

ORGANIZATION OF AMERICAN STATES

The Organization of American States (OAS) was created in Bogotá, Colombia, in 1948. Its history can be traced to 1889 with the formation of the international Union of American Republics at the First International Conference of American States in Washington, D.C. The Pan American Union, which acts as OAS general secretariat, was founded in 1910. OAS is made up of twenty-five member nations, with ten nations acting as permanent observers. Member governments are represented by ambassadors and special delegations. The general assembly, meeting annually, decides general action and policy.

Since 1910 the Pan American Union has organized studies, seminars, congresses, conferences, and meetings on a variety of aspects directly connected with universities. These activities, however, were seldom part of an ongoing program; instead, they were mainly isolated efforts sponsored by the union. A more coordinated approach was attempted in 1956 during the second meeting of the OAS *Consejo interamericano cultural* (CIC: Inter-American Cultural Council). CIC recommended, as an overall, long-range goal, the development of integráted educational planning and the establishment of permanent educational statistics. It recommended also that research on higher education be conducted, and the results disseminated, and that periodic meetings among university authorities be organized on various university matters. The landmark Seminar on Over-All Planning for Education, organized by OAS in Washington, D.C., in 1958, was a result of these recommendations. In a series of volumes touching on all educational levels, the seminar made several recommendations concerning university planning. As a result, the United States Department of State, with the aid of the University of Kansas (Lawrence, Kansas), began a project to bring together Latin and North American university authorities for several weeks each year to discuss common problems.

In 1961, under the administration of United States President John F. Kennedy, the Alliance for Progress set up a special committee to study Latin American higher education and inter-American cooperation. The committee, composed of ten well-known hemisphere leaders in university education, proposed important innovations for regional cooperation and integration and university improvment., Nothing came of the project because the proposals emphasized outright United States grants to Latin American universities, instead of devising conditions that would promote specific goals for institutions.

In 1962 OAS collaborated with UNESCO and the Economic Commission for Latin America (ECLA), in Santiago, Chile, to set up the Conference on Education and Economic and Social Development in Latin America, which strengthened the principle of inter-American cooperation in higher education propagated by the Alliance for Progress. The humanist position on education was supplanted by the proposition that education must be a function of socioeconomic progress, even at the university level.

The widespread implementation of this materialistic concept of education had a strong effect on Latin American higher education, as symbolized by gradual alterations in the charter of the *Unión de universidades de América latina* (UDUAL: Union of Universities of Latin America. In its original charter document, formulated in 1949 in Gratemala, UDUAL stipulated that the Latin American university should ensure human rights, promote friendships among peoples of all nations, and contribute to the esteem of Latin American communities. Furthermore, the university should recognize national and world problems; encourage academic freedom; and develop social consciousness among students. Finally, the university should keep its courses and research attuned to the latest knowledge—but, at the same time, make sure that technical knowledge serves human interests and needs. In the 1960s, instead of furthering the ideals of the charter, UDUAL asked for a special Inter-American Fund for universities south of the United States border. When this proposition failed to materialize, one of the indirect consequences was that UDUAL changed its charter, turning the university away from the humanist position.

During that decade OAS agencies, commissions, conferences, and meetings continued to make global recommendations about continental university improvement. In 1967, at Punta del Este, Uruguay, the heads of the states in attendance asked OAS to organize meetings among experts who could recommend measures to harmonize national study programs and curricula with the goals of Latin American integration.

Contemporary Programs

In 1968, at Maracay, Venezuela, CIC established regional development programs for education, science, technology, and culture. Through the OAS Departments of Educational, Scientific, and Cultural Affairs, CIC administered large-scale technical assistance programs, involving multimillion budgets financed by member states. The Department of Educational Affairs was reorganized and expanded to absorb the new responsibilities placed on it by the *Programa regional de educativo desarrollo* (PREDE: Regional Educational Development Program). The department's activities concentrate on educational administration and planning, basic studies, technical education, adult education, educational research, curriculum improvement, preparation and dissemination of educational material, educational technology, and higher education.

University modernization. OAS, through PREDE, has promoted technical assistance in the fields of university organization and administration, directed specifically toward the establishment of more efficient university structure and management.

University administration. OAS suggested short or graduate courses and national or multinational seminars on principles and techniques of university administration. These activities were organized at the request of interested institutions and/or approved PREDE projects, to clarify concepts, arouse interest on a continental scale, promote exchanges of ideas and experiences, facilitate interinstitutional cooperation, publish specialized texts, stimulate research, and help new institutions.

Seminars. A multinational seminar, U.S.

College and University Curriculum Improvement Toward Increased International Awareness, Interest, and Understanding, was organized by the American Association of State Colleges and Universities and held at the Autonomous University of Guadalajara in 1972, in Gradalajara, Mexico. Two national seminars for rectors of Mexican universities, promoted by the University of Monterrey, were held in Monterrey, Mexico, in 1970: one on university structure and the other on university administration. A multinational seminar on universities in transition was held by the University of Florida in Gainesville, Florida, in 1970. A multinational seminar on university administration was organized by the *Federación de universidades privadas de América central y Panamá* (FUPAC: Federation of Private Universities of Central America and Panama) in Guatemala in 1970. A First Seminar on University Modernization was promoted in 1972 by the University of Houston, Texas; a multinational First Seminar on University Administration was organized by the Autonomous University of Guadalajara in 1973. An institutional seminar on University Administration was held in 1973 at the Federal University of Santa Maria in Santa Maria, Brazil; and a regional seminar on Principles of University Administration was held in 1973 at the Pontifical Catholic University of Rio Grande do Sul in Pôrto Alegre, Brazil.

These and similar activities received support from university authorities and institutions of higher learning concerned with qualitative and structural improvement. Since higher education has a vital part in the cultural and socioeconomic development of a community, it appears that OAS will increase its efforts in this direction.

University management. In 1975—at the request of the *Asociación de universidades e institutos de investigación del Cariobe* (UNICA: Association of Caribbean Universities and Research Institutes) and with the support of the appropriate agencies of the general secretariat—OAS began a five-year, multinational project in university management in the Caribbean area. The project is designed to help the universities improve their structure, academic content, planning, and administration. In addition, OAS has contributed to the professional improvement of Latin American university staff through exchange programs, including both fellowships for advanced study abroad and noninterest loans provided by the Leo S. Rowe Pan American Fund.

Representative Publications

The organization has published *Latin American Studies in American Institutions of Higher Learning* (1938–39); *Courses on Latin America in Institutions of Higher Education in the United States* (1948–49); and *Latin American Higher Education and Inter-American Cooperation Report* (also published in Spanish), prepared by a special committee in 1961, as a cooperative effort between the United States government and OAS. It also publishes annual lists of universities and university courses in Latin America. Other publications include *la educación superior en América latina,* (1963); *Corrientes de la educación superior en América* (1966); *Inter-American University Cooperation,* a survey of programs of cooperation between institutions of higher education in the United States and Latin America (1968); and *Can Man Transcend His Culture* (1972); also published in Spanish). As a result of the First Seminar on University Administration, cosponsored by OAS and the *Universidad autónoma de Guadalajara* at Lake Chapala, Mexico, in 1973, OAS published *Teoría sobre administración universitaria, 03Administración académica,* and *Financiamiento de la universidad.*

17th Street/Constitution Avenue NW
Washington, D.C. 20006 USA

See also: Agriculture in Higher Education: International Cooperation in Agriculture; Aid to Other Nations; Exchange, International.

ORGANIZATION OF CATHOLIC UNIVERSITIES IN LATIN AMERICA
(Organización de universidades católicas de América latina)

The *Organización de universidades católicas de América latina* (ODUCAL: Organization of Catholic Universities in Latin America) was founded at Santiago, Chile, in September 1953 to promote the activities of Catholic universities in Latin America, to encourage the study of their common problems, and to assist in the cultural and educational progress of the area. Membership in the association consists of some thirty-five Catholic universities in fifteen Latin American countries and Puerto Rico: Argentina, Bolivia, Brazil, Chile, Colombia, Dominican Republic, Ecuador, El Salvador, Guatemala, Mexico, Nicaragua, Panama, Paraguay, Peru, Venezuela, and Puerto Rico. Its executive board consists of a president, two vice-presidents, two counselors who are rectors of universities, and a secretary general. Congresses of the organization are held every two years.

ODUCAL publications include *Anuario, Sapientia,* and *Universitas.*

Pontificia universidad católica argentina
Juncal 1912
Buenos Aires, Argentina

ORGANIZATION OF CENTRAL AMERICAN STATES
(Organización de estados centroamericanos)

Founded in 1951, the *Organización de estados centroamericanos* (ODECA: Organization of Central American States) aims to reestablish the unity of Central America; establish friendly relations by mutual consultations; provide for peaceful settlement of disputes; promote and take joint action for economic, social, cultural, and economic development; and seek common solutions for common problems. Member states are Costa Rica, El Salvador, Guatemala, Honduras, and Nicaragua.

A conference of the heads of government of the five member states makes up the supreme organ of ODECA. Meetings of the Conference of Foreign Ministers take place every year to initiate and consider proposals and to elect a secretary general. At the July 1973 meeting held in San Salvador, the Conference of Foreign Ministers decided to abolish the post of secretary general and to set up a commission to reorganize ODECA.

The executive council, composed of

the foreign ministers of the five republics, is responsible for the policy of the organization and the election of the president each year. This council may meet as often as once a week. The legislative council, composed of three members of the legislative assemblies of each of the member states, advises on legislative matters and studies the possibilities of uniform legislation in the Central American States. Other councils in the structure of ODECA are the Central American Court of Justice, composed of the presidents of the supreme courts of each member state; the Economic Council, which plans and coordinates the economic integration of Central America; and the Monetary Council, composed of the presidents of the central banks of the member countries, which operates the Central American Clearing Houses.

Among the other bodies that bring together the ministers of the member countries for their particular concerns are various councils or commissions for culture and education, defense, labor and social welfare, tourism, government, migration and internal affairs, agriculture, health, infrastructure, geography, cartography, and communications.

Publications include *Boletín informativo laboral, Boletín informativo de salud, Boletín informativo de educación* (all quarterly), and *Memoria,* an annual.

Pino Alto, Paseo Escalón
San Salvador, El Salvador

ORIGINS OF HIGHER EDUCATION
See History of Higher Education; Philosophies of Higher Education, Contemporary and Historical; Religious Influences in Higher Education.

OSTEOPATHIC MEDICINE
(Field of Study)

A meaningful definition of osteopathic medicine must clarify the similarities and differences between it and allopathic medicine. Doctors of osteopathy (D.O.s) and doctors of medicine (M.D.s) have the same goals—to diagnose, treat, cure, and prevent diseases, relieve pain, and improve and preserve health. Osteopathic and allopathic physicians are licensed in the United States to employ any recognized modality in the treatment of disease, including pharmaceuticals, X ray, and surgery.

Webster's *New World Dictionary* defines allopathy as the "treatment of disease by remedies that produce effects different from or opposite to those produced by the disease." The principles of osteopathic medicine are consistent with this definition, but the osteopathic physician would add the following principles about the structural integrity of the musculoskeletal system and its effects upon health and illness in the human body: (1) the human body is a unit in which structure and function are interdependent; (2) the body, through a complex equilibrial system, tends to be self-regulatory and self-healing; (3) adequate function of body systems depends upon the unimpeded flow of blood and nerve impulses; (4) the musculoskeletal system is one of the several body systems, and its importance far exceeds that of framework and support; and (5) local or distant components of disease, which not only manifest the disease but also contribute to and/or maintain it, should be treated. These principles of osteopathic medicine result in a "holistic" view, attributed to Hippocrates, which recognizes that the body is a complexly interrelated community of organs and systems, each dependent upon the other, each contributing to the other, each compensating to meet the demands of internal and external stress. A specific organ may become the central focus of illness, but the effects of the illness are felt in varying degrees throughout the body.

The osteopathic profession recognizes that the musculoskeletal system (bones, joints, connective tissues, skeletal muscles, and tendons) plays an important role in the body's continuous effort to resist and overcome illness and disease. This largest body of systems reflects internal illness and may actually aggravate or accelerate the process of disease. The use of manipulative therapy or biomechanics in diagnosis and treatment, therefore, is an integral part of the osteopathic concept.

The American Osteopathic Association (AOA), the national political and accrediting organization for the osteopathic profession, is recognized by the United States Office of Education and the Commission of Postsecondary Education as the only official accrediting body for all educational programs within the osteopathic profession. In 1975 there were fourteen separate boards of certification for osteopathic specialties in anesthesiology; dermatology; general practice; internal medicine (cardiologists, gastroenterologists, urologists, or nephrologists); neurology and psychiatry (neurologists and psychiatrists, neurologists, pediatric psychiatrists, and psychiatrists); nuclear medicine; obstetrics and gynecology (obstetricians and gynecologists, obstetrical-gynecological surgeons); ophthalmology and otorhinolaryngology (ophthalmologists, otorhinolaryngologists, and otolaryngologists); pathology (anatomic pathologists, and laboratory medical specialists, cytopathologists, forensic pathologists); pediatrics; proctology; radiology (diagnostic roentgenologists, radiologists, and roentgenologists); rehabilitation medicine; and surgery (general surgeons, neurosurgeons, thoracic surgeons, plastic surgeons, cardiovascular surgeons, and urological surgeons). These recognized fields of specialty and subspecialty practice in osteopathic medicine correspond generally to their allopathic counterparts. More than 75 percent of osteopathic physicians are general practitioners, and colleges of osteopathic medicine stress general practice, its importance, and the shortage of primary care physicians in America.

The American Association of Colleges of Osteopathic Medicine represents the nine colleges of osteopathic medicine located in the United States: Chicago College of Osteopathic Medicine (Chicago, Illinois); College of Osteopathic Medicine and Surgery (Des Moines, Iowa); Kansas City College of Osteopathic Medicine (Kansas City, Missouri); Kirksville College of Osteopathic Medicine (Kirksville, Missouri); Michigan State University College of Osteopathic Medicine (East Lansing, Michigan); Oklahoma College of Osteopathic Medicine and Surgery (Tulsa, Oklahoma); Philadelphia College of Osteopathic Medicine (Philadelphia, Pennsylvania); Texas College of Osteopathic Medicine (Fort Worth, Texas); West Virginia School of Osteopathic Medicine (Lewisburg). There are also 224 osteopathic hospitals in the United States.

Osteopathic medicine and allopathic medicine share many concerns with the following professions: dentistry, optometry, pharmacy, podiatry, veterinary medicine, nursing, physical therapy, paramedical personnel, clinical psychology, public health, social work, occupational therapy, and speech therapy. Relationships among these professional groups vary. Some may be employed by others to provide a special service for patients. Some may join together in a partnership or group practice.

Because of the relatively limited financial resources and the comparatively small number of practitioners of osteopathic medicine, extensive research programs have not been undertaken. Osteopathic medical research tends to concentrate in the basic sciences on topics which ordinarily would not be studied outside the field; for example, the various phases of interrelationship between structure and function, the anatomy and function of nerve-muscle junctions, the transmission of nervous impulses, somatic reflex functions, renal (kidney) growth and function, and blood flow dynamics. There are, moreover, clinical studies of structural findings in hospitalized patients, the effects of manipulation under anesthesia for specific orthopedic problems, the effect of osteopathic manipulation on hypertension, and management of chronic obstructive lung disease by regular medical means, with and without osteopathic manipulation.

Within the area of osteopathic medical research are many basic scientists—biologists, biochemists, physiologists, pharmacologists, microbiologists, and anatomists. Furthermore, principles of osteopathic medicine have been incorporated into educational programs for allopathic physicians and other health professionals.

Osteopathic medicine began in the United States as a movement against the rather primitive and limited drugs and surgical techniques employed in the nineteenth century. Serving as an army physician during the Civil War, Andrew Still Taylor was appalled by the number of patients for whom nothing could be done. He began an intensive study of the muscular and skeletal systems, and returned to the Hippocratic concept of the whole man—when one body system is in dysfunction, it affects another system. The solution, he concluded, was to treat the initial problem instead of the symptoms. He approached various medical colleges, hoping to incorporate his ideas into the current medical curriculum; after repeated rejection, he decided in 1892 to establish a new medical college in Kirksville, Missouri, where, with an enrollment of eighteen, he began conferring the Doctor of Osteopathy degree. Although osteopathic medicine struggled against the opposition of other medical and health professions, it now has equal recognition and benefits with allopathic medicine in the United States. There were more than 14,000 osteopathic physicians licensed and practicing in America in 1975.

The Michigan State University College of Osteopathic Medicine and the Philadelphia College of Osteopathic Medicine are involved in interdisciplinary programs. At Michigan State University, the College of Osteopathic Medicine is located on the same campus with a college of allopathic medicine and a college of veterinary medicine, and cross registration between the health professional schools is encouraged. The Philadelphia College of Osteopathic Medicine participates in the Philadelphia Interdisciplinary Health and Education Program, established in 1972–73 to "develop multiple and effective use of existing facilities, faculties, and curriculum programs and educational programs among the disciplines for interdisciplinary and team health care delivery purposes." Other participants are the Medical College of Pennsylvania, Pennsylvania College of Optometry, Philadelphia College of Pharmacy and Science, Pennsylvania College of Podiatric Medicine, Temple University (health records and administration, medi-

cal technology, occupational therapy, pharmacy, and physical therapy), and the University of Pennsylvania (dental medicine, nursing, social work).

Some of the colleges offer an accelerated program. The undergraduate osteopathic medical curriculum normally requires four academic years for completion, but under the accelerated program a student completes all required courses in thirty-six months of continuous study. Persons with Ph.D. degrees in one of the basic sciences are sometimes awarded advanced credit in osteopathic medical education programs.

Osteopathic medicine developed in the United States, and the largest numbers of schools and physicians are located within its boundaries. Doctors of osteopathy practicing in Canada receive their education at one of the colleges of osteopathic medicine in the United States. The Canadian Osteopathic Association was recognized in 1970, and the scope of practice of osteopathic physicians varies from province to province.

In the United Kingdom there are two schools of osteopathic medicine. Entrants to the British School of Osteopathy require only a secondary school education; their four-year course is limited to manipulative therapy and diagnosis, and their practice is limited to these areas. The London College of Osteopathy limits its entrants to those with an M.D. degree; the fourteen-month course is a postgraduate training program that stresses the musculoskeletal system and manipulative therapy. Graduates are accepted into the British system of socialized medicine and have unlimited practice rights. Both groups may belong to the British Osteopathic Association.

In other countries, regulation varies greatly. While the practice of osteopathic medicine as such is not provided for by law outside the countries already discussed, osteopathic physicians practice in many other places, including Africa and India. In addition, osteopathic medical research has been undertaken in the United Kingdom and the Federal Republic of Germany, as well as in the United States.

The minimal basic science and clinical educational requirements for graduation from a college or osteopathic medicine are the satisfactory completion of courses in the following: history, basic theory, and practice of osteopathic medicine; human anatomy; biochemistry; pharmacology; physiology; pathology; microbiology; physical diagnosis; clinical and laboratory diagnosis; medicine; pediatrics; obstetrics and gynecology; preventive medicine; public health; psychiatry; surgery; radiology; medical ethics; and legal medicine. The education of clinical clerks in facilities specifically approved by the American Osteopathic Association is included in the four-year undergraduate osteopathic medical program.

WILLIAM B. STRONG

Major International and National Organizations

American Association of Colleges of
  Osteopathic Medicine
Suite 609, 4720 Montgomery Lane
Washington, D.C. 20014 USA

American Osteopathic Association
212 East Ohio Street
Chicago, Illinois 60611 USA

Australian Osteopathic Association
4 Collins Street
Melbourne, Victoria, Australia

British Osteopathic Association
24–25 Dorset Square
London NW1, England

Canadian Osteopathic Association
575 Waterloo Street
London, Ontario, Canada N6B 2R2

Principal Information Sources

GENERAL

For a general discussion of osteopathy and related fields and the educational requirements for the field see:

Blake, J. B., and Roos, C. (Eds.) *Medical Reference Works 1679–1966: A Selected Bibliography.* Chicago: Medical Library Association, 1967. *Supplement I* (1967–1968), compiled by M. V. Clark, 1970; *Supplement II* (1969–1972), compiled by J. S. Richmond, 1973; *Supplement III* (1973–1974), compiled by J. S. Richmond, 1975.
Fact Sheet. Chicago: American Osteopathic Association, 1970. Supplies statistical information on physicians, education, research, and hospitals for the field.
Heffel, L. E. *Opportunities in Osteopathic Medicine Today.* Louisville, Kentucky: Data Courier, 1974.
Norton, L. T. *The Use of Medical Literature.* Ham-

den, Connecticut: Archon, 1974.
World Health Organization. *Publications: Catalog 1947–1973.* Geneva: WHO, 1974. Supplement, 1974–75.

For a history and overview of the field see:

Northrup, G. W. *Osteopathic Medicine: An American Reformation.* Chicago: American Osteopathic Association, 1966.

Introductions to the field include:

Cayce, H. T., and Still, A. T. *Osteopathy: Comparative Concepts.* Virginia Beach, Virginia: A.R.E. Press, 1973.
Hoag, J. M., and others. (Eds.) *Osteopathic Medicine.* New York: McGraw-Hill, 1969.
Stoddard, A. *Manual of Osteopathic Practice.* London: Hutchinson, 1969.

CURRENT BIBLIOGRAPHIES

The following journals publish indexes to the literature for the field:

D.O.: A Publication for Osteopathic Physicians and Surgeons. Chicago: American Osteopathic Association, 1927–.
Journal of the American Osteopathic Association. Chicago: American Osteopathic Association, 1901–.

In addition see:

Excerpta Medica. Amsterdam: Excerpta Medica Foundation, 1947–.
Index Medicus. Bethesda, Maryland: National Library of Medicine, 1960–.

PERIODICALS

A sampling of the important journals for the field includes *D.O.: A Publication for Osteopathic Physicians and Surgeons* (US), *Health* (US), *Journal of the American Osteopathic Association* (US), *Osteopathic Annals* (US), *Osteopathic Hospitals* (US), *Osteopathic Physician* (US), *Osteopathic Symposium* (US).

For related journals in the field see:

Ulrich's International Periodicals Directory. New York: Bowker, biennial.
World Medical Periodicals. (3rd ed.) New York: World Medical Association, 1961. Supplement, 1968.

DICTIONARIES, ENCYCLOPEDIAS, HANDBOOKS

Among the most respected English-language medical dictionaries are:

Dorland's Illustrated Medical Dictionary. (25th ed.) Philadelphia: Saunders, 1974.
Stedman, T. L. *Stedman's Medical Dictionary.* (23rd ed.) Baltimore: Williams & Wilkins, 1976.

DIRECTORIES

American Osteopathic Association Yearbook and Di-

rectory of Osteopathic Specialists. Chicago: American Osteopathic Association, annual. A biographical directory that includes a list of all colleges of osteopathic medicine and organizations for the field.

Journal of the American Osteopathic Association (JAOA) Education Annual. Chicago: American Osteopathic Association, annual. A discussion of all aspects of osteopathic education and licensure.

RESEARCH CENTERS, INSTITUTES, INFORMATION CENTERS

A. T. Still Osteopathic Foundation and Research Institute
212 East Ohio Street
Chicago, Illinois 60611 USA

Also see:

Medical Research Index. (4th ed.) Guernsey: Francis Hodgson, 1971. Contains general information on medical research.

OVERSEAS ACADEMIC PROGRAMS

See Exchange, International: Study Abroad.

OVERSEAS DEVELOPMENT COUNCIL, United States

The Overseas Development Council (ODC) is an independent, nonprofit organization established in 1969 to increase American understanding of the economic and social problems confronting the developing countries and the importance of these countries to the United States in an increasingly interdependent world. ODC seeks to promote consideration of development issues by the American public, policymakers, specialists, educators, and the media through research, conferences, publications, and liaison with United States mass media membership organizations interested in relations with the developing world. The ODC staff works closely with newspapers, radio, television, and several major opinion groups.

The council is not a grant-making or project-funding organization. Its program is funded by foundations, corporations, and private individuals. Policies are determined by a board of directors.

At the request of the Agency for International Development and a number of private voluntary agencies, the council conducts a series of workshops to enhance the development capability of these agencies. With the support of the Lilly Endowment, the council is making a study of the longer-range potential of voluntary agencies—both individually and in cooperation with one another and other organizations—to help programs of developing countries.

ODC has conducted meetings on such subjects as the world food crisis, energy, and international agricultural research. With the Carnegie Endowment for International Peace the council cosponsored a series of meetings on international economics for private specialists, government officials, members of the United States Congress, and United Nations representatives. With the support of the Aspen Institute for Humanistic Studies, the council convened a meeting of American religious groups on issues of global poverty and social justice. In addition, ODC has initiated a seminar series for representatives of nongovernmental organizations in Washington, D.C., to provide current information and a forum for the exchange of ideas; established a program of visiting fellows to enable specialists from government and universities to spend a year or more in Washington doing research on policy issues; and worked closely with national and international groups such as the Society for International Development, World Council of Churches, and Overseas Development Institute in Great Britain.

Publications of the council include *Agenda for Action,* annual assessment of American relations with low-income countries; *By Bread Alone,* study of the world food problem; *In the Human Interest,* used as a background document for United Nations Population Conference; *Overseas Development Council Studies,* compilation of ODC monographs; *Focusing on Global Policy and Development: A Resource Book for Educators,* book-length set of materials for use in secondary schools; *Global Justice and Development,* report of an interreligious meeting held at Aspen, Colorado; and *Beyond Dependency: The Developing World Speaks Out,* by scholars from developing countries.

1717 Massachusetts Avenue NW
Washington, D.C. 20036 USA

P

PAINTING

See Drawing and Painting (field of study).

PAKISTAN, ISLAMIC REPUBLIC OF

Population: 64,900,000 (1972 census). Student enrollment in primary school: 4,440,000; secondary school (academic, vocational, technical): 1,415,000; higher education (university): 302,900. Student enrollment in higher education as percentage of age group (18–21): 2%. Language of instruction: Urdu and English. Academic calendar: September to June. Percentage of gross national product (GNP) expended on education: 1.7% (1972). [Unless otherwise indicated, figures are for 1973.]

The history of education in the Islamic Republic of Pakistan can be traced to the rise of Islamic culture on the Indian subcontinent. After the formal founding of Islam in A.D. 622, Muslim Arabs spread its teachings from the Middle East to Central Asia. Scholarship started in religious schools there for interpretation of the Muslim holy book, the Koran. These religious schools were the source of Islamic education on the Indian subcontinent until in 1875, Sayyid Ahmad Khan established the Anglo-Oriental College in Aligarh to provide higher education based on the British model. By the year 1920 this college had become a leading institution for the training of British government workers and the

nucleus of the early leadership of the country. When Pakistan achieved independence from England in 1947, the country had two universities, twenty professional colleges, and eighty-three colleges of arts and science, with a total enrollment of 37,102 students. By 1960 Pakistan had developed its system of higher education into 6 universities, with an enrollment of about 7400, and 209 colleges, with an enrollment of 110,000. In order to improve the output of technical manpower, thirteen polytechnical institutions were opened between 1958 and 1963.

But along with this growth, many problems became noticeable during the developmental period. Specific problems noted in 1959 by the Commission on National Education, a government advisory body, were (1) an overemphasis on memorization at the expense of mastery of principles and (2) student and parent prejudice against manual labor, which impeded acceptance of higher technical learning. Moreover, a major disruption of the system of higher education occurred in 1971, when the eastern part of the country separated from Pakistan to become Bangladesh.

By the end of 1972 Pakistan had 8 universities, 354 colleges of arts and science, and 172 professional colleges. However, when assessing educational development in 1972, the government criticized Pakistan's educational progress. On March 15,

1972, in a speech announcing the introduction of a new educational policy, President Z. A. Bhutto stated that "ever since we gained independence, education has remained almost the most neglected sector in the body politic of our country. For a long time, the obsolete idea of producing an educated class from amongst the privileged few to constitute the elite in the country remained the cornerstone of our educational system. This was a heritage of colonialism" (quoted in Baloch, 1972, p. 2).

The new policy for the period 1972 to 1980 was designed to rectify past failings. More than 50 percent of the age group had remained without formal schooling; as a result, the country had almost forty million illiterate citizens. The new plan incorporated a number of literacy programs outside the formal school system but also included provision for universal education until grade 5 for boys by 1979 and for girls by 1984.

The plan also was designed to correct the imbalance of graduates in the higher education sector. Some 61 percent of graduates had been enrolled in arts programs, to the detriment of technological study. To provide the manpower needed for a developing nation, the government proposed to increase enrollments in technological study to 42 percent of total enrollments, while 30 percent of students would be enrolled in science. Accordingly, the plan called for the establishment of new universities: the Agriculture College of Tandojam was to be raised to university status, as were the engineering colleges in Sind and Karachi. In addition to existing university centers, new universities were planned for Multan, Saidu, and Sukkur. Open universities on the pattern of the British Open University also were envisioned.

Due to a lack of financing, the timetable for this ambitious program has not been followed. However, steps have been taken to achieve a more coordinated planning of higher education by the establishment of a University Grants Commission, and standards in the universities have been raised

by the introduction of university centers of excellence and university area study centers.

National Educational Policy

Educational policy in Pakistan must be understood within the framework of a socialistic state based on Islamic ideology. Included in this ideology are the beliefs that all are equal in the eyes of Allah, that education is necessary for everybody, that man is free to develop his own potential, and that all are entitled to the necessities of life.

Higher education policy is determined by the 1972–1980 Education Policy set forth by the federal government. This policy includes the following provisions: access to education is to be more equitable; academic freedom is to be accorded to the higher institutions within a structure of national security; faculty, students, and community are to be allowed to participate in the administration of higher institutions; college enrollment is to be directed into fields such as science, agriculture, and technology; youth are to be taught respect for physical labor and are to be trained as leaders of environmental and social improvement programs.

Legal Basis of Educational System

A number of legal measures have been introduced to implement the educational plan for 1972–1980. The legal acts and ordinances establishing the universities were amended during 1972 and 1973. In addition, legal measures established the University Grants Commission (1973), university centers of excellence (1973), university area study centers (1974), and the National Educational Council (1974).

Types of Institutions

Higher education in Pakistan is available in eight universities, seven of which are under provincial control: University of Karachi (1951), University of Sind in Jamshoro, Hyderabad (1947), University of Baluchistan in Quetta (1970), University of the Punjab in Lahore (1882), University of Peshawar (1950), Pakistan University of Engineering and Technology in Lahore (1961), Pakistan Agricultural University in Lyallpur (1961). The University of Islamabad (1965) is administered by the federal government.

Nonuniversity higher education is offered by polytechnics, Oriental-language colleges, religious *madrassa*, institutions for the training of technical and primary teachers, and vocational schools.

Relationship with Secondary Education and Admission Requirements

After five years of elementary school, students enter one of four types of secondary school programs leading to postsecondary education: comprehensive high schools, pilot schools, public/cadet schools, and general high schools. Their curricula emphasize Islamic studies as well as science, vocational, and technical subjects. Upon successful completion of secondary school, students receive the Secondary School Certificate. Graduation from secondary school generally is at age fifteen. Students may then enter a two-year intermediate college, which serves to prepare them for university study; or they may enter technical institutes, which offer a three-year program. At the end of intermediate college, those students, who wish to enter a university, sit for the Higher Secondary School Certificate examination.

The Secondary School Certificate is the minimum requirement for admission to all types of formal nonuniversity institutions of higher education and to the intermediate colleges. For admission to colleges of Oriental languages and *madrassa*, no fixed criteria are prescribed. For professional and degree study the minimum entrance requirement is the Higher Secondary School Certificate.

Administration and Control

Education has been the responsibility of the provinces in the past. However, according to the 1973 constitution, a number of important matters in the educational sphere have been placed on the Concurrent Legislative List, which gives the federal parliament the power to make laws related to policy, planning, curriculum, syllabi, books, centers of excellence, standards of education, and Islamic education. As in the time before the new constitution was established, the federal government continues to be the overall policymaking, coordinating, and advisory authority.

The University Grants Commission and the National Educational Council assist the federal Ministry of Education in planning and execution of educational policies. The University Grants Commission, as envisioned under the Education Policy, is designed to guide and control university development and, as a body distinct from the national government, to protect universities from undue political interference. It distributes government grants to the universities, gives advice on the establishment of new institutions or the expansion of older ones, and has the power to inspect faculties and accounts and to withdraw funding.

The provincial governors are the chancellors, and the provincial ministers of education are the pro-chancellors of the provincial universities. The president of the Islamic Republic of Pakistan is chancellor of the federal University of Islamabad. Chancellors appoint the university vice-chancellors and may preside over the convocation meetings of the university senates. The chancellors also appoint the treasurers and exercise financial control over revision of staff salary scales.

Direct administration and control of the general arts and science and some professional colleges (medical and agricultural) is exercised by the Provincial Departments of Education through the directors of education. Generally, however, the professional colleges are run by the respective provincial departments, such as Health and Agriculture. For departmental institutions of higher learning there is a board of governors for each institution to supervise the standards of education and other matters.

Internally, the vice-chancellor of each university exercises the administrative authority. He is guided by the university senate and by the main executive body of the university, the syndicate; the senate and the syndicate are composed of the representatives of university teachers, affiliated colleges, students, registered graduates, and nominees of the chancellor. Academic councils and boards of studies lay down the policies of admission, prescribe courses of study, and deal with other related academic matters subject to approval by the syndicate.

Constituent colleges of universities are directly controlled by the university, while the affiliated colleges are under the administrative control of provincial governments, the federal government, or their respective administrative boards. The academic council of the university appoints an affiliation committee, which makes annual inspections of each institution, evaluates the standard of education, and recommends improvements for granting further affiliation. Internally the university colleges are administered by principals.

As a result of the implementation of the Education Policy, there are no longer any private colleges, with one or two exceptions, since all education in the country has been nationalized and private institutions have been taken over by the government.

Programs and Degrees

Broad fields of study at institutions of higher education in Pakistan are arts and humanities, social sciences, natural sciences, medical science, education, engineering, agriculture, technology, and religion. Academic programs end with an award of the Bachelor of Arts (B.A.) or Bachelor of Science (B.Sc.) degree after two years of study or the bachelor's degree with honors after three years of study. Subsequent to receiving a bachelor's degree, a student may go on to two years of study for the Master of Arts (M.A.) or Master of Science (M.Sc.) degree; upon successful completion of either of these programs, he may then pursue three to five years of additional study for the doctoral degree.

Study for professional degrees includes the one-year program for the bachelor's degree in education, which a student may pursue after receiving the Bachelor of Arts or Bachelor of Science degree; the one-year program for the master's degree in education, for those who have received the bachelor's degree in education; and the doctoral programs in education offered by the University of Sind and the University of the Punjab. Others are the four-year program for the Bachelor of Science degree in agriculture; the two-year program for the master's degree in agriculture, which demands the Bachelor of Science degree in agriculture as a prerequisite; the four-year program for the bachelor's degree in engineering; and the five-year program for the bachelor's degree in medicine and surgery.

Students who are pursuing a bachelor's or master's degree must pass an examination each year in order to graduate into the next-higher class. This means that while taking four years of courses in academic programs toward the two degrees, students must pass four examinations in their subject area.

In addition to the above university programs, diploma courses in different fields are offered by the universities and departmental boards of education. The duration of these programs is one to three years. The *madrassa* offer instruction in Islamic law and literature to prospective *imams* (spiritual leaders) of Islam.

Financing and Student Financial Aid

The main sources of financing higher education are the annual grant from the provincial government, specific grants from the University Grants Commission, and student fees. Private contributions are negligible. Grants-in-aid for specific projects may be arranged by the national government through UNESCO and friendly foreign countries.

There are different types of scholarships instituted by the federal and provincial governments for talented students; in addition, interest-free loan schemes are provided. Certain philanthropic agencies and enterprises award scholarships to special categories of students, such as minorities, children of deceased army officers, and employees' children.

Loans advanced to the students by the federal government are to be paid back in easy installments after the students are employed. Each recipient of a scholarship for foreign study must serve the country for at least three to five years upon returning from abroad.

Student Social Background and Access to Education

Although the population of Pakistan is predominantly Muslim, there are some Hindus, Buddhists, and Christians. Languages include the universally spoken Urdu and the regional languages: Punjabi, Baluchi, Pashtu, and Sindhi.

Higher education is open to all students, irrespective of caste, creed, or color. Participation of women in higher education is comparatively low; in 1972–73, only 2.17 percent of the age group was enrolled at the secondary level.

Each institution of higher learning has a student union composed of elected representatives. The main activities of the student union are educational, social, and cultural. Under the new university acts, students have been given representation on the university syndicate and senate.

Teaching Staff and Research Activities

Teaching personnel in educational institutions from primary schools to colleges, including professional colleges, are government servants. University teachers are employees of autonomous bodies. Thus, the appointing authority at the college level is the secretary of education in the province, whereas the university teaching staff are appointed by the syndicate upon the recommendation of the university selection board.

Generally, the initial appointment in the institutions of higher learning is made in the capacity of a lecturer; but initial appointment to the higher grades of assistant professor, associate professor, and profes-

sor can be made by the appropriate authority on the basis of qualifications. In colleges promotions generally are made on the basis of seniority. In the universities appointment to a higher rank is made on the basis of qualifications and research experience; seniority is not the main criterion.

Pay scales for different categories of teachers are set by the government on a time scale, but for a new entrant the appointing authority may set salary up to the maximum of the salary grade.

To qualify as a university lecturer, a candidate must have a master's degree (M.A. or M.Sc.); a university assistant professor must have a master's degree and six years of experience; a university associate professor must have a doctoral degree and ten years of experience, whereas a full professor must have a doctoral degree and thirteen years of experience. At the college level a lecturer must have a master's degree; an assistant professor and full professor must have a master's degree and seniority.

The tenure of service is twenty-five years of continuous employment, or to the age of fifty-eight; however, the period is extendable. If the work or the conduct of an employee is not satisfactory, he or she can be removed from service.

University teaching staff are required to undertake individual research to obtain promotion and the annual raise in salary. The University Grants Commission and international agencies for education, including the World Health Organization (WHO) and the United Nations Children's Fund (UNICEF), provide funds to individual teachers and institutions for educational research of national importance.

Current Problems and Trends

A chronic problem within the universities is overemphasis on the end-of-the-year external examinations. They sometimes have become more important than the research and teaching functions of the institutions; students tend to focus on examinations and fail subsequently to apply learning to practical activities.

Access of women to higher education has

been limited by the institution of *purdah* (seclusion of women). Although coeducation exists at the primary and tertiary levels, it is less common at the secondary level.

A lack of vocational guidance has resulted in failures, low academic achievement, and an imbalance between the manpower needs of the country and the output from the universities. The high percentage of arts graduates has resulted in unemployment for graduates. Pakistan has also been affected by a large migration of manpower to industrialized countries.

All these problems have been recognized in a number of studies undertaken by various government commissions since independence. Reforms similar to those proposed in the 1972–1980 Education Policy have been proposed by previous administrations but have not been implemented. The present Education Policy, however, has led to extensive innovations, including the establishment of the University Grants Commission, nationalization of all private colleges, creation of new universities, a planned expansion of existing colleges into universities, revision of higher educational curricula to emphasize science and agrotechnical subjects, and institution of the National Service Corps of Youth to provide education to illiterates. Other planned changes include the use of the national language at higher institutions; increase in enrollments; extension of more financial aid to students; promotion of more in-country research; and reforms in examination and evaluation, libraries, book production, instructional technology, and teacher education.

The new university facilities are planned eventually to serve all geographical areas of the country. They are planned to include new institutions at Multan, Saidu, and Sukkur; and new agriculture and engineering universities established on existing agriculture and engineering college sites at Tandojam, Karachi, Sind, Jamshoro, and Peshawar. Moreover, establishment of centers of excellence in the natural and social sciences and area study centers is projected for existing universities. Thus, the University of the Punjab is to be a center of excellence in solid-state physics and mathematics and will focus on the Indo-Pak subcontinent as an area of study; the University of Karachi is planned as a center of excellence in marine biology and will focus on Europe as an area of study; the University of Sind will specialize in analytical chemistry and the Far East and Southeast Asia; the University of Peshawar, on geology and Central Asia; the University of Baluchistan, on mineralogy and the Middle East and Arab countries; and the University of Islamabad, on Africa and North and South America.

Relationship with Industry

Until recently, there was no cooperation between industry and educational institutions. However, under the National Development Volunteer Program scheme, educational institutions and industrial concerns cooperate in providing on-the-job training.

Very little financial aid has been given by industry to the educational institutions, except in the form of occasional donations. Nevertheless, the considerable impact of industrial development has resulted in increased enrollment in scientific and technical courses.

International Cooperation

Under bilateral programs, scholarships are awarded to scholars for higher education in a number of countries abroad and substantial exchanges of professors and students are taking place. For instance, more than three thousand Pakistani students attended universities in the United States in 1973–74. UNESCO has extended assistance to the University of Islamabad. The organization has awarded fellowships as well as the services of experts in fields such as topography and computer applications.

Pakistan is a member of the Colombo Plan for Co-operative Economic Development in South and Southeast Asia. Under the plan, Pakistani students may study abroad in advanced technology programs; equipment also is provided for domestic technical training and research.

[Information supplied by N. A. Baloch, Vice-Chancellor, University of Sind, Hyderabad, Pakistan.]

Educational Associations

All-Pakistan Federation of University Academic
    Staff Associations
University of the Punjab
Lahore, Pakistan

Association of University Professors
8 Zafar Ali Road
Lahore, Pakistan

All-Pakistan Federation of University Women
Frere Road
Karachi, Pakistan

Bibliography

Baloch, N. A. (Ed.) *The Education Policy 1972: Implications and Implementation.* Hyderabad: University of Sind Press, 1972.
Bulletin of the UNESCO Regional Office for Education in Asia. No. 14. Bangkok, Thailand: UNESCO Regional Office, 1973.
Development of Education in Pakistan. Islamabad: Ministry of Education and Scientific Research, Central Bureau of Education, 1971.
Education in Pakistan 1971–73. Islamabad: Ministry of Education, Central Bureau of Education, 1973.
Education Policy 1972–1980. Islamabad: Ministry of Education, 1972.
Further Education of Teachers in Service in Asia: A Regional Survey. Bangkok, Thailand: UNESCO Regional Office, 1973.
Pakistan Education 1974—A Sector Assessment. Islamabad: Ministry of Education, Bureau of Educational Planning, 1974.
Progress of Education in Sind. Karachi: Government of Sind, Education Department, 1973.
Year Book for 1972–1973. Islamabad: Ministry of Education and Provincial Coordination (Education Division), Central Bureau of Education, 1973.
Year Book for 1974. Islamabad: Ministry of Education and Provincial Coordination (Education Division), Research and Evaluation Unit, 1974.

See also: Archives: Africa and Asia, National Archives of; Financing of Higher Education: University Grants Committee; Manpower Planning: Role of International Agencies; South Asia: Regional Analysis.

PANAMA CANAL ZONE

Population: 45,200 (1974 estimate). Student enrollment in primary school: 8000; secondary school: 3000; higher education: 1675. Language of instruction: English and Spanish. [Figures are for 1974–75. Sources: Grant and Lind, 1976; Wade, 1975.]

The Panama Canal Zone, under United States jurisdiction, consists of a strip of land, ten miles wide, five miles on each side of the Panama Canal, which extends through the southern portion of the Central American isthmus. The population of the Canal Zone consists of United States citizens and Panamanian and other Caribbean peoples.

Free schools are operated by the Canal Zone government. These schools are divided into two groups: United States children follow a United States curriculum in English, while the rest of the students follow a Panamanian program and are instructed in Spanish.

The only institution of higher education is Canal Zone College, a coeducational institution operated by the United States government. Students must be residents of the Canal Zone or the Republic of Panama.

Three degrees are granted, two associate degrees and one bachelor's degree. The Associate in Arts in art, behavioral sciences, English, foreign languages, and history is intended for students who will transfer into a Bachelor of Arts program. An Associate in Science is offered in biology, engineering, science, mathematics, physical science, physical education, accounting, business administration, or secretarial administration. This program also is a transfer program preparing for a Bachelor of Science or a terminal scientific degree. A Bachelor of Science in medical technology is offered. Under this program the student is required to serve a one-year internship at an approved school of medical technology.

One-year certificate programs in data processing and secretarial study also are available.

Bibliography

Grant, W. V., and Lind, C. G. *Digest of Education Statistics.* Washington, D.C.: U.S. Government Printing Office, 1976.

Wade, G. H. *Fall Enrollment in Higher Education, 1974.* Washington, D.C.: U.S. Government Printing Office, 1975.

PANAMA, REPUBLIC OF

Population: 1,631,000 (1974 estimate). Student enrollment in primary school: 319,000 (1973); secondary school (academic, vocational, technical): 111,900 (1973); higher education: 22,000 (1973). Language of instruction: Spanish. Academic calendar: April/May to December/ February. Percentage of national budget expended on all education: 22% (1974).

The Republic of Panama, the most southern of the Central American countries, was part of the Spanish empire from the early days of the sixteenth century until 1821, when it broke with Spain and became a province of Colombia. The relationship existed until 1903, when Panama, supported by the United States, declared its independence. Although Panama is geographically part of Central America, its political and economic situation have made it an anomaly in that region. The development of its educational system, therefore, does not reflect the strong regional character manifest in the other five Central American states. During the colonial period Panama was not under the captaincy-general of Guatemala but was part of the viceroyalty of New Granada. In 1749 King Ferdinand VI of Spain authorized the creation of its first institution of higher learning—the Royal and Pontifical University of Saint Xavier, established by the Society of Jesus—which served the country until 1767, when the Jesuits were expelled. During the nineteenth century, when Panama was part of Colombia, a second institution with university status, *Colegio del Ismo* (School of the Isthmus), existed briefly. In 1907, after the separation of Panama from Colombia, a secondary school, the *Instituto nacional* (National Institute), was opened.

After World War I, authorities pressed for the establishment of a Pan-American university in Panama. Although their efforts failed, a school of law was attached to the *Instituto nacional* in 1918. The school closed in 1930, but three years later two new schools—a school of pharmacy and an institute of pedagogy—were opened; and in 1935 a national university, the *Universidad de Panamá* (University of Panama), was founded.

The *Universidad de Panamá* opened in 1936, temporarily utilizing the old facilities of the *Instituto nacional.* Its founder and first rector, Octavia Méndez Pereira, planned for it to become an international university; and in 1943, after a meeting of the Latin American ministers of education, Panama's congress authorized the name change from *Universidad de Panamá* to *Universidad interamericana* (Inter-American University). The true international standing of the institution, however, was never realized; and the constitution of 1946, which granted the university its autonomy, reconfirmed the official name of *Universidad de Panamá.* For the next twenty years it served as the country's only institution of higher learning. In 1965 *Universidad Santa María la Antigua* (Santa Maria la Antigua University) was opened by the authority of the archbishop of Panama.

In the late 1960s Panama was in a state of political and economic turmoil, which was also reflected in higher education. In 1968 the autonomy of the university suffered a serious blow when the grounds were occupied by the military and the authorities stripped of their power. A decree by the *Junta provisional de gobierno* (Provisional Governing Board) in December 1968 temporarily abolished the university and its autonomy. Six months later it was reopened as the official *Universidad de Panamá* by Decree 144 of June 3, 1969, and its reorganization was clarified. In June 1970 the *Estatuto de la Universidad de Panamá* (Statute of the University of Panama) specified in 292 articles the function and structure of the university. The 1970s have seen a growing acceptance of current ideologies, a careful adherence to government policy, and a greater concern for social welfare.

Legal Basis of Educational System

The basic constitutional rights of the 1946 constitution were suspended in 1968 but were restored the following year. The Provisional Governing Board, in its Decree 144 of June 3, 1969, reopened the university, recognized it as the official university of the republic, conceded its autonomy, and granted it control of its own administration and structure. On June 16, 1970, these principles were sanctioned in 292 articles by the *Estatuto de la Universidad de Panamá*. Article 97 of the new constitution of October 11, 1972, reaffirmed the autonomy of the *Universidad de Panamá*, while Article 93 authorized the university to supervise the private universities. Article 98 established the state's financial responsibility toward the university. Article 99 reaffirmed academic freedom in accordance with the rules of the *Estatuto de la Universidad de Panamá*. Decree 16 of July 1963 regulated the constitution and structure of private universities and determined that they should follow the same standards as the *Universidad de Panamá*.

Types of Institutions

Higher education is provided by two universities: the *Universidad de Panamá*, founded 1935, and the private *Universidad Santa María la Antigua*, founded 1965. The state university is divided into faculties, each comprised of one or more schools. The faculties are engineering; architecture; law and political science; medicine; natural sciences and pharmacy (which includes nursing); philosophy, letters, and education; public administration and commerce; and agriculture. *Universidad Santa María la Antigua* consists of departments such as administration, social science, technology, humanities and fine arts, foreign languages, law and political science, natural sciences, religious studies, and physical education.

Relationship with Secondary Education and Admission Requirements

Article 78 of the constitution of 1946 provides that education shall be free and compulsory for children between seven and fifteen years. Private schools are also available and are subject to constitutional provisions in terms of subjects taught and admissions policies.

Primary education consists of six years of basic education. The secondary program is divided into two three-year cycles. The first cycle consists of general education; the second cycle is divided into three programs: an academic program; a professional program in primary teaching and commercial studies; and a vocational program in home economics, agriculture, and trades. The programs lead to a *bachiller* or an equivalent title such as *maestro de primaria* (primary teacher), *perito* (expert), or *bachiller mercantil* (business title).

Admission to the universities is determined by available space and by national needs for human resources (Article 7 of Decree 144). A *bachiller* or the equivalent is required for entrance into the regular faculties and professional schools. In addition, faculties require entrance examinations in specific subjects.

Administration and Control

The administrative structure of the *Universidad de Panamá* is specifically set forth in the university statutes and Decree 144. Article 9 of Decree 144 recognizes the *consejo directivo* (directive council) as the highest administrative authority. The council, which meets once a month, consists of the minister of education, who presides; the rector of the university; one dean elected annually by the academic council; one student elected annually; and three citizens named by the president of the republic for a six-year term. In case of absence, the vice-minister of education substitutes for the minister, the academic vice-rector for the rector. The functions of the council are to elect the rector, approve appointment of the vice-rectors and secretary, supervise the institution, consider the budget, formulate policy, and solicit the opinion of the academic council.

The *consejo universitario* (university council), in accordance with Article 11 of Decree 144, consists of the rector or, in his absence, the academic vice-rector; the deans of the faculties; two full professors from each faculty, elected by the corresponding faculty council by secret ballot during the first five days of the academic year (or by the rector if the election does not take place); and the student with the highest scholastic average from each faculty. The council, which is convened by the rector, reforms statutes, confers degrees, and resolves matters submitted for consideration by the rector.

Article 13 of Decree 144 establishes the structure of the *consejo académico* (academic council). The council consists of the rector, who presides; the academic vice-rector, who presides in the absence of the rector; a representative of the minister of education; the deans of the faculties; the director of the planning office of the university; and two student representatives selected from the ten students with the highest academic average in the university. The function of the council is to supervise teaching effectiveness, authorize teaching staff, approve plans of study, and decide on sabbatical leaves and benefits.

As provided by Article 15 of Decree 144, each faculty has a *junta de facultad* (faculty council), made up of the dean, vice-dean, secretary of the faculty, directors of the schools and departments within the faculty, full-time professors, and one student representative to every ten professors or fraction thereof. The council designs plans of study to be submitted to the academic council, recommends professors for appointment, and formulates regulations for the faculty.

The highest single authority and legal representative of the university is the rector (Article 16 of Decree 144). Elected for a period of five years and eligible for one more term, he directs and coordinates the administration of the university. His specific duties include presiding over sessions of the university and academic councils; supervising the political development of the university; naming the vice-rector, deans, and administrative secretary; appointing teaching staff, on the recommendation of the academic council; formulating budget proposals for consideration of the directive council; and imposing general discipline. The other administrative officers of the university include two vice-rectors, the director of students, and the deans. The deans are appointed by the rector for three-year terms; they represent the faculty and preside over faculty council meetings.

The *Universidad Santa María la Antigua,* which was created as a dependency of the Confederation of Catholic Bishops of Panama and is under the authority of the Archbishop of Panama, has a roughly similar structure. The grand chancellor serves as the highest single administrative authority, and the rector reports directly to him. The administrative structure also includes a *junta de directores* (board of directors) consisting of seventeen members who name the vice-rector, general secretary, and other university officers; a university council; and an academic council. The university is divided into departments rather than faculties, each under a dean.

Programs and Degrees

The declared goal of the universities' programs is to provide professional training. There is a growing movement, however, to also develop general education courses, particularly in humanities, basic sciences, and languages (Benjamin, 1965, p. 99).

The University of Panama awards the first degree or title, the *licenciado,* after approximately four years of study. Professional or subprofessional titles such as civil engineer, electromechanical engineer, and medical laboratory technician also are awarded. The doctoral degree is awarded to licentiates who pass qualifying examinations and present approved dissertations. The doctoral degree is also awarded for the completion of professional courses. Such degrees—including Doctor of Dentistry, Doctor of Economics, and Doctor of Medicine and Surgery—require six or seven years. The university's extension division runs a summer school and also offers diplomas and certificates in short programs.

At Santa Maria la Antigua University the *licenciado* is awarded after five years of study, and professional qualifications are also available.

Financing and Student Financial Aid

Article 84 of the constitution states that education will have priority over all other governmental expenditures. Decree 144 of June 3, 1969, reaffirms the state's financial commitment to the university. Thus, the University of Panama is financed almost entirely by government grants. These are supplemented by fees and by monies received for services that the university renders. Santa Maria la Antigua University is supported by the founding authority and student fees.

In accordance with the constitution, the state may grant scholarships or economic assistance to students whose level of achievement makes them worthy of state assistance. In addition, fees may be reduced for students from low-income families.

Teaching Staff and Research Activities

Members of the teaching staff at the university are divided into two categories: regular and special staff. Regular professors have the ranks *profesor titular* (full professor), *agregado* (associate), and *auxiliar* (assistant). Full professors obtain their position through competitive examinations and are appointed by the rector for five years, after which they are evaluated; the

appointment then may become permanent. Associate and assistant professors are appointed for three years after a competitive examination and may then be promoted to the next rank. In addition to examinations, the institutions take into account the candidates' degrees, professional preparation, teaching and other experience, and publications and research.

Special staff members include extraordinary professors, who are generally eminent professors appointed without the usual examinations; temporary professors, who must fulfill the usual qualifications and who serve when a regular professor cannot serve or has not been appointed; contingent professors, whose qualifications are specified according to Article 132 of the statutes; and visiting professors, who teach regular or postgraduate courses.

Sabbaticals are regulated according to Article 31 of Decree 144. Retirement is at age sixty-five for men and fifty-five for women (Decree 144, Article 41).

Scientific research is conducted in two research institutes connected to the University of Panama: the Institute of Juridical Investigation, which is connected to the law school; and the Institute of Anthropology and Historical Research.

Current Problems and Trends

Many of the problems facing Panama stem from the relationship of the Canal Zone to the country. Panama City is a highly cosmopolitan urban center with a well-developed educational system. The outlying rural districts of the country, however, are poor, and far fewer students can avail themselves of educational opportunities.

The tension between the United States and Panama has exacerbated educational problems. The political dominance of the area by the United States made it difficult in the past for the country to realize its own national aspirations. In 1967 the United States ceded its sovereignty over the canal to Panama. Since then an attempt has been made to develop an educational system that will tap human resources of the country and fulfill the manpower needs required by the country's new sovereignty

International Cooperation

Panama belongs to the *Consejo superior universitario centroamericano* (CSUCA: Central American Higher University Council; it seeks to develop a unity of curricula in Central American universities and promotes the exchange of students and professors. It also participates in other regional organizations, such as the *Unión de universidades de América latina* (UDUAL: Union of Latin American Universities), the *Federación de universidades privadas de América central y Panamá* (FUPAC: Federation of Private Universities of Central America and Panama), and the *Organización de universidades católicas de América latina* (Organization of Catholic Universities in Latin America), and in the cultural and educational efforts of the *Organización de estados centroamericanos* (ODECA: Organization of Central American States). Panama also participates in faculty and student exchange programs, such as the exchange program established between the University of Panama and the College of Arts and Sciences of Florida State University in the United States.

Bibliography

Benjamin, H. R. *Higher Education in the American Republics.* New York: McGraw-Hill, 1965.

Censo universitario latinoamericano, 1971. Mexico City: Unión de universidades de América latina, 1974.

Constitution of the Republic of Panama 1946. Dobbs Ferry, New York: Oceana, 1973.

Estatuto de la Universidad de Panamá. Panama: Imprenta universitaria, 1971.

García Laguardia, J. M. *Legislación universitaria de América latina.* Mexico City: Universidad nacional autónoma de México, 1973.

Inter-American University Cooperation. Washington, D.C.: Pan American Union, General Secretariat of the Organization of American States, 1968.

Penna, C. V. "Seminar on Educational Documentation and Information in Latin America." *Panama,* November 1971, pp. 8–13.

La supresión de la autonomía y la intervención militar de la Universidad de Panamá. San José, Costa Rica: Secretaría permanente del Consejo superior universitario centroamericano, 1969.

Waggoner, G. R., and Waggoner, B. A. *Education in Central America.* Lawrence: University of Kansas Press, 1971.

See also: Academic Dress and Insignia; Archives: Mediterranean, the Vatican, and Latin America, National Archives of; Central America: Regional Analysis.

PANCYPRIAN FEDERATION OF STUDENTS AND YOUNG SCIENTISTS

The Pancyprian Federation of Students and Young Scientists was formed after the first Pancyprian Conference of Students and Young Scientists, held in Nicosia in July 1973. The federation believes in democracy, freedom, peace, justice, equality, and independence of people. The group encourages international solidarity in struggles against colonization and racial discrimination and in defense of human rights. Membership includes fourteen thousand Cypriot students and young scientists in fifteen unions in Cyprus and all over the world.

Seeking security and unity for the Cypriot student movement, the federation encourages the political and intellectual growth of Cypriot students and young scientists, promotes international friendship and cooperation to create a link between students and young scientists of Cyprus and other countries, and upholds the national interest of Cyprus people and United Nations principles.

The Pancyprian Federation of Students and Young Scientists works on a volunteer basis. Support is derived from union membership; fund-raising activities; and financial help from other student unions, such as the International Union of Students.

The federation publishes an information bulletin as well as a magazine, pamphlets, and posters.

P.O. Box 4126
Nicosia, Cyprus

PAPUA NEW GUINEA

Population: 2,718,000 (mid 1975). Student enrollment in primary school: 237,715; secondary school (academic, vocational, technical): 38,296; higher education—university: 2350; higher education—nonuniversity: 3422; higher education—total: 5772. Language of instruction: English. Academic calendar: February/ March to November, two or three semesters. Percentage of gross national product (GNP) expended on higher education: approximately 3%. Percentage of national budget expended on higher education: approximately 9%. [All figures are for 1975–76.]

On September 16, 1975, the Trust Territory of New Guinea and the non-self-governing Territory of Papua, both of which had been administered by Australia since World War I, became the independent state of Papua New Guinea. Papua New Guinea's higher education system is more broadly defined than that of many other countries, where higher education generally refers to education commencing after the student has completed twelve years of schooling. In Papua New Guinea, only ten years of previous schooling are required for entry into higher education, and a number of institutions have accepted students with as little as eight years of schooling. It was not until 1975 that the primary teachers colleges obtained all their new enrollments from form 4 (grade 10) school leavers. Thus, although some Papua New Guinean higher education institutions accept students with less than the traditional ten to twelve years of prior schooling, these institutions are still considered part of the higher education system. To omit them would distort their value to a country which relies on them to supply much of its lower- and middle-level manpower needs. Further, such institutions offer full tertiary programs as well as higher vocational studies, and plans are under way for a ten-year admission requirement.

The development of the postsecondary education system is recent. The first post-secondary institutions in the country, the Papuan Medical College and the Port Moresby School of Nursing, were not established until 1958; and the two universities, the University of Papua New Guinea and the Papua New Guinea University of Technology, were founded in 1965. The main reason for this late development was that after eighty years of essentially colonial status there were no suitably qualified school leavers to be enrolled at postsecondary institutions. As the high school system expanded, the postsecondary and tertiary sector was also able to expand; at the same time, however, an increase in direct employment of school leavers, particularly in the public sector, has reduced the supply available for entry into higher education.

As the demand for a rapid replacement of expatriates with national manpower has grown and the number of school leavers has increased, the need to coordinate and plan the further growth of all postsecondary institutions in Papua New Guinea has become apparent. However, to date no completely satisfactory machinery or institution with directive powers has been established to undertake this task.

National Educational Policy

In a country such as Papua New Guinea, where there has been a rapid change from a position of colonial dependence to national independence, the whole social fabric, of which the educational system is a part, is undergoing rapid change. The roles of the various institutions, their objectives, and the means by which they achieve their objectives are thus subject to frequent changes. In 1975 a five-year education plan proposing some far-reaching changes was prepared. A Committee of Enquiry into University Development has presented its report, which recommends several significant changes. The basic policy underlying the provision of postsecondary education is that there must be a viable manpower need before new courses are introduced.

Types of Institutions

There are three basic types of higher education institutions: the two autonomous universities established by legislative act, the departmental institutions set up by various government departments and not governed by specific legislation, and the teacher training colleges. The autonomous universities are the liberal arts/science-oriented University of Papua New Guinea and the technical Papua New Guinea University of Technology. Departmental institutions include five schools of nursing, a dental college, and the College of Allied Health Sciences, under the Department of Public Health; Vudal Agricultural College, Highlands Agriculture Training Institute, and Popondetta Agriculture Training Institute, under the Department of Agriculture, Stock and Fisheries; the Nautical Training School and Civil Aviation Training College, under the Department of Transport; the Administrative College, under the Public Service Board; the Joint Services College, governed by a council consisting of the uniformed services departments; the Police Training College, under the Royal Papua New Guinea Constabulary; the Corrective Institution Training Centre, responsible to the Department of Social Development and Home Affairs; the Posts and Telegraphs Training Centre, under the Department of Posts and Telegraphs; and the Cooperative College, under the Cooperative Education Trust. The eleven primary teachers colleges, some of which are administered by missions (Roman Catholic, Protestant, and especially Seventh-Day Adventist missions have been active in Papua New Guinea), are responsible to the National Education Board.

Relationship with Secondary Education

Secondary education in Papua New Guinea consists of high schools offering programs for forms 1–6 (grades 7 through 12). By 1972 the number of these schools had increased to sixty-six, from ten in 1962; but in 1975 only three schools led to the sixth-form level (grade 12). Primary education now consists of six years, standards 1–6.

The educational award made on completion of ten years of schooling is the School Certificate, and after twelve years the Higher School Certificate.

Admission Requirements

It is likely that in the late 1970s undergraduate enrollment of nonnational students at the universities will not be permitted except in exceptional circumstances. The enrollment of persons from South Pacific nations other than Papua New Guinea, however, will continue on the basis of regional cooperation. Within Papua New Guinea there is a policy to attempt to enroll students in proportion to population levels in each province.

Although admission requirements have become more demanding, they vary from institution to institution. While it would be incorrect to state that they are arbitrarily determined, it cannot be denied that to fill quotas some institutions have recruited over a wide ability and performance range. Teachers colleges, for instance, prefer to take only students who have completed form 4 (grade 10) but will admit form 3 (grade 9) graduates if necessary. Nevertheless, the rising level of admission requirements is undeniably a function of the gradually increasing number of school leavers from form 4 and form 6. The overall objective is eventually to require ten years of schooling prior to entry into all postsecondary institutions.

The universities set their own standards of admission. They require at least twelve years of schooling at entry. Both conduct a predegree year of study for students with ten years of schooling; during this year a student's suitability to undertake degree-level studies in technical or nontechnical programs is assessed. There is no conclusive evidence, however, that students who commence degree studies after completing the preliminary year perform very differently from students who have completed twelve years of schooling.

The assessment of university applicants is based on data available through the National School Leavers Program. The data include a student's past academic performance, assessed performance, psychological profile, and comments by headmaster, teacher, and guidance officer. During the 1970s, approximately 70 percent of all new students at the two universities have been recruited from the top three deciles of ability, as measured by a national compound figure based on psychological tests and past academic performance. A final important item in selection is the terminal school examination, taken at the end of form 4 or form 6.

Administration and Control

The control of postsecondary education is not vested in any one government or statutory agency. The existing postsecondary institutions are governed by the organization that established them, or according to specific legislation. There is no legislation that binds them all together into one system. The largest single subsystem within this informal collection of institutions is formed by the teachers colleges under the National Education Board and staffed by the Teaching Service Commission. The board, which is advised by each college's governing council, is an advisory body to the minister for education; it is chaired by the director of education and has representation from the missions and the community. For day-to-day operation, the teachers colleges refer to the Department of Education, or to the department in conjunction with a church mission, or, in one case, solely to the Seventh-Day Adventist Mission. The two universities are autonomous bodies. Most other institutions are individually controlled by the government department that established them, in order to satisfy their own needs for trained manpower. It is only since the 1970s that the

functions of these institutions have included the training of persons from other South Pacific countries, as well as persons entering private, as distinct from public, employment in Papua New Guinea.

To formalize the planning and administration of higher education, the Brown Report (1971) recommended the establishment of a permanent Commission of Higher Education, which was never organized, although its secretariat, the Office of Higher Education, was created as an interim measure. Today, the office functions very much as the commission was intended to function; it is a coordinating and advisory body to government. The report also recommended the establishment of a Tertiary Education Finance Board, which was not established; instead, a Universities Finance Review Committee (UFRC) was created. It meets annually to consider university finances and is serviced by the office. Both the office and the UFRC participate in coordinating the planning and organization of the universities; no other postsecondary institutions come effectively under their jurisdiction. The office, however, is usually consulted on matters relating to higher education. Departmental institutions of higher education receive much closer supervision than the two universities, and the lines of control and supervision are much more direct than between government and the universities. The internal administration of the universities is autonomous, while departmental institutions have to follow normal public service regulations.

Internally, most postsecondary institutions are governed by councils, generally composed of a balanced representation of government, political interests, the public at large, students, and academic and administrative staff. The exceptions are departmental colleges, such as Vudal Agricultural College, which is governed by its principal and by the Department of Agriculture; some departmental colleges, however, have unofficial councils.

Faculty and students generally have no direct control of national or institutional policy making, although faculty are frequently consulted. The major pressure that students can bring to bear is through Student Representative Councils, the recently formed National Union of Students (NUS), and the mass media. In the recent past, student solidarity has influenced government on national issues. Moves have been made to establish formal communications through periodic meetings between the minister for education and the NUS executive. Students are represented on the major institutional committees and governing bodies. They are a minority group in such bodies; the extent to which they can control policy is limited.

Programs and Degrees

The degree-conferring authority for the universities is the chancellor. He confers degrees, diplomas, and certificates. Arrangements in departmental institutions vary. Generally, diplomas and certificates are awarded by the particular institution. For the teachers colleges, the Department of Education registers graduates or teachers after they have received their certificates.

The emphasis in Papua New Guinea is on training at the first degree and below degree levels. Postgraduate study in many fields is possible but limited by staff resources; the two universities have a charter enabling them to award such degrees in all fields in which undergraduate teaching is provided. However, enrollment in postgraduate master's degree and doctoral studies is very much an exception; those who are enrolled are largely staff members. The highest award possible in the following broad fields of study is the Doctor of Philosophy: agriculture, accountancy, architecture, business administration, biological sciences, education, engineering, humanities, law, physical science, surveying. The Doctor of Dental Science and Doctor of Medicine are the highest degrees in dentistry and medical programs. The highest award possible in teacher training is

the Bachelor of Education. A diploma is awarded in the following fields of study: health science and technology, library science, public administration, police studies, journalism. A certificate is the highest award conferred in the nursing programs.

In departmental institutions, curriculum and standards are determined by specific government department requirements for trained personnel. Teachers colleges are a major exception, since they serve the public at large. Here, programs of study, standards, and curricula are changed—generally at the initiative of college boards of studies—through the college governing council; coordinated at departmental level by the superintendent of curriculum and teacher education; and finally approved by the National Education Board.

At the two universities, very much the same process is followed. Initially program changes are prepared by the teaching departments and submitted to their faculty or school boards. Final approval is given by the academic board. If it is a completely new program of study leading to a new award, government approval is needed for extra funds. Standards, degree requirements, and levels of achievement are internal university matters.

Financing

The vast bulk of expenditure on postsecondary education is allocated in the national budget. For 1975–76 the total national budget was K408,000,000 (US $1 = .7257 kina), of which approximately 31 percent was supplied by Australia. The total proposed expenditure on postsecondary education was K32,000,000. Of this figure, K15,000,000 was for university education (including Goroka Teachers College, which since 1975 has been an integral part of the University of Papua New Guinea) and K2,400,000 for teacher (primary) education.

For all sectors of higher education, 76 percent of the total expenditure was on recurring expenditure, 16 percent for scholarships, and 8 percent for capital expenditure.

The departmental institutions receive their funds through the normal budgetary process of government, in which each department competes for funds. The department is permitted to distribute the funds among its various divisions, including its training institutions. Thus, the departmental institutions do not compete directly with each other for funds, as do the departments themselves.

The universities are expected to expend funds in accordance with the detailed plan set out in their biennial estimates, as adjusted and accepted by the government. Financial control is effected through the annual review of the universities' finances by the government-appointed Universities Finance Review Committee (UFRC). The Office of Higher Education (OHE) functions as the secretariat to the UFRC; during the year when the UFRC is not in session, the universities are required to submit claims for supplementary funds through the OHE, which advises the National Executive Council (cabinet) on the salient aspects of the request. No new programs can be established during the year without the recommendation of the OHE and the approval of the minister. This procedure is not based on legislation and applies only to the two universities.

Student Financial Aid

All students who are accepted by the universities or departmental institutions are assured of financial support from the government. In addition, many students are sponsored by industry, especially in technical fields. Some student wastage occurs due to financial pressures from families. At present, the cost of income forgone by students is a worthwhile investment in view of the great demand and good opportunities for graduates of all types.

Student Social Background and Access to Education

Access to higher education in Papua New Guinea must be understood in relation to the number of primary and secondary students available for progression to tertiary study, the country's ability to finance higher education, and manpower needs.

The ultimate objective in primary education is to achieve universal enrollment. Barriers to this objective are the shortage of teachers and lack of finance. Progression from the first level to the second level of education is by examination; only 30 percent of the sixth-grade students are allowed to progress to secondary study. The noncompletion rate at secondary schools is high; fewer than 20 percent of the starters in 1969 reached form 4 (grade 10) in 1972, while just over 1 percent of the starters in 1967 reached form 6 (grade 12) in 1972. Form 4 graduates will, for some time, continue to be the major source of input into postsecondary education. In spite of the level of wastage, there is an excess of form 4 school leavers, for whom neither employment nor further training and education are available.

The general age of students at a comparable level of education tends to be higher than that in more advanced countries. Age statistics, however, are not reliable. As far as can be assessed, in 1974 the 15–19 age group at the two universities was 41 percent of all those enrolled; the 20–24 age group was 36 percent; the 25–29 age group was 11 percent; and older persons were 12 percent.

Not a great deal is known about the male/female ratio of the student population at institutions other than the two universities, where, in 1974, 11.8 percent of the student body were females. At coeducational teachers colleges females constitute, at most, 25 percent of the student body. At other institutions this figure may vary considerably. Until 1975 some institutions, notably the agricultural colleges, made no provision for female students. There is, however, an active policy of encouraging females to participate in all aspects of life in Papua New Guinea, including their enrollment in postsecondary educational institutions. In 1975, for the first time, forty women enrolled in the

Vudal Agricultural College in East New Britain.

Small numbers of students from other South Pacific nations are enrolled, particularly at teachers colleges and agricultural colleges; but enrollment is overwhelmingly Papua New Guinean.

The present postsecondary Papua New Guinean student population is the first generation of a nontraditional, nonagricultural urban middle class. It will be some time before differences in the social background of students will markedly affect educational mobility in Papua New Guinea.

Teaching Staff

The ranks of teaching staff at the universities are professor, associate professor or reader, senior lecturer, lecturer, senior tutor, and tutor. The colleges have the ranks of principal lecturer, senior lecturer, lecturer, and tutor.

All areas of employment in Papua New Guinea are subject to a vigorous process of localization. That is, the deliberate policy is to replace expatriate employees with citizens. In the selection of personnel, therefore, some consideration is always given to the applicant's adaptability to the Papua New Guinea environment and ability to carry out a training task. No expatriate academic is given tenure at either departmental institutions or the universities. All are employed on contracts. Nevertheless, promotion is possible at the two universities from the level of tutor to senior tutor, and from lecturer through to associate professor, without the need to apply for a vacant position. At departmental institutions, however, all vacant positions must be advertised, and normal public service selection procedures are followed; thus, the departmental institutions have very little autonomy with regard to appointment of faculty and staff. Vacancies at departmental institutions are frequently filled by promotion from within the public service. Where governing bodies or depart-

mental institutions exist, they make recommendations on the applicants for positions to the Public Service Selection Committee.

Within the constraint of overall government policy to replace expatriate with national staff, both universities are quite autonomous in the appointment of administrative as well as academic staff.

Salaries of national employees of government department institutions are determined by the Public Service Commission. In cases of dispute, a process of conciliation and arbitration based on legislation is used. Salaries are generally set at a level that the country can afford; they are well below those payable to expatriate employees. Salaries payable to expatriate employees of government department institutions are based on the salaries payable to occupants of similar positions in the Australian (federal) Public Service. Where no similar position exists in the service, the relevant Australian State Public Service is used as the model. In general, when there is a salary increase in Australia, the increase is passed on to the expatriate employee in Papua New Guinea, although there have been variations to this pattern because of the employment of citizens of nations other than Australia.

The salaries of national employees of the universities are generally similar to salaries payable to national Papua New Guinea public service employees, but there are at present very few national academic staff.

Expatriate university academic and administrative staff are employed by the university councils, and their salaries are paid from grants to the universities from the national budget. In the past, academic salaries increased in accordance with those in Australia. This arrangement has recently been changed. Academic salaries in Papua New Guinea are now below those in Australia but compare favorably with those in many other countries. The universities may themselves set academic salaries within the government guidelines. In case of dispute, the process of conciliation and arbitration is provided by law. Regular reviews are undertaken.

Research Activities

The amount of officially sanctioned research carried out by the institutions varies. Teachers colleges, for instance, have no charter to conduct research, although minor projects of an applied nature are conducted. The Department of Education has its own research branch, however, and produces regular bulletins.

The bulk of research funds at the two universities is obtained from the government as part of general university financing. The universities control these funds and allocate them through their own research committees, once the general research grant has been made available by the government. Small amounts of money are made available for research by industry. In 1973, 3.4 percent of the total recurrent expenditure of the universities was available for research.

At both universities some 80 percent of research is applied. For instance, the school of accountancy and business studies at the Papua New Guinea University of Technology carries out research in areas such as small-business development, shipping practices, and retail distribution methods and outlets; the school of engineering is investigating ways of developing village technology; and the school of architecture and building studies is experimenting with low-cost housing designs. In addition, basic research programs are being conducted in fields such as seismology and food chemistry. Very much the same situation prevails at the University of Papua New Guinea, where approximately 115 projects were under way in 1974. In 1975 the New Guinea Research Unit of the Australian National University was transferred to the Papua New Guinea government and renamed the Papua New Guinea Institute of Social and Economic Research. The institute will have its own research program and also keep a record of all ongoing and completed social research.

Current Problems and Trends

Many of the problems facing the higher education system in Papua New Guinea are endemic to all aspects of the society at present. In addition to the changing patterns of world affairs that affect the country, it is experiencing the multitude of changes that occur when a nation becomes politically independent. Thus, the system of higher education, like the public and private sectors of the economy, is experiencing some difficulties in recruiting adequately qualified and experienced staff. The country is well away from the mainstream of academic life, and the universities do not offer positions with tenure to expatriates.

Another problem that is difficult to overcome is that of elitism. The universities particularly have the image of luxury establishments where a very small number of privileged students are preparing to consolidate and maintain their privileged positions for the rest of their working lives. In contrast to fee-paying students at primary and secondary schools, students at teachers colleges, the universities, and other postsecondary institutions pay no fees and receive government scholarships providing them with pocket money and fares to travel home each year. As a result, the postsecondary institutions are under continual pressure to minimize their expenditure. This, especially at the universities, is beginning to affect staff morale.

One proposal designed to reverse the elitist tendencies in tertiary education is the plan to change program structures to incorporate work experience. Under this proposed innovation, the undergraduate bachelor's degree may be broken into three modules. At the end of each, an award may be made: from certificate to diploma to degree. Before proceeding to the next module, a student must not only complete the previous module with above-average performance but must also show motivation and full capability to complete the next module. Students will be encouraged to undertake two years of work, preferably in their chosen vocation, before they undertake the next module. During work they would be able, and indeed encouraged, to continue their studies on a part-time and/or external basis. Preference for enrollment in advanced modules would be given to those students who undertake such part-time study. The proposal has its problems but is supported by the government and will be implemented where feasible.

A number of side effects would result from the implementation of this scheme. The most obvious is that it would take considerably longer to produce a full graduate and that the number of dropouts would increase. However, a considerable number of students have had great difficulty in completing degrees, while others fail to do so altogether. The proposed program will allow such students to get an academic qualification. A second major side effect would be the tendency to produce far more persons with diplomas than persons with degrees. This is regarded as desirable, since the level of operation in most areas of Papua New Guinea is highly practical; training to degree level is not essential and may be counterproductive.

Still another plan to remove elitist connotations from higher education is implicit in the *Report of the Committee of Enquiry into University Development* (1974), which recommended a major move into the field of extramural activities. The intention is to enable a wider cross section of the population to partake in, and benefit from, postsecondary education. In addition, a vigorous program of extension activities of value to village people is to be implemented.

A recent innovation related to the financing of postsecondary education was the establishment of the National Tertiary Scholarship (NATSCHOL). Under this scheme, which abolished other more expensive schemes, any student who gains admission to a postsecondary institution is assured of government financial support while he studies. It is intended that commercial firms that provide private sponsorships align the benefits of their awards with NATSCHOL.

One of the most far-reaching innovations to improve coordination between institutions has been the development of the National Education Board and the Teaching Service Commission. Prior to the development of these bodies, there were two parallel teacher training systems. One consisted of three colleges operated by the Department of Education, and the other consisted of seven colleges operated by the various denominational missions, each of which conducted its own program and was responsible for raising its own finance. With the establishment of the board and the commission, teacher training is still the responsibility of agencies such as the Department of Education and the various church organizations, but all programs are coordinated by the board and the commission. The exception is the Seventh-Day Adventist Mission.

A further important example of coordination is the method by which the universities cooperate to provide degree-level studies. A good example is the degree program in agriculture and forestry. Each university teaches that part of the degree which it is best equipped to teach. In this way, a minimum of duplication occurs. In the medical program, all students are required to spend a considerable time in rural areas.

The trend toward cooperation and coordination was also manifest in the establishment of the Joint Services College in Lae, in 1974. In a common first year at one location, the college trains the officer ranks of the defense force (land, maritime, air) the police, and the correctional service. After the common year, each service provides its own unique training for a further year at its own institution.

Relationship with Industry

Relations between postsecondary institutions and industry are good but vary depending on the institution. Industry involvement in teachers colleges, for instance, is minimal; it is largely confined to the awarding of prizes for achievement. In other institutions, particularly the University of Technology, participation is more significant. The major area of industry cooperation in tertiary education is provision of sponsorships for students; the unsponsored student in his third or fourth year at the University of Technology is rare, and there is strong industry representation on its boards of study to ensure program relevance.

Departmental colleges, such as the Vudal Agricultural College, have a direct relationship with the agricultural industry; they were established in order to provide extension services to its various branches.

International Cooperation

Through significant general and unspecified aid to the national budget, the government of Australia indirectly provides funds to the institutions of higher education in Papua New Guinea. In 1974 14.5 percent of the students enrolled at the universities in Papua New Guinea were from Australia, New Zealand, and other European-colonized nations; and 2.5 percent were from other Pacific nations and territories, excluding Australia and New Zealand.

Papua New Guinea is a member of the Colombo Plan for Co-operative Economic Development in South and Southeast Asia. Under the plan, study abroad in higher technology programs is available to Papua New Guineans, as well as equipment for domestic technical training and research.

The University of Technology participates in the University of Hawaii's Peacesat Satellite Programme.

Since Papua New Guinea achieved self-government in 1973, the New Zealand government has become increasingly involved in providing aid funds for specific higher education projects; it also provides an unlimited number of scholarships in New Zealand for Papua New Guinean students.

W. J. OOSTERMEYER

Educational Associations

Papua New Guinea Teachers Association
P.O. Box 6546
Boroko, Papua New Guinea

National Union of Students (NUS)
University of Technology
P.O. Box 793
Lae, Papua New Guinea

Bibliography

Collated Comments on the Report of the Committee of Inquiry into University Development. Konedobu: Office of Higher Education, 1975.

Five-Year Education Plan. Konedobu: Department of Education, 1975.

Report of the Commission on Higher Education in Papua New Guinea. (The Currie Report.) Canberra: Government of Australia, 1964.

Report of the Committee of Inquiry in Higher Education in Papua New Guinea. (The Brown Report.) Canberra: Government of Australia, 1971.

Report of the Committee of Inquiry into University Development. (The Gris Report.) Port Moresby: Cabinet of the Government of Papua New Guinea, 1974.

Smith, G. *Education in Papua New Guinea.* Carlton South, Australia: Melbourne University Press, 1975.

See also: Oceania: Regional Analysis.

PARAGUAY, REPUBLIC OF

Population: 2,350,000 (1972 census). Students enrolled in primary school: 462,449; secondary school: 70,986; higher education: 9083. Student enrollment in higher education as percentage of age group (18–22): 4%. Language of instruction: Spanish. Academic calendar: March to December, one semester. Percentage of gross national product expended on all education: 1.8%; higher education: .29%. [Figures are for 1974 unless otherwise noted. Source: Ministry of Education and Culture, Department of Educational Planning.]

From the middle of the sixteenth century until the declaration of its independence in

1811, Paraguay was a Spanish colony. Its capital city, Asunción, was the first stable settlement in the Spanish-dominated Río de la Plata region. The province enjoyed a central position of power until 1776, when Río de la Plata was separated from Paraguay and the viceroyalty established its center in Buenos Aires.

Even in the earliest years of Paraguay's colonial existence, its governors were preoccupied with education. They organized a system of primary education and in 1598 petitioned the Spanish crown for a university college in Asunción that would rival other prestigious institutions, such as the university in Lima. Although a lack of funds doomed the effort, in 1622 King Philip IV of Spain and Pope Gregory XV, responding to the demands of the Paraguayan priest, Friar de Trejo y Sanabria, granted a charter to the College of Córdoba del Tucuman in the nearby Río de la Plata. For a while the college serviced the entire area and played an important role in focusing the cultural life of Paraguay, but in the eighteenth century new efforts were launched for a college in Asunción. Again the efforts were in vain. At first feuds between the city council and the Society of Jesus delayed the project, then a populist revolution swept the province from 1715 to 1735, and finally the rivalry between Asunción and Buenos Aires, then the capital of the viceroyalty of Río de la Plata, resulted in Asunción's receiving only a secondary institute, which was established in 1783.

In May 1811 Paraguay, severing its political ties with Spain and Buenos Aires, declared its independence. From 1814 to 1840 the new republic was under the dictatorship of José Gaspar Rodríguez Francia, whose efforts to preserve the country's independence were at the expense of educational and cultural development. He was succeeded by the progressive Carlos Antonio López, and attempts were made to right the balance by founding a new high school and seminary and by encouraging scholars to pursue further study in Europe. In 1864 Paraguay became engaged in a devastating war against the triple alliance of Argentina, Brazil, and Uruguay. It emerged in 1870 having lost 55,000 square miles and half of its population, but even during the difficult years of reconstruction intense efforts were made to restructure and develop a sound educational system. The constitution of 1870 promised free primary education; in 1877 a stable secondary school, *Colegio nacional de la capital* (National High School of Asunción), was opened; and in 1878 the *Seminario mayor del Paraguay* (Theological Seminary), now the Higher Institute of Theology at the Catholic University, was established to prepare priests and deacons for the Catholic church.

In 1883 a law school, the precursor of the future national university, was incorporated into the *Colegio nacional de la capital.* Six years later, largely as a result of the efforts of Senator José Decoud, a bill was passed in the Paraguayan congress chartering the establishment of the *Universidad nacional de Asunción* (UNA: National University of Asunción) and was signed into law by President General Patricio Escobar. In March 1890, three centuries after it had been initially proposed, the National University of Asunción opened its doors.

During the next eighty years the university developed from three original faculties—law and social sciences, medicine, and mathematics—and a first graduating class of four lawyers into an autonomous institution of thirteen faculties, schools, and institutes and more than six thousand students. The development was not without setbacks. Although the faculty of law had only one brief disruption, during the Chaco war with Bolivia (1932–1935), the faculty of medicine was less secure and was even forced to close in 1909; it reopened, however, in 1910 with enlarged laboratories and hospital affiliation. The faculty of mathematics faltered shortly after it opened; but in 1926 it became firmly reinstated as the faculty of physical and mathematical sciences, offering majors in civil engineering and surveying. An important step forward was Law 1048 of 1929, which granted the university full autonomy. In the next decades the National University of Asunción opened several new faculties, schools, and institutes, including the faculties of economic sciences (1937); dentistry (1937); chemistry and pharmacy (1938); philosophy (1948); agriculture and veterinary science (1956); architecture (1957); and the *Instituto "Dr. Andrés Barbero,"* which encompassed the former schools of obstetrics, nursing, and social service. In 1948 the government intervened in the university, overriding its autonomy; but the charter of the National University of Asunción, promulgated in Law 356, reestablished the prerogatives and aims of the institution.

The 1940 constitution of Paraguay had recognized the right of the church to found institutions of higher learning, but it was not until February 1960 that a decree of the *Conferencia episcopal del Paraguay* (Paraguayan Conference of Bishops) authorized the opening of a second university in the country, the *Universidad católica "Nuestra Señora de la Asunción"* (Catholic University of Our Lady of Asunción). The state granted recognition to the institution in September 1960.

The newest institution offering postsecondary education is the *Instituto superior de educación* (Higher Institute of Education), founded by decree of January 1968 for the training of teachers and educational personnel.

National Educational Policy and Legal Basis of Educational System

National educational policies are stated in the national constitution of August 25, 1967. Article 89 declares: "All inhabitants of the republic have the right to develop their mental and physical capabilities." It goes on to say: "The state shall maintain the public schools necessary to assure all inhabitants, free of charge, the opportunity to learn, and it shall endeavor, by all the means at its disposal, to provide equality of opportunity for students in all of them. It shall also maintain and promote, on the same basis of equality and freedom, secondary, vocational, agricultural, industrial, and technical education, and higher or university education, as well as scientific and technological research."

Article 91 states: "The law shall establish the educational system at all levels as well as determine the extent of university autonomy. It will determine for which professions degrees are required, the requirements to be met in order to obtain such degrees, the authority empowered to issue them, and the controls to which these professions shall be subject."

The structure and organization as well as the aims, rights, and privileges of the university were determined by Law 356, promulgated in July 1956. According to this law, the National University of Asunción is a corporation with academic and administrative autonomy. Supported by the state, it is devoted to the cultivation of teaching and to the diffusion of knowledge in the sciences, humanities, arts, and physical education. Its responsibility is to educate professionals and researchers and to extend its offerings into the community. Article 5 of the law explicitly forbids any partisan politics or political maneuvering within the university and gives the executive branch of government the power to intervene in the university whenever its aforementioned purposes are perverted or whenever the university authorities are unable to maintain the normal functioning of the institution.

The legal bases of the Catholic university are Law 663, enacted by the chamber of representatives in 1960, and Decree 11079 of June 1960. These laws require the Catholic university to maintain a curriculum comparable in quality to that of the National University of Asunción and authorize it to grant degrees and diplomas. The Ministry of Education and Worship is commissioned to inspect and supervise the curricula; the qualifications of the teaching staff; the examination system; and the observance of the laws, decrees, and resolutions pertinent to the private institutions.

Types of Institutions

Two institutions in Paraguay have full university status: the National University of Asunción and the Catholic University of Our Lady of Asunción. The Higher Institute of Education offers nonuniversity advanced courses in education.

The National University of Asunción is divided into ten faculties: law and social sciences, philosophy, medicine, physics and mathematics, economics, odontology, chemistry and pharmacy, agriculture, veterinary medicine, and architecture. There is also a School of Fine Arts; an Institute of Sciences; and the new *Instituto "Dr. Andrés Barbero,"* which offers health-related programs.

At its inception the Catholic university had only faculties of juridical, political, and social sciences; philosophy; and science of education. Since then, it has expanded its curricula and offers programs not only in the usual liberal arts fields—humanities and natural sciences—but also in professional fields—law, diplomacy, and business administration. Because of financial limitations it avoids the more expensive technological programs and those requiring expensive laboratories and equipment. The Catholic university has absorbed the former *Seminario mayor del Paraguay* (theological seminary), which is now associated with it as the Higher Institute of Theology and Religion. The Catholic university has proved to be progressive both in its response to national social change and in the development of its curricula.

The Higher Institute of Education certifies teachers and educational personnel and offers many practicing educators the opportunity to update their knowledge.

Relationship with Secondary Education

The constitution of August 1967, Article 89, makes it the duty of the state to provide free and equal elementary education and requires that every child in the republic, seven years or older, attend and complete six years of elementary schooling. The law, however, cannot be enforced, particularly in the rural areas, where many children must leave school before completion to help on the farm and where some districts do not even have the requisite number of grades in the elementary schools.

Secondary education is under the jurisdiction of the Ministry of Education and Worship, which proposes and standardizes curricula. It is not compulsory and is offered at both public and private institutions, with more than half of the students attending the private institutions. It is divided into two three-year cycles: the first, or basic, cycle has a common curriculum in all schools; the second cycle is provided in three standard programs. The academic program concentrates on the humanities and sciences, is designed to prepare the student for further study at the university, and leads to the diploma *bachillerato en ciencias y letras.* The commercial program introduces the student to business-related disciplines; offers preparation for continued studies at the university in accounting, economics, and administration; and leads to the diploma *bachillerato comercial.* The teacher training program, taught in normal schools, regional centers, and private schools, prepares students for elementary teaching or for further study in education, philosophy, and letters. It leads to the title *maestro normal* (primary school teacher).

The projected school-leaving age is eighteen; but, because many students must suspend their studies for financial reasons, the average school-leaving age is actually nineteen. During the 1960s the Ministry of Education and Worship introduced an equivalency secondary school-leaving examination and certificate for students over seventeen who were not able to complete the three-year upper cycle. The concept has not been abandoned, although it is being reassessed to counter criticism that it accredited students who were inadequately prepared.

Admission Requirements

The two universities have different entrance requirements and standards, although both require a *bachillerato* or equivalent diploma, approved and authenticated by the Ministry of Education and Worship. The Higher Institute of Education requires the title *maestro normal* or equivalent.

At the National University of Asunción satisfactory performance in an entrance examination is required in addition to the diploma. This practice was instituted when the reforms of the 1950s caused an enormous increase in the number of high school graduates. Each faculty, school, or institute administers its own examination, which is prepared, supervised, and graded by a special committee selected by the faculty council. High school class rank is usually not taken into account as an admission prerequisite, although applicants who ranked first or second in their high school graduating class are awarded a bonus 10 percent on their examination scores. Some faculties—such as medicine, dentistry, agronomy, and veterinary medicine, which have space limitations and entrance quotas—accept only those with the highest scores in the examination. A student at the National University of Asunción is considered a member of a particular faculty, institute, or school. Admission by transfer is possible, but in general a student must reapply for admission to his desired faculty, even in the same university. Depending on his previous record and on the particular faculty, the entrance examinations may be waived and credit given for some subjects.

In 1971 the Catholic university abandoned the practice of entrance examinations and adopted a policy of open admission. An entering student is admitted first to a probation year and upon successful completion automatically becomes eligible for the second and all subsequent years.

Administration and Control

Higher education in Paraguay is largely self-governed, since both the universities have autonomous governing bodies and enjoy the status of legal corporations. The administration of the National University of Asunción, usually heeds the directives of the national government. For important changes, state consent is required. The Catholic university is totally independent of the government but is supervised by the Department of Higher Education and Cultural Diffusion of the ministry, which has no authority over the national university.

The highest governing body of the National University of Asunción is the *consejo superior universitario* (higher university council), which consists of the rector, the deans, one full or associate professor from each faculty, one nonteaching alumnus, and one student representative. The professors and the alumnus serve for two years, the student for one; they may be reelected. The minister of education serves as the honorary president and has voice but no vote. The council is empowered to formulate general policy and rules, approve programs, appoint full and associate professors, establish faculties, grant honorary titles, elaborate the budget, control and allot funds, impose discipline, suggest to the president removal of the rector, and intervene in faculty matters when necessary.

The administrative head of the university is the rector, appointed by the government from three candidates proposed by the higher council; he serves for a five-year term with eligibility for reelection. To be considered for appointment, candidates must be Paraguayan and at least thirty-five years old and must have the highest degree and teaching experience as a full or associate professor. The rector is the legal representative of the university. He appoints the deans of the faculties; grants titles and honors; prepares the budget for presentation to the council; appoints administrative personnel, assistant professors, and other persons in charge; and presides over the council.

Each faculty is headed by a dean and a faculty council (*consejo directivo de las facultades*); each institute and school is headed by a director with the same responsibilities as the dean. The dean is appointed by the rector, on the advice of the faculty council, for a term of five years and may be reelected. His principal duties are to represent the faculty, oversee its general administration, propose nominations and dismissal of administrative personnel, propose to the rector the names of professors for appointment, and give permission for sabbaticals. The faculty council is composed of the dean, five professors, a graduate, and a student. The duties of the council include proposing to the rector the nominees for the position of dean, formulating faculty rules, proposing nominees for teaching positions within the faculty, designing plans of study to be submitted to the university council for approval, and drawing up the budget for the faculty. It also recommends to the university council the dismissal of the dean.

Each faculty has a *claustro docente* (teachers' assembly), which is composed of all the professors. It considers questions relative to plans of study and university development, and its decisions are brought to the attention of the university authorities. Meetings are called and presided over by the rector or dean at the proposal of the university and directive councils.

The Catholic university is under the jurisdiction of the church, with the Archbishop of Asunción as the grand chancellor entrusted with duties by the Paraguayan Conference of Bishops through its special commission on the Catholic university. In practice, the administrative and academic management structure is similar to that of the National University of Asunción. The rector is appointed by the Holy See.

The teaching staff in both universities participate in the governance of the institutions through representatives on the faculty council and the higher university council, where they compose the overwhelming majority. The students are very active in proposing new policies, even though they have only one representative in the councils.

Programs and Degrees

Both the national university and the Catholic university offer standard pro-grams in the fields of humanities and social sciences; both also offer programs in the professional fields of law, education, and business administration, but the National University of Asunción is the only institution in the nation that provides programs in technological and health-related fields.

The Catholic university has four faculties at its main campus in Asunción: accountancy and business administration, law and diplomatic studies, political and social sciences, philosophy and education, and the Higher Institute of Theology and Religion. The *licenciado* is awarded in all of these fields, in programs that range from four to six years. The university also operates three semiindependent branches at Concepción, Encarnación, and Villarrica. Each branch offers programs in accountancy and administrative sciences, juridical sciences, and philosophy and education, but none provides full degree programs. The doctoral degree is available at the main campus in administration and accounting, law, and the disciplines offered by the faculty of philosophy and education: philosophy, history, humanities, mathematics, modern communication, education, and psychology. According to the regulation approved on October 21 and November 4, 1972, a candidate for the doctorate must (1) be a graduate of the Catholic university or the National University of Asunción or of any foreign pontifical Catholic university or faculty, or of any college or university of a foreign country having educational exchange agreements with Paraguay; (2) have a minimum grade point average of 3.5 out of 5.0 (remedial examinations are available if this requirement is not fulfilled); (3) show proficiency in at least one foreign language; (4) have successfully completed four four-month courses at the postgraduate level; and (5) submit and orally defend an original thesis of at least 150 pages in Spanish.

The National University of Asunción offers a wider variety of programs and degrees. The *licenciado* is awarded after three years of study in philosophy, journalism, mathematics, letters, education, and the

English language. Four years are required for pharmacy, history, physio-chemistry, exact sciences, natural sciences, and social service. The doctorate is awarded on the submission and acceptance of a thesis. The length of time varies with the discipline. One additional year after the *licenciado* is required in history; two additional years are demanded in philosophy, letters, mathematics, and education. The Doctor of Odontology and the Doctor of Veterinary Science require five years. A doctorate in medicine and surgery, biochemistry, economic science, and industrial chemistry is awarded after six years. In addition to these degrees, the university awards the titles of surveyor (three years), notary public (four years), nurse (four years), agronomic engineer (five years), architect (six years), and civil and industrial engineer (six years and a thesis).

The *Instituto "Dr. Andrés Barbero"* offers two kinds of curricula: a two-year graduate program in obstetrics for physicians and a three-year midwifery program leading to an *obstetricia diplomada*.

The Higher Institute of Education offers programs and titles for teachers of elementary education (two years), secondary education (two years), and industrial arts (one year) and for school directors (two years). It also offers full university courses in guidance, supervision, and evaluation (two years).

Financing and Student Financial Aid

The National University of Asunción derives most of its revenue from the government's appropriations in the general budget. A smaller amount comes from the very nominal tuition fees. In 1975 approximately 97 percent of the budget of the national university was provided by state appropriations. Three percent was raised through student fees and tuition. The Catholic university is funded mainly through tuition and fees, which are not very large, and by minimum state contributions. In 1975, 95 percent of its funds came from tuition and fees; the remaining five percent was provided by the state, gifts, and

collections. The Institute of Theology operates on a separate budget. Three fourths of its funds are provided by the Paraguayan Conference of Bishops; the remainder by the state. The income for the Higher Institute of Education is derived from the Ministry of Education.

Private contributions are not a substantial part of the financing of higher education; one or two buildings have been donated to the National University of Asunción, and there is small church support for the Catholic university and the Institute of Theology. However, the Paraguayan church is not wealthy, and any contribution constitutes a sizable sacrifice.

Coordinated and extensive student financial aid is urgently necessary in Paraguay. Although tuition and fees are low at the universities, many prospective students are still not able to afford them, much less the necessary maintenance and books. For those who live outside the capital city, access to higher education is almost impossible. Although Article 90 of the national constitution states that the law shall take into account provision of funds for fellowships, scholarships, and other aid to enable Paraguayans who demonstrate outstanding aptitude—preferably those who lack financial resources—to receive advanced scientific, technological, artistic, or intellectual training, there is no structure to implement this article. Grants are insufficient, too few, and apt to be awarded only to an elite who study abroad.

Some scholarships are available at the National University of Asunción, and tuition is waived for children of veterans of the Chaco war. The Catholic university also waives all tuition and fees for students lacking financial resources; the number of these scholarships (over three hundred) is substantial for an institution deriving 95 percent of its revenues from student fees. All students in the Institute of Theology are interns and receive room and board, as well as tuition scholarships.

The rector's office of the National University of Asunción is allowed to grant a few supplemental aid scholarships, but their extent is not known, and little publicity is given to them. The ruling party, the *Asociación nacional republicana,* grants some cash-aid scholarships to its members who attend either university; it also operates a small residence facility.

Student Social Background and Access to Education

The majority of students in higher education are from urban and upper-middle-class or upper-class backgrounds. Although the law assures that entrance to the National University of Asunción is open to all qualified applicants without regard to economic or social background, in effect access to higher education is limited for three major reasons. (1) Academic preparation varies in accordance with the students' socioeconomic background. In spite of efforts being made to correct the situation, the quality of secondary education is better in Asunción than in other parts of the republic, and even in Asunción astonishing differences exist between the better and more expensive private high schools and the cheaper ones. Although public high schools maintain fairly rigid standards, they are too few to absorb poorer students. (2) The concentration of most higher education facilities in Asunción and neighboring areas poses still another problem to prospective students from outside Asunción. A lack of residence halls and a shortage of financial aid, which the rural poor need to defray their living expenses, militate against their enrollment at the universities. (3) Students lacking other means of support must seek full- or part-time employment. At both universities all the humanities and social sciences courses are scheduled in the evenings; but all the technical, scientific, and health-related programs are held during the day. As a result, the proportion of lower-class students in these courses is low. The problem of access is compounded for the poorer students by more stringent entrance examinations in these disciplines.

Because the population of Paraguay is racially homogeneous, with a strong national conscience and sense of unity, there is no specific minority awareness in the nation. Women are given equal rights by the constitution, and they form a sizable percentage of the student body. The Higher Institute of Education enrolls mainly women.

Each faculty and school of both universities has a *centro de estudiantes* (student union), to which all eligible students belong; all the unions are members of the *Federación universitaria del Paraguay* (FUP). The unions play an important role in the social life of the students, by organizing sport competitions and social parties, and in the political life of the community. Most students participate in the election of their representatives for the faculties and university councils and through them participate in the decision-making process. In addition, a sizable part of the student body is strongly committed to either the official party or the opposition.

The strike, a powerful weapon at the disposal of the student body, is sometimes used to protest against academic measures or to demonstrate against the status quo. Compared with students in other Latin American countries, however, Paraguayan students rarely have resorted to striking.

Teaching Staff

Members of the teaching staff at both universities are classified as *profesores titulares* (full professors), *profesores adjuntos* (associate professors), and *profesores auxiliares* (assistant professors). In addition, there are the following special categories: *contratados* (contracted professors), who teach particular courses for a limited period; *libres* (free professors), who teach partial or full courses; *encargados de cátedra* (professors in charge), who hold interim positions for an academic year when a permanent staff member is not available; and *auxiliares de la enseñanza* (teaching assistants), who aid the professors. Honorary professorships are awarded on retirement to full or associate professors who have served the university for ten years.

A full professor must be a Paraguayan who holds the highest degree and has been an associate professor for five years or a free professor for ten years. His obligations are to direct and teach courses. He is appointed after a competitive examination, which takes into account his titles, merits, and aptitudes. A professorship is for ten years and may be renewed for an equal period after an assessment. Associate and assistant professors are appointed in the same manner as the full professor. The associate rank requires three prior years on the assistant level or four prior years as a free professor. The assistant may serve in that rank for three years and may be confirmed for another three years without competitive examination. The standard requirements for this post may also be waived by the higher university council. Requirements are not as rigid for appointments in the special categories.

Professors are not granted tenure at the National University of Asunción, although their positions are protected by law. Remuneration is determined by the faculty council when a particular professorship is being considered. The criteria for determining salary tend to be arbitrary and vary considerably from one faculty to another and from one professorship to another within the same faculty. At the Catholic university salary is regulated in accordance with hours of lectures per week and rank. Although Paraguayan society holds teaching in high regard and the position offers prestige and respect, salaries are low; and, since the laws limit a professor to two professorships, most faculty members can teach only part time and must depend on outside professional careers for their living; consequently, they can give only limited attention to the university.

Retirement with a pension is possible if a professor is over forty-five and has served twenty years or if he is sixty and has taught ten years and has ten more years in public service.

Academic freedom (*libertad de cátedra*) is guaranteed and protected by the law; that is, the professor is protected from outside interference while presenting material in class relevant to the discipline. At the National University of Asunción, the professor is free to set the method, course contents, and regulations for his department.

Research Activities

One of the goals stated in the charter of the National University of Asunción is to prepare researchers in various fields of human knowledge. Research programs, however, involve large expenditures, and neither university can afford to divert substantial resources to this end. As a result, little research is done at the university level. At the National University of Asunción, some research is conducted with the cooperation of the Ministry of Agriculture and Livestock by the faculty of agriculture and veterinary science. The faculty of medical sciences and the Institute of Sciences are also engaged in some scientific research. At both universities, individual research on Paraguayan values and problems is conducted in the fields of humanities.

Current Problems and Trends

In the 1970s Paraguay is undergoing profound changes in many areas. The population is increasing rapidly (2.5 percent annually), which makes it difficult to provide all the educational services and opportunities that a youthful population requires. In addition, since the 1950s there has been an unprecedented internal migration away from the city of Asunción to new outlying areas of the nation. At the same time, the nation is beginning to realize some of its vast potentials in agriculture, cattle raising, and hydroelectric power. The migration and the new economic situation are both factors that will require new educational policies.

International Cooperation

Many of Paraguay's international educational contacts are with the United States.

The faculty of agriculture and veterinary science of the National University of Asunción cooperates with the college of agriculture and home economics at New Mexico State University (in Las Cruces) in a project to develop curriculum, administration, and laboratory facilities at the faculty. The program is largely financed by the United States Agency for International Development. The National University of Asunción also cooperates in three programs with the State University of New York at Buffalo. Under a contract with AID, a specialist in higher education from the State University of New York serves as a consultant to the rector of the National University of Asunción on problems of reorganization and reform. In the second program, the school of nursing at the State University of New York provides instruction and assistance to the staff of the nursing school at the national university. The third program involves technical assistance in curriculum, organization, and administration provided by the faculty of medicine at the State University of New York to its counterpart at the National University of Asunción.

Paraguay also participates with other Latin American countries in activities to develop the education and culture of the region. It is a member of the Council on Higher Education in the American Republics (CHEAR), and the *Unión de universidades de América latina* (UDUAL: Union of Latin American Universities). The Catholic university is a member of the *Organización de universidades católicas de América latina* (ODUCAL: Organization of Catholic Universities of Latin America), which promotes Catholic higher education activities and regional cultural programs in Latin America.

DOMINGO A. POLETTI LIUZZI

Bibliography

América en cifras, 1972. Situación cultural: Educación y otros aspectos culturales. Washington, D.C.: Secretaría del Instituto interamericano de estadística, 1974.

Censo universitario latinoamericano, 1971. Mexico City: Unión de universidades de América latina, 1974.

Current and Future. New York: International Council for Educational Development, 1973.

García Laguardia, J. M. *Legislación universitaria de América latina.* Mexico City: Universidad nacional autónoma de México, 1973.

Monge Alfaro, C. *La universidad y la integración de América latina.* San José, Costa Rica: Universidad de Costa Rica, 1968.

Ocampo Londoño, A. *Higher Education in Latin America: Current and Future.* New York: International Council for Educational Development, 1973.

Socio-Economic Progress in Latin America. Ninth Annual Report. Washington, D.C.: Social Progress Trust Fund, 1969.

See also: Archives: Mediterranean, the Vatican, and Latin America, National Archives of; South America: Regional Analysis.

PARALLEL COOPERATIVE EDUCATION

See Cooperative Education and Off-Campus Experience: Cooperative Education in the United States.

PARTICIPATORY DEMOCRACY

The form of governance, administration, and decision making in the world's colleges and universities has remained relatively unchanged for many years. In the United States, for example, policymaking has long been in the hands of lay boards of trustees, which, by choosing the president and delegating to him control of the institution's budget and personnel policies, are assured at least a modicum of control over educational policy and institutional direction. Faculty participation in, or power over, the educational policy, admission practices, tenure decisions, and even budget priorities, varies widely among institutions. The faculty tends to have substantial educational policymaking authority but little fiscal authority in the more well-known colleges and less overall power in the lesser-known colleges. Student participation in decision making was virtually nonexistent in most universities in the United States before the 1960s.

European and South American universities have traditions of control and participation different from those of institutions in the United States. In the early 1960s in Europe, control of the universities ranged from the full professor's chair in France, to the vice-chancellor in Britain, to the relatively democratic committees of Swedish universities. South American universities derive from fifteenth and sixteenth century European models and have a history of student participation in governance that was carried over into the early colonial universities. However, the general stability in government and society that characterized the United States immediately following World War II was also evident in European and South American countries.

Impact of Increased Political Activity on University Policymaking

Political activity increased worldwide in the late 1960s. The Cultural Revolution in the People's Republic of China, general strikes in France, intensification of leftist activity in Latin America, anti–Vietnam War activities in the United States, the rise of a youth culture in Japan, and the civil war in Bangladesh are examples of increased involvement in the political system by a broader range of people. Increased political activity was mirrored in one way or another in colleges and universities. In the United States opposition to federal government and university policies was manifested in the taking over of university buildings, the bombing of army and war matériel centers, riots, student strikes, and other active resistance.

College and university authorities responded in a variety of ways, from bewilderment, surrender, and passive resistance, to summoning civil and military authorities. In the early 1970s university response began to harden. The agitation reached its peak in the campus riots of May 1970, protesting the United States invasion of Cambodia. The Ohio National Guard,

called to the Kent State University campus to maintain order during student demonstrations, shot and killed four students.

It was during this period that radical student organizations, some dedicated to violent resistance, were formed on many American campuses. Among them were Students for a Democratic Society and the Weathermen. These organizations often had members or even leaders who, although of student age, were not university students.

The influence of such groups and the esteem in which they were held by nonparticipating students declined in the 1970s. The gradual winding down of the Vietnam War and a reassessment of the effectiveness of violent tactics resulted in a reduction of active resistance on campuses.

In response to the politics of confrontation, resistance, and violence of the late 1960s and early 1970s, higher education institutions dramatically changed the nature of the decision-making process. People whose views on the life and the direction of college and university communities had been previously ignored were consulted, and those previously uninvolved in the politics of the university—junior faculty, students, political party members, and custodial staff—began to serve on advisory and decision-making councils. In France since 1968, junior faculty have become more powerful in university decision making, a basic democratic change in institutional structure. In the United States and Great Britain, on the other hand, where students won only token representation or gained and then lost interest in more substantial representation, signs of participatory democracy might be political faddism or perhaps expediency on the part of administrators sensitive to the explosiveness of the period.

From the perspective of the mid 1970s, participatory activity has achieved little substantive change in institutional operations or in decision-making processes. Although greater input is achieved, the basic hierarchical patterns remain. In the

United States and in other industrial nations, particularly the Federal Republic of Germany and Japan, the power of the university presidency continues to grow. In Great Britain the vice-chancellor retains the same executive leadership as before the National Union of Students successfully negotiated for increased representation in 1968. Internal dialog is increased, lower-level decision making is more widely shared, but effective control of universities is no more in the hands of students and junior faculty than it was in the 1960s. In fact, internal reforms, innovations, and redistribution of power have contributed to strengthening the chief executive, who alone is accountable to the public and the trustees for increasingly adventurous programs and procedures of the faculty and students.

On the other hand, educational executives are becoming more sensitive to process and the means by which many voices may be heard and considered in decision making. So, in fact, the quality of decisions is changed and improved by the attitudinal shaping of executive leadership that resulted from the difficult decade beginning in 1965.

The most sought-after participatory roles for students in college and university governance are as trustees, voting members of educational policymaking bodies, and voting members of appointment, promotion, and tenure-deciding bodies. These are obvious and important objectives for anyone wishing to influence the outcome of university decisions. The trustees are ultimately responsible for university policy, the choice of chief executive, and many major decisions. Educational policymaking, however, is generally delegated to faculty and administration, as are decisions about faculty appointments, promotion, and tenure. In these cases and in educational policy, though, the trustees retain the power of approval. Faculty ambitions were directed primarily at participation as trustees and in institutional budget-making councils.

Developments Since the Late 1960s

South America, Central America, and Mexico. The history of student participation in governance of Latin American universities was cited as a precedent by students demanding the return of rights that had been eroded as the universities grew larger and more hierarchical. In 1966 it was estimated that in Latin American universities "generally about one-third of the governing body are students" (Lipset, 1964, pp. 144–145).

In 1971 there was violence at universities in Colombia. In response, the government proposed legislation which, among other things, included students and faculty on all levels of university governance. A political expedient to restore order, this bill was still unpassed in 1972 because of opposition from the Catholic church, industry, and private universities (which would have had their disproportionate representation on government boards reduced).

Elsewhere in Latin America student and faculty participate in university governance in varying degrees. As of 1972 students at the Ibero-American University in Mexico had five voting members on a governing board of thirty. In Brazil the university council, chief decision-making body at each university, includes heads of schools, deans of faculty, representatives of all ranks of teaching faculty, an alumni representative, and several students. Each faculty or department within the university is governed by a congregation, which includes lower-rank teachers and students as well as full professors and deans. University governance in Guyana provides for a form of input that appears unique to countries whose educational system was influenced by Great Britain. Each university has a guild of graduates, which contributes to academic policy decisions in an advisory capacity; in some universities members of the guild of graduates sit on governing boards.

Europe. In France the *Loi d'orientation de l'enseignement supérieur* (Orientation of

Higher Education Act) of 1968 removed the full professor's chair as the basic unit of power and inaugurated participatory government. The faculties of all universities were reorganized into interdisciplinary units called *Unités d'enseignement et de recherche* (UER: Units of Teaching and Research). UERs were later regrouped into universities and assimilated institutions. The chief governing units are boards of no more than eighty members, composed of equal numbers of students and faculty, plus researchers, nonteaching staff, and laymen, equal to as much as one third of the total membership. University presidents are elected by these boards.

Three factors provoked the establishment of the UER boards: student agitation, an anachronistic central administration, and pressure from junior faculty for a release from their patriarchal relationship to the professorial chairs. The conditions of the Orientation of Higher Education Act provided that student representation should be directly proportional to student voter turnout. In 1969 only 52 percent of the students voted, and by 1971 this figure had dropped to 32 percent. Beginning in 1970 government amendments began eroding the power of the orientation act.

In Great Britain a 1968 agreement between the Committee of Vice-Chancellors and Principals and the National Union of Students (NUS) called for more student participation in decision making. Although the reforms allowed student views to be taken into account in curricular and university management and planning, they were relatively ineffective as a serious challenge to the vice-chancellor's powers. An NUS survey showed that in 1968–1969 the number of universities with students on their university councils increased from six to seventeen. In late 1969 there were twenty-nine universities with student-staff committees making recommendations to the councils and senates. In 1965 there had been none with student-staff committees (Burn, 1971). In July 1970 twenty-six London colleges adopted a procedure by which students would be elected to boards of governors. However, under the procedure students would be asked to leave meetings when matters they were "not meant to know about" were under discussion.

In the Federal Republic of Germany there is no single pattern of university governance, but many interesting moves toward participation have resulted from continuing student pressure for *Drittelparität*—one-third representation on all legislative committees and administrative bodies. In July 1969 West Berlin instituted reforms to break down the traditional hierarchical powers of the faculties, place universities under strong executive administration, and give students a voice in all levels of decision making. Legislative authority within institutions is given to university councils that are empowered to elect presidents and determine educational policy. Students have one third of the vote on these committees.

By 1970, in the Lippe Colleges in North Rhine–Westphalia, with a student body of five thousand, students were heavily represented on appointment committees and on all other governing councils, to the point where most decisions cannot be made without them. This was cited as being similar to the trend in all the socialist-governed federal states (including the city-states of Berlin, Hamburg, and Bremen), where considerable administrative power is in the hands of students and younger staff. In a 1973 ruling the federal court at Karlsruhe held that the Landau states must allow professors at least 50 percent of the seats on the main decision bodies and more than 50 percent on appointment and research funding committees. In 1970 at the Free University in Berlin, secretaries, caretakers, and charwomen were brought into decision-making administrative councils.

In Sweden students have been represented on curriculum committees since 1957 (by election through student unions) and on departmental advisory boards since 1964. In 1969 a series of ongoing experiments were set up to evaluate possibilities for further cooperation between teachers, staff, and students at the department and institute level. Councils were established on which students and teachers had equal representation and on which administrative and technical staff were also represented. Councils were delegated anywhere from partial power on educational matters to complete decision-making capacity. A provision for continuing evaluation was part of the project.

In the Netherlands the university council (the highest decision-making body) at some universities is comprised of five sixths university members and one sixth lay persons. The five sixths is further designated as a minimum of one third academic staff, a maximum of one third students, and a maximum of one third nonacademic staff.

In Hungary in 1969 reforms were instituted specifically to decentralize university decision making and to include noneducational personnel, including members of the Hungarian Socialist Workers Party, on university councils.

In Finland the representation of students in authoritative bodies is growing, and a government proposal to revamp internal university administration to achieve "one person-one vote" was under discussion in 1976.

The Far East. In the People's Republic of China wide representation is achieved through "three in one committees," composed of faculty, students, and Chinese Communist Party representatives, which advise the state Chinese Communist Party University Committees.

In Burma the universities' central councils include representatives of the Burma Socialist Program Party, the People's Workers Council, the People's Peasant Council, prominent educators, and journalists.

In Hong Kong only one of the three universities, the University of Hong Kong, has a great degree of student and faculty participation. The main managerial council of the university selects 50 percent of its members from the academic staff. Aca-

demic policy is controlled closely by a senate composed of staff and six students.

In Bangladesh the University Orders of 1973 supported the autonomous nature of universities and democratized their activities. The national assembly passed a bill limiting the power of university officers by providing for increased student and faculty participation in administration. Five students are now represented on the university senate of the University of Rajshahi. Since 1973 students at all universities have been members of some committees, among them those that deal with establishing regulations and conducting examinations.

In Japan students have rarely participated in university decision making, but they are increasingly demanding participation. At some private institutions students participate indirectly in the preliminary stages of presidential selection, and students now vote for deans at several facilities. However, a subcommittee report of the Japanese Central Council for Education recommends against student participation in "organs which are de facto final decision making organs of universities" (Burn and others, 1971, p. 249).

In the Soviet Union student influence has been limited to passive resistance to certain requirements.

North America. In Canada the traditional form of government in universities is the two-tier system: a board of governors and an academic council, with the president or principal as chief executive officer. Corporate power by statute rests with the board of governors, usually composed of lay persons but often including faculty and students. In a few cases, students serve on appointments and promotion committees. Lowering the voting age to eighteen increased student agitation for involvement in university governance. A controversial experiment in Canada is the adoption of a one-tier system of government, sometimes including representation from all interested groups including administrators, teachers, and students. Laval University experimented with one-tier structures as early as 1852, under its initial charter; the University of Toronto has done so more recently (Johnston, 1973).

In the 1960s in the United States student, faculty, and minority representation increased on boards of trustees but still remained a small fraction of board membership. In 1964, 4 percent of the trustees of institutions surveyed were faculty members serving their own institutions, and 25 percent of the institutions surveyed had trustees selected by faculty on their boards (Hartnett, 1969; Hartnett, 1970).

According to a 1972 national survey of 430 colleges and universities by the American Council on Education, 25 percent of public four-year colleges and about 14 percent of all institutions had students on their governing boards. In 58 percent of the institutions student members of governing boards were not allowed to vote and functioned only in an advisory capacity. Of the institutions that did not have students on their governing boards, 63 percent did not plan to include students at a future date. At the institutions that responded to the survey, 45 percent of the nonstudent board members were either "unfavorable" or "highly unfavorable" to student membership. From these two surveys it would appear that student and faculty trusteeships are both uncommon and unpopular.

Forty junior colleges were polled as to their practices in selecting presidents and trustees. Faculty were reported involved in 51 percent of the colleges; 48 percent reported either outside consultants, outgoing presidents, or both, involved; 6 percent reported alumni participation; 21 percent reported community leaders involved; and 22 percent reported that students were involved (Carpenter, 1972, p. 27). A later Indiana University Student Association poll revealed that, at 110 out of 139 large universities responding, students were not represented on committees making tenure decisions (Carpenter, 1972, p. 28).

In North America, then, progress was made in the late 1960s and early 1970s in achieving wider student and faculty participation and representation on key institutional decision-making bodies, including boards of trustees; presidential selection committees; appointment, promotion, and tenure committees; and educational policy committees. In no case cited in the literature is there an example of faculty or student control of a board of trustees, presidential search committee, or budget-making body. In most cases participation in those three areas is token or advisory in nature, even though the representatives may have voting power. Student and faculty representatives usually are less experienced in the matters under consideration and are greatly outnumbered by unsympathetic committee colleagues.

Moreover, such representatives may be viewed with suspicion by the president or chief executive officer of the institution. The suspicion emanates from the unavoidable possibility of conflict of interest that attends faculty participation in bodies responsible for policy or decisions affecting individual faculty, including the faculty representative on the body. There is no easy way for a faculty trustee to avoid the awkwardness of participating directly or indirectly in matters from which he may benefit.

A further complication and challenge for faculty representatives is to maintain integrity and confidentiality in the face of pressures from their constituencies. Lay trustees, by contrast, represent the general public and have a sufficiently distant relationship to their constituencies to afford independent action. The problems of conflict are less apparent for student trustees, although they, too, may be personally affected by policy decisions on fees, financial aid, and other pocketbook issues.

Given the history of participation in these critical decision areas, the trend since 1970, and the inherent problems in such participatory governance, it is unlikely that there will be widespread change or growth in student and faculty participation in the immediate future.

Bibliography

Bereday, G. Z. F. (Ed.) *Comparative Education Review.* Special Issue on Student Politics, 1966, *10*(2).

Burn, B. B., and others. *Higher Education in Nine Countries: A Comparative Study of Colleges and Universities Abroad.* New York: McGraw-Hill, 1971.

Carpenter, D. A. "The Role of Nontrustees in Selecting Presidents." *Junior College Journal,* 1972, *42*(9), 27–29.

Froese, L. "University Reform: A Comparative Analysis of the United States, USSR, and Germany." *World Yearbook of Education, 1971–72.* New York: International Publication Services, 1971.

Hartnett, R. T. *College and University Presidents: Their Backgrounds, Roles and Educational Attitudes.* Princeton, New Jersey: Educational Testing Service, Princeton University, 1969.

Hartnett, R. T. *The New College Trustee: Some Predictions for the 1970s.* Princeton, New Jersey: Educational Testing Service, Princeton University, 1970.

Havinghurst, R. "Latin American and North American Higher Education." *Comparative Education Review,* 1961, *4*(3), 176.

Hoffman, S. "Participation in Perspective." *Daedalus,* Winter 1970, *99,* 177–221.

Jenks, R. S. "Student Participation in University Government: A Case History." *Education Record,* 1973, *54,* 236–242.

Johnston, B. (Ed.) "News Highlights." *Education Yearbook, 1973–74.* New York: MacMillan Educational Corporation, 1973.

Lipset, S. M. "University Students and Politics in Underdeveloped Countries." *Minerva,* 1964, *3*(1), 15–56.

Niblett, W., and Butts, R. (Eds.) "Higher Education in Latin America in an Era of Change." *World Yearbook of Education, 1972–73.* New York: International Publication Services, 1972.

Patterson, M. "French University Reform." *Comparative Education Review,* 1972, *16*(2), 281–302.

Pelczar, R. "University Reform in Latin America: The Case of Colombia." *Comparative Education Review,* 1972, *16*(2), 230–250.

Perlman, D. H. "Faculty Trusteeship." *Education Record,* 1973, *54,* 115–129.

Whiting, C. "Battle of the New Freedoms: West Germany." *Times* (London) *Educational Supplement,* 1970, *2881,* 8.

Whiting, C. "London Students Will Elect Governors." *Times* (London) *Educational Supplement,* 1970, *2877,* 6.

CHARLES R. LONGSWORTH

See also: Accountability; Autonomy; Faculty Unionism: the United States and Great Britain; Governance and Control of Higher Education; Unrest, Campus.

PATENTS

See Legal Aspects of Higher Education.

PAX ROMANA

Pax Romana was founded in Fribourg, Switzerland, in 1921 under the name of Pax Romana—International Secretariat of Catholic Students. At its Rome assembly in 1947, the organization established two autonomous branches: (1) Pax Romana —International Movement of Catholic Students and (2) Pax Romana—International Catholic Movement for Intellectual and Cultural Affairs.

The student branch of Pax Romana, made up of sixty-five national federations in sixty countries, aims to develop understanding among federations of Catholic students in different countries, to see that members receive a sound grounding in Christian principles, to spread Christian doctrines in the university milieu, and to undertake international projects. The student movement's highest organ is the interfederal assembly, composed of two delegates from every national federation, which meets every two years. The directing committee and the general secretariat (in Fribourg, Switzerland) are the other two important organs of the movement. Regional secretariats are located in Hong Kong; Lima, Peru; and Fribourg, Switzerland. Specialized secretariats exist for specialized fields of study such as engineering.

The graduate branch, Pax Romana —International Catholic Movement for Intellectual and Cultural Affairs, aims to unite Catholic university graduates so that they can find solutions to problems of modern life in keeping with Christian faith and ethics. Furthermore, the movement provides contact and mutual aid to Catholic intellectuals and their oganizations. Comprising sixty federations in fifty countries, the graduate branch is guided by a plenary assembly, which meets every two years. The executive organ of the graduate branch is the council, which meets twice a year. The president, two vice-presidents, the secretary general, and fourteen members elected by the assembly make up the council. There are specialized secretariats for artists, teachers, jurists, engineers, and scientists. The general secretariat is located at Fribourg, Switzerland.

The two branches of Pax Romana have a common organ, the Committee of Pax Romana, consisting of the president, secretary general, and two members of the directing committee/council of each movement. Every six years, the two movements conjointly organize a world congress.

Pax Romana publishes a quarterly, *Convergence,* in two editions, English and French.

1 route du Jura
1701 Fribourg, Switzerland

Among the report's general recommendations concerning the pay and pay structures in postsecondary education are periodic review of teachers' pay independent of their negotiating bodies, improvement of data available to negotiators on the impact of pay structures, and increased effort to simplify salary scales. The committee specifically recommends a common salary grade structure for the polytechnics and colleges of education in England and Wales, and a separate but common structure for postsecondary institutions in Scotland.

The report assesses the impact that these recommendations, if implemented, would have on negotiating machinery and estimates the average annual percentage pay increases under the proposed common salary grade structures. The immediate average annual percentage increase in pay, retroactive from May 1974, for postsecondary teaching staff in England and Wales would be 26 percent, while the long-term average annual increase would be 30 percent. In Scotland the increase would be 24 percent immediately and 31 percent in the long run.

PAY OF NON-UNIVERSITY TEACHERS, THE (Higher Education Report), United Kingdom

The Pay of Non-University Teachers (London: H. M. Stationery Office, 1974)—a report of the special Committee of Inquiry appointed by the secretary of state for education and science of the United Kingdom and the secretary of state for Scotland, under the chairmanship of D. Houghton— examines the compensation of nonuniversity teachers in England, Wales, and Scotland. The committee considered the salaries of teachers in postsecondary institutions, including polytechnics and colleges of education. Materials are also included on the compensation of primary and secondary school teachers.

PEDAGOGICAL RESEARCH CENTER OF HIGHER EDUCATION
(Felsöoktatási pedagógiai kutatóközpont), Hungary

The Pedagogical Research Center of Higher Education was founded in 1963 as a research unit at Eötvös Loránd University, Budapest. An independent research center since 1967, it conducts studies in higher and adult education with a national or international focus. Research topics in higher education include the following: economics of higher education, educational planning, educational technology, history of higher education, curricula and instruction, methodology of research, and reform in higher education. In addition to research activities, the center develops evaluation tools such as tests and measurements, trains researchers, holds conferences and seminars, and provides a documentation service.

Directed and funded by the Ministry of Education, the center has a staff of thirty research professionals, four paid consultants, twenty administrative personnel, two secretaries, four editorial personnel, and eight printers. The staff has access to libraries and computers.

Eötvös Loránd tudományegyetem
Rigó u. 16
1431 Budapest VIII, Hungary

PERIODICALS, HIGHER EDUCATION

For those concerned with the world of higher education, its journal literature—conceived as one element of a system of information transfer—serves an infinite variety of purposes. It is probably the most widely used instrument for recording and disseminating information. In the context of rapid, worldwide growth and change in higher education, the ever increasing number of periodicals has been represented as a print format that meets the practitioner's need for up-to-date information and serves the professional's need for a channel of publication and dissemination. More particularly, the journal literature meets the user's need for creative stimulation as well as retrospective searching. In addition, periodicals record and circulate reports presented to professional meetings in every part of the world. Paisley (1968, pp. 1–30) has noted that the professional staffs of the influential higher education journals and their circles of contributors and consultants literally govern the flow of information in their subject areas.

As yet there is no single access tool, no single comprehensive bibliography of the journal literature in higher education. The neglect of this subject is apparent in the fact that the index to Winchell's (1967) monumental American *Guide to Reference Books* and its several supplements does not include any reference to higher education other than a single monograph. And Burke and Burke's (1967) standard aid to bibliographical access in the field of education does not include the term *higher education* in its index at all. Hardly more explicit in its treatment of the periodical literature of higher education is White's (1973) *Sources of Information in the Social Sciences.* However, relevant and important writing is being done by people outside the field of higher education and their work appears in a wide range of popular, technical, and social science journals. For access to and identification of this information in so many different kinds of journals, the abstract and index publications are invaluable.

Computer technology, microform publishing, and new modes of printing and publication have created new styles of information storage and retrieval, affecting the format of journal literature as well as raising questions about the timeliness of the content of the established media. Some of the new formats (for example, journal articles accompanied by abstracts) suggest a future melding and integration of print and computer technology. This trend is anticipated in the European Documentation and Information System for Education (EUDISED) sponsored by the Council of Europe (Strasbourg, France) and in *New Serials Titles* (1975). Some enthusiasts for the potential of computer technology as a tool of information science criticize the conventional journal literature and hold that "information has only archival value by the time it reaches print in primary journals" (Farbisoff and Ely, 1974, p. 58).

Inseparably linked to periodicals that appear at regular intervals are serial publications and continuations, such as proceedings, transactions, advances, progresses, reports, yearbooks, annual reviews, and handbooks, which fill the vaguely defined area of information dissemination between monographic publications and the journal literature. For those who seek and use information, the division of the literature by formats and categories is somewhat artificial.

Taken together, the periodical-serial literature is, with its accompanying abstracts and indexes, basic to planning and to the policymaking and decision-making processes essential to the continued development of institutions of higher education. Access to educational documentation is vital to planners, administrators, researchers, teachers, and to the general public concerned with the development of the educational institutions of the world.

The various ideological currents, impulses, interest groups, and concerns at work in the enterprise of higher education are reflected in related journal literature. Although these vary from country to country, common human aspirations have given rise to an array of periodicals referred to as international.

Obvious approaches to the identification of international periodicals are found in the published output of international organizations, such as UNESCO (Paris), Organization of American States (Washington, D.C.), International Association of Universities (Paris), Council of Europe (Strasbourg, France), and International Institute for Studies on Education (Brussels). Some journals that are international in character deal with undergraduate study abroad, student exchange, and the problems of aid to new nations; others deal with the informational needs of the most advanced specialists—in particular disciplines as well as in area studies. A few simply have the word *international* in the title or subtitle, an aspiration hardly reflected in the content. Most deal with postsecondary schooling in more than one culture. The international orientation has also influenced the format of a few journals: some represent translations from one language to another; in others the contents are produced in more than one language, although English appears to be most prevalent. It is notable, however, that the ideology of internationalism as essential to the survival of mankind and

integral to the idea of a university is predominant in the entire range of journal literature.

National journals of higher education mirror academic life and, more particularly, professional affairs and the traditional discipline orientation of the college and university; local journals usually reflect the academic life and concerns of a single institution—although some exhibit a special or regional concern. The national journal literature reflects not only established change but also change brought on by the impact of political and social forces. A social and economic order of growing complexity, combined with the pressures of egalitarian philosophies, has brought new populations into the arena of the teaching/learning process in the industrial as well as in the developing countries, and this in turn has introduced problems of access. The closely related phenomenal expansion of higher education has raised questions of finance: Who will pay and who will benefit? Political, social, and economic change is forcing a redefinition of higher education as lifelong education—formal and informal—embracing adult, technical, vocational, and professional education. For each area of concern and specialization, new interest groups are formed and new journals established. The expansion of the academic structure itself and the impact of technology have brought into being new problems of operation, administration, and pedagogical strategy, each giving rise to one or more journals as a medium of communication for the interest groups concerned.

The significance of the whole range of journal literature—international, national, and local—was felicitously described by Ross (1972) in a statement of editorial policy launching the journal *Higher Education* in the United Kingdom. He described the new publication as a place in which problems may be discussed, objectives refined, ideas shared, and strategies compared.

Substantively this article deals with higher education as it appears in the traditional academic enterprise. Other segments of postsecondary education—such as those represented by theological institutions, the military, civil service, business and industry, nursing schools, labor unions' educational programs, and proprietary schools—are not explicitly covered, and only a selection of the most recently published bibliographies are included.

Types and Sources of Periodicals

To impose some order on the diversity of literature published for and by various sectors of the educational community throughout the world, the following discussion of the types and sources of periodicals is divided into several categories: general education, indexing and abstracting publications, government publications, administrative information, research literature, contemporary problems and developments, lifelong education, and special-purpose journals.

General education. There are many periodicals covering the several aspects and levels of education. In the United States two such journals are sponsored by prominent schools of education: the *Teachers College Record* (Columbia University; New York) and the *Harvard Educational Review* (Harvard University, Cambridge, Massachusetts). Both are wide ranging in content and appear to involve a circle of contributors and readers far beyond their institutional constituencies. The *Record*, however, devotes more space to educational activities in other countries. Another source of general comment on education is interest groups, such as the Society for the Advancement of Education, which publishes *Intellect* (New York), a monthly that blends news reporting and professional comment on a wide variety of subjects, of which education is only one. Another kind of interest group, the Federation of Australian University Staff Associations, publishes *Vestes* (Melbourne). A disciplinary approach is also apparent in the journal literature, as exemplified by *Sociology of Education,* published by the American Sociological Association; it responds to the fact that the theoretical perspectives of anthropology, economics, history, political science, psychology, and sociology are being used in the analysis of educational institutions. A more specific disciplinary orientation, but general in character, may be found in the *History of Education Quarterly* (New York), the official organ of the History of Education Society, published in cooperation with the School of Education, New York University. Although predominantly American in its emphasis, it also publishes articles dealing with education elsewhere in the world.

Other countries also publish comprehensive journals. For example, the new *Oxford Review of Education,* linked to Oxford University's Department of Educational Studies and published three times a year, publishes papers on the theory and practice of education from scholars throughout the world writing from a variety of disciplinary viewpoints. It also proposes to publish articles on matters of educational policy, administration, and planning. Similarly broad in coverage is the *West African Journal of Education,* published by the University of Ibadan's Institute of Education on behalf of participating West African universities and Ministries of Education.

Revue française de pédagogie, sponsored by the *Institut national de recherche et de documentation pédagogiques,* publishes articles that are national in character and serve interests at every level. A German equivalent, *Bildung und Erziehung* (Stuttgart), also includes abstracts of the articles in English. The Italian bimonthly, *I problemi della pedagogia* (Rome), exemplifies a scholarly philosophical and historical approach. Japan's educators produce a number of important journals little known in other countries. However, the English-language *Education in Japan,* published by the International Educational Research Institute of Hiroshima University, is a showcase journal that brings to the world Japanese educational history, philosophy, and practice.

The socialist countries publish a considerable range of educational journals with a pervasive political orientation. A major Soviet publication is *Sovetskaia pedagogika* (Moscow); the Institute of Pedagogy of the University of Warsaw is represented by *Kwartalnik pedagogiczny;* and *Pedaggiai szemli* is published in Budapest. Considered as a group, their concession to English-language readers is limited to an English table of contents and an occasional brief article summary. For such readers, the editors of *Soviet Education,* a monthly journal of translations published by the International Arts and Sciences Press (White Plains, New York), select material from more than thirty-five Soviet periodicals, newspapers, and, occasionally, books. The same publishers also market a companion translation quarterly, *Chinese Education.*

International organizations and interest groups also publish general journals. For example, the Council of Europe's Council for Cultural Co-operation publishes *Education and Culture* three times a year in English, French, and German editions. This periodical is concerned with all of the media of communication and represents the widest possible conceptualization of education; it is offered as an instrument of practical cooperation among European educationists. Another example is *Universidades,* a Spanish-language bimonthly representing the member institutions affiliated to the Union of Universities of Latin America (including Cuba and Puerto Rico) in an open forum of thought and opinion. *Paedagogica Historica,* an international journal of history published in Ghent, Belgium, has an editorial board that is international in representation; the journal itself is quadrilingual, with English, French, German, and Dutch texts. Integrative elements of *Paedagogica Historica* are its "Index Bibliographicus," a list of recent acquisitions of the Centre for the Study of the History of Education, also located in Ghent, and its "List of Periodicals Mentioned," helpful to those interested in identifying journals that publish historical articles.

Indexing and abstracting publications. In-separably linked to the professional literature—and part of the systematic effort to analyze and coordinate access to it—are the indexing and abstracting publications. Probably the best-known American publication in this field since 1929 is the *Education Index.* A more comprehensive publication (since 1969) is the *Current Index to Journals in Education* (CIJE) published by Macmillan Information in New York. It covers more than seven hundred journals, all of which are indexed by one of the eighteen Educational Resources Information Center (ERIC) clearinghouses operated by the United States Office of Education. CIJE is also converted to magnetic tape for access via computer. Such tapes are marketed under the trade names Dialog/ERIC (Lockheed Corporation) and SDC/ERIC (Systems Development Corporation). Other well-established indexing publications are the *Australian Education Index* (Victoria), the *British Education Index* (London), and the *Canadian Education Index* (Toronto).

Dissemination of the contents of the professional literature is also facilitated through the publication of summaries or abstracts, such as the *Indian Education Abstracts* (New Delhi). In addition there are compilations of abstracts for special-interest groups, such as *Research into Higher Education Abstracts* (London) and *Educational Administration Abstracts;* the latter, published by the University Council for Educational Administration (Columbus, Ohio) is based on nearly one hundred American, British, French, and Australian journals.

Another technique of speeding user access to the periodical literature is provided by *Current Contents; Behavioral, Social and Educational Sciences,* a weekly publication of the Institute for Scientific Information (Philadelphia), which reproduces in original format the tables of contents of more than seven hundred education journals published in United States and abroad.

Government publications. In the various countries around the world there is no uniform relationship between government and education. In some instances, higher education is outside the realm of government; in others, it is under ministry control. Communication between a ministry and those concerned with any particular level of education takes place through directive or nondirective publications. Directive issuances generally take the form of bulletins, circulars, instructions, gazettes, notices, notes, orders, and regulations; nondirective communications take the form of announcements, informational bulletins and letters, newsletters and newspapers, research studies, and professional journals of general and specialized types.

Trends in Education is a Ministry of Education quarterly published by Her Majesty's Stationery Office in London. Although its emphasis is on educational process and teacher training, it covers all levels of education, including vocational, technical, and adult education. When the United Kingdom joined the European community, a special 1973 Europe issue was devoted entirely to European educational themes. *Education Quarterly,* published by the Ministry of Education and Social Welfare of the government of India, is broader and more speculative in content, containing articles on "Academic Freedom in Universities" (October 1973, *25*), "The Open University" (July 1973, *25*), and "Examination Reforms in Technical Education" (April 1973, *25*). The United States counterpart is *American Education,* which is published ten times a year by the Office of Education and reflects the federal interest at all educational levels. Its format is that of a popular magazine and differs from other ministerial publications in its nonprofessional and informal character. *Annali della publico istruzione* is a general quarterly under the egis of the Italian Ministry of Public Instruction. The *Tasmanian Journal of Education* is another government periodical that deals with all levels of schooling.

Exclusively higher education periodicals published by ministries of education are the *Message of the Teacher* of Jordan (printed in Arabic and English), *Vestnik vysshei shkoly* of the Soviet Union, and *Lycie szkoly wyzszej* of Poland. One ministry publication, the *Pakistan Educational Review* (Islamabad), is published under the joint auspices of the Central Bureau of Education and the Pakistan National Commission for UNESCO.

Administrative information. College administrators find journals sponsored by commercial firms useful for their advertising as well as for their information content. For example, *College Management,* one of the Macmillan professional magazines, blends informative advertising with useful current information. *American School and University,* published monthly in Greenwich, Connecticut, by the Educational Division of the North American Publishing Company, contains advertisements dealing with the widest array of products needed for plant maintenance and support of a college population. Indeed, a number of publishers—Academic Press, Elsevier, and Pergamon, among others—maintain stables of journals pertinent to higher education.

There is also a wide range of professional journals that deal with academic administration. One is *College and University,* published in Philadelphia, the quarterly journal of the American Association of Collegiate Registrars and Admissions Officers (Washington, D.C.), whose articles from contributors around the world promote education and the offices of admission, financial aid, institutional research, records, registration, and related functions. The Standing Conference of Rectors and Vice-Chancellors of the European Universities (CRE) publishes the quarterly *CRE Information* (Geneva, Switzerland) in English and French texts. A more catholic approach to both administration and education is represented in the University of Leeds' (England) *Journal of Educational Administration and History.*

Research literature. A most useful listing of the research literature in periodical form appears in the "Source Journal Index" section of the annual cumulation to the *Current Index to Journals in Education,* primarily because of the broad coverage given to ERIC documents distributed through clearinghouses, each of which is responsible for a particular subject area. Higher education is well covered since there are clearinghouses for higher education, junior colleges, adult education, and vocational and technical education. Although the bulk of the journal literature indexed in CIJE is American, many periodicals with an international orientation, as well as some foreign journals, are analyzed under appropriate subject headings.

Similarly, in the United Kingdom the reporting medium on recent or current research, *Research into Higher Education Abstracts* (London), provides comprehensive coverage together with selected coverage of appropriate "overseas" work. A companion publication is the *Register of Research into Higher Education.* Both are published quarterly by the Society for Research into Higher Education (London). Abstracts are based on a regular survey of more than 160 periodicals, including the *Alberta Journal of Educational Research* (University of Alberta, Canada), *American Educational Research Journal* (Washington, D.C.), *Bulletin of the International Association of Universities* (Paris), *Higher Education* (Amsterdam), and *Vestnik vysshei shkoly* (Ministry of Higher and Secondary Specialized Education of the Soviet Union).

An explicit international orientation is represented by *Scientia Pedagogica Experimentalis,* published twice a year by the Center for Experimental Educational Research in Ghent, Belgium. Its table of contents is in English and French, and articles may appear in any of several languages. A periodical with more limited scope is the University of Western Australia's (Nedlands) *Educational Research and Perspectives,* which includes both scholarly articles and research reports for all levels. The New Zealand Council for Educational Research publishes the biannual *New Zealand Journal of Educational Studies* (Wellington), which despite its sponsorship includes general articles from any of the major fields of educational study in New Zealand and the Pacific area.

Contemporary problems and developments. Change, published in New Rochelle, New York, is a broadly conceived journal that deals with current information and issues in higher education. Its objective is embodied in its explicit title. Funded by the Exxon Education Foundation, the Ford Foundation, and the Lilly Endowment, it appears in a general as well as a community college edition. Perhaps more staid in content and opinion is the *Educational Record,* published quarterly by the American Council on Education (Washington, D.C.). Its pages provide "a platform for the presentation of ideas and information of importance to colleges and universities in the United States." The *British Journal of Teacher Education,* published three times a year by Methuen in Hampshire, England, is a platform for discussion of change endemic in teacher education. It has a panel of overseas correspondents that helps reflect developments in teacher education on an international scale. An older journal, *Improving College and University Teaching,* suggests a narrower focus of interest in innovation and is directed toward the teacher at two- and four-year higher education institutions. Sponsored by the Graduate School of Oregon State University (in Corvallis), the journal reaches educators in more than forty countries. The concern with change and orientation toward the future has deeply affected the content of almost all of the journal literature, no matter what the area of specialization.

Lifelong education. The journal literature dealing with adult and continuing education, vocational and technical education, and the community college—with some notable exceptions—is generally national and even parochial in character. One exception is the *Journal of the International Congress of University Adult Education* (Ontario, Canada), which provides opportunities for the publication of substantial articles and research papers on aspects of university adult education; another is *Convergence* (Toronto, Canada), which is an international journal in the fullest sense. Established for the "sharing of achievements and failures, of innovations and demonstrations of hopes, dreams and affirmations," it is printed in the languages first used by UNESCO: English, French, Spanish, and Russian. While *Adult Education,* the journal of the Adult Education Association of the United States (Washington, D.C.), does invite articles on comparative adult education, the few international references found in recent (1974, 1975) issues were restricted to the book reviews. Similarly, Britain's *Adult Education,* published by the National Institute of Adult Education in London, evidences an effort to facilitate international contact through sections of the journal titled "Information and Events" and "Reviews." *The Indian Journal of Adult Education* (New Delhi), although focused on national concerns, does reflect a strong interest in the experience of the developing countries as well as the industrial areas of the world.

Many other adult education journals can be identified by turning to any of the numerous bibliographies in the field, such as Savicky (n.d.) or *Bibliographie sur l'éducation permanente* (1973), which defines lifelong education as a global concept that integrates different aspects and educational processes in a coherent continuum.

The journal literature that deals with vocational and technical education is also largely national in character, although there are several exceptions—for example, the *International Journal of Electrical Engineering Education* (Wrexham, England), the *International Journal of Mechanical Engineering Education* (London), and *Industrial Training International* (London). More typically, the journal of the technical colleges of education, *Vocational Aspect of Education* (London), deals largely with the British scene, although some comparisons with concepts, theory, and practice in other cultural settings are included. The essential international role is not fulfilled by the specialized journal literature but is accomplished by *CIRF Abstracts,* published by the International Labour Office in Geneva, Switzerland. (CIRF is an acronym for *Centre international d'information et de recherche sur la formation professionnelle.*)

The predominantly American junior and community college literature reflects the model of postsecondary education whose main characteristics have spread to many countries, including Canada, Japan, Yugoslavia, and Norway. The major periodical is *Community and Junior College Journal* (Washington, D.C.), published eight times a year by the American Association of Community and Junior Colleges; it supports the entire range of junior and community college program goals. *Community College Frontiers,* a quarterly published in Springfield, Illinois, under the sponsorship of Sangamon State and Governors State Universities, gives special attention to students and teachers in technical and vocational curricula. *Community College Review* is a regional quarterly linked to North Carolina State University. *Tankidaigaku kyoiku* (Junior College Education) is published in Japan.

Special-purpose journals. The *Times Higher Education Supplement* (THES), published in London, is the most widely read weekly newspaper devoted exclusively to higher education. Essentially British in content, each issue includes American as well as world university news; THES forthrightly regards academics as members of an international community. Tabloid in format, its articles are largely written by professional journalists, although its pages offer an open forum on major academic, social, and political issues facing higher education throughout the world. The periodical is read by an estimated 23,400 academics in the United Kingdom and 5000 readers overseas. Similar in format but more popular in style and content is the *Chronicle of Higher Education,* published weekly during the academic year in Washington, D.C.

Filled with news of the American campus scene, it includes occasional articles about academic life and activities elsewhere in the world.

Another special category of journal is essentially a public relations and fund-raising vehicle for colleges and universities. For example, the purposes of the *West Virginia University Magazine,* published quarterly by West Virginia University Foundation, Inc., a nonprofit corporation dedicated to the advancement of West Virginia University, are to inform alumni and friends of major developments at the university and to share a variety of ideas with them. A broader cultural appeal is represented in *University; A Princeton Quarterly,* a journal that professes to reflect a modern university's progress toward its two objectives: the education of men and women and the development of knowledge. The *University of Chicago Record,* which emanates from that institution's office of the vice-president for public affairs, includes a variety of official and formal notices and articles. A more general journal is the quarterly *Columbia Today,* which is circulated to the widely scattered graduates of Columbia University (New York), with information about sports, programs, libraries, faculty accomplishments, and achievements of graduates. The *Israeli Technion,* which adheres to the same pattern, is an English-language quarterly of the public relations department of the Technion—Israel Institute of Technology (Haifa) addressed to a worldwide circle of supporters.

Many other journals deal with such special subject matter as teacher preparation, teacher organizations, student organizations, and academic libraries.

Bibliography

Berdahl, R. O., and Altomare, G. *Comparative Higher Education.* Occasional Paper No. 4. New York: International Council for Educational Development, 1972.

Bibliographie sur l'éducation permanente. Paris: UNESCO, 1973.

Burke, A. J., and Burke, M. A. *Documentation in Education.* New York: Teachers College Press, Columbia University, 1967.

Camp, W. L., and Schwork, B. L. *Guide to Periodicals in Education and Its Academic Disciplines.* (2nd ed.) Metuchen, New Jersey: Scarecrow Press, 1975.

Diener, T. J., and Trower, D. L. *An Annotated Guide to Periodical Literature: Higher Education.* Athens: University of Georgia Institute of Higher Education, 1969.

Dimitrov, T. D. (Comp. and Ed.) *Documents of International Organizations: A Bibliographic Handbook.* London: International University Publications, 1973.

Educational Periodicals. Paris: UNESCO, 1963.

Educational Press Association of America. *America's Education Press.* Syracuse, New York: Syracuse University School of Journalism, 1971.

Educator's World. Philadelphia: North American Publishing Company, 1972.

Farbisoff, S. G., and Ely, D. P. *Information and Information Needs.* Washington, D.C.: U.S. Office of Education, 1974.

International Guide to Educational Documentation. (2nd ed., 1960–1965.) Paris: UNESCO, 1971.

Irregular Serials and Annuals. (3rd ed., 1974–1975.) New York: Bowker, 1974.

Katz, B. *Magazines for Libraries.* New York: Bowker, 1969.

Lins, L. J., and Rees, R. A. *Scholars' Guide to Journals of Education and Educational Psychology.* Madison, Wisconsin: Dembar Educational Research Service, 1965.

New Serials Titles 1950–1970. (4 vols.) Washington, D.C.: Library of Congress, 1973.

New Serials Titles 1950–1970. (2 vols.) New York: Bowker, 1975.

New Serials Titles 1971–1973. Washington, D.C.: Library of Congress, 1974.

Paisley, W. J. "Information Needs and Uses." In C. A. Cuandra (Ed.), *American Society of Information Science and Technology.* Vol. 3. Chicago: Encyclopaedia Britannica, 1968.

Ross, A. M. "Editorial." *Higher Education,* February 1972, *1,* 3.

Savicky, I. *European Selective Bibliography on Adult Education (1966–1971).* Prague: European Centre for Leisure and Education, n.d.

Ulrich's International Periodicals Directory. (16th ed., 1975–1976.) New York: Bowker, 1975.

White, C. M. *Sources of Information in the Social Sciences.* Chicago: American Library Association, 1973.

Willingham, W. W. *Source Book for Higher Education.* New York: College Entrance Examination Board, 1973.

Winchell, M. *Guide to Reference Books.* Chicago: American Library Association, 1967.

SIDNEY FORMAN
NORMAN WADHAM

[With special acknowledgement to Florence B. Wilkinson, Teachers College Librarian, Columbia University.]

See also: Documentation and Information Centers in Higher Education; International Directory of Documentation and Information Centers in Higher Education; Literature of Higher Education, Sources of and Access to; Publications, Higher Education.

PERU, REPUBLIC OF

Population: 15,383,000 (1974 estimate). Student enrollment in primary school: 2,750,000 (1970); secondary school (academic, vocational, technical): 985,300 (1970); university: 165,000 (1974). Language of instruction: Spanish. Academic calendar: April to December, two semesters, with some variation. Percentage of national budget expended on all education: 19.9% (1971–72); higher education: 2.7% (1971–72).

Peru's first university, San Marcos, was founded in 1551, eighteen years after the Spanish under Francisco Pizarro had conquered the Incas. (San Marcos is generally considered to be the first university in all of Latin America, although the Autonomous University of Santo Domingo makes a similar claim.) Modeled on the University of Salamanca in Spain, it was essentially theological and ecclesiastical, and it was reserved for the sons of the *conquistadores.* At the end of the nineteenth century some secularization took place when law, natural sciences, and medicine were added to the curriculum. The changes were made to provide the sons of the nobility access to status denied them by the Spanish crown because of their colonial birth. At the same period, university financing passed from the clergy to the crown, and governance came directly into the hands of the viceroy. For over 140 years, until the Catholic university of San Antonio Abad was established in Cuzco in 1692, San Marcos remained the only university in the region now known as Peru. It was not until Peru became independent of Spain in 1824 that education began to receive greater attention. Twenty-five years after independence, public secondary and normal schools were founded; control of public education was centralized; two more universities were established, in Trujillo and Arequipa.

By the twentieth century, approximately one thousand students were enrolled in the four universities and in the national schools of engineering and agriculture. In 1917 the Catholic University of Peru, which later became the Pontifical Catholic University of Peru, was founded in Lima. In 1955 one more university was added, the National Engineering University, which had been founded in 1875 as the School of Civil Engineering and Mining. The same year the total enrollment among the five institutions reached eighteen thousand. Since then, dramatic growth, including the opening of over twenty-five new institutions, has characterized Peruvian higher education, and coping with this growth has been a major factor in recent reforms. By 1960 there were eight universities with an enrollment of thirty-one thousand students, while in 1975 there were thirty-three universities (twenty-two national and eleven privately supported) with total enrollment estimated at one hundred seventy thousand. Fifteen institutions are located in the Lima area alone, which has over 60 percent of the country's student population.

Legal Basis of Educational System

The current legal basis for higher education in Peru is complex and enigmatic. The system is in the midst of what is designed to be a profound reform, compatible with the sweeping reforms of the revolutionary government of General Juan Velasco Alvarado, established in 1968. It is, however, politically and structurally operating within a legal double standard. In 1969 the revolutionary government took a firm stand against Peruvian university autonomy, as reflected in Decree-Law 17437 and subsequent modifications in

Decree-Laws 17833 and 17843. These laws established vast structural changes, with a clear hierarchical and authoritarian system of governance and control.

Almost universal dissatisfaction among students and faculty with the 1969 reform led to continued unrest and instability within universities. As a consequence, a commission was established to redesign the reform and produce a new one which would embrace all levels of education and receive support from crucial educational sectors. By 1971 it was clear that the new educational reform would differ substantially from that of 1969 by being more open, participatory, and representative. Finally, in March 1972 the General Education Law (Decree-Law 19326) was passed; however, it provided only the general framework for the new reform. The law established the *Comisión estatuaria nacional* (CEN: National Statute Commission) to prepare a statute which would apply to the entire system and, in effect, activate the law.

Several attempts have been made to present completed statutes to the government, which has failed to approve them because the statutes cannot appease all political factions, and the government is unwilling to risk renewed unrest. The result has been a legal if not philosophical vacuum, in which educational policy has been developed within the context of both the 1969 and the 1972 reforms, so that attributes of both laws are found in the current system. The government of General Francisco Morales Bermúdez, who took office in August 1975, has indicated that a resolution to this problem, a new university statute, would appear soon.

Types of Institutions

In 1975 there were thirty-three universities in Peru. Of these, twenty-two were *nacionales* (public) and eleven *particulares* (private) universities. Technical institutes and professional schools are not considered equivalent to universities, but many of them provide alternative forms of post-secondary training for individuals who are unqualified for or do not wish to engage in university training. With some exceptions the quality of these institutions is relatively low. All programs are terminal and do not qualify graduates for university admission.

As a result of the law of 1972, higher education, together with initial education, will represent a radical departure from precedent and tradition. Higher education is to be viewed as an integral aspect of the total educational process and system. The new system provides three cycles in higher education. Cycle one creates a new type of institution, *Escuela superior de educación profesional* (ESEP: Higher School of Professional Education). Distinct from the traditional university or professional school, the ESEP offers a six- to eight-semester course to prepare students for the *bachillerato profesional,* which certifies them for middle-level professional activities and is required for entrance into a university academic program. The ESEP will serve as a channeling device to determine which students will continue on to more advanced education and which will terminate their professional studies at this level. Designed to be a sophisticated professional education center, the ESEP includes general studies as well as professional training. It is also designed to alleviate the political pressures upon the government as well as the physical pressures upon the universities which stem from the great demand for admission to university studies and from the vast numbers of young people who are denied admission. About a half-dozen ESEPs are already in operation.

Cycle two consists of university-level studies, leading to the professional *licenciatura* and the postgraduate *maestria* degrees, and studies in other parallel institutions leading to equivalent degrees.

Cycle three includes all advanced studies and research activities leading to the doctoral degree. Study and research activities at this level are carried out by the universities but are coordinated by the *Instituto nacional de altos estudios* (National Institute of Graduate Studies).

Relationship with Secondary Education and Admission Requirements

Until the 1972 law comes into full force, public secondary education will consist of two cycles for youths between the ages of twelve and sixteen. The first cycle consists of three years of highly structured general studies. This is followed by a two-year cycle of specialized studies, such as in letters and sciences, industry/commerce, or agriculture. Students who complete the specialized cycle of secondary studies are then eligible to apply to a university-level institution, but final admission is granted only after successful achievement on the entrance examinations given in March of each year. Only about 10 percent of new graduates from secondary schools score in the acceptable range for a particular institution and academic program. Since applicants cannot apply to more than one institution or major field of study, those who are unsuccessful must wait a full year before reapplying. A number of private academies provide programs of study to prepare these persons for subsequent examinations.

Basic education for children from age six to fifteen consists of nine grades, which correspond approximately to the existing primary and secondary system. Basic education is oriented toward personal development of the individual and toward the acquisition of occupational skills.

Administration and Control

In 1969 the *Consejo nacional de la universidad peruana* (CONUP: National Council of Peruvian Universities) was created, bringing the great number of autonomous universities under centralized authority and control. Prior to 1969 cooperative agencies, such as an Inter-University Council and Planning Office, did exist; but their powers were modest in comparison to those of CONUP. All universities presently operate under the supervision of CONUP, which oversees all budgets, plans, curricula, and, in some instances, the actual governance of public institutions. Private universities receive a relatively minor subsidy via CONUP but are nevertheless included within the general purview of the council's influence.

Under the 1972 reform, CONUP is to be replaced as the highest authority within higher education by the *Asamblea universitaria nacional* (National University Assembly), made up of university officials, teachers, and students, each group having a one-third representation. Included in this body are two nonteaching university employees with voting membership. The executive body is the *Consejo representativo del sistema universitario* (CRESU: Representative Council of the University System), made up of university officials, teachers, and students. Its president will also be the president of the National University Assembly. The membership of the executive body will not exceed fifteen. A general secretariat will serve in an advisory capacity, with technical responsibilities. Until a statute is written for the 1972 law, however, CONUP will continue to function as the highest authority for the university system.

The 1969 law ratified the reform movement of the mid 1960s, which—at least in theory—promoted liberalization of the highly professional curricula and departmentalization of the disciplines. The law called for the organization of universities into departments and academic programs within departments. Further, each university was obliged to establish a general studies program for all first- and second-year students. The 1972 law reverses that of 1969 by specifically leaving internal academic organization to the discretion of each institution.

The *asamblea universitaria* (university assembly) is the highest internal authority of a university and it consists of the rector, who presides; the vice-rector(s); the university directors; the directors of academic programs; the heads of academic divisions (when applicable); the heads of departments, in a proportion of one for every four departments; representatives of professorial ranks, according to carefully stated regulations; and representatives of graduates and of students, equal to one third of all members. The private universities include, in addition, three representatives of the founding authority. The functions of the council include approval and modification of the general regulations of the university, election of the rector and vice-rector(s), approval of the university's plans of operation and development, election of the university's directors, and ratification of the directors of academic programs. The rector, who is the administrative head of the university, is elected for a term of five years; reelection requires 80 percent of the vote of the assembly.

Day-to-day administration of the university is handled by university directors appointed by the assembly; they form the membership of an executive council and are in charge of specific areas, such as planning, research, and student welfare. The university is further divided into academic departments, each administered by a department head.

Programs and Degrees

Upon matriculation, students in many Peruvian universities enter a two-year general studies curriculum before entering the actual *carrera* (professional faculty) into which they have been accepted. In most cases, after four or five successful years of studies, the student is awarded the academic title of *bachiller*. A student may then choose to continue university studies (usually consisting of the preparation of a thesis) for an additional year or more to earn the professional *título* or *licencia* (title or license) normally required for practice of a profession. The academic *maestria* (master's) degree and the *doctorado* (doctorate) are offered on a limited basis.

The thirty-three Peruvian universities offer a total of ninety possible professional degree programs. Those most frequently offered are economics (found in 22 universities), accounting (21), secondary education (21), business administration (17), sociology (15), agronomy (12), nursing (11), social service (11), and law (10); these constitute over 40 percent of the total number of degree programs in the country. Another 20 percent are found in the engineering fields, and just over 5 percent of the programs are in the basic sciences. Eleven universities offer programs leading to the *maestria* degree, and two institutions offer doctoral programs.

Financing

Financial resources for higher education are derived from three major sources. The national government through the Ministry of Education (or occasionally through other ministries) provides from 75 to 85 percent of the total annual budget for higher education. Between 7 and 15 percent of the budget is derived from income from property, goods, services, special taxes, or legal arrangements of the institutions themselves; and from 2 to 8 percent of the budget is financed by loans.

In 1971 Peru's total expenditures on education comprised almost 20 percent of the national budget for that year. Expenditures for higher education represented almost 20 percent of the education budget (and, correspondingly, 5 percent of the national budget). Although in 1966 total education costs had reached almost 30 percent of the national budget, the share of education in national expenditures normally oscillates around 20 percent.

Private institutions are financed differently from public ones in that over 50 percent of the funds for operating costs are derived from income generated by the institution itself, usually in the form of tuition and related fees. In some private universities as much as 95 percent of the budget is derived from tuition payments. Donations received by private institutions also constitute a significant source of funding; in a very few institutions such funds represent as much as 40 percent of an annual budget, but more frequently that proportion is 25 to 30 percent. Finally, the national government contributes subsidies to private universities; these subsidies may represent from 5 to 35 percent of an institution's budget.

Student Financial Aid

Within the budgets of each national university, funds are designated for *bienestar estudiantil* (student welfare). These funds include scholarships to needy students for housing, meals, and medical services. Private universities also have scholarship and loan programs for needy and academically qualified students.

Two Peruvian agencies provide scholarships and educational loans to students at all levels: the *Instituto nacional de becas y crédito educativo* (INABEC: National Institute of Scholarships and Educational Credit) and the private *Instituto peruano de fomento educativo* (IPFE: Peruvian Institute for Educational Development).

Student Social Background and Access to Education

The dramatic increase in university enrollment since 1960 (about 250 percent between 1960 and 1970) and in the numbers of institutions has unquestionably made higher education accessible to historically neglected social and economic sectors. A 1970 survey by CONUP shows that about 5 percent of the total population attends secondary school, but less than 1 percent attends the universities (excluding alternate forms of postsecondary education). However, metropolitan Lima, which has 25 percent of the total population, enrolls over 36 percent of all secondary students and 60 percent of university students. The six departments of northern Peru, with almost 30 percent of the population, provide 25 percent of the total secondary enrollment and 9 percent of university enrollment. These data show that access to higher education is significantly more available to the inhabitants of Lima than to the secondary school graduate in the provinces.

Teaching Staff

University teachers within the national universities are considered public servants and have the same rights as persons in other civil service positions in Peru. Regulations within the university system, however, pertain to the teachers in private as well as national institutions.

The ranks of professors are *ordinarios* (ordinary), *extraordinarios* (extraordinary), and *contratados* (contracted). Ordinary faculty fall within one of three categories: *profesor principal* (full professor), *profesor asociado* (associate professor), or *profesor auxiliar* (assistant professor). Extraordinary faculty are either emeritus or honorary or have visiting status. The services of contracted faculty are engaged for specific periods of time, while the other two classes enjoy tenured status.

Other categories are *instructor, ayudante* (assistant), and *jefe de práctica* (laboratory section head). These positions can fall into the ordinary or contracted category and are frequently reserved for the newest faculty members or for top students in their final years of study.

Faculty appointments may be for *dedicación exclusiva* (exclusive dedication), which requires the services of the professor at the university for eight hours per day and prohibits outside paid employment; for *tiempo completo* (full time), requiring the professor's presence for a minimum of five hours per day; or for *tiempo parcial* (part time), a variable period of dedication to university activities under five hours per day.

According to law, the minimum requirement for *principal* or *asociado* status is an academic doctorate or an equivalent professional degree. For *auxiliar* status, a lower academic or professional degree is required. Faculty appointments are awarded on the basis of merit, as judged through a public *concurso* (competition), after which the professor becomes *nombrado* (literally, "named" to his position). The appointment is ratified after one year of satisfactory service. Promotion is based upon years of service and evaluation of the faculty member's merit.

Current Problems and Trends

The Peruvian revolutionary government believes that its objectives—social and economic integration, equalization of opportunity, direct participation of all citizens in the revolutionary processes, and achievement of an integrated Peruvian cultural identity—cannot be realized through the traditional educational framework. The university, because of its historical ties to the aristocratic and elitist segments of society, is viewed as especially inadequate in furthering the development goals of Peru; therefore, the government has attempted to redirect the university and to place it at the service of all Peruvians. Because such a reform has been difficult to achieve in Peru, and because the transitional process is slow, some time will pass before the reform is implemented and many years before its impact can be measured and evaluated.

International Cooperation

The National Council of the Peruvian Universities channels programs of technical cooperation between the country's universities and foreign universities and organizations. The cooperation takes many forms, such as student and teacher exchange, exchange of information, and technical assistance agreements. Scholarships have been awarded to Peruvian students by Argentina, Brazil, Great Britain, Mexico, and the United States. Technical assistance agreements have been concluded with countries such as Hungary, the Netherlands, and Switzerland. A number of Peruvian institutions have initiated information exchange with countries such as Argentina, Chile, Cuba, France, the Federal Republic of Germany, Great Britain, Japan, Tanzania, and the United States. Peru is a member of most of the Latin American educational associations, including *Unión de universidades de América latina* (Union of Latin American Universities), Inter-American Educational Development Program of the Organization of American States, Ibero-American Bureau of Education, and *Organización de universidades católicas de América latina* (Organization of Catholic Universities in Latin America).

[Information provided by the Consejo nacional de la universidad peruana.]

LEWIS A. TYLER

Bibliography

The Admission and Academic Placement of Students from Selected Countries of Latin America—A Workshop Report on Argentina, Chile, Ecuador, Peru. Washington, D.C.: National Association for Foreign Student Affairs, American Association of Collegiate Registrars and Admissions Officers, 1971.

Estadísticas de la educación, año: 1974. Lima: Ministerio de educación, Unidad de estadística, n.d.

Estudio de recursos humanos universitarios. Lima: Dirección de planificación universitaria, Departamento de estudios socio-económicos, January 1975.

"Grados y titulados en la universidad peruana, decada 1960–1969." In *Boletín estadístico No. 6.* Lima: Dirección de planificación universitaria, Oficina de estadística, December 1972.

"Grados y títulos que otorga la universidad peruana (programas y departamentos académicos)." In *Organo de difusión No. 4.* Lima: Consejo nacional de la universidad peruana (CONUP), October 1973.

Reforma de la educación peruana, informe general. Lima: Ministerio de educación peruana, 1970.

Waggoner, G. R. (Ed.) *Seminar Reports from the Yearly Seminars in Higher Education in America.* Lawrence: University of Kansas Press, n.d.

See also: Academic Dress and Insignia; Archives: Mediterranean, the Vatican, and Latin America, National Archives of; Science Policies: Advanced Developing Countries: Andean Common Market Countries; South America: Regional Analysis.

PETROLEUM ENGINEERING
(Field of Study)

Petroleum engineering is the application of geology, chemistry, and the principles of engineering to the production of liquid and gaseous hydrocarbons. It is a narrow and well-defined field concerned with oil, from its initial discovery to its delivery to a refinery. The petroleum engineer is bounded on one side by the geologist and the geophysicist, who discover the oil, and on the other by the chemical engineer, who refines it into the petroleum products crucial to modern technology.

The branches of petroleum engineering are drilling, petroleum processing, reservoir engineering, and economic forecasting. *Drilling* involves surveying the location; providing roads, fuel, and water; designing the well to fit the geological structure; and supervising the drilling. The type of drilling fluid (mud) and the pressure are critical in the prevention of wasteful and ecologically harmful "blowouts." Installing steel well casings and cementing them in place are also delicate operations. *Petroleum processing* involves getting the oil from the wellhead to the refinery. Gas-oil separators remove the dangerous gases dissolved in the oil. Highly volatile gasoline elements are also removed. The remaining oil is then transported through pipelines and via oil tankers to the refineries. Depending upon the economics, the gases are reinjected into the oil reservoir, burned wastefully in flares, or piped separately to consumers. The oil from some reservoirs has water mixed with it, which is separated out by heating, filtering, or deemulsifying. Corrosion is a continuous problem, and special materials must be used to withstand such reagents as hydrogen sulfide. *Reservoir engineering* involves the management of the oil reservoirs. It includes the selection of the optimum number of wells, the optimum rate at which the reservoir can be drained, and the method for driving the oil out of the ground. Sometimes the internally dissolved gases can be used, sometimes gases are reinjected to provide a pressure drive, and sometimes water is injected to flush out the oil. Complex computer programs are written to simulate the mathematical equations which describe the reservoirs and to derive optimum strategies. *Economic considerations* are central to the oil business. The mathematical models for reservoirs predict the volume of oil delivered as a function of time for various operating conditions and can be used to select

the most economically attractive ones. Even a small percentage change in the total yield from a large reservoir can amount to billions of dollars. The overall economics of oil is complicated by political and social factors on an international scale. A petroleum engineer must therefore understand the laws and social customs of many countries before he can make a production forecast in any one of them.

The fields most closely related to petroleum engineering are geology and chemical engineering; petroleum engineering is, in fact, a hybrid between these two. The geologist enters the petroleum field primarily as a prospector; once the oil has been discovered, it becomes the province of the petroleum engineer. The chemical engineer, who enters the petroleum field primarily in the area of refining, accepts the crude oil from the petroleum engineer and processes it into the products required by modern society. Since the fields overlap, however, geologists and chemical engineers often work on petroleum engineering problems.

The modern oil industry is generally conceded to have begun with the drilling of a well at Titusville, Pennsylvania, by Edwin L. Drake in 1859. The production and the use of oil have increased dramatically since that time, particularly since the introduction of the internal-combustion engine in the early 1900s. For some time the international oil business has been dominated by seven major companies: Standard Oil of New Jersey, Standard Oil of California, Gulf, Texaco, Mobil, Royal Dutch/ Shell, and British Petroleum. These are integrated companies with production, transportation, refining, and marketing facilities. Their position is being challenged, however, by the growth of additional companies (the independents), the formation of government-sponsored companies in Europe, and the formation of the Organization of Petroleum Exporting Countries (OPEC) in 1961.

The early workers in the petroleum field were trained as geologists, miners, or civil engineers. The first courses in petroleum engineering were offered by the University of Pittsburgh in 1910. The first degrees in petroleum engineering were granted in 1915 from the school of mines at the University of Pittsburgh; bachelor's degrees in petroleum engineering were also available at the University of California. Many other universities were offering courses in petroleum engineering and eventually developed degree programs. In 1975 there were approximately thirty such programs in the United States, twenty having curricula accredited by the Engineers' Council for Professional Development. Similar developments have occurred in the other countries where petroleum is important. In France and the Soviet Union training programs are associated with government-sponsored research institutes rather than general universities, but the level of material taught is comparable to master's degree programs in the United States.

In the United States twenty-one of the petroleum engineering curricula have been extended to the graduate level. In addition, six schools offer two-year associate degree programs in petroleum engineering technology. In 1975 there were 309 Bachelor of Science, 74 Master of Science, and 20 Ph.D. degrees granted in petroleum engineering in the United States.

Many of the developing countries with oil resources—including Venezuela, Colombia, Indonesia, Iraq, Libya, Saudi Arabia, Turkey, and Nigeria—are starting their own petroleum engineering programs. As the ownership of production gradually shifts to the producing countries, locally educated petroleum engineers will be in great demand, and the domination of the field by United States educational institutions may be expected to decrease.

Levels and Programs of Study

Programs in petroleum engineering generally require as a minimum prerequisite a secondary education with an emphasis on science and lead to the following degrees: bachelor's, master's, the doctorate, or their equivalents. Programs deal with the principles and practices of petroleum engineering and consist of classroom and laboratory work and, on the advanced levels, seminars and research.

Programs that lead to an award not equivalent to a first university degree are concerned with the production of oil, from the drilling of the wells to the delivery of oil to the refinery. Programs usually last two or three years. Basic courses are required in mathematics, physics, chemistry, and geology. Specialized material is given in the properties of porous rocks, petroleum production, drilling and logging of wells, and surface operations in petroleum engineering.

Programs that lead to a first university degree in petroleum engineering (Bachelor of Science) include courses in the basic sciences; mathematics and engineering sciences are taken with the other engineering disciplines. Specialized material is added in the properties of rocks, fluid flow in porous media, drilling methods, petroleum production, reservoir engineering, and the economics evaluation of reservoirs.

Programs that lead to a postgraduate university degree deal with advanced studies in specialized areas of petroleum engineering. The emphasis is on original research as demonstrated by the preparation and defense of a graduate thesis. Course work specializes in drilling techniques, remedial operations, production problems, reservoir modeling, oil from shale and coal, natural gas, secondary recovery, PVT (pressure-volume-temperature) relationship of oil and gas at extreme values, and rock mechanics.

Major International and National Organizations

INTERNATIONAL

Arab League
Tahrir Square
Cairo, Egypt
   Sponsors the Arab Congress on Petroleum.

Organization of the Petroleum Exporting
Countries (OPEC)
1010 Vienna, Austria
A trade organization of the major exporting
countries; supports research in oil-related
fields.

Society of Petroleum Engineers of the
American Society of Mechanical Engineers
6200 North Central Expressway
Dallas, Texas 75206 USA
Sponsors the annual International Offshore
Technology Conferences.

World Petroleum Congresses
61 New Cavendish Street
London W1M 8AR, England
The major international organization in its
field; sponsors congresses every four years.

NATIONAL

United Kingdom:
    Institute of Petroleum
    61 New Cavendish Street
    London W1M 8AR, England

United States:
    American Institute of Mining,
        Metallurgical and Petroleum Engineers
    345 East 47th Street
    New York, New York 10017

Principal Information Sources

GENERAL

Guides to the literature on petroleum engineering include:

Fundaburk, E. L. *Reference Materials and Periodicals in Economics: An International List in
Six Volumes.* Vol. 4: *Four Major Manufacturing
Industries—Automotive, Chemical, Iron and
Steel, Petroleum and Gas.* Metuchen, New
Jersey: Scarecrow Press, 1972. See Section
4, "Petroleum and Gas Industry," for bibliographies, indexing and abstracting services,
and periodicals in the field.

Guide to the Literature of Petroleum. Houston,
Texas: Science Information Associates,
1959.

Sell, G. (Comp.) *Fifty Years of Petroleum Technology: A Guide to the Scientific and Technical
Publications of the Institute of Petroleum, 1914–
1964.* London: Institute of Petroleum, 1968.

Introductory works to various aspects of the
field include:

Dunstan, A. E. (Ed.) *The Science of Petroleum: A
Comprehensive Treatise of the Principles and
Practice of the Production, Refining, Transport*

and Distribution of Mineral Oil. London: Oxford University Press, 1938–1955.

Hobson, G. D., and Pohl, W. (Eds.) *Modern
Petroleum Technology.* (4th ed.) Barking,
Essex, England: Applied Science Publishers,
1973.

For historical accounts of the field see the
following:

American Petroleum Institute, Division of
Production. *History of Petroleum Engineering.* Dallas, Texas: Boyd Printing, 1961.
A history of American petroleum engineering.

Giddens, P. H. *The Beginnings of the Petroleum
Industry: Sources and Bibliographies.* Harrisburg, Pennsylvania: Historical Commission, 1941. Includes early sources of information.

For general works dealing with petroleum
engineering education see:

International Petroleum Abstracts. Barking, Essex,
England: Applied Science Publishers,
1973–. Published quarterly. Formerly *Institute of Petroleum Abstracts,* 1969–1972.

CURRENT BIBLIOGRAPHIES

The significant abstracting and indexing services which provide current information in the
field are:

*Abstracts of Petroleum Substitutes Literature and
Patents.* New York: American Petroleum
Institute, Central Abstracting and Indexing
Service, 1969–.

Engineering Index. New York: Engineering Index, Inc., 1884–.

International Petroleum Abstracts. Barking, Essex,
England: Applied Science Publishers,
1973–. Covers the literature of the petroleum industry as well as sources dealing with
education and training in the field.

Petroleum Abstracts. Tulsa, Oklahoma: University of Tulsa, College of Petroleum Sciences
and Engineering, 1961–.

Petroleum Literature Index. Amarillo, Texas: National Petroleum Bibliography, 1956–.

Petroleum Sourcebook. Amarillo, Texas: National
Petroleum Bibliography, 1958–. Annual
international bibliography of petroleum
information, arranged by countries and
regions.

*Referativnyĭ zhurnal. Khimicheskoe, nefteperer-
abatyvayushchee i polimernoe mashinostroenie.*
Moscow: Akademiia nauk, SSSR, Institut
nauchnoĭ informatsii, 1970–. The outstanding Russian abstracting service.

PERIODICALS

Journals dealing with petroleum engineering are *Bulletin of the American Association of Petroleum Geologists (AAPG), Bulletin of Canadian Petroleum Geology, Chemical and Petroleum Engineering* (US), *Drilling Contractor* (US), *Erdöl-Erdgas-Zeitschrift* (FRG), *Ingeniería petrolera* (Mexico), *Iranian Petroleum Institute Bulletin, J.P.T. Journal of Petroleum Technology* (US), *Middle East Economic Survey* (Lebanon), *Offshore Technology* (UK), *Oil and Gas Journal* (US), *Oil, Gas, and Petrochemical Equipment* (US), *Petróleo y petroquímica internacional* (US), *Petroleum and Petrochemical International* (UK), *Petroleum Chemistry* (USSR), *Petroleum Engineer* (US), *Petroleum Review* (UK), *Petroleum Times* (UK), *Proceedings of the American Petroleum Institute (API), Ropa a uhlie* (Czechoslovakia), *Sekiyu gakkai/Bulletin of the Japanese Petroleum Institute, Society of Petroleum Engineers of AIME Journal* (US), *Techniques du pétrole* (France), *World Oil* (US), *World Petroleum Congresses, Proceedings* (UK).

For a more complete listing of journals dealing with petroleum and gas see: *Ulrich's International Periodicals Directory.* New York: Bowker, biennial.

ENCYCLOPEDIAS, DICTIONARIES, HANDBOOKS

Frick, T. C., and Taylor, R. W. *Petroleum Production Handbook.* New York: McGraw-Hill, 1962.

Institut français du pétrole. *Dictionnaire pétrolier des techniques de diagraphie, forage et production: Russe, français, anglais, allemand.* Paris: Technip, 1965.

International Petroleum Encyclopedia. (2nd ed.) Tulsa, Oklahoma: Petroleum Publishing, 1975.

Moltzer, J. (Ed.) *Elsevier's Oilfield Dictionary: English/American, French, Spanish, Dutch, and German.* Amsterdam: Elsevier, 1965.

The Petroleum Handbook. (5th ed.) London: Shell International Petroleum, 1966.

Sell, G., and Dossett, H. A. (Eds.) *Handbook of the Petroleum Industry.* London: Newnes, 1958.

Zaba, J., and Doherty, W. T. *Practical Petroleum Engineers' Handbook.* (5th ed.) Houston, Texas: Gulf Publishing, 1970.

DIRECTORIES

Oil and Gas International Year Book. London: Financial Times, 1910–. A directory to the petroleum industry.

Peterson's Annual Guides to Graduate Study, 1976.

Book 5: *Engineering and Applied Sciences.* Princeton, New Jersey: Peterson's Guides, 1975. The section on minerals and petroleum engineering provides a directory to petroleum engineering programs in the United States.

Petroleum Engineering Schools. Dallas, Texas: Society of Petroleum Engineers, 1975. Lists colleges and universities offering programs in petroleum engineering in the United States.

Wöhlbier, H., and others. (Eds.) *Worldwide Directory of Mineral Industries Education and Research.* Houston, Texas: Gulf Publishing, 1968. The most comprehensive international directory to universities offering programs and degrees in petroleum engineering (as well as other mineral industries); includes descriptions of departments of petroleum engineering, research institutes, special facilities, libraries, and publications of the universities.

The following is a listing of non–United States universities offering degrees in petroleum engineering:

Africa:
   The Polytechnic
   Ibadan, Nigeria

   University of Benin
   Benin, Nigeria

   University of Tripoli
   Box 3932
   Tripoli, Libya

Asia:
   Bandung Institute of Technology
   Bandung, West Java, Indonesia

   University of Tokyo
   Bunkyo-ku, Tokyo, Japan

Canada:
   Northern Alberta Institute of
      Technology
   Edmonton, Alberta
      Diploma programs only.

   Southern Alberta Institute of Technology
   Calgary, Alberta
      Four-year engineering technology
   degree.

   University of Alberta
   Edmonton, Alberta

Europe:
   Delft University of Technology
   Mijnbouwstraat 20
   Delft, Netherlands

Ecole nationale supérieure du pétrole
92 Rueil-Malmaison, France

Institute of Petroleum Geology
Saint Jerome
Marseille 13397, France

Rogaland Regional College
N-4000 Stavanger, Norway

Technische Universität Clausthal
3392 Clausthal-Zellerfeld
Federal Republic of Germany

University of Mining and Metallurgy
Leoben 8700, Austria

Latin America:
Universidad Industrial de Santander
Bucaramanga, Santander, Colombia

Universidad del Zulia
Maracaibo, Zulia, Venezuela

Universidad de Oriente
Puerto La Cruz
Anzoátegui, Venezuela

Universidad nacional
Medellín, Antioquia, Colombia

Middle East:
Middle East Technical University
Ankara, Turkey

University of Baghdad
Baghdad, Iraq

University of Petroleum and Minerals
Dhahran, Saudi Arabia

University of Riyadh
Riyadh, Saudi Arabia

Soviet Union:
Azerbaijan Institute of Petroleum
and Chemistry
pr. Lenina 20, Baku
Azerbaijan SSR

Grozny Institute of Petroleum
Technology
pl. Ordzonikidze 100, Grozny
Russian SFSR

Moscow Institute of Petroleum and
Gas Technology
pr. 65 Leninsky, Moscow
V-296 Russian SFSR

Ufa Institute of Petroleum Technology
ul. Kosmonovtov 1, Ufa 62
Bashkir SSR

Ukraine Institute of Petroleum and
Gas Technology
ul. Lenina 28, Ivano-Frankovsk
Ukrainian SSR

United Kingdom and Commonwealth:
Royal School of Mines
Imperial College
London SW 7, England

University of Queensland
St. Lucia, Brisbane
Queensland, Australia

RESEARCH CENTERS

France:
Institut français de pétrole
4 avenue de Bois Preau
Rueil-Malmaison 92502

Lebanon:
Arab Petroleum Research Center
P.O. Box 7167
Beirut

United States:
American Petroleum Institute
1271 Avenue of the Americas
New York, New York 10020

RONALD E. SCOTT

PHARMACY (Field of Study)

Pharmacy is concerned with all aspects of medicinal agents, including their discovery, isolation and characterization, formulation, distribution, and utilization for the treatment of diseases and disorders in man. The beginnings of pharmacy occurred well before the dawn of history, and its development parallels that of the human race. The need for drug therapy stems directly from man's constant struggle to control and overcome disease. The earliest record of a prescription dates back more than five thousand years, to Egypt at the time of the construction of the pyramids. There is also evidence that pharmacy was practiced in ancient Babylonia, China, and Greece. Frequent references to medicinals appear in the Bible, and they were also known to the Romans. Pharmacy and medicine were tightly intertwined until the establishment of the first apothecaries in the eighth century in Baghdad, when pharmacy was clearly delineated as a separate profession. The Arabian apothecary shops spread westward to Europe, where the first legal division of pharmacy from medicine occurred in 1224, when an edict by Frederick II of Germany and Sicily initiated the establishment of the first educational program for pharmacists. Such programs have proliferated and encompass the entire world.

The modern practices of pharmacy and pharmacy education have markedly changed from these humble beginnings. Since pharmacy has become a highly structured, multifaceted profession, the potential pharmacist needs a broad educational background at the collegiate level in many scientific, clinical, administrative, and legal subjects. The curriculum in pharmacy is expected to represent a composite of educational experiences which will produce a well-educated person and a well-trained professional. Usually a balance is sought between general education, preclinical sciences, and the professional studies. Professional studies may be represented by the pharmaceutical sciences (pharmacognosy, pharmacology, medicinal/pharmaceutical chemistry, pharmaceutics, and pharmacy administration), biomedical sciences (pathology, physical diagnosis, biostatistics, and clinical pharmacology), the social and behavioral sciences (medical sociology and health care economics), and the clinical sciences and practice (clinically applied courses in pharmacy practice and clinical clerkship and externship).

The major branches of the pharmaceutical sciences comprise pharmacognosy, medicinal or pharmaceutical chemistry, pharmacology, and pharmaceutics. Pharmacognosy relates to the discovery, isolation, purification, and characterization of drugs from plants, animals, and other natural sources. Prior to the development of synthetic drugs, all medicinals were of natural origin, and drugs from biological systems or their metabolites are still important as a source of new pharmaceutical agents. Medicinal or pharmaceutical chemistry is concerned with the chemical modification of naturally occurring drugs, the design and preparation of synthetic agents, and

the correlation of chemical structure with biological activity. Chemistry is important in pharmaceutical development because every drug has some undesirable side effects and thereby possesses therapeutic limitations, so that minor changes in chemical structure may be beneficial; for example, a compound may be produced that retains activity and yet is devoid of those poor qualities that are found in the parent structure. Pharmacology is the science that deals with the action of drugs and other chemicals upon living systems and their integral component parts. Knowledge of this discipline is vital for the pharmacist, since he needs a complete understanding of how drugs function in the prevention, diagnosis, and treatment of disease. Closely related is toxicology, the systematic study of the detection and control of the harmful effects elicited by all chemical agents, including drugs, on mammalian systems. Both of these areas require a firm foundation in anatomy, physiology, biochemistry, and microbiology. Pharmaceutics is concerned with the physicochemical factors, methodology, and techniques that affect (1) drug formulation, dispensing, and assay; (2) rates of dissolution and release from drug preparations of active principals; and (3) absorption, distribution, and elimination characteristics of those components. The scientific evolution and fragmentation of this discipline has spawned such areas of study as biopharmaceutics, pharmacokinetics, and radiopharmaceutics. Biopharmaceutics is concerned with the study of determinants that affect the therapeutic agent's true availability at the site of action (that is, bioavailability). Pharmacokinetics relates to the rates of transport, biotransformation, and concentration and compartmentalization of drugs and their metabolites in mammalian systems. Radiopharmaceutics or nuclear pharmacy, an area of recent development, focuses on the synthesis, formulation, analytical criteria, distribution, utilization, and action of radioactive drugs for diagnostic and therapeutic purposes.

This professional science background is essential for the education of the practitioner, whether he functions in a community, hospital, ambulatory care, industrial, educational, or governmental environment. Knowledge from these diversified science areas serves as a solid basis for the clinical component of the education of the pharmacist. Clinical pharmacy has become a major part of the educational background of every pharmacist. This area of study —patient-oriented pharmacy—places the student in a clinical milieu, where he gains a practical understanding of drug medication as applied to man. The student acquires an appreciation of the influence of different routes of administration on drug effectiveness; drug interactions and toxicity; the influence of the patient's condition upon the medication regimen; the effect of physical and psychological factors on patient compliance in the drug therapy; the importance of the pharmacist as a member of the health team; and the relationship of the pharmacist to other health professionals, such as physicians, dentists, nurses, and allied health professionals.

The roles of the practicing pharmacist are so diverse that knowledge and expertise in modern business management and administrative techniques are essential. Competency in such an area requires instruction in the principles of basic economics, accounting, statistics, management, marketing, and merchandising. Also, because the control and dispensing of medications have legal restrictions and ramifications, the pharmacist requires specific pharmaceutical jurisprudence background. For example, national, sectional, and local political bodies protect the public from the misuse and abuse of drugs through controls which vary with the culture and customs of an area. National controls also stem directly from the increasing involvement of all governments in health care delivery and, thereby, the dispensing of medications. Health insurance plans, whether private or governmental, directly affect the practice of pharmacy; therefore, knowledge

of insurance is also important to the pharmacist.

To assure the public that quality practitioners are ministering to their health needs, internship programs with a carefully prescribed minimum duration are frequently established by legislative edict. Such requirements must be completed before an applicant can take a state examination for professional licensure. In this manner a practical training and performance period provides the incipient practitioner with the applied experience necessary for the development of the pharmacist.

In addition to undergraduate programs which lead to the Bachelor of Science in pharmacy, several programs in the United States lead to the Doctor of Pharmacy (Pharm.D.). In some schools this program is considered the first professional degree. The goal of such a program is to prepare the pharmacist to function as a clinical practitioner with extensive knowledge about the effects of drugs in man and their contraindications. His knowledge and expertise qualifies him uniquely as the drug information specialist within the health care delivery system. Unlike the normal five-year baccalaureate program, the Pharm.D. program requires a minimum of six years beyond the secondary level. There is a great deal of discussion in academic pharmaceutical circles as to whether this program should be the sole professional degree or an advanced professional degree program which follows a more general undergraduate course of study.

Established graduate programs in pharmaceutical education, which lead to Master of Science and Doctor of Philosophy degrees, are structured about the fields of pharmacognosy, pharmaceutical or medicinal chemistry, pharmacology, pharmaceutics, hospital pharmacy, and pharmacy administration. Though there may be areas of overlap, each division is a recognized discipline. As in all graduate study, these programs build upon the undergraduate curriculum, but only the latter three— pharmaceutics, hospital pharmacy, and pharmacy administration—generally require an undergraduate pharmacy background. Graduate programs in pharmacognosy, medicinal chemistry, and pharmacology are also attractive to students who have matriculated in biology and chemistry programs. In addition, there are programs in industrial pharmacy, which may be closely associated with related studies in pharmaceutics and require similar background and expertise.

Internationally, at least eighty-six countries have schools or programs in pharmacy. Some nations have multiple programs that eventually lead to licensure. Education time ranges from one to six years following primary and secondary school programs. Generally, schools of pharmacy with an administrative officer and faculty are responsible for the academic content and control. In some schools, however, the program may be divided between preprofessional and professional schools; in others, schools other than pharmacy have the academic responsibility. Courses and content are also highly variable, but they generally include anatomy and physiology, biology, botany, general chemistry, analytical chemistry, biochemistry, inorganic chemistry and organic chemistry, medicinal chemistry or pharmaceutical chemistry, mathematics, microbiology, pharmaceutics, pharmacognosy, pharmacology, pharmacy, pharmacy administration, forensic pharmacy, physics, and toxicology. The amount of time required to complete such a course of study is highly variable, but the average is between four and five years. After completion of the academic program, more than half of the nations require a period of apprenticeship prior to licensure. Here, also, the time is quite variable, ranging from two months to three years, with an average of nearly one year.

Finally, because of the dynamic state of pharmacy and the need to incorporate new knowledge into the academic background, continuing education becomes essential, if not mandatory, for the contemporary practitioner. It is becoming apparent that the education for such health professionals as the pharmacist is no longer limited to a finite period but is an ongoing process.

The major international pharmacy organization, the *Fédération internationale pharmaceutique* (FIP), was established in 1912. Its purpose is to develop the profession and science of pharmacy internationally and to expand the role of the pharmacist in the field of public health. In 1975 its membership included sixty-three associations from countries around the world, with over 3700 individuals or organizations as associate members and over one hundred collective associate members. Much of the work of FIP is carried out by permanent sections and commissions representing the various disciplines of pharmacy, including an academic section. FIP holds an annual international congress and publishes an information bulletin, which contains details of the activities of FIP and articles about pharmacy in various parts of the world.

ALBERT H. SOLOWAY

Major International and National Organizations

INTERNATIONAL

Federation of Asian Pharmaceutical
  Associations (FAPA)
40 Soi Santisuk, Sukhumvit Rd.
38 Bangkok, Dhonburi Metropolis II, Thailand

International Academy of the History of
  Pharmacy
Académie internationale d'histoire de la
  pharmacie
Postbox 2250
Rotterdam 3015, Netherlands

International Pharmaceutical Federation
Fédération internationale pharmaceutique
  (FIP)
11 Alexanderstraat
The Hague, Netherlands
  FIP is in the process of building a world pharmacy, which will be staffed by 10,000 pharmacists from countries throughout the world.

International Pharmaceutical Students'
  Federation
% Peter Sharott, Pharmaceutical Department
General Hospital
Nottingham, England

International Society for the History of
Pharmacy
Internationale Gesellschaft für Geschichte
der Pharmazie
Hohenheimerstrasse 48
7 Stuttgart S., Federal Republic of Germany

Latin-Mediterranean Society of Pharmacy
Société de pharmacie de la méditerranée latine
9 rue Vallence
13 Marseille 8e, France

Pan American Pharmaceutical and Biochemical
Federation
Division of Communications
American Pharmaceutical Association
2215 Constitution Avenue NW
Washington, D.C. 20037 USA

NATIONAL

Canada:
Canadian Pharmaceutical Association
175 College Street
Toronto, Ontario M5T IP8

Soviet Union:
All-Union Pharmaceutical Society
Kolobovsky per 19
Moscow

Switzerland:
Société suisse de pharmacie
Marktgasse 52
Ch-3011, Bern

United Kingdom:
Pharmaceutical Society of Great Britain
17 Bloomsbury Square
London WC1, England

United States:
American Association of Colleges of
Pharmacy
8121 Georgia Avenue
Silver Spring, Maryland 20910

American Council on Pharmaceutical
Education
One East Wacker Drive
Chicago, Illinois 60601

American Pharmaceutical Association
American Institute of Pharmacy
2215 Constitution Avenue NW
Washington, D.C. 20037

For information on national and international pharmacy associations see:

*Medical Research Index: A Guide to World Medi-
cal Research.* Guernsey, Channel Islands:
Francis Hodgson, 1971.
Minerva, Wissenschaftliche Gesellschaften. Berlin,
Federal Republic of Germany: de Gruyter,
1972.

Pharmaceutical Directory. Washington, D.C.:
American Pharmaceutical Association,
annual.
World Guide to Scientific Associations. New York:
Bowker, 1974.
The World of Learning. London: Europa, annual.

Principal Information Sources

GENERAL

Guides to the literature include:

Brunn, A. L. *How to Find Out in Pharmacy: A
Guide to Sources of Pharmaceutical Information.*
Oxford, England: Pergamon Press, 1969.
Drug Literature. Washington, D.C.: 88th Congress, 1st session. Senate, Committee Print,
1963. Provides a selected list of monographs
on pharmacy, a world list of pharmacy
journals, and drug information sources
throughout the world.
Jackson, E. C. "Books for Pharmacy Colleges,
1962–68." *American Journal of Pharmaceutical Education,* 1969, *33,* 246–267, 411–458.
Bibliography of reference works for pharmacy college libraries.
Pasztor, M., and Hopkins, J. *Bibliography of
Pharmaceutical Reference Literature.* London:
Pharmaceutical Press, 1968.

More specialized guides include:

"Drug Information Sources: A World List."
American Journal of Pharmacy, 1964 (136),
52–70, 152–164, 257–267; 1965 (137),
35–40, 69–81. Provides lists of books for
identifying drugs in countries throughout
the world; updated periodically.
Millis, J. S. *Pharmacists for the Future: The Report
of the Study Commission on Pharmacy.* Ann
Arbor, Michigan: Health Administration
Press, 1975.
Reilly, M. J. *Drug Information: Literature Review
of Needs, Resources and Services.* Washington,
D.C.: United States Health Services and
Mental Health Administration, 1972.

The following provide a good introduction
to and basic history of the field:

Deno, R. A. *Profession of Pharmacy: An Introductory Textbook.* (2nd ed.) Philadelphia:
Lippincott, 1966.
Kremers, E., and Urdang, G. *History of Pharmacy.* (3rd ed.) Philadelphia: Lippincott,
1963.

For information on the field internationally
see:

"International Pharmacy: Current Perspectives." *Journal of the American Pharmaceutical
Association,* 1975, NS *15* (12), entire issue.

CURRENT BIBLIOGRAPHIES

The most important bibliographical and abstracting services in pharmacy are:

Bulletin signalétique. Part 330: *Sciences pharmacologiques–toxicologie*. Paris: Centre national de la recherche scientifique, 1961–.

CC-LS. Philadelphia: Institute for Scientific Information, 1958–. Formerly *Current Contents: Chemical, Pharmaco-Medical and Life Sciences*. Lists tables of contents of approximately one thousand international journals.

Derwent Pooled Pharmaceutical Literature Documentation. Ringdoc. Abstracts Book. London: Derwent Publications, 1964–.

Drug Literature Index. Amsterdam: Excerpta Medica Foundation, 1969–.

Excerpta Medica. Section 30: *Pharmacology and Toxicology*. Amsterdam: Excerpta Medica Foundation, 1948–.

Index Medicus. Bethesda, Maryland: National Library of Medicine, 1960–.

International Pharmaceutical Abstracts. Washington, D.C.: American Society of Hospital Pharmacists, 1964–.

Pharmacognosy Titles. Chicago: University of Illinois at the Medical Center, 1966–. Provides coverage of the literature for specialized branches of the field.

Psychopharmacology Abstracts. Washington, D.C.: U.S. Government Printing Office, 1961–. Provides coverage of the literature for specialized branches of the field.

Referativnyĭ zhurnal. Farmakologiya. Moscow: Akademiia nauk, SSSR, Institut nauchoĭ informatsii, 1963–.

Sciences et techniques pharmaceutiques. Paris: Edition S.E.P.E., 1947–. Formerly *Technique pharmaceutique*. Lists tables of contents of pharmaceutical journals.

PERIODICALS

Some of the important pharmacy journals are *American Journal of Hospital Pharmacy, American Journal of Pharmaceutical Education, Annales pharmaceutiques françaises, Biochemical Pharmacology* (UK), *Canadian Journal of Pharmaceutical Sciences, Chemotherapy* (Switzerland), *Clinical Pharmacology and Therapeutics* (US), *Current Therapeutics* (Australia), *Deutsche pharmazeutische Gesellschaft Mitteilungen* (FRG), *Drug and Cosmetic Industry* (US), *Drug Intelligence and Clinical Pharmacy* (US), *Facts and Comparisons* (US), *Internationale Zeitschrift für klinische Pharmakologie, Therapie und Toxikologie/Journal of Clinical Pharmacology, Therapy and Toxicology* (FRG), *Journal of the American Pharmaceutical Association, Journal of Pharmaceutical Sciences* (US), *Journal of Pharmacology and Experimental Therapeutics* (US), *Journal of Pharmacy and Pharmacology* (UK), *Molecular Pharmacology* (US), *Pharmaceutica Acta Helvetiae* (Switzerland), *Pharmaceutical Journal* (UK), *Pharmaceutical Society of Japan Journal, Pharmacological Reviews* (US), *Pharmacology* (Switzerland), *Pharmazie* (GDR), *Toxicology and Applied Pharmacology* (US).

The following provide lists of pharmacy periodicals:

Andrews, T., and Oslet, J. "World List of Pharmacy Periodicals." *American Journal of Hospital Pharmacy*, 1975, *32*, 85–124. An updated and enlarged list.

Drug Literature. Washington, D.C.: 88th Congress, 1st session. Senate, Committee Print, 1963.

Shilling, C. W. *Pharmacology, Toxicology and Cosmetics Serials*. Washington, D.C.: George Washington University, Biological Sciences Communication Project, 1965.

ENCYCLOPEDIAS, DICTIONARIES, HANDBOOKS

Elsevier's Dictionary of Pharmaceutical Science and Techniques, in Five Languages. New York: American Elsevier, 1968.

International Encyclopedia of Pharmacology and Therapeutics. Oxford, England: Pergamon Press, 1966–.

Marler, E. E. J. *Pharmacological and Chemical Synonyms: A Collection of Names of Drugs and Other Compounds Drawn from the Medical Literature of the World*. Amsterdam: Excerpta Medica Foundation, 1973.

Modern Drug Encyclopedia. (11th ed.) New York: Donnelley, 1970.

Roth, H. J. and others (Eds.) *Hager's Handbuch der pharmazeutischen Praxis*. New York and Berlin, Federal Republic of Germany: Springer-Verlag, 1967.

Steinbichler, E. *Lexikon für die Apothekenpraxis in sieben Sprachen, mit fünf selbstständigen Alphabeten und einer pharmazeutischen Phraseologie*. Frankfurt/Main, Federal Republic of Germany: Govi-Verlag, 1963.

DIRECTORIES

Blacon, N. W. (Ed.) *Extra Pharmacopoeia*. (26th ed.) London: Pharmaceutical Press, 1972. A comprehensive guide to drugs and medicine.

Greffenhagen, G. *Pharmacy Museums*. Madison, Wisconsin: American Institute of the History of Pharmacy, 1956. Provides a discussion of pharmacy museums and collections in the United States and Europe.

Guide Rosenwald médical et pharmaceutique. Paris: L'expansion scientifique française, 1971. Lists schools, associations, and laboratories for pharmacy in France and in colonies.

Pharmaceutical Directory. Washington, D.C.: American Pharmaceutical Association, annual. Provides lists of national and international associations, colleges of pharmacy, and journals.

World Directory of Schools of Pharmacy. Geneva: World Health Organization, 1966. Provides information on pharmacy education throughout the world.

RESEARCH CENTERS, INSTITUTES, INFORMATION CENTERS

Medical Research Index: A Guide to World Medical Research. Guernsey, Channel Islands: Francis Hodgson, 1971.

Minerva, Forschungsinstitute. Berlin, Federal Republic of Germany: de Gruyter, 1972.

The World of Learning. London: Europa, annual.

PHILANTHROPY AND FOUNDATIONS

Philanthropy as discussed here involves the giving of private property to serve public interests such as health, welfare (charity), education, and science; it is defined as voluntary gift support provided by individuals, foundations (including charitable trusts), and business firms, but excluding contributions by governments and religious groups.

The extent of voluntary philanthropy for higher education or for any other purpose on an international level is rather difficult to determine, due to the absence of any central agency to accumulate and publish such information. For example, the Association of Commonwealth Universities, based in London, is unable to accurately describe the extent to which philanthropic activities of individuals, foundations, and corporations are involved in financing higher education within the British Commonwealth. A representative of the association has indicated that acquiring such data would involve extensive research into official Ministry of Education publications in each country. An analogous situation exists in Japan, where the supervision of foundations is divided among a number of ministries and prefectural governments.

Similar difficulties exist in many other nations throughout the world.

In the United States, such information must be provided to the government according to the laws requiring the documentation of contributions that are excluded from taxation. The legal requirements for reporting, together with established data-collection mechanisms and a rather precise definition of philanthropy for tax purposes, is not widely duplicated elsewhere.

Philanthropy in the United States amounted to about $25,200,000,000 in 1974. This total sum consisted of $22,000,000,000 given by individuals directly and by wills (bequests) or other deferred gifts; $2,100,000,000 given by foundations; and $1,100,000,000 given by business corporations. Of this total, $3,900,000,000 was allocated for health programs; $6,700,000,000 for civic, cultural, welfare, and other activities; $10,900,000,000 for religious purposes; and $3,700,000,000 for all levels of education (Lundberg, 1975).

Voluntary support received by colleges and universities in the United States during fiscal year 1974 totaled an estimated $2,240,000,000. Of this total sum, $1,950,000,000 was given by individuals, foundations, and corporations, and the balance came from religious denominations and associations. This amount includes an estimated $1,070,000,000 given by both alumni and nonalumni. The magnitude of individual support may be further demonstrated by the fact that, in 1974, foundations provided $535,000,000 and corporations $354,000,000. Thus, individuals contributed substantially more than foundations and corporations together, and twice the total sum of foundation support (*Voluntary Support of Education*, 1975).

Independent (non-tax-supported) colleges and universities in the United States received more than three fourths of all the voluntary support provided for higher education in fiscal year 1974 (*Voluntary Support of Education*, 1975). Although data are not complete, it appears likely that private contributions will be of relatively less importance in those nations where higher education is considered primarily the domain of the state.

The dominance of American philanthropy by individuals is a long-standing national phenomenon encouraged by the wealth accumulation opportunities provided for by the private enterprise system, by national tax policies encouraging charitable gifts, and by the aggressive solicitation of college and university fund-raising staffs. Contributions by individuals take many forms and utilize several mechanisms for a variety of purposes: cash, investment securities, and personal and real property, all given through outright contribution, bequests or deferred gifts, and used for current operations or capital purposes. The greatest source of funding is outright contributions; individuals prefer giving capital gifts for endowment or facilities rather than for operating support. An individual is also more inclined to support institutions attended by the donor or his family, those in which he serves as a trustee or director, or those located near his residence. Support is also given to domestic or foreign institutions conducting instructional, research, and service programs of special interest to the donor.

Corporate Support

Significant corporate giving in the United States began after a provision of the Internal Revenue Act of 1935 was passed, exempting certain charitable gifts up to 5 percent of pretax net income from taxation. Although this act has increased corporate giving, average contributions are still only in the range of 1 percent of net income. A report of the Commission on Private Philanthropy and Public Needs, published in the United States in 1975, noted that in 1970 only 20 percent of all corporations reported any contributions and only 6 percent made gifts of more than $500 *(Giving in America,* 1975).

A major portion of corporate philan-thropic gifts are a direct function of the size of private business operations and the existence of tax policies encouraging contributions. Corporations are probably less motivated by altruism than either individuals or foundations. Prospective grantees must usually show how an award to an institution will directly or indirectly benefit the firm, its field of concentration, or the general business community. With the occasional exception of the largest firms, a rather direct benefit must be shown; for example, in terms of the numbers of the institution's graduates employed; relationships between the business area of the firm and the school's focus of research activity; and the availability of part-time, job-related programs, especially for the company's professional-level staff. Service to the firm's employees or customers and an indication that the firm's assistance will be publicized also provide a rationale.

The forms and specific purposes of corporate support are too diverse for complete enumeration. The New York–based Council for Financial Aid to Education has shown that United States firms prefer gifts for current operations against contributions for capital purposes. Grants for student financial aid, research projects, experimental programs, and unrestricted current operating purposes are more common than support for construction or renovation of buildings, equipment, or endowment. Especially where tax motivations exist, corporations also provide gifts of their products or other property in addition to, or as an alternative to, direct financial support. Depending upon the firm's area of business and the extent of its relationships with the educational institution, contributions range from expendable supplies to real estate or expensive and highly sophisticated equipment.

The Council for Financial Aid to Education notes that, in fiscal year 1974, 988 reporting institutions obtained 15.8 percent of all voluntary support from business corporations; 71.9 percent of this support was for current operations *(Voluntary Sup-*

port of Education, 1975). This same preference for operating support has been discerned by the Conference Board in a 1973 study of the international public service activities of 218 headquarter companies of American-based multinational corporations *(U.S. Business Support,* Part I, *1973).* The analysis also discloses that education and research are the most common beneficiaries of support (often closely followed by health/welfare programs and business education), but the majority of surveyed companies limit their direct funding to American and international organizations based in the United States. Assistance to foreign educational institutions and other charitable causes is usually provided through foreign affiliates or American-based intermediary organizations.

In a related study *(U.S. Business Support,* Part II, *1973),* the Conference Board surveyed the overseas public service activities of 606 affiliated companies in sixteen countries (five in Europe, four in Latin America, three in Asia, three in Africa, and one in Canada). This report also showed that education and research are the most commonly cited recipients of funding, with 495 firms reporting contributions in this category. Most affiliates tend to give small grants to each of a large number of causes within the host nations, with $1,000 to $10,000 as the most common range of public service expenditures. A sampling of average support per affiliate reveals that consumer product firms lead all others by a wide margin. This undoubtedly reflects their very broad customer constituency.

Most companies report that only informal guidelines are used for proposals and that these are based on their own experience or patterned after those of United States parent companies. Only seven reporting firms have established written policies. Also, where guidelines do exist, they often differ in specifics from domestic American practices to accommodate dissimilar national traditions. An example is the willingness of certain affiliates to assist educational institutions operated by religious organizations.

Foundations

Foundations of at least a rudimentary type appear to have flourished in ancient Egypt, Rome, Greece, and China. The tradition and seeming universality of the motivation to establish such formal structures for charitable giving has been dramatized by Nielsen (1972, p. 3): "In all probability if the anthropological data were available, it would be found that the red Mayans, the white Norsemen and the black Benin made their own appropriate arrangements to serve the universal impulse of altruism."

No official or internationally accepted definition of the term *foundation* is available. The *Foundation Directory,* considered by many to be an authoritative source in the field, defines a foundation as "a nongovernmental, non-profit organization, with funds and program managed by its own trustees or directors, and established to maintain or aid social, educational, charitable, religious, or other activities serving the common welfare, primarily through the making of grants" (Lewis, 1975, p. xi). In a somewhat modified form, this same definition has been adopted by the Hague Club (established at The Hague in 1970 to provide an informal forum for the discussion of foundation programs and administration by various European foundation officials) to facilitate discussions among European foundations. Variations of it are employed in the *Guide to European Foundations* (Giovanni Agnelli Foundation, 1973), the *International Foundation Directory* (Hodson, 1974), and elsewhere.

This definition is intended to include grant-making trusts and charitable corporations, but it excludes operating foundations whose basic purposes are formally limited to supporting only specific beneficiaries. It is sufficiently broad, however, to include all those philanthropic organizations called corporations, funds, endowments, or trusts, which are subsumed under the rubric *foundations.*

F. Emerson Andrews (1973), president emeritus of the Foundation Center in New York and a "foundation watcher" of international reputation, has suggested that there are five types of foundations: general-purpose, special-purpose, family, community, and company sponsored, with considerable overlapping among these categories.

General-purpose foundations. Such foundations operate under the broadest mandates, permitting maximum grant-making flexibility in both geographical area and field of interest. These institutions, first established on a large scale in the United States about the turn of the twentieth century, usually consist of large permanent endowments available for various humane causes. The basic purpose of the Rockefeller Foundation, to promote the well-being of mankind throughout the world, is often cited as an example of the scope of interests of such foundations. Within these broad aims, specific fields of current interest and actual grant decisions are determined by a board of directors or trustees, often with the administrative and technical support of a professional staff. The Ford Foundation, the Carnegie Corporation of New York, the Lilly Endowment, and many other giants of American philanthropy are included in this category, as would be the Leverhulme Trust (United Kingdom), Sir Dorabji Tata Trust (India), and Calouste Gulbenkian Foundation (Portugal).

The phrase *general-purpose foundation,* although common parlance for those actively engaged in the business of philanthropy, is somewhat misleading in that these organizations are selective in their donations. Most have specific eligibility guidelines, and, except for relatively small sums set aside for special situations, program emphases are clearly defined in keeping with evolving societal needs and changing foundation leadership. Also, foundations are not usually inclined to give support for ongoing operating costs, preferring instead to make short-term planning and "start-up" grants for ventures that will eventually become self-sustaining. In addition, most foundations specifically exclude grants to individuals.

Special-purpose foundations. Using the term in its broadest sense, special-purpose foundations are probably the most numerous internationally. They are limited by charter or long established practice to a specific field, purpose, or geographical area, such as medical research, student financial aid, or particular city, state, or regional institutions. Examples of this type of foundation are the Max Planck Society for the Advancement of Science (Federal Republic of Germany), devoted to basic science research; the Hindemith Foundation (Switzerland), limited to music education and musicology; and the Moody Foundation (United States), which supports only organizations in the state of Texas.

Family foundations. Such foundations are established by living persons rather than through bequest, and their activities are directed by the donor or members of his or her family and their close associates. Family foundations generally reflect the personal interests of their founders and may base decisions for major awards less on established guidelines and staff recommendations than upon the interests of the key individual. A few of the world's largest foundations, such as the Rockefeller Brothers Fund (United States) and the Giovanni Agnelli Foundation (Italy), fall into this category.

Community foundations. Community foundations, which do not exist to any extent outside the United States, are a sort of "umbrella" mechanism for strengthening the administration of a number of separate charitable funds, each with a similar and rather limited geographical focus, usually a metropolitan area. The assets of such a foundation consist of the pooled resources of the various accounts. The reasoning behind such an arrangement is to permit the efficiently centralized and professional management of the funds in accordance with the wishes of the donors. The principal sum of the endowment, provided by gift, by bequest, or through the liquidation and transfer of assets from small family foundations, is generally administered by the trust department of a local bank; grant policies and award decisions are made by a board, which is broadly representative of the community served.

Suomen kulttuurirahasto (Finnish Cultural Foundation) is a European counterpart to the American community foundation. Established in 1939 at the urging of several young intellectuals, its original resources were contributed by more than two hundred thousand individuals and business organizations. A central governing board and staff oversee the administration of one hundred separate funds, provided by gift or bequest. A number of regional subdivisions have been created to benefit specific provinces within Finland.

Company-sponsored or corporate foundations. These foundations are one of the principal mechanisms used by business firms to disburse funds to charity. Other disbursement avenues include the chief executive officer and contributions committees that are usually comprised of senior company executives from areas such as general management, finance, and public relations, who meet periodically to make grant decisions. Foundations operated by corporations may be either conduits for annual gifts equal to yearly contributions received from the parent company, or they may have substantial permanent endowments of their own.

While corporate foundations are separate legal entities, their boards are either exclusively or primarily composed of corporate officials. Some foundations also have professional staffs, however. Grant decisions usually relate to corporate interests, sometimes broadly defined. Special consideration usually is given to activities that benefit employees, their families, the communities in which the corporation's

plants or offices are located, and also services that enhance the company's business operations and image. The endow corporate foundation offers the advanta of ensuring a relatively stable level of co tributions, irrespective of fluctuating cor pany earnings. In addition, such perm nent resources encourage the use of fu time staff to review applications, to ma informed recommendations on fundin and to administer awards.

The fifth edition of *The Foundation L rectory* (Lewis, 1975) lists the twenty-fi largest company-sponsored Americ: foundations by the amount of grants. 1974 these organizations made gran totaling slightly more than $70,000,00 with the most abundantly endowed org nization reporting assets of $107,000,00 The total sum awarded is less than th annual amount of Ford Foundation gran and the largest corporate foundation ran about thirtieth among all American fou dations in terms of assets. Thus, althoug they represent a very important eleme of American philanthropy in the aggr gate, corporate foundations in the Unite States do not, generally, have the large pe manent endowments characteristic of th best-known general-purpose foundatior

Corporate giving exists widely throug out the world, but some of the most signi cant recent developments have occurre in Japan, as reported by Tadashi Yam moto, director of the Japanese philan thropy project (Yamamoto, 1975). Infl enced by extraordinary economic grow and mounting social pressure to ameliora the unfavorable impacts of rapid industri expansion, several large Japanese firm such as the Tokyu Corporation, Toyo Motors and Toyota Motor Sales, Nissa Motors (Datsun), and the Japan Broa casting Corporation, have recently esta lished foundations. Previously establishe Japanese corporate foundations such . Mitsubishi, Toray Science Foundation, an several others are increasing their contr butions and diversifying their progra interests.

Many firms have also recently established or expanded charitable activities through direct contributions. Substantially larger sums are being allocated to corporate responsibility programs. Some of the larger international companies such as Mitsui and Sumitomo have recently made a series of sizable overseas grants, especially to eminent American universities. As in many other nations, the expansion of private philanthropy in Japan is inhibited by such constraints as tax policies discouraging wealth accumulation and a tradition of exclusive government support in fields that might otherwise attract individual contributions for voluntary support. However, the combination of substantial corporate resources and the demands of enlightened self-interest have stimulated a reassessment of the role of corporate philanthropy.

International Foundations

There is no widely accepted definition of "international foundation." For purposes of this essay, an international foundation is construed as any foundation that makes grants on a significant scale beyond its own nation's frontiers.

A study (Meagher, 1976) of international giving activities of the 262 largest United States foundations, included in the 1974 *Foundation Grants Index* of the Foundation Center, showed that these international foundations made grants for all purposes totaling $701,000,000, or one third of the total sum awarded in 1974. The research further disclosed that eighty-three, or 32 percent, of these organizations made at least one grant of $5000 or more to such international activities as education, technical assistance, health and welfare, cultural relations, peace and international cooperation, relief and refugees, international studies, or exchange of persons.

The international grants of these eighty-three organizations have accounted for about 10 percent of the value of grants made by larger foundations in recent years, totaling $76,000,000 in 1974. Eight foundations each contributed $1,000,000 or more, for a total of $67,000,000. This sum, comprising 88 percent of international grant dollars, was provided through 457 grants. The Ford Foundation, which contributed $41,000,000, accounted for 54 percent of the total. Education received $16,656,000, or 22 percent, of the total allocated to international activities by these foundations. This proportion was exceeded only by support for technical assistance programs, which received 23 percent of the total. In terms of numbers of grants, education was the leading beneficiary by a substantial margin, with 161 awards.

In a study prepared for the Institute of International Education, Meagher (1974) noted that the field of international activities attracted the greatest dollar volume of support in 1966, when a peak level of $141,000,000 was achieved. The 1973 level of $66,000,000 represents an even more dramatic reduction in real terms. The Council on Foundations has shown that, during the period from 1951 to 1970, the costs of activities supported by foundations experienced a 3 percent average rate of increase above the general price level. The rate varied from 3 percent for general operating costs to 3.9 percent for student financial aid and 5.3 percent for university and other scholarly research projects. Thus, using 1966 as the base year, international funding for 1973 was about half the absolute dollar total, with a real value of 31.5 percent of the 1966 funding level.

Phillips (1976) has estimated that private foundations contributed about $45,000,000 of the $2,350,000,000 in international assistance for education in developing countries spent during 1973. This international foundation total included $29,500,000 given by the Ford Foundation; $13,300,000 given by the Rockefeller Foundation; and $1,000,000 provided by the Carnegie Corporation. Thus, all other foundations in the United States and in other nations contributed only about $1,200,000, or 2.7

percent of the total. Although Phillips reports that statistics are not available, it appears that an important fraction of this small remaining balance was provided by the Nuffield Foundation (United Kingdom), Calouste Gulbenkian Foundation (Portugal), and *Stiftung Volkswagenwerk* (Federal Republic of Germany), which have a variety of foreign educational aid programs.

In sharp contrast to this level of foundation spending, an estimated $2,300,000,000 additional assistance was provided by direct government-to-government aid programs, intergovernmental organizations and agencies, and by the private voluntary sector. About $1,400,000,000 of this sum was provided by members of the Development Assistance Committee of the Organisation for Economic Co-operation and Development (OECD), but half of this amount was comprised of French educational assistance to its former African colonies. Such non-OECD countries as the Soviet Union, the People's Republic of China, and the Eastern European nations gave an estimated $200,000,000.

The World Bank, the Inter-American Development Bank, and the World Food Program have provided $435,000,000 in educational assistance; agencies such as UNICEF, UNESCO, the United Nations Development Programme, and others have contributed $150,000,000; and church-affiliated donors and other nongovernmental sources have devoted approximately $400,000,000 to the effort. Thus, private foundations play only a minor role in educational funding, with virtually all support during 1973 given by American-based or Western European organizations.

As observed in a Rockefeller Foundation staff review of the Phillips report, the preparation of that study disclosed that "in the busy business of international assistance to higher education, everyone was flying blind. There was, in short, no central index in which the activities of various agencies were recorded and analyzed. There was not even a central record of the dollar amounts of aid involved" (Wolff, 1976,

p. 2). The designation of an appropriate international organization, such as OECD or UNESCO, to establish uniform definitions and to accumulate data in this field would be an extraordinarily useful contribution to better understanding and more effective action in this critically important area of international cooperation for development.

Foundations do not, in aggregate terms, provide a major fraction of the total sums allocated to international higher education programs. However, they do represent a major source of support for certain regional and international organizations concerned with higher education and related issues, such as associations, institutes, research centers, and postsecondary institutions, which are of worldwide interest or renown. In addition, they often contribute importantly to domestic higher education activities in many nations.

The bibliography includes several references—*Guide to European Foundations* (1973), *International Foundation Directory* (1974), *Trusts and Foundations in Europe* (1972), *Philanthropic Foundations in Latin America* (1968)—that provide multinational data regarding foundations and their interests, resources and management. In addition to these reference works, *Foundation News* (Foundation Center, New York) has published many articles on philanthropy abroad in recent years. These include descriptions of specific foundations, discussions of philanthropy in various nations and regions, and lists of directories.

Bibliography

Andrews, F. E. *Philanthropic Foundations.* New York: Russell Sage Foundation, 1956.

Andrews, F. E. *Foundation Watcher.* Lancaster, Pennsylvania: Franklin and Marshall College, 1973.

Arlett, A. (Ed.) *A Canadian Directory to Foundations and Other Granting Agencies.* (3rd ed.) Ottawa, Ontario: Association of Universities and Colleges of Canada, 1973.

Commission on Foundations and Private Philanthropy. *Foundations, Private Giving and Public Policy.* Chicago: University of Chicago Press, 1970.

Corson, J. J., and Hodson, H. V. *Philanthropy*

in the 70s: An Anglo-American Discussion. A Report on the Anglo-American Conference on the Role of Philanthropy in the 1970s. New York: Council on Foundations, 1973.

Directory of Grant-Making Trusts. (3rd compilation.) Tonbridge, Kent, England: Charities Aid Fund, 1974.

Directory of Philanthropic Trusts. Wellington: New Zealand Council for Educational Research, 1964.

Foundation Grants Index. New York: Foundation Center, 1974.

Giovanni Agnelli Foundation. *Guide to European Foundations.* Milan: Franco Angeli Editore, 1973.

Giving in America: Toward a Stronger Voluntary Sector. Washington, D.C.: Commission on Private Philanthropy and Public Needs, 1975.

Hart, E. D., and Brown, C. A. *Directory of Philanthropic Trusts in Australia.* (2nd rev. ed.) Hawthorn, Victoria: Australian Council for Educational Research, 1974.

Hodson, H. V. (Ed.) *The International Foundation Directory.* London: Europa, 1974.

Lehsmann, K., and Odelberg, W. *Svenska kulturfönder.* (3rd ed.) Stockholm: Norstedt & Söners Förlag, 1970.

Lewis, M. O. (Ed.) *The Foundation Directory, Edition 5.* New York: Foundation Center, 1975.

Lundberg, J. M. (Ed.) *Giving USA, 1975 Annual Report.* New York: American Association of Fund-Raising Counsel, 1975.

Meagher, S. K. "Foundation Giving to International Programs." Unpublished study prepared for the Institute of International Education, New York, 1974.

Meagher, S. K. "Foundation Grants in International Activities." Unpublished study prepared for the Institute of International Education, New York, 1976.

Newhoff, K., and Pavel, V. (Eds.) *Trusts and Foundations in Europe: A Comparative Survey.* London: Bedford Square Press, 1972.

Nielsen, W. A. *The Big Foundations.* New York: Columbia University Press, 1972.

Phillips, H. M. *Higher Education: Cooperation with Developing Countries.* New York: Rockefeller Foundation, 1976.

Spear, N., III. "Corporate Philanthropy in Japan." *Foundation News,* 1970, *11*(5).

Stromberg, A. *Philanthropic Foundations in Latin America.* New York: Russell Sage Foundation, 1968.

Sutton, F. X. *American Foundations and U.S. Public Diplomacy.* New York: Ford Foundation, 1968.

U.S. Business Support for International Public Service Activities. Part I: *Support from U.S. Headquarters.* Part II: *Support from Overseas*

Affiliates. New York: Conference Board, 1973.

Voluntary Support of Education, 1973–1974. New York: Council for Financial Aid to Education, 1975.

Wolff, A. "Upfront." *RF Illustrated,* March 4, 1976.

Yamamoto, T. "Philanthropy in Japan." *Foundation News,* 1975, *16*(1).

DONALD G. PORTER

See also: Development, College and University.

PHILIPPINE ASSOCIATION OF COLLEGES AND UNIVERSITIES

Founded in 1932 by eminent Filipino educators, the Philippine Association of Colleges and Universities (PACU) is a national, nonpolitical, voluntary, nonstock, and nonprofit organization of schools, colleges, and universities. Originally named Association of Filipino Private Universities and Colleges, it changed its name when it began to admit both public and private schools. Although original members were nonsectarian private schools, colleges, and universities, PACU has since admitted sectarian institutions of learning that share its policies and subscribe to its ideals, aims, and objectives.

The association aims to pursue the nation's development goals and educational objectives provided in the new constitution of the Philippines. Specifically, it seeks quality standards at all levels of education and institutional autonomy and academic freedom in institutions of higher learning. It is also committed to work for tax exemption and other privileges and incentives for private schools.

PACU's membership of seventy is composed of private schools, colleges, and universities in the Philippines with an estimated total student enrollment of more than 300,000 students. More than two thirds of the nation's college and university students are in PACU-member institutions. Schools applying for membership in the Philippine Association of Colleges and Universities are carefully screened. To be admitted, an applicant school must be sponsored by a school which is already a member of PACU. It must be an institution of reputable standing in the community, must have its own site and buildings, must have democratic administrative and teaching staffs, must pursue the goals and objectives of Philippine education as embodied in the Philippine constitution, and must be financially stable.

Members are charged membership fees in accordance with a schedule approved by the board of directors of PACU. These fees constitute PACU's main source of funding; in addition, a special assessment may be levied on members as the need arises.

PACU is governed by a board of directors composed of fifteen members who are elected annually in a general meeting. A president, two vice-presidents, and a secretary-treasurer are elected.

PACU has links with educational associations in the Philippines and abroad. It has been and continues to be consulted by the Department of Education and Culture, the National Board on Education, and other educational agencies, both governmental and nongovernmental, in policy formulation and decision making on matters relating to Philippine education.

PACU initiated the organization of the Coordinating Council of Private Educational Associations (COCOPEA), which has since been recognized as a force in Philippine education and as a sounding board in the formulation of basic educational policies and programs. COCOPEA is a combination of the Philippine Association of Colleges and Universities (PACU), the Catholic Educational Association of the Philippines (CEAP), and the Association of Christian Schools and Colleges (ACSC).

PACU organizes workshops, conferences, and seminars and maintains a liaison staff to represent its member schools before the offices of the Secretary of Education and Culture, the Bureau of Private Schools, the National Board on Education, and the Fund for Assistance to Private Education, a foundation specifically founded to assist private education in the country and funded from the war-damage funds authorized by the Congress of the United States. Member schools receive PACU technical assistance on various matters such as planning and development, curriculum development, standards for faculty salaries, and faculty rankings and classification. It also assists members in the recruitment and placement of faculty members and administrative personnel; conducts studies and research on education; and draws up position papers, whenever necessary, on any fundamental issue confronting Philippine education.

PACU has an independent commission for accrediting its members. The commission, composed of seven members, is set up along the American model of voluntary accreditation.

244 Isabel Building
España Street
Manila, Philippines

PHILIPPINES, REPUBLIC OF THE

Population: 41,517,000 (1974 estimate). Student enrollment in primary school: 6,764,000; secondary school (academic, vocational, technical): 1,723,300; higher education: 1,125,000 (1975 estimate). Student enrollment in higher education as percentage of age group (17–20): 17%. Language of instruction: English. Academic calendar: June/July to March/April, two or three terms. Percentage of national budget expended on education: approximately 33%. [Unless otherwise indicated, figures are for 1972–73.]

In the sixteenth century, shortly after Spain occupied what is today the Philippines, Roman Catholic missionaries began to open parish schools, which eventually developed into a widespread system of primary education. The missionaries also later opened colleges, including the College of Our Lady of the Rosary (1611), which became the College of Santo Tomas in 1616 and received university status in 1629. These missionary colleges permitted children of Spanish colonists as well as local inhabitants to receive higher education.

During the next two centuries more colleges were opened. The curricula included Latin, Greek, Spanish grammar, poetry, rhetoric, history, philosophy, theology, astronomy, physics, chemistry, natural history, and mathematics (geometry, algebra, and trigonometry).

In the nineteenth century the Spanish organized a number of professional technological institutions for marine and agricultural sciences. In addition, scientific and technological faculties in such fields as medicine, pharmacy, engineering, and basic sciences were added to the University of Santo Tomas. Medicine and pharmacy were the major scientific disciplines. Basic science and engineering technologies did not grow to any significant degree, except for those connected with seafaring. On the whole, emphasis was on classical studies, the humanities, and law.

By the end of the nineteenth century, the local intelligentsia, influenced by the French and American revolutions, organized a revolt against the Spanish rule. In 1898 intervention by the United States resulted in the defeat of both the Spanish colonists and the Filipino revolutionaries. Until 1946, except for a brief period of Japanese occupation (1942–1945), the Philippines were under the direct control of the United States. During the United States domination primary education expanded widely, and university and professional education was strengthened. In 1908 the University of the Philippines was established at Manila. By 1926 it had affiliated colleges of agriculture, medicine, hygiene and public health, and teacher training. From 1898 to the Japanese occupation, a great number of colleges were founded. Six institutions achieved university status: National University (1921), University of Manila (1921), Philippine Women's University (1932), Silliman University (1938), Far Eastern University (1933), and Adamson University (1947).

In 1946 the Philippines declared its independence, and in the next quarter century the number of colleges and universities increased approximately 125 percent over the previous 334 years (1611–1945). The rate of growth of privately owned universities and colleges was particularly dramatic. Prior to independence, the ratio of private to state institutions on the national level was 3:1; in 1970 it was 5:1. On the regional level it varied from 15:1 in Manila to 1:1 in the Cagayan Valley–Batanes region (*Higher Education in the Philippines*, 1972, p. 1). By 1973 there were 32 state colleges and universities and 610 private universities and colleges, the latter serving about 90 percent of the students.

The rapid proliferation of higher education has been attributed to a pursuit of excellence and academic freedom; it has also been attributed to a pursuit of vested interest by businessmen and politicians. Whatever the reason, the rapid growth in the number of universities has introduced problems of standards, and the great output of graduates has caused employment problems; graduates unable to find employment have been forced to go abroad. Since the early 1970s there has been a concerted effort by the government to formulate a policy on the expansion of higher education and to increase opportunities for postsecondary-level technical training while maintaining a moratorium on the establishment of new universities and on student enrollments. A national system, with the University of the Philippines as the core, is envisioned but has yet to be implemented (Tenmatay, 1974, p. 83).

Legal Basis of Educational System

The legal authority for higher educational policy and administration rests in the 1973 Philippine constitution and in acts, ordinances, and presidential decrees. The acts include Act 1459 (1906), or the Corporation Law, which required private institutions to register as stock or nonstock corporations with the Securities and Exchange Commission; Act 2706 (1917, amended 1923), or the Private School Law, which established state regulation of private institutions; Republic Act 1124 (1954, amended 1965), which created the National Board of Education and specified its composition; Republic Act 6055 (1969), which granted private institutions the right to nonprofit status; and Republic Act 6139 (1970), which regulated tuition and fees charged by private institutions. After the declaration of martial law in 1972, several presidential decrees were issued to provide guidelines for government assistance to educational programs. This assistance is tied to an accreditation scheme, but its implementation is contingent upon reorganization of the bureaucracy of the national educational system (*Final Report of the Committee on Higher Education,* 1974).

Types of Institutions

Higher education is provided in nearly 650 institutions: 7 state universities, 25 state colleges, 35 private universities, and approximately 575 private colleges. State-supported institutions mainly offer teacher education, agriculture and related sciences, and technology training. Over 90 percent of the students attend institutions in the private sector.

Although the state-supported colleges and universities are distributed almost evenly in the eleven regions of the country, the distribution of private institutions closely corresponds with the density of the population. Thus, Luzon, which has approximately 50 percent of the population, has 58 percent of the higher education institutions. Most of the institutions are small: approximately 75 percent have an enrollment of less than 1000 students, and those with enrollments exceeding 20,000 are found only in Manila (*Higher Education in the Philippines,* 1972, p. 2).

Relationship with Secondary Education

Primary education is compulsory and lasts six years. It is followed by four years of secondary education, which may be taken at either a general or a vocational high school. General secondary education follows a 2–2 plan: two years of general studies and two of either academic studies or vocational studies. Completion of secondary studies leads to a school-leaving certificate. Students from vocational high schools generally enter the labor market. Those from the vocational stream of the general high school often proceed to higher vocational/technical colleges, while those in the academic sector continue into the university.

Admission Requirements

Admission to higher education is based on the secondary school-leaving certificate. In addition, since 1974 all high school graduates have been required to pass a National College Entrance Examination (NCEE) for admission to postsecondary academic or professional degree programs. The purpose of the examination is to maintain the highest quality of education through regulation of admission, to promote national development, and ultimately to help maintain a healthy balance of all types of personnel in the manpower pool of the nation. Although passing the examination is necessary to qualify for college study, it does not assure admission. Colleges and universities may still impose additional requirements for specific programs.

Administration and Control

The Philippines has no unitary organization for higher education, although all educational institutions except the University of the Philippines are under the supervision of the Department of Education and Culture, which is assisted by the National Board of Education. The board consists of eight members, including the secretary of education, who directs the board and is the chairman ex officio; the chairman of the house and senate education committees; the president of the University of the Philippines; and a representative from each major educational association.

The twenty-five state colleges and seven universities are governed by special charters, legislated by congress. Each college or university is autonomous and is under a board of regents. The secretary of education and culture generally is the chairman of the board. Other members of the board vary from institution to institution. They generally include the president of the institution and may include the chairmen of committees on education of the senate and house of representatives, the director of public schools, the director of vocational training, the presidents of graduate associations, and a number of representatives appointed by the regents or by the president of the republic. Generally the board of regents elects the university president, who is assisted by an executive vice-president for academic affairs. There may also be a university council, composed of the president of the university and academic professorial staff. Universities can be subdivided into colleges under the control of a dean or director and further subdivided into departments under a department head.

The 35 private universities and 575 colleges are, like the state institutions, under the overall supervision of the Department of Education and Culture. Their specific governance is the responsibility of the Bureau of Private Schools, and they are supervised by its director. Each private institution operates under authority granted by the secretary of education on the recommendation of the director of private schools. The authority is usually in the form of a permit or recognition. A permit to open represents the government's judgment that the institution is in the public's interest and that it can offer satisfactory instruction. The initial permit approves programs for one year. Recognition may then be accorded by the government and is permanent unless canceled or revoked.

Changes in accreditation for both public and private institutions were recommended by the National Board of Education in a report of April 18, 1974. According to the report, a National Accreditation council should be established to standardize evaluation procedures for all higher education institutions.

Each private institution is expected to conform to rules and regulations as well as curricular programs designed and revised from time to time by the Department of Education and Culture. There are twenty regional superintendents; under each are area supervisors, who are responsible for ensuring that the individual institutions meet the requirements of the Bureau of Private Schools. Internal administration is generally controlled by a board of regents, trustees, or directors.

Programs and Degrees

The state and private universities grant undergraduate degrees in all the major disciplines of social and natural sciences and humanities. In addition, the professional colleges award diplomas, certificates, and degrees in their respective areas of specialization, such as agriculture, business administration, dentistry, education, engineering, law, medicine, public health, pharmacy, and veterinary medicine. In the 1970s by far the largest number of students in higher education are in some form of teacher training, and the next-largest enrollment is in business and commerce (*Higher Education in the Philippines,* 1972, p. 2).

The first degree is usually a bachelor's and requires four to five years of study. In medicine, pharmacy, and veterinary medicine, however, the first degree is the doctor's degree, which requires six years of study.

Graduate programs are offered at only a few institutions and mainly in the field of teacher education. Graduate degrees include the master's, generally awarded after two years of study beyond the bachelor's. The doctoral degree requires two to three years beyond the master's. Certificates and diplomas may be awarded on the undergraduate level or advanced level and take from one to eight years. In addition, many higher education institutions offer an associate degree, which is obtained at the end of two years of postsecondary study.

Financing

The constitutional commitment to free, universal elementary education, which consumes two thirds of the government's educational funds, has prevented a more active government role in the financing of higher education. However, state colleges and universities are funded by government contributions and by tuition, fees, production income, alumni support, and public donations. The public institutions submit a yearly budget to the Department of Education and Culture for approval. Chartered public institutions receive appropriations directly from congress, according to provisions in their legislation; construction at these institutions is financed separately under the Public Works Act.

Private institutions are financed largely by tuition and fees. Private donations and income from auxiliary sources provide less than 5 percent of their operating costs (Tenmatay, 1974, p. 86). They receive no government funds directly but have some tax exemptions, which assure their profitability. It is estimated that, after taxes, return on equity at proprietary private institutions is 17.3 percent, as compared to 14.9 percent for large manufacturing companies in the republic (Miao, 1971). Although they are not yet an important source of assistance, foreign agencies extend grants to some of the nonprofit institutions run by churches or foundations.

Student Social Background and Access to Education

Because tuition and fees are charged, and because most higher education institutions are located in urban areas, a large percentage of students in higher education come from urban middle- and upper-middle-class families. Private institutions enroll more students from higher socioeconomic classes than the state institutions.

Fees for courses vary. Teacher education and business and commerce are low-cost programs and attract most of the lower-income students. In 1970, 44 percent of undergraduate and graduate students were enrolled in education programs, 25.3 percent in business, 4.7 percent in engineering, 4 percent in agricultural sciences, 3.6 percent in medical sciences, 1.5 percent

in physical sciences, and .8 percent in biological sciences. The remaining 16.1 percent were divided among all remaining programs (*Higher Education in the Philippines*, 1972, p. 9).

Although most institutions of higher education are coeducational, there is a women's university, Philippine Women's University, originally opened in 1919 as Philippine Women's College. Women students tend to enroll in teacher education, humanities, and fine arts. Engineering, law, and political science are almost exclusively reserved for men.

Teaching Staff

The ranks of teaching staff at institutions of higher education are full professor, associate professor, assistant professor, instructor, and lecturer. There are no uniform qualifications required for appointments. Public colleges and universities determine their own criteria; private institutions follow guidelines determined by the Bureau of Private Schools. A graduate degree is usually requested, although in 1971–72 some 20 percent of those teaching on the master's level held only the bachelor's, and of those teaching on the doctoral level only 65 percent held the bachelor's (*Higher Education in the Philippines*, 1972, p. 3). Appointments of professorial staff are generally made by the board of regents or directors on the recommendation of the institution's president. Instructors are generally appointed by the president. Appointments are secured by a contract for one month, one semester, or a full year. In 1971 there were three times as many instructors as assistant, associate, or full professors; and tenured faculty amounted to only about 5 percent of the total.

Members of the teaching staff may be appointed to full- or part-time positions. The proportion of part-time faculty members in private universities and colleges is three times the number of part-time faculty in public institutions (*Higher Education in the Philippines*, 1972, p. 3). Many private institutions pay teaching staff on an hourly basis, which gives little encouragement for course improvement or for participation in administrative functions. It also encourages many to seek supplementary outside employment.

Research Activities

The universities have no uniform policy on research. Because of financial restrictions, few institutions are able to provide their teaching staff with research incentives such as a reduction of teaching load and sabbatical leaves. There is also no established policy on research and publications as a factor in promotions. Moreover, emphasis in graduate study is on teaching rather than research. Except at the college of agriculture at the University of the Philippines, there is no existing practice of engaging faculty members exclusively for research.

Current Problems and Trends

In its final report in 1974, the Committee on Higher Education stated that the major problems in the system of higher education in the Philippines were the very large number of universities and colleges with no consistency in basic policy, direction, or academic standards; the overcrowding of programs in education, commerce, and liberal arts, graduates of which have difficulty in obtaining employment; and the serious lack of graduates in the sciences, technological fields, and engineering. The committee also noted a geographical maldistribution of colleges and universities which deprives many deserving students of an opportunity for higher education. While stressing the need for financial assistance to higher education, the committee took into account the lack of funds for such assistance (*Final Report*, 1974, pp. 3–4).

The Philippines loses one of every five graduates of higher education through migration to other countries. This has especially affected the medical, academic, and engineering professions. It has also affected the supply of middle-level executives and technicians (*The Brain Drain*, 1971, pp. 99–103).

International Cooperation

The Philippines is an active member of the Association of Southeast Asian Nations (ASEAN). The association promotes an exchange of teachers and students between member nations and encourages the development of facilities to teach the language, history, and geography of member countries. The Philippines also participates in the South-East Asia Treaty Organization (SEATO). Through SEATO's cultural program, awards are granted to post- and undergraduate students of the member nations. As a member of the Colombo Plan for Co-operative Economic Development in South and Southeast Asia, the Philippines cooperates in programs that train technical manpower from South and Southeast Asia and that supply special equipment for technical training and research. In 1971–72 the Philippines enrolled over 12,000 foreign students in its institutions of higher education.

[Information supplied by the Ministry of Education and by Eleanor T. Elequin, Director, College of Education, University of the Philippines System, Quezon City, Philippines.]

Bibliography

The Brain Drain from Five Developing Countries. New York: United Nations Institute for Training and Research, 1971.

Brown, H., and Tellez, T. *National Academy of Sciences: International Development Programs of the Office of the Foreign Secretary.* Washington, D.C.: National Academy of Sciences, 1971.

Carson, A. L. *Higher Education in the Philippines.* Washington, D.C.: U.S. Government Printing Office, 1961.

Case, H. L. *The University of the Philippines: External Assistance and Development.* East Lansing, Michigan: Institute for International Studies in Education, 1970.

Educational Statistics School Year 1971–1972. Manila: National Board of Education, 1974.

Final Report of the Committee on Higher Education. Manila: National Board of Education, 1974. Mimeographed.

Frey, J. "Philippines." In *The Evaluation of Asian Educational Credentials: A Workshop Report.* New York: National Association for Foreign Student Affairs, 1966.

Further Education of Teachers in Service in Asia: A Regional Survey. Bangkok, Thailand: UNESCO Regional Office for Education in Asia, 1973.

Hayden, H., and others. *Higher Education and Development in Southeast Asia.* Vol. I: *Director's Report.* Vol. II: *Country Profiles.* Paris: UNESCO, 1967.

Higher Education in the Philippines 1970–1971. Manila: Higher Education Research Council, 1972. Mimeographed.

Hsueh, S. S. (Ed.) *Recent Trends in Administration in Southeast Asian Universities.* Bangkok, Thailand: Association of Southeast Asian Institutions of Higher Learning, 1970.

Laya, J. C. "The Government as an Environmental Factor in Philippine Private Enterprise Management." In Y. H. Yip (Ed.), *Role of Universities in Management Education for National Development in Southeast Asia.* Singapore: Regional Institute for Higher Education and Development, 1972.

Legaspi, L. Z. "Planning and Managerial Systems and Techniques for Private Philippine Colleges and Universities." In P. Chomchai (Ed.), *Meeting the Challenges of the Seventies: Managing the University.* Bangkok, Thailand: Association of Southeast Asian Institutions of Higher Learning Secretariat, 1973.

Miao, E. C. "The Structure and Performance of the Proprietary Institutions of Higher Education in the Philippines." Unpublished doctoral dissertation, University of Wisconsin, Madison, 1971.

Morales, A. T. "Higher Education in the Philippines." *Bulletin of the UNESCO Regional Office for Education in Asia,* 1972, 7(1), 114–124.

Smail, R. W. *Contribution of Education to the Development of Human Resources in the Republic of the Philippines.* Manila: United States Agency for International Development, 1965.

Tenmatay, A. L. "Country Report (Philippines)." In A. Tapingkae (Ed.), *The Growth of Southeast Asian Universities: Expansion Versus Consolidation.* Singapore: Regional Institute of Higher Education and Development, 1974.

See also: Academic Standards and Accreditation: International; Agriculture in Higher Education: Agribusiness Education; Archives: Africa and Asia, National Archives of; Cooperative Education and Off-Campus Experience: Cooperative Education Worldwide; Courts and Higher Education; Graduate and Professional Education: General History and Contemporary Survey; Military Training and Higher Education; Science Policies: Advanced Developing Countries: Asian Countries of the Philippines, Indonesia, Republic of Korea: Southeast Asia: Regional Analysis.

PHILOSOPHIES OF HIGHER EDUCATION, HISTORICAL AND CONTEMPORARY

To study properly the beginnings of the philosophy of higher education, one must go back to the extant sacred texts belonging to the ancient civilization of India: the Vedas, a collection of religious hymns, and Upanishads, a prose commentary on these sacred poems, belonging to the first millennium B.C.; the Bhagavad Gita, a philosophical poem, probably originating in the fourth century B.C.; and the somewhat later Ordinances of Manu, the moral code of the Brahmans, formulated approximately A.D. 500. These texts do not address themselves specifically to the subject of education, because early man did not categorize his life into various and manifold components. They do, however, provide the moral precepts and religious and legal codes that express the aspirations and ideals from which educational philosophy has been derived. In both the Hindu and the Buddhist attitudes toward human existence, life itself is considered an emanation from the Divine Essence, and the goal of life is the return of the self to everlasting peace or nirvana. The aim of education, therefore, is to help the individual realize this process, which is highly individual (because each soul has its own specific destiny, or *dharma*), yet common to all (for it is fulfilled through the natural and universal processes of life, the stages in human development from childhood to adult community responsibility). Although not specifically a philosophy of higher education, in their emphasis on the inner development of the individual, such views prepared the ground for a spiritual and intellectual conception of education which dominates Indian thought even to the philosophy of nonviolence preached by Mahatma Gandhi.

Another ancient civilization—China—introduced for the first time differing views on the purpose of education that reappear in the entire subsequent history of educational thought. This difference in emphasis may be seen in two of China's most important early philosophers: Confucius (c. 551–479 B.C.), who stressed education as the socialization of the individual, the acquisition of knowledge for the sake of harmony in society; and Lao-tse (c. 604–531 B.C.), founder of Taoism, who emphasized internal growth, learning for the sake of understanding. Although these philosophies are not mutually exclusive, the contrast they provide is intrinsic to almost all later discussions of the aims and objectives of higher education. The theories of Confucius provide the foundation for those systems of education that aim at producing good citizens and productive people, whereas the philosophy of Lao-tse aims at the cultivation of the individual and considers the fruits of such civilization as secondary. According to the philosophy of Confucius, the ideal man is the cultivated man, the man who combines wisdom with courtesy. Education, therefore, should be in *li*, or propriety, the learning of the proper conduct for one's role in life. In contrast, Taoism teaches individualism, the cultivation of inner harmony and peace. Man should seek not his ideal role in society, but his union with nature. This Taoist belief nurtured spontaneity and simplicity, a precursor to the romantic movement in eighteenth-century Western thought. By no means confined to China and Eastern culture, this divergence in objectives expressed by Confucius and Lao-tse also characterizes much of Western thought. Indeed, most fruitful educational theories have tried to combine them while tending to stress one aspect or another.

Ancient Greek and Roman Philosophies

The influence of the ancient Greek and Roman philosophers on the systematic development of education was extensive. The most notable contributions were those of Plato, Aristotle, Plutarch, and Quintilian.

Plato. In the Western world the first comprehensive and systematic philosophy of education is to be found in the writings of Plato (427–347 B.C.). So much of Western philosophy is indebted to this one thinker, it is not surprising that he should also provide the fundamental questions that have engaged the philosophers of educational theory since his time. Although many of Plato's proposals now seem antiquated and authoritarian, he did see with astonishing clarity and profundity most of the basic issues of higher education still with us today.

First and foremost, Plato perceived higher education as cultivation of the individual for the sake of the ideal society, the just state, as well as for the inner happiness and harmony of the individual. In the Platonic system, the individual who learns to exhibit in his own life the beauty and harmony of the universe is the individual who will make the best citizen; he will know "how both to rule and be ruled righteously" (*Laws*, 1942, *1*, 65).

With this end in view, Plato presented a system of education aimed at the cultivation of those virtues that help the individual achieve inner harmony and allow the state to benefit from the harmony of satisfied citizens fulfilling their proper roles. Early education in this system included the cultivation of the body and the acquisition of good habits. Since Plato believed that only the intellectually elite could benefit from higher education, those who, in the early years of their training, demonstrated capability only for becoming producers (workers) for the appetitive needs of society or warriors had their education curtailed in late adolescence. For those capable of further education, Plato developed a course of study designed primarily to inculcate the ideals of service and political leadership and to train the mind to grasp the more difficult concepts of the notion of good itself and the underlying reality beyond the flux of sensory experience.

The central idea that motivates Plato's philosophy of higher education is the conviction that knowledge of that which really is cannot be discovered by the evidence of our senses; it can be attained only by long and rigorous training in dialectic, and only he who has gone through this training will be able to discern the true and the good and hence will be qualified to rule the state. Plato's philosophy thus presupposes innate inequalities in the capabilities of men (and women). Indeed, it proposes to capitalize upon such inequalities by differentiating the length and type of education by those individual differences. Plato, unlike most of his successors, conceived of higher education as a prerogative of the aristocracy of the intellect, not of birth or position. Thus, this philosophy views the ultimate purpose of higher education as the creation of a just and harmonious society.

Aristotle. Aristotle (384–322 B.C.), like Plato, wrote no formal treatise on the subject of education, but the principles he delineated in the *Ethics* and the *Politics* both implicitly and explicitly express his educational ideals. He shared with Plato the conviction that the end of life for the individual is the development of *arete*, virtue, which is at one and the same time moral goodness and human excellence. According to Aristotle, "The good of man is the active exercise of his soul's faculties in conformity with excellence or virtue, or, if there be several human excellences or virtues, in conformity with the best and most perfect among them" (*The Nicomachean Ethics*, 1945, *1*, 33). This good can be best accomplished by first habituating children to like that which is beautiful, noble, and good and to eschew the opposite; at a later stage in their education reliance upon reason is introduced as the guiding principle for human conduct, and thereafter learning to live in harmony with the *logos*, the rational principle, becomes the means of both education and the good life. Both the early training, which encourages good habits, and the more advanced training of the mind presuppose a lifelong stress on sound physical conditioning of the body.

Aristotelian and Platonic theory thus agree in stressing the development of the rational aspect of human nature and in insisting that the aim of education is production of the good citizen. It is not surprising, therefore, that most of what Aristotle has to say about the higher stages of education appears in the *Politics,* although he transcends this somewhat narrow conception of education as a political and social instrument and introduces a more profound and influential concept of the responsibility of higher education for the creative and intelligent use of leisure. The ultimate aim of education, he claims, is to prepare the individual for the active enjoyment of leisure *(Politics,* 1932, pp. 609–617). And just as Aristotle believed that the highest activity of all is the active use of one's intellectual faculties, he was convinced that the activity best suited to leisure is *theoria,* or the disinterested search for truth, not for utilitarian or economic motives but purely as an activity in itself. In the Aristotelian view, education, even when it is professional or practical, must always include the awareness that man is truly free only when he is not earning a living but creatively using his leisure. In his own day, Aristotle's philosophy was relevant only for a small and highly favored aristocratic class whose existence depended on a slave economy; in advanced industrial societies, his words, if heeded, could have relevance for a far more significant portion of the population. The concept of higher education as a means of learning the creative use of leisure time rather than providing a way to earn a living or to develop a responsible citizen is just beginning to enter the mainstream of educational thought.

Plutarch. Plutarch (C. A.D. 46–120) is the next thinker who properly belongs to this historical sketch, principally because of his influence on Renaissance humanism. A syncretic and largely derivative thinker, Plutarch blended the central tenets of Greek educational thought—namely, the emphasis on physical health and hygiene, acquisition of noble habits, and cultivation of a rational mind. Aristocratic by birth and inclination, Plutarch designed a model for the young gentleman entailing the acquisition of culture interlaced with a liberal dose of high moral principles. "For to receive a proper education is the source and root of all goodness," he claimed (*Moralia*, 1927, *1*, 19). His importance lies not in the originality of his thought but in the felicity with which he expressed his ideas, so that he preserved for Western culture the ideals and contributions of classical Greek thought. His essay *On the Guidance of Children* reentered the Western world in 1411 through a Latin translation by Guarino da Verona (1370–1460), and it exerted great influence for several centuries.

Quintilian. One other thinker of the ancient world, the Roman orator Quintilian (c. A.D. 35–100), deserves mention here. In contrast to the largely theoretical thrust of Greek thought, Quintilian concerned himself principally with the practical side of education, especially the education of the orator. He saw the discipline of oratory as central to the education of the individual, and instead of the empty formulations of the philosophers, Quintilian wished the content of education to be style—the eloquence of rhetoric, the art of expression and persuasion. He also developed theories, many still of value today, about the methods and curriculum of elementary education, which he believed should provide a general education. According to Quintilian, when a youth was approximately sixteen years of age and had completed his general studies (music, arithmetic, geometry, gymnastics, and oratory), he should specialize in rhetoric. Yet Quintilian believed that the study of the art of public speech required not only a thorough knowledge of grammar and literature but also training in philosophy, ethics, civil law, and the custom and religion of the state; a truly eloquent and persuasive style, which in Quintilian's system took precedence over content, would not be possible without a fundamental knowledge of the traditional curriculum. His emphasis on formalism, however, became an important aspect of

Renaissance thought, when the humanist Giovanni Francesco Poggio discovered the *Ars Oratoria* in 1410. Those who criticize the classic humanist education with its emphasis upon literature, the study of ancient authors, and the development of the art of expression in both oral and written communication are, in part, objecting to the ideal of Quintilian.

Medieval Thought

In turning from the classical world to that of medieval Christianity, one finds that the ancient ideal of the development of the individual in all his various faculties—physical, emotional, mental—was supplanted by the Christian ideal of humility and self-abnegation. The classical ideal of individual self-realization gave way to the worship of God; the concept of the importance of life on earth was belittled compared with the vision of the life to come, and knowledge attained through reason was considered subordinate to that attained through revelation. With such a basic shift in philosophical orientation, it is to be expected that the philosophy of higher education would assume a new posture, and indeed it did. At the same time, Christianity had to interact with the educated pagan world, and since many of the early fathers of the church were Greek and thoroughly imbued with their classical heritage, elements of pagan thought were bound to be assimilated by the early Christian church.

Christianity. The first great period of Christian thought was formative: both the Greek and Latin fathers of the church in the first six centuries A.D. were clearly struggling with the reconciliation of the gospel of Jesus and the philosophical tradition of Plato and Aristotle. In opposition to the guiding ideal of classical thought on higher education—the self-realization of the individual, the educated and hence the good citizen of the state—the Christian believed that the end of man was salvation. Since this life was only a preparation for the life beyond the grave, the function of the state was only of peripheral interest.

Rather than education for responsible citizenship, the Christian philosophy advocated education for the sake of the life to come, through inculcation of the Christian virtues of faith, hope, and charity.

It should be remembered that all the writers of this period presupposed an already existing system of secular education. Although some held that secular learning was to no avail due to the imminence of the Kingdom of God, others, such as St. Augustine (A.D. 354–430), believed that pagan learning and culture could be used by the Christian in his progress toward an understanding of God *(Works,* 1934, *2,* 14). Treatises dealing specifically with the subject of education, however, were rare.

al-Ghazzali. During the same period, a decisive step in the history of higher education was taken by the Muslim theologian al-Ghazzali (1058–1111). Just when the Western world was challenging the authority of revelation with the authority of reason, al-Ghazzali challenged the rationalist tradition itself with a mystical philosophy, which was thereafter characteristic of Islamic thought. Starting with the philosophical intuition of the unity of all knowledge al-Ghazzali focused Islamic education on the unity of the cosmos, which in turn was a revelation of the unity of the Divine Principle. This basic philosophical premise led to an entirely different attitude toward learning, an attitude that does not seek the accumulation of new facts or stress the importance of originality but rather values stability and knowledge of the permanence of unity. Muslim philosophy seeks the One, and the highest level of thought, the contemplative, is the conscious participation of the individual in the unity of nature. The acquisition of knowledge in Islamic tradition has always been considered a religious duty, since ultimately he who knows is he who sees things as they really are. The Western ideal of progress, therefore, is foreign to this Muslim philosophy that knowledge is stable and truth is one and unchanging. Indeed, this Eastern concept of higher education precludes the notion of specialization so prevalent in the Western world (see Nsar, 1970, pp. 59–90).

Origins of universities. What higher education in the West owes, above all, to medieval culture is the origin of universities and the compelling belief that the goal of higher education is the pursuit of truth and learning. All subsequent Western thought on the philosophy of higher education finds its source in the growth of universities in the twelfth century. Although their actual origins are obscure, the universities of this period began with groups of learners, both students and faculty, who were often connected with a cathedral or a famous teacher.

The importance of these early centers of scholarship lies in the legacy they bestowed, particularly in their concept of the role of the university and its organizational structure, details of which are still retained by universities today (such as curriculum, formal instruction, awarding degrees, and examinations). Of greatest significance was the view of the university as an organization dedicated to the advancement of knowledge and to the training of scholars for future generations. Not still the same today is the belief in the comparative purity of the university as an entity dedicated to the pursuit of truth independent of political and economic institutions and free to follow its own line of inquiry. Nevertheless, the medieval European conception of the university has influenced education in North and South America, in India, and in Africa, and it has provided the aims and objectives that the modern world still holds central to its basic philosophy of education.

Humanist and Renaissance Philosophies

The ideal of education cherished by the medieval universities was to be challenged in the centuries that followed. Even before the Renaissance of the sixteenth century, the humanist movement had redirected the minds of people toward the question of learning and its acquisition. Scholasticism had perpetuated the medieval concept of higher education as consisting of the seven liberal arts (the *trivium*—grammar, rhetoric, logic—and the *quadrivium*—music, arithmetic, geometry, and astronomy), heavily interspersed with the Christian virtues. Although the humanist philosophy did not abandon this curriculum, it did give new expression to the ancient tradition by claiming that learning is for the express purpose of life in this world and that the goal of education is the well-rounded development of the individual. Moral exhortation had not diminished, but it was now accompanied by practical advice to men on how to win glory, attain worldly success, or rule advantageously.

Like the ancient authors whom the humanists so often quoted—Plato, Aristotle, Plutarch, Quintilian—these fifteenth century thinkers presumed that higher education belonged to an aristocratic elite, and their advice concerning both subject matter and pedagogical method was directed toward enabling the student to have a full and accomplished life. Implicit in their writing, with its frequent use of quotations from classical and medieval scholars, is the belief that what is necessary to the good life has already been found and has, indeed, already been recorded in those works perceived as classic texts. This philosophy of higher education focuses on the teaching of values rather than facts and considers the training of the mind, not the teaching of a specific skill or vocation, its central concern. As such, humanistic philosophy is the direct ancestor of the liberal arts education and provides the basis for modern thought on this type of education.

The Reformation. Another challenge to medieval concepts of education came from the Protestant Reformation, particularly from the pen of Martin Luther (c. 1483–1546). Although the relationship in Luther's thinking between freedom and authority is an intricate and complicated one, his decisive break with the authority of the Catholic church and his insistence on the primacy of the individual relationship between man and God clearly promoted individual self-reliance. Because he believed

in the importance of reading the Gospels in their original language, he urged the study of Latin, Greek, and Hebrew, not for the sake of individual self-cultivation but for the sake of individual piety. As he says, "We will not long preserve the Gospel without the languages. The languages are the sheath in which this sword of the Spirit is contained" (*Luther's Works,* 1962, *45*, 360). As salvation depends, at least in part, in Luther's philosophy on knowledge of the Bible, the indirect function of higher education is to bring man closer to God. Luther also believed in the responsibility of education, at whatever level, to teach the role of the Christian citizen. Seeing civil government as a divine institution, Luther felt that the educational process should imbue Christians with a strong sense of social obligation. Another and perhaps the most original element in Luther's philosophy is his belief in the vocation or "calling" of man, and his concomitant conviction that advanced schooling should address itself to the needs of an individual's vocation. Thus, in Luther the purposes of higher education are advancement of individual piety, provision of an intelligent and informed citizenry, and, of particular interest to the modern world, encouragement of the individual to follow his calling. His influence on later thought is particularly evident in the writings of John Locke and Immanuel Kant, who expressed Luther's concept of the "inner liberty" of the Christian as the doctrine of the individual worth of every human being and the need for tolerance of others.

Erasmus. Another thinker of this period to focus on the needs of the individual was Desiderius Erasmus (c. 1466–1536). An avowed humanist and Christian, Erasmus combined Plato's educational ideals with Christian values into a system that had for its objective the living of a good and worthwhile life. Erasmus held scholarship in high esteem, yet always placed the highest priority on piety and the moral life. As he says in *De Civilitate Morum Puerilium,* "The first and most important part of education is that the youthful mind may receive the seeds of piety; next, that it may love and thoroughly learn the liberal studies; third, that it may be prepared for the duties of life; and fourth, that it may from the earliest days be accustomed to the rudiments of good manners" (Woodward, 1971, p. 73). Although most of his treatises on education center on the methods and content of early childhood education, Erasmus's concept of intellectual culture as the fusion of antiquity and Christianity (as opposed to Luther's contempt for Aristotle and most pagan thought) did much to preserve the educational ideals of the ancient world. The antiintellectualism implicit in Reformation philosophy with its stress on individual piety found a healthy counterbalance in Erasmus's conviction that the human being, by virtue of the possession of reason, has both the duty and the privilege of education as the means to a wise and virtuous life.

Montaigne. The same strain runs through the writings of Michel Eyquem de Montaigne (1533–1592), who wrote two treatises on education. It was Montaigne's belief that education should teach the art of living, and the measure of education is the behavior of those who have received it. The educated man, he claims, "will not so much say his lesson as do it. He will repeat it in his actions" (Montaigne, [1948] 1957, p. 124).

According to Montaigne, neither the schoolroom nor the library but the world itself is the best source of instruction: "This great world . . . is the mirror in which we must look at ourselves to recognize ourselves from the proper angle" (Montaigne, [1948] 1957, p. 116). He considered observation, travel, and moral example the best teachers and believed that the process of education should cultivate the whole person, thereby avoiding an artificial division of mind and body which is detrimental to both. Montaigne, it should be noted, was not averse to book learning; he believed, however, that the reading of books without the experience of the real world produced a shallow and limited mind.

In one other respect Montaigne is a precursor of those modern philosophies of education no longer based on religious premises but on human psychology. Education in the Western world since the time of the early church fathers had been built on a Christian foundation, but Montaigne, in his philosophies both of man and education, adhered to a secular conception of man as an autonomous and self-responsible being. Indeed, it is with this psychology that the modern history of the philosophy of higher education may be said to have begun.

Philosophers of the Seventeenth and Eighteenth Centuries

The seventeenth century, the age of the great scientific revolution, did much to foster the more secular view of education introduced by Montaigne. Such key thinkers as Francis Bacon (1561–1626) and Galileo Galilei (1564–1642) urged abrogation of discussion in favor of observation and experimentation. This led to a new emphasis on both the utilitarian and the scientifically demonstrable aspects of learning. Galileo scorned the professors at the University of Padua who refused to look through his telescope and who referred instead to the authority of Aristotle; Bacon, in turn, advocated the inductive method in science—the systematic and discriminating gathering of facts, free from the tyranny of preconceived ideas.

The scientific revolution of the seventeenth century, although not addressing itself directly to problems of educational theory, did much to undermine the role of tradition and revelation as the ultimate sources of authority and thus severed medieval educational theory from its philosophical premises. Substituted were the new and equally uncompromising standards of truth, mathematical demonstration, and empirical evidence. Without such a major philosophical transition, it is impossible to conceive of the enormous emphasis on the experimental method and the role of the mathematical model so much in evidence in the modern educational curriculum.

Bacon. Bacon was particularly modern in his view of the ends of higher education; in his writing (1605) he deprecates the trend toward professional studies in university work and calls for thorough training in the arts and sciences by saying, "This dedicating of foundations and dotations [*sic*] to professory learning hath not only had a malign aspect and influence upon the growth of sciences, but hath also been prejudicial to states and governments. For hence it proceedth that princes find a solitude in regard of able men to serve them in causes of estate, because there is no education collegiate which is free; where such as were so disposed might give themselves to histories, modern languages, books of policy and civil discourse, and other the like enablements unto service of estate" (*Advancement of Learning*, 1957, pp. 78–79).

Another germinal idea in Bacon is the usefulness of knowledge. "Knowledge and human power are synonymous," he states, "since the ignorance of the cause frustrates the effect" (*Novum Organum*, 1889, p. 192). The emphasis on the almost veneration of utility permeates all Bacon's writings. More than the worldliness of Montaigne, who preached the cultivation of knowledge for the sake of the complete man, Bacon's utility is the pursuit of knowledge to attain mastery over nature to improve the condition of man. As such, Bacon's theories represent the inchoate beginnings of a philosophy of higher education seeking to control rather than to understand, to produce practical results rather than theoretical structures.

Comenius. John Amos Comenius (1592–1670), another thinker of the seventeenth century, contributed an equally modern idea: education for all regardless of birth or wealth. In *The Great Didactic*, Comenius states, "Not only the children of the rich and powerful but all children ought to be educated in the same way whether they are nobles or commoners, rich or poor, boys or girls, or whether they come from cities, towns or villages" (1896, p. 218). The old ingredients of Roman virtue, Christian piety, and the utilitarian notion of higher education as seen in Bacon, are happily merged in Comenius with a belief in the universal brotherhood of man. However, he was firmly convinced of the aristocracy of the intellect and believed that the highest learning—university scholarship—should be reserved only for those who have proved themselves capable, by public examination, of profiting from it. According to Comenius, "only select intellects, the flower of mankind" (1896, p. 432) are suitable for university study and "care should be taken to admit to the university only those who are diligent and of good moral character" (1896, p. 434).

For the average individual, Comenius advocated more moderate educational goals: "But do not imagine that we demand an exact or thorough knowledge of all the arts and sciences from all men. This would neither be useful of itself, nor on account of the shortness of life can it be attained by anyone. It is the principles, the causes, and the purposes of all the main facts about the world that we wish everyone to learn. For we must do all in our power to ensure anything so unknown to him that he cannot pass a sober judgment upon it, and turn it to its proper use without serious error" (1896, p. 222). Although this idea was not practiced for several centuries, the concept of higher education as training the student to cope with any eventuality with intelligence and good judgment became an important component of modern higher education theory.

Comenius also provided the seventeenth century with a philosophical statement of the ultimate aims of education combining religious piety, morality, and the advancement of learning. Beginning with the premise that "the ultimate end of man is eternal happiness with God," Comenius argues that in erudition, virtue, and religion "is situated the whole excellence of man, for they alone are the foundation of the present and of the future life. . . . Under erudition we comprehend the knowledge of all things, arts and tongues; under Virtue, not only external decorum, but the whole disposition of our movements, internal and external; while by Religion we understand that inner veneration by which the mind of man attaches and binds itself to the supreme Godhead" (Keatinge, 1931, pp. 23–25).

Although by no means identical to the sole reliance placed upon religious authority by medieval thinkers, Comenius's ultimately theological conviction that man is created to strive for eternal happiness with God did establish for his own and successive generations the religious purposes that were to dominate higher education both in Europe and the New World for many years. John Milton (1608–1674) echoed his very words when he proclaimed in his *Treatise on Education,* "The end then of learning is to repair the ruins of our first parents by regaining to know God aright, and out of that knowledge to love Him, to imitate Him, to be like Him, as we may the nearest by possessing our souls of true virtue, which being united to the heavenly grace of faith, makes up the highest perfection" (*Prose Works,* 1959, pp. 366–367).

Locke. The intellectual successor of Comenius was the English empirical philosopher John Locke (1632–1704), who, although never directly quoting from Comenius, clearly stated with him the view that one of the principal aims of higher education is the cultivation of the mental faculties themselves. Like Comenius, Locke stressed the importance of wide experience, particularly before forming philosophical or religious judgments. As he explains in the *Conduct of the Understanding,* "I do not say to be a good geographer that a man should visit every mountain, river promontory, and creek upon the face of earth, view the buildings and survey the land everywhere as if he were going to make a purchase; but yet everyone must allow that he shall know a country better that often makes sallies into it and traverses up and down, than he that like a mill horse goes round in the same track" (1890, pp. 11–12). Locke also agreed with Comenius in opposing specialization; both saw the main function of higher education in the preparation of students "to open and dispose their minds as may best make them capable of any [subject] when they shall apply themselves to it" (1890, p. 44).

There is, however, another aspect of Locke's thought concerning education, not to be found in Comenius, which should be mentioned even though it is largely concerned with primary education. That is his emphasis on the individualism of the child, on the unique qualities, interests, and motivations each young child brings to the classroom. Locke was quick to stress the need to adapt teaching methods and philosophy to the individual student, for what encouraged one young mind might be ineffective with another.

Rousseau. It may have been Locke's ideas that influenced Jean Jacques Rousseau (1712–1778); it is certain that Rousseau was familiar with Locke's writings and with those of Thomas Hobbes, Montaigne, and early thinkers of the French Enlightenment. Predominant in Rousseau's thinking is the idea, though not itself original, that individualism, the growth and development of the person, is the end of education. Throughout the history of the philosophy of higher education, the differing views of education for the sake of individual self-development, as opposed to education for the sake of the development of the good citizen, have found expression. The difference in emphasis was first noted in the ancient Chinese philosophies of Confucius and Lao-tse. In Rousseau the emphasis falls almost exclusively on individualism, an individualism unequivocally opposed to corrupting effects of civilization. Widely read and highly influential, Rousseau was neither a consistent nor a clear exponent of his own ideas, yet even in its inchoate and confused form, his concept of "back to nature" had important consequences in educational theory. Rousseau was particularly influential in his emphasis on the natural self-development of the individual and the need to tailor educational content and methods to the gradual changes in the growing person; he reminded theorists and practitioners alike that educational philosophy must always take account of a kinetic, not a static, individual. Also significant was his view of the child not as an adult in miniature but as a personality at a different stage in development, with different needs and ways of looking at the world.

Pestalozzi. In his own day Rousseau was the source of many almost revolutionary reforms; since that time his work has been reflected in such diverse thinkers as Pestalozzi and John Dewey.

Of immediate impact was Rousseau's book *Emile* (1762), which dealt largely with the education of the young child. The book led Johann Heinrich Pestalozzi (1746–1827) to seek in education a remedy for the universal ills of society. Although Pestalozzi stressed the individual needs of the growing child and the need for educational theory to address itself to the unique capacities of each person, he also placed equal emphasis on the importance of individual self-development for the social good. This belief found expression in his program for equality of educational opportunity for all children, which was coupled with differentiation of educational content based on individual ability and interest. What children need most, according to Pestalozzi, is not the acquisition of skills, but individual development: "It is all very well and good for [children] to learn something, but the really important thing is for them to *be* something—for them to become what they are meant to be" (1892, p. 152). Although his writings focus on childhood education, Pestalozzi did not rigidly compartmentalize the educational process; rather, he perceived learning as

a lifelong process and higher education as an extension of the ideals of individual nurture begun in childhood.

Herbart. More philosophical than Pestalozzi but nevertheless influenced by him, the German scholar Johann Friedrich Herbart (1776–1841) offered to educational theory an alliance of metaphysical premises with educational objectives reminiscent of Plato. For Herbart, "the term virtue expresses the whole purpose of education" (1901, p. 7). "Man's worth," according to Herbart, "does not . . . lie in his knowing, but in his willing." However, "volition has its roots in thought," and, accordingly, the development of character depends upon the activity of the mind and the active engagement of the pupil's interest (1901, p. 40). To accomplish the development of character and to engage the entire emotional attitude or attention of the student, Herbart advocated introducing new material carefully related to that already learned. This approach reappears in the twentieth century with John Dewey's definitions of spontaneous and reflective attention.

Herbart was the first to make a systematic, formal analysis of the best way to acquire knowledge and to encourage the will to learn. He believed that only when a pupil is voluntarily involved in the learning process will he retain and integrate into his personality the information he has newly acquired, for "interest means self-activity" (1901, p. 60). Herbart had the opportunity to put his educational ideals into practice at the University of Königsberg, where he was called to the chair of philosophy and pedagogy in 1809. Here he anticipated the contemporary two-culture controversy by establishing a demonstration school with a two-sided curriculum: the one, mathematical and scientific, to teach the observation of natural phenomena; the other, classical, to cultivate human sympathy. According to Herbart's philosophy, both sides are necessary and decidedly not antithetical; indeed, education should develop the "many-sided individual," whose interests are empirical, speculative, esthetic, sympathetic, social, and religious (1901, pp. 76–92). With this emphasis on the multifaceted individual, Herbart introduced yet another modern note into his complete and systematic theory of education.

Froebel. Another disciple of Pestalozzi, Friedrich Froebel (1782–1852), shared Herbart's conviction that educational philosophy should stem from a more general philosophical position. Evolutionary theory had not yet been formulated, but the study of evolution was emerging, and it provided the philosophical backdrop for Froebel's educational ideals, which included the then novel philosophical conviction that life is an evolutionary process in which man moves toward even higher stages of development. Although best known for his creation of the kindergarten and his theory of early childhood education, Froebel's guiding notion of the evolutionary process did have implications for higher education as well. All individual existence, according to Froebel, is a single step in the development of mankind as a whole, and the development of mankind is inextricably related to the plant and animal world. In his autobiography he relates how he was particularly impressed by two principles enunciated by his teacher of natural history: "The first was the conception of the mutual relationship of all animals, extending like a network in all directions; and the second was that the skeleton or bony framework of fishes, birds, and men was one and the same in plan, and that the skeleton of man should be considered as the fundamental type which Nature strove to produce even in the lower forms of creation" (1908, p. 31). From this insight—the unity in diversity and the interconnection of all living things—Froebel derived a theory of education aimed at enhancing the inner "natural" development of man. In his approach, the instructional method, curriculum, and progression of studies at every level should stress the unity of life and accelerate the process of development,

innate in man, which had already brought about progress in the human race.

Nineteenth-Century Views

German thought dominated educational theory in the seventeenth and eighteenth centuries. During that period, English thought tended to concentrate on more practical problems—school organization, curriculum, method of instruction. But in the nineteenth century, English attention turned to the theory of liberal education as presented in two quite different philosophies: utilitarianism and classical humanism.

Utilitarianism. Utilitarianism is generally associated with Jeremy Bentham (1748–1832), its founder, and with James Mill (1773–1836) and his son John Stuart Mill (1806–1873). Bentham postulated that men are so constituted that all human behavior is determined by the desire to seek pleasure and avoid pain. He argued that morality should depend not upon teaching people what they ought to do, but upon the recognition that all men are subject to the principle of utility, which determines human actions through the consequences of pleasure and pain. According to this principle, one would not steal, for example, not because it is wrong, but because the consequence of stealing—prison—would be more painful than the pleasure obtained from the spoils of the crime.

The principle of utility proved to be a powerful concept in educational philosophy of the nineteenth century. Equally important was the theory of the association of ideas, a psychological concept contributed by James Mill. Mill argued that the entire mental life of man can be explained by a process in which learning is made possible by the formulation of connections among sensations, ideas, and memories. His educational theory, therefore, was devoted exclusively to the cerebral activity of man, with almost no attention to emotional factors. He had the opportunity to put his theory into practice with the purely intellectual education of his son John Stuart

Mill. Nonetheless, both James Mill and John Stuart Mill agreed that the aim of this intellectual education was to provide for the happiness of each individual and increase his measure of general culture. As John Stuart Mill states in his "Inaugural Address at St. Andrew's," "Men are men before they are lawyers, or physicians, or merchants, or manufacturers; and if you make them capable and sensible men, they will make themselves capable and sensible lawyers and physicians" (Cavenogh, 1931, p. 134).

John Stuart Mill contributed in yet another way to the nineteenth-century debate on the nature of a liberal arts education. In response to Herbert Spencer (1820–1903), who had given priority to scientific studies, and because he was well aware of the virtues of his own classical education, Mill emphatically asserted that the idea of a liberal education inextricably includes training in both the classics and the sciences.

Classical humanism. Classical humanism, particularly as exemplified in the writings of Cardinal John Henry Newman (1801–1890), is the other nineteenth-century theory of liberal education that was of particular influence. The most important statement concerning the idea of a liberal education can be found in Newman's *Idea of a University,* originally delivered as a series of lectures in 1852. In Newman's view, the university is, above all, an institution created for the express purpose of teaching and of cultivating the mind. Its function is not research, which belongs to other institutions, but the dissemination of knowledge, which, Newman says, is not the acquisition of facts nor the development of useful skills but "a state or condition of mind; and since cultivation of mind is surely worth seeking for its own sake, we are thus brought once more to the conclusion which the word 'Liberal' and the word 'Philosophy' have already suggested, that there is a Knowledge, which is desirable though nothing come of it, as being of itself a treasure, and a sufficient remuneration of years of labour" (1947, p. 101).

One other theme dominates Newman's discussions of the aims and principles of higher education—namely, his belief in universal knowledge and his consequent conviction that religion must always be part of the university curricula: "A University . . . by its very name professes to teach universal Knowledge: how then is it possible for it to profess all branches of Knowledge, and yet to exclude from the subjects of its teaching one which, to say the least, is as important and as large as any of them" (1947, pp. 18–19).

These two ideas—the vision of the university as the imparter of knowledge, and knowledge as the cultivation or enlargement of the mind—are the crux of Newman's discussion. Newman's philosophy also emphasizes the importance of the residential college, an association of students for the advancement of learning. If he had to choose between a "university which dispensed with residence and tutorial superintendence, and gave its degrees to any person who passed an examination in a wide range of subjects, and a university which had no professors or examinations at all, but merely brought a number of young men together for three or four years," Newman says he would "have no hesitation in giving the preference to that university which did nothing, over that which exacted of its members an acquaintance with every science under the sun" (1947, p. 128). In essence, he reasons that if one brings together a group of intelligent, sympathetic, and intellectually curious people, they are bound to learn from one another.

Other writers of the nineteenth century addressed themselves to the nature and aims of a liberal arts college, but Newman's lectures represent the most articulate theoretical defense of the acquisition of knowledge for the development of the mind, which for him was obviously the goal and ultimate principle of all higher education.

Whitehead. One of the most eloquent observers of the university since Newman was Alfred North Whitehead, British mathematician, scholar, and philosopher (1861–1947), who concurred with the nineteenth-century ideal of the cultivation of the mind but who protested against the teaching of dead knowledge, which he characterized as "inert ideas," ideas that are "merely received into the mind without being utilised, or tested, or thrown into fresh combinations" (1947, p. 1). Instead of the accumulation of such inert ideas, Whitehead believed that the standard of university education must be activity of thought.

In his insistence on active thought, Whitehead, like Newman, inveighed against the learning of facts without an understanding of their relation to one another and without the capacity to use facts for purposeful thought. The aims of education, according to Whitehead, should be expert knowledge and the acquisition of culture, culture being "activity of thought, and receptiveness to beauty and humane feelings" (1947, p. 1). This view of the mind as an active, functioning instrument rather than as a passive storehouse of information stands at the core of Whitehead's philosophy and provides the basis for all his suggestions on the objectives and methods of higher education.

He defined education as the art of the *utilization* of knowledge, with the emphasis again on function, and he suggested a methodology of higher education that similarly recognizes active stages of mental development which the good teacher would respect. This philosopher conceived of three general stages in the development of mental life—romance, precision, and generalization. Although he did not intend this scheme to be interpreted rigidly, Whitehead believed that if the curriculum were adapted to these naturally occurring periodic stages of development, the growing child would learn more and enhance his pleasure in the mastery of his environment.

In the final analysis, however, Whitehead's philosophy of education is highly intellectual. He believed firmly in the need for an educated mind, a mind thoroughly imbued with the culture of its historical heritage, the living past, while also rigorously trained in the best scientific knowledge of the present. His view is unequivocal: "In the conditions of modern life, the rule is absolute: the race which does not value trained intelligence is doomed" ([1932] 1947, pp. 22).

German research-oriented institutions. As Whitehead was writing, universities in Europe and the United States were feeling the influence of quite another model—that of the German research-dominated institution in which teaching was subsidiary to research. The great German universities of the nineteenth and early twentieth centuries, all research oriented, had such widespread influence that they shaped the idea of the modern university, which was described by Abraham Flexner as "an institution consciously devoted to the pursuit of Knowledge, the solution of problems, the critical appreciation of achievement, and the training of men at a really high level" (1930, p. 42). The Germans also contributed the idea of *Lernfreiheit* (freedom of the student to choose his own program) and *Lehrfreiheit* (freedom of the professor to teach what he wished and to engage in research). This philosophy influenced Charles W. Eliot, who, upon assuming the presidency of Harvard in 1869, launched a program of curricular reform, including the famous free-elective system, which penetrated most United States colleges and universities in the twentieth century.

Twentieth-Century Developments

In both France and the Soviet Union, university education since the nineteenth century has been part of a national system, and the philosophy governing instruction in these countries is largely subservient to national purposes. In general, both countries have tended to separate technical and professional training from research activities. In contrast, universities in the United States have tried to accommodate the many, sometimes conflicting, roles and functions of higher education, including instruction in the liberal arts and research as well as vocational and professional training. These manifold functions have led Clark Kerr to describe the modern American university as the "multiversity" (1973, p. 6).

Other countries have followed a variety of educational paths. Contemporary higher education in the People's Republic of China has been guided by a philosophy that seeks to eliminate the ancient Confucian tradition, which revered harmony and stability, and the mandarin ideal of the scholar-bureaucrat. Contemporary Chinese education has virtually replaced the notion of the liberal arts with that of vocational-technical training, a policy instituted in part to effect deep social changes. By combining physical labor with mental theory, as is the practice in the universities of the People's Republic, the establishment of a new educational elite is precluded. The universities themselves are charged with the task of helping to implement an economy run almost exclusively according to the Maoist philosophy of frugality, self-reliance, and independence. Education is thus viewed as an instrument of the state, designed not so much for the discovery of truth as for the propagation and maintenance of socially valued ideals.

In Latin America the philosophy of higher education has been closely related to the history and cultural development of each country. The Spanish colonies of the sixteenth, seventeenth, and eighteenth centuries shared with their European ancestors the belief that higher education should provide training for members of the professions, specifically theology, law, medicine, and the liberal arts (chiefly philosophy). But by 1850 the Spanish-American educational system was beginning to welcome the inclusion of scientific research. Many Latin American universities now include among their aims the concept of public service—an objective that is characteristic of institutions in both North and South America—in addition to professional preparation and scientific research.

The development of higher education in Africa was a subject of an international conference of that same name in 1962 organized by the government and people of Madagascar in cooperation with the United Nations Economic Commission for Africa. The role of the African university, the conference concluded, is a multifaceted one: the university must teach, advance knowledge through research, raise the intellectual standard of the population at large, and provide trained personnel in a variety of fields. In addition, the conference found that "to avoid a neo-fragmentation of the African society, the university must encourage and support elucidation of and appreciation for African culture and heritage" and "should further contribute to a synthesis of national, regional and African unity by adapting curricula to African needs for enriching both the individual and the nations of Africa" (UNESCO, 1963, p. 18). The social function of higher education, which dates back to Plato, here assumes a new and unique role. The university is not only perceived in terms of its traditional functions and obligations, but it also must transcend tribal barriers, overcome age-old conflicts and prejudices, and bring about the unification of a nation through the process of edification.

Universities throughout the world have not thus far, however, been the prime source of educational ideas in the twentieth century. The giant of contemporary educational thought has been John Dewey (1859–1952). Like his predecessors, Dewey's educational ideals grew from his philosophical thought, which has often been characterized as pragmatism but is in reality a more complex philosophical world view combining the sociological theory of Karl Marx with the biological evolutionary ideas of Charles Darwin. According to Dewey, man is a social animal whose development cannot be explained in abstract metaphysical terms but which must be seen as a concrete endeavor to respond to problematic situations in his environment. Thus abstract ideas, such as truth, being, goodness, do not exist in themselves but are conditioned by and developed from individual experience. In this system, thought is personal, not abstract, and it must be recognized that thinking and reasoning are essentially the human organism's way of solving immediate experiential problems.

The implications of Dewey's psychology for educational theory and practice are far reaching. Indeed, Dewey claims that at every level, from early childhood through adulthood, "education is not a means to living, but is identical with the operation of living a life which is fruitful and inherently significant" (1916, p. 281). Furthermore, "since life means growth, a living creature lives as truly and as positively at one stage as at another, with the same intrinsic fullness and the same absolute claims. Hence education means the enterprise of supplying the conditions which insure growth, or adequacy of life, irrespective of age" (1916, p. 61). In his view of growth as the characteristic of life, Dewey was influenced by evolutionary theory, and he considered the function of education to be the understanding of man's natural development and the enhancement of that process.

Dewey also emphasized education as a process of socialization and claimed that if the enhancement of the quality of individual life is a key element in the ultimate end of education, equally important is the recognition that education must help bring about the creation of a democratic community. He felt that if each individual, through the educational process, becomes a free and autonomous person, then society will be free of irrational conflicts. Individual freedom in Dewey's thinking is thus naturally compatible with the social good, and individuals correctly instructed should recognize the rational harmony of the community and its members.

In contrast with the philosophy of pragmatism that underlies Dewey's concept of education is the metaphysical philosophy redoubtably presented in the lectures and program of Robert M. Hutchins (1899–1977), former president of the University of Chicago. Hutchins, one of the foremost contemporary philosophers of education, argued the intellectual and educational validity of the pursuit of such questions as the nature of man, the nature of truth, and the nature of value. Knowledge of these metaphysical first principles is, Hutchins contended, the foundation stone of all education: since the nature of man is to be rational, the proper aim of education is the cultivation of the intellect. In his essential return to the nineteenth-century concept of a liberal education, which focuses on the creation of a rational and humane man, Hutchins has had many advocates, particularly those who have opposed the "learning by doing" philosophy of Dewey.

Another major thrust in twentieth-century educational philosophy has been the influence of the psychological principles of William James (1842–1910). Although James was emphatic in his belief that teaching is an art, not a science, his psychological theory makes evident the need for an educational philosophy based upon scientific knowledge of the nature of human development and learning. He himself denied that "psychology, being the science of the mind's laws, is something from which you can deduce definite programmes and schemes and methods of instruction for immediate schoolroom use" (1929, p. 7). Even so, James provided so-called laws for the art of teaching: the teacher must first activate an intense state of undivided attention in his pupil, then reveal the subject matter to be taught, and finally create a state of compelling curiosity about the next step in the learning process. James conceived of the human mind as essentially an associating machine: his *Talks to Teachers* explains how the laws of association can be utilized by the teacher so that learning occurs naturally and less arduously. But he was always careful to point out that education could not be programed, and he, if not his more enthusiastic disciples, saw the laws of psychology as providing only the framework, not the whole edifice, of the educational process. Early writers had pointed to the need for understanding the human mind before attempting to teach it; only in the twentieth century have thinkers tried to develop a science of human development and laws of learning.

The current philosophy of higher education manifests its historical lineage; indeed, many of its assumptions and presuppositions can be traced to an earlier period. But modern educational philosophy also provides a distinctive character of its own. Vocational preparation, a minor note in the seventeenth century, constitutes an increasing part of the curriculum of higher education; the vast and rapid movement of worldwide industrialization has created a demand for skilled labor and advanced scientific and technical training, which must be met by educational institutions. Coextensive with vocational education but less structured are modern ideas for the broadening of higher education—education for leisure, continuing education, and education for a greater proportion of the population. Finally, the growth of democracy has necessitated the creation of an educated populace, a citizenry able to vote intelligently. The notion that education should be used for the creation of a just state goes back to Plato, but today the number of persons affected is infinitely greater. Thus, the current philosophy of higher education has been shaped both by long historical exchanges and by contemporary needs. Modern philosophers have imparted to higher education its traditional responsibility for the transmission of culture and the discovery of new knowledge; they now also perceive higher education's role as an important creator and reservoir of public policy.

Bibliography

Aristotle. *The Politics.* (H. Rackham, Ed. and Trans.) London: Heinemann, 1932.

Aristotle. *The Nicomachean Ethics.* (H. Rackham, Ed. and Trans.) London: Heinemann, 1945.

Augustine, Saint. *Works.* (15 vols.) (M. Dods, Ed. and Trans.) Edinburgh: T. & T. Clark, 1872–1934.

Bacon, F. *The Advancement of Learning.* (W. A. Wright, Ed.) Oxford, England: Clarendon Press, [1605] 1957.

Bacon, F. *Novum Organum.* (T. Fowler, Ed.) Oxford, England: Clarendon Press, 1889.

Barendsen, R. D. *The Educational Revolution in China.* Washington, D.C.: U.S. Government Printing Office, 1973.

Cavenogh, F. A. *James and John Stuart Mill on Education.* Cambridge, England: Cambridge University Press, 1931.

Comenius, J. A. *The Great Didactic.* (M. W. Keatinge, Ed.) London: Black, 1896.

Dewey, J. *Democracy and Education.* New York: Macmillan, 1916.

Flexner, A. *Universities, American, English, German.* New York: Oxford University Press, 1930.

Froebel, F. W. *Autobiography.* (E. Michaelis and H. K. Moore, Trans.) Syracuse, New York: C. W. Bardeen, 1908.

Herbart, J. F. *Outlines of Educational Doctrine.* (A. F. Lange and C. de Garmo, Trans.) New York: Macmillan, 1901.

James, W. *Talks to Teachers on Psychology.* New York: Holt, Rinehart and Winston, 1929.

Keatinge, M. W. (Ed.) *Comenius.* New York: McGraw-Hill, 1931.

Kerr, C. *The Uses of the University.* New York: Harper & Row, 1973.

Locke, J. *Conduct of the Understanding.* (T. Fowler, Ed.) Oxford, England: Clarendon Press, 1890.

Locke, J. *The Educational Writings of John Locke.* (J. L. Axtell, Ed.) Cambridge, England: Cambridge University Press, 1968.

Luther, M. *Luther's Works.* (55 vols.) (J. Pelikan, Ed.) Vol. 45, edited by W. I. Brandt and H. T. Lehman. Philadelphia: Muhlenberg Press, 1962.

Milton, J. *Complete Prose Works of John Milton.* (7 vols.) (D. M. Wolfe, Ed.) Vol. 2, edited by E. Sirluck. New Haven, Connecticut: Yale University Press, 1959.

Montaigne, M. de. *The Complete Works of Montaigne.* (D. M. Frame, Trans.) Stanford, California: Stanford University Press, [1948] 1957.

Newman, J. H. *The Idea of a University.* New York: Longmans, Green, [1873] 1947.

Nsar, S. H. *Science and Civilization in Islam.* New York: New American Library, 1970.

Pestalozzi, J. H. *Leonard and Gertrude.* (E. Channing, Trans.) Boston: Ginn, Heath, [1885] 1892.

Plato. *Laws.* (2 vols.) (R. G. Bury, Ed. and

Trans.) Loeb Classical Library. London: Heinemann, 1942.

Plato. *The Republic*. (2 vols.) (P. Shorey, Ed. and Trans.) Loeb Classical Library. London: Heinemann, 1943.

Plutarch. *Moralia*. (14 vols.) (F. C. Babbitt, Ed. and Trans.) Vol. 1: *The Education of Children*. Loeb Classical Library. London: Heinemann, 1927.

Quintilian (Marcus Fabius Quintilianus). *The Institutio Oratoria of Quintilian*. (4 vols.) (H. E. Butler, Trans.) Loeb Classical Library. Cambridge, Massachusetts: Harvard University Press, 1921.

Rousseau, J. J. *Emile*. London: J. M. Dent, [1762] 1938.

UNESCO. *The Development of Higher Education in Africa*. Paris: UNESCO, 1963.

Whitehead, A. N. *The Aims of Education*. London: Williams & Norgate, [1932] 1947.

Woodward, W. H. *Desiderius Erasmus Concerning the Aim and Method of Education*. New York: Burt Franklin, [1904] 1971.

MAUD CHAPLIN

See also: History of Higher Education; Religious Influences in Higher Education; Scholarship, Classification of in the Curriculum.

PHILOSOPHY (Field of Study)

In its beginning, philosophy denoted all reflective thinking about the world and man's experience. As human knowledge increased, however, classification of the physical world became more detailed; methodological tools, such as the experimental method in the Renaissance, developed; and specialized areas of knowledge began to be consolidated. Physics and astronomy were first to separate from philosophy, later biology, and then the social sciences and psychology. The branches of academic philosophy today are a residuum of what at one time included the natural sciences, mathematics, and the social sciences.

The traditional branches of philosophy are (1) esthetics (the analysis of art, the artistic process, and esthetic experience, including theories of art, beauty, and standards of artistic excellence); (2) epistemology (the sources and nature of knowledge; their relation to belief, experience, and language; and the evaluation of claims to knowledge of the world, ourselves, and other persons); (3) ethics (a systematic and critical inquiry into theories of the good life and the principles which should guide human conduct); (4) history of philosophy, which includes classical Greek and Roman philosophy, medieval philosophy, and modern philosophy; (5) logic, dealing with deductive and inductive reasoning; (6) metaphysics (an investigation of the nature and structure of reality), usually divided into ontology and cosmology; (7) social and political philosophy (analysis and evaluation of beliefs about the structure, aims, and functions of society and political organization, actual or proposed).

Other general divisions of philosophy in academic departments are area studies (for example, American philosophy and Indian philosophy); special topics or issues (for example, alienation, freedom and determinism, rationalism, and empiricism); and individual philosophers.

Additional branches of philosophy are philosophical anthropology, philosophy of education, philosophy of history, philosophy of law, philosophy of language, philosophy of mathematics, philosophy of the social sciences, philosophy of mind (or philosophical psychology), philosophy of religion, and philosophy of science.

Other disciplines in the sciences, social sciences, and humanities retain the philosopher's interest because of the questions that can be raised about their interrelationships, key concepts, methodological problems, and value or normative assumptions. For example, the philosophy of science raises issues from man's attempt to obtain systematic and reliable knowledge of the natural world. Furthermore, philosophy attempts to define common concepts among the sciences, such as scientific inference, theory, explanation, law, causality, classification, confirmation, proof, induction, probability, measurement, and prediction. In physics, philosophers have written on quantum theory, theories of relativity, and definitional problems of space and time. In biology, special problems are the definition of life and whether mechanical laws adequately explain the activities of organisms.

Unlike the West, philosophy in the Near and Far East has been inseparable from religious metaphysics and cosmology. Religious texts, such as the Upanishads for the Hindu and the Pali Canon for the Buddhist, were the focus of philosophical activity. Discussion of these sacred texts, along with those of the Jainists, however, led to problems in logic, linguistics, perception, and materialism, which have corollaries in Western philosophy. Although religious concerns remain dominant in India, the establishment of British-style universities in the late nineteenth century introduced Western philosophy, especially the British absolute idealism.

The major philosophies or religions of Confucianism, Taoism, and Buddhism have contended with each other throughout Chinese history. At the beginning of the twentieth century, neo-Confucianism was challenged by the ideas of Henri Bergson, Charles Darwin, René Descartes, Friedrich Nietzsche, Immanuel Kant, Karl Marx, and the American pragmatists William James and Charles Sanders Peirce and their followers. Since World War II, most Chinese universities have confined themselves to Marxist interpretations of traditional Chinese philosophy and a study of the works of Mao Tse-tung.

In Japan, T'ang Confucianism became prevalent in the fifth century and Buddhism and Taoism in the tenth century. In the ancient Far East, teaching often took the form of masters expressing themselves aphoristically to their disciples. Master and disciples were often itinerant, but congresses, lectures, and disputations took place at kings' courts and monasteries. Japan was receptive to Anglo and German idealism and to American pragmatism at the end of the nineteenth century, and to existentialism, phenomenology, and Marxism after World War II. Today Japan is influenced by most of the contemporary trends in Western philosophy.

The type of philosophy emphasized in Africa depends upon the language the country adopted during colonization. There are few graduate programs in philosophy, and philosophy in secondary education is within Muslim or Christian education. In Libya, Islamic theological philosophy is stressed, along with Greek and medieval texts; Morocco provides a standard *lycée* training with a required course in philosophy; Somalia emphasizes the Koran, theology, religious history, and ethics; and in the Sudan, Islam and Christianity are taught, but there is no higher education in philosophy.

Philosophy in the non-African Arab states also reflects the area's religion. Most of the philosophy arose out of Islam and its sacred text, the Koran. Ancient Greek and neo-Platonic philosophy influenced Islamic philosophy, which in turn influenced medieval Western philosophy. Jewish philosophers throughout history have also made major contributions to philosophy. Philosophy in Israel today focuses on logic, the philosophy of science, and the religious existentialism of Martin Buber.

Western academic education in philosophy began with the pre-Socratic Pythagoreans in ancient Greece. The Pythagoreans (followers of the Greek mathematician and philosopher Pythagoras, who flourished around 540–510 B.C.) were the first to use the term *philosopher* for one who seeks truth about natural phenomena and their causes through contemplation, as opposed to those who seek fame and fortune. During the fifth century B.C., a group of itinerant teachers of oratory and rhetoric, known as the Sophists, also taught Greek history, law, and elementary logic; the most famous of them, Protagoras, taught some natural science. Instruction took place in small circles or seminars and public lectures. The curriculum was neither systematically developed nor well established. However, "higher education" was in the hands of these Sophists before the advent of Plato's school, the academy.

Plato (c. 427–347 B.C.), inspired by the Socratic search for truth through careful analysis, was, like his mentor, critical of the

Sophists' overemphasis on rhetoric and their abuse of forensic techniques to win arguments by any means. Philosophy aims at direct access to reality and true knowledge, which, for Plato, can only be of realities which are eternal and immutable. The central purpose of the academy, for Plato, was ultimate philosophical truth about the world, and, following Socrates, the method used was question and answer.

Aristotle (384–322 B.C.), who had been a pupil at Plato's academy, founded formal logic and developed many of the issues in the philosophy of science. As a naturalist, he systematically investigated biological phenomena, and he also lectured on psychology, ethics, literary criticism, physics, and metaphysics. Aristotle's classification of the sciences was an important influence on future curricula in higher education. He divided knowledge into theoretical, practical, and productive. The theoretical sciences embrace metaphysics (or first philosophy), mathematics, physics, and the philosophy of nature (encompassing biology and psychology); the practical sciences include ethics and politics; and the productive sciences (poetics) comprise the fine and useful arts. Logic was considered preparatory to any search for knowledge and hence was not, strictly speaking, a part of the sciences.

During the Hellenistic-Roman period, Stoicism (founded by the Greek philosopher Zeno in the early third century B.C.) and Epicureanism (founded by the Greek Epicurus [c. 342–270 B.C.]) emphasized moral wisdom as the central concern of the philosopher, who took on the popular meaning of moral guide or teacher of the art of life, especially of imperturbability in the face of life's adversities.

With the introduction of Greek culture into Roman civilization, philosophy became a part of its educational system, and instruction was carried out mainly by parents or tutors. In the Greco-Roman world, the chief purposes of education were the socialization of the individual and preparation for practical affairs through economics and military and political training.

An important event in the history of philosophy occurred in the third century B.C., in the library and museum at Alexandria, where the religious philosophies of the East and the speculative philosophies of classical Greece were merged and argued. In Syria, the study of philosophy was carried over into Arabic and Saracen cultures.

The development of philosophy was not continuous, however. Philosophy and culture were generally eclipsed in the early Middle Ages in the West, although some logic was taught in the monastic schools. The Arabs and Jews of Spain made major contributions to philosophy in Moorish centers of learning, through Arabic translations of Aristotle. These translations, along with Arabic commentaries, reached the West around the end of the twelfth century and were translated into Latin.

Aristotle's influence on philosophy continued. For example, in the thirteenth century science and natural philosophy followed his treatises on nature. The University of Paris was a major center of theology and philosophy, and the problem in the great medieval universities was how to cope in a Christian way with the pagan Greek and Arabic learning being introduced into the West. St. Thomas Aquinas (c. 1225–1274) solved this problem by synthesizing these pagan sources with Christian theology. In general, philosophy was used for Christian apologetics and the elucidation of Christian doctrine. In the medieval university philosophy extended over practically the whole field of liberal studies: the arts, sciences, and letters.

During the Renaissance interest revived in mathematics, Plato, Aristotle, Stoicism, Epicureanism, and some of the schools of the ancient Greek Skeptics, previously relatively unknown to the Western world. Italy was the focus of this renewed interest in classical philosophy and a major contributor to the beginnings of natural science. Although many of the innovative scholars and philosophers of the sixteenth and seventeenth centuries received university training, there was often tension between the new learning and the ecclesiastical doctrines and methods prevalent at the universities; Galileo (1564–1642), who held a chair at the University of Padua, is a famous example. Consequently, many philosophers worked outside the university, and later thinkers found support in the scientific academies of the seventeenth and eighteenth centuries.

Another important influence upon philosophy was the rise of modern science. The implications of the new view of nature and the reconciliation of these views with the traditional religious world view occupied most of the seventeenth-century philosophers; for example, René Descartes (1596–1650). The hold of ecclesiastical authority on higher education was weakened by the French revolution, and French philosophy began to be centered in the universities. Gradually the universities, which were still largely under ecclesiastical control, included the new philosophy of nature. Around 1659, Cambridge opened itself to the study of the new mathematical physics of Galileo and Descartes. What used to be called "natural philosophy," which often meant Aristotle's treatises on motion, gradually came to refer to the works of Galileo and Isaac Newton (1642–1727). "Moral philosophy" or "moral science," by contrast, encompassed all else except logic: ethics, politics, psychology.

With the eighteenth-century "Age of Reason," critical reason further weakened the prevalent religious cultural outlook. Philosophy was profoundly altered by Newton and others, who showed that the universe could be explained by the new mechanics. Through the influence of the German philosopher Immanuel Kant (1724–1804), Newton was introduced into the German universities. In France in the nineteenth century, Auguste Comte (1798–1857) applied the scientific method to problems in the social sciences, and Emile Durkheim (1858–1917) based his study of society and ethics on close observation of social behavior. In addition, through the idealism of Georg Wilhelm Friedrich Hegel (1770–1831), the dialectical materialism of Karl Marx (1818–1883), and the evolu-

tionary naturalism of Herbert Spencer (1820–1903), speculative metaphysics was renewed. German philosophy, especially the systems of Kant and Hegel, began to dominate academic philosophy throughout the Western world in the last quarter of the nineteenth century, although British thinkers (such as John Locke, George Berkeley, and David Hume) have been a major influence in the United States since the eighteenth century.

Philosophy in the twentieth century is marked by a plurality of schools and movements: existentialism; phenomenology; logical positivism; ordinary-language philosophy; pragmatism; process philosophy; philosophies which have their major impetus from political ideologies, such as Marxism-Leninism and Maoism; and philosophies which have their major impetus from religious traditions and beliefs, such as Thomism (the system of St. Thomas Aquinas) and the religious philosophies of the Near and Far East. Work is being done in all of the major branches and topics of philosophy, especially esthetics, epistemology, ethics, the history of philosophy, logic, Marxism, metaphysics, oriental philosophy, phenomenology, philosophy of language, philosophy of mind, philosophy of religion, and philosophy of science.

Two concerns of American philosophers are logical positivism and linguistic analysis. Probably the most influential thinker in this area was the Austrian philosopher Ludwig Wittgenstein (1889–1951). Logical positivism, or logical empiricism, dominant in the second quarter of the twentieth century, was partly a reaction to the speculative excesses of nineteenth-century German idealism. The concerns of logical positivism are the analysis of meaning and the function of language and symbols. Other interests of United States philosophers include Thomism and neo-Thomism, Marxist and Soviet thought, and Asian philosophy. Pragmatism, the one philosophy indigenous to the United States, was at its height during the first quarter of the twentieth century. However, despite the interest in analytic philosophy and scholarly activity in logic, the philosophy of science, and linguistics, most of the graduate programs at the larger institutions in the United States do not restrict themselves to any particular trend or movement in contemporary philosophy.

Unlike philosophy in the United States, Canadian universities focus on British analytic philosophy and stress historical, interdisciplinary, and international studies. Notable are the studies in eighteenth-century philosophy at York University in Toronto and the historical studies at McGill University in Montreal, as well as the new master's program in post-Kantian thought, especially German and French phenomenology and existentialism, at Brock University in St. Catharines, Ontario. There are many interdisciplinary studies at the University of Toronto, including an M.A. program in the history and philosophy of science and technology. McGill University is also noted for its international emphasis, and Brock University has an M.A. program in comparative studies of Western and Asian (especially Indian) philosophy.

The general focus of British philosophy in modern times has been epistemological. With a few exceptions, its drift has been toward empiricism. There are programs in logic and the philosophy of science at the Universities of London, Bristol, Manchester, and Leeds, and, in Scotland, there are programs at the Universities of Aberdeen, Edinburgh, Glasgow, and St. Andrews.

Descartes' stress upon skepticism, doubt, and methodology is characteristic of French philosophy. But his belief that reason independent of the senses yields knowledge has not been characteristic. Rationalism has had much opposition by French philosophers, who deemphasize deductive reasoning and appeal to faith, intuition, common sense, sentiment, and "nature." These historical factors may partly account for the prevalence in France of phenomenology and existentialism, whose practitioners separate philosophy, its methods and questions, from science and mathematics. Existentialism enjoyed some popularity inside and outside France after World War II, but many French philosophers are equally insistent on the dependence of philosophy on the natural and social sciences.

Using methods opposite those of the French phenomenologists and existentialists, many modern German philosophers have turned their attention to science and its methods. For example, Hans Vaihinger's (1852–1933) early work and the writings of Ernst Cassirer (1874–1945) in the epistomology of science have attracted attention. In addition, although German philosophy is diverse, it continues the line of idealism. An interest in Hegel is being revived by those holding positions as diverse as existentialism, phenomenology, and Thomism. Hegel's work generated the young (or left) Hegelians, who accepted his dialectical methods but rejected his absolute idealism and his view of philosophy. Karl Marx was the foremost left Hegelian; and Marxism-Leninism, as the official orthodoxy of communism, remains the dominant movement in the German Democratic Republic in the late 1970s.

Although contemporary German philosophy reflects an interest in science, one of the two major philosophical influences in German universities in the first half of this century was phenomenology. The other was the existential ontology of Martin Heidegger (1889–1976) and Karl Jaspers (1883–1969). In Germany, existential Protestant theologians and existential psychoanalysts have been directly influenced by Heidegger.

In Italy in the early twentieth century, various systems of philosophy prevailed: Comtean positivism; Kantianism; Hegelian idealism; and an interest in mathematical logic and the philosophy of science, influenced by British empiricists and United States pragmatists. However, the dominant philosophy was Benedetto Croce's (1866–1952) neo-Hegelianism and his interest in esthetics and the philosophy of history. After World War II, existentialism gained popularity, and recently an interest in the philosophy of language has drawn many Italian philosophers toward logical positivism and linguistic analysis.

As one might expect, philosophy and ideology have been closely connected in the Soviet Union, which has been mainly concerned with social philosophy, ethics, and the philosophy of history and culture. However, the major thinkers of the eighteenth and nineteenth centuries mainly worked in "circles" outside the framework of universities. The writings of Tolstoy and Dostoyevsky were literary rather than argumentative, but they raised social and political issues. Since the eighteenth century, Russian intellectual life has been influenced by most of the philosophical trends in Europe. The popularity of Hegel paved the way for the influence of Karl Marx in the early 1890s. Since the Revolution, Marxism-Leninism has been the ideology of the Communist Party. As early as 1921 there were efforts to remove non-Marxist professors, and much of the philosophy in Soviet Russia has been energetic commentary on Marxist-Leninist orthodoxy.

After the Stalinist era, the Soviet Union opened its doors to outside influences; and, since detente, this has increased, mainly in nonpolitical philosophy: philosophical logic, information theory, cybernetics, and the philosophy of science. There is also a renewed interest in idealism, existentialism, empiricism, and the history of philosophy.

In Bulgaria, dialectical materialism is the official philosophy, and neo-Marxist ideas have been suppressed. Similarly, Marxism-Leninism is the official philosophy in Czechoslovakia. In Poland Marxism-Leninism has been somewhat transformed by Gyogy Tamas, who has done work on comparisons of formal logic and Marx's dialectical logic, and by the revisionists Adam Schaff and Leszek Kolakowski. After the break with Stalin in 1949, Yugoslavia continued its diverse philosophical movements. Especially strong are positivism; existentialism; orthodox Marxism; and nonorthodox Marxism, which stresses the independence of philosophy from ideology and points to the humanistic background of Marxist philosophy.

Despite regional differences in philosophy, there have been efforts toward international cooperation. The International Institute of Philosophy, founded in 1937, has organized many congresses and cooperative efforts among philosophers throughout the world. Since 1948 the International Federation of Philosophical Societies (*Fédération internationale des sociétés de philosophie*) has promoted cooperation among national and international organizations.

There is also an increasing interest in interdisciplinary work. For example, the philosophy of language may touch upon linguistics and anthropology; and the philosophy of mind may involve cybernetics, the use of computers, and mathematics. Interest is high in the biomedical sciences, not only because of the theoretical and logical interest they present but also because of the moral issues mankind is confronting in biomedical technology. Existential psychoanalysis indicates new approaches to psychoanalytic theory related to man's being in the world. Modern philosophy is interested in applying philosophical skills to everyday human problems (for example, medical ethics) and also in the theory of action, applied logic (including deontic logic, decision theory, and the theory of political decisions), and the relation of philosophical analysis to human justice and welfare.

Another trend is the increasing interest in the teaching of philosophy. Many graduate programs offer a teaching internship that provides certification for junior college teachers of philosophy. Other graduate programs offering an M.A. degree are designed to prepare teachers of community colleges, as well as providing a basis for doctoral study. Philosophy is also being introduced at earlier educational levels—

for example, at the precollege level—in many lyceums in Europe and in many independent preparatory schools and church-affiliated high schools.

WALTER FOGG

Levels and Programs of Study

Programs in philosophy generally require as a minimum educational prerequisite a secondary education and lead to the following degrees: bachelor's (B.A.), master's (M.A.), the doctorate (Ph.D.), or their equivalents. Programs deal with the nature of reality, human consciousness, human values, and esthetics and consist of classroom sessions, group discussions, and research.

Programs that lead to a first university degree deal with such subjects as introduction to philosophical thinking, classical and modern logic, history of philosophy, one or more types of classical philosophy, ethics and morals, epistemology, and esthetics. Optional courses include the philosophy of science, religion, and language. Frequently there is concentration on a particular school, such as Marxism, existentialism, scientific humanism, or empiricism. Programs are often combined with programs in history, political science, or classical language. Background courses usually include history, fine and applied arts, religion and theology, social sciences, and foreign languages.

Programs that lead to a postgraduate university degree usually emphasize research work as substantiated by the presentation and defense of a scholarly thesis or dissertation. Principal course content and areas within which research projects tend to fall are epistemology, logic, semantics, esthetics, moral philosophy, the works of a particular philosopher or school of philosophy, history of philosophy at a particular period, a comparative study of Western and Eastern philosophy, or philosophy of science or mathematics.

[This section was based on UNESCO's *International Standard Classification of Education (ISCED)* (Paris: UNESCO, 1976).]

Major International and National Organizations

INTERNATIONAL

Comité international des professeurs de philosophie dans l'enseignement du second degré
Gerhart Hauptmann Strasse
44 Munich, Federal Republic of Germany

International Association for Philosophy of Law and Social Philosophy
Casella postale 157
10100 Turin, Italy

International Committee for Aesthetics
Instituut voor esthetica
Nieuwe Achtergracht 170 IV
Amsterdam, Netherlands

International Council for Philosophy and Humanistic Studies (ICPHS)
UNESCO
1 rue Miollis
75732 Paris, France

International Council of Scientific Unions (ICSU)
51 boulevard de Montmorency
75016 Paris, France

Internationale Hegel Gesellschaft
Richard Strele Strasse 16
A-5020 Salzburg, Austria

International Federation of Philosophical Societies (IFPS)
Fédération internationale des sociétés de philosophie (FISP)
123 Institut des sciences exactes
Sidlerstrasse 5
3012 Bern, Switzerland
There are 33 national societies and 11 international societies and institutes affiliated with IFPS.

International Institute of Philosophy (IIP)
Institut international de philosophie
173 boulevard Saint-Germain
75272 Paris, France

International Phenomenological Society
State University of New York at Buffalo
Buffalo, New York 14226 USA

International Society for the History of Ideas
Findley Center, City College
New York, New York 10031 USA

International Society of Logic and the Philosophy of Science
% F. Gonseth, Goldaurstrasse 60
Zurich, Switzerland

International Union of the History and
Philosophy of Science (IUHPS)
12 rue Colbert
Paris II, France

Société internationale pour l'étude de la
philosophie médiévale (SIEPM)/
International Society for the Study of Medieval
Philosophy (ISSMP)
Kardinaal Mercierplein 2
3000 Louvain, Belgium

World Union of Catholic Societies of
Philosophy
Aigner Strasse 25
A-5026 Salzburg, Austria

NATIONAL

For information on the numerous national
philosophical organizations throughout the
world see:

Cormier, R., and others. (Eds.) *International
Directory of Philosophy and Philosophers 1974–
1975.* Bowling Green, Ohio: Bowling Green
State University, Philosophy Documentation
Center, 1974.
Minerva, Wissenschaftliche Gesellschaften. Berlin,
Federal Republic of Germany: de Gruyter,
1972.
The World of Learning. London: Europa, 1947–
Published annually.

Principal Information Sources

GENERAL

Guides to the literature in the field include:

Bochenski, I. M. (Ed.) *Guide to Marxist Phi-
losophy: An Introductory Bibliography.* Chicago:
Swallow Press, 1972.
Borchardt, D. H. *How to Find Out in Philosophy
and Psychology.* Elmsford, New York: Per-
gamon Press, 1967. Updated by "Recent
International Documentation in Philosophy:
A Survey of Select Reference Works," *Inter-
national Library Review,* 1972, *4,* 199–212.
Chan, Wing-Tsit. *An Outline and an Annotated
Bibliography of Chinese Philosophy.* New Ha-
ven, Connecticut: Yale University Press,
1969.
De George, R. T. *A Guide to Philosophical Bib-
liography and Research.* New York: Appleton-
Century-Crofts, 1971.
deRaeymaeker, L. *Introduction à la philosophie.*
Louvain, Belgium: Publications universi-
taires de Louvain, 1964.
Klibensky, R. (Ed.) *Contemporary Philosophy: A
Survey.* Montreal, Quebec: Mario Casalini,
1968–1971. Includes discussions of phi-
losophy in Eastern Europe, Asia, and Latin
America.

Lachs, J. *Marxist Philosophy: A Bibliographical
Guide.* Chapel Hill: University of North
Carolina Press, 1967.
Plott, J. C., and Mays, P. D. *Sarva-Darsana-
Sangraha: A Bibliographical Guide to the Global
History of Philosophy.* Leiden, Netherlands:
E. J. Brill, 1969. Attempts global coverage
in the bibliographies.
Potter, K. H. *Bibliography of Indian Philosophies.*
Delhi: Motial Banarsidass for the American
Institute of Indian Studies, 1970.
Rogers, A. R. *The Humanities: A Selective Guide
to Information Sources.* Littleton, Colorado:
Libraries Unlimited, 1974. See pages 34–73.
Varet, G. *Manuel de bibliographie philosophique.*
Paris: Presses universitaires de France, 1956.

Among the many introductions to the field
are:

Carritt, E. F. *The Theory of Beauty.* New York:
Barnes & Noble, 1962.
Croce, B. *Aesthetic as Science of Expression and
General Linguistic.* (2nd ed.) New York:
Macmillan, 1922. A classic.
Magill, F. N. *Masterpieces of World Philosophy in
Summary Form.* New York: Harper & Row,
1961. Summarizes two hundred major works
from ancient times to the middle of the
twentieth century.

Histories of philosophy are offered by:

Beck, L. M. A. *The Story of Oriental Philosophy.*
New York: Holt, Rinehart and Winston,
1928.
Bréhier, E. *Histoire de la philosophie.* Paris:
Presses universitaires de France, 1926–1932.
(Translation: *The History of Philosophy.* Chi-
cago: University of Chicago Press, 1963–
1969.)
Brinton, C. C. *Ideas and Man: The Story of Western
Thought.* (2nd ed.) Englewood Cliffs, New
Jersey: Prentice-Hall, 1963.
Copleston, F. C. *A History of Philosophy.* West-
minster, Maryland: Newman Press, 1946–
1966.
Russell, B. *A History of Western Philosophy.* New
York: Simon & Schuster, 1945.
Ueberweg, F. *Grundriss der Geschichte der Phi-
losophie.* Herford, Federal Republic of Ger-
many: E. S. Mittler, 1923–1928.

Sources dealing with philosophy education
are:

*La enseñanza de la filosofia en la universidad his-
panoamericana.* Washington, D.C.: Pan
American Union, 1965. A survey of the
teaching of philosophy at Latin American
universities.
O ensino da filosofia nas universidades brasileiras.
Washington, D.C.: Pan American Union,

1968. Discussion of the teaching of philosophy at Brazilian universities.

The Teaching of Philosophy: An International Enquiry of UNESCO. Paris: UNESCO, 1953. Contains individual essays on the teaching of philosophy in the following countries: Cuba, Egypt, France, Germany, India, Italy, the United Kingdom, and the United States.

The Teaching of Philosophy in Universities of the United States. Washington, D.C.: Pan American Union, 1965.

CURRENT BIBLIOGRAPHIES

Bibliographie de la philosophie/Bibliography of Philosophy. Paris: Vrin, 1937–.

Bibliographie Philosophie mit Autoren und Sachregister. Berlin, German Democratic Republic: Zentralstelle für die philosophische Information and Dokumentation, 1967–. Covers Marxist philosophy.

Bulletin signalétique. Section 519: *Science humaines: Philosophie.* Paris: Centre national de la recherche scientifique, 1947–.

Philosopher's Index: International Index to Philosophical Periodicals. Bowling Green, Ohio: Bowling Green State University, Philosophy Documentation Center, 1967–.

Répertoire bibliographique de la philosophie. Louvain, Belgium: Editions de l'Institut supérieur de philosophie, 1949–. Comprehensive coverage of books and articles in Dutch, English, French, German, Italian, Portuguese, and Spanish.

PERIODICALS

Lists of philosophy journals may be found in the following:

Dennison, A. T. "Philosophy Periodicals: An Annotated Select World List of Current Serial Publications." *International Library Review,* 1970, *2,* 355–386.

Hogrebe, W., Kamp, R., and König, G. *Periodica Philosophica: Eine internationale Bibliographie philosophischer Zeitschriften von den Anfängen bis zur Gegenwart.* Düsseldorf, Federal Republic of Germany: Philosophia Verlag, 1972.

Ulrich's International Periodicals Directory. New York: Bowker, biennial.

World List of Specialized Periodicals in Philosophy. The Hague: Mouton, 1967.

Some important philosophical journals are *American Philosophical Quarterly, Analysis* (UK), *Archiv für Geschichte der Philosophie* (FRG), *Das Argument* (FRG), *Australian Journal of Philosophy, Bulletin de la Société française de philosophie, British Journal for the Philosophy of Science, British Journal of Aesthetics, Deutsche Zeitschrift für Philosophie* (GDR), *Dialogue: Canadian Philosophical Review (Revue canadienne de philosophie), Diogenes: An International Review of Philosophy and Humanistic Studies* (Italy), *Ethics: An International Journal of Social, Political and Legal Philosophy* (US), *Inquiry* (Norway), *IPA: International Philosophical Quarterly* (US), *Journal of the History of Philosophy* (US), *Journal of Symbolic Logic* (US), *Man and World* (Netherlands), *Mind: A Quarterly Review of Psychology and Philosophy* (UK), *The Monist* (US), *The Personalist* (US), *Philosophia: Philosophical Quarterly of Israel, Philosophical Books* (UK), *Philosophical Quarterly* (UK), *Philosophical Review* (US), *Philosophical Studies* (US), *Philosophy East and West* (US), *Phronesis: A Journal for Ancient Philosophy* (Netherlands), *Ratio* (UK), *Revue internationale de philosophie* (Belgium), *Second Order: An African Journal of Philosophy* (Nigeria), *Soviet Studies in Philosophy* (US), *Studies in Soviet Thought* (Netherlands), *Synthèse* (Netherlands), *Theoria: A Swedish Journal of Philosophy.*

ENCYCLOPEDIAS, DICTIONARIES, HANDBOOKS

Baldwin, J. M. *Dictionary of Philosophy and Psychology.* New York: Macmillan, 1901–1905. (Reprinted, New York: Peter Smith, 1960.) A classic in the field.

Ballestrem, K. G. *Russian Philosophical Terminology.* Dordrecht, Netherlands: D. Reidel, 1964. Provides English, French, and German equivalents for Russian terms.

Edwards, P. (Ed.) *The Encyclopedia of Philosophy.* New York: Macmillan, 1967.

Enciclopedia filosofica. (2nd ed.) Florence, Italy: Sansoni, 1968–1969.

Filosofskaia entsiklopediia. (5 vols.) Moscow: Sovet-skaia entsiklopediia, 1960–1970.

Inoue, T. *Dictionary of English, German, and French Philosophical Terms with Japanese Equivalents.* Tokyo: Maruzen Kabushiki-Kaisha, 1912.

Lalande, A. *Vocabulaire technique et critique de la philosophie.* (10th rev. ed.) Paris: Presses universitaires de France, 1968. Provides German, English, and Italian equivalents.

Ritter, J. (Ed.) *Historisches Wörterbuch der Philosophie.* Basel, Switzerland: Schwabe, 1971–.

Runes, D. D. *Dictionary of Philosophy.* (16th rev. ed.) New York: Philosophical Library, 1969.

DIRECTORIES

Directories which provide information on philosophical study are:

American Universities and Colleges. Washington, D.C.: American Council on Education, 1928–. Published quadrennially.

Bahm, A. (Ed.) *Directory of American Philosophers.* Bowling Green, Ohio: Bowling Green State University, Philosophy Documentation Center, biennial. Provides information on philosophical activities in the United States and Canada, including lists of philosophers, colleges and universities, periodicals, publishers, organizations, and assistantships and fellowships in philosophy.

Commonwealth Universities Yearbook. London: Association of Commonwealth Universities, 1914–. Published annually.

Cormier, R., and others. (Eds.) *International Directory of Philosophy and Philosophers 1974–1975.* Bowling Green, Ohio: Bowling Green State University, Philosophy Documentation Center, 1974. Provides lists of universities, institutes and research centers, organizations, periodicals, and publishers of philosophical books. The 1965 edition of this directory (New York: Humanities Press) contains brief essays on the philosophical activities of specific countries throughout the world, with particular attention paid to the teaching of philosophy.

International Handbook of Universities. Paris: International Association of Universities, 1950–. Published triennially.

The World of Learning. London: Europa, 1947–. Published annually. Lists colleges and universities, research institutes, and learned societies throughout the world.

RESEARCH CENTERS, INSTITUTES, INFORMATION CENTERS

A few of the important information centers for philosophy are:

Centre national de la recherche scientifique
Centre de documentation, Sciences humaines
54 boulevard Raspail
Paris 6, France

Institut international de philosophie
173 boulevard Saint-Germain
75272 Paris, France

Philosophy Documentation Center
Bowling Green State University
Bowling Green, Ohio 43403 USA

Philosophy Information Center
Philosophy Institute
University of Düsseldorf
Düsseldorf, Federal Republic of Germany

Zentralstelle für die philosophische
Information und Dokumentation
Taubenstrasse 19/23
108 Berlin, German Democratic Republic

For additional information and research centers see:

Minerva, Forschungsinstitute. Berlin, Federal Republic of Germany: de Gruyter, 1972.

PHOTOGRAPHY AND CINEMATOGRAPHY
(Field of Study)

Photography and cinematography are intimately related arts/crafts. Both were nineteenth-century inventions, and both depend on the same basic photochemical process for recording images, although photography renders its images in "still" form while cinematography captures images "in motion." The two arts share an almost parallel history and development, with photography slightly the senior of the two. Cinematography, however, has been more widely used in education around the world because of its broad appeal and potential for communication and artistic creation.

Photography and cinematography programs share basic courses. For example, courses in history and appreciation are generally used as introductions to the disciplines and are followed by courses in specific periods or forms as well as studies of individual artists or creators. Production courses for photography and cinematography, which are thought to be more advanced than the broad overviews, cover basic technical procedures, darkroom methods, camera technique, lighting, and composition. Cinematography also requires additional training in editing and in sound and camera movement.

The teaching of photography began in 1839, with the publication of an instructional booklet by a French painter, Louis Daguerre. Daguerre and an associate, Joseph N. Niepce, pioneered the photographic technique. In the United States the first formal instruction began the same year, with a course offered by D. W. Seager, who used the daguerreotype process, at the Stuyvesant Institute of New York City. By the 1850s photography schools had been established in Germany, France, and England. The University of London introduced the subject into its curriculum in 1856. Early education in photography emphasized the technical and vocational aspects of the medium; indeed the photograph was more science and invention than art until the turn of the century.

During the first years of the twentieth century, higher education in photography began to underscore and explore some of the artistic aspects and potentials of the medium. Clarence H. White developed a photography program at Teachers College, Columbia University, in New York City, which offered students an esthetic approach to the study and practice of photography. Clarence White, Jr., later followed his father's inclination and developed a broadly conceived and imaginative photography curriculum at Ohio State University; that curriculum still stands as a model for teaching and study of the photographic technique and its allied crafts and arts.

Cinematography education has had a similar history and course of development. As early as 1903, cinematography was offered in colleges and universities in the eastern United States while the major European nations and the Soviet Union began to develop film schools that have eventually become prestigious and powerful. In the United States cinematography education developed rapidly on the West Coast, near the center of the film industry, at the University of Southern California and the University of California at Los Angeles. Other programs in cinema technique quickly grew in the major urban centers of the East Coast and again at Ohio State University. In other countries the teaching of cinematography developed within a conservatory atmosphere, where masters banded together with apprentices to practice their skills.

In the mid 1970s photography and cinematography are taught as fine arts, communication media, and vocational skills. Students may pursue academic degrees at all levels and in all varieties, from diploma courses to doctoral study. In all countries and in most programs of study, however, there remains a fundamental split between the creative elements of the media and their technical-vocational aspects, although in the future this split will probably close. In countries such as the United Kingdom, the Soviet Union, and India, the major film schools are closely allied with the film industry.

Both photography and cinematography are specialty areas of a number of academic fields. Within the fine and applied arts, photography is taught as an aspect of art and art history, design, and graphics. Photography is also studied as both a vocational process and a documentary technique in the communications field. In the sciences, courses are offered in meteorological photography, astronomical photography, and microscopic photography. Career possibilities range from the most meticulous of scientific-technological photo techniques to commercial journalistic or portrait photography. Cinematography also is studied within a number of academic contexts. Again, art and art history courses are often related to the history and esthetic development of the cinematographic arts. Motion picture production is taught as artistic expression, journalistic recording, and communications technology. Cinematographic technique has also become an intrinsic aspect of the biological sciences in such areas as marine biology and physiological cinematography. There is hardly an academic discipline that has not been touched by the effects and principles of photography and cinematography, and both arts/crafts are being studied and learned in a variety of contexts and disciplines. The trend toward interdisciplinary programs is especially apparent in cinematography. Though both fields are still young in the educational hierarchy, they are growing rapidly and are developing a large body of literature.

The arts of image recording and image making are very important both culturally and educationally, and thus almost every country has a major and central source or institution concerned with the preservation and advancement of the photographic and cinematographic arts. Higher education is on the verge of embracing the vast potential of these two transcultural media.

SAM L. GROGG, JR.

Levels and Programs of Study

Programs in cinematography and photography usually require as a minimum prerequisite a secondary education and/or demonstrated skill or talent in the chosen field and lead to the following awards: certificate or diploma, bachelor's degree, master's degree, the doctorate, or their equivalents. Programs are designed to develop skill in photography or cinematography for professional, cultural, or recreational purposes and consist of lectures, group discussions, and studio practice sessions. Students normally devote themselves to one aspect of photography or cinematography.

The chief aim of most programs is the development of creativity and skill in the chosen field of study, but related courses such as art history, animation, design, visual fundamentals, color, and the camera may be included. Programs in cinematography usually include study of the various forms of film (documentary, avant-garde, comedy, animation) and the styles of various directors. Course content may include the following: film direction, editing, production, screen writing, animation, graphics, film history, and criticism. In addition, most programs generally include liberal arts courses such as literature, history, philosophy, languages, or social sciences.

On the advanced levels, students acquire comprehensive knowledge of some specialty within the broad area of cinematography. Doctoral programs require the preparation and defense of a thesis or dissertation based on original research into a particular problem within the major subject and the achievement of a professional standard in the specialization.

[This section was based on UNESCO's *International Standard Classification of Education (ISCED)*. Paris: UNESCO, 1976.]

Major International and National Organizations

INTERNATIONAL

International Animated Film Association
45 rue Olteni
Bucharest 4, Romania

International Association of Documentary
Film Makers
Groeselenberg 93B
1180 Brussels, Belgium

International Center of Films for Children
and Young People—Cinema and Television
Centre international du film pour l'enfance et
la jeunesse
11 rue Notre-Dame des Champs
75006 Paris, France

International Committee for Diffusion of Arts
and Literature Through the Cinema
Comité international pour la diffusion des
arts et des lettres par le cinéma
9 bis rue Magdebourg
75116 Paris, France

International Committee of Film Education
and Culture
18 rue Marboeuf
Paris 8e, France

International Committee on Ethnographical
and Sociological Films
Musée de l'homme
place du Trocadéro
75016 Paris, France

International Congress of Film and Television
Centre international de liaison des Ecoles de
Cinéma et de Télévision (CILECT)
Rue Thérèsienne 8
1000 Brussels, Belgium

International Council for Educational Films
(Also known as International Committee for
Advancement of Audio-Visual
Media in Education)
Conseil international du film d'enseignement
Institut pédagogique national
29 rue d'Ulm
75005 Paris, France

International Experimental and Art Films
Theatres Confederation
Bureau 22
92 Champs-Elysées
75008 Paris, France

International Federation of Film Producers'
Associations
Fédération internationale des associations de
producteurs de films
33 Champs-Elysées
75008 Paris, France

International Federation of Film Societies
42 rue de Cardinal Lemoine
75005 Paris, France

International Federation of Photographic Art
Spiserwis 9
CH-9030 Abtwil–St. Gall, Switzerland

International Film and Television Council
via Santa Susanna 17
00187 Rome, Italy

International Scientific Film Association
38 avenue des Tornea
Paris, France

International Union of Amateur Cinema
Union internationale du cinéma d'amateurs
Rubenslei 1
Antwerp, Belgium

International Union of Cinematographic
Exhibitions
92 Champs-Elysées
75008 Paris, France

International Union of Technical
Cinematographic Associations
92 Champs-Elysées
75008 Paris, France

NATIONAL

Austria:
Österreichische Gesellschaft für
Filmwissenschaft
Rauhensteingasse 5
1010 Vienna

Belgium:
Fédération nationale de la photographie
professionnelle
19 rue de l'Aurore
1050 Brussels

Canada:
Canadian Film Institute
1762 Carling Avenue
Ottawa, Ontario

Federal Republic of Germany:
Deutsche Gesellschaft für Film- und
Fernsehforschung
Findelgasse 7
Nuremberg

Finland:
Central Association of Finnish
Photographic Organizations
Korkeavuorenkatu 2 B F72
SF 00140 Helsinki 14

France:
Confédération française de la
photographie
8 rue Montyon
75 Paris 9

Fédération nationale des industries
techniques du film, cinéma et
télévision
92 Champs-Elysées
75 Paris

Hungary:
Magyar fotomuveszek szovetsége
Bathoryh 10
Budapest

Italy:
Associazione nazionale industrie
cinematografie ed affini
viale Regina Magherita 286
00198 Rome

Japan:
Society of Photographic Science and
Technology of Japan
Honcho 2-9-5
Nakano-ku, Tokyo

Netherlands:
Stichting Nederlands filminstituut
Nieuwezijds, Voorburgwal 345
Amsterdam

Poland:
Zwiazik polskich artyston fotografikow
Sniadeckich 10
Warsaw

Sweden:
Svenska film institutet
POB 27126
S-10252 Stockholm

United Kingdom:
British Film Institute (BFI)
81 Dean Street
London W1, England

Photographic Society of Great Britain
14 South Street
London W1Y 5DP, England

Society for Education in Film and
Television
63 Old Compton Street
London W1V 5PN, England

United States:

American Film Institute
Kennedy Center for the Performing Arts
Washington, D.C. 20566

Educational Film Library Association, Inc.
17 West 60th Street
New York, New York 10023

Photographic Society of America
2005 Walnut Street
Philadelphia, Pennsylvania 19103

For additional national and international organizations in photography and cinematography see:

Directory of European Associations. Detroit: Gale Research, 1971.
The World of Learning. London: Europa, 1947–. Published annually.

An international listing of national organizations in photography may be obtained from the International Federation of Photographic Art.

Principal Information Sources

GENERAL

Guides to the literature in the field include:

Boni, A. *Photographic Literature, An International Bibliographic Guide to General and Specialized Literature on Photographic Processes, Techniques, Theory; Chemistry; Physics; Apparatus; Materials and Applications; Industry History; Biography; Aesthetics.* Dobbs Ferry, New York: Morgan and Morgan, 1962.

Boni, A. *Photographic Literature 1960–1972.* 1st supplement. Dobbs Ferry, New York: Morgan and Morgan, 1972. A subject listing of books, pamphlets, and periodicals relating to photography in English, German, and French.

Bukalski, P. J. (Comp.) *Film Research: A Critical Bibliography with Annotations and Essay.* Boston: Hall, 1972. A partially annotated, classified bibliography of books relating to film; contains an introductory essay.

Gerlach, J. C., and Gerlach, L. *The Critical Index: A Bibliography of Articles on Film in English, 1946–1973, Arranged by Names and Topics.* New York and London: Teachers College Press, Columbia University, 1974. Contains bibliographies of books, reviews, archives, periodicals, and articles about film, some annotated briefly. An excellent source for articles concerning film activities in each country of the world.

Gottesman, R., and Geduld, H. M. *Guidebook to Film: An Eleven-in-One Reference.* New York: Holt, Rinehart and Winston, 1972. Contains lists of books and periodicals, theses and dissertations, museums and archives, film schools (United States and abroad), equipment and supplies distributors, publishers, and organizations.

Limbacher, J. L. *A Reference Guide to Audiovisual Information.* New York: Bowker, 1972. An annotated bibliography of reference books and periodicals. Contains a glossary.

Writers' Program, New York. *The Film Index, A Bibliography.* Vol. 1: *The Film as Art.* New York: Museum of Modern Art Film Library and H. W. Wilson, 1941. Reprinted New York: Arno Press, 1966. Classified, annotated bibliography which includes history, technique, and types of film. Index contains authors, titles (of books and films), and persons connected with production.

Useful introductory and historical works in the field include:

Arnheim, R. *Film as Art.* Berkeley: University of California Press, 1957. An important work.

Bardeche, M., and Brasillach, R. *The History of Motion Pictures.* (Edited and translated by I. Barry.) New York: Arno Press, 1970. Covers period from 1895 to 1935.

Braive, M. F. *The Era of the Photograph: A Social History.* (Translated by D. Britt.) New York: McGraw, 1966.

Clerc, L. P. *Photography, Theory and Practice.* (3rd ed.) London: Focal Press, 1954.

Eisenstein, S. M. *Film Form, and Film Sense.* (Edited and translated by Jay Leyda.) New York: Meridian Books, 1957.

Gassan, A. *A Chronology of Photography: A Critical Survey of the History of Photography as a Medium of Art.* Rochester, New York: Handbook Company, 1972.

Gernsheim, H., and Gernsheim, A. *The History of Photography from the Earliest Use of the Camera Obscura in the Eleventh Century up to 1941.* New York: Oxford University Press, 1955.

Jacobs, L. *The Rise of the American Film: A Critical History.* New York: Teachers College Press, Columbia University, 1968.

Jacobs, L. (Ed.). *The Emergence of the Film Art.* New York: Hopkinson and Blake, 1969.

Jacobs, L. *The Documentary Tradition: From Nanook to Woodstock.* New York: Hopkinson and Blake, 1972.

Knight, A. *The Liveliest Art.* New York: New American Library, 1959.

Madsen, R. *The Impact of Film.* New York: Macmillan, 1973.

Newhall, B. *The History of Photography from 1839 to the Present Day.* New York: Museum of Modern Art, 1964.

Ramsaye, T. *A Million and One Nights.* New York: Simon & Schuster, 1964. Covers period to 1925.

For a listing of national histories consult:

Gottesman, R., and Geduld, H. M. *Guidebook to Film: An Eleven-in-One Reference.* New York: Holt, Rinehart and Winston, 1972. Pp. 14–18.

Books and journal articles dealing with education and careers in the field are:

Bolen, F. "Les écoles du cinéma en Belgique." *Cinéma,* March 1973, *174,* 26é29.

Bukalski, P. J. (Comp.) *Film Research: A Critical Bibliography with Annotations and Essay.* Boston: Hall, 1972. Consult "Careers in Film," pp. 193–194.

"Film Study Abroad: The London School of Film Technique." *Cineaste,* Summer 1969, *3*(1), 4–, 31.

Horell, C. W. *A Survey of Motion Picture, Still Photography, and Graphic Arts Instruction.* Rochester, New York: Eastman Kodak, 1974. Canvasses higher education in the United States and Canada for developments in photographic and cinematographic instruction.

Horwitz, M. "Petite Géographie de l'enseignement du cinéma dans les universités parisiennes." *Cinéma,* January 1973, *172,* 14–17. A survey of film courses given in Paris universities.

International Index to Film Periodicals. New York: Bowker, 1972–. Subject section "Film Education" lists articles with full citation by country and includes brief annotations.

Katayeve, Y. "Soviet School of Cinematography." *Filmmakers Newsletter,* December 1971, *8* (2), 42–44.

Maben, A., and Jacobson, G. "The Centro Sperimentale di Cinematografia." *Cineaste,* Summer 1969, *3*(1), 8–10. On the Italian film school.

Neblette, C. B. *Careers in Photography.* Rochester, New York: Rochester Institute of Technology, 1965.

Toeplitz, J. "Film Scholarship: Present and Prospective." *Film Quarterly,* Spring 1963, *16* (3), 27–36. Observations of the director of the Polish State Film School.

CURRENT BIBLIOGRAPHIES

Abstracts of Photographic Science and Engineering Literature. Boston: Society of Photographic Scientists and Engineers, 1962–. Monthly.

Artbibliographies Modern. Santa Barbara, California: ABC-Clio, 1970–. Published quarterly.

Art Index. New York: Wilson, 1933–.

Current Video Abstracts. Amsterdam: Douglas Bulls, 1973–. Published quarterly.

Film Literature Index: A Quarterly Author-Subject Periodical Index to the International Literature of Film. Detroit: Information Coordinators, 1973–. International coverage.

Film Review Index. Pasadena, California: Audio-Visual Associates, 1970–.

International Index to Multi-Media Information. Pasadena, California: Audio-Visual Associates, 1970–. Published quarterly.

Nye boeger om film/New Books on Film. Copenhagen: Dansk filmmuseum, 1967–. Published semiannually.

Photographic Abstracts. London: Science and Technical Group of the Royal Photographic Society of Great Britain, 1921–.

PERIODICALS

The following are representatives of the many journals in the field: *Afterimage* (US), *Amaetur Photographer* (UK), *American Cinematographer, American Film: Journal of the Film and Television Arts, Aperture* (US), *Art fotographique* (France), *Audio-Visual Communications* (US), *Avant-scène 'cinéma* (France), *Bianco e nero* (Italy), *British Journal of Photography, Bulgarsko foto* (Bulgaria), *Cahiers du cinéma* (France), *Camera* (Switzerland), Camera palet (Netherlands), *Cineaste* (US), *Cineforum* (Italy), *Film Comment* (US), *Film Literature Quarterly* (US), *Film Quarterly* (US), *Film World* (India), *Films and Filming* (UK), *Industrial and Commercial Photographer* (UK), *International Photographer* (US), *Landers Film Reviews* (US), *Modern Photography* (US), *Premier plan* (France), *Officiel de la photographie et du cinéma* (France), *Photo-Ciné-Review* (France), *Rangefinder* (US), *Research Film/Film de recherche/Forschungsfilm* (FRG), *Screen* (India), *Screen* (UK), *Sight and Sound* (UK), *SMPTE Journal* (US), *Soviet Film/Sovetski film, Technicien du film* (France), *Zhurnal nauchnoĭ i prikladnoi fotografii i kinematographii* (USSR).

For more comprehensive listing of journals consult:

Film Literature Index. Albany, New York: Filmdex, 1973–. Published quarterly.

International Index of Film Periodicals. New York: Bowker, 1972–. Published irregularly.

Photographic Abstracts. London: Royal Society, 1921–. Published monthly.

Répertoire mondial des périodiques cinématographiques/World List of Film Periodicals and

Serials. (2nd ed.) Brussels: Cinémathèque de Belgique, 1960. An annotated listing of periodicals and serials related to film, arranged by country.

Ulrich's International Periodicals Directory. New York: Bowker, biennial.

ENCYCLOPEDIAS, DICTIONARIES, HANDBOOKS

Boussinot, R. *L'encyclopédie du cinéma.* Paris: Bordas, 1967.

Clason, W. E. (Comp.) *Elsevier's Dictionary of Cinema, Sound and Music in Six Languages: English/American, French, Spanish, Italian, Dutch, German.* Amsterdam: Elsevier, 1956.

Eder, J. M. *Ausführliches Handbuch der Photographie.* (4 vols. in 19 parts.) Halle, german Democratic Republic: Mitteldeutscher Verlag, Halle, 1892–1932. A standard work.

Fenner, F., Jr. *Glossary for Photography Defining over 3000 Words Having a Photographic Significance.* New York: A. S. Barnes, 1939.

Focal Press Encyclopedia of Photography. London: Focal Press; New York; Macmillan, 1956. Combination dictionary/encyclopedia; defines terms and contains articles on photographic history, technology, and photography as art. International orientation, with emphasis on British influences.

Jonas, P. *Manual of Darkroom Procedures and Techniques.* Radnor, Pennsylvania: Chilton, 1971. Processing of film and equipment through advanced techniques.

Malkiewicz, J. K. *Cinematography: A Guide for Film Makers and Film Teachers.* New York: Van Nostrand Reinhold, 1973. A useful handbook; includes glossary and bibliography and discusses practical problems.

Roberts, K. and Sharples, W., Jr. *A Primer for Film-Making: A Complete Guide to 16mm and 35mm Film Production.* Indianapolis, Indiana: Pegasus, 1972. Professional approach to filmmaking; includes discussions on basics of cinematography.

Sadoul, G. *Dictionary of Films.* (Translated by Peter Morris.) Berkeley: University of California Press, 1972.

Santen, J. M. van. *Amalux fototolk: Viertalig, verklarend woordenbook voor fotografie en cinematografie.* Bloemendaal, Netherlands: Focus, 1948. In Dutch, English, French, and German.

Schreyer, R., and others. *Dictionary of Photography and Cinematography.* London: Focal Press, 1961. In English, French, German, and Russian.

Spottiswoode, R. *The Focal Encyclopedia of Film and Cinematography.* New York: Hastings House, 1969. Combination encyclopedia/dictionary; a classic work.

DIRECTORIES

American Art Directory. New York: Bowker, 1974. Lists art schools in United States, Canada, and abroad; contains names, addresses, admission requirements, and major courses of study (photography, movie design, film, television, audiovisual arts, and cinematography).

Gottesman, R. and Geduld, H. M. *Guidebook to Film: An Eleven-in-One Reference.* New York:Holt, Rinehart and Winston, 1972. Includes a list of film schools in United States and abroad.

Guide to College Courses in Film and Television. Washington, D.C.: American Film Institute, biennial. Offers extensive information on United States programs and courses in cinematography and video.

International Film Guide. New York: A. S. Barnes, 1964–. Published annually. A directory of directors, schools, and film festivals.

Rose, E. D. *World Film and Television Study Resources: A Reference Guide to Major Training Centers and Archives.* Bonn, Federal Republic of Germany: Friedrich-Ebert-Stiftung, 1974. Provides basic information on cinematography (and partially on photography) schools in seventy-five countries.

RESEARCH CENTERS, INSTITUTES, INFORMATION CENTERS

The following are important international centers of information and/or research in the field:

International Federation of Film Archives
Fédération internationale des archives du film
74 Galerie Ravenstein
1000 Brusels, Belgium

International Federation of Photographic Art
Spiserwis 9
CH-9030 Abtwil–St. Gall, Switzerland
Acts as an international information exchange on photographic knowledge and developments within the field.

International Liaison Center for Cinema TV
TV Schools
92 Champs-Elysées
75008 Paris, France
Aims to improve knowledge about and standards in the cinema and coordinates actions of higher education in this field.

International Scientific Film Library
Cinémathèque scientifique internationale
31 rue Vautier
B-1040 Brussels, Belgium
Promotes study of the scientific film, preservation of materials of outstanding merit in the scientific and technological area.

The following are among the most important national archives and libraries in the world:

American Film Institute
Kennedy Center for the Performing Arts
Washington, D.C. 20566 USA

Centraine archiwun filmowe
61 Pulawska
Warsaw, Poland

Ceskoslovensky film vstav-filmoteka
V-jame 1
Prague 1 [Nové Mesto], Czechoslovakia
(Major European film archive and library.)

Cinémathèque Française
82 rue de Courcelles
Paris 8e, France

Gosfilmofund
Slancia Bielye Stolby
Moscow, Soviet Union

Jugoslavenska kinoteka
Knez Mihailora 19/1
Belgrade, Yugoslavia

Museum of Modern Art Film Library
11 West 53rd Street
New York, New York 10019 USA

National Film Archive
81 Dean Street
London W1, England

Staatliches Film Archiv der DDR
Köne Strasse 108
Berlin 8, German Democratic Republic

For a more extensive listings of film archives and libraries throughout the world consult:

Directory of Film Libraries in North America. New York: Film Library Information Council, 1971.
Gottesman, R. and Geduld, H. M. *Guidebook to Film: An Eleven-in-One Reference.* New York: Holt, Rinehart and Winston, 1972.

[Bibliography prepared by Susan Johnson.]

PHYSICAL EDUCATION
(Field of Study)

The term *physical education* generally connotes a broad program which includes skill in, knowledge about, and appreciation of human movement as it contributes to the quality of life. However, to use the term this way, in a historical sense, is misleading, because organized physical education (as opposed to body building, military training, physical activity, physical culture, physical training, gymnastics, hygiene, sports, play, recreation, athletics, sports education, physical fitness, and calisthenics) is a twentieth-century phenomenon. In the 1970s physical education is the art and science of human movement as it relates to the theory and practice of sport, dance, play, games, and exercise. The unity of man, recognized and practiced by the Athenian Greeks, is a basic tenet of the discipline. It is this concept that binds physical education to aspects of such diverse fields as anatomy, physics, physiology, history, sociology, and psychology. The body of knowledge basic and unique to physical education is found in these disciplines and focuses on man's engagement in motor performances. Specialized and systematic study of the related disciplines has led to a body of knowledge inherent in the areas of kinesiology and body mechanics, physiology of exercise, neuromuscular coordination, perceptual-motor development and learning, psychosocial aspects of physical performance, the historic and contemporary role of sport, exercise, and dance in the culture, and the interaction of these areas with human development and functional motor abilities.

Physical education as a discipline has a multitheoretical framework: process, product, and media. The process is human movement; the product is the quality of human movement and well-being; and the media are games, sport, play, exercise, and dance. As the theoretical framework expands, the scholars of the discipline have created subdivisions within the field: exercise physiology, kinesiology and biomechanics, sports medicine, sociology of sport, sports psychology, perceptual-motor development and learning, adaptive and corrective physical education, history and philosophy of physical education, sport, and dance. Scholars are involved in basic and applied research directed at the process, product, and media of physical education. The researchers are increasingly approaching human movement not only from an interdisciplinary framework but also from an international one. Practitioners in the field of physical education are applying the results of research as they practice the art and science of human movement.

Physical education varies among and within countries around the world. Some programs have developed from a philosophical or ideological base and others from a scientific one. Regardless of existing differences in program and philosophy, physical education in institutions of higher learning is directed at the development of health, fitness, lifetime sports, skills, and/or the preparation of teachers of physical education.

In the United States physical education for the general college student is directed at the development of lifetime sports skills and recreational activities. The trend is toward elective physical education and away from required programs. Since physical education is considered a basic subject taught in elementary and secondary schools, the preparation of teachers is the responsibility of four-year colleges and universities. Approximately 700 institutions provide curricula for physical educators. Although there is no standard national curriculum, there is some degree of uniformity and regulation by the National Council for the Accreditation of Teacher Education. Most curricula provide a base in general education, with foundation courses in biological, social, and physical sciences. Applied sciences and specialized courses related to method and significance usually comprise 50 percent of the curriculum. Personal skill and knowledge in a variety of physical skills are also provided. At the present time, an oversupply of physical education teachers has resulted in many young teachers' leaving the profession or going to other countries to teach.

In the United Kingdom university undergraduate physical education consists of sports organized, financed, and coached by the students themselves. There is a trend toward organized physical education programs and instruction in several institutions. Physical education teachers become qualified by completing a three-year specialized course at a college or university. All classroom teachers in England and Wales take a professional course in physical education; thus, many schools attempt to conduct physical education without a full-time specialist. Many physical educators serve as supervisors of and consultants to the classroom instructors who teach public school physical education.

The oldest department of physical education in Latin America was established at the University of Chile (in Santiago) in 1905; a year later the Institute of Physical Education was established in Buenos Aires. The publications and work from these departments have influenced the physical education programs throughout Latin America. Modern programs in physical education have also been introduced in Brazil, Uruguay, and Venezuela, and reform commissions have been active in Peru and Colombia. Reports published by the Pan American Physical Education Congresses indicate the activity in curriculum revision, methods of teaching, and organizational and administrative problems in teacher training programs in Latin America. Some teacher colleges are introducing master's degree programs in physical education, and the ministries of various countries in Latin America have formed a council for the development of sport science.

Diverse systems with national labels characterize physical education in Europe. The Scandinavian and German countries have had teacher training programs for physical education since about 1850, and an increasing number of academic degrees have been awarded since 1925. The programs generally require four years of study, but master's and doctoral degree programs are also available. Research institutions for sports medicine have been developed in Stockholm, Sweden; Leipzig, German Democratic Republic; and Cologne and Freiburg, Federal Republic of Germany. Some European countries have autonomous sports colleges or *Hochschulen* (for example, the *Deutsche Sporthochschule* in Cologne, Federal Republic of Germany), which have standards equivalent to those of a university.

In India physical education is not an academic subject. Poor economic and social conditions are a deterrent to education in general and physical education in particular. A student can acquire certification for teaching physical education by completing a one-year course after high school. To teach at the college level, one must have a bachelor's degree plus one year of study in professional preparation courses, which leads to a diploma in physical education.

Japan is at the other end of the continuum in Asia. Four academic credits in health and physical education are required of every college student prior to graduation. Course work for the general student includes scientific, psychosocial, and philosophical aspects of physical education in addition to sport and dance activities. Approximately forty-seven national universities and several private and public institutions provide curricula in professional preparation. Japan—along with the United States, Sweden, and the Soviet Union—is noted for research in sport and sports medicine.

Nigeria is representative of the emerging African nations, where physical education is almost nonexistent at the secondary and college levels. Although Africa is becoming increasingly sports conscious, as seen by participation in international competitions, only Nigeria, Liberia, Ghana, and Ethiopia have a degree-offering institution of physical education. As in India, physical education in Africa is in the process of fighting for recognition and survival.

University and college physical education in Egypt is an extracurricular activity. Students have opportunities for participation in intramural and intercollegiate sports programs instead of instructional physical education. The need for professionally prepared personnel is supplied by four institutions, which offer a bachelor's degree in health, physical education, and recreation. Egypt is building on a scientific base as it studies and assimilates world developments in physical education.

Physical education, known as physical culture, enjoys an enviable position in the Soviet Union. Considered an important avenue for national security, productivity, and health, it is viewed as important for the entire population as well as for school-age children. Prospective physical educators in the Soviet Union are screened by examination before being admitted to government-subsidized institutions. The three levels of professional preparation correspond to primary, secondary, and college levels. On the highest level are the physical education institutes of higher learning, with undergraduate and postgraduate schools. These institutes specialize in research and theory related to physical education and sports. The salaries of researchers are usually better than those of teachers, physicians, and engineers. The Academy of Pedagogical Sciences supports a number of research institutes, such as the Research Institute for Physical Education and Hygiene. Because physical education is taken seriously, its instruction is not relegated to the untrained or ex-athlete but is reserved for those who are potential scholars. The influence of the Soviet Union's physical education is noticeable in most other Communist countries, and the results are conspicuously evident in international athletic competition.

International exchange in educational research and process has resulted in improved programs in physical education for both youth and adults. Although philosophies differ, awareness of the need for physical education is almost universal; consequently, it has received support from most governments, medical associations, and educational institutions.

Sports and activities common to most countries of the world are soccer, basketball, track and field, volleyball, gymnastics, rhythmic activities and dance, cultural games, hiking, and cycling. Physical education is required in most developed countries at the primary and secondary school levels, but it is elective in institutions of higher learning. Most countries require some degree of specialized preparation for physical education teachers and view research in physical education and sport as prerequisite to the realization of individual and national potential.

CARL S. CHRISTENSEN

Levels and Programs of Study

Programs in physical education generally require as a minimum prerequisite a secondary education and lead to the following awards: certificate or diploma, bachelor's degree, master's degree, the doctorate, or their equivalents. Programs that lead to an award not equivalent to a first university degree are designed to increase physical strength, agility, and grace of movement; athletics and sports are also developed. The aim in some cases may be spiritual and moral improvement in the individual through physical excellence and control of the body. The theoretical part of the programs includes study of human anatomy and physiology, natural science, social and behavioral science, and first aid. Attention may be paid to the history of physical education in different cultures. Stress is laid on sports of all kinds and on field athletics, as well as on gymnastics and eurhythmics. Students are normally expected to select two or three areas in which they attempt to achieve excellence—for example, football, running, jumping, dancing, hockey, kendo, and judo. Competitive sports may or may not be encouraged. Programs are usually at least two years in duration, part time or full time, and they are normally offered in colleges of physical education, community colleges, or technical colleges, and sometimes in universities.

Programs that lead to a first university degree or its equivalent consist primarily of classroom instruction and gymnasium exercises dealing with the essentials of physical education. Principal course content usually includes some of the following: adaptive physical education; analysis of physical education activities for the elementary schools; statistical methods in health, physical education, and recreation; physical fitness appraisal; methods and principles of athletic coaching; human anatomy and physiology; principles of body mechanics; kinesiology; and organization and administration of health and physical education in schools. Much attention is paid to the achievement of competence and skill in athletics such as running and jumping; in sports such as football and hockey; in gymnastics and games; in activities such as boxing, wrestling, and judo; and in the achievement of rhythmic excellence—for example, in dancing.

[This section was based on UNESCO's *International Standard Classification of Education (ISCED): Three Stage Classification System, 1974* (Paris: UNESCO, 1974).]

Major International and National Organizations

INTERNATIONAL

Arbeitskreis für zeitgemässe Leibeserziehung
Laar van Meerdervoort 691
The Hague, Netherlands

Asian Association of Physical Education
12 Shah Jahan Street
Takteh Jamshid
Tehran, Iran

Association internationale des écoles
    supérieures d'éducation physique (AIESEP)
Université de Liège au Sart Tilman
4000 Liege, Belgium

Association internationale d'histoire de
    l'éducation physique et du sport
Deutsche Sporthochschule
Postfach 450327
D-5 Cologne 41, Federal Republic of Germany

Catholic International Federation for Physical
    and Sports Education
Fédération internationale catholique
    d'éducation physique et sportive (FICEPS)
5 place Saint-Thomas d'Aquin
Paris 7e, France

Fédération internationale de médecine sportive
(FIMS)
18 rue Général Lotz
Brussels, Belgium

Fédération internationale du sport universitaire
101 boulevard de Tervuren
Louvain, Belgium

International Amateur Athletic Federation
(IAAF)
Windsor House
46 Victoria Street
London SW1, England

International Association of Physical Education
and Sports for Girls and Women (IAPESGW)
Deutsche Sporthochschule
Postfach 450327
D-5 Cologne 41, Federal Republic of Germany

International Council of Sport and Physical
Education (ICSPE)
Conseil international pour l'éducation
physique et le sport (CIEPS)
Université de Liège au Sart Tilman
400 Liège, Belgium
    Headquarters at UNESCO House, Place de
Fontenoy, 75007 Paris, France.

International Council on Health, Physical
Education and Recreation (ICHPER)
1201 16th Street NW
Washington, D.C. 20036 USA

International Federation for Physical
Education
Fédération internationale d'éducation physique
(FIEP)
65 Arreau, France

International Olympic Committee
Mon Repos
Lausanne, Switzerland

International Recreation Association (IRA)
345 East 46th Street
New York, New York 10017 USA

International Society for Sports Psychology
P.O. Box 200
Toledo, Ohio 43602 USA

Internationaler Arbeitskreis Sportstättenbau
(IAKS)
Bundesinstitut für Sportwissenschaft
Hertzstrasse 1
5023 Lövenich/Cologne, Federal Republic of
Germany

Internationales Büro für Dokumentation und
Information des Sports
Nederlandse sport federatie
Karnebeeklaan 6, Burg V, Netherlands

Latin Group for Physical Medicine and Sports
145 rue de la Pompe
Paris 16e, France

Society on the History of Physical Education
in the Asian and Pacific Area
Institute of Physical Education
Keio University
Mita
Minato-ku, Tokyo, Japan

South American Union of Sport Medicine
981 Arenales
Buenos Aires 3, Argentina

NATIONAL

Canada:
    Canadian Association for Health,
        Physical Education and Recreation
    Association canadienne pour la santé,
        l'éducation physique et la récréation
    333 River Road
    Vanier, Ontario K1L 8B9

Federal Republic of Germany:
    Deutscher Sportbund e.V.
    Quellenbusch 97
    425 Bottrop

Japan:
    Nippon taiiku gakkai
    % School of Education
    University of Tokyo
    Tokyo

United Kingdom:
    Central Council of Physical Education
    26–29 Park Crescent
    London W1N 4AJ, England

United States:
    American Alliance for Health, Physical
        Education and Recreation (AAHPER)
    1201 16th Street NW
    Washington, D.C. 20036

For a more complete listing of international
and national organizations see:

*Physical Education and Sport: A Handbook on Insti-
tutions and Associations.* Strasbourg, France:
Council for Cultural Co-operation of the
Council of Europe, 1964.
Vendien, C. L., and Nixon, J. E. *The World
Today in Health, Physical Education, and Rec-
reation.* Englewood Cliffs, New Jersey:
Prentice-Hall, 1968.
*Who's Who in Physical Culture: List of Institutions,
Research Centers, Schools, Persons and Period-
icals in Sports and Physical Education.* Warsaw:
Institute for Research in Physical Culture,
1967.

Principal Information Sources

GENERAL

For guides to the literature see:

Hendry, L. B. *A Bibliography of Studies in Physical Education.* (3rd ed.) London: Physical Education Association of Great Britain and Northern Ireland, 1973.

Hubbard, A. W. (Ed.) *Research Methods in Health, Physical Education, and Recreation.* (3rd rev. ed.) Washington, D.C.: AAHPER, 1973. An up-to-date approach to research methods in the field; includes selected bibliographies.

Miller, B. (Comp.) "Bibliography on International Relations." In *Proceedings of the National Conference on International Relations Through Health, Physical Education, and Recreation: International Understanding: Challenge and Action.* Washington, D.C.: AAHPER, 1972. Pp. 84–91.

Pahncke, W. *Geschichte der Körperkultur: Eine Auswahlbibliographie deutschsprachiger Veröffentlichungen.* Leipzig, German Democratic Republic: Bibliothek der deutschen Hochschule für Körperkultur, 1967.

Ziegler, E. F., Howell, M. L., and Trekell, M. (Eds.) *Research in the History, Philosophy, and International Aspects of Physical Education and Sport: Bibliographies and Techniques.* Champaign, Illinois: Stipes, 1971.

The following are histories of physical education:

Diem, C. *Weltgeschichte des Sports.* Stuttgart, Federal Republic of Germany: Cotta Verlag, 1967.

Hackensmith, C. W. *History of Physical Education.* New York: Harper & Row, 1966.

Seurin, P. *L'éducation physique dans le monde.* Bordeaux, France: Éditions Bière, 1961.

Van Dalen, D. B., and Bennet, B. L. *A World History of Physical Education.* (2nd ed.) Englewood Cliffs, New Jersey: Prentice-Hall, 1971.

Vendien, C. L., and Nixon, J. E. *The World Today in Health, Physical Education, and Recreation.* Englewood Cliffs, New Jersey: Prentice-Hall, 1968.

For other information on comparative physical education see:

Bennett, B. L., Howell, M. L., and Simri, U. *Comparative Physical Education and Sport.* Philadelphia: Lea & Febiger, 1975.

Comparative Physical Education and International Sport. Vol. 1: *European Countries;* Vol. 2: *Asian Countries.* Washington, D.C.: AAHPER, 1972–. Research guides to comparative and international physical education.

International Conference on Sport and Education. *Sport and Education.* Liège, Belgium: Université de Liège, 1969.

Jokl, E., and Simon, E. (Eds.) *International Research in Sport and Physical Education.* Springfield, Illinois: Thomas, 1964. A collection of papers on research in countries around the world.

Physical Education Around the World. Washington, D.C.: ICHPER, n.d. A monograph series developed by Phi Epsilon Kappa.

Physical Education in the School Curriculum, Teacher Training in Physical Education. Washington, D.C.: AAHPER, 1962–1968.

The Place of Sport in Education. Paris: UNESCO, 1956. A study of fourteen countries.

Status of Teachers in Physical Education. Washington, D.C.: AAHPER, 1962–1968. A study of physical education in more than eighty countries.

CURRENT BIBLIOGRAPHIES

The following publications provide bibliographies and abstracts of physical education scholarship:

Completed Research in Health, Physical Education and Recreation. Washington, D.C.: AAHPER, Research Council, 1959–.

Health, Physical Education and Recreation Microform Publications. Eugene: University of Oregon, School of Health, Physical Education and Recreation, 1949–. Publications out of print and unpublished research are made available in the form of microfiche.

H.P.E.S.R. Abstracts: Revue analytique d'éducation physique et de sport. Liège, Belgium: Conseil international pour l'éducation physique et sportive, 1959–.

Index and Abstracts of Foreign Physical Education Literature. Indianapolis, Indiana: Phi Epsilon Kappa, 1955–. Provides English translations of research published in other languages.

PERIODICALS

Acta Physiologica Scandinavica (Sweden), *American Journal of Physiology, Canadian Journal of History of Sport and Physical Education, Child Development* (US), *Educational and Psychological Measurement* (US), *Ergonomics* (UK), *Gymnasium: International Journal of Physical Education* (FRG), *International Review of Sport Sociology* (Poland), *Journal of the American Medical Association, Journal of Applied Physiology* (US), *Journal of Applied Psychology* (US), *Journal of Biomechanics* (US and

UK), *Journal of Bone and Joint Surgery* (US and UK), *Journal of Educational Research* (US), *Journal of Health Education* (US), *Journal of Leisure Research* (US), *Journal of Motor Behavior* (US), *Journal of Physical Education* (US), *Journal of Physical Education and Recreation* (US), *Journal of Sports Medicine and Physical Fitness* (Italy), *Lancet* (US and UK), *Medicine and Science in Sports* (US), *Parks and Recreation* (UK), *Perceptual and Motor Skills* (US), *Phi Delta Kappan* (US), *The Physical Educator* (US), *Physiological Reviews* (US), *Quest* (US), *Research Quarterly* (US), *Sociological Review* (UK), *Sport and Recreation* (UK), *Sportsworld* (UK), *Trans-American Journal of Sports Psychology* (US).

Who's Who in Physical Culture provides a list of physical education periodicals published in countries throughout the world.

ENCYCLOPEDIAS, DICTIONARIES, HANDBOOKS

The following provide useful information:

College and University Facilities Guide for Health, Physical Education, Recreation and Athletics. Washington, D.C.: AAHPER, 1968. Provides information for planning and building physical education facilities; a bibliography of literature dealing with construction of facilities is available from the Sports and Recreation Facilities Department at the Bundesinstitut für Sportwissenschaft in Cologne, Federal Republic of Germany.

Hyman, A. S. *Encyclopedia of Sports Science and Medicine.* New York: Macmillan, 1971.

Menke, F. G. *The Encyclopedia of Sports.* (4th ed.) South Brunswick, Federal Republic of Germany: A. S. Barnes, 1969.

Recla, J. *Moderne Sportdokumentation.* Graz, Austria: Internationaler Lehrgang für Sportdokumentation, 1967.

Recla, J. *Sportdokumentation im Durchbruch.* Bad Honnef, Federal Republic of Germany: Internationaler Kongress für Dokumentation der Sportwissenschaften, 1970.

Stanley, D. K., Waglow, I. F., and Alexander, R. H. *Physical Education Activities Handbook for Men and Women.* (3rd ed.) Boston: Allyn & Bacon, 1973. Provides a discussion of the fundamentals of forty-one sports; includes bibliographies and a source list of official rules for a variety of sports.

Watman, M. F. (Comp.) *The Encyclopedia of Athletics.* (2nd ed.) London: Robert Hale, 1967.

DIRECTORIES

The HPER Directory of Professional Preparation Institutions. Washington, D.C.: AAHPER, 1974. Lists colleges and universities offering major programs in physical education at the undergraduate and graduate levels in the United States.

Physical Education and Sport: A Handbook on Institutions and Associations. Strasbourg, France: Council for Cultural Co-operation of the Council of Europe, 1964. Lists organizations in sport and gives information on the training of instructors in physical education and the important publications on physical education in eighteen European countries.

Who's Who in Physical Culture: List of Institutions, Research Centers, Schools, Persons and Periodicals in Sports and Physical Education. Warsaw: Institute for Research in Physical Culture, 1967. Provides international information on physical education.

RESEARCH CENTERS, INSTITUTES,
INFORMATION CENTERS

Federal Institute for Sport Science
Hertzstrasse 1
5023 Lövenich/Cologne, Federal Republic of Germany
Important for international documentation in sports.

National Documentation Centre for Sport,
Physical Education, and Recreation
University of Birmingham
P.O. Box 363
Birmingham B15 2TT, England

There are some fifty-two information and documentation centers in the world concerned with sports. For lists of research centers see *Who's Who in Physical Culture,* listed above.

PHYSICAL PLANT

See Business Management of Higher Education: Facilities, Physical Plant.

PHYSICAL THERAPY (Field of Study)

Physical therapy is a specialized health profession that uses physical agents and procedures to treat and prevent a wide variety of disorders. Patients are referred for treatment by physicians from general practice and many different specialties; and the physical therapist often works closely with other health professionals, such as nurses, social workers, and occupational therapists, in providing comprehensive rehabilitation services. Frequently used forms of treatment include therapeutic exercise, heat, cold, ultraviolet light, water, various types of electrical current, massage, training in adapted functional activities such as walking with crutches or using an artificial limb, and training in self-care activities. As a part of treatment, the therapist performs various evaluative procedures as the basis for an individual plan of instruction and therapy for each patient.

Although natural physical agents like hot baths and sunlight have been used for centuries to relieve common ailments, physical therapy as a specialized health service has developed largely since 1900. Formal training in physical therapy was first offered in the late 1890s in European countries; in England, for example, early instruction was provided by nurses specializing in therapeutic massage, and in Sweden training developed as a special branch of physical education or remedial gymnastics. The profession in the United States received much of its early impetus from the need for rehabilitation services for the many severely handicapped patients from the two world wars and from the widespread outbreaks of poliomyelitis that occurred prior to development of the polio vaccine during the 1950s.

Throughout its development physical therapy has been closely associated with orthopedic surgery in the treatment of fractures, joint injuries, back pain, bony deformities, and amputations. However, therapists now also treat such diverse ailments as stroke, arthritis, spinal cord injuries, burns, cerebral palsy and developmental disorders, circulatory problems, and breathing problems such as asthma and emphysema. By 1975 preventive programs were also receiving growing attention.

Physical therapists require from one to four years of full-time study at the postsecondary level or above. Instruction includes courses in three general areas: basic sciences, such as anatomy, physiology, chemistry, physics, and psychology; medical sciences, such as neurology and pathology; and treatment and evaluation procedures. Didactic work is supplemented by a substantial period of required supervised clinical experience. There is considerable variation in the structure of physical therapy schools and in their relationship to other institutions of higher education. Three basic patterns are most common.

The first pattern—followed in many countries, particularly those of northern Europe and the United Kingdom—has schools of physical therapy located within major teaching hospitals and forming an integral part of those institutions. Students receive two to three years of theoretical classroom and laboratory instruction and the major part of their supervised clinical experience at the hospital, but they may be assigned to other hospitals or rehabilitation centers for part of this practical work.

A second pattern is that of the independent school, often operated by the Ministry of Health or some other governmental agency. These schools have a close working association with one or more hospitals, in which students receive their clinical experience. In some countries—for example, Poland—the school is associated with a school of physical education. In others, such as Chile and several other Latin American countries, the program is affiliated with a university. However, students in physical therapy meet a somewhat different set of admission requirements from those entering the university's academic programs, and upon completion of training they receive a diploma or professional certificate rather than an academic degree.

Only a relatively small number of countries follow the third pattern: education of physical therapists in programs that are an integral part of a university and award an academic bachelor's degree as well as professional certification upon graduation. Even among these schools there is considerable variety in the relationship between professional studies and general education. In the United States, where university degrees have been the standard since the 1950s, and in Canada and Australia, where in the 1970s diploma schools have converted to university degree programs, professional studies in physical therapy represent the student's undergraduate major or field of academic concentration during a four-year course of study. However, at least half of the student's work during those four years is devoted to general education in language, literature, history, the arts, and the basic social and natural sciences. By contrast, bachelor's degree programs in some other countries, such as India, Pakistan, and Nigeria, consist entirely of scientific and technical studies directly related to professional preparation.

The pattern in the United States is further complicated by two other types of programs, both for students who have already received a university degree in an academic discipline such as biology or psychology. These are the professional certificate programs, which last twelve to eighteen months, and the two-year basic professional master's degree programs. Despite their differences in length and starting level, all three programs (bachelor's degree, postbachelor's certificate, and master's degree) comply with the same set of standards for professional training and provide graduates with equal credentials for licensure or registration. It is primarily the breadth of general education and the degree of formal preparation for special responsibilities in teaching, administration, and research that vary rather than the degree of competence as a practitioner.

Because of these wide variations in program organization and curriculum structure, international comparisons among physical therapy training programs are difficult to make. There is no single international standard for physical therapy education, and the therapist who has trained in one country and wishes to work in another may be required to take additional training, pass a special examination, or work under supervision for a period of time to become eligible for licensure. In many countries the therapist must be licensed or registered by the government. In some countries this recognition is given automatically to all

graduates of approved schools of physical therapy in the country. In others, such as the United States, graduates of approved schools must also pass a special examination given by the state to become licensed or registered. Eligibility for licensure is usually determined by the government in close consultation with the professional organization representing physical therapists in the country.

International sharing of information on physical therapy education has been greatly facilitated by the establishment in 1951 of the World Confederation for Physical Therapy (WCPT). This organization, with headquarters in London, is a federation of national associations, each recognized within its own country as representing a majority of that nation's qualified physical therapists. By 1975 the WCPT included thirty-seven member organizations. The confederation organizes international scientific congresses every three or four years, provides consultation on physical therapy education and practice to a variety of international agencies, and publishes a number of informational documents.

Although the World Confederation for Physical Therapy has done a great deal to advance communication within the profession, it is not an academic or educational body as such, and admission to membership does not confer any official recognition by the WCPT of the standard of professional education in the countries represented in membership. The confederation has published a pamphlet of guidelines for training of physical therapists, but these are intended as general suggestions rather than international standards. In fact, confederation policy suggests that a single standard for training in all countries would be inappropriate, since physical therapy education must be responsive to national differences in overall educational systems, economic resources, health problems, and patterns of health care.

Most countries provide formal training for, and recognition of, only one level of worker in physical therapy—the professional general practitioner. However, in a small but growing number of countries two additional levels of training are offered: programs for therapist assistants and advanced programs. The physical therapist assistant or technician, who ordinarily works under the supervision of a professional therapist, is trained, usually in junior or community colleges, in programs approximately two years in length. In comparison with the curriculum for the professional therapist, the assistant's training includes less advanced study in the sciences and less training in evaluative procedures and complex forms of treatment. These programs are most widely established in the United States, but they are also developing in other places, such as the Canadian province of Quebec, Finland, and Poland. Considerable controversy exists concerning the desirability of establishing this additional level of training and practice.

Formal training at an advanced or specialized level is also limited to a few countries, and here again the pattern is varied. A few countries, such as Canada, the United States, and Poland, have university graduate programs in which already qualified therapists may study for a master's degree. (These are not the same programs as those referred to earlier for basic training in physical therapy at a master's degree level.) The advanced professional master's programs emphasize advanced clinical theory and methods, as well as aspects of clinical research, teaching, and administration applicable to physical therapy. Although a number of therapists have completed doctoral studies, there is no doctoral program in the field of physical therapy itself; such advanced study must therefore be done in special programs of physical education or in any of a wide variety of traditional academic disciplines. Several countries, such as the United Kingdom and Finland, have advanced programs in which qualified therapists may earn a special diploma or certificate as a teacher; and in a very few countries, such as Norway, formal recognition is given therapists who complete ad-

vanced courses or an apprenticeship and examination in a specialized treatment method, such as joint mobilization. However, formal certification of specialists in a particular area of clinical practice is uncommon, and in many countries in the 1970s it is viewed as highly controversial.

NANCY T. WATTS

Major International and National Organizations

INTERNATIONAL

European Confederation for Physical Therapy
Confédération européenne pour la thérapie physique
9 rue des Petits-Hôtels
75010 Paris, France

Pan American Health Organization (PAHO)
525 23rd Street NW
Washington, D.C. 20037 USA

Rehabilitation International
122 East 23rd Street
New York, New York 10010 USA

World Confederation for Physical Therapy (WCPT)
Confédération mondiale de physiothérapie
20/22 Mortimer Street
London W1, England

World Health Organization (WHO)
1211 Geneva 27, Switzerland

NATIONAL

The following organizations are members of the World Confederation for Physical Therapy and provide a sampling of organizations in the field:

Australia:
Australian Physiotherapy Association
201 Balaclava Road
Caulfield 3161, Victoria

Austria:
Verband der Diplomierten Assistenten für physikalische Medizin Österreichs
Alserstrasse 4, Hof 7
Vienna IX

Belgium:
Association des kinésithérapeutes de Belgique
15 rue d'Albanie
Brussels 6

Brazil:
  Associação brasileira de fisioterapeutas
  Rua Frei Caneca 1407 8°, Sala 809
  Jardim Paulista, São Paulo

Canada:
  Canadian Physiotherapy Association
  Canadian Hospital Association Building
  25 Imperial Street
  Toronto 7, Ontario

Chile:
  Colegio de kinesiólogos de Chile
  Casilla 9317, Correo Central
  Santiago

Colombia:
  Asociación colombiana de fisioterapia
  Apartado Aéreo 16560
  Bogotá

Denmark:
  Danske fysioterapeuter
  Nannasgade 28
  DK Copenhagen N

Federal Republic of Germany:
  Zentralverband Krankengymnastik e.V.
  Viktor-Scheffel Strasse 10/11
  Munich 23

Finland:
  Finnish Physical Therapy Association
  Töölöntullinkatu 8
  Helsinki 25

France:
  Fédération française des masseurs
    kinésithérapeutes rééducateurs
  9 rue des Petits-Hôtels
  Paris 10e

Greece:
  Panhellenic Physical Therapy Association
  12 Gilfordou Street
  Athens

Iceland:
  Félag Islenzkra sjúkrapjálfara
  P.O. Box 5023
  Reykjavik 5

India:
  Indian Association of Physiotherapists
  35 Chowpaty Sea-Face
  Bombay 400-007

Israel:
  National Union of Physiotherapists in
    Israel
  Histadrut Building, 93 Arlosoroff Street
  Tel Aviv

Jamaica:
  Jamaica Physiotherapy Association
  P.O. Box 167
  Mona, Kingston 7

Japan:
  Japanese Physical Therapy Association
  % School of Rehabilitation
  1-2-7 Umezono, Kiyoseshi
  Tokyo 180-04

Malaysia:
  Malaysian Physiotherapy Association
  Rehabilitation Department, University
    Hospital
  Petaling Jaya, Selangor

Mexico:
  Asociación mexicana de terapia física
    y rehabilitación
  Apartado Postal 66-633
  Mexico 12, D.F.

Netherlands:
  Nederlands genootschap voor
    fysiotherapie
  Van Hogendorplaan 8
  Amersfoort

New Zealand:
  New Zealand Society of Physiotherapists
  P.O. Box 2399
  Wellington

Nigeria:
  Nigeria Society of Physiotherapy
  Lagos University Teaching Hospital
  P.M.B. 12003
  Lagos

Norway:
  Norske fisioterapeuters forbund
  Motzfeldsgate 3
  Oslo

Pakistan:
  Pakistan Physiotherapy Society
  % Post Bag 3997
  Karachi 4

Philippines:
  Philippine Physical Therapy Association
  % School of Allied Medical Professions
  College of Medicine, University of the
    Philippines
  547 Pedro Gil Street
  Manila

Poland:
  Magistrów wychowania fizypracujacych
    w rehabilitacji
  (Section for the Disabled)
  Zarzad Glowny, ul. Partyzantów 4 m, 10
  00-629 Warsaw

Portugal:
  Associação portuguêsa de fisioterapeutas
  % Escola de reabilitação
  Alcoitao, Estoril

Republic of Korea:
Korean Physical Therapy Association
% Dept. of Physical Therapy, Woo Sok
University
42nd Street
Myung Yoon-Dong
Chong Ro-ku, Seoul

Rhodesia:
Rhodesian Physiotherapy Association
P.O. Box A 147
Avondale, Salisbury

South Africa:
South African Society of Physiotherapy
P.O. Box 11151
Johannesburg

Spain:
Asociación española de fisioterapeutas
Apartado Postal 50696
Madrid 14

Surinam:
Surinaamse vereniging voor
fisiotherapie
P.O. Box 719
Paramaribo

Sweden:
Legitimerade sjukgymnasters
riksförbund
Birger Jarlsgatan 13
111 45 Stockholm

Switzerland:
Fédération suisse des physiothérapeutes
Hinterbergstrasse 106
Zurich 8044

Turkey:
Physical Therapy Association "Turkey"
Kubilay Sok 8/2
Maltepe, Ankara

United Kingdom:
Chartered Society of Physiotherapy
14 Bedford Row
London W1R 4ED, England

United States:
American Physical Therapy Association
1156 15th Street NW
Washington, D.C. 20005

For additional listings of physical therapy
and related organizations consult:

List of Member-Organisations. London: World
Confederation for Physical Therapy, up-
dated regularly.
Wasserman, P., and Giesecke, J. (Eds.) *Health
Organizations of the United States, Canada and
Internationally.* (3rd ed.) Washington, D.C.:
McGrath, 1974.

Principal Information Sources

GENERAL

The following are general guides that provide information about the field:

Blake, J. B., and Roos, C. (Eds.) *Medical Refer-
ence Works 1679–1966: A Selected Bibliography.*
Chicago: Medical Library Association, 1967.
Supplement I (1967–1968), compiled by M. V.
Clark, 1970; *Supplement II* (1969–1972),
compiled by J. S. Richmond, 1973; *Supple-
ment III* (1973–1974), compiled by J. S. Rich-
mond, 1975.
*Books and Periodicals for Medical Libraries in Hos-
pitals.* (4th ed.) London: Library Association,
Medical Section, 1973.
Morton, L. T. *The Use of Medical Literature.*
Hamden, Connecticut: Archon, 1974.

Overviews and texts for the field include:

Cash, J. E. *Textbook of Medical Conditions for
Physiotherapists.* London: Faber & Faber,
1971.
Cash, J. E. (Ed.) *Chest, Heart and Vascular Disorders for Physiotherapists.* Philadelphia: Lippincott, 1975.
Downer, A. H. *Physical Therapy Procedures: Selected Techniques.* (2nd ed.) Springfield, Illinois: Thomas, 1974.

The following two compilations contain valuable articles discussing physical therapy training worldwide:

*Proceedings of the 7th International Congress of the
World Confederation for Physical Therapy, Mon-
treal.* London: World Confederation for
Physical Therapy, 1974.
*Proceedings of the 6th International Congress of the
World Confederation for Physical Therapy,
Amsterdam.* Assen, Netherlands: Van Gor-
cum, 1971.

Other comparative education and training
sources include:

*Conferencia latinoamericana sobre rehabilitación de
inválidos.* Publicación cientifica No. 224.
Washington, D.C.: Organización panameri-
cana de salud, 1971. Includes suggested
guidelines for training of physical therapists.
Decker, R. "Physical Therapy Education: The
Past." *Physical Therapy,* 1974, *54,* 27–31.
Hogue, R. E. "Physical Therapy Education:
The Present." *Physical Therapy,* 1974, *54,*
32–36.
Reid, D. C., and Pickles, B. "Undergraduate
Physiotherapy Programmes in Canada."
Physiotherapy, 1971, *57,* 582–584.
Saldias, E. G. "Paramedical Education in Re-
habilitation in South America." *Archives of
Physical Medicine,* 1969, *50,* 704–708. An

overview of the educational trends in South America; lists courses of training available.

Histories of the field include:

Coulter, J. S. *Physical Therapy.* New York: Hoeber, 1932.

Physical Therapy. Washington, D.C.: American Physical Therapy Association, 1921–. See January 1976, *56* (1), for a discussion of the historical development of the field in the United States.

CURRENT BIBLIOGRAPHIES

Current Catalog. Bethesda, Maryland: National Library of Medicine, 1955–.

Excerpta Medica. Section 19: *Rehabilitation and Physical Medicine.* Amsterdam: Excerpta Medica Foundation, 1958–.

Hospital Literature Index. Chicago: American Hospital Association, 1945–.

Index Medicus. Bethesda, Maryland: National Library of Medicine, 1960–.

Rehabilitation Literature. Chicago: National Easter Seal Society for Crippled Children and Adults, 1940–.

PERIODICALS

A listing of important journals in the field includes *Australian Journal of Physiotherapy, Danske fysioterapeuter* (Denmark), *Fysioterapeuten* (Norway), *Journal of the Japanese Physical Therapy Association, Journal of the Nederlands genootschap voor fysiotherapie, Journal of the Nigerian Society of Physiotherapy, Journal of the Pakistan Physiotherapy Society, Kinésithérapie* (France), *Krankengymnastik* (FRG), *Laakintavoimistelija fysioterapeuten* (Finland), *New Zealand Journal of Physiotherapy, Physical Therapy* (US), *Physiotherapy* (Canada), *Physiotherapy* (US), *Sjukgymnasten* (Sweden), *South African Journal of Physiotherapy, Tijdschrift voor fysische therapie* (Belgium).

For further listings of physical therapy journals and related journals see:

Ulrich's International Periodicals Directory. New York: Bowker, biennial.

DICTIONARIES, ENCYCLOPEDIAS, HANDBOOKS

Glossary of Terms and Phrases Commonly Used by Physical Therapists. London: World Confederation for Physical Therapy, 1968–. Available in various combinations of languages.

Hickok, R. J. (Ed.) *Physical Therapy Administration and Management.* Baltimore: Williams & Wilkins, 1974.

Shestack, R. *Handbook of Physical Therapy.* (2nd ed.) New York: Springer-Verlag, 1967.

DIRECTORIES

Allied Medical Education Directory. Chicago: American Medical Association, 1974. Lists the essentials of an accredited educational program along with actual accredited programs in the United States.

Courses of Training, Scholarships and Bursaries in Countries Represented in the World Confederation for Physical Therapy. London: World Confederation for Physical Therapy, 1972.

Physical Therapy, 1976, *56,* 428–436. Lists educational programs leading to professional qualifications in physical therapy, graduate programs, physical therapist assistant programs, short-term courses for graduate physical therapists, and state board examinations for the United States; updated regularly.

Registration Requirements and Working Conditions in Countries Represented in the World Confederation for Physical Therapy. London: World Confederation for Physical Therapy, n.d.

[Bibliography prepared by Marion Levine.]

PHYSICIAN'S ASSISTANTS, PROGRAMS FOR (Field of Study)

The physician's assistant—a person educated to perform tasks and functions traditionally performed by physicians —works in a dependent relationship with a physician. The term *physician's assistant* is principally generic, encompassing individuals identified by such other terms as *physician's associate, MEDEX, primary care associate, health associate, health assistant, community health medic, surgeon's assistant, pathologist's assistant, radiologist's assistant, dermatology assistant,* and *urologic physician's assistant.* Although the physician's assistant concept has occasionally been likened to that of the *feldsher* in the Soviet Union and the "barefoot doctor" of the People's Republic of China, they remain remarkably different concepts within their unique cultures.

The principal object of the field is to help the physician in data collection, treatment, and management of the health, injury, and illness processes experienced by individuals. Fundamentally, the physician's assistant is trained (1) to elicit a comprehensive health history, (2) to perform a comprehensive physical examination, (3) to perform selected diagnostic laboratory tests and to understand and use their results, (4) to perform basic treatment procedures, and (5) to make an appropriate clinical response to commonly encountered emergency care situations.

The principal educational effort in the preparation of the physician's assistant is focused on preparing individuals who are competent in dealing with the broad dimensions of primary care. In the United States there are approximately sixty institutions sponsoring programs of study with major focus on preparing assistants to primary care physicians. Approximately ten institutions educate and train assistants to surgeons, with only one or two institutions conducting programs for the development of assistants to other medical specialties.

The National Academy of Sciences of the United States has defined three principal categories of physician's assistant as simply types A, B, and C. The assistant to the primary care physician is a Type-A assistant, with competencies and knowledge related to the identification and management of commonly encountered clinical health requirements and problems of individuals from conception until death. The Type-B or "other specialty" physician's assistant has less breadth of clinical knowledge and competence than the Type-A assistant but considerably more depth of knowledge and competence in his given area of specialty. The surgeon's assistant is one such example; his knowledge of surgery often exceeds that of physicians who are not surgeons. The Type-C assistant is fundamentally a technical aide, either to the physician or to a physician's assistant. It might be said that the Type-C assistant is to the physician as the nursing aide is to the professional nurse.

By the end of 1975 there were an estimated 3300 formally educated physician's assistant graduates in the United States. This relatively small number is estimated to increase by 1100 a year within the immediate future. Yet physician's assistants will remain a minority group for some time, in view of the 350,000 physicians and over 1,000,000 nurses in practice throughout the United States.

There is no direct relationship between the physician's assistant and the nurse practitioner, yet there are substantial similarities in the range of their clinical competencies and responsibility. One major difference is that the physician's assistant accepts his or her dependent relationship with the physician, whereas nurses are striving to expand the scope of independent nursing practice and to establish an interdependent relationship with medicine in addressing patients' health needs.

The concept of the physician's assistant began to manifest itself in the United States in demonstration projects in the mid 1960s. These early demonstrations were established in the middle Atlantic seaboard, the northwest Pacific coast, and the Rocky Mountains. Each of these efforts first occurred within well-established academic medical centers. The federal government of the United States underwrote the principal costs of demonstration and evaluation of the validity of the physician's assistant concept and that of the nurse practitioner/clinician as means of addressing the primary care deficits in the early 1970s.

Since the inception of physician's assistant education, the majority of educational programs have been developed under the egis of medical schools or academic medical centers. Programs of study are all postsecondary and not infrequently are designed to build upon earlier education in the behavioral and biological sciences and/or earlier education and training for a health services occupation. About half of the programs award a baccalaureate degree; approximately one fifth award an associate degree; and the remainder award a certificate. One program awards a master's degree.

Course content of physician's assistant curricula is similar to that commonly taught in medical education. There is remarkably less focus on theory and greater emphasis on the application of knowledge from the behavioral and biological sciences to clinical problem identification and problem solving, within the parameters of commonly encountered manifestations of physical and mental disease. By and large, the physician and other medical educators involved in this innovative effort have capitalized on contemporary advances in educational theory and technology and have developed curricula designed around stated behavioral objectives for all components of the instruction and supervised practice experience. For the education of assistants to primary care physicians, the curriculum includes courses in anatomy, applied physiology, chemistry, bacteriology, pharmacology, and the behavioral sciences. The behavioral science courses deal with the development of listening and interviewing skills; personality development; mechanisms for coping with stress in daily living; and a broadened understanding of individual values relating to such dimensions of human experience as sexuality, death, and dying. In the second year, students receive much greater applied content and supervised practice in dealing with the commonly encountered demands for primary health care of individuals from infancy through childhood, adolescence, and the various phases of adulthood.

The AMA has recognized four types of physician's assistant: the orthopedic physician's assistant, the primary care physician's assistant, the urologic physician's assistant, and the surgeon's assistant.

The minimum educational standards for the orthopedic physician's assistant were adopted by the AMA House of Delegates in 1969 upon recommendation from the American Academy of Orthopaedic Surgeons. In January 1974 the academy announced its withdrawal from the accreditation effort due to reported problems of graduates' finding employment and some concern within the profession regarding "overtraining." As a consequence, the AMA Council on Medical Education announced a moratorium on accreditation of any additional programs, and after substantial consultation with the academy, it informed the eight accredited programs that accreditation would be discontinued upon graduation of classes in the spring of 1976. (The AMA does not conduct accreditation efforts without the expressed support and involvement of the medical specialty societies and allied health organizations most closely associated with the occupation.) Five of the eight accredited programs have been discontinued.

Minimum standards for the education of the assistant to the primary care physician were developed under the auspices of the American Academy of Family Physicians, the American Academy of Pediatrics, the American College of Physicians, and the American Society of Internal Medicine and adopted by the AMA House of Delegates in December 1971. The accreditation effort became operational in late spring of 1972; at the end of 1975 fifty-three programs in twenty-nine states had been accredited.

In June 1972, on recommendation from the American Urological Association, the AMA House of Delegates adopted minimum standards for the education of the urologic physician's assistant. Two programs have been accredited. In June 1974, on recommendation of the American College of Surgeons, minimum standards for the education of the surgeon's assistant were adopted by the AMA House of Delegates. Two surgeon's assistant programs were accredited during 1975.

Programs educating assistants to primary care physicians and to surgeons are reviewed and recommended for accreditation by a review body of representatives of the American Academy of Family Physicians, the American Academy of Pediatrics, the American Academy of Physician's Assistants, the American College of Physicians, the American College of Surgeons, and the American Society of Internal Medicine. In February 1974 the AMA Council on Medical Education received the maximum four-year award of recognition from the United States Office of Education as the national accrediting agency for physician's assistant education.

As a result of joint planning by several national organizations and support from the federal government, the National Board of Medical Examiners developed and administered the first national certification examination for assistants to primary care physicians in November 1973. This is the only certification by examination currently available to the physician's assistant. Within the following year, the National Commission on Physician Assistant Certification was established as an independent body, with support from the AMA, the Federation of State Boards of Medical Examiners, the American Nurses' Association, the American Academy of Family Physicians, the American College of Physicians, the American Academy of Physician's Assistants, the American Academy of Pediatrics, the American College of Surgeons, and the American Society of Internal Medicine. The commission's policies and programs are determined by a board of individuals who are appointed by the organizational sponsors of the commission. The third administration of the national examination was conducted in November 1975.

L. M. DETMER

Major International and National Organizations

INTERNATIONAL

World Health Organization (WHO)
1211 Geneva 27, Switzerland
    Especially the Committee on Professional and Technical Education of Medical and Auxiliary Personnel.

NATIONAL

United States:
    American Academy of Physician's
        Assistants
    2120 L Street NW, Suite 210
    Gelman Building
    Washington, D.C. 20037

    Association of Physician Assistant
        Programs
    2120 L Street NW, Suite 210
    Gelman Building
    Washington, D.C. 20037

Principal Information Sources

GENERAL

Some guides to the literature include:

Backs, M., and Bicknell, W. J. *The Medical Assistant: A Compendium.* San Francisco: Office of Health Affairs, Office of Economic Opportunity, 1969.

Gish, O. (Ed.) *Health Manpower and the Medical Auxiliary: Some Notes and an Annotated Bibliography.* London: Intermediate Technology Development Group, 1971.

Overviews to the field include:

Ad Hoc Panel on New Members of the Physician's Health Team. *New Members of the Physician's Health Team: Physician's Assistants, Report.* Washington, D.C.: National Academy of Sciences, 1970.

Kane, R. L. (Ed.) *New Health Practitioners.* Bethesda, Maryland: National Institutes of Health, 1974. DHEW Publication No. (NIH) 73–875.

Pitcairn, D. M., and Flahault, D. "The Medical Assistant: An Intermediate Level of Health Care Personnel." WHO *Public Health Papers,* 1974, *60,* 1–171.

Sadler, A. M., Sadler, B. L., and Bliss, A. A. *The Physician's Assistant, Today and Tomorrow.* Cambridge, Massachusetts: Ballinger, 1972.

Studies in comparative education include:

Fendall, N. R. E. *Auxiliaries in Health Care: Programs in Developing Countries.* Baltimore: Johns Hopkins University Press, 1972. Discussion of the need, training, and utilization of auxiliary personnel in the health care systems in developing countries.

Proger, S. "A Career in Ambulatory Medicine." *New England Journal of Medicine,* 1975, *292* (25), 1318–1324. A proposal for a different type of primary medical education.

Quinn, J. R. (Ed.) *Medicine and Public Health in*

the People's Republic of China. Bethesda, Maryland: National Institutes of Health, 1973. DHEW Publication No. (NIH) 76–67.

Sidel, V. W. "The Barefoot Doctors of the People's Republic of China." *New England Journal of Medicine,* 1972, *286,* 1292–1300. The delivery of health care in China is reviewed; also covers the *feldsher* type of medical personnel.

"The Training and Utilization of Feldshers in the USSR." WHO *Public Health Papers,* 1974, *56,* 1–52. A descriptive review of the *feldsher* system, including the training and utilization of these intermediate-level health care personnel.

"Training of Medical Assistants and Similar Personnel: Seventeenth Report of the WHO Expert Committee on Programs and Technical Education of Medical and Auxilliary Personnel." *WHO Technical Report Series,* 1968, *385,* 1–26.

CURRENT BIBLIOGRAPHIES

Cumulated Index Medicus. Bethesda, Maryland: National Library of Medicine, 1960–. Especially under the subject headings "Physician's Assistants," "Health Manpower," and "Health Occupations."

Excerpta Medica. Amsterdam: Excerpta Medica Foundation, 1947–. Especially section 17: "Public Health, Social Medicine and Hygiene," and section 36: "Health Economics and Hospital Management."

PERIODICALS

Journals important to the field include *American Journal of Nursing, American Journal of Public Health, British Medical Journal, Community Mental Health Journal* (US), *Dimensions in Health Service* (Canada), *Ethiopian Medical Journal, Health Services Reports* (US), *Hospitals* (US), *International Journal of Health Services* (US), *Journal of the American Medical Association, Journal of Medical Education* (US), *Lancet* (US and UK), *Medical Care* (US), *New England Journal of Medicine, P. A. Journal: A Journal for New Health Practitioners* (US), *Public Health Papers* (Switzerland), *Social Science and Medicine* (US and UK), *WHO Technical Report Series* (Switzerland).

ENCYCLOPEDIAS, DICTIONARIES, HANDBOOKS

Medical dictionaries and handbooks would be most useful to physician's assistants. A selection of some of the more widely used works includes:

Current Medical Diagnosis and Treatment. Los Altos, California: Lange, annual.

Dorland's Illustrated Medical Dictionary. (25th ed.) Philadelphia: Saunders, 1974.

Merck Manual of Diagnosis and Therapy. (12th ed.) Rahway, New Jersey: Merck, 1972.

Passmore, R., and Robson, J. S. (Eds.) *A Companion to Medical Studies.* (3 vols.) Oxford, England: Blackwell, 1968–1974.

Stedman's Medical Dictionary. (22nd ed.) Baltimore: Williams & Wilkins, 1972.

DIRECTORIES

American Medical Association. *Allied Medical Education Directory, 1976.* Chicago: American Medical Association, 1976.

American Medical Association. Department of Allied Health Evaluation. *Educational Programs for the Physician's Assistant.* Chicago: American Medical Association, 1973. A listing of AMA-approved educational programs for the allied medical occupations of assistant to the primary care physician, orthopedic physician's assistant, and urologic physician's assistant.

Selected Training Programs for Physician Support Personnel. Bethesda, Maryland: National Institutes of Health, 1972. DHEW Publication No. (NIH) 72–183. A compilation of 125 programs for training new physician support personnel in 35 states. Listed are institutions, program directors, stage of development of the program, curriculum, entrance requirements, duration of study, tuition, and availability of financial aid.

[Bibliography prepared by Marion Levine.]

PHYSICS (Field of Study)

Physics is the study of the behavior of inanimate matter and energy. In a simplified outline we may say that the activity of physics proceeds thus: Suppose a new phenomenon is observed during an experiment which is inexplicable under the known laws of physics. The laboratory work will be repeated by others (experimentalists) to be sure no observational error has been made. If the experimental facts are verified, and they disagree with the known laws of physics, then the laws *must* be changed. It is a basic assumption in physics that a theory which disagrees with experiment must be modified or abandoned. Some physicists (theoreticians) next make theoretical speculations about changes that might be made in the laws to accommodate the new experimental facts. For example, small factors previously ignored might be added to the laws. The rules of mathematics are then applied to see if the newly observed phenomenon and *all* previously observed phenomena are now permitted by the proposed new laws. If the new laws cannot successfully describe *all* known phenomena, they are rejected. If they can pass this test, they are accepted. (They are accepted, that is, until a new phenomenon shows them to be inadequate.) Thus the central activity of physics continually expands our range of experience (experiment). Of course, since physics is a human activity, it does not always proceed flawlessly. Sometimes a flash of insight advances a theory before many phenomena have been observed. The theoretical advance will then predict new experimental results. Sometimes theories are temporarily rejected, not because they fail to agree with experiment but because of preconceived notions of how matter must behave. But in general the field proceeds quasi-rationally.

Elementary-particle physics studies very small objects, the constituents of the nucleus and other subnuclear constituents produced in energetic collisions of nuclear constituents. This field includes the study of baryons (for example, the proton), mesons (for example, the pi meson), and leptons (for example, the electron). The experimental activity in this field is often called high-energy physics because very high-energy phenomena are also pursued in elementary-particle physics. The theory of elementary-particle physics includes the study of "symmetries" in nature. Another significant branch is field theory, which studies the forms a theory may take for energy which is extended over space and time.

Knowledge about large aggregates of atoms is the subject of solid-state physics, a somewhat misleading name, since this field includes the study of liquids and even high-pressure gases. It has many subfields. Low-temperature physics deals with phenomena observed at very low temperatures (generally near $-273°C$); one practical result of these studies has been the development of superconducting wire. The phenomenon of magnetism in large clusters of atoms is still not well understood, and its study is the object of solid-state magnetism. Other active fields in solid-state physics include studies of gases at high pressure, thin-film studies, surface phenomena, and the propagation of energy packets through solids. The theory of solid-state physics includes many-body theory and thermodynamics.

Astrophysics concerns the universe of stars. Observations of the stars (astronomy) may be made via visible light, using telescopes, but they are also made by observing radio waves with radio telescopes and by observing gamma rays (nuclear radiation) with gamma ray telescopes. The theory used in astrophysics includes general relativity, which is Albert Einstein's twentieth century advance on Newton's theory of gravitation. Modifications of this theory are also being worked on by some theorists. The theory needed to understand astrophysics, our frontier of large objects, also depends upon the newest discoveries in elementary-particle physics, our frontier of small objects.

Plasma physics studies very hot gases in electric and magnetic fields. One aim of this field is to learn how to contain these ionized gases whose thermal motion causes large energy releases from nuclear fusion (nuclei sticking together). As a result, by the year 2000 we will probably enjoy fusion power, with fuel derived from seawater.

Other fields of physics active in the mid 1970s include psychophysics, which deals with the boundary of psychology and physics, and other boundary subjects such as chemical physics, biophysics, and medical physics.

As physics proceeds, it generates knowledge and techniques useful in an applied sense. The application of well-understood laws of physics comprises several fields of engineering. Thus, relatively well-understood portions of physics are the basis of electrical and mechanical engineering and metallurgy. A study of the related physics fields is a prerequisite for these engineering studies. Physics provides techniques and a theoretical basis for chemistry, chemical engineering, microbiology, and experimental psychology. Physics itself makes use of the results of mathematics, and occasionally it motivates the development of mathematics. (Newton was a major contributor to the development of calculus as well as mechanics and optics.) In more remote fields, like medical physics, the findings of physics are applicable. For example, the study of fluids in the physics of fluid dynamics is important to understanding the flow of blood. The use of radioactive tracers in diagnosis and therapy for cancer victims also involves physics.

Technology and physics have always advanced hand in hand. Physics has developed special devices, sometimes as tools for experiments (for example, vacuum pumps) and sometimes as the central object of the experiment itself (for example, radio transmission, superconductivity, and fission). Many new devices, although still being developed, are applied to the problems of physics research. In the mid 1970s the particle accelerators used in high-energy physics are extremely high-technology devices which encouraged the development of superconducting magnets (a product of low-temperature solid-state physics), high-power klystrons, and on-line minicomputers. The laser, a product of physics research, was applied immediately in further physics research.

In general, physics at any time involves studying the limits of knowledge. For example, in the early eighteenth century the laws of motion of ordinary matter (rocks and cannonballs) were not fully known, and their study was the activity of physicists and mathematicians. By the nineteenth century, the laws of ordinary matter,

as encountered in ordinary experience, were reasonably well known. The major activity of physicists had by then moved on to the study of puzzling phenomena of electricity and magnetism.

Galileo Galilei (1564–1642) is generally recognized as the first modern physicist. Many of the rules he established are still guidelines of the field, for example, a theory must agree ("reasonably well") with experiment, and an experiment must be reproducible. Galileo wrote about his experiments in sufficient detail that they can be reproduced. He, and the great theorist who followed him, Isaac Newton (1642–1727), dealt most successfully with mechanics, the motion and interaction of ordinary pieces of matter. Newton not only proposed fundamental laws of mechanics (which were not modified until the early 1900s by Albert Einstein), but he also discovered the universal law of gravitation. In the century after Newton, scientists used Newton's method to study the behavior of sound and heat, liquids and gases.

Electricity and magnetism were the next major phenomena reduced to formal laws by physicists. In 1873 James Clerk Maxwell (1831–1879) published his laws of electromagnetism, which are the basis of radio, radar, television, and related engineering fields. His theoretical laws unified the empirical laws of Charles A. de Coulomb (1736–1806) on the force between static charges; Jean Baptiste Biot (1774–1862) and Félix Savart (1791–1841) on magnetic field; and Michael Faraday (1791–1867) on changing magnetic field creating electric field. Maxwell also predicted the phenomena of electromagnetic radiation (radio and radar) and showed that light is an electromagnetic wave.

By the beginning of the twentieth century physics had turned away from electromagnetism and was studying very small objects (atomic physics), very large objects (astrophysics), and very fast objects (relativity). This was an extremely exciting time because these discoveries showed that our preconceptions of what "must" be were based on our everyday experience and were only a dim reflection of the richness of the real world. Albert Einstein (1879–1955) showed that measured length, time, and mass depends on the relative motion of the object and its observer. Ernest Rutherford (1871–1937) showed that most of the volume of an atom is empty. Louis Victor de Broglie (1892–) and Erwin Schrödinger (1887–1961) showed that matter does not move in simple paths but behaves like a wave.

Atomic physics and special relativity dominated the first thirty years of the twentieth century. General relativity started during the same period, but it is a much slower-moving field because of the difficulty of doing experimental work. Nuclear physics was the dominant field from about 1930 until about 1950, when high-energy (elementary-particle) physics blossomed. Solid-state physics also developed rapidly during this period. In 1975 elementary-particle physics was the most prolific field, followed closely by solid-state and astrophysics.

The mathematical laws and many of the practical procedures of physics continue to be of great use. For example, almost all engineering curricula include a year or two of studies of eighteenth- and nineteenth-century physics. Almost always, these courses are taught by physicists to introduce the engineering student to the motivation and techniques of exploration in physics. In addition, a significant amount of the knowledge gained by nuclear physics is now being applied by nuclear engineering to power plant development and, unfortunately, by weapons engineers to methods of mass destruction.

In antiquity, centers of learning usually had concentrations available in mathematics and in "natural philosophy." The teaching of "physics" dates from the post-Newtonian era. In modern physics education, a Ph.D. is a virtual necessity to perform front-line research. In fact, the typical physicist extends his training two or three years beyond the Ph.D. in postdoctoral research before he is fully trained.

Physics has, since the late nineteenth century, been almost totally international. Centers of modern physics exist in the United States, Europe, the Soviet Union, the People's Republic of China, and to some extent in Africa and South America. Problems and techniques are internationally recognized. There is considerable cross publication except in Soviet and Chinese journals, which are still highly national. Centers of study of elementary-particle physics particularly tend to be international, partly because of the enormous cost of the particle accelerators required in this field. The European Organization for Nuclear Research (CERN), in Geneva, Switzerland, was a joint undertaking of several European countries which could not separately afford the cost of the facility. When one country does build its own accelerator, the next accelerator is usually an improvement on the first and is built by another country. For example, the highest-energy accelerator in 1975 was in the United States at the National Accelerator Laboratory near Chicago. Before that, the accelerator at Serpukhov, in the Soviet Union, held that position, and before that, the CERN accelerator was the leader.

Meetings on forefront problems in physics are almost always international. For example, in 1975 the Fourth International Conference on Meson Spectroscopy was held at Northeastern University, with over 200 physicists attending, from thirteen different countries. There is a biannual conference in high-energy physics which cycles among the Soviet Union, the United States, and Europe. The only geographical boundaries in physics appear in times of international tension or war.

Training facilities in physics exist in most major countries; and wherever physics is well developed, there is a striking similarity of problems and techniques. The Arabic countries, Africa, and portions of South America are developing physics programs, but less industrialized countries generally do not participate much in the forefront of physics research. The dividing line, however, appears to be partly cultural as well as economic. It takes a couple of generations and much money to develop a physics center. Where physics is starting, but less developed, the portions of the field nearest to applied physics or engineering as well as the less expensive areas of physics research start up first. Thus, a Third World nation may stress nuclear engineering, or research in optics, or electromagnetism, rather than the more central front-line problems of particle physics, solid-state physics, and astrophysics. Generally the first front-line field attacked by a nation newly engaged in physics is solid-state physics.

ROY WEINSTEIN

Levels and Programs of Study

Programs in physics generally require as a minimum educational prerequisite a secondary education and lead to the following awards: certificate or diploma, bachelor's degree (B.S.), master's degree (M.S.), the doctorate (Ph.D.), or their equivalents. Programs deal with the principles and practices of physics and consist of classroom and laboratory instruction.

Programs that lead to an award not equivalent to a first university degree stress the practical applications of physics. Principal course content usually includes some of the following: evolution of modern physics, physical measurements, geometrical optics, wave theory, heat, statics, light, electrostatic and electromagnetic forces, thermodynamics, thermoelectricity, spectrometry, quantum mechanics, relativity, solid-state physics, and nucleonics. Background courses often included are geophysics, metrology, logic circuits, control systems, mathematics, chemistry, applied mechanics, drafting, photography, computer programing, and instrumental analysis.

Programs that lead to a first university degree stress the theoretical and funda-

mental principles of the subjects studied, although practical application is not ignored. Some programs may also include physical metallurgy. Principal course content usually includes some of the following: general physics, optics, physical optics, electricity, magnetism, theoretical mechanics, electromagnetic theory, electric circuits, atomic and nuclear physics, optical instruments, electrical measurements and measuring instruments, electronics, advanced mechanics, classical thermodynamics, theoretical physics, statistical mechanics, quantum mechanics, relativity, solid-state physics, physical metallurgy, structure of metals, and corrosion. Background courses often included are general chemistry, cosmology, astronomy, astrophysics, history of science, mathematics, humanities, social sciences, and languages.

Programs that lead to a postgraduate university degree deal with advanced subjects in the field of physics (or physical metallurgy). Emphasis is placed on original research work as substantiated by the presentation of a scholarly thesis or dissertation. Principal subject matter areas within which courses and research projects tend to fall include advanced subjects related to the physics field—for example, the quantum theory of solids, statistical mechanics, advanced thermodynamics, theoretical acoustics, applied group theory, advanced nuclear physics, advanced electricity and magnetism, quantum mechanics, atomic physics, advanced electronics, Fourier optics, physical metallurgy, the structure of metals, X-ray diffraction in metals, relativity and cosmology, fluid mechanics, superconductivity, advanced geophysics, and physics of the earth. Subject areas within which background studies tend to fall include appropriate specialties in chemistry, biology, geology, mathematics, statistical analysis, and social sciences.

[This section was based on UNESCO's *International Standard Classification of Education (ISCED)* (Paris: UNESCO, 1976.)]

Major International and National Organizations

INTERNATIONAL

European Physical Society
Association européenne de physique
% Dr. L. Etienne-Amberg, Executive Secretary
P.O. Box 39
CH-1213 Petit-Lancy 2, Switzerland

International Commission on Physics
Education
Science Department, Malvern College
Malvern, Worcestershire, England

International Institutes of Physics and
Chemistry
Instituts internationaux de physique et de
chimie
Université libre de Bruxelles
50 avenue Franklin Roosevelt
1050 Brussels, Belgium

International Union of Pure and Applied
Physics (IUPAP)
Union internationale de physique pure et
appliquée (UIPPA)
Université Laval
Quebec 10, Canada

Latin American Centre for Physics
Centro latinoamericano de física (CLAF)
avenida Wenceslau Braz 71
20,000 Rio de Janeiro ZC 82, Brazil

NATIONAL

A sampling of the many national physics
organizations is:

Australia:
    Australian Institute of Physics
    Clunies Ross House
    191 Royal Parade
    Parkville, Victoria 3052

France:
    Société française de physique
    12 place Henri Bergson
    75008 Paris, France

Italy:
    Società italiana di fisica
    Istituto di fisica
    via Irnerio 46
    Bologna 40126

United Kingdom:
    Institute of Physics
    47 Belgrave Square
    London SW1, England

United States:
    American Physical Society
    335 East 45th Street
    New York, New York 10017

For extensive listings of international and
national physics organizations consult:

*Guide to World Science: A New Reference Guide to
Sources of World Scientific Information.* (2nd
ed., 25 vols.) Guernsey, Channel Islands:
Francis Hodgson, 1974–1975.
*International Physics and Astronomy Directory
1969–70.* Reading, Massachusetts: W. A.
Benjamin, 1970.
Minerva, Wissenschaftliche Gesellschaften. Berlin,
Federal Republic of Germany: de Gruyter,
1972.
World Guide to Scientific Organizations. Pullach/
Munich, Federal Republic of Germany: Ver-
lag Dokumentation; New York: Bowker,
1974.
The World of Learning. London: Europa, 1947–.
Published annually.

Principal Information Sources

GENERAL

Guides to the literature include:

*Check List of Books for an Undergraduate Physics
Library.* (2nd ed.) New York: American Insti-
tute of Physics, 1966.
Coblans, H. *Uses of Physics Literature.* London:
Butterworth, 1975.
Parke, N. G. *Guide to the Literature of Mathematics
and Physics.* (2nd ed.) New York: Dover,
1958.
Roll, P. G. "Introductory Physics Textbooks."
Physics Today, 1968, *21,* 63–71.
Whitford, R. H. *Physics Literature: A Reference
Manual.* (2nd ed.) Metuchen, New Jersey:
Scarecrow Press, 1968.
Yates, B. *How to Find Out About Physics: A Guide
to Sources of Information.* Oxford, England:
Pergamon Press, 1965.

A sampling of the overviews and introductions to the field include:

Alonso, M., and Finn, E. J. *Fundamental Uni-
versity Physics.* (3 vols.) Reading, Massachu-
setts: Addison-Wesley, 1967–1968.
Beiser, A. *The Foundations of Physics.* Reading,
Massachusetts: Addison-Wesley, 1964.
The Berkeley Physics Course. (5 vols.) New York:
McGraw-Hill, 1965–1973. Vol. 1: C. Kittel,
W. D. Knight, and M. A. Ruderman, *Me-
chanics,* 1973; Vol. 2: E. M. Purcell, *Electricity*

and Magnetism, 1965; Vol. 3: F. S. Crawford, *Waves and Oscillations,* 1968; Vol. 4: E. H. Wichmann, *Quantum Physics,* 1971; Vol. 5: F. Reif, *Statistical Physics,* 1967.

Feynman, R. P., and others. *The Feynman Lectures on Physics.* (3 vols.) Reading, Massachusetts: Addison-Wesley, 1964–1965. Vol. 1: *Mainly Mechanics, Radiation, and Heat;* Vol. 2: *Mainly Electromagnetism and Matter;* Vol. 3: *Quantum Mechanics.*

Harnwell, G. P., and Legge, G. J. F. *Physics.* New York: Van Nostrand Reinhold, 1967.

Kip, A. F. *Fundamentals of Electricity and Magnetism.* (2nd ed.) New York: McGraw-Hill, 1969.

Resnick, R., and Halliday, D. *Physics.* (2 vols.) New York: Wiley, 1966.

Sears, F. W., and others. *College Physics.* (4th ed., 2 vols.) Reading, Massachusetts: Addison-Wesley, 1974.

Sears, F. W., and Zemansky, A. W. *University Physics.* (4th ed., 2 vols.) Reading, Massachusetts: Addison-Wesley, 1970.

Weber, R. L., and others. *College Physics.* (5th ed.) New York: McGraw-Hill, 1974.

Weinstein, R. *Atomic Physics and Nuclear Physics.* New York: McGraw-Hill, 1964.

Young, H. D. *Fundamentals of Optics and Modern Physics.* New York: McGraw-Hill, 1968.

Young, H. D. *Fundamentals of Mechanics and Heat.* (2nd ed.) New York: McGraw-Hill, 1973.

Sampling of the histories of the field:

Cajori, F. A. *A History of Physics in Its Elementary Branches, Including the Evolution of Physical Laboratories.* (Rev. and enl. ed.) New York: Macmillan, 1929.

Greider, K. *Invitation to Physics.* New York: Harcourt Brace Jovanovich, 1973.

Wilson, W. *A Hundred Years of Physics.* London: Duckworth, 1950.

Education in the field is discussed in:

Brown, S. C., and Clarke, N. (Eds.) *International Education in Physics.* Cambridge, Massachusetts: MIT Press, 1961. Results of the International Conference on Physics Education held in Paris in 1960.

Brown, S. C., and Clarke, N. (Eds.) *The Education of a Physicist.* Cambridge, Massachusetts: MIT Press, 1966. From the International Conference on Education of Professional Physicists held in London in 1965.

Hanle, W., and Scharmann, A. *The Teaching of Physics at University Level.* Strasbourg, France: Council for Cultural Co-operation, Council of Europe, 1967.

Lewis, J. L. *Teaching School Physics: A UNESCO Source Book.* Paris: UNESCO, 1972.

Lewis, J. L., and others. (Eds.) *New Trends in Physics Teaching.* Vol. 3. Paris: UNESCO, forthcoming.

Nagy, E. (Ed.) *New Trends in Physics Teaching.* Vol. 2. Paris: UNESCO, 1972.

A Survey of the Teaching of Physics at Universities. Paris: UNESCO, 1966. Covers United States, Soviet Union, United Kingdom, France, Federal Republic of Germany, and Czechoslovakia.

Warren, J. W. *The Teaching of Physics.* London: Butterworth, 1966.

CURRENT BIBLIOGRAPHIES

Bulletin signalétique. Part 130: *Physique.* Paris: Centre national de la recherche scientifique, 1940–.

CC-PCS (Current Contents: Physical and Chemical Sciences). Philadelphia: Institute for Scientific Information, 1961–.

Current Physics Index. New York: American Institute of Physics, 1975–.

Physical Review Abstracts. New York: American Physical Society, 1970–.

Physics Abstracts. London: Institution of Electrical Engineers, 1898–.

Physikalische Berichte. Brunswick, Federal Republic of Germany: Vieweg, 1920–.

Quarterly Checklist of Physics, Including Astronomy and Astrophysics. Darien, Connecticut: American Bibliography Service, 1960–.

Referativnyĭ zhurnal. Fisika. Moscow: Akademiia nauk, SSSR, Institut nauchnoĭ informatsii, 1954–.

The following journals keep physicists abreast of current information in the field:

Current Papers in Physics. London: Institution of Electrical Engineers, 1966–.

Physical Review Letters. New York: American Physical Society, 1958–.

Physics Letters. Amsterdam: North-Holland Publishing, 1962–.

PERIODICALS

A sampling of the important journals internationally for the field includes *Acta Physica* (Hungary), *Annalen der Physik* (GDR), *Arkiv för fysik* (Sweden), *Australian Journal of Physics, Canadian Journal of Physics, Chinese Physics/Acta Physica Sinica, Czechoslovak Journal of Physics, Helvetica Physica Acta* (Switzerland), *Indian Journal of Pure and Applied Physics, Journal de physique* (France), *Journal of Applied Physics* (US), *Journal of Chemical Physics* (US), *Journal of the Physical Society of Japan, Journal of Physics (A, B, C, D, E, F, G)* (UK), *Nuovo cimento (AB)* (Italy), *Physical Review (A, B1, B15, C, D1, D15)* (US), *Physical Review Letters* (US), *Physics Education* (UK), *Pro-*

ceedings of the Royal Society—A (UK), *Reviews of Modern Physics* (US), *Soviet Physics—Doklady, Soviet Physics—JETP, Zeitschrift für Physik* (FRG).

For listings of physics journals consult the following:

Maizell, R., and Siegel, F. *The Periodical Literature of Physics: A Handbook for Graduate Students.* New York: American Institute of Physics, 1961.
Ulrich's International Periodicals Directory. New York: Bowker, biennial.

DICTIONARIES, ENCYCLOPEDIAS, HANDBOOKS

Besancon, R. M. (Ed.) *The Encyclopedia of Physics.* (2nd ed.) New York: Van Nostrand Reinhold, 1974.
Clason, W. C. *Elsevier's Fachwörterbuch der Physik in sechs Sprachen: Englisch (amerikanisch)-französisch-spanisch-italienisch-niederländisch-deutsch.* Amsterdam and New York: Elsevier, 1962.
De Vries, L., and Clason, W. C. (Comps.) *Dictionary of Pure and Applied Physics.* Amsterdam and New York: Elsevier, 1963–1964. Volume 1 is German-English; volume 2 is English-German.
Ebert, H. *Physics Pocketbook.* London: Oliver and Boyd, 1967.
Fizicheskii entisiklopedicheskii Slovar. Moscow: Izdatelstvo "Sovetskaya Entsiklopediya," 1960–1966.
Gray, D. E. (Ed.) *American Institute of Physics Handbook.* (3rd ed.) New York: McGraw-Hill, 1972.
Madelung, E. *Die mathematischen Hilfsmittel des Physikers.* (7th ed.) Berlin, Federal Republic of Germany: Springer-Verlag, 1964.
The McGraw-Hill Dictionary of Scientific and Technical Terms. New York: McGraw-Hill, 1974.
Skibicki, W. (Comp.), and Jezenski, M. (Ed.) *Slownik terminow fizyenych: Polsko-angielsko-francusko-niemiecko-rosyjski.* Warsaw: Państwowe Wydawnictwo Naukowe, 1961.
Sube, R., and Eisenreich, G. (Eds.) *Wörterbuch Physik: Englisch, deutsch, französisch, russisch.* (3 vols.) Frankfurt am Main, Federal Republic of Germany: Harri Deutsch, 1974.
Thewlis, J. (Ed.) *Encyclopedic Dictionary of Physics.* Oxford, England: Pergamon Press, 1961–1964 and Supplements (1966–). Volume 9 of this work, *Multilingual Dictionary* (1964), contains physics terms in English with French, German, Spanish, Russian, and Japanese equivalents.
Weast, R. C. (Ed.) *Handbook of Chemistry and Physics: A Ready Reference Book of Chemical and Physical Data.* Cleveland, Ohio: Chemical Rubber Publishing Co., annual.

Westphal, W. H. (Ed.) *Physikalisches Wörterbuch.* Berlin, Federal Republic of Germany: Springer-Verlag, 1952.

DIRECTORIES

Graduate Programs in Physics, Astronomy, and Related Fields. New York: American Institute of Physics, 1971.
Guide to World Science: A New Reference Guide to Sources of World Scientific Information. (2nd ed., 25 vols.) Guernsey, Channel Islands: Francis Hodgson, 1974–1975. Includes descriptions of science policies and structures in various countries as well as a directory of scientific establishments worldwide.
International Physics and Astronomy Directory, 1969–1970. Reading, Massachusetts: W. A. Benjamin, 1970.
List of Colleges and Universities Offering Physics Majors. New York: American Institute of Physics, 1972.
Minerva, Forschungsinstitute. Berlin, Federal Republic of Germany: de Gruyter, 1972.
The World of Learning. London: Europa, 1947–. Published annually.

PLAN EUROPE 2000
See Education Project of Plan Europe 2000.

PLANNING, DEVELOPMENT, AND COORDINATION

1. OVERVIEW

2. INSTITUTIONAL PLANNING

3. STATE PLANNING IN UNITED STATES HIGHER EDUCATION

4. REGIONAL PLANNING OF HIGHER EDUCATION

5. NATIONAL PLANNING OF HIGHER EDUCATION

6. INTERNATIONAL EDUCATIONAL PLANNING AND DEVELOPMENT

1. OVERVIEW

Systematic planning of institutions of higher education has largely developed since World War II. Even in the industrialized nations, the development and maintenance of colleges and universities did not represent a major call on their human and physical resources until the 1950s, so that the need for long-range comprehensive plans was not generally recognized. Since then, however, planning has become an important feature of higher education throughout the world.

At the level of the political state, the need for planning is being felt from several quarters. Because higher education is increasingly seen by many as the means for becoming part of the social and political elite, those aspiring to this status for themselves or their children press for the establishment of new universities or the expansion of existing ones. Because higher education furnishes the primary avenue to professional occupations, both those wanting to enter these occupations and those seeking to expand professional services demand more resources for professional education. Increasingly, too, political leaders, as well as those in business and industry, are recognizing needs of the state for highly educated persons in various categories, such as economists, agriculturists, engineers, and scientists. Some political leaders are also sensing the value of having a supply of educated citizens who can provide informed guidance to help the nation solve the critical problems it faces.

In the developing nations, these demands for higher education are in competition with demands for universal literacy and for greatly expanded and reformed secondary education. The tremendous global expansion of radio and television has created an awareness of the value of literacy in nations where elementary education has been available only to a small fraction of the population. To build schools, train and employ teachers, and provide instructional supplies, far more resources are required than these nations have previously spent on education. At the same time, many opportunities for national economic development are dependent on the training of workers at the secondary school level, creating a strong demand for secondary education.

In the industrialized nations, the competition for resources comes largely from other public services: health, welfare, housing, and law enforcement. But in both the developing and the industrialized states, efforts to meet the demands for higher education and other services place a strain on the available resources. As the strain becomes apparent, initial steps are usually taken to obtain the information required for intelligent planning. A common first step is to estimate the demands in quantitative terms; that is, to translate the goals of the state's social, political, and economic development plan into the number of educated persons needed in each major occupational field and the costs for providing the education. This equation often gives a figure that is much greater than foreseeable resources could provide; consequently, several alternatives are considered in seeking to develop a plan that can be followed. One is to establish priorities among the demands by setting a balance among the competing social forces pressing the demands. A second is to establish priorities by trying to estimate in monetary terms the relative benefits to be obtained from each major program in relation to cost. For most programs that prepare professionals, however, the cost-benefit analysis is difficult, if not impossible, to make with sufficient reliability to justify the effort. A third alternative is to lengthen the time span for the development of programs and thus reduce the annual cost. Frequently, however, this procedure does not relieve the political pressure because the results the proponents desire are too long delayed.

As these financial estimates show costs for some programs or institutions that are far higher than the state can meet, the alternative of participation in developing regional resources and institutions and coordinating the use of them by the several states becomes attractive. This alternative is particularly important for states with limited resources. For these same states, however, national pride is not as well satisfied by being a part of a regional group as by having its own institution. Conflicts growing out of local pride are likely to plague regional arrangements and coordinating activities for many years, even while their value is being increasingly demonstrated.

Another alternative now recognized by most countries is the establishment and development of educational institutions and programs that seem likely to meet some of the pressing demands at lower cost. Two-year technical institutes and community colleges are illustrations of relatively new institutions that are now found in the plans of most nations. The creation of educational programs jointly conducted by educational institutions and industrial organizations (cooperative education) is another alternative. The design and establishment of new occupations requiring less than four-year college preparation to reduce unfilled demands for professionals in the health and education fields is a further illustration of plans that seek to maximize the use of scarce resources.

There are many indicators of how important planning for higher education has become at the level of the nation-state. For example, UNESCO and its subsidiaries and other specialized agencies of the United Nations, such as the Food and Agriculture Organization (FAO) and the World Health Organization (WHO), have furnished ideas and opportunities for cooperation in educational planning at the global level. The Organisation for Economic Co-operation and Development, the South-East Asian Ministers of Education organization and the Association of African Universities are examples of regional organizations formed to promote cooperation that includes planning for higher education. The foreign aid programs of several of the industrialized nations have included the provision of technical assistance in planning, as well as assistance in obtaining human and physical resources to implement plans. Finally, loans from the World Bank to aid the development of higher education require the formulation of long-range plans.

The international organizations are furnishing assistance for both national and regional planning; most of the latter, however, has involved plans for educational resources to be used jointly by several nations rather than an educational institution that is designed to serve and to be managed by several nations or a regional organization. Education appears to be viewed as having a local or national form and content by many people who fear that an international educational institution would lack the local or national ethos that colleges and universities have instilled, consciously or unconsciously. However, experiences with regional institutions are too limited to predict their ultimate survival and development.

At the institutional level, the need for planning arises from conditions similar in some respects to those at the national level. Pressures from business, industry, agriculture, and the civil service to provide college graduates with the appropriate background to meet their employment needs, combined with those from prospective students and their families to furnish educational opportunities to serve a range of occupational, social, and personal goals, produce demands for expansion and development that would require a substantial increase in resources. Furthermore, many of these pressures are for programs with which the institution has had no previous experience. For example, a college designed to offer a liberal education is pressed to provide programs in business administration and in nursing; a college that has focused its efforts primarily on the preparation of teachers is pressed to offer programs in the administration of justice and in engineering. In such cases, to meet the demands would involve not only the acquisition of increased financial support but also the building of new faculties and the development of appropriate curricula.

At the same time, most colleges and universities are being asked by the present staff to increase salaries, add personnel and new courses, and furnish more and more up-to-date equipment. The effort to meet these demands from without and within produces a strain on the available resources that results in the university administration's realization that all the requests and pressures cannot be met. Some means must be devised to establish priorities and a plan formulated to guide a long-range program of institutional development.

Like the nation-state, the institution usually explores several procedures for obtaining the information needed for intelligent planning. Most colleges and universities have depended on the several departments to produce initial educational plans. These plans, however, have usually reflected the viewpoints and special interests of existing departments and faculty members, giving little or no consideration to new needs and new areas of educational effort and no valid basis for making quantitative estimates of numbers of graduates needed in various categories and numbers of students required to produce the needed number of graduates. From the piecing together of departmental proposals to obtain an institutional plan, a second stage has been that of seeking to formulate a definite role for the institution and then to derive from this role model the programs to be offered, the numbers to be graduated, and the numbers of faculty members required in each program. But this procedure is also very limited since it fails to produce and consider dependable information about important factors external to the institution that should be considered in plans that can actually be implemented and achieve constructive results. Institutional planning that is conducted

by the staff of the institution based only on its experience, beliefs, and goals is likely to be seriously inadequate. When this inadequacy is recognized, the planning procedures are changed in an attempt to take into account the external environment in which the institution exists, depending as it does on the larger society to provide the resources of students, faculty, and finances, while it serves the larger society through its educational and knowledge-seeking activities. This symbiotic relationship to the larger society is easier to state and to recognize in general terms than it is to specify in relatively precise planning of what the institutional priorities are for a given time period and how these priorities are to be implemented. The problem is even more complex when consideration is given to rapid changes in some societies. In spite of these difficulties, many institutions are developing plans that seek to take into account relevant features of the external environment and that estimate what they will be like over the planning period. In the light of this outline of the external environment, an attempt is made to set major educational goals for the planning period. The plans usually include a proposed strategy designed to attain the goals by the end of the planning period. Finally, the plans specify what is to be undertaken in the immediate future, usually the next year. From this specification of environment, institutional goals, strategy, and immediate operating plan is derived an estimate of the resources to be obtained and their utilization, including staff, students, space, equipment, and financial support.

The results of these planning efforts appear to be mixed. Rarely have they been precise predictions in quantitative terms; usually they have served to make explicit the aspirations of the institution and its chief problems. Usually, too, those participating in the planning report that they have learned much and appear to be wiser for it. Institutional planning is likely to be a permanent feature of higher education, since the unplanned interaction among students, faculty, and sources of support does not furnish a comprehensive and informed basis for the maintenance and development of the multipurpose college and university system that has evolved.

One reason for the greater complexity of higher education today is its significant role in economic development. Earlier notions of development included as major factors the amount of capital invested in land and equipment, the quantity of available labor, and the quantity of useful raw materials. The agricultural colleges, which combined research, demonstration, and education to produce tremendous development in agricultural productivity, led the way to the contemporary belief in the importance of education and research in other fields as well as a major factor in economic development. In both industrialized and developing countries, this belief is strongly influencing both national and institutional planning for higher education. Planning boards are no longer comprised almost wholly of academic people; representatives from industry, business, and agriculture are now to be found in considerable numbers. But educational planning for economic development is still in infancy and takes several directions and many forms throughout the world.

Although there appears to be no consensus regarding specific planning procedures, certain basic principles are generally recognized. Most nations and institutions seek to involve representation on the bodies responsible for planning that includes persons from without as well as those employed within colleges and universities. The purposes of broad representation are to obtain first-hand information about the educational needs and attitudes of significant sectors of the society, to furnish communication channels from the planning body to these sectors both to inform them and to gain their support, and to obtain a range of informed judgments regarding proposed policies. The breadth of this outside representation varies greatly among nations and institutions, from those with only one or two public members to those that include representation from business, industry, labor, agriculture, the professions, government, and students.

A second widely recognized principle is that planning must be carried to the point of establishing a calendar specifying the times at which the several stages will be implemented and specified resources will be needed. The lack of a time schedule has caused many planning efforts to flounder or bog down completely.

A third recognized principle is that the information needed for effective planning includes both data regarding the kinds and amounts of human and physical resources required to implement the plan and corresponding information about their availability. A planning procedure that estimates for a certain program the requirements in numbers and training of faculty members in classrooms, libraries, and laboratories, in kinds and amounts of specialized equipment, and in numbers of qualified students to be enrolled but does not ascertain the probable availability of these factors is not likely to be a plan that can be effectively implemented.

A principle that is now slowly gaining recognition is that an effective plan must provide for the education or training of those responsible for its interpretation and implementation. Experiences with national plans demonstrate many misunderstandings of a plan that is turned over to colleges and universities to implement. Even though some of the university administrators and faculty members were involved in developing the plan, it is likely to be misinterpreted in the initial presentation to many who were not directly involved, and the resulting efforts at implementation do not produce the programs as planned. Even institutional plans developed by bodies on which the local faculty and administration are well represented are often grossly misunderstood, and the implementation is far different from the program as conceived.

As far as time is concerned, it appears to take three to five years of education and training for a new program—that is, a program very different from previous practice—to be implemented with reasonable similarity to the plan as developed and recorded. It is estimated that the cost of the initial education and training in such cases is about twice the annual operating cost of the program. Few groups have taken these factors of time and cost into account when they have developed their plans.

The several articles that follow describe planning organizations and procedures at the international level, the regional level, the national level, and the institutional level. They also identify some of the particular problems that emerge when realistic planning is undertaken and suggest the importance of evaluation as part of the planning procedure.

Evaluation is an essential part of the planning process in higher education, just as it is in other fields. The term *evaluation* was first used in education to refer to the process of ascertaining the degree to which students were attaining the educational objectives that had been established for the educational course or program. Now, however, the term *educational evaluation* is used to refer more broadly to a comparison of the actual features of the educational program with those assumed or expected in the plan. Thus, evaluation may check on the assumption of a national plan that five hundred qualified applicants will enroll annually in the nation's engineering schools if provision is made for teaching five hundred students. The evaluation in this case might show that only four hundred qualified applicants enrolled when the plan was put into operation.

Evaluation may also compare the actual results of a program with those expected. An institutional plan, for example, may expect that graduates of its program in political science will understand the ways in which the nation's legislative and executive departments operate and will be able to devise procedures for more efficient operations, but performance tests of the graduates' competencies may indicate that only 34 percent of them can devise practicable procedures.

These illustrations are only two of many possible examples to suggest that systematic evaluation is helpful in planning and operating educational programs to keep them in accord with reality. Evaluation is useful at various stages in planning, from the effort to identify educational needs through the development of educational objectives, the design of programs, the implementation of plans, and the estimation of results. In many cases, evaluation is difficult, because education is concerned with helping students to develop not only overt habits and skills but also ways of thinking and feeling that are not readily observable. Furthermore, the long tradition of evaluation has focused on testing the individual student to find out what he has remembered—a procedure that is only a small part of the evaluation needed to assist higher education.

Bibliography

Anderson, C. A. "The University of East Africa Plan, 1967–70: A Commentary." *Minerva,* 1969, 7(1-2), 35–51.

Anderson, C. A. "Sweden Re-examines Higher Education: A Critique of the U68 Report." *Comparative Education Review,* 1974, *10*(3), 167–179.

Anderson, C. A., and Bowman, M. J. "Theoretical Considerations in Educational Planning." In D. Adams (Ed.), *Educational Planning.* Syracuse, New York: Syracuse University Press, 1965.

Anderson, C. A., and Foster, P. "The Outlook for Education in Middle Africa." In F. S. Arkhurst (Ed.), *Africa in the Seventies and Eighties: Issues in Development.* New York: Praeger, 1970.

Beeby, C. E. *Qualitative Aspects of Educational Planning.* Paris: UNESCO, 1969.

Cowan, L. G. *Recent Developments of Higher Education in Francophone Countries.* Washington, D.C.: Overseas Liaison Committee, American Council on Education, 1969.

Foster, P. "Dilemmas of Educational Development: What We Might Learn from the Past." In *Education and Development.* Port Moresby: University of Papua New Guinea, 1975.

Foster, P. "False and Real Problems of African Universities." *Minerva,* 1975, *13*(3).

Foster, P. "The Political Economy of Universities in Anglophonic Africa." In *African University Development.* Berkeley: University of California Press, 1975.

International Institute of Educational Planning. *Fundamentals of Educational Planning.* Paris: UNESCO, 1969.

Laska, J. A. *Planning and Educational Development in India.* New York: Teachers College Press, Columbia University, 1968.

Lockwood, G. *University Planning and Management Techniques.* Paris: UNESCO, 1972.

Lyons, R. F. (Ed.) *Problems and Strategies of Educational Planning: Lessons from Latin America.* Paris: UNESCO, 1965.

Mendes, D. T. *Toward a Theory of Educational Planning: The Brazilian Case.* East Lansing: Latin American Studies Center, Michigan State University, 1972.

Myers, R. G. "Peruvian Educational Development and United States Policy." In D. Sharp (Ed.), *Peru: A Case Study of U.S. Foreign Policy.* Austin: University of Texas Press, 1972.

Nozhko, K., and others. *Educational Planning in the U.S.S.R.* Paris: UNESCO, 1968.

Onushkin, V. G. (Ed.) *Planning and Development of Universities.* Paris: UNESCO, 1971.

Organisation for Economic Co-operation and Development: Directorate for Scientific Affairs. *Educational Policy and Planning: France.* Paris: OECD, 1972.

Organisation for Economic Co-operation and Development: Directorate for Scientific Affairs. *Educational Policy and Planning: Germany.* Paris: OECD, 1972.

Organisation for Economic Co-operation and Development: Directorate for Scientific Affairs. *Educational Policy and Planning: Japan.* Paris: OECD, 1973.

United Nations Educational, Scientific, and Cultural Organization. *Educational Planning: A World Survey of Problems and Prospects.* Paris: UNESCO, 1970.

RALPH W. TYLER

See also: Manpower Planning; Trends in Higher Education.

2. INSTITUTIONAL PLANNING

Planning is not a set of complex techniques, a panacea, or an end in itself. It is the making of decisions, wherever possible, in a structured sequence and on the basis of all available information and relevant data. As such it is practiced in all universities, partly because decisions are normally deliberate and public acts and partly because they usually have to be taken well in advance of implementation due to the time scales on which such institutions operate. Since all universities are dependent on the societies in which they function, they have to plan in order to accommodate to changes in those societies. The increasing development of national systems and plans, for example, requires any institution to increase its own planning if it wishes to maximize its influence on its future. Thus, the immediate questions about institutional planning concern its nature and organization. The answers to these questions depend on a large number of variables affecting each individual institution: its size and rate of growth, the national system of which it is a part, the number of roles it performs, its governmental structure, its history, and the characteristics and attitudes of its members. Whatever the effects of those variables, institutional planners must utilize internal skills and enterprise in order to maximize their capacity for development as external events create the opportunity for change.

Basic Principles

Three basic planning principles are likely to have validity in all universities:

First, if the overall planning system is to remain effective, the approach to planning and the machinery for planning should be flexible and kept under regular review. At some time or for some areas of the university, student enrollment may be a prime criterion; at other times or for other areas, the prime criterion may be the balance of staff within or among disciplines. In either case, the mechanisms must be adjusted accordingly. The task of meeting these criteria can be aided by a regular turnover of the personnel responsible for organizing the planning process.

Second, all members of a university should participate in some aspect of planning, partly for internal political reasons, partly for their own benefit, but mainly to improve the quality and effectiveness of the planning process. To limit participation would be to restrict the range of experience and ideas brought to bear on the analysis of problems and the formulation of alternative solutions. More important, planning is a useless exercise unless the institution has the ability and the opportunity to change. Both of these prerequisites depend on a complex of factors. The ability to change is related to the institution's degree of structural flexibility, which in turn is related to the attitudes of its members. The opportunity to change partly turns on external judgments of the university. It is of little benefit, for example, to plan for the expansion of the university if the responsible national or state agency is not prepared to finance it. The task of management is to maximize these two prerequisites, both of which depend heavily on the attitudes of university members and their sense of being a party to the decisions. In the long run, therefore, planning can rarely be effective unless affected members are involved in the formulation of proposals.

Planning is not an activity that should be conducted by a few representatives aided by specialists and surrounded by a technical mystique. Those elements may be ingredients of the overall process, but to treat them as anything more is to misunderstand the nature and purpose of planning. Planning should be the collective exercise of foresight aimed at purposeful change; planning problems are mainly those of human relations. Any dangers resulting from unstructured involvement, such as an emphasis on equity planning (equal shares of resources for each existing group), can be counteracted with a carefully structured planning process. Each planning cycle should, for example, be guided by a set of assumptions that state the parameters within which the discussions should be held and that contain specific recommendations for action. The head of the institution should prepare

these assumptions and clarify the parameters throughout the cycle of discussions. In the absence of a clear framework of guidelines, participants can waste considerable time and energy. The members of an institution need to face the realities of planning, for example, by having to forecast the repercussions of their proposals or by suggesting ways in which resources can be released from existing activities to meet the costs of their development proposals. Individual groups may rightly seek to maximize their resources, and individual members may do so to enhance their career prospects. One of the functions of the framework of assumptions should be to ensure that they do so in ways that are not prejudicial to the development of the university as a whole.

Third, planning activity should be integrated both in terms of specialties and levels. Academic, financial, social, and physical factors should be interrelated at all points of the planning process, since they are not distinct activities that can be conducted in isolation or merely coordinated at certain times and stages in the process. Departmental, faculty, and university planning are not disparate activities and should be carried out in concert within an agreed framework, so that their interactions can be continually taken into account. The allocation of one additional academic faculty post will affect the educational, financial, spatial, and social aspects of the university, and the planning process must be able to accommodate all such decisions and their effects without stunting initiative or centralizing decision taking.

Theoretical Model

Although the way in which sound principles and practices are built into the organization of planning varies with the institution, the following theoretical model illustrates some of the main features of the planning process. For descriptive purposes, the model is divided into elements (strategic planning, operational planning, budgeting); contents (student and staff numbers, space, and social); levels and units (departments or faculties); cycles (annual or periodic); and supporting inputs (information, evaluation, and staff).

Elements. In considering elements it is helpful to distinguish among strategic, operational, and budgetary planning. Strategic planning is concerned with the setting of objectives and the selection of strategies to meet those objectives. This type of planning might be done through the explicit statement of the overall mission and of formal goals stemming from that mission or through concentration on specific issues, such as the rate of growth, the balance between main characteristics (roles, faculties, undergraduates/graduates), site capacity, and extension. Whatever the style, the primary focus of strategic planning should be to identify long-term issues and major decisions that could change the character, balance, or direction of the university's development. Strategic time scales will differ from university to university, depending on the particular critical problems or restraints involved. The time scale for an urban university contemplating significant expansion could be twenty years, since a critical problem is likely to be the purchase and clearing of nonuniversity property. On the other hand, the time scale for a rural university with extensive areas of unused land could be as short as five years. In this respect, the stage of development of the institution is the important variable. The foundation of a new institution (formation planning), the development of an institution in a strategic phase of growth (additive planning), the continuous renovation of an institution in a phase of no growth (steady-state planning), and the reorientation of a declining institution (subtractive planning) can be included in the model, but the emphasis of each will be vastly different. For example, the need to maintain flexibility over the use of marginal resources is paramount

in steady-state planning but of less importance in formation planning; the virtues of participation are stronger in additive than in subtractive planning.

Operational planning is the translation of strategic planning into specific action programs concerned, for example, with the forward allocation of staff posts; the determination of student intakes by course and major; the allocation of space; the introduction of new departments, courses, or research programs; major changes in curricula or teaching methods; forward financial estimates; and patterns of development of residential facilities. It should be conducted on a rolling basis, as far as is possible within any fixed national system. Forward plans should be amended each year in light of changed circumstances. A university cannot afford the time and effort of involving every one of its parts in a review of all its plans every year, and for this reason the annual cycle should be concerned with marginal change, leaving major replanning to the periodic cycle.

Budgetary planning involves the translation of the operational plan into a fixed plan for the year ahead. The degree to which the plan is fixed will depend on the methods adopted by the individual university. The plan could, for example, be fixed at the university level but, using the principle of devolution, the areas and units in the university could have authority to change their parts within agreed limits as circumstances change during the year. Although it is called budgetary, this level of planning covers all the contents of planning, such as agreement for the year ahead on the allocation of finances, the manpower budget, student intakes by course and subject, space allocation, and curriculum change.

Contents. The contents of planning include all of the activities of the university and all categories of resources within the planning function. Planning is often equated with means rather than ends, since it is expressed in resource and logistical terms, dealing with such items as unit costs, staff/student ratios, and space utilization. Even if planning in a particular institution is not directly concerned with ends (for example, the setting of role priorities and the specification of objectives for programs), there are means that need to be included in the planning process (for example, teaching methods, staff recruitment, admissions criteria, counseling procedures) other than those purely logistical in character.

Levels and units. The levels (tiers) and units involved in the planning process will depend on the organizational structure of the university. For purposes of description, the model defined here has three levels: university, faculty or equivalent, and department or equivalent. The university is represented by the governing body and the president or vice-chancellor. The faculty level is referred to as "areas," since *faculty* is not a term that can cover nonacademic equivalent units such as a community services group; ideally, the number of areas should not exceed ten, even though that may involve combining some existing faculties into a new joint area (for example, amalgamating theology and arts or law and social sciences). The departmental level is referred to as "units" for the same reason. The department of history may be a unit within the faculty of arts area in the same way as a residential accommodation service may be a unit within the community services area.

In planning functions the need for boundaries does not necessarily lead to rigidity in operational activity, but it does require a more complex process of resource allocation. The department of economics may provide teaching for the faculties of arts, social sciences, and applied sciences. The assignment of this department to the faculty of social sciences for organizational purposes should not lead to a reduction in the amount of cross-faculty teaching done by the department, but the resources needed for teaching have

to be calculated and then transferred from the departments of arts and applied sciences to the department of social sciences or directly to the department of economics.

Cycles. The planning process should require each unit, each area, and the university to produce strategic, operational, and budgetary planning documents for discussion and modification by the decision-making bodies of the institution. For this purpose the planning process should have an annual and a periodic cycle. The annual cycle, which would structure the flow of business through the levels over the academic year, might commence in August or September with the preparation by the leadership of the planning assumptions for the year. These planning assumptions are key to the cycle, incorporating comments on the strategic and operational plans from the previous cycle and containing the budgetary assumptions for the following year (for example, suggested allocation of resources to each area). The assumptions should also inject into the discussions information on external changes or pressures and on internal performance and should indicate the chief topics for discussion. The planning assumptions might then be discussed and approved by the governing body in the September/October period, being publicized (for example, in the university magazine) and passed to the unit level for action. They need not pass through the area level, partly to save time but mainly because comments and ideas ought to be generated from the level closest to the point of action. The unit members should be asked to revise their unit plans and to forward the updated version to the area level by the end of January, after consulting any other unit that might be affected by the proposed changes. For instance, an academic department should be required to consult with the library before it proposes the introduction of a new course that would involve library development in a new subject area. The area level should then use the planning assumptions and the amended unit plans to revise the area plan for presentation to the governing body in March. From March to May the governing body should revise the strategic, operational, and budgetary plans of the university, prior to implementation. Although the strategic and operational plans may be fed back into the following year's annual cycle, they should remain valid for purposes of action until they are again revised by the governing body.

In practice, many adjustments need to be made to this part of the model. First, a university must retain the capacity to take urgent decisions quickly. Second, it is not necessary that all the elements and contents of the planning process involve all areas and units each year. The annual planning assumptions need to allow room for assessment of how much business the participants in the cycle can and should bear in any given year. The purpose of a cycle is not to inculcate a reverence for planning but to ensure that decisions are taken at the right time by the right people, to integrate the several strands of planning (academic, physical, social), and to increase the openness of the planning system. It is unfortunately the case that in large and complex institutions such aims require bureaucratic organization for their achievement.

The periodic cycle should occur at intervals set by the institution (for example, a three- or five-year period). It should follow the same procedural format as an annual cycle, using the same bodies and the same flow but with an emphasis, particularly in terms of evaluation, that marks it as a significant break point in the planning process. In the periodic cycle discussions should concentrate on the reappraisal of the strategic plan and on the formulation of the next operational plan.

Supporting inputs. One administrative officer should be responsible for assisting the vice-chancellor or the president in the coordination of the planning process as a whole. The designated officer should work with the area (faculties, institutes) and specialist offices (finance, buildings) to ensure the smooth functioning of the process, to keep in touch with the dispersed planning activities throughout the annual cycle, to maintain schedules, and to sort out frictions caused by conflicting or overlapping proposals and discussions.

Coordination of analytical and developmental work within the planning process should be the responsibility of the chief administrator. Also, as much as possible, the analytical work should be conducted by the offices responsible for operational activity. For example, the finance office should be responsible for analyses of financial planning, the admissions office for student demand projections, the social studies area office for the analysis of course and option selection patterns and forecasts. Officers and administrators should not be divided into "planners" and "implementers." Removal of planning and analytical work from the operational offices not only stunts the development and motivation of the personnel in those offices but also removes the planning team from the forces of reality.

However, some analytical work cuts across operational office boundaries: correlating and manipulating the various sets of data and analyses from the operational offices (for example, using student numbers, recurrent costs, and capital cost projections to determine costs per student in each department or course); conducting analyses and development exercises specially requested by planning bodies that themselves cut across the operational divisions; evaluating planning effectiveness; and analyzing external factors and changes for insertion into the internal process. There are several ways in which such categories of staff work can be undertaken, and solutions will depend on the staffing strengths and structures at each institution; however, unless all of this work is given to the management information office, each of the functions should be allocated clearly.

The importance of accurate and relevant

information in decision making is obvious; the full range of data cannot be listed here. However, it needs to be stressed that information must be sifted and structured to be of use in the planning process. Over-provision of information can be as inefficient as underprovision. The management information in decision making is obvious; annually produce critical-indicator profiles for each unit, each area, and the university as a whole. These profiles should include a categorized analysis of income and expenditure, space occupied, space per student or unit of activity, model teaching methods and average class size, and number of research workers, as well as more specialized items for particular units (for example, material usage indicators in the library).

Evaluation should be an integral part of the planning process. The work of the management information office or its equivalent (for example, in the production of critical indicators) represents a limited form of evaluation, since the information it provides serves only as a checklist for generating more searching questions. Although every activity of the university cannot be scrutinized each year, some should be selected for annual evaluation to provide relevant assessments for the periodic cycle. A small budget should be available for this purpose, and the exercises need not require a permanent planning office; they could be conducted on a contract basis by project teams, by academic groups within the university, or by external agencies. Evaluation exercises should include surveys of consumer satisfaction (for example, student feedback on courses of study, staff comment on library service, employer attitudes toward ex-students in employment); quantitative analyses of a more detailed nature than those conducted routinely each year (for example, use of staff time); and behavioral studies (for example, the effects of budgetary devolution). The examples given assume that the university has made changes in these fields, since evaluation should be concerned with attempting to ascertain the effects of previous decisions.

Techniques

The focus of this article is on the nature and processes of planning rather than on the repertoire of available planning techniques, partly because techniques are of secondary importance, since their effective use depends on the existence of an efficient process for the making of planning decisions. Moreover, techniques are less lasting than processes and have less common applicability in that they must be selected to meet the particular problems of the individual university. Experience has shown that there is a long acceptance time attached to many techniques; for example, it may take a few years before a university can fully utilize a computerized model for relating staff posts to student numbers, so that there will be sufficient time to train staff in the use of the technique and to develop a "home-grown" formula that can be accepted with greater confidence.

The techniques available for planning include computerized simulation models of the whole institution, forecasting mechanisms, replacement theory, cost-benefit analysis, systems analysis, program budgeting, policy analysis, critical path and PERT (Program Evaluation and Review Technique) methods, regression analysis, marginal costing, and linear programing. However, one must keep in mind that some techniques, such as computer-based mathematical models, are extremely expensive in terms of manpower and equipment, and their applications have not been the subject of conclusive cost-effectiveness studies. In addition, such models are largely static in concept, having to operate on the assumption that trends of the present will continue into the future, whereas universities operate in an increasingly dynamic environment.

The selection of techniques has to depend on the size and history of the particular institution and on the skills, experience, and resources it has available. However, the main advantage of most techniques lies in their scientific or systematic base, which requires specificity of inputs, the need to state assumptions and aims, an understanding of the effects of decisions, and the need for feedback. Such techniques impose a discipline on decision making; their output also supplies a starting point for discussion on a particular issue— that is, the application of a technique concerning the optimization of the use of resources within a unit does not provide an objective answer but a set of figures on which judgment or political debate can be based. Simple and inexpensive techniques can afford the same basic advantages as computer-based models; for example, the annual production of a profile of critical indicators for a unit will impose systems discipline and serve as a starting point for discussion; moreover, such a profile is more easily understood than a computerized, mathematical optimization model.

Planning in a university community should be phrased in terms that fall within the experience of the members. Those members should be given the opportunity to understand and absorb the techniques that will allow them to participate in the planning process.

Formal Models

The previous discussion has concentrated on a theoretical model of the planning process that can be easily and inexpensively implemented. While no one single working system can be transferred from one institutional environment to another, the aims and organizational principles of the system can. Formal models embodying those aims and principles do exist in the literature of planning; for example, PPBS (Program Planning and Budgetary System) and PAR (Policy Analysis Review). Any institution preparing to invest intensively in planning would be well advised to study those models in depth. For further infor-

mation on PPBS, see the last two references in the following bibliography.

Bibliography

Beeby, C. E. *Planning and the Educational Administrator*. Paris: UNESCO, 1967.

Bolin, J. G. *Institutional Long-Range Planning*. Athens, Georgia: Institute of Higher Education, 1969.

Budgeting, Programme Analysis and Cost-Effectiveness in Educational Planning. Paris: Organisation for Economic Co-operation and Development, 1968.

Dressel, P. L., and Associates. *Institutional Research in the University: A Handbook*. San Francisco: Jossey-Bass, 1971.

Dressel, P. L., and Pratt, S. B. *The World of Higher Education: An Annotated Guide to the Major Literature*. San Francisco: Jossey-Bass, 1971.

Fielden, J., and Lockwood, G. *Planning and Management in Universities: A Study of British Universities*. London: Chatto and Windus (for Sussex University Press), 1973.

Knowles, A. S. (Ed.) *Handbook of College and University Administration*. Vol. 1. New York: McGraw-Hill, 1970.

Menges, G., and Elstermann, G. *Capacity Models in University Management*. Proceedings of the Seventeenth International Conference, Institute of Management Science. Saarbrücken, Federal Republic of Germany: Universität des Saarlandes, 1970.

Parden, R. J. (Ed.) *An Introduction to Program Planning, Budgeting and Evaluation for Colleges and Universities*. Santa Clara, California: Office of Institutional Planning, University of Santa Clara, 1970.

Program Planning-Budgeting-Evaluation System Design: An Annotated Bibliography. Chicago: Research Corporation of the Association of School Business Officials, 1969.

G. LOCKWOOD

See also: Financial Affairs: Budgeting, Cost Analysis; Institutional Research; Statistics in Higher Education; Steady State.

3. STATE PLANNING IN UNITED STATES HIGHER EDUCATION

Those who would understand American higher education must look first to the crucial role played by the states in the United States federal pattern of government. Even before the states formally existed, some of the colonies were giving public aid to the private colleges within their territory. The Tenth Amendment to the United States constitution of 1789 made it clear that all powers not delegated to the national government or prohibited to the states were to be reserved to the states and to the people. The power over education was one of these reserved powers.

Given a primary role both by history and by the constitution, all states have created a state university and such additional institutions as the particular state conditions might seem to require. Some states had established public universities by the end of the eighteenth century; most states did so during the course of the nineteenth century; and a few established systems as recently as the twentieth century. The diversity in the size, cost, and complexity of state systems is very large: on the one hand, in 1973–1974 a small state like Delaware educated some 25,000 students in its public institutions (one university, one state college, and three community colleges), with state appropriations totaling about $31,300,000; on the other hand, a state like California educated some 1,300,000 students in about 125 public campuses (9 university campuses, 19 state colleges, and nearly 100 community colleges), with state appropriations totaling $1,230,000,000. States like California, New York, Pennsylvania, Michigan, and Texas operate systems of higher education easily equivalent in size, cost, and complexity to all but a relatively few foreign national systems. Thus, the analysis of state planning efforts is no mere academic exercise.

The United States national government, through the use of its spending powers since the end of World War II, has come to play a major role in higher education, especially in funding university research and student access on a broad scale. Nevertheless, the primary responsibility for planning, coordinating, and financing higher education remains at the state level. Originally, much of this state responsibility was delegated to the governing boards of the public institutions. The trustees of these boards were publicly appointed or elected and were presumed to govern not only in the interests of the institutions in question but also with some sensitivity to the protection of the public interest. Prior to the middle of the nineteenth century, problems that occasionally emerged about finances or programs could usually be worked out directly between the university and the state government. Student numbers were then relatively low, state costs were still relatively modest, and curriculum issues during the period of classical studies were relatively straightforward.

However, during the century following the end of the Civil War in 1865, basic changes occurred in American society and in higher education that caused the states to modify their original practice of deferring to institutional boards. A rural, agricultural society shifted toward an urban, industrial one; government at both the state and national levels moved away from laissez-faire toward extensive regulatory and welfare activities; and access to higher education broadened from approximately 2 percent of the college-age group in 1869 to approximately 52 percent in 1972. With these changes came increases in the number and diversity of institutions, in costs, and in complexity of curricular issues.

In addition to the state university, most states subsequently added some or all of the following higher education institutions: (1) Land-grant institutions, based on the Morrill Act of 1862, featured the agricultural and mechanical arts but later began to move into curricular areas overlapping those of the state university. In many states, land-grant institutions also evolved into state universities. (2) Normal schools, two-year institutions for teacher training, began as a result of the movement toward compulsory secondary education. These institutions usually evolved into state teachers colleges. Some then became state colleges offering bachelor's and master's degrees in liberal arts and business administration as well as in education. Finally, increasing numbers have been designated as state universities, with expansion into doctoral-level work occasionally permitted. (3) Junior colleges were based on the need to extend access to higher education to urban youth, relatively neglected by the placement of many nineteenth-century state institutions. As time passed, these institutions broadened their functions and became community colleges offering college-transfer, two-year technical, and adult education programs. Although most of these institutions began as products of local government, problems connected with their funding, planning, and coordination (for example, efforts by some to become four-year colleges) have brought them more and more into the state systems.

Because of this growth and diversification, the states' traditional pattern of dealing with (and largely deferring to) institutional governing boards in a bilateral context gradually gave way to the establishment of statewide agencies that dealt with higher education institutions on a multilateral basis. Such statewide agencies seemed necessary because institutional governing boards, which tended to push aggressively for bigger, better, and more expensive facilities and programs, did not always seem to be working in the public interest. In addition, governors and legislators, despite considerable experience in working through even bitter budgetary fights, lacked a frame of reference by which to judge the increasingly complex questions of allocations of programs and changing institutional missions. Thus, statewide agencies of higher education were established to provide advice more specialized than that available from the regular legislative and executive staff of the state and more disinterested than that available directly from the institutions. Through time, it was found that this agency advice was more meaningful if given in the context of broader planning guidelines. Thus, agency functions gradually turned from emphasis on ad hoc program and mission recommendations to long-range planning.

While some state planning preceded the establishment of these statewide boards of higher education, and while some state planning now occurs in places other than these boards, by and large they have come to play a major role in state efforts to plan higher education. More recently, the establishment of State Post-Secondary Education Commissions (known as 1202 Commissions) has made the situation more complicated. The national Education Amendments Act of 1972 included a Section 1202, which provided that states could create a state commission broadly representative of all units of postsecondary education, public and private. These commissions would receive some earmarked federal funds for the improvement of comprehensive statewide planning. Although the funds thus earmarked were extremely modest (around $26,000 per state the first year, then graduated up to $100,000 for the largest states), forty-six states had established such planning agencies by the second year. In thirty states the authorities either designated an existing state agency as a 1202 Commission or augmented the membership of an existing agency to make it more broadly representative. In sixteen other states, however, new 1202 Commissions were created.

The Nature of State Planning

An idealized model of comprehensive statewide planning would include "the identification of key problems, the accumulation of accurate data about those problems, the analysis of their interrelationships, the extrapolation of future alternatives which might emerge out of present conditions, the assessment of the probable consequences of introducing new variables, the choice of the most desirable (or least undesirable) modified alternatives as the basic goals, a sequential plan for implementing the desired goals, and a built-in feedback system for periodically reevaluating both the goals selected and the means used to achieve them. Naturally, the broader the problems analyzed and the longer the time span covered, the more difficult the planning job" (Berdahl, 1971, p. 74). Until relatively recently most state planning efforts fell considerably short of this comprehensive model. Eells, in a 1937 study, *Surveys of American Higher Education,* found that the earliest state studies were made in 1912, in North Dakota, Pennsylvania, and Virginia. In 1936 alone, Eells identified fifty-one different surveys. However, these early surveys were mostly fact finding and limited in scope. The first state reports to be called master plans appeared only after World War II. One of the better known of these master plans was the *Report on the Needs of California in Higher Education* (University of California Committee, 1948), followed by the *Restudy of the Needs of California in Higher Education* (Liaison Committee, 1955) and the widely heralded *Master Plan for Higher Education in California 1960–1975* (California Master Plan, 1960). During the 1950s many states, lacking the internal planning capabilities required, turned to outside consultants for their educational planning.

By the 1960s it had become much more common for states to turn to their statewide boards of higher education for planning, although some used governors' ad hoc commissions and state legislative committee studies. Contracts by the states with consulting firms also began to have an impact on educational planning during this period. A survey of statewide planning in 1969 found that twenty-three states had master plans; eight others were in the process of completing them; and an additional seven were expected to develop such a plan (Abrahams, 1969). A preliminary survey conducted in 1975 indicated that perhaps as many as thirty-five states had completed some kind of long-range plan.

However, there has been some movement away from the concept of undertaking one comprehensive master plan at infrequent intervals in favor of an approach that uses more continuous planning based on strategic and tactical dimensions (Task Force on Statewide Comprehensive Planning for Postsecondary Education,

1971.) Using this approach, strategic planning, undertaken every five to seven years, would set out the state's fundamental assumptions about postsecondary education. These would include long-range societal objectives and goals and the principal missions, roles, and functions of all educational institutions and agencies. In other words, strategic planning establishes the fundamental premises, value judgments, philosophies, and purposes for which tactical planning then devises the means toward achievement. Tactical planning involves both short- and intermediate-range analysis of priority problems, within the established strategic framework. Tactical planning is continuous (in the sense that the planning process is never terminated) and rolling (in the sense that other cycles may be begun while earlier ones are continuing).

The Concerns Addressed in Current State Plans

State plans written in the mid 1970s reflect the emergence of new problems and public demands in American higher education: the slowing of enrollment growth in traditional higher education institutions, the leveling off of state funding for higher education at the same time that public demand for greater institutional accountability is increasing, and increased pressure to extend greater educational opportunities to segments of the population unable to participate in traditional full-time study.

A reading of twelve state plans, written since 1971, reveals that these concerns are common to all, although individual plans differ in comprehensiveness, scope, and sophistication of treatment. The twelve plans, chosen because they represent efforts at fairly broad planning by an interesting cross section of states, come from California, Connecticut, Florida, Illinois, Michigan, Montana, New Jersey, New York, Pennsylvania, Texas, Virginia, and Washington. All of these state plans include planning for a stabilizing system and for an increase in accountability and efficiency. In addition, they call for a broadening of the public higher education system to include consideration of the needs and resources of private and vocational-technical institutions and of increasing equality of opportunity. At the student level, this goal would be aided by special programs for disadvantaged students and by development and support of programs for adult learners. At the faculty and staff level, equality would be advanced through affirmative action programs to promote the hiring of qualified women and minority group members.

Planning for a stabilizing system. In the 1960s most state plans dealt with expansion of state systems of higher education. In the 1970s state plans were concerned with ways to undertake orderly slowdowns or even retrenchment in higher education systems. The leveling off of enrollments, with decline probable in the 1980s, and a corresponding leveling off of state funding in some states, necessitated this reorientation in planning.

In states such as Connecticut, Texas, and Washington, state plans have advocated a moratorium on the construction of conventional four-year campuses. However, some states' plans noted unmet needs, such as the need for additional community colleges in New Jersey or for off-campus facilities in Washington. In Montana, where enrollments had already begun declining, a 1974 report called on the state regents to consider closing a state college where enrollments had dropped significantly. But closure of institutions is an extreme measure, and few state plans have advocated it. More planning for the possibility of institutional closure may be expected by the early 1980s, when total enrollments may begin to fall.

Another response to the need for orderly scaling down and retrenchment in higher education is an increased emphasis in state plans on review of academic degree programs. For example, by linking its review of certain proposed new programs to evidence of institutional reallocations in existing programs, the Washington state plan would hold down the number of degree programs. More important, a number of state plans, such as those for Illinois and Montana, advocate that existing programs be subject to statewide review—and possible termination. Some states, such as New York, had begun such action by 1975.

In a period of slowing growth in enrollments and funding, a concern for the maintenance and promotion of diversity and flexibility is expressed in many state plans. The policy guidelines for the Florida plan recommend that faculty and administrative personnel be provided opportunities for professional retraining. State plans in Connecticut and Virginia recommend that the statewide boards be given funds to be used in awarding grants to institutions for the development of nontraditional programs. And, as noted below, several states recommend statewide development of flexible and nontraditional approaches to higher education. Yet, although there has been some sharp differentiation of functions among institutions (notably in Illinois), state plans by and large have not recommended significant changes in the roles and scope of existing institutions. In California, for example, the 1976–1981 state plan reaffirms the differentiation of function among the three public segments of higher education (the state research university, the comprehensive state colleges and universities, and the community colleges) established by the state's 1960 master plan. The California plan and many other state plans suggest that existing institutional roles and the differentiation of functions among institutions are essentially adequate to meet the requirements of the coming period of stabilization and retrenchment.

Increasing accountability and efficiency. Although almost all of the twelve state plans present enrollment projections, several (for example, Montana and Washington) do not present projections of the financial costs—to the state, the student, and the institution—of their expected and recommended future systems. Most of the plans emphasize the need for greater efficiency in the use of funds and other resources and increased accountability to the public and to the student-consumer.

One way toward increased accountability is regular program review. Suggested criteria for program review include efficiency and lack of duplication among programs, manpower requirements and quality of the program.

Also important in increasing efficiency are interinstitutional agreements for the coordination or sharing of programs, facilities, faculty, and students. These are suggested in a number of state plans, including those for Connecticut, Illinois, and Massachusetts. In Illinois, Phase III of the Master Plan for Higher Education in Illinois (Illinois Board of Higher Education, 1971) recommends study of the feasibility of a collegiate common market that would enable the pooling of all educational resources, public and private. A number of plans, such as those for California and Pennsylvania, have suggested the idea of intrastate regionalization of planning as a means of reducing unnecessary duplication of programs among institutions in the same geographical area. Similarly, several state plans, such as that for Washington, advocate reciprocity agreements between states when similar programs on both sides of a state border cannot be supported; to date, most interstate agreements have involved high-cost programs such as veterinary medicine. The development of statewide computerized information systems for finance and budget (Connecticut) or for student aid (Washington) have also been advocated for increased efficiency.

Finally, a new theme that emerges in state plans is a concern for student-consumer protection. The Washington state plan, for example, recommends legislation prescribing minimum standards of quality, safety, and fair business practices in proprietary institutions (institutions run for profit). It also notes its intention to study the effectiveness of vocational programs in both public and private institutions and requests institutions to examine their consumer practices with regard to students.

Broadening the higher education system. In the 1960s state plans tended to encompass only the public institutions of higher education in the state. In the 1970s several factors have led to the inclusion in state plans of private as well as public institutions and of vocational-technical institutions as well as those in the traditional higher education area. Among these factors are the need to utilize all resources at a time of increasing financial pressures, the precarious position of private institutions in some states, and social and public pressure to expand the range of programs considered as postsecondary.

The extent to which state plans actually include these elements, however, varies widely. In the Montana report, for example, private institutions are only marginally addressed. However, enrollments in private institutions in Montana are a rather small part of total higher education enrollments in the state. At the opposite extreme is New York, where a relatively large proportion of students (about 40 percent) are enrolled in private institutions and the state board for higher education exercises greater control over private institutions than in any other state in the United States. The 1974 New York progress report (on the 1972 state plan), *Postsecondary Education in Transition* (Regents of the State of New York, 1974), has thus incorporated private institutions even into its recommendations for review of doctoral programs, and the state undertook a study for the "orderly closure" of failing institutions, public or private. Although other state plans do not appear to encompass the private institutions to the extent that New York does, many seek to encourage interinstitutional arrangements between public and private institutions (for example, Illinois) and to provide for aid to students in private institutions or even direct aid to private institutions (for example, New Jersey). Others have recommended studies of the financial condition of private institutions (for example, California).

State plan attention to public vocational-technical institutions and to proprietary institutions also varies widely. For example, the 1972 New York plan, *Education Beyond High School* (Regents of the State of New York, 1972), not only addressed the role and resources of proprietary institutions at some length but also briefly examined the contributions of non–school-based training and educational programs, such as those offered by business and industry. Other state plans do not mention these institutions and programs at all. No state plan has yet been able to gather adequate data on such noncollegiate postsecondary institutions and programs as postsecondary educational courses, programs, and opportunities offered by proprietary and public vocational-technical institutions, by non-school-based training programs in industry, and by libraries and museums. However, many states are developing inventories to include such data.

Extending equality of opportunity. A final theme of state plans of the mid 1970s has been the extension of greater opportunities both to those denied opportunities because of their economic, social, or ethnic situation and to those whose life situation prevents them from attending traditional, full-time study on college campuses—that is, working and homemaking adults.

Continuing education programs (that is, generally part-time day and evening programs that may or may not offer college credit), in which most working and homemaking adults are enrolled, are given priority in many state plans. In California adult education ranks second (behind a statewide information system) in the plan's list of priority problems to be addressed. Other state plans recommend that continuing education courses given by universities count for degree credit and be fully transferable (Virginia); that continuing education programs leading to a degree, di-

ploma, or certificate receive state funding at a level comparable to that provided for regular on-campus programs (Washington); that part-time students, including those in the continuing education division, be eligible for (prorated) student aid (Connecticut).

In extending educational opportunities to those who cannot attend a traditional college program, some state plans have proposed programs that differ from regular on-campus programs not only in the hours in which they are conducted but in the methods of learning and/or assessment of learning which are utilized. Credit by examination, credit for appropriate work experience, and compilation and documentation of an individual's various educational experiences through a centralized "credit bank" are among the assessment methods being recommended or implemented in current state plans. The most important of these state programs is the New York Regents External Degree Program, which has developed a series of proficiency exams that test individuals' self-acquired knowledge and thus enable individuals to obtain a college degree without their having to attend any formal college classes; the New York program strongly influenced the planning of somewhat similar programs in such states as New Jersey and Connecticut.

In addition to extending greater educational opportunities to working adults, increasing educational opportunities for those of college age remains a primary concern of all state plans. In particular, state plans are concerned with the need for increasing the availability of student aid to low-income students at a time when both state and institutions tend to be under financial pressure. Many plans recommend initiating or expanding financial assistance to students in private institutions, in order partially to offset the higher tuition costs such students must pay (for example, Connecticut). State plans also urge that institutions or the state provide adequate counseling and other supportive services to students, especially to disadvantaged students. On the other hand, state planners seem uncertain just how much of his educational costs the college student should pay. Most plans do not recommend immediate substantial increases in tuition charges at public institutions, but several states (for example, Washington) note that they intend to study further what share of costs should be paid by the student.

Finally, many state plans are concerned with promoting affirmative action, that is, the hiring of qualified women and minority-group members for college faculties and staffs. While some plans simply state affirmative action as a goal, one state plan, that for Connecticut, recommends that public institutions not currently under federal regulations to prepare affirmative action plans prepare such plans for the state.

Major Problems in State Planning

In the 1960s state planning was essentially "means-oriented," quantitative planning for expansion in a context of relative affluence. Planning in the 1970s has become more "ends-oriented," an effort to improve quality during a period of slow growth and fiscal austerity.

Furthermore, the effort to broaden the planning of higher education to include many types of students, programs, and institutions not traditionally included has engendered several problems. Among these are the need to identify new types of students (for example, adult learners, including senior citizens) and their special program needs; the greater difficulty of constituent participation in statewide planning when the constituency has been thus broadened; the need to adapt the planning information system to include categories and definitions that apply to all included units; the necessity to reexamine the concept of differentiation of function (that is, certain institutions undertaking certain functions) in the light of the inclusion of

more and different types of institutions; and the thorny issue of the degree of accountability to be expected of the private sector in exchange for its increasing receipt of state monies.

In addition to these new problems, there still remain some unresolved problems from the earlier era—establishing closer linkages between the planning process and state budgeting and program review and integrating planning for student access when separate jurisdictions exist for admissions policies, state student aid programs, and institutional tuition policies.

The increasing importance of meshing federal and state programs in postsecondary education creates another planning problem. Federal programs in the student aid and university research areas, for example, have an important impact on state institutions, and ways must be found for state planning to take them into account more successfully than at present.

State plans, it is sometimes charged, are too often unrealistic public relations documents. Especially when the planners have little or no authority to implement them, state plans may have little impact on public policy. Unfortunately, few states have sought to assess the extent to which the recommendations of their state plans have been implemented.

Even when the apparent correlation between recommendations and actions is high, the question of the impact of state planning remains. In *Long Range Planning for Higher Education,* for example, Mayhew (1969, p. 102) noted: "Typically, master plans have been initiated through political desire for greater efficiency in higher education, social desire to extend its opportunities, and economic desire to produce the skilled workers needed for a technological society. It is difficult to say whether master plans have in fact facilitated this Indiana and Illinois have populations of about the same educational attainment, but one has an elaborate master plan and the other has none. Michigan has no master plan and California has a complex one, but both have distinguished systems of higher education universities of the highest quality." The problem is, of course, that there are so many intervening variables between the planning that occurs and the results that seem to follow.

Bibliography

Abrahams, L. *State Planning for Higher Education.* Washington, D.C.: Academy for Educational Development, 1969.

Berdahl, R. O. *Statewide Coordination of Higher Education.* Washington, D.C.: American Council on Education, 1971.

California Master Plan Survey Team. *A Master Plan for Higher Education in California, 1960–1975.* Sacramento, California: State Department of Education, 1960.

California Postsecondary Education Commission. *Planning for Postsecondary Education in California: A Five Year Plan 1976–81.* Sacramento: California Postsecondary Education Commission, 1975.

Connecticut Commission on Higher Education. *Master Plan for Higher Education in Connecticut, 1974–79: Quality and Equality.* Hartford: Connecticut Commission, 1974.

Coordinating Board, Texas College and University System. *Texas Higher Education, 1968–1980; A Report to the 64th Texas Legislature.* Austin, Texas: Coordinating Board, 1975.

Eells, W. C. *Surveys of American Higher Education.* New York: Carnegie Foundation, 1937.

Florida Board of Regents. *Assumptions, Commitments and Policy Guidelines for Preparation of the 1975–76 Six Year Plan for the Educational and General Operations of the State University System of Florida.* Tallahassee: Florida Board, 1974.

Illinois Board of Higher Education. *Master Plan—Phase III for Higher Education in Illinois: An Integrated State System.* Springfield: Illinois Board, 1971.

Liaison Committee of the Regents of the University of California and the State Department of Education. *A Restudy of the Needs of California in Higher Education.* Berkeley, California: Liaison Committee, 1955.

Mayhew, L. *Long Range Planning for Higher Education.* Washington, D.C: Academy for Educational Development, 1969.

Michigan Department of Education. *The State Plan for Higher Education in Michigan.* Lansing: Michigan Department of Education, 1973.

Montana Commission on Postsecondary Education. *Final Report.* Helena: Montana Commission, 1974.

New Jersey Board of Higher Education. *A Development Plan for Higher Education in New Jersey: Phase II of a Master Plan for Higher Education in the State of New Jersey.* Trenton: New Jersey Board, 1974.

Pennsylvania State Board of Education. *The Master Plan for Higher Education in Pennsylvania.* Harrisburg: Pennsylvania State Board, 1971.

Regents of the State of New York. *Education Beyond High School: The Regents Statewide Plan for the Development of Postsecondary Education 1972.* Albany: State University of New York, 1972.

Regents of the State of New York. *Postsecondary Education in Transition: The Regents 1974 Progress Report on Education Beyond High School; the Regents Statewide Plan for the Development of Postsecondary Education, 1972.* Albany: State University of New York, 1974.

Task Force on Statewide Comprehensive Planning for Postsecondary Education. *Comprehensive Planning for Postsecondary Education.* Denver, Colorado: Education Commission of the States, 1971.

University of California Committee on the Conduct of the Study. *A Report of the Needs of California in Higher Education.* Berkeley: University of California Committee, 1948.

Virginia State Council for Higher Education. *The Virginia Plan for Higher Education.* Richmond: Virginia State Council, 1974.

Washington Council for Postsecondary Education. *Planning and Policy Recommendations for Washington Postsecondary Education: 1976–1982.* Olympia: Washington Council, 1975.

ROBERT O. BERDAHL

AMI ZUSMAN

See also: Accountability; Adult Education; Consortia in the United States; Financing of Higher Education; Governance and Control of Higher Education; Statistics in Higher Education; Steady State.

4. REGIONAL PLANNING OF HIGHER EDUCATION

There are diverse views on the need for or desirability of regional planning for higher education within countries. In geographically large countries where the population is concentrated in one area, the need to provide opportunities for higher education and to extend the public services of higher education institutions to more remote areas makes regional planning essential. In countries with large numbers of diverse institutions of higher education, regional or subregional planning may be the best means of relating these institutions (providing for student transfer, sharing resources, or preventing wasteful overlapping) without the management problems inherent in a single central control. In some countries, however—especially the smaller ones—the more prestigious institutions consider themselves national or international centers, recruiting from all parts of the nation and from other countries, and resist regional planning in the fear that it will reduce their status.

Students belong predominantly to a highly mobile age group, and many of them positively welcome the chance to leave home and see new places. Why then is any sort of regional location or planning policy for universities needed? There are several relevant arguments for decentralizing higher education. First, study at distant locations leads to less efficient use of housing space and furniture and is likely to involve additional costs for services that would be provided free in the family. Admittedly, a student wanting a particular course may have to leave home to get it, since it may not be worthwhile to provide such a program in more than one center. In general, however, leaving home should not be encouraged when there is no large advantage to offset the cost. Second, many part-time students are unable to travel great distances for higher education. Local institutions would stimulate part-time study by reducing costs, extending opportunities to social groups that would otherwise miss them, and allowing for periodic retraining during working life. Moreover, full-time students of mature age may also be tied to a particular locality by spouses' jobs, children's schools, and the possession of property. Third, the presence of a higher education institution brings particular benefits to its locality beyond its direct

and indirect economic contribution—for example, better supplies of educated manpower (students often take jobs close to their university or college); a fuller cultural life (a concentration of staff and students stimulates enterprises in drama, music, the visual arts, sports, and adult education that might otherwise not exist); research services to local firms, strengthening their economic contribution and conceivably attracting new enterprises; other forms of public service through wider use of the institution's library, the availability of testing facilities, support of local social work agencies and public service organizations, and training of better qualified candidates for public office. Thus, even countries where the idea of regional planning of higher education is unpopular—of which the United Kingdom is a leading example—have not been unmindful of the need to obtain a proper regional distribution of universities, polytechnics, and colleges of education (Perkin, 1969, p. 64).

However, the idea of a centrally determined location policy is regional only in a rudimentary sense; the main interest of this essay is policy planning, which, in addition to securing a fair location of facilities, involves some degree of control, cooperation, or coordination at the regional level.

Representative National Plans

The Swedish U 68 report (*Higher Education*, 1973) proposed a division of the country into nineteen higher education areas, combined into regions, in each of which state higher education programs would be jointly organized under a board of higher education, representative of local interests and occupations as well as of staff and students. The reasons underlying this proposal included the need to increase opportunities for students previously unable to enroll at higher education institutions for geographical reasons, the desire to develop higher education in line with local needs, the need to anchor decision making in the local community (public representatives thus being in a majority on each board), and the opportunity to save resources by cooperation and concentration of facilities. The need for better supplies of educated manpower in the various regions was also influential. The report suggested arrangements to stimulate a two-way flow of students between local institutions and the large universities, which would remain national institutions, though it assumed that further expansion of higher education would be provided outside the present concentrations around major cities. Twelve of the nineteen areas would provide basic higher education only, and seven would provide for research and research training as well (Bergendahl, 1974).

A corresponding development in Norway has involved the creation of regional community-oriented two-year colleges, some of whose students would transfer to the national universities, while others would go directly into their careers. The emphasis of the Norwegian plan has been on the extension of educational opportunity and the improvement of the life and protection of interests of rural and remote areas. The two-year colleges were not intended to become substitute universities but to develop their own regional identities, for instance, by an emphasis on fishery economics at Bodø, on environmental conservation at Bø, and on oil technology at Stavanger (Kintzer, 1974).

The Norwegian experiment relates to only part of the system—the universities being unaffected except for possible student transfers. The difficulties encountered by more fundamental reforms can be illustrated in the experience of Colombia. Here the planning division of the *Asociación colombiano de universidades—Fondo universitario nacional* (ACU—FUN: Association of Colombian Universities—National University Fund) prepared in 1968 a feasibility study for the coordinated development of higher education in three regions, the purposes being cooperation in the use of dispersed resources, avoidance of duplication in programs, and regional specialization in particular disciplines. The plans were implemented by ACU—FUN's successor body, the *Instituto colombiano para el fomento de la educación superior* (ICFES: Colombian Institute for the Development of Higher Education), with some significant progress, especially in the Atlantic coast region. The four participating universities created common programs of general studies, transfer arrangements, and plans for the elimination of duplicate courses and specialization in particular fields. The ground was also prepared for bringing these universities under a single administration. But there were "numerous setbacks . . . due to financial difficulties, resistance from independent deans, and lack of support from some university trustees" (Pelczar, 1974, p. 51). Following the university riots in 1971, the Colombian government proposed a general reorganization of higher education along regional lines, having in mind particularly the need to lessen the concentration of students in Bogotá and other large cities, which (as in other South American countries) tends to concentrate opportunities on the middle class. Up to the time of Pelczar's (1974) report, however, the proposals had made no headway; the universities jealously guarded their autonomy and repudiated state intervention in their affairs. Pelczar comments— and the point has a wider application—that it was easier to make progress with planning on a small scale or regional level than to promote progress as part of a national plan.

What, however, is a region? It could be defined as a political subdivision of a national state, existing for purposes other than higher education: a state of the United States, a province of Canada, a German *Land.* If that subdivision also has full responsibility for public higher education, its problems are not distinct from those of a nation-state exercising that responsibility. Thus, the universities of Canada have long been predominantly a provincial responsibility, and since the reforms of the 1960s, far-reaching measures have been taken to integrate the whole postsecondary education systems in some of the provinces (Harris, 1975). In Canada reform is regional policy; the federal responsibility is mainly to transfer resources to meet half the operating costs of postsecondary education and to support research, but the significant problems are not different from those that would arise if the provinces of Quebec or Ontario had full national independence.

Nevertheless, a special interest attaches to the developments in Quebec as a consequence of the recommendations of the Parent (1963–1966) report. All students wishing to proceed to further education must now spend two years in a *collège d'enseignement général et professionnel* (CEGEP: general and professional school) or a *collège privé* (private school) offering a preuniversity course; the CEGEPs offer terminal vocational courses but are also the route to the universities. The University of Quebec is a public federal institution comprising not only university colleges but also research institutes and "superior" schools. Its flexibility of organization enables it to give special assistance in remote areas; for instance, the *Direction des études universitaires dans l'ouest quebecois* (Office of University Studies in Western Quebec) operates at Rouyn, 570 miles from Quebec, providing degree courses for teaching and administration and a range of certificate courses.

In Ontario the main function of the Council on University Affairs is to advise government on methods of allocating funds; while it has recommended a continuation of the formula method, it has also concerned itself with its own regional planning problem, well described in the following extract:

Nothing in its brief experience has impressed Council more profoundly than the naked appearance of what are indeed extraordinary geographic circumstances in Northern Ontario. . . . There is simply no southern counterpart to the nature of the extension offerings disseminated over tens of thousands of square miles by Lakehead, Laurentian and the latter's affiliated colleges. The Northern environment generates particularly intense needs for regionally oriented research and services applied to sectors that range from the problems of native peoples to those of natural resource industries. There is the sheer weight of the community contribution of northern universities to an enormous area that can never have access to the full spectrum of cultural and social amenities available in the South. Then there are less cosmic yet severely practical problems, such as the added institutional costs of fuel and travel that are a direct legacy of the environment, and the costs of attracting and retaining qualified personnel in the area (OCUA, 1975, p. 19).

The council in consequence proposed supplementary grants to the northern universities.

For an analogous problem in Africa, the best example is perhaps Nigeria. Here the Ashby (1960) report recommended the creation of four universities, including one in the north to cater to the very different needs of its predominantly Muslim community. While this report recommended that each university should be national in outlook, regionalism was already a significant force; a minority report from the western minister of education (Federation of Nigeria, 1960), which was accepted by the federal government, proposed an additional university and indicated that the west government was already planning it. Since that time the Institute of Technology in Benin has become a university, and in other regions a number of higher education institutions have appeared that may later wish to become universities. The federal structure of Nigeria has (quite apart from the great size of the country) produced demands that each state should make its own contribution to higher education (Fafunwa, 1975). This situation serves as a reminder that, in addition to the other reasons for regional location or planning policies, an important factor may be the desire of partly autonomous political units to have their own institutions.

It is possible, of course, that a region for the planning of higher education might be defined quite differently from any other political or administrative unit. No examples have yet been identified, but there are certainly cases in which regional planning of higher education appears to be quite independent of any other planning system. Thus, the location of teacher education institutions in England is controlled by the Department of Education and Science (in dialog with the administering local authorities and other bodies) in order to secure an adequate local supply of teachers; the economic and cultural impact of the college and its effect in training persons other than teachers does not appear to receive any attention. But, before proceeding to the conclusion that higher education should be related to general economic, physical, and cultural planning, it is worth observing that whatever may be done for the convenience of administrators, regions defined for different purposes should not in fact have the same boundaries. The point is well illustrated by some splendid maps of student catchment areas for institutions in the Federal Republic of Germany (Geissler, 1965).

Another justified conclusion is that any planning system should cover "education beyond school" as a whole. In countries surveyed for this essay, the overlap of function among universities, colleges, and other institutions is substantial; thus, any plan that omits or deals only with universities is likely to miss some fundamental problems. The leading example of a comprehensive plan for higher education can be found in California. Dating back to the powers given in the Donahoe Act of 1960, this plan has provided a model for similar master plans in other states. The California plan is hierarchical: the University of California, a multicampus institution, selects freshmen from the top eighth of the state's public high school graduates; the state colleges select from the top third; and the community or junior colleges (located within commuting distance of nearly all entrants) admit any graduate from a California high school. The university undertakes high-level research and training for prestige occupations, such as law and medicine; the state colleges have an interest in a further range of occupations, especially school teaching; the junior colleges train for what might be termed the lower vocations. Freedom of movement up the ladder of the system is of course provided (under the supervision of the Coordinating Council for Higher Education), but it can be said that the California system assumes and supports a social stratification based on occupation. While the plan has had some success in eliminating duplication and utilizing resources, the orderliness of the system may make it open to political interference by the state legislature (Perkins and Israel, 1972).

Alternate Approaches

A comprehensive regional plan covering several types of institutions almost certainly has to have legislative backing; the number of participants and the divergence of their interests are too numerous for a voluntary planning agreement to survive or succeed. Even the forty-four universities of the United Kingdom, though in many respects a homogeneous group, find it very difficult to agree on any significant common action that may abridge the autonomy of any one university. Nevertheless, some significant partial forms of planning have appeared by voluntary agreement. For instance, consortia of colleges in the United States— such as the Associated Colleges of the Midwest, the Kansas City Regional Council for Higher Education, the Great Lakes Colleges Association, and the association of state universities known as the University of Mid-America—exist to foster various types of cooperative enterprise—the interchange of students and faculty members and the sharing of facilities and publicity efforts (Henderson and Henderson, 1975, pp. 218–235). The Northern Universities Conference in England provides not only for the discussion of common problems but also for the interchange of forward plans, so that members can judge for themselves whether a greater degree of coordination is needed in the interests of the region.

It is impossible to prove that the existing examples of regional planning are cost-effective. Some involve spending more money to produce a benefit in a region like Northern Ontario, where the rewards are certainly identifiable but impossible to quantify; others provide for orderly development and uniformity of access. Whether or not individual schemes prove to be cost-effective, various experiments in regional planning will continue to develop as a consequence of the increasing educational needs of society throughout the world.

Bibliography

Ashby, E. *Investment in Education: Report of the Commission on Post-Secondary School Certificate and Higher Education in Nigeria.* Lagos, Nigeria: Federal Ministry of Education, 1960.

Bergendahl, G. "U 68—A Reform Proposal for Swedish Higher Education." *Higher Education*, 1974, *3*(3), 353–364.

Fafunwa, A. B. "The Universities of Nigeria." In *Commonwealth Universities Yearbook.* London: Association of Commonwealth Universities, 1975.

Federation of Nigeria (Sessional Paper No. 3). *Educational Development 1961–70.* Lagos, Nigeria: Gebrüder Jänecke Verlag, 1961.

Geissler, C. *Hochschulstandorte. Hochschulbesuch.* Hanover, Federal Republic of Germany: Gebrüder Janecke Verlag, 1965.

Harris, R. S. "The Universities of Canada." In *Commonwealth Universities Yearbook.* London: Association of Commonwealth Universities, 1975.

Henderson, A. D., and Henderson, J. G. *Higher Education In America: Problems, Priorities, and Prospects.* San Francisco: Jossey-Bass, 1975.

Higher Education: Proposals by the Swedish 1968 Educational Commission. (The U 68 Report.) Stockholm: Allmänna förlaget, 1973.

Kintzer, F. C. "Norway's Regional Colleges." *Higher Education,* 1974, *3*(3), 303–314.

OCUA (Ontario Council on University Affairs). *First Annual Report, 1974–75.* Toronto, Ontario: Ministry of Colleges and Universities, 1975.

Parent, A-M. *Report of the Royal Commission of Inquiry on Education in the Province of Quebec.* (5 vols.) Quebec: Government of Quebec, 1963–1966.

Pelczar, R. S. "University Reform in Latin America: The Case of Colombia." In P. G. Altbach (Ed.), *University Reform: Comparative Perspectives for the Seventies.* Cambridge, Massachusetts: Schenkman, 1974.

Perkin, H. J. *Innovation in Higher Education: New Universities in the United Kingdom.* Paris: OECD, 1969.

Perkins, J. A. and Israel, B. B. (Eds.) *Higher Education: From Autonomy to Systems.* New York: International Council for Educational Development, 1972.

The Reform of Higher Education in Sweden. Strasbourg, France: Council of Europe, 1975.

CHARLES F. CARTER
DAVID J. HOUNSELL

See also: Central America: Regional Analysis.

5. NATIONAL PLANNING OF HIGHER EDUCATION

Planning is all efforts to deal purposefully with conflict. National planning for higher education may be defined in correspondingly inclusive terms as all efforts to deal purposefully with the conflicts associated with the options pertaining to a nation's higher education policies.

Planners and social scientists addressing themselves to educational policy studies conventionally speak of national planning for higher education as a generic phenomenon. To do so is to accept, implicitly, a rather specific set of institutional arrangements as social realities common to all or most nations. It is also to elect, quite arbitrarily, a starting point for, and to limit the range of, studies of higher education policy options.

An anthropologist, however, might choose to point out that the institutional arrangements implied by "higher education" are peculiar to modern Western culture and were established to deal with some conflicts inherent to the polities that culture has produced. Among the most important of such conflicts are those that pertain to the relationships between monopoly over certain means to legitimating, certifying, promoting, and preserving knowledge, and the distribution of power. An anthropologist might also note that conscious efforts to promote national development, and indeed any consensus as to what national development is to mean, are also cultural phenomena peculiar to modern states and, perhaps, to only a portion of them.

An advantage of the conventional acceptance of planning as a generic phenome-

tion, in planning for higher education, is that it encourages concentration on the consequences of specific policy options and on modest policy adjustments. A possible disadvantage is that the planning literature, and most efforts at policymaking for higher education, concentrate only on short- and intermediate-range consequences of policy. The concern is for the future measured in years, sometimes in decades, almost never in generations.

It is not feasible to define educational planning by listing an exhaustive set of planning operations. However, a partial list of those operations can give some notion of the variety and range of activities subsumed. In planning for higher education, it is appropriate to say that planning includes the formulation of proposed projects, programs, and policies. Planning is also the designing and executing of policy studies with immediate relevance to the formulation of policies. It is sustained efforts at accumulating social, demographic, educational, and economic information of direct or indirect relevance to educational policymakers and political authorities. It can even be sustained or intermittent efforts to educate political authorities, or whole populations, as to the range of alternative policies for higher education they may choose from and the most likely consequences of their choices.

To some degree, the range of activities that planning for higher education can imply is determined by the institutional peculiarities of the polity and economy concerned. It can be efforts to influence, indirectly, the behavior of private not-for-profit and for-profit institutions and firms in market economies with either unitary or federal political systems. It can mean the preparing of very specific directives to operations that are the immediate agencies of public policy in highly centralized states.

The locations of authority and responsibility for planning for higher education are almost as varied as the activities themselves. This planning is sometimes the work of special government committees, such as the Robbins Committee, 1961–1963, in En-

gland; the National Commission on the Financing of Postsecondary Education, 1972–1973, in the United States; or the Commission on Post-Secondary Education in Ontario, 1969–1972, in Canada. It is sometimes the undertaking of a part of government, such as the French Ministry of Education, or a more-or-less permanent agency of government, such as India's University Grants Commission. The actual research and writing associated with educational planning can be primarily the work of civil servants, as was the preparation of "U 68" by Sweden's Educational Commission of 1968–1973. Sometimes, as with the *Wissenschaftsrat* (Science Council) of the Federal Republic of Germany, planning for higher education is the product of both government officials and educators. The Carnegie Commission on Higher Education in the United States is a private foundation that has repeatedly mobilized educators and laypeople to research and write on aspects of planning for higher education. In many countries this planning, particularly the related policy studies, is the work of university-based researchers in several faculties and, in a few cases, of academic departments or units specializing in educational planning. Finally, institutional or bureaucratic locations of authorities who can plan for, or deliberately influence, higher education are typically less centralized than the locations of authorities who plan for elementary and secondary education.

Not surprisingly, librarians and bibliographers have not been very successful in delimiting the literature of educational planning as it pertains to higher education or in producing a taxonomy of the literature. Moreover, major efforts to better organize the literature would likely be an uneconomic use of resources. The literature relating education, higher education in particular, to national development is in a state of flux. It is probable that in the next decade there will be less motivation than now to link the topics of planning for higher education and national development. If present trends continue, future writers on national development will be reluctant to make assumptions about direct and continuous relationships between development and educational variables, particularly those pertaining to higher education. Increasingly education is being relegated to the status of one among several institutional complexes, such as financial institutions and labor organizations, with important influence upon national development.

It is universally recognized that making policy for higher education is part of nation building and that planning for higher education is a component of the art and science of statecraft. Contemporary literature of educational planning and development planning concedes that these statements are not less true because there is not a universally appropriate definition or description of higher education. Increasing appreciation for the variation in the institutional arrangements among nations is, however, changing the character of the literature on educational planning very rapidly.

Despite the seeming homogeneity of problems bearing upon the more rational organization of industry in the less developed nations, a uniform set of institutions as the locations of higher education in those states is not emerging. Although the rich nations face a nearly identical set of problems bearing on the perpetuation of high living standards, the institutions of education in those states are not following markedly similar evolutionary paths. Statements about national planning of higher education as a generic phenomenon, therefore, require some remarkable qualifiers. First is that, depending on the nature of nationalist movements in the states of the world and the institutional arrangements that evolve in each of those states, it may or may not be appropriate for policymakers in one state to look at what policymakers in another state are doing to and with higher education. For example, it may be as appropriate for policymakers for higher education in one state to study what their counterparts in other states are doing as it is for

environmental protection policymakers to watch their foreign counterparts. On the other hand, it may be no more appropriate for higher education policymakers to study what their counterparts in other states are doing than it is for those authorities making policy for the Lutheran Church in Sweden to study what policies are being made regarding the Roman Catholic Church in Quebec, the Southern Baptist Church in Mississippi, or Islam in Iran. In the present literature of planning, higher education policy is being treated a bit less like policy for environmental protection and a bit more like policy for religious institutions.

As recently as the mid 1960s it was appropriate to speak without much qualification of national educational systems generally, and national systems of higher education in particular, as belonging to the same species or as interesting variations on a single theme. Until the 1960s, also, one could speak of national development as if it were the same phenomenon in all nations. It took no unusual level of self-confidence for students of education and economic development to speak with authority about national planning for higher education or the place of higher education policy in national economic development plans. The actual or apparent consensus from about 1947 to 1967 was undoubtedly partly caused by the relatively homogeneous origins of those who wrote about educational policy or planning and national development. The writers were overwhelmingly Westerners and Westernized, or Western-educated members of non-Western societies. In addition, Americans were predominant among those students of education and development. American influence would have been predominant, of course, even if Americans had been represented among those writers only in proportion to their numbers among people in the rich, industrialized states. Not only were Americans represented out or proportion to their numbers, however, but even non-American students of comparative education, economic development, and education as a factor of national economic development were still operating under the influences of then prevailing notions of the causes of American hegemony.

Since approximately 1967 writers dealing with any aspects of educational policy and statecraft have been rapidly losing their propensity to accept the set of assumptions for relating education to national development that had become the conventional frame of reference during the early 1960s. In the 1970s, so far no new set of assumptions has appeared that can be called the conventional frame of reference.

The frame of reference that came to characterize the literature of educational planning and national development in the post–World War II years and that had become a very powerful convention among educational planners by the early 1960s was an economic rationale. More specifically, it was a set of assumptions about the economic nature of education. The basic assumption was that expenditures on education are investments in the industrial capacity of a nation. A second assumption, which linked educational investment to national economic policy, was that observed statistical relationships between educational expenditures and such economic indexes as gross national product can be used to measure the return on educational investment.

A second approach to rationalizing educational policies, an alternative to the educational investment rationale, is manpower planning. Manpower planning depends on assumptions about the predictability of future demand for workers with specific qualifications and the educational experiences that will be appropriate to the training of those workers. Manpower planning is not simply an example of the application of economics to educational policymaking; it pertains to planning for operations and institutions outside a nation's educational sector. Manpower planning implies a multisectoral approach to planning for national development and a corresponding deemphasis of education as an independent deter-

minant of economic development. There is no recognizable turning point in the literature of manpower planning in the late 1960s, although precursors of some of the new emphases in contemporary approaches to conceptualizing educational planning are found in the early 1960s literature of manpower planning. Manpower planning remains, however, an area of activity and literature separate from and complementary to educational planning for higher education.

The Economic Rationale

With some exceptions, the literature of the economics of education and education and development in the decade before 1967 was a grand polemic for the rising public expenditures for education in most nations. Some of that literature was candid reporting of results from research intended to exploit contemporary econometric techniques, improving data sources in many nations (that were in turn the results of electronic data storage-retrieval-processing capacities and several decades of sustained efforts at national accounting), and theories of economic growth, to help us speak with more authority about the relationship of the human conditions in a nation to the productivity of its population. In some cases education was acknowledged, implicitly or explicitly, as a variable that pertains to several aspects of the human condition. Across nations, or across ethnic or class groups within a nation, education measures may be expected to be correlated to health conditions, attitudes toward consumption and saving, propensities to accept industrial discipline, and urbanization. No empirical research on education and productivity has ever made convincing claims to have measured the contribution of education, in isolation, to productivity or any other aspect of national development. Nevertheless, research attempting to relate quantities of education in a society, or levels of educational expenditures in a society, to national product usually had results that could be used to rationalize expansionary educational policies, high levels of public expenditures, and even budget deficits.

Origins. Notions that public education can be a contributing factor to a nation's productivity and its efficacy in international economic competition were well-established elements in the mainstream of economic literature as it evolved in the century 1775–1875. In particular, the writings of the Anglo-Saxon political economists accommodated the demand for a rationalization of public expenditures on education as sound public policy and for a rationalization of the infringements on liberty and economic freedom that are necessary to public education policy.

Rudolph Blitz's article "Some Classical Economists and Their Views on the Economics of Education" is perhaps the best examination of the treatment of education in the writings of (Anglo-Saxon) classical political economists; it is certainly the most succinct. Blitz reviewed the works of Adam Smith, Thomas Malthus, Nassau Senior, John McCulloch, and John Stuart Mill, whose writings spanned the first century of the industrial revolution. In his conclusion, Blitz says, "Smith was the most reluctant advocate of public education; his successors advocated it with increasing zeal" (1961, p. 46). Blitz also notes, however, that these philosophers were frequently very critical of public education and offered caveats with their endorsements of state education systems, and that there were other people he might have selected who never endorsed or explicitly denounced education as any sort of public undertaking.

At the very least, however, by the last quarter of the nineteenth century it was quite generally conceded that educational policy could be exploited to promote economic development. And in the closing decades of the century it was already recognized that the differentials in the products of national education systems were a major contributor to the structure of international trade and the relative advantages of the industrializing states in world trade

(Jonathan Chambers, in *The Workshop of the World: British Economic History from 1820 to 1880,* notes that before 1880 education was already credited with important effects upon relative national advantages in the new chemical industry).

The economics of education that so influenced educational policy and planning in the 1950s and 1960s was not, then, a new departure, only a new emphasis. Earlier generations of economists and political philosophers had struggled to conceptualize the nature of education's contribution to economic development. Relying more on intuition than on empirical evidence, students of American social and economic history had long claimed that America's propensity to spend on education and to afford unusual levels of educational opportunity to its citizens had been an important positive influence on American productivity. Early efforts to study the effects of educational expenditures on American productivity had not been efforts at analyzing or measuring the returns to educational expenditures at all. Rather, they had been quite primitive demonstrations of the high correlations between quantities of education and industrial productivity of individuals, classes, and geographic groupings. A U. S. Bureau of Education bulletin, written by A. Caswell Ellis, a professor of educational philosophy, titled *The Money Value of Education* (1917), was, if not the first, one of the very early efforts to deal quantitatively with the relations between varying levels of education and earnings and was an archetype of many studies to come. However, the only relationships between quantities that Ellis offered were correlational. Such a simplistic approach was potentially misleading and invited more rigorous treatment of the available data.

The investment consensus. The quantification of education-productivity relationships became a minor but recurring theme in the American literature of economics in the decades of the 1920s and 1930s. Solomon Fabricant's *Employment in Manufacturing 1899–1939,* published in 1942, may be considered the outstanding work attempting to explain the contribution of technological change and its behavioral implications to productivity of the years before the post–World War II period. Fabricant demonstrated that the increments in physical capital explain a relatively small part of the rapid growth in per capita production in the United States.

After World War II, the preeminent position of the United States economy motivated more studies of the relationships between education and productivity in that country. More important, perhaps, the increasing quantity and improving quality of data on the American economy, advances in the techniques of econometrics, and the availability of computers facilitated the new efforts at quantifying the contributions of education to productivity. The bases of these studies (national in most cases) and the style and format of the related reports suggested immediate relevance of these studies to national educational and economic planning. In particular, for developed societies that already had an approximation of universal elementary education and abundant opportunities for secondary education, they seemed of especial relevance for national planning for higher education.

Perhaps the most influential research supportive of expansionary education policies was Edward Denison's study, *The Sources of Economic Growth in the United States and the Alternatives before Us* (1962). It became the model for many good, indifferent, and poor studies to follow. Denison and his disciples proceeded on the assumption that to understand or ensure progress, we must identify the factors which, as complements of a growing population and accumulating capital, assure increasing productivity even under conditions of diminishing per capita resources. The facts that increasing productivity (of labor) has accompanied growing populations in the past and was often in excess of that presumed to be caused by incremental capital accumulation offer apparent justification for the assumption that such complementary factors exist. Using equations that they regarded as acceptable mathematical expressions of the relationships of the total product of an economy to the several factors committed to the processes involved, these researchers identified a residual factor—that is, something other than labor and capital. Careful definition of terms can make plausible the assumption that the residual factor represents changing technology and labor value. Still more assumptions and some faith are required to connect that residual to education, however. Research of this genre is quite uniformly associated with such assumptions, some researchers attributing most or nearly all of that residual to education, others attributing only some substantial part of it to education.

In simplified terms, the policy-research results of the postwar years to about 1967 can be expressed as a frame of reference for national educational planning in the following ways: (1) It is possible to identify the "extra" factors (other than constant-quality labor and capital) that have allowed continuing progress in the past, even in the face of declining per capita natural resources. Whether progress is taken to mean only an increase in per capita (or per worker) product, or that increase plus a decrease in the proportion living in poverty, the extra factors are the same: improvement in the quality of labor and technology. A behavioral variable related to these improvements, a variable perceived as particularly amenable to influence in the form of public policy, is investment in education, or more correctly, the propensity to invest more—in absolute and relative terms—in education over time. (2) It can be assumed that per capita product and the erosion of poverty can still be served through public policy that promotes increasing educational investment and, indirectly, improvement of labor quality and technology. The high correlation between progress and educational investment across nations attests to this, as does the obvious relationship (over time) between productivity and educational investment in the United States.

The results of most empirical research relating education to development can be appropriated by those preparing briefs for expanding educational budgets and rising public expenditures. Considering the patronage, timing, and assumptions vital to the results and associated implicit or explicit recommendations of this research, it would be difficult not to assume that some of it was part of general sustained efforts in many nations to rationalize expansionary educational policies, high public expenditures, and budget deficits. In Canada, Gordon Bertram's *The Contribution of Education to Economic Growth* (1966) is a particularly appropriate example of a piece of policy research that cannot be disassociated from the interests of policymakers already committed to the policies its results supported. As an Economic Council of Canada study, it was doubtlessly intended to have relevance for public policymaking. Because Bertram concluded that the residual component in Canada's production function for the half century ended in 1961 was substantial, and because he attributed a considerable portion of it to education, but more importantly because he attributed much of the per capita income differential between Canada and the United States to educational investment differentials, Bertram and the Economic Council contributed to the rationalization of public policies that led to Canada assuming first place among the developed nations as a spender on public education (as a percent of GNP).

There were sound and compelling reasons for Americans and non-Americans alike to be especially interested in the determinants of American productivity levels, particularly in the first two decades after World War II. As the preeminent world economy, the United States had performed or experienced an organization of its industrial processes that all nations wanted to emulate, at least partly. If education had in fact been an important independent influence in that reorganization, the implication that education was a potential control variable for national economic planners was inescapable. In addition, it was appropriate, and probably inevitable, that in the post–World War II period the newly important methodology of econometrics be used to offer quantitative statements of education's contribution to the economy (or to the economies of the world). However, the econometric studies of education and the economy were probably not accompanied by all the appropriate qualifiers that economic research results should have. In particular, it should have been emphasized that no matter how great the returns to educational investment in the past (or on the average), it is difficult to relate that rate of return to new increments of investment (at the margin).

It should be noted, however, that even those researchers most enthusiastic about their own research results seldom accompanied the results with the bold recommendations for expansionary educational policies which some policymakers did. These policymakers appropriated those research results into their briefs for rising educational expenditures and expanding educational opportunities. Indeed, some economists quite explicitly pointed out the probable disappointing returns to investments in expanded systems of education, particularly in very rapid expansions. Fritz Machlup, in *The Production and Distribution of Knowledge in the United States*, commented at length on the inability of school systems, national or local, to get constant returns on investments for educational expansion. He maintained that a major expansion in a nation's educational institutions results in most of the marginal product being lost to "inflation." For example, the expansion associated with the changing of the normal duration of education from eight to twelve years results in a rising price, in years of students' time (and taxpayers' money) needed to acquire a given amount of knowledge, with marginal returns to the incremental years being nearly nil (1962, p. 128).

Significance. Several points should be

made about the effects of the consensual acceptance of this frame of reference upon planning for higher education in the nations of the world. Because the econometric studies associated with this frame of reference dealt with grand aggregations, they did not raise questions about the comparability of public and private educational investments or educational investments in centrally planned economies and educational investments in market economies.

So long as the policy research of most relevance to planners supported the claim that the returns to investment in education in general would continue to be high, it was not necessary to emphasize the difference between highly developed and developing societies or between federal and unitary states. It was of minimal importance that the historical model for educational planning in most societies was a rich, federal political system, with most investments market determined (that is, the United States).

The emphasis upon general relationships between education and economic development suggested that educational cooperation between developed and developing nations required only that the developed nations help the developing nations raise their levels of educational expenditures to more closely approximate those in developed societies. The implicit (sometimes explicit) assumptions that economic development in every nation meant, first and foremost, an improving standard of living for an increasing proportion of a growing population, that GNP as conventionally measured is an appropriate index of that improvement in any nation, and that education is an independent factor influencing economic development, suggested that simple expansion of higher education of the types in industrialized societies would further national policies for prosperity in any nation.

Manpower Planning and Higher Education

Perhaps the most difficult obstacle to delineating the domain of national planning for higher education in any society is

making the proper allowance for the overlapping areas of higher education (also vocational education and sometimes secondary education) policy and manpower planning. Manpower planning is sometimes regarded as an activity separate from, but complementary to, national planning for education. Manpower-planning-oriented students of higher education and development, even in the 1950s and 1960s, did not accept, and offered an alternative to, the above mentioned econometric frame of reference for educational planning. It is claimed here that manpower planning in the years before 1967 was not actually an alternative to that frame of reference. It was, more correctly, a separate aspect of planning for national development or an important source of qualifiers to the assumptions sometimes made for education-development relationships.

A conference on educational planning was held in 1964 at Syracuse University. *Educational Planning* (Adams, 1964) presents six papers from that conference. It is an effort to describe the state of the art of educational planning as educational planners saw it in the mid 1960s. In each of the six papers presented it is clear that the author's first concern was for education as the prime instrument for more effective exploitation of human resources for national development, meaning essentially economic growth. Manpower planning was mentioned repeatedly as the technique for better educational investment strategies, but the basic rationalization for higher levels of educational expenditure (either assumed or recommended) was education's contribution to human resources development in some more general sense. There are two national studies reported, both concerning Thailand. William Platt's "Manpower Planning in Thailand" emphasized the importance of educational policies to accommodate the projected manpower requirements of the Thai economy. Platt did not say or imply that manpower studies can be used to determine the scale of educational expenditures. Cole Brembeck, in "Educational Planning in

Thailand," acknowledged the importance of Platt's manpower study. He also recommended a manpower-requirements basis for many educational policy decisions to be made. However, his basic rationalization of the educational expansion he called for was an assumed relationship between education and human resources development of a much more general nature.

In the 1960s there was some hope that manpower studies could become the basic policy studies for relating human resources development policies to economic development policies. Manpower studies did not develop into the fine instruments of policy design their most enthusiastic advocates had hoped for. Nor were they the futile or irrelevant efforts the harder critics of manpower planning had expected they would be. Of more importance to the subject at hand, manpower planning has neither subsumed planning for higher education nor offered a basic new frame of reference for that planning.

The Organization for Economic Cooperation and Development's (OECD) definition of the "active manpower policy" they advocate leaves no doubt that manpower policy is one thing and higher education policy is another and that the policy studies related to the former will be of only limited utility to the latter:

Active manpower policy has had a very specific function as an adjunct of broad economic policy and programmes as well as a tool for the attainment of the social values which have been broadly accepted by most countries in the postwar world. Through its services and programmes it seeks to promote the availability, mobility and quality of the human resources needed by the economy and to assure the smooth adjustment of people to the changing geographical and occupational patterns of employment. By means of its administrative measures directly affecting the actual or potential work force, or through its advocacy of general and specific economic policies and its influence on private action, it tries to promote the full employment of those willing to work within the framework of a free society, with its emphasis on the free choice of jobs (OECD, 1965, p. 8).

Perhaps the greatest weakness of manpower studies as a potential replacement for education-investment studies is that both types of studies share the same flaw. However well or poorly we can measure the contributions of education to economic development (or any other kind) historically, we are quite incapable of specifying how education of one kind might have been substituted for another (for example, to what degree might nonuniversity technical training have been substitutable for university applied-science training had the latter not been available). We are even less capable of saying what will be the contributions to development of the next increment of education. Similarly, whatever we can say about the qualified manpower requirements of specified levels of production in the past, we are less able to estimate the degree to which one type of qualified labor might have been substituted for another (a technician for an engineer, a nurse for a physician) and still less able to say what the qualified manpower requirements of new levels of production will be.

Current Approaches

There have been no renunciations of education investment-returns studies by their qualified critics; there has only been an increasing tendancy to discount their relevance to policymaking. Nor has there been any repudiation of manpower studies, only an increasing tendency to stress their limitations and the narrow range of policy questions concerning education that they help to answer.

Special mention should be made of one development that has contributed to the deemphasis of investment-return studies. To some degree, appreciation of the studies depended on infatuation with the phenomenon of economic and social development in the United States. For the greater part of two decades now, attention has been drawn to other exciting stories of national economic development, notably, but not exclusively, Germany and Japan. In neither case is the hypothesis that education has been a powerful independent determinant of development very compelling. It is interesting to note that the 1976 study by Edward Denison and William Chung, *How Japan's Economy Grew So Fast*, places much less importance upon education's contribution to development than does Denison's 1962 study.

The OECD's Review of National Policies for Education series of recent years are fine critiques of the state of education reform in the countries studied. The one titled *Germany* (1972) is a particularly interesting study of ongoing reform. It is worth noting that neither the international study team nor German state policymakers think that the relatively modest rate of educational reform and expansion in the postwar Federal Republic of Germany has retarded that nation's economic development.

In regard to higher education particularly, the reforms Germany has pursued, the reforms that nation is now committed to, and indeed, even the further reforms the OECD Examiners endorse, recall the contests between the supporters of the elitist, traditional university system in Germany and the supporters of new styles of higher education more appropriate to a modern, democratic republic, which Abraham Flexner described so well in 1930 (*Universities: American, English, German*), more than they do arguments of the last generation about the proper economic bases of educational planning. Of more importance, the Examiners seem to accept with equanimity the necessity of slowing the rate of reform under the new economic difficulties facing Germany at the time they were writing. This is hardly an assumption that they would be expected to make if they believed that increased investments in higher education would lead certainly and immediately to increased productivity.

In the industrialized, non-Marxist states, the changing orientations and emphases in policy research and policymaking bearing on education can be summarized as a deemphasis of "the economics of growth" and a reemphasis of "the economics of public finance." More particularly, the emphasis is on issues related to the size and growth of public expenditures, the efficiency and effectiveness of government programs, and the distribution of both income and public services. An interesting indication of this shifting emphasis in the developed nations is the reorientation of the Ontario Economic Council in Canada. In the 1974–1975 Annual Report of the Council it was pointed out that "[when] the Council was formed [1961] it was conceived principally as a body which would investigate and report on problems related to achieving a high level of industrial growth and employment for the Province. The primary emphasis was on economic development: indeed, there was some suggestion that the new body might be named the Ontario Productivity Council or the Ontario Economic Development Council" (p. 1). In an October 1974 news release, the Chairman of the Council said: "Research on public expenditure, rather than economic development, will be the main priority of the Ontario Economic Council for the next few years. . . . The program will focus on the size and growth of public expenditures. . . . Particular emphasis will be placed on spending in the health, education, community and social services fields. These make up about two thirds of the provincial budget" (*Toronto Globe and Mail*, October 11, 1974, p. B1).

The shifting of emphasis from the economics of growth to the economics of public finance as the frame of reference of educational planning in the developed nations is a return to more traditional orientations toward education's role in national life and social development. It is more difficult to generalize about the effects of deemphasizing the economics of growth as the frame of reference for educational planning in the developing nations.

For developing nations that share, to an important degree, the cultural and intellectual heritage of the richer, more developed states, the emerging styles of educational policy and policy studies demonstrate the same propensities to view education in the context of general public finance issues that are observable in the developed countries, but to a more modest degree. There is also more reluctance to make the assumption that educational policies are not of direct and immediate consequence to economic conditions. *Education in OECD Developing Countries* (1974) surveys the state of educational reform and recent educational policy developments in Greece, Portugal, Spain, Turkey, and Yugoslavia. Clearly, and probably quite correctly, those nations are more concerned about the impact of educational policy on the economy than are the wealthier OECD nations. Just as clearly, they do not make the case as strongly as they would have in the mid 1960s. The study notes that existing plans in those countries "point to the need for reducing unit costs of education" and "agree that educational expansion should not take place at the expense of the quality of education" (p. 61). More importantly, there is a reluctance in those countries to present plans for expansion out of context of plans for its financing that would not have been expected a decade or more ago, and education is increasingly viewed as only one of a set of services which must be expanded to accommodate expanding, urbanizing populations.

In the developing nations outside Europe, some more radical departures from the higher educational policy norms of the developed nations are being considered and attempted. In some revolutionary societies, notably Cuba and the People's Republic of China, it is possible that no institutions which will be the recognizable counterparts of universities and other Western institutions of higher education will survive. In many more ex-colonial societies, new emphases and interpretations are being placed upon the teachings of Karl Marx and other reformers bearing on the dysfunctionality of formal education, or non-work-related education, to other than bourgeois, capitalist societies. To date, however, no generalization about new orientations for planning in the developing countries is justified beyond the observation that individually, and sometimes collectively, these nations are looking for new intellectual and ideological frames of reference for rationalizing higher education policy development. The general purport of such essays as W. Arthur Lewis' "The University in Less Developed Countries" (1974) and Kenneth Thompson's "Higher Education for National Development: One Model for Technical Assistance" (1972) appears to be that the developing nations of the world have joined the most developed nations in the continuing and exciting task of fashioning appropriate policies for their universities and other institutions of higher education appropriate to their own particular problemts in a changing, uncertain world.

Bibliography

Adams, D. K. (Ed.) *Educational Planning.* Syracuse, New York: Syracuse University Press, 1964.

Bertram, G. *The Contribution of Education to Economic Growth.* Ottawa: Queen's Printer, 1966.

Blitz, R. C. "Some Classical Economists and Their Views on the Economics of Education." *Economia* (Santiago, Chile), 1961, 72, 34–60. Reprinted, in part, in *Readings on Education and Economic Development.* Paris: UNESCO, 1964.

Brembeck, C. S. "Educational Planning in Thailand." In D. K. Adams (Ed.), *Educational Planning.* Syracuse: Syracuse University Press, 1964, 127–152.

Chambers, J. D. *The Workshop of the World: British Economic History from 1820 to 1880.* London: Oxford University Press, 1968.

Denison, E. F. *The Sources of Economic Growth in the United States and the Alternatives before Us.* New York: Committee for Economic Development, 1962.

Denison, E. F., and Chung, W. K. *How Japan's Economy Grew So Fast.* Washington, D.C.: The Brookings Institute, 1976.

Ellis. A. C. *The Money Value of Education.* Washington, D.C.: U.S. Government Printing Office, 1917.

Fabricant, S. *Employment in Manufacturing 1899–1939.* New York: National Bureau for Economic Research, 1942.

Flexner, A. *Universities: American, English, German.* London: Oxford University Press, 1930.

Lewis, W. A. "The University in Less Developed Countries." Occasional Paper No. 11. International Council for Educational Development. New York: 1974.

JOHN HOLLAND

6. INTERNATIONAL EDUCATIONAL PLANNING AND DEVELOPMENT

This discussion focuses on international planning mechanisms and activities that affect institutions and systems of higher education in developing societies—those which are predominantly poor and nonindustrialized or semiindustrialized, and which, in many cases, were until recently colonies of rich industrialized states. "Higher education" refers primarily to universities and to other formal teaching institutions (colleges, institutes) for which completion of secondary education is normally a condition of admission.

The network of national and international agencies whose activities—organizing conferences, providing direct financial aid and technical assistance, providing training for local personnel, conducting or sponsoring research, and disseminating information—affect the development of higher education in developing nations has been an effective international planning mechanism. This massive international effort to aid higher education has produced a relatively common view of the educational future in most recipient societies; internationally agreed-upon targets for growth; standard methodologies used widely by national planners in determining how their own resources can best be used for higher education; and a relatively common set of second-order problems, which have been created or exacerbated by the very success of the international aid effort. This analysis of the predominant characteristics and trends of international planning provides illustrative examples but not an exhaustive catalog of all agencies and activities involved in the effort.

Development of the Planning System

For as long as there have been colonial systems and missionary activities, there have been attempts by agents of one nation to influence the development of higher education in other nations. Indeed, when most of the newly independent states of Africa and Asia entered the postcolonial era, such institutions or systems of higher education as they possessed were the direct products of the influence of colonizing powers or religious missionaries (the latter often a substitute for the former). Thus, current and recent activities have a long, if not altogether honorable, heritage.

During the late 1950s and early 1960s, international planning for higher education changed markedly, both in scale and organizational style. Many new actors, principally national aid agencies and international organizations, entered the field; the flow of money and technical advice increased dramatically; and attempts were made to better coordinate the separate and often highly idiosyncratic efforts to "develop" higher education in poor nations as part of the effort to "develop" the nations themselves. These marked changes were the product of the confluence of several phenomena.

First, the simple fact of many colonies becoming independent states within a brief time brought forcibly to the attention of the richer nations the fact that most of the people in the world live in exceedingly poor nations. To some extent, the advent of independence for so many nations transferred responsibility for their poverty (or at least responsibility for doing something about it) from the few overtly colonial powers to the entire rich and industrial world.

Second, by the late 1950s the "Cold War" had developed to a point where these new nations were perceived by both sides as a prime field for economic and ideological warfare. Among the principal weapons were foreign aid and technical assistance. Thus, throughout much of the rich portion of the world, moral imperative to help the poor converged with perceived economic and ideological necessity.

Third, something of a revolution in the

science of economics occurred at roughly this same time—the so-called "Human Investment Revolution." This revolution produced both a message and a tool for exploiting it. The message was that investment in "human capital" (investment in formal education) was sure to pay off in increased economic development. Moreover, the greatest returns accrued to investment in higher education. Thus, the message went, if money invested in education is good, money invested in higher education is especially good. The tool provided was manpower planning. With this technique long-term plans for the development of the economy could be converted into detailed prescriptions for the kinds of highly qualified manpower the economy would require. If the message said to invest in higher education, the tool told planners in what kinds of higher education to invest, and for how many students. Thus, markedly increased aid to education generally, and to higher education in particular, was provided with a moral rationale, a politicoeconomic rationale, and a scientific rationale.

It is important to note that the enormous international effort called forth by this triple rationale aimed at *change*—both quantitative expansion of educational systems and qualitative reorientation. Although it may have been indirect, it was most certainly *planning*. In this effort to help the less developed nations, higher education was seen as a particularly crucial leverage point. The general spirit of the time was well expressed by Ladislav Cerych (1965, p. 49), writing under the auspices of the Atlantic Institute: "Since the importance of external aid to education increases as the scale of levels of education is mounted, it is easy to see that aid to higher education is a top priority from every point of view. It is at this level that the longest time is needed to train nationals of developing countries in adequate numbers and to find the necessary material and equipment on the spot. It is at this level also that internal effort alone, without the support of external aid, will have the greatest difficulty in succeeding. . . . Higher education is the apex of the pyramid of all educational systems, and therefore action which affects it should, by definition, have the widest and deepest possible effect."

UNESCO. Among the earliest and most influential responses to the generally perceived need for greater educational development, and more aid to stimulate it, were a series of regional conferences sponsored by UNESCO. These conferences produced regional plans, which were basically targets for the quantitative expansion of educational systems in the regions involved; estimates of resources required to meet the targets; and general commentaries on needed qualitative changes. African targets were established at a conference in Addis Ababa in 1961 and partly revised at Tananarive, Madagascar, in 1962. For Asia, conferences in Karachi, Pakistan (1959–1960); in Tokyo (1962); and in Bangkok (1965) prepared and revised regional educational plans. Targets for Latin America were set at a conference in Santiago, Chile, in 1960 and revised in Bogotá, Colombia, in the following year. The scale of quantitative increases in higher education forecast (or at least hoped for) in these regional plans can be seen in the Addis Ababa plan, which projected an increase in higher education enrollment in Africa from 25,000 in 1961–62 to 328,000 in 1980–81, raising the percent of the relevant age group enrolled in school from 0.2 to 2.0. The Santiago plan projected an enrollment increase in higher education for Latin America from 521,000 in 1960 to 905,000 in 1970, raising the percentage from 3.1 to 4.0 (Cerych, 1965, pp. 11, 18).

Whether or not the targets were eventually met, these conferences were extremely important events. Cerych (1965, pp. 3–4) has labeled the plans produced by the first three conferences as "basic international charters of educational development." He notes: "The political and psychological importance of the three UNESCO documents is unquestionable. Because of them many countries became more conscious of their real situation and of the necessity for increased educational efforts. The plans have the additional merit of being the only comprehensive documents available. They cover more than 70 of the underdeveloped countries of the world, with a total population of approximately 1,150 million (in 1960). This figure represents between 80 and 85% of the population of all non-Communist underdeveloped countries." A decade after the early conferences, the following comment was made in a technical staff paper prepared for the secretariat of the Organisation for Economic Co-operation and Development (1971, p. 3): "The 'objectives' or 'targets' established at various regional meetings were both a declaration of principle and a model methodology for long term expansion of the educational systems of the individual countries. They played an important role in focusing attention on the implications for domestic expenditure and foreign aid requirements of the objectives at the different educational levels which were considered feasible by the Ministers of Education and the overall planning authorities of the developing countries. Another useful result was that they stimulated the establishment of *national* educational plans" (emphasis added). Finally, even when the targets themselves were not met, they became international benchmarks in terms of which the failure was measured.

Although many other agencies have entered, or increased their activity in, the area of international aid to higher education since those conferences, UNESCO remains a preeminent force in furthering the development of higher education. In carrying out its mission to stimulate and organize international and regional cooperation, UNESCO can call on a number of specialized agencies within or associated with the United Nations system. The International Bureau of Education, in Geneva, is primarily responsible for documentation and dissemination of information. The UNESCO Institute for Education (Hamburg) deals chiefly with research. The International Institute for Educational Planning (Paris) has undertaken or commissioned a great deal of research and carries out an extensive program of specialized training in educational planning.

This centralized international machinery is paralleled by a network of cooperative bodies at the level of geographical or cultural regions. Ministers of education in each major region meet regularly under UNESCO auspices to compare notes, exchange views, isolate common problems, and, at times, plan joint action. In each of the four principal geographical regions of the underdeveloped world there is a UNESCO Regional Office for Education (in Dakar for Africa, in Santiago for Latin America and the Caribbean, in Beirut for the Arab countries, and Bangkok for Asia), whose duties include carrying out studies and surveys to analyze the educational situation in states of the region; collecting and disseminating information in collaboration with the International Bureau of Education; and providing training for specialized educational personnel.

In collaboration with the two major funding agencies of the United Nations system, the World Bank and the United Nations Development Programme, UNESCO has undertaken a number of activities in the area of higher education. Coombs (1973, p. 276) cites some of these: "It has helped a number of developing nations to plan, build, and staff new higher educational institutions and to add new components to existing institutions. It has helped, for instance, with teacher training colleges, science and engineering departments, and full universities. Again, UNESCO has provided U.N. fellowships and arranged foreign study opportunities for large numbers of young and mid-career people from virtually every developing nation. In addition, it has conducted international studies and provided an international forum to investigate important problems such as university admissions policies, the equivalency of higher education credits and degrees among different countries, and the role and responsibilities of universities in national development."

World Bank. Although the World Bank is part of the United Nations system and frequently works in collaboration with UNESCO, it is in itself a sufficiently powerful and influential agency to merit separate consideration. Prior to the early 1960s the World Bank had devoted its resources exclusively to economic projects. However, by 1971 the bank had concluded that "the lack of qualified manpower in developing countries was a serious obstacle to the successful implementation of many of its own projects in particular and to the process of economic development in general" (World Bank, 1974, p. 49). This led the bank to undertake its first education project in 1963, with close to one hundred projects having been started in the years following (World Bank, 1974, pp. 66–68). Following from its diagnosis of the problem (which dovetailed with the message from economics alluded to earlier), the Bank has concentrated its efforts on support of institutions and programs for the development of highly qualified manpower, with particular emphasis on secondary education (general comprehensive and technical) and, increasingly, on higher education. Between 1963 and 1971 the Bank loaned $99,320,000 to higher education projects, this being 23 percent of its total expenditure for education during those years. In the following three years, it provided $257,170,000 for higher education, comprising 41 percent of its total budget for education (World Bank, 1974, p. 64).

National aid agencies. Also important are national aid agencies such as the Agency for International Development (AID) of the United States, the Canadian International Development Agency (CIDA), the Ministry of Overseas Development of the United Kingdom, and the Swedish International Development Authority (SIDA). It is difficult to obtain reliable and comprehensive figures concerning the aid flows from such national agencies to the educational sector as a whole, let alone to a particular subsector such as higher education. However, some indication of the level of effort may be obtained from the following data regarding the activities of the members of the Development Assistance Committee (DAC)—those member states of the OECD that have foreign aid programs. Just prior to 1974 DAC countries financed 211 educational aid projects in fourteen of the least advanced developing countries (Botswana, Burundi, Chad, Dahomey, Ethiopia, Guinea, Lesotho, Malawi, Mali, Nepal, Rwanda, Somalia, the Sudan, and the Yemen Arab Republic). Of these projects, seventy-two are related to higher education; almost 75 percent of these either financed expatriate teachers or provided fellowships for local teachers to improve their qualifications by studying abroad (UNESCO, 1974a, Table 3). In one year, 1968, these same DAC countries were providing overseas training for 2,690 educational professionals for all less developed nations and were financing 5,909 expatriate teachers in institutions of higher education (Organisation for Economic Co-operation and Development, 1971, Tables 7 and 8).

Private foundations. Still another influence in the aid-to-education field has been large private foundations. The Ford Foundation, for example, has long provided substantial funds to develop institutions in less developed nations, either directly or by contracting with United States universities to supply assistance. The foundation also supports research projects or programs that have often had as an outcome an institutionalized university-based research capacity within developing nations. An idea of the scale of the Ford Foundation's operations may be gained by noting that in 1968 it spent $34,000,000 on research in educational institutions and training in less developed nations (Organisation for Economic Co-operation and Development, 1971, p. 13). The Rockefeller Foundation has also had a major program of aid to higher education, although it operates on a smaller scale (devoting $9,000,000 to educational aid in 1968). Its most notable activity in this area is the University Development Program, started in 1963. This program aims to develop key faculties, particularly in medicine, agriculture, and economics, by providing grants for advanced study and research abroad for local professors; by supplying teachers from Canada, the United Kingdom, and the United States for one- or two-year periods; and by providing foundation staff members for long-term assignments. It also provides support for teaching and research equipment.

Efforts at coordination. The picture that emerges from such efforts is that of a number of actors, all responding to a set of general pressures, but in uncoordinated and idiosyncratic ways; that is, of a great deal of planning, in the sense of much activity consciously intended to change higher education in poor nations, but of very little systematic or coordinated planning. During the decade of the 1960s this was very much the case. However, in 1972 a significant attempt at coordinating and systematizing effort among various agencies began when a group of the major donor agencies (called the Bellagio Consortium because major meetings of the group are held in Bellagio, Italy) started a series of discussions aimed at better focusing and coordinating their separate efforts in the field of educational assistance. The agencies involved are CIDA, the Ford Foundation, the French Ministry of Foreign Affairs, the Inter-American Development Bank, the World Bank, the International Development Research Center (Canada), the Ministry of Overseas Development of the United Kingdom, OECD, the Overseas Economic Cooperation Fund of Japan, the Rockefeller Foundation, SIDA, the United Nations Children's Fund (UNICEF), the United Nations Development Programme, UNESCO, and AID. To support this effort a series of background studies has been commissioned. The International Council for Educational Development was funded by the consortium to provide a series of studies indicating the role that higher education can play in national development and the role that the donor agencies may play in assisting higher education in poor nations.

Effects of Planning

Direct results. Quantitatively, the growth in higher education as a result of this international effort has been remarkable. Many new institutions of higher education have been established; new programs, departments, and faculties have been established within existing institutions; and existing programs have expanded their enrollment capacity. For all developing nations the total student enrollment in higher education increased between 1960 and 1972 from 2,200,000 to 7,492,000 (UNESCO 1974b, pp. 89–90). During roughly the same period—1960 to 1970—the percent of the age group enrolled in these nations doubled, going from 1.9 to 3.9 (UNESCO, 1974b, pp. 102–104). In most cases the enrollment targets set for higher education at the UNESCO regional conferences have been met or exceeded.

Although by far the largest proportion of funds required for this expansion has come from the budgets of the developing nations themselves, the role of foreign assistance has been critical. Many new institutions or faculties would not be in existence at all if they were not originally supported by external aid. Many institutions, especially in the poorest nations, could not function at all or could not function at anything approaching their current scale, if it were not for aid-supported expatriate teachers and local teachers trained abroad under the sponsorship of aid agencies. The importance of aid-financed expatriate teachers, and the need for training of nationals to replace them, can be seen by noting, for example, that, in 1972, 64.9

percent of all higher education teaching posts in Rwanda were held by foreigners; in Somalia in 1971, 72.6 percent of such posts were held by foreigners (UNESCO, 1974a, Table 12).

A very few foreign advisers, bringing with them the prestige of the rich industrialized world, can have a profound effect upon the direction taken by an institution or a system. Even a small amount of aid (as a proportion of a nation's total domestic investment in higher education), if strategically used, may exert a great deal of leverage in changing an institution or a system. An example of this "leverage" effect is the work of the Rockefeller Foundation with universities in Uganda, Kenya, and Tanzania. Thompson and others (1974, p. 201) have described the foundation's role as follows:

The Foundation's contribution has always been minor, first to the three independent national colleges, then to the federated University of East Africa, and most recently to the three national universities bound together by numerous functional ties and a common Inter-University Committee. However, 66 percent of all East African faculty have been Rockefeller Foundation scholars or holders of Special Lectureships established with Rockefeller Foundation funding for returning national scholars for whom an established post was not yet available. If the sample is limited to East Africans who are full professors and deans, 80 percent have had assistance. The Agricultural Faculty at Makerere College in Uganda reoriented its curriculum with greater emphasis on crop production during the leadership of Dean John Nickel, Rockefeller Foundation staff member. The Institute of Development Studies in Nairobi reached maturity in the years of Dr. James S. Coleman's directorship. For a far-flung multinational university in these countries, help at crucial points can affect the entire university even though the total resources provided from outside may be small relative to the overall educational budget.

Perhaps the main testimony to the effectiveness of the massive attempt to develop university institutions in poorer nations is the fact that practically all universities in developing countries have been modeled, both in structure and function, after older institutions in richer countries. For example, Todaro and others (1974, p. 205) have noted: "By long and powerful tradition the universities of the Western World are structured by disciplines or professions, as they have been since the medieval period. This structure, departments (disciplines) and their grouping (faculty) was exported on a large scale to universities in the developing countries, with little thought or effort given to questions of how this mode of academic organization would fit to serve existing conditions."

Second-order problems. Toward the end of the 1960s, a number of observers began to point with increased concern to problems emerging among institutions of higher education in developing nations. Malcolm Adiseshiah (1970, p. 251), then deputy director general of UNESCO, provided this view of the situation:

The current university situation in the under-developed world can only be described as bleak. The prevailing syndrome of wastage, dropouts, inefficiencies, repetitions, uninspired teaching, prescription of pre-digested and erroneous 'bizarre notes' as texts, overcrowded classrooms, lack of time for reflection and research, examination systems—all these inhibit thought and act as superficial classification machines. . . . Add to this the lack of relation between employment opportunities and development demands for skills on the one hand, and the streams and specialization offered in the colleges and universities on the other. Crown it with the moral confusion and material corruption creeping into university administrations and staff life, the atmosphere of terrible boredom and shiftless unreality, and one then sees the whole sad picture."

A few years later, Todaro and colleagues from the Rockefeller Foundation (1974, p. 205) wrote: "Universities in the developing countries have been found by practically all informed observers to be as dysfunctional and disoriented as educational institutions in lower levels. Many of the problems basic to primary and secondary education recur in more or less aggravated form in universities: annual increases in the order of 10 percent in student enrollment, rising costs, declining pupil-teacher ratios, deficient facilities, inappropriate curricula, administrative inertia, and ever more serious problems of unemployment or malemployment for university graduates."

Some have claimed that these problems arose despite international planning, arguing either that the volume of external aid has been insufficient to overcome such problems or that no amount of external aid could alleviate conditions until the political, social, and economic conditions in the recipient nations change (see Phillips, 1976, p. 124). The position taken here, however, is that many of the most critical problems of higher education in developing nations are a direct product of the success of the effort to implant what are essentially Western institutions in recipient societies. (Indeed, readers who work within universities in developed nations will have heard most of the criticisms noted above leveled at their own institutions.) Among the problems most clearly created for recipient nations by this massive export of traditional Western university forms and practices, the following are most frequently noted.

First, the "excellence" of university work is measured in terms of international academic standards, rather than in terms of its contribution to national development. Professors gain prestige by publishing in international scholarly journals or in local journals patterned after international journals. To gain access to the pages of those journals, scholars must focus their work on problems that are of interest to the international scholarly community (or at least that segment of it which controls journals) and devote much effort to developing in their work an internationally acceptable standard of methodological and theoretical rigor. Instructional quality is judged by the extent to which local credentials are regarded by prestigious universities in rich nations as equivalent to their own credentials. For example, will a student with a locally earned undergraduate degree be able to enroll in a postgraduate program in a rich nation? This continuing

reference to external role models reinforces a long-standing tendency for curricula, methods of instruction, and even the language of instruction in transplanted universities to be typically Western. These tendencies are particularly troublesome among the poorest and least developed nations. A recent UNESCO document refers to educational aid to what are classified by UNESCO (1974a, p. 15) as the twenty-five least developed countries: "The bulk of the aid streams is being utilized for paying expatriate teachers, who often teach a 'Western' type curriculum in a foreign language. The value to the recipient of such type of cooperation is likely to be only a fraction of its cost to the donor."

Second, universities in rich countries are, in the main, elitist institutions. Transplanted to poor societies, they have served either to ratify and enhance the status of existing elites or to create elites where none (or very small ones) existed. Thus, their presence has contributed to an increase in structured social inequality.

Third, universities have been preparing too many of the "wrong" types of graduates. Many development efforts are impeded by a lack of many types of qualified manpower, though the societies have large numbers of unemployed university graduates who either can find no jobs at all in their fields or cannot find jobs which provide the levels of salary and working conditions they have been led to expect are appropriate for university graduates. In some cases this criticism reflects the "irrelevant curriculum" argument noted above; in other cases it reflects the manpower planning exercises done a decade or more ago. Planners then based their forecasts of required manpower on estimations of what the society would, in an ideal sense, "need" rather than on estimations of what the developing economy would "demand" in terms of available employment opportunities; they placed too much faith in what has proven to be a very imprecise technique.

Fourth, universities are extraordinarily expensive institutions to maintain, primarily because faculty salaries, responding to some extent to the pressures of an international marketplace, are, in poorer nations, higher in relation to national per capita income than they are in rich countries. Almost everywhere the cost of instruction per student is far higher at the university level than at any lower educational level. Thus, after an institution has been established with international cooperation and the initial aid is withdrawn, the recipient nation is left with the necessity of continuing to support the institution, whose very high recurrent costs represent a very heavy drain on a limited public budget. Thus, universities in poor nations are often means by which the already very poor subsidize the high living styles of the already well-to-do elite.

Finally, the presence and rapid expansion of institutions of higher education has created a heavy social demand for their continued expansion. Having observed that positions of power and wealth are predominantly occupied by university graduates, students in lower levels of the educational system aspire in large numbers to enter the university. In few developing nations have governments been able politically to resist this pressure. There is thus a built-in expansionary dynamic to university systems in most developing nations which aggravates the problems noted above.

Current Trends

Although not all of these problems characterize every system of higher education in poor nations, they are sufficiently common to have led to a substantial rethinking of the appropriate role of international aid to higher education. It is as yet too early to predict what the outcome of that rethinking will be. One argument is that although these problems were very evident a few years ago, some progress has been made toward solving them, and continuing relatively modest adjustments in the kinds of aid given and the way it is given will be sufficient to eventually solve the problems.

Another argument suggests that these problems are inherent in aid to higher education, and that what is required is a massive redeployment of international aid, away from higher education and toward forms of education (and other projects) that will directly and immediately help the vast majority of people in developing nations who are desperately poor and predominantly rural. A third general approach claims that these problems are only manifestations of the fact that all aid to education (indeed all aid) is part of an international neocolonial and imperialist system in which the poor are made poor and kept poor by the rich for the benefit of the rich. Thus, problems can be solved only by a complete reordering of the international political and economic systems. Whichever view eventually predominates, it seems clear that the last years of the 1970s will bring at least some, perhaps substantial, changes in the levels and types of aid provided for the development of higher education. Indeed, as of 1976 there is an observable tendency among major donor agencies to decrease the proportion of their aid funds devoted to higher education projects.

Bibliography

Adiseshiah, M. *Let My Country Awake.* New York: UNESCO, 1970. A powerful and compelling statement, by a well-known international statesman from the developing world, of the problems and dilemmas confronting developing nations and of the effects of international aid programs.

Cerych, L. *Problems of Aid to Education in Developing Countries.* New York: Praeger, 1965. A useful statement of the views prevalent in the early 1960s regarding aid to education.

Coombs, P. "The Role of International Organizations in the Field of Higher Education." In J. A. Perkins (Ed.), *Higher Education: From Autonomy to Systems.* Washington, D.C.: Voice of America, Forum Series, 1973.

Harbison, F. H. "The Strategy of Human Resource Development in Modernizing Economics." In *Policy Conference on Economic Growth and Investment in Education.* Paris: Organisation for Economic Co-operation and Development, 1962. A good statement of the "investment in human resources" rationale for providing aid to education as perceived in the early 1960s.

Harbison, F. H., and Myers, C. A. *Education, Manpower and Economic Growth.* New York: McGraw-Hill, 1964. A classic and highly influential work emphasizing the need for developing highly qualified manpower for national economic development.

International Development Research Center. *The IDRC Task Force Report on Education Research.* Ottawa, Ontario: International Development Research Center, April 1975. Concentrating on research needs regarding education in developing nations, this report clearly reflects current trends in thinking about refocusing educational assistance.

Organisation for Economic Co-operation and Development (OECD). *Aid to Education in Less-Developed Countries (Note by the Secretariat).* Paris: Organisation for Economic Co-operation and Development, April 1971. A useful collection of data regarding aid flows.

Perkins, J. A. *Higher Education: From Autonomy to Systems.* Washington, D.C.: Voice of America, Forum Series, 1973. A collection of papers which provides a useful picture of the agencies involved in the international educational planning system for development of higher education.

Phillips, H. M. *Educational Cooperation Between Developed and Developing Countries.* New York: Praeger, 1976. A highly useful analysis of the development of the international planning system for educational development and a "middle of the road" analysis of current trends. Chapter 7 deals specifically with higher education.

Simmons, J., and Others. *Investment in Education: National Strategy Options for Developing Countries.* Working Paper No. 196. Washington, D.C.: World Bank, February 1975. A very good recent collection of papers discussing current problems and trends in educational development. A wide range of views, from moderately reformist to radical critiques, are presented.

Thomas, J. *World Problems in Education: A Brief Analytical Survey.* Paris: UNESCO-IBE (International Bureau of Education), 1975. A relatively recent survey of current problems in educational development.

Thompson, K. W., and others. "Higher Education and National Development: One Model for Technical Assistance." In F. C. Ward (Ed.), *Education and Development Reconsidered: The Bellagio Conference Papers.* New York: Praeger, 1974.

Todaro, M. P., and others. "Education for National Development: The University." In F. C. Ward (Ed.), *Education and Development Reconsidered: The Bellagio Conference Papers.* New York: Praeger, 1974.

UNESCO. *International Cooperation in Education with Special Reference to the 25 Least Developed Countries.* Paris: UNESCO, IDC/REF. 1, April 1974a. A pointed analysis of problems created or exacerbated by educational aid efforts, containing useful data regarding aid flows.

UNESCO. *UNESCO Statistical Yearbook, 1974.* Paris: UNESCO, 1974b. An annual international compendium of statistics.

Ward, F. C. (Ed.) *Education and Development Reconsidered: The Bellagio Conference Papers.* New York: Praeger, 1974. A very useful collection of papers analyzing the current state of education in developing nations, and the role international aid has played and may play in the future.

World Bank. *Education: Sector Working Paper.* Washington, D.C.: World Bank, December 1974. Reflects the current viewpoint regarding aid to education of one of the most influential agencies in the international planning system.

JOSEPH P. FARRELL

See also: Science Policies: Overview.

PLANNING UNIVERSITY DEVELOPMENT: GENERAL REPORT

See Organisation for Economic Co-operation and Development.

PLANT PATHOLOGY (Field of Study)

Plant pathology is a biological science concerned with the nature, epidemiology, and control of diseases that threaten the productivity of plants. Research plant pathologists study the complex interactions between plants and their destructive pathogens: viruses, bacteria, fungi, nematodes, mycoplasma-like organisms, and parasitic seed plants. In addition, plant pathologists investigate the physiological effects on plants of abiotic (nonliving or nonparasitic) agents such as air pollutants, various toxic agents, and adverse environmental conditions. Unlike human medicine and veterinary science, plant pathology seeks to prevent disease in large populations rather than to cure individual sick plants. Combating disease may require diverse approaches such as (1) exclusion of pathogens by quarantines or use of disease-free seed and planting material; (2) eradication of pathogens through the use of chemicals prior to planting, modification of cultural practices, or direct removal of plants; (3) protection against infection through the application of sprays or dusts; (4) prophylaxis by postinfection treatment with systemic fungicides; and (5) development of resistant varieties through cooperation with plant breeders and geneticists, the major emphasis in the mid 1970s.

Branches in plant pathology include phytobacteriology, plant virology, plant nematology, disease physiology, genetics of plant pathogens in relation to disease resistance, epidemiology, soil microbiology in relation to soil-borne pathogens, and chemical control. Forest pathology is usually also identified as a separate area, based on the distinctive approaches to disease control for forest trees. A developing area is the study of air pollution damage to plants. A second developing area is the role of plant pathogens and related fungi in the formation of potent mycotoxins injurious to farm animals and man.

Principles and concepts distinctive to plant pathology have been developed; however, the field remains dependent on basic biological and physical sciences and on applied agricultural disciplines such as agronomy, horticulture, weed science, and soils. Specific related fields are the botanical sciences (plant physiology, morphology, anatomy, mycology, and ecology), cell biology, cytology, microbiology, virology, zoology (nematology and parasitology), genetics, and biochemistry. Development of effective, safe chemicals for plants and soils requires information from agricultural engineering, chemistry, meteorology, soil science, computer science, and crop science. Entomology also is important, since insects disseminate many plant pathogens

and may also injure plants directly. Finally, disease-resistant varieties can be developed only with knowledge of the principles of genetics and plant breeding, as well as those of agronomy and horticulture.

Until the nineteenth century, the causes of plant disease eluded man; hence, he was unable to prevent crop losses, damage to forests, and famine. From 1845 to 1848 millions starved from epidemics of the blight disease of potatoes in Ireland and northern Europe, a disaster which gave strong impetus to studies on disease causation in Europe. Anton De Bary, a German physician turned botanist, provided the first conclusive evidence that a fungus was the causal agent of the late blight disease. From 1880 to 1920, through applications of the pure culture techniques of Robert Koch and Oskar Brefeld, the causal relationship of many fungi to specific plant diseases was determined. In 1885 a French scientist, Alexis Millardet, discovered the effectiveness of a copper sulfate–lime fungicide (Bordeaux mixture) for controlling downy mildew of grape; the fungicide also was useful for controlling the late blight disease of potatoes. In the 1890s Erwin F. Smith of the United States Department of Agriculture showed that certain bacteria can cause disease in plants. D. Ivanovski in Russia (1890) and Adolph Mayer (1885) and M. W. Beijerinck (1898) in the Netherlands demonstrated that ultramicroscopic infectious agents (the viruses) also induce plant diseases. Finally, in 1935 the tobacco mosaic virus was first crystallized by Wendell Meredith Stanley; and from 1914 until his death in 1932, Nathan Augustus Cobb, who worked initially in Australia and then in the United States, explored the importance of parasitic nematodes to plant diseases. The discovery and availability of inexpensive soil fumigants caused an upsurge in research and training in nematology in the United States after World War II.

In the United States, teaching and research in plant pathology developed slowly in agricultural state universities and experiment stations, which employed the first plant pathologists. Educational programs designed for professionals were established in the early 1900s at the University of California, the University of Minnesota, Cornell University, and the University of Wisconsin. The greatest growth and expansion occurred after World War II, mainly in the United States but also in other developed countries. Undergraduate courses were mycologically oriented and stressed disease recognition and methods of control. Second-level courses usually covered diseases of specific groups of crops. Emphasis has shifted to more fundamental aspects of the science, both in undergraduate and advanced courses.

In recent years plant pathologists have encountered new and more complex diseases. For example, outbreaks of disease such as the corn leaf blight in the United States in 1970 emphasized the genetic vulnerability of major food crops. Greater emphasis, consequently, is being placed on the need to maintain genetic diversity of crop plants and to understand the genetic variability of pathogens, as well as the factors causing epidemics. Curricula at major institutions reflect the need for more depth in genetics and plant breeding for plant pathologists who will be working in a team approach with plant breeders. Another trend has been the application of computer technology to disease epidemics. If disease outbreaks can be predicted accurately, fungicide applications can be reduced; thus, many universities in the United States are developing programs in epidemiology. Other recent developments are (1) a shift in student interest—from biochemical or physiological aspects of disease to more ecological concerns; (2) availability of more opportunities for individuals in applied areas of plant pathology; and (3) the initiation of undergraduate programs with a multidisciplinary approach, where more emphasis is placed on plant pathology, entomology, and weed science than on the crop sciences.

As an outgrowth of these trends, centers of advanced training and basic research in plant pathology have developed, mainly in North America, Western Europe, Japan,

and Australia. Furthermore, research in tropical areas was conducted primarily by Western-trained scientists and directed to the control of diseases of plantation and export crops, such as coffee and bananas, with little emphasis on basic food crops. However, the emphasis has changed rapidly since the 1950s, particularly after the dramatic increases in yield following the development of disease-resistant dwarf wheat and rice by the international institutes in Mexico and the Philippines.

From 1945 to 1965 expansion in graduate training programs occurred in the developed countries, particularly in the United States. Furthermore, many students from developing countries, who were provided with advanced training, returned to their respective countries and developed advanced training programs. In addition, through the technical assistance programs of the Food and Agriculture Organization of the United Nations, large numbers of Western-trained plant pathologists were sent to new or expanding agricultural colleges and institutes in Africa, Asia, and Central and South America. The influence of these scientists is felt in the expanded number of educational programs, research publications in plant pathology, and countries with national societies for plant pathology.

The recent establishment of the Technical Advisory Committee of the Consultative Group on International Agricultural Research initiated coordinated funding of international agricultural research institutes of the world. These institutes emphasized cooperative efforts between plant pathologists, breeders, and other researchers in developing resistant varieties. As training centers, the institutes strengthen plant pathology and other related sciences in developing countries.

Levels and Programs of Study

Programs in plant pathology usually require as a minimum prerequisite a secondary education and lead to the following degrees: bachelor's (B.S.), master's (M.S.), the doctorate (Ph.D.), or their equivalents.

Programs deal with the principles and practices of plant pathology and consist of classroom, seminar, and research. In-depth instruction in plant pathology is usually not required in many of the two-year programs designed for plant protection specialists.

Programs that lead to a first university degree usually consist of basic training in biological sciences rather than specialization in plant pathology. Course content usually includes introduction to botany; advanced botanical science subjects (physiology, ecology, taxonomy, morphology, and anatomy); introduction to zoology and entomology; genetics; microbiology; and one or more crop science courses, including weed science. Other basic courses usually required are chemistry (inorganic and organic), biochemistry, physics, mathematics, and statistics. Because basic background courses in biological and related agricultural sciences must have priority, relatively few courses in plant pathology are offered at this level. Courses in communication skills and general education are usually also required.

Programs that lead to a postgraduate university degree or the equivalent vary in requirements for course work. The Ph.D. degree requires in-depth study and completion of an original research project on some special topic in plant pathology. In some institutions the Master of Science degree or equivalent does not require completion of a research thesis or project; adequate mastery of course work may satisfy the requirement.

Subject areas for an advanced degree in American universities include courses on plant pathogens (virology, nematology, mycology, phytobacteriology) and courses in advanced plant pathology, covering such topics as soil-borne pathogens, disease diagnosis, epidemiology, breeding for disease resistance, control by chemical and other methods, and disease physiology. Special courses concerned with diseases of specific crops may also be covered. Forest pathology is usually treated in a separate course. This system for advanced training has been adopted in many developed and developing countries, including India and Japan. Additional courses in other fields are chosen according to the subject of a student's research project and specific employment interests. Major background courses may include advanced genetics, cytogenetics, plant breeding, biochemistry and biochemical methods, microbial physiology and ecology, molecular biology, soils, and other areas.

Major International and National Organizations

INTERNATIONAL

Asociación latinoamericana fitopatología
Centro internacional de agricultural tropical
Apartado Aéreo 5813
Bogotá, Colombia

International Organization of
  Mycoplasmatologists
Building 7
National Institutes of Health
Bethesda, Maryland 20014 USA

International Society for Plant Pathology
Phytopatologisch Laboratorium
Javalaan 20
Baarn, Netherlands
  Major international organization in the field.

Mediterranean Phytopathological Union
Istituto di patologia forestale
University of Florence
Piazza delle Cascine 28
Florence, Italy

In addition to the organizations listed above, there are a number of specialized organizations concerned with specific areas of the field. For a listing, consult:

Yearbook of International Organizations. Brussels: Union of International Associations, 1974.

NATIONAL ORGANIZATIONS

Australia:
  Australian Plant Pathology Society
  Plant Pathology Branch
  Department of Primary Industries
  Meiers Road
  Brisbane, Queensland 4068

Canada:
  Canadian Phytopathological Society
  Research Branch, Agriculture Canada
  Box 1210
  Charlottetown, Prince Edward Island
  C1A 7M8

Chile:
Sociedad chilena de fitopatología
Instituto de investigaciones agropecuarias
Estación experimental La Platina
P.O. Box 5427
Santiago

Denmark:
Dansk plante patologisk selskab
Staten plante patologiske forsøg
Lottenborguet 2
Lyngby

Federal Republic of Germany:
Deutsche phytomedizinische Gesellschaft
Otto Sanderstrasse 5
7 Stuttgart 70

India:
Indian Phytopathological Society
Indian Agricultural Research Institute
New Delhi 12

Iran:
Iranian Phytopathological Society
Plant Pests and Diseases Research Institute
P.O. Box 3178
Tehran

Ireland:
Society of Irish Plant Pathologists
Agricultural Institute
Oak Park Research Centre
Carlow

Italy:
Società italiana di fitopatologia
Istituto di patologia
via Celoria 2
20133 Milan

Japan:
Phytopathological Society of Japan
National Institute of Agricultural Sciences
Nishigahara, Kita-ku
Tokyo 114

Netherlands:
Nederlandse planteziektenkundige
vereniging
Postbus 31
Wageningen

Peru:
Asociación peruana de fitopatología
Departamento de fitopatología
Universidad nacional agraria
Apartado 456
Lima

Philippines:
Philippine Phytopathological Society
Department of Plant Pathology,
College of Agriculture
University of the Philippines
Los Baños

South Africa:
South African Society for Plant Pathology
and Microbiology
P.O. Box 11446
0011 Brooklyn

United Kingdom:
Federation of British Plant Pathologists
Department of Agricultural Botany
Welsh Agricultural College
Aberystwyth, Cardiganshire, Wales

United States:
American Phytopathological Society
Department of Plant Pathology
University of Georgia
Athens, Georgia 30601

Principal Information Sources

GENERAL

Guides to the literature in the field include:

Barnes, H. V., and Allen, J. M. *A Bibliography of Plant Pathology in the Tropics and Latin America.* Washington, D.C.: U.S. Government Printing Office, 1951.

"A Bibliography of Lists of Plant Diseases and Fungi." *Review of Applied Mycology,* 1968, *47,* 553–558; 1970, *49,* 108; 1971, *50,* 1–7; 1972, *51,* 1–7; 1975, *54,* 963–966. Each article is devoted to one geographical area: (1) Africa, (2) Asia, (3) America, (4) America, (5) Australia.

Bush, E. A. R. *Agriculture: A Bibliographic Guide.* (2 vols.) London: Macdonald, 1974. Includes information on plant pathology and plant diseases.

Commonwealth Mycological Institute. *Plant Pathologist's Pocketbook.* Reading, England: Lamport Gilbert, 1968.

Plant Sciences in East Africa: Bibliography. Morgantown: West Virginia University Library, 1971.

Selected List of American Agricultural Books in Print and Current Periodicals. Beltsville, Maryland: National Agricultural Library, 1975. An extensive listing of books on various aspects of agriculture and related subjects published by United States publishers; contains a section on plant pathology.

General introductory texts are:

Agrios, G. N. *Plant Pathology.* New York: Academic Press, 1969.

Roberts, D. A., and Boothroyd, C. W. *Fundamentals of Plant Pathology.* San Francisco: W. H. Freeman, 1972.

Roger, L. *Phytopathologie des pays chauds.* (3 vols.) Paris: Lechavalier, 1951–1954.

Stakman, E. C., and Harrar, J. G. *Principles of Plant Pathology.* New York: Ronald Press, 1957.

Stevens, R. B. *Plant Disease.* New York: Ronald Press, 1974.

Tarr, S. A. J. *Principles of Plant Pathology.* London: Macmillan, 1972.

Walker, J. C. *Plant Pathology.* (3rd ed.) New York: McGraw-Hill, 1968.

Wheeler, B. E. J. *An Introduction to Plant Diseases.* Chichester, Sussex, England: Wiley, 1969.

Selected advanced texts are:

Baker, K. F., and Cook, R. J. *Biological Control of Plant Pathogens.* San Francisco: W. H. Freeman, 1974.

Baker, K. F., and Snyder, W. C. *Ecology of Soil-Borne Pathogens.* Berkeley: University of California Press, 1965.

Bawden, F. C. *Plant Viruses and Virus Diseases.* (4th ed.) New York: Ronald Press, 1964.

Day, P. *Genetics of Host-Parasite Interaction.* San Francisco: W. H. Freeman, 1974.

Horsfall, J. G., and Dimond, A. E. (Eds.) *Plant Pathology: An Advanced Treatise.* (3 vols.) New York: Academic Press, 1959–1960.

Matthews, R. E. F. *Plant Virology.* New York: Academic Press, 1970.

Thorne, G. *Principles of Nematology.* New York: McGraw-Hill, 1961.

Van der Plank, J. E. *Principles of Plant Infection.* New York: Academic Press, 1975.

Wood, R. K. S. *Physiological Plant Pathology.* Oxford, England: Blackwell Scientific Publications, 1967.

Histories of the field are offered by:

Carefoot, G. S., and Sprott, E. R. *Famine on the Wind, Man's Battle Against Plant Disease.* Chicago: Rand McNally, 1967.

Holton, C. S. (Ed.) *Plant Pathology: Problems and Progress 1908–1958.* Madison: University of Wisconsin Press, 1959.

Large, E. C. *The Advance of the Fungi.* New York: Holt, Rinehart and Winston, 1940.

Parris, G. K. *A Chronology of Plant Pathology.* Starkville, Mississippi: Johnson & Sons, 1968.

Walker, J. C. "Some Highlights on Plant Pathology in the United States." *Annual Review of Phytopathology,* 1975, *13,* 15–29.

Whetzel, H. H. *An Outline of the History of Phytopathology.* Philadelphia: Saunders, 1918.

A work dealing with plant pathology education is:

Broadbent, L. (Ed.) *Symposium on Higher Education for Crop Protection in Europe.* British Crop Protection Council Monograph 13. Nottingham, England: Boots Company, 1974.

CURRENT BIBLIOGRAPHIES

Agrindex. Rome: Food and Agriculture Organi-

zation (FAO), 1975–. Includes information on plant production and protection as well as on agricultural education.

Bibliographie der Pflanzenschutzliteratur. Berlin, Federal Republic of Germany: Biologische Bundesanstalt für Land und Forstwirtschaft, 1914–. Comprehensive bibliography of plant protection.

Bibliography of Agriculture. Scottsdale, Arizona: Oryx Press, 1942–. International coverage; monthly index to literature on agriculture and related sciences; includes information on plant science.

Helminthological Abstracts. Series B, Plant Nematology. St. Albans, England: Commonwealth Institute of Helminthology, 1970–.

Refererativnyĭ zhurnal. 55: Rastenievodstvo. Moscow: Akademiia nauk, SSSR, Institut nauchnoĭ informatsii, 1969–.

Review of Plant Pathology. Kew, England: Commonwealth Mycological Institute, 1922–. (Formerly *Review of Applied Mycology.*) Compiled from world literature.

PERIODICALS

Annales de phytopathologie (France), *Annals of Applied Biology* (UK), *Annals of the Phytopathological Society of Japan, Annual Review of Phytopathology* (US), *Archiv für Phytopathologie und Pflanzenschutz* (FRG), *European Journal of Forest Pathology* (FRG), *Fitopatología* (Peru), *Indian Phytopathology* (India), *Mikologiya i fitopatologiya* (USSR), *Nematologica* (Netherlands), *Netherlands Journal of Plant Pathology, Notiziario sulle malattie delle piante* (Italy), *Philippine Phytopathology, Phytopathologische Zeitschrift* (FRG), *Phytopathology* (US), *Plant Disease Reporter* (US), *Transactions British Mycological Society* (UK), *Virology* (US).

For a more extensive listing of journals dealing with plant pathology see:

List of Serials Currently Received by the Food and Agriculture Organization of the United Nations Library. Rome: FAO, 1973.

"List of Serial Publications Regularly Seen." In *Review of Plant Pathology.* Kew, England: Commonwealth Mycological Institute, annual January issue.

Ulrich's International Periodicals Directory. New York: Bowker, biennial.

ENCYCLOPEDIAS, DICTIONARIES, HANDBOOKS

Ainsworth, G. C. *Ainsworth & Bixby's Dictionary of the Fungi.* (6th ed.) Kew, England: Commonwealth Mycological Institute, 1971.

American Phytopathological Society. *Sourcebook of Laboratory Exercises in Plant Pathology.* San Francisco: W. H. Freeman, 1967.

Diakova, G. A. *Phytopathological Dictionary: Russian-English-German-French.* Moscow: Itayka, 1969.

Merino-Rodríguez, M. *Elsevier's Lexicon of Plant Pests and Diseases.* Amsterdam: Elsevier, 1966. In English, Latin, French, Italian, Spanish, and German.

Plant Pathologist's Pocketbook. Kew, England: Commonwealth Mycological Institute, 1968.

Shurtleff, M. C. *How to Control Plant Diseases in Home and Garden.* (2nd ed.) Ames: Iowa State University Press, 1966.

Tuite, J. *Plant Pathological Methods.* Minneapolis: Burgess, 1969.

Westcott, C. *Plant Disease Handbook.* (3rd ed.) New York: Van Nostrand Reinhold, 1971.

DIRECTORIES

Educational directories which include information on agricultural study are:

American Colleges and Universities. Washington, D.C.: American Council on Education, 1928–. Published quadrennially.

Commonwealth Universities Yearbook. London: Association of Commonwealth Universities, 1914–. Published annually.

International Handbook of Universities. Paris: International Association of Universities, 1959–. Published triennially.

The World of Learning. London: Europa, 1947–. Published annually. Lists universities, colleges, institutes, research centers, learned societies, and libraries throughout the world.

Directories of plant pathologists include:

American Phytopathological Society Directory of Members. Athens, Georgia: American Phytopathological Society, 1974.

Fisher, F. E. *World Directory of Plant Pathologists.* Lake Alfred, Florida: n.p., 1973.

RESEARCH CENTERS, INSTITUTES, INFORMATION CENTERS

Directories to research and information in the agricultural sciences include:

Boalch, D. H. *World Directory of Agricultural Libraries and Documentation Centers.* Oxford, England: International Association of Agricultural Librarians and Documentalists (IAALD), 1960. Records nearly two thousand libraries in more than one hundred countries; a revised edition is being planned.

Index of Agricultural Research Institutions and Stations in Africa. Rome: FAO, n.d.

National Agricultural Library. *Directory of Information Resources in Agriculture and Biology.* Washington, D.C.: U.S. Government Printing Office, 1971.

ARTHUR KELLMAN

PLANT SERVICES

See Business Management of Higher Education: Facilities, Physical Plant.

PODIATRY (Field of Study)

Podiatry is a branch of the health fields that deals with the examination, diagnosis, treatment, and prevention of diseases and disorders of the human foot. Treatment may be by medical, mechanical, physical, or surgical means. Among the foot disorders that cause pain and disability are corns and callosities; hypertrophied, deformed, and ingrown nails; verrucae; and various other infections and inflammations. General disease processes are also manifest in the feet, for example, neurological and vascular deficiencies, diabetes, and rheumatic diseases. The scope of practice thus includes physical examination of the feet and legs, diagnoses and their medical and surgical management, application of medicine and drugs, heat therapy, padding and strapping, and the prescription and fabrication of corrective and protective appliances and modifications to footwear.

The podiatrist, an independent, licensed practitioner, works in association with other specialists in the medical and related professions in a variety of settings: government institutions, hospitals, colleges of podiatric medicine, or private practice. In hospitals, podiatrists may serve in departments of orthopedic surgery, peripheral vascular disease units, diabetic units, or geriatric divisions.

In the United Kingdom, the term *chiropody* is used to describe this field, whose scope is more limited than in the United States. For example, chiropodists in the United Kingdom do not treat foot disorders by surgical means; rather, the chiropodist is chiefly concerned with nonsurgical treatment of corns, warts, callosities, and bunions of the feet.

The roots of podiatry, like those of other medical professions, can be traced to antiquity. References to foot remedies were recorded in the Ebers medical papyrus as early as the sixteenth century B.C., and Hippocrates referred to foot treatments in 400 B.C. Later, during the fourteenth to seventeenth centuries, foot care was provided by individuals in guilds of barbers-surgeons. The first work devoted exclusively to foot care, *Chiropodologia,* written by an Englishman, D. Low, in 1774, gave rise to the term *chiropody.*

The original scope of chiropodiatric practice was confined to minor and superficial disorders of the feet. In the mid 1800s foot treatment was performed in the United States by "corncutters." During the twentieth century, however, podiatry-chiropody has evolved into a complex, skilled profession which applies scientific principles to the diagnosis and treatment of a wide variety of disorders and deformities of the foot.

In the United States the first office devoted exclusively to chiropody was established in Boston in 1846. In 1868 there were only 25 chiropodists in the United States; by 1912 there were approximately 1500. The first professional organization in the field was established in 1912 as the National Association of Chiropodists; in 1958 its name was changed to the American Podiatry Association. The first professional chiropodial society in the United Kingdom was established in 1913 as the Incorporated Society. In 1946 the Incorporated Society merged with other professional societies to form the Societies of Chiropodists.

The first schools of chiropody, the New York School of Chiropody and the Illinois College of Chiropody and Orthopedics, were established in 1912. In 1976 there were six accredited colleges of podiatric medicine in the United States: California College of Podiatric Medicine in San Francisco, Illinois College of Podiatric Medicine in Chicago, New York College of Podiatric Medicine in New York City, Ohio College of Podiatric Medicine in Cleveland, Pennsylvania College of Podiatric Medicine in Philadelphia, and the School of Podiatric Medicine at the Health Services Center of the State University of New York (SUNY) at Stony Brook.

The accrediting agency for colleges of podiatric medicine in the United States is the Council on Podiatry Education of the American Podiatry Association. Graduates of colleges of podiatric medicine can further their training through postgraduate and residency programs at several medical centers in the United States, which offer specialties in different areas of podiatry; for example, foot surgery or orthopedics. Canadian podiatrists receive their training in the United States.

In the United Kingdom there are eight recognized training schools for chiropody (five in England, two in Scotland, and one in Wales): Chelsea School of Chiropody (London), London Foot Hospital and School of Chiropody, Birmingham School of Chiropody, Durham School of Chiropody, Northern College of Chiropody (Salford), Edinburgh Foot Clinic and School of Chiropody, Glasgow School of Chiropody, and Cardiff School of Chiropody. The Society of Chiropodists is the qualifying body that controls professional examinations in the United Kingdom.

The scope of podiatric licensure and practice in the United States is the most extensive in the world. In the United States the podiatrist is licensed to perform a variety of surgical operations; British chiropodists, however, may not undertake bone or joint surgery, nor may they take X rays.

The college teaching staff in the United States and the United Kingdom consists mainly of podiatrists or chiropodists, who are responsible for classroom and clinical instruction of podiatric/chiropodic theory and practice. Teaching assistance is also provided by biologists, anatomists, physiologists, physicians, and surgeons. Several areas of study are of particular importance: the structure and function of the human foot and its relationship to the body; the origin and cause of foot abnormalities; and the methods of treatment for such disorders.

Programs include study of the life sciences, particularly anatomy and physiology, since a general knowledge of these areas is necessary for further studies in microbiology and pathology. Emphasis is placed on those aspects of anatomy and physiology that relate to the foot in health and disease. Anatomy of the lower limb and the study of the nervous and vascular systems are of particular importance. Courses in the principles of medicine and surgery in relation to disorders of the lower limbs provide the student with knowledge of systematic disease and locomotor dysfunction of the foot and leg.

Usual length of the professional podiatry curriculum is four academic years or the equivalent. The first two years consist mainly of classroom instruction and laboratory work, although in the second year students begin to gain some experience in the college clinics. During the last two years students spend most of their time obtaining clinical experience in two phases: didactic and laboratory courses, and supervised treatment of patients in cases of varying complexity. Service may be in clinics and hospitals which are either a part of the college or separately organized and affiliated with the college. Clinical instruction and practice cover all phases and aspects of podiatric service.

In countries other than the United States and the United Kingdom, training for practitioners in the area of foot care ranges from little or no formal education to three years of technical schooling.

There are no institutions devoted exclusively to podiatry in the Soviet Union or Eastern Europe. Consequently, foot care is treated within the general scope of surgery, particularly orthopedic surgery. Likewise, in the Middle East podiatric medicine as a specialty does not exist on a large scale, and foot surgery is generally handled by orthopedists. There are, however, some British-trained chiropodists in Israel.

Several schools of podology (the study of the human foot in health and disease) exist in Western Europe, but they deal with its nonsurgical, relatively minor aspects. An example is the Institute of Podology in France, which offers a two-year course. A third-year program is also available for special training in foot prosthesis. However, as in all countries except the United States, major aspects of foot care and foot surgery are the responsibility of orthopedic surgeons.

While foot problems are universal, adequate attention to such problems does not universally exist. Therefore, the scope and standards of podiatric practice and education vary significantly throughout the world.

[Material provided by American Podiatry Association, Louis G. Buttell, Marvin W. Shapiro, and Society of Chiropodists.]

Levels and Programs of Study

Programs in podiatry/chiropody generally require as a minimum educational prerequisite a secondary education, and lead to the doctor of podiatric medicine (D.P.M.) degree or its equivalent. Programs deal with the diagnosis and treatment of pathological conditions affecting the foot, including both functional and structural disturbances.

The professional curriculum in podiatry/chiropody comprises three or four years of study and consists of classroom sessions, laboratory work, and clinical instruction. Programs usually include instruction in the basic medical sciences, physiological sciences, microbiology, biochemistry, pathology, pharmacology, and principles of surgery. In addition, principal course content generally includes dermatology; podology, with emphasis on the anatomy, physiology, and pathology of the foot; chiropodial therapeutics; general diagnostic procedures, such as physical and roentgenologic diagnosis; therapeutic procedures, such as pharmacology, orthotics and prosthetics, surgical procedures, anesthesia, and operative podiatry. Related background courses often include biology, zoology, chemistry, physics, mathematics, humanities, ethics and jurisprudence, and the social sciences.

Major International and National Organizations

INTERNATIONAL

International Federation of Podology
Fédération internationale de podologie
Netherlands Congress Centre
P.O. Box 9000
10 Churchillplein
The Hague, Netherlands

NATIONAL

Argentina:
  Asociación argentina de pedicuros
  Pte Luis Saenz
  Pena 1119
  Buenos Aires

Australia:
  Australian Chiropody Association
  446 Elizabeth Street
  Sydney, New South Wales

Austria:
  Verband österreichischer Fusspfleger
  Salzburg-Stauffeneggstrasse 25a
  A-5020 Salzburg

Belgium:
  Chambre nationale des chiropodistes
  97 avenue Crockaert
  Brussels 15

Brazil:
  Associação brasileira de pedicuros
  Caixa Postal 2701
  São Paulo

Canada:
  Canadian Podiatry Association
  1648 Victoria Park Avenue
  Scarborough, Ontario

Chile:
  Asociación nacional de podologistas de
    Chile
  Abdon Cifuentes 82
  Santiago

Ireland:
  Irish Association of Chiropodists
  21 North Frederick Street
  Dublin

Italy:
  Associazione nazionale italiana pedicure
  via Ramazzini #3
  20129 Milan

Netherlands:
  Nederlandse vereniging voor
    voetverzorging
  Dacostakade 3 bix A
  Utrecht

New Zealand:
  New Zealand Society of Chiropodists
  Box 387
  Christchurch

Paraguay:
  Asociación de podiatras del Paraguay
  Estrella 976
  Ascunción

Peru:
  Asociación peruana de pedicuros
  Luna Pizarro 1155 Dto. 3 La Victoria
  Lima

Spain:
  Agrupación de podologos de España
  Coso 77
  5° Saragossa

Sweden:
  Sveriges fotvårdsspecialisters
    riksförbund
  Box 7147
  Göteborg 7

United Kingdom:
  Society of Chiropodists
  8 Wimpole Street
  London WIM 8BX, England

United States:
  American Podiatry Association
  20 Chevy Chase Circle NW
  Washington, D. C. 20015

Uruguay:
  Asociación podologos del Uruguay
  Casilla de Correo 200
  Montevideo

For a listing of the American Podiatry Association's "Component Societies," listed alphabetically by state, consult the monthly issues of the *Journal of the American Podiatry Association*. Washington, D.C.: APA, 1907–.

Principal Information Sources

Guides to the literature of podiatry include:

Krausz, C. E. (Ed.) *Chiropody Index. 1907–1920.* Philadelphia: The Editor, 1943.

Reed, S. E. *Catalog of the Reed Library of the Foot and Ankle.* (2 vols.) Des Moines, Iowa: The Author, 1974. Lists books and journals in the field of podiatry.

Reed, S. E. "Review of American Podiatric Literature." *Journal of the American Podiatric Association*, 1974, *64*, 302–311. A bibliography of texts between 1847 and 1974.

Introductions and overviews to the field include:

Altman, M. I. (Ed.) *Modern Therapeutic Ap-*

proaches to Foot Problems. Mt. Kisco, New York: Futura Publications, 1973.

American Podiatry Association. *Podiatry in Today's Hospital.* Washington, D.C.: Block, McGibony, 1973. Includes a list of courses offered by the California College of Podiatric Medicine which is typical of podiatric curricula in the United States.

Charlesworth, F. *Chiropodial Orthopaedics.* (2nd ed., rev. and ed. by L. C. Gibbard) London: Baillière, Tindall, 1968.

Hass, F. J., and Dolan, E. F., Jr. *The Foot Book.* Chicago: Regnery, 1973.

Walker, M. *Your Guide to Foot Health.* New York: Arc Books, 1972.

Weinstein, F. *Principles and Practices of Podiatry.* Philadelphia: Lea & Febiger, 1968. A general text which includes a brief history of the field in Canada, the United Kingdom, and the United States.

Weinstein, F. *Principles and Practices of Foot Roentgenology.* St. Louis, Missouri: Green, 1974.

Yale, I. *Podiatric Medicine.* Baltimore: Williams & Wilkins, 1974.

Histories of the field include:

Dagnall, J. D. "The History of Chiropodial Literature." *Chiropodist,* 1965, *20,* 173–184.

Dagnall, J. D. "Notes on the History of Chiropody-Podiatry." Presented at the Region 6 convention of the American Podiatry Association, Des Moines, Iowa, April 1967.

Taub, J. "The Ancient Art of Podiatry." *Journal of the American Podiatry Association,* 1967, *57,* 555.

Valentin, B. *Geschichte der Fusspflege: Pedicurie, Chiropodie, Podologie.* Stuttgart, Federal Republic of Germany: Thieme, 1965.

Sources dealing with podiatric education are:

Blauch, L. E. *The Podiatry Curriculum.* Washington, D.C.: American Association of Colleges of Podiatric Medicine, 1970. A classic in the field of podiatry in the United States; provides a comprehensive view of the podiatric curriculum for the future; the only extensive cooperative study of podiatry and podiatric education on a nationwide basis.

Criteria, Guidelines, and Procedures for Accrediting Podiatry Colleges. Washington, D.C.: American Podiatry Association, Council on Podiatry Education, 1967.

Dalton, K. D. K., and Dalton, M. J. T. *Essentials of Chiropody for Students.* (6th ed.) London: Faber & Faber, 1968.

General Information and Outline of Courses, Regulations and Syllabus of Training. London: Society of Chiropodists, 1974.

"Podiatric Medicine, Function and Education." *Journal of Podiatric Education,* March 1973, *63,* 6–13. Discusses licensure, scope of practice, role in quality health care, and education in the United States (schools, requirements, and postgraduate education).

Podiatry Education, General Information for Prospective Students of Podiatric Medicine. Washington, D.C.: American Podiatry Association, 1972.

Podiatry Education in the 1960s: Status and Opportunities. Washington, D.C.: American Podiatry Association, Special Commission on Status of Podiatry Education, 1961.

Shangold, J. *Opportunities in a Podiatry Career.* New York: Educational Books, Division of Universal Publishing and Distributing Corp., 1971.

CURRENT BIBLIOGRAPHIES

Excerpta Medica. Amsterdam: Excerpta Medica Foundation, 1947–.

Hospital Literature Index. Chicago: American Hospital Association, 1945–.

Index Medicus. Bethesda, Maryland: National Library of Medicine, 1960–. Preceded by *Quarterly Cumulative Index Medicus,* 1927–1956.

Science Citation Index. Philadelphia: Institute for Science Information, 1961–.

PERIODICALS

Periodicals in the field include *British Journal of Chiropody, Canadian Journal of Podiatric Medicine, Chiropodist* (UK), *Chiropody Review* (UK), *Current Podiatry* (US), *Hospital Podiatrist* (US), *Journal of the American Association of Foot Specialists, Journal of the American Podiatry Association, Journal of Podiatric Medical Education* (US), *Podiatric Medicine and Surgery* (US), *Podiatry Management Letter* (US), *Podología* (Argentina), *Podologie* (France), *New Zealand Podiatrist.*

For additional titles see:

Index of NLM Serial Titles: A Keyword Listing of Serial Titles Currently Received by the National Library of Medicine. Bethesda, Maryland: National Library of Medicine, 1972.

DICTIONARIES AND HANDBOOKS

Alamilla, J. R. *Manuel de quiropodía: Malos de los pies.* (3rd ed.) Madrid: Paraninfo, 1970.

Guide to the Health Care Field. Chicago: American Hospital Association, annual.

Helfand, A. E. "Practice Guide for Podiatric Programs in Extended Care Facilities." *Journal of the American Podiatry Association,* 1966, *56,* 22.

Le Rossignol, J. N., and Holliday, C. B. *A*

Pharmacopoeia for Chiropodists. (8th ed.) London: Faber & Faber, 1971.

Radiological Health Training Guide for Podiatry Programs. Rockville, Maryland: Department of Health, Education and Welfare, Bureau of Podiatric Health, 1974.

"Standard Podiatric Nomenclature of Diseases and Operations." In *Desk Reference.* Washington, D.C.: American Podiatry Association, annual.

DIRECTORIES

Annual Directory (of United States and Canadian Boards of Examiners in Podiatry). Boston: Federation of Podiatry Boards, 1975.

Desk Reference (and Directory with Catalogue of Audio-Visual, Informational and Educational Materials, Formulary, Pharmaceutical and Therapeutic Index). Washington, D.C.: American Podiatry Association, annual.

Directory of Special Libraries and Information Centers. (3rd ed., 3 vols.) Detroit: Gale Research, 1974. Lists podiatric libraries in the United States.

Journal of the American Podiatry Association. Washington, D.C.: American Podiatry Association, 1907–. See monthly issues for a listing of colleges of podiatric medicine.

[Bibliography prepared by Deborah Tobin.]

PODOLOGY

See Podiatry (field of study).

POIGNANT REPORT

See Education in the Countries of the Common Market (Higher Education Report), Multinational.

POINT FOUR PROGRAM AND HIGHER EDUCATION

See Public Service Role of Higher Education.

POLICE AND LAW ENFORCEMENT TRAINING (Field of Study)

Formal police training is primarily a development of the twentieth century. During the greater part of their history, police services relied upon on-the-job training with some degree of supervision to prepare their recruits for their new responsibilities. Most professional civil police forces were created in or after the nineteeth century, and the major impetus in police training occurred after World War II —although police training establishments were founded in the 1880s and 1890s in centers as far apart as Paris, France, and Vellore, India. The importance and complexity of the police task are now more widely recognized, especially in the increasingly urbanized societies of the modern world.

Police training may be divided into three main divisions: basic, specialist, and higher. Basic training, its nature being determined by the level of induction, is given to the newcomer to the service and is designed to prepare him or her for the immediate performance of duty. It usually consists of police academy instruction combined with practical experience under tutelage. Similarly, specialist training, such as that provided for detectives, consists of academic and practical work. Higher training is concerned with the supervision, management, and command of the service. Elements of higher training are necessarily included in the basic training of people recruited directly to senior grades. Police officers take advantage of university and other extramural education, and university teachers and others from a wide variety of occupations frequently participate in the instruction given under police auspices. Police training establishments are commanded and staffed by police officers, though teachers from the academic community are often employed to work with them.

The content and emphasis of police training programs are established according to the duties for which trainees are being prepared. Police duties are quite varied and include the following: preventive patrol; criminal investigation; road-traffic work; crowd and riot control; fingerprinting; community and race relations; airport security; frontier guard; political, social, and economic intelligence; counter-espionage; protection of embassies, consulates, and important personages; administration and organization; narcotics; art thefts; fraud; and juvenile delinquency. New problems and changes in society as well as new forms of criminality dictate changes in police training.

Several other factors determine the nature of a police service's training system. One of these is the kind of control under which the police operate: national or local (state, city, county, township) or constituted by a partnership between national and local authority. The most common kind is national control, which is found in many European, African, Asian, and South American countries. The control in the United States is predominantly local, though there are a number of strong federal law enforcement agencies; local control is also predominant in Australia. In Great Britain a dual control is held by both central and local government bodies. National police services have unified training systems. Where national and local government are in partnership, systems are largely unified; where local authorities are in sole control, training systems are apt to be diverse and multifarious.

The manner of recruitment to the police force is another factor governing police training. For example, if highly educated people are inducted directly to supervisory and command ranks, they must be trained at a very different level from that which is provided when all recruits enter in the patrolman grade. Also, if a country is policed by both civil and military (*gendarme*) police forces, completely separate training systems are required. The military style of several civil police services also influences the character of their training.

Another highly significant factor governing police training is the proportion of the resources which a country is able or willing to allocate to its police. Training is expensive in money, manpower, installations, and equipment; the operational needs of undermanned forces and the in-

ability to provide the necessary facilities still result in minimal training in many areas.

In many countries the police career attracts too few of the better educated. In an age when many more people than ever before are receiving a higher education, this is a serious problem for the police administrator, who ideally seeks to recruit from a representative cross section of the community. One measure used to remedy this problem has been to require higher educational qualifications, but such a requirement could exclude many people of potential value to the police. Another measure that has been employed is the provision of in-service training programs with educational components appropriate for the adult trainee, who often proves to be a "late developer." For services that recruit exclusively through the patrolman grade, such programs are essential to the development of the higher supervisory and the command personnel.

International conferences for heads of police training establishments are held from time to time under the auspices of the International Criminal Police Organization (Interpol). Increases in transnational and international crime give impetus to international liaison in training as well as in operations; many of the more advanced training systems, for example, accept officers from other countries as trainees.

At the Fifth United Nations Congress on the Prevention of Crime and the Treatment of Offenders (Geneva, 1975), the emerging role of the police was one of the principal topics. The delegates concluded that police training should include, in addition to technical subjects, comprehensive instruction in such fields as ethics, human rights, and social science. The delegates also thought that training should be thorough and should be renewed throughout the police career. These deliberations reflect the great progress made since the 1950s in those countries with training programs that aim to implement the ideal of the integration of police and community.

There exists a worldwide movement toward police professionalism. This movement—and all that it implies by way of expertise, service, and ethics—is evident in the greater quantity of police training in many parts of the world.

PHILIP JOHN STEAD

Levels and Programs of Study

Programs in police and law enforcement usually require as a minimum prerequisite a secondary education, though mature applicants with relevant experience may be admitted with lower educational qualifications. The usual award is a certificate or diploma. Programs deal with specialized training in police work, law and security administration, and enforcement, and consist of classroom sessions, simulation and practical exercises, and group discussion. Principal course content for programs that lead to awards not equivalent to a first university degree usually includes introduction to law enforcement, drill, physical education, unarmed combat, firearms instruction, first aid and rescue operations, the use and care of police equipment, narcotics and drug abuse, laws of evidence and court procedures, report writing, criminal investigation, traffic control and administration, police administration, criminal law and legal procedures, crime and delinquency, police operations, language and communications, social and behavioral sciences, human relations, and ethics of the police profession.

[This section was based on UNESCO's *International Standard Classification of Education (ISCED): Three Stage Classification System, 1974* (Paris: UNESCO, 1974), with revisions by Jean Nepote, Secretary General, International Criminal Police Organization, Saint-Cloud, France.]

Major International and National Organizations

INTERNATIONAL

Fédération internationale des fonctionnaires supérieurs de police
% Prévention Routière
91-Linas Montlhery, France

Forensic Science Society
P.O. Box 41
Harrogate
North Yorkshire, HG1, 2LF, England

International Association of Chiefs of Police, Inc.
11 Firstfield Road
Gaithersburg, Maryland 20760 USA

International Association of Coroners and Medical Examiners
2121 Adelbert Road
Cleveland, Ohio 44106 USA

International Association of Women Police
6655 N. Avondale Avenue
Chicago, Illinois 60631 USA

International Conference of Police Associations, Inc.
1239 Pennsylvania Avenue SE
Washington, D.C. 20003 USA

International Criminal Justice Association
168–01 Jamaica Avenue
Jamaica, New York 11432 USA

International Criminal Police Organization (ICPO—Interpol)
26 rue Armengaud
92210 Saint-Cloud, France

International Federation of Senior Police Officers (IFSPO)
Norbertstrasse 165
D-43 Essen 1, Federal Republic of Germany

International Juvenile Officers' Association, Inc.
1005 West Main Street
St. Charles, Illinois 60174 USA

International Narcotic Enforcement Officers Association
178 Washington Avenue
Albany, New York 12210 USA

International Police Association
% Kent County Constabulary, Sutton Road
Maidstone, Kent ME15 9BZ, England

International Prisoners Aid Association
436 W. Wisconsin Avenue, Room 307
Milwaukee, Wisconsin 53201 USA

International Society for Forensic Odonto-Stomatology
Parkvej 2
4250 Fuglebjerg, Denmark

International Society for Social Defence
28 rue Saint-Guillaume
Paris, France

United Nations Congress for Social Defense
United Nations Plaza
New York, New York 10017 USA

NATIONAL

Canada:

    Canadian Association of Chiefs of
      Police, Inc.
    116 Albert Street, Suite 304
    Ottawa, Ontario K1P 5G3

    Canadian Section, International Police
      Association
    416 Vermont Avenue
    London, Ontario N5Z 3E5

United Kingdom:
    Police Federation
    15–17 Langley Road
    Surbiton, Surrey KT6 6LP, England

United States:

    National Association of State Directors of
      Law Enforcement Training
    11 Firstfield Road
    Gaithersburg, Maryland 20760

    National Sheriffs' Association
    1250 Connecticut Avenue NW
    Washington, D.C. 20036

    United States Section, International
      Police Association
    3403 NW 37th Street
    Fort Lauderdale, Florida 33309

National police associations and organizations are listed in:

Cramer, J. *Uniforms of the World's Police.* Springfield, Illinois: Thomas, 1968.

The yearly October issue of *Police Chief* contains a listing of international law enforcement associations and related organizations, national associations from Canada and the United States, and the members of the International Association of Chiefs of Police (some 11,000 members in 63 countries).

Principal Information Sources

GENERAL

General guides to police and law enforcement literature include:

Becker, H., and Felkenes, G. *Law Enforcement: A Selected Bibliography.* Metuchen, New Jersey: Scarecrow Press, 1968.

International Bibliography of Selected Police Literature. (2nd ed.) London: International Police Association, 1968. A country-by-country listing of police literature classified into police history and biography; personnel; police organization; administration and operations; investigations and field operations; identification and laboratory technique; traffic safety and investigation; ca-

nine police; national laws, rules, and regulations; and periodicals and journals.

Wright, M. *Use of Criminology Literature.* Hamden, Connecticut: Shoe String Press, 1974. See the chapter on police literature, pp. 160–176.

Introductions to the field include:

Eldefonse, E., Coffey, A., and Grace, R. C. *Principles of Law Enforcement.* New York: Wiley, 1968.

Germann, A. C., Day, F. D., and Gallati, R. R. J. *Introduction to Law Enforcement.* Springfield, Illinois: Thomas, 1968.

Hormachea, C. R. *Sourcebook in Criminalistics.* Reston, Virginia: Reston Publishing, 1974. An introduction to the field of criminalistics, showing the application of technological advances to crime prevention.

Sullivan, J. L. *Introduction to Police Science.* New York: McGraw-Hill, 1966.

Several useful books for understanding the development of European and American law enforcement systems are:

Chapman, S. G., and St. Johnston, T. E. *The Police Heritage in England and America.* East Lansing: Michigan State University, Institute for Community Development and Services, Kellogg Center, 1962.

Fosdick, R. B. *American Police Systems.* Montclair, New Jersey: Patterson Smith, 1969.

Fosdick, R. B. *European Police Systems.* Montclair, New Jersey: Patterson Smith, 1968.

CURRENT BIBLIOGRAPHIES

Abstracts on Police Science, Deventer, Netherlands: Kluwer B. V., 1973–. An international abstracting service covering police science, the forensic sciences, and forensic medicine.

Semi-Annual List of Selected Articles. Saint-Cloud, France: International Criminal Police Organization, 1949–. Brief notes of articles in police periodicals of member countries.

PERIODICALS

The following are the principal police science journals internationally: *Australian Police Journal, Chroniques internationales de police/ International Police Chronicle* (France), *Deutsche Polizei* (FRG), *Enforcement Journal* (US), *F.B.I.* (US), *Gendarmerie nationale* (France), *Illustrierte Rundschau der Gendarmerie* (Austria), *International Criminal Police Review* (France), *International Police Chronicle* (France), *International Review of Criminal Policy* (Switzerland), *Journal of Police Science and Administration* (US), *Kenya Police Review, Kriminalistik* (FRG), *Law and Order* (US), *Law Officer* (US), *L'officier de police* (Belgium), *National Police Journal* (US), *Neue*

Polizei (FRG), Nordisk kriminalteknisk tidsskrift (Norway), Police (UK), Police Chief (US), Police College Magazine (UK), Police Journal (UK), Police Review (UK), Police World (UK), Policía española, Polizia moderna (Italy), Revue de la police nationale (France), Revue internationale de criminologie et de police technique (Switzerland), Royal Canadian Mounted Police Gazette, Royal Canadian Mounted Police Quarterly.

A current country-by-country list of periodicals in police and forensic science can be found in the previously mentioned:

Abstracts on Police Science. Deventer, Netherlands: Kluwer B. V., 1973–.

ENCYCLOPEDIAS, DICTIONARIES, HANDBOOKS

Martin, J. A. Law Enforcement Vocabulary. Springfield, Illinois: Thomas, 1973.
Salottolo, A. Modern Police Service Encyclopedia. (2nd ed.) New York: Arco, 1970. Handbook defining more than 2000 terms of concern to the police officer.

DIRECTORIES

Agate, J. M. (Ed.) International Security Directory. London: Security Gazette, 1973. Provides details of top personnel in police forces throughout the world.
Cramer, J. Uniforms of the World's Police. Springfield, Illinois: Thomas, 1968. The police organizations of 174 countries are listed and briefly described.
Cramer, J. The World's Police. London: Cassell, 1964.
Kobetz, R. W. Law Enforcement and Criminal Justice Education Directory 1975–76. Gaithersburg, Maryland: International Association of Chiefs of Police, 1975. Lists law enforcement and criminal justice degree programs offered in colleges and universities in the United States and Canada.

POLICY CONFERENCE ON HIGHLY QUALIFIED MANPOWER

See Organisation for Economic Co-operation and Development.

POLISH PEOPLE'S REPUBLIC

Population: 33,636,000 (1974). Student enrollment in primary school: 4,605,800; secondary school (academic, vocational, technical): 2,661,800; higher education: 426,700. Student enrollment in higher education as percent- *age of age group (19–24): 9.2%. Language of instruction: Polish. Academic calendar: October 1 to September 30, two semesters. Percentage of national budget expended on all education: 7.35% (1974); higher education: 1.66%.*

Schooling in Poland had its origins in the thirteenth century, when the first institutions were started primarily to train future members of the clergy. The founding of the University of Cracow (Jagiellonian University) by Kazimierz the Great in 1364 heralded the beginning of higher education. The school system, which had been set up by the Jesuits and Piarists, remained under the control of the Catholic church until 1773, when the Commission of National Education (*Komisja edukacji narodowej*), the first Ministry of Education in Europe, unified the educational system from the elementary to the university level.

During the years when Poland was partitioned by foreign powers (1795–1918), most of the universities were closed. They were not reopened until after World War I, when Poland once again became an independent nation-state. However, the Jagiellonian University in the Austrian sector of Poland and a university in Lwów remained open during the partition. Although submitting to temporary Germanization, the universities once again became centers of Polish culture and science. In 1870 the Polish language regained its status as the language of instruction.

When Poland gained its independence in 1918, the first compulsory seven-year elementary school system was established. There was also a revival of higher education.

Although World War II disrupted education once more, an underground educational system, which included university-level studies, provided some educational continuity for Polish students. It has been estimated that as much as 60 percent of the potential prewar university population was lost in World War II.

Since World War II and the establishment of the Polish People's Republic, the educational system has been completely reorganized. Considerable emphasis has been placed on the development of higher education, particularly to provide opportunities for increasing numbers of the population. In this respect there has been marked progress. Between 1944 and 1974, about 687,400 students graduated from Poland's institutions of higher education, 48.7 percent of them between 1966 and 1973. The annual number of graduates has increased from about 6000 during 1945 to 1950, to about 53,000 during 1971 to 1973. In addition, the proportion of women students has increased from 29.8 percent during 1945 to 1950, to 40.2 percent during 1966 to 1970, to 46.5 percent in 1973.

In 1971 a committee of experts, headed by Polish sociologist Jan Szczepanski, was formed to examine insufficiencies and inequities in the educational system. The committee's recommendations, which were presented to the Polish government in 1973, included consideration of the nation's population growth and economic needs to the year 2000. The parliament of the Polish People's Republic, on October 10, 1973, decided to introduce a compulsory ten-year school system—that is, eight years of elementary school and two years of secondary school. The ten-year system is expected to be fully operational by 1985. Also adopted was a plan to channel 25 percent of the eighteen to twenty-five age group into three-year technical programs at the tertiary level, and about 30 percent of that age group into the universities for five-year programs leading to a first degree. Advanced scientific degrees would continue to be organized in the traditional European pattern of study, which consists of research beyond the first degree level.

National Educational Policy and Legal Basis of Educational System

All Polish citizens are guaranteed the right to an education. The aim of the educational system is to provide opportunities for all to obtain the skills and training needed to develop and support the Polish culture and economy, and to develop in youth a respect for work and the socialist foundations of the state.

The constitution of the Polish People's Republic, passed on July 22, 1952, guarantees the right of each person to an education; provides for a universal, free, and compulsory elementary school program; guarantees state aid in upgrading the skills of the citizens employed in industry; provides scholarships and grants; and establishes living quarters for students.

The act of November 5, 1958, relating to higher education, specifies the tasks, competency, and structure of colleges and universities and the duties and privileges of the staff and students. Two amendments to this act were made on March 31, 1965, and December 20, 1968.

Also important is the act of March 31, 1965, concerning academic titles and degrees. It determines the requirements and the procedure of awarding academic degrees and titles. An amendment to this act was made on December 20, 1968.

The act of March 22, 1972, also called "the Teachers' Charter," determines the rights and duties of teachers.

Types of Institutions

There are 111 institutions of higher education in Poland, twice the number in 1946–47. They consist of universities, technical universities, higher schools of engineering, higher agricultural schools, higher schools of economics, higher teacher training colleges and higher teachers schools, medical academies, higher schools of fine and applied arts, higher schools of physical education, higher schools of marine study, theological academies, as well as a large number of higher schools for officers.

There is also a private institution in Lublin, *Katolicki uniwersytet Lubelski* (KUL: Catholic University of Lublin). It was founded in 1918 and authorized to award academic degrees in 1938. Four faculties exist at KUL: divinity, canon law, Christian philosophy, and the arts.

Higher studies are conducted in four forms: normal day studies, night classes, extramural studies, and external studies, where the student does not attend classes but only takes the examinations. This type of program is available only in certain fields of study. Higher schools also conduct classes for those who would like to increase their working qualifications or gain a new specialty in their area of endeavor.

A nonuniversity type of higher education is available primarily in 283 vocational colleges, which are similar to the junior colleges in the United States. These institutions accept students from secondary college preparatory schools. Their level of education is subprofessional, and their course of study lasts from two to two and a half years. Upon completion of this program, the student is prepared primarily for a career in the medical field as a nurse, midwife, or laboratory technician. Some of the schools also offer programs in economic and technical fields.

Relationship with Secondary Education

Elementary education in Poland lasts eight years and is compulsory for children between the ages of seven and sixteen. Graduates receive a diploma, which allows them to apply to a secondary school. The three principal types of secondary schools in Poland are college preparatory, technical engineering, and basic vocational. In addition to these three types, there are also secondary schools of applied arts.

The program in college preparatory schools lasts four years, while the studies in technical engineering schools last from four to five years. Upon completion of the programs at these schools, the student receives a diploma known as a Certificate of Maturity, which entitles him to apply for admission to an institution of higher education. A Certificate of Maturity from a secondary school of technical engineering also allows the student to work in his chosen field and confers upon him the title of technician. Programs at basic vocational schools last from two to three years,

depending upon the area of specialization. A primary school graduate can go to secondary vocational school, where the course of study lasts three years.

Preparations are presently under way to implement a ten-year compulsory education system by 1985. This system will be divided into primary education (grades 1–3) and secondary education (grades 4–10). Following the compulsory program, students who wish to continue into higher education may attend two-year specialized schools. Provision is also made for vocational education of varying duration.

Admission Requirements

Persons who have received a Certificate of Maturity upon completion of their secondary-level studies and who are twenty-five years of age or younger (thirty years if applying to study philosophy) are eligible to apply for admission to an institution of higher education. Applicants must have maintained a good overall grade point average while attending secondary school and must pass an entrance examination. The procedure for taking the entrance examination and the requirements for acceptance to the first year of studies is published annually in the *Information for Candidates to Higher Schools*. Applicants who pass the entrance examination are accepted on the basis of the number of points received on the examination.

Access to higher education for persons of worker or peasant origin, for persons who have worked in an industry corresponding to their chosen field of study, or for persons who have distinguished themselves academically in secondary school is facilitated by awarding them additional points. Applicants receiving national recognition in a nationwide competition involving fields such as mathematics, physics, chemistry, technology, and knowledge about Poland are exempted from taking an entrance examination. Each competition produces from ten to twenty winners.

There is no age limit for persons applying to evening or extramural programs.

Students, other than those receiving special scholarships, are required to fulfill a government work requirement of two years upon completion of their studies. They are assigned their positions by the Plenipotentiary Committee of the Ministry of Labor situated at each institution.

Following the implementation of the ten-year compulsory school system, admission to higher education will be based upon a certificate, which is awarded by (1) ten-year secondary schools, if the student has excelled in a national competition, or "subject olympiad"; (2) schools offering two-year specialized programs; (3) vocational schools; (4) ten-year schools to students who have completed a practical program of two years or who have completed their military service (Kuberski and Wolczyk, 1975, p. 308).

Administration and Control

According to Article 2 of the act of November 5, 1958, every institution of higher education in Poland is individually formed, transformed, or closed by a separate decree of the Council of Ministers (*Rada ministrów*). The Ministry of Science, Higher Education and Technology is the principal organ of administration and control over all institutions of higher education in Poland. It exercises general authority in administration and planning, including financial planning, curricular planning, and determination of teaching methodology. Of the 111 state institutions of higher education, 55 fall under the direct responsibility of the Ministry of Science, Higher Education and Technology, while 10 are under the Ministry of Public Health and Social Welfare, 16 are under the Ministry of Culture and Art, 18 are under the Ministry of National Defense, 6 are under the Central Committee of Physical Culture and Tourism, 2 are under the Ministry of Foreign Trade and Navigation, and 4 are under the Ministry of Internal Affairs. The ministries having direct control over an institution determine the program of studies, the degrees to be offered, and the schedule (that is, whether the programs will be offered in day sessions, evening courses, and/or extramural studies). In the 1970s there has been discussion regarding the advisability of separating science and technology from the Ministry of Science, Higher Education and Technology and creating a Ministry of Education and Higher Education, thus placing responsibility for elementary, secondary, and postsecondary education in one ministry.

Institutions are headed by a rector, who is appointed for a three-year term by the minister and has direct responsibility over the institution. Rectors are chosen from among the professors. The rector may be assisted by a pro-rector(s), appointed by the governing minister after consultation with the rector, and by a rector's council composed of the pro-rector(s), an administrative director, a representative of the Polish United Workers Party, and a representative of the trade unions.

The internal structure of each institution is determined by the minister in cooperation with the rector. Institutions may have one or more faculties, which constitute major fields of study such as medicine and are composed of various organizational units such as departments and/or institutes.

Institutes were formed in 1972, when it was found that the chairs (the previous organizational units for an academic discipline) were too limited in size to carry out serious research work. Within the framework of the faculties, chairs that had similar roles were combined to form institutes (these would correspond to departments in Anglo-Saxon countries). The managing directors of the institutes are responsible for research work, while the dean of the faculty is responsible for didactics.

The various units of a faculty may also exist (1) independently of, but associated with, one or more institutions of higher education or (2) under the joint sponsorship and jurisdiction of various ministries. Faculties are headed by a dean, who is appointed by the rector for a three-year term.

A dean may be assisted by assistant deans, appointed by the rector after consultation with the appropriate dean, and by a dean's council established with the rector's consent.

Both rectors and deans are assisted by advisory councils with regard to didactic, academic, and behavioral matters. The senate also advises the rector and is composed of the rector's council; deans of all of the faculties; one representative of each faculty council; directors of interdepartmental programs and services, such as the library and physical education facilities; representatives of the teaching staff other than full professors; heads of permanent rectoral commissions, such as the Commission on Educational Research and Educational Staff Development (an advisory body to the Minister of Science, Higher Education and Technology); and representatives of the Socialist Polish Students' Association. The law of 1958 empowered the rector to set up two permanent commissions: one to deal with the area of research and the other to handle staff problems. When necessary, other permanent or temporary commissions may be established to prepare various matters for the rector's decision.

The corresponding council assisting the dean is the faculty council, comprised of the dean's council; all full and/or associate professors in the faculty; the heads of various organizational units within a faculty, such as the director of the Faculty Council on Student Matters; representatives from the Polish United Workers Party and the Polish Teachers Association; and representatives of the remaining teaching staff. The faculty council is also responsible for awarding the degrees of Doctor and Doctor Habilitated.

Rectors are also assisted by additional councils. The School Council on Student Matters, made up of specially appointed teachers (two thirds of the membership) and representatives of student organizations (one third), serves as an important advisory council. The Faculty Council on Student Matters plays a corresponding role within each faculty. The governing minister may also appoint a School Community Council, composed of political, economic, social, and cultural activists, to establish good relations between the institution and the surrounding community.

Programs and Degrees

Four degree levels exist in the Polish higher education system. Professional studies lasting four years lead to a university degree in the field of specialization upon completion of the program. A master's degree, which is the basic degree program in higher education institutions, requires four or five years of study and completion of a master's thesis. Postgraduate academic degrees consist of the Doctor and the Doctor Habilitated, which is an advanced degree received after the doctorate. Students must obtain permission from the appropriate Faculty Academic Council to engage in doctoral-level studies.

At the universities the program of study for full-time day students lasts four or five years, depending on the particular field, while at the technical colleges and higher schools of agriculture they last from four and a half to five and a half years. In teacher training colleges and higher teachers schools, higher schools of economics, and higher schools of physical education, the program is primarily four years, with a few exceptions requiring four and a half to five years. Medical studies last six years, with the exception of dentistry and pharmaceutical studies, which last five years. Programs at higher schools of fine and applied arts, depending on the major field, last from four to six years, while those at higher schools of military education last four years. Successful completion of any of the above programs leads to a master's degree, with the exception of technical studies, where the actual title of the degree is Master of Engineering (*magister inzynier*), and medical studies, where graduates receive the title of *physician* (of medicine or dentistry).

There are three types of vocational secondary schools in Poland. The first admits primary school graduates and has a course of study lasting five years. The second type of school enrolls technical school graduates and has a three-year course of study. The last type is considered a postsecondary school and offers a course of study that lasts for two years.

Between 1945 and 1973, one out of every three graduates received a degree in a technical field, whereas 12.6 percent received degrees in a medical field of study. Graduates in the humanities and economics accounted for 10.8 and 10.4 percent, respectively, of the total number of graduates during that same period. Other fields accounted for lower percentages: mathematic-scientific study, 9.3; agriculture, 7.9; law and administration, 7.3; and teacher education, physical education, fine and applied arts, and others, 8.4.

In addition to regular full-time day programs, various institutions offer evening classes, extramural studies, and/or external studies. In the latter two programs, students from outside a school are granted the diploma after they have passed all examinations. Extramural students sit for various tests and go to regular laboratory sessions (Tymowski and Januszkiewicz, 1975). Students enrolled in evening courses attend about fourteen hours of classes per week. All universities, technical colleges, higher schools of engineering, higher schools of economics, higher teacher training colleges and higher teachers schools, and higher schools of music offer evening classes. These institutions also conduct extramural classes, as do the higher agricultural schools and higher schools of physical education. External studies are minimal and are conducted only in specified fields at various times. Graduates of these three types of study programs receive the same degree or title as persons completing the regular day programs. Approximately 164,000 persons have recieved degrees through evening and extramural programs, comprising almost 24 percent of the total number of persons who received degrees from higher education institutions between 1945 and 1973. Between 1951 and 1970, the percentage of graduates who received their degrees through evening and extramural programs increased from 7.1 percent to 34.8 percent.

In 1968 the doctoral-level programs were reorganized due to the growing need for persons with an advanced education (Januszkiewicz, 1973). Three-year programs of full-time study, supported by twelve- to eighteen-month scholarships and monthly grant programs, were introduced; during planning, special consideration was given to persons aged thirty-five or under who had worked for at least one full year. In 1970 there were at least 132 separate programs for doctoral-level studies, operated primarily by faculties within institutions of higher education. Doctoral-level studies were also conducted by the Polish Academy of Sciences and various research institutes.

Financing

The institutions of higher education are completely financed by the state. The Catholic University of Lublin is privately supported through tuition fees, church collections, and other church funds.

Student Financial Aid

There are no tuition charges for students. Financial assistance for living expenses is available primarily through state and special scholarships. State scholarships provide financial assistance for the ten months of the school year. During 1972–73, approximately 48 percent of the students were recipients of state scholarships. All entering students may apply. Students having good grades are eligible for scientific scholarships from the state.

Special scholarships are sponsored by industries and institutions. The monthly allotments are generally higher than those of state scholarships, and funds are provided for the entire twelve months of the year. Students may apply after completion of their second year of studies and are obligated to work for the sponsoring industry or institution for a period of three years after receiving their degree.

Teaching Staff

Teaching staff are grouped into two levels: junior staff (assistants, senior assistants, and adjuncts) and senior staff (docents, extraordinary professors, and ordinary professors). The senior staff are appointed by the minister in charge of the research facility or institution of higher education.

Appointments to the positions of assistant and senior assistant are made by the rector of the institution after consultation with the respective dean and faculty council. Gifted students are generally given an appointment as an assistant after receiving a master's degree. Within one to two years after appointment as an assistant, the rector must decide whether to promote the teacher to the position of senior assistant or dismiss him. An appointment as a senior assistant lasts from three to six years, during which time the teacher must work for, and receive, a doctoral degree in order to be promoted to a position as adjunct. An instructor may remain at the level of adjunct until retirement, which is permissible at age sixty-five and mandatory at age seventy.

To be promoted to the position of docent, a person should generally have received the advanced degree of Doctor Habilitated and must have conducted research beyond the doctoral level. If a docent makes a major contribution to his field of study, he may be promoted to the position of extraordinary professor, which generally takes about five years. An additional major contribution to his field of study is a prerequisite for an extraordinary professor to be promoted to ordinary professor.

Salaries are established by a decree of the cabinet and are based upon the position, the degree(s) held, and the teacher's pedagogical experience.

Research Activities

Higher education institutions are involved in both basic and applied research. Specific research projects may be financed by the state, especially in conjunction with the Polish Academy of Science and other institutions financed by the state in the areas of management and cultural problems. In fields such as technological planning, institutions may directly engage in research agreements with particular industries or businesses. Institutions of higher education play a significant role in resolving existing problems in technology and management. Students may participate in research projects.

Current Problems and Trends

As a result of the reorganization of the compulsory education cycle and attendant changes in the structure of all postprimary education, access to higher education will be affected. The extent of the changes will not be known until the new structures are fully implemented in 1985.

Some of the problems facing educational planners include (1) the expansion of basic and applied research activities, (2) the development of additional training programs for specialists, (3) the improvement of cooperation among the various academic disciplines, and (4) the coordination of educational programs and extracurricular activities in the context of consideration for the total development and growth of Polish youth.

Relationship with Industry

Industry and higher education in Poland enjoy a cooperative relationship through which industry plays an educational and supportive role. Various industries provide special scholarships from their own operating budget to help support students who are attending institutions of higher education. In addition, for some fields of study, work assignments constitute part of the degree requirements. Students pursuing a degree in engineering, for example, must complete a total of four months of work experience to receive their degree; one month must be completed after the first year of studies, one month after the second year, and two months just before receiving the degree. The requirements are similar for students enrolled in agricultural programs. Persons who are working and at the same time pursuing an education are also given special consideration. Many receive paid holidays prior to, and during, examination periods, while many attending evening schools are granted a reduced workday.

International Cooperation

Polish universities engage in educational activities internationally through cooperative efforts and programs with individual countries or under the sponsorship of international organizations such as UNESCO, in an effort to promote understanding, international cooperation, and learning opportunities. They are members of the International Association of Universities, the Standing Conference of Rectors and Vice-Chancellors of the European Universities, and many other specialized organizations.

International cooperation in the field of higher education is realized in Poland by cooperation within the Council for Mutual Economic Assistance (CMEA), by bilateral intergovernmental agreements, and by bilateral interuniversity agreements.

[Information supplied by the Research Institute of Science Policy and Higher Education and by Janusz Tymowski, Professor, Warsaw, Poland.]

Educational Associations

Polish Teachers' Union
ul. Spasowskiego 6/8
00-950 Warsaw, Poland

Federation of Socialist Unions of
  Polish Youth
Nowy Świat 18/20 Str.
00-920 Warsaw, Poland

Bibliography

Agoston, G., and others. *Case Study on the Development of Higher Education in Some East European Countries.* Paris: UNESCO, 1974.

Apanasewicz, N., in collaboration with W. Medlin. *Educational Systems in Poland.* Washington, D.C.: Department of Health, Education and Welfare, 1959.

Hartman, R. *Hochschulwesen und Wissenschaft in Polen 1918–1960.* Frankfurt/Main, Federal Republic of Germany: Alfred Metzner Verlag, 1962.

Januszkiewicz, F. *Education in Poland.* Warsaw: Interpress Publishers, 1973.

Kozakiewicz, M. "Higher Education: Quantity into Quality." *Polish Perspectives,* February 1972, *15*.

Kuberski, J., and Wolczyk, J. "The Bases of the Reform of the Educational System of Poland." *Prospects,* 1975, *5*(3), 301–311.

Parnowski, Z. *Education in Poland.* Warsaw: Polonia Publishing House, 1958.

Ratuszniak, Z. *L'enseignement supérieur en Pologne.* Etudes et documents d'éducation, No. 49. Paris: UNESCO, 1964.

Searing, M. E. *Estimates of Educational Attainment in Poland: 1950–1969.* International Population Reports, Series P-95, No. 68. Washington, D.C.: Bureau of the Census, U.S. Department of Commerce, 1970.

Suchodolski, B. *Edukacja narodu: 1918–1968.* Omega Series. Warsaw: Wiedza Powszechna, 1970.

Suchodolski, B. "The Future of Higher Education." *Polish Perspectives,* March 6, 1973, *16*.

Szczepanski, J. "The State and the Planning of Higher Education." *Poland,* January 1969.

Szczepanski, J. "The New Shape of Education." *Polish Perspectives,* June 6, 1973, *16*.

Tymowski, J. *Organizacja szkolnictwa wyższego w Polsce.* Warsaw: Państwowe wydawnictwo naukowe, 1975.

Tymowski, J., and Januszkiewicz, F. *Postsecondary Education of Persons Already Gainfully Employed in European Socialist Countries.* Warsaw: Study Prepared for UNESCO, 1975. Mimeographed.

See also: Academic Dress and Insignia; Eastern European Socialist Countries: Regional Analysis; Library Administration Outside the United States; Science Policies: Industrialized

Planned Economies: Eastern European Socialist Countries.

POLISH TEACHERS UNION—
SECTION OF SCIENTIFIC WORKERS
(Związek nauczycielstwa polskiego—
Sekcja nauki)

Founded in 1905 by elementary school teachers, the *Związek nauczycielstwa polskiego* (Polish Teachers Union) did not assume its present name until 1930. After World War II the *Towarzystwo nauczycieli polskich szkół srednich i wyższych* (Society of Polish Secondary and Higher School Teachers) joined the *Związek nauczycielstwa polskiego.* In 1947 the *Sekcja szkół wyższych* (Section of Higher Education Institutions) of the union was organized and later renamed *Sekcja nauki* (Section of Scientific Workers). The union aims to improve the quality of work and the working conditions of academic teachers and research workers within the socialist system.

In 1975 the union had workers in sixty-seven higher education institutions and about one hundred research institutes. A total membership of 90,000 members represented 40,000 academic teachers and 10,000 research workers. The ten medical academies and twelve schools of art have their own unions. In 1952 the section joined the World Federation of Scientific Workers. A membership fee of 1 percent is deducted from the monthly salaries of workers.

Union congresses and section conferences are held every three years to elect local, regional, and central executive committees. Committees then elect their praesidia and chairmen.

From 1946, when the socialist principle "One union in one shop" was introduced into institutions of higher education in Poland, the union organized specialized bodies for work on particular topics, such as improvement of teaching methods, or groups to represent interests of librarians, teachers, technical staff, and administrative staff.

Union publications include *Głos nauczycielski,* weekly; and *Życie szkoły wyższej,* monthly.

Mostowa 4, m. 7
00–260 Warsaw, Poland

HENRYK SZARRAS

POLITICAL PERSECUTION
OF ACADEMICS

In this article academics are defined as individuals who are members of, or are associated with, an organized community of scholars, usually in an institution of higher education. They may be graduate students, fellows, or temporary or permanent members of the teaching staff of an institution. They may also be independent scholars engaged in intellectual pursuits related to higher education although not, themselves, members of any institution. Purposely excluded from this discussion are novelists, playwrights, actors, and artists who have no academic affiliations.

Role of Academics in Society

As thus defined, academics constitute a group of potential power and influence in society. The possibility that they will individually or collectively exercise this power and influence can create tension between them and political leaders who regard themselves as the legitimate custodians of law and order. This tension, when positive, has a creative effect by stimulating academics to make contributions in their various disciplines, while encouraging political authorities to facilitate and support the work of intellectuals in the academic community. On the other hand, if either group begins to feel that the other is encroaching on its own special rights and prerogatives, a negative tension develops, with the result that academics become the object of varying degrees of political pressure. A refusal to yield to pressure or to accept demands for conformity with the values and ideas currently being promulgated by the political authorities can lead to persecution—that is, the continual harassment of individuals or groups intended to cause them economic loss, social discomfort and annoyance, or even physical and mental injury.

This negative tension between academics and politicians arises from a basic conflict over the insistence by academics that in their teaching and research they can acknowledge only that authority which conforms with the highest good—that of truth. If the state, represented by politicians who exercise authority on its behalf, betrays the values that the academic accepts, it becomes the academic's duty to challenge, condemn, or even to resist the authority claimed by the state. The search for the highest values in the discipline to which the academic has devoted himself can be conducted only in an atmosphere of academic freedom. The insistence on this right to academic freedom—in the exercise of which the authority of the state may be accepted or denied, affirmed or rejected—is the root cause of the various kinds of countermeasures taken by the state to assert the supremacy of its authority. Persecution is the most drastic of measures that politicians believe they can legitimately use to maintain the order and conformity threatened by the challenge of academic freedom.

Academic Freedom Versus State Authority

Academic freedom as a concept originated in Germany during the nineteenth century. It was not intended as a means of providing immunity to academics from accountability for their actions. Academics share with their fellow citizens civic responsibilities as well as those freedoms to which all men have a right—freedom of speech, worship, thought, and assembly. But another freedom came to be seen as necessary for members of the academic community: the freedom to seek and disseminate knowledge, including the freedom to analyze in an objective manner any and all aspects of the social environment, such as the government.

Historically the first discernible associa-

tion between academics and authorities of the state occurred in China. Emperor Hsüan Tsung founded the Hanlin Academy of Letters in 725, and by the time of the Sung cultural period (960–1279) academic communities had developed in every region of China. Intellectuals from these communities who passed the very difficult qualifying examinations were admitted to the national and state civil services and wielded considerable authority in government as long as they remained in favor with the ruling emperor.

Toward the end of the fifteenth century, academic communities helped answer the need for well-trained administrators in the civil service of the Ottoman Empire, as they did similar needs in the civil services of France and the United Kingdom. More recently, the Indian civil service, which was modeled after the British service, also recruited heavily from the universities, both before and after independence. Because of this close link between academic communities and the civil administration, academics were not likely to be persecuted by their colleagues in positions of authority in the state.

Western Europe and North America. Generally speaking, in the democratic states in Europe and in Canada and the United States, the role of the intellectual community in influencing social change by analyzing the causes of current problems and proposing solutions to them has become commonly accepted. In order to understand the many processes at work in society, political authorities may commission studies to obtain a better insight into adjusting or controlling these processes to achieve certain objectives. Academics derive satisfaction by placing their professional expertise at the service of the state. In many cases they are amply rewarded either by enhanced social status, by appointment to positions of influence, or by increased support from public funds of their institutions. Notable examples of personal reward to academics are John Maynard Keynes, the British economist, mathematician, and fellow of King's College, Cambridge, who was rewarded with a peerage as Baron Keynes of Tilton in 1942, and Henry Kissinger, the American political scientist and Harvard University professor, who has served as secretary of state in the cabinets of Presidents Richard Nixon and Gerald Ford.

The experience of academics in the United States has been unusual in some respects. Both in absolute numbers and in proportion to the population, there are more academic institutions and therefore more academics than in other countries. Most of the leaders in government and industry are alumni of leading colleges and universities who generally respect and support the academic community. However, in spite of the generally high status of American academics, occasionally those who either do not conform or are suspected of not conforming with so-called American economic and political ideas are subject to persecution. For example, in the early 1950s, under the leadership of Senator Joseph McCarthy of the Senate Permanent Investigations Subcommittee, persons who were suspected of being communists, or of belonging to organizations that communists had infiltrated, or who had expressed in their writing or their teaching ideas that could be interpreted as being critical of laissez-faire capitalism and free enterprise, were subjected to harassment and persecution. Pressures were placed on their institutions to deprive them of their faculty positions or to silence them in one way or another.

The Soviet Union and Eastern Europe. In the Soviet Union and the communist Eastern European countries, academic intellectuals have not generally been able to play a role in the civil service similar to their counterparts in Western Europe and North America. Academics may be propaganda theorists of the regime, or may make important scientific and technological contributions to the development of communist society, but any attempt to expose inhumane use of power by the state or to challenge or criticize the authority of the

state brings about speedy repercussions, ranging from minor harassment to imprisonment or, worse, to permanent confinement in an institution for the mentally ill. A celebrated example of the fate of dissidents is Andrei Sakharov, a leading nuclear physicist and member of the Soviet Academy of Sciences, who was subjected to harassment and threats of arrest by Soviet authorities when he began in 1973 to criticize the policy of his government to deny the rights of Soviet citizens—especially Jews—to emigrate freely.

Academic freedom in the communist states is as restricted as other freedoms. The Soviet Union does not tolerate the expression of any thought or the pursuit of any intellectual activity that would result in a challenge to the government's authority in any sphere of national life. Literature, the arts, and the sciences must conform to the ideology of the state. An academic may continue to live and work in the academic community only so long as he does nothing to contradict, criticize, or challenge the authority of the state. On the other hand, the "conforming" academics enjoy special privileges and advantages and are given a place in the social hierarchy next in status to the leaders of the ruling party.

Asia and Africa. The situation in the new nations of Asia and Africa, which achieved independence from colonial rule after World War II, is not encouraging. During the preindependence liberation movements, members of the academic institutions, representing the professions and students, joined forces with trade unionists and other nationalists in the struggle for independence. In both the British and the French colonies, educational opportunities had generally been available to only a small segment of the population. It was therefore inevitable that the spokesmen of the independence movements were usually intellectuals who had received at least part of their academic training in the universities of the metropolitan power. However, when independence was achieved and the former colonial power withdrew, the absence of a long tradition of academic leadership soon resulted in the ascendance of other groups to power. In Africa, for example, only ten years after Ghana, the first colonial country to be liberated, had gained independence in 1957, the majority of the newly independent countries had succumbed to military coups d'etat. In countries under military rule, members of the academic community are often suspected of being nonrevolutionaries, and because of their natural links with universities abroad, of which they are usually graduates, they are often accused of being agents of neo-colonialism. In some instances, individual academics have lost their university appointments, while others have suffered arbitrary arrest and imprisonment without trial under emergency regulations set up by the military regime.

The real reason behind such persecution, however, is the intolerance of the new regimes to criticism by intellectuals about the betrayal of the independence movement, the suppression of human rights, and the corruption and nepotism that appear to be an inevitable result of the transfer of power to those who have neither the inclination nor the discipline to resist the material temptations of high political office.

Latin America. Although the academic communities in the Latin America countries are no larger than their counterparts in the newly independent countries of Asia and Africa, they have been in existence much longer. Academics have made significant contributions to the leadership of several countries and constitute an elite of about equal importance with the military and the industrialists. This status has not, however, spared them persecution. In Brazil, for example, where there has been virtually a dictatorship since the military coup d'etat ousted President João Goulant in 1964, successive governments have not tolerated any challenge to their authority and have harassed and imprisoned scores of intellectuals for opposing the suppression of human rights. Similar occurrences

have taken place in Chile under the jurisdiction of the military junta. Rectors of the eight universities have been replaced by men drawn from the ranks of the armed forces; approximately one third of the university staff has been dismissed; and an estimated 20 percent of the student body have been suspended. A massive exodus of intellectuals, particularly in the faculties of engineering and science, has been taking place (Knight, 1975).

Responses to Persecution

An important result of persecution or the threat of persecution is the flight of many academics from their mother countries. Although academic persecution may not be the most important cause of the brain drain, political incompatibility accounts for the permanent emigration of many academics with the consequent loss to their original country of its investment in their training. As serious as the problem is to all countries, the developing ones can least afford to be deprived of individuals whose knowledge and skills are needed for the country's economic and social development.

In many countries, the persecution of academics has led either to the formation of special support organizations or to existing organizations adding this concern to their other activities. The United States has groups, such as the American Civil Liberties Union and the American Association of University Professors, which have not been silent when political harassment and persecution have affected the academic community. Elsewhere, organizations that champion the rights of persecuted academics as part of their program include Amnesty International and World University Service.

Amnesty International, with headquarters in London, acts principally, and with considerable success, by mobilizing individuals and groups in several countries to send letters and telegrams to the governmental authorities of any country where academics have been imprisoned without fair trial or are being tortured during imprisonment. Amnesty International groups in each country are encouraged to adopt certain "prisoners of the month" and to concentrate their appeals on behalf of these prisoners. Most countries, in the face of the wide publicity engendered by the intervention of Amnesty International, yield to these pressures and appeals and either release the prisoners or lessen their sentences.

World University Service, with international headquarters in Geneva, was organized to provide scholarships and other forms of financial support for needy students and teachers, particularly in the developing countries, but more recently has undertaken to support the defense of persecuted members of the academic community. National chapters in some forty countries receive funds from their own academic communities in support of the worldwide program.

In the final analysis, the most certain guarantee of the freedom of academics from political persecution is the public advocacy of political rights of free speech and assembly and the judicious control by academics themselves of the exercise of academic freedom. The conflict between the right to acquire and disseminate knowledge and the duty to submit to lawfully constituted authority will never be resolved, and members of the academic community must decide for themselves when they must follow their consciences and challenge the authority of the state during attempts to suppress fundamental human rights and essential freedoms. In such cases, the support of their colleagues and of the public at large may considerably influence their fate.

Bibliography

American Association of University Professors. "1940 Statement of Principles on Academic Freedom and Tenure." *Bulletin,* 1959, *45,* 107.

Goldston, R. C. *The American Nightmare.* Indianapolis, Indiana: Bobbs-Merrill, 1973.

Hofstadter, R., and Metzger, W. P. *The Development of Academic Freedom in the United States.* New York: Columbia University Press, 1955.

Knight, P. "Campus Purges Grow as Brain Drain Continues." *Times* (London) *Higher Education Supplement,* December 26, 1975, p. 7.

Salisbury, H. E. (Ed.) *Sakharov Speaks.* New York: Knopf, 1974.

Seltzer, R. J. "Dissident Soviet Scientists Under Attack." *Chemical and Engineering News,* 1976, *54*(13), 18–20.

JOHN KAREFA-SMART

See also: Academic Freedom; Due Process and Grievance Procedures.

POLITICAL SCIENCE (Field of Study)

The term *political science* is derived from roots in Greek and Roman antiquity. To the Latin *scientia* (to know) is affixed the original notion of the Greek public life, which centered on the *polis* (the city-state) and on the Aristotelian concept of the *zoon politikon* (the political being). Thus, political science may be defined as a systematic study of the microscopic and macroscopic forces which determine the relations between man and government. Specifically, the political scientist studies institutions, theory, political systems, and political behavior. Developing from history, public law, and political philosophy, political science has expanded its scope and modernized its methods since 1950 under the influence of behavioralism and empiricism. Ideas and techniques from anthropology, economics, management sciences, mathematics, psychology, and sociology have also contributed to political science—giving rise, for example, to the subfields of political psychology, political socialization, methodology, voting behavior, and empirical political theory—fields that either did not exist or were in infancy as recently as the early 1950s. Contributions to political understanding also have been made through studies of personality in decision making, psychohistorical studies of the human uses of power, motivation in politics, and effective political appeals to specified political "mind sets."

Apart from its subfields (discussed below), political science recognizes a number of analytical components:

1. *Power focus.* All branches of political science acknowledge the centrality of power in political decision making. Some branches, notably traditional studies of international relations, accept power as the sole determining ingredient.

2. *Institutional focus.* Once regarded as the principal element of politics but now in declining stature as a focal point of political science research are the formal institutions of politics. While it is still accepted that much decisional manipulation occurs through institutionalized politics, the behavioral focus has diminished institutionalism.

3. *Behavioral focus.* From individual motivation and political socialization to mass public opinion, individual choice and resulting actions are seen as the microscopic initiatives of politics. Personality factors affecting individual choice, the costs and benefits of political activity, and propaganda and other political communications are crucial elements in a comprehensive understanding of political science.

4. *Group focus* (a prebehavioral concept). The political scientist who focuses on political allegiance through group formation and group activity explores the formation and actions of small communities of interest and follows their contribution to political decision making.

5. *Functional focus.* As much a reaction to institutionalism as behavioralism is, functionalism seeks to explain political phenomena as products of capabilities and actions rather than as institutionally formalistic outcomes. It abandons structure for function, system for process.

6. *Policy-relevance focus.* Sensitive to charges that scientific abstraction is explanatory rather than predictive or useful for decisional choice, political science strives for techniques that will give its conclusions practical utility in the making of public policy.

For the most part, the principal branches of political science were defined prior to the empirical and behavioral revolutions, though these new trends have affected substantial second-order divisions of the discipline. The emphasis on policy orientation in recent decades has resulted in the identification of policy science as a separate division of political science. The principal divisions of political science are political theory, domestic studies, comparative and cross-polity studies, international and foreign policy studies, and policy science and public choice.

Like other social sciences, political science is rich in theories to explain political phenomena. The three most useful categories of political theory are political philosophy, empirical theory, and methodology. Political philosophy (or political thought) is regarded by traditionalists as the heart of political understanding and by others as the antecedent of modern political science. Political philosophy, which traces political ideas from antiquity to the present, is concerned with descriptive analysis of such fundamental concepts as authority, legitimacy, sovereignty, social contract, sociopolitical belief systems, and justice. Whereas political philosophy attempts to *explain* political phenomena, empirical theory seeks to *demonstrate* their characteristics by the scientific method; that is, the empiricist strives to reduce political ideas to testable hypotheses. In this sense empiricism, a major component of behavioralism, involves the application of methodology. Modern political analysis requires increasing scientific and/or mathematical instruments for testing and measuring political observations. Rooted mainly in statistics, methodology as a branch of political theory comprises the discovery and study of tools for the collection and quantitative analysis of data.

Most political analysis is addressed to domestic studies. Both institutional and behavioral, these studies subdivide as follows: (1) studies of national government and politics, which examine structure and function of national institutions and political parties, opinion and voting behavior, political communications, legal analysis, practical politics and violence, and theories of national politics; (2) studies of subnational government and politics, which examine state, local, and provincial politics.

Comparative and cross-polity studies compare and contrast methods and performances in disparate places in order to enlarge political understanding. In addition to examining the aspects of politics familiar to domestic studies, cross-polity analysis gives greater attention to comparative ideologies and political cultures. Development politics also falls in this category.

International and foreign policy studies —examinations of interaction among political systems, whether similar or dissimilar—represent the ultimate macroscopic level of political analysis. Concern is with the causes of war and the conditions of peace, as well as analysis of the international political system and efforts to transform it by controlling interstate conflict. Foreign policy studies link domestic phenomena with the external behavior of governments as a further aspect of conflict control. Among the principal subdivisions are international law and international organization, which investigates the restructuring of world politics through international and supranational institutions. Newer aspects of international studies include international political economy (the causes and effects of international economic practice, including imperialism and neoimperialism, upon world politics) and peace studies (a multidisciplinary look at alternatives for maintaining international peace).

Finally, policy science and public choice has emerged as a distinct empirical subdivision of political science. Spawned by public administration and economic theories of politics (particularly those of Anthony Downs, 1957) and armed with sophisticated methodology and computer capability, this subdivision delineates logical policy choices by the most objective available means.

Other organizational schemes emphasize the many second-order institutional and behavioral divisions of political science applicable to domestic, cross-polity, and international studies. The subfields of institutionalism are legislative systems, executive systems, judicial systems, political parties, revolution and change, public law, national security policy, comparative ideologies, and political cultures. The subfields of behavioralism include legislative behavior, executive behavior, judicial behavior, voting behavior, mass political behavior, political socialization, political psychology, comparative political behavior, and political action and reaction.

Political science is related to many other fields of study in the humanities, the physical sciences, and the social sciences. Cultural anthropology, in particular, has given the political scientist an improved understanding of political cultures, within multinational states and among nation-states, which has modernized cross-polity studies and increased ethnic political studies. Physiology has contributed to political theory by providing an analogy of a political system: the notion that politics is a continuous dynamic of competing inputs (interests, objectives); interactions (debate, violence, compromise); outputs (decisions, rules, costs, benefits); and feedbacks (revised inputs) in a structural-functional environment of interdependent parts. From contemporary economic theory political science has derived many of its quantitative methods. Economics has also contributed to the political scientist's understanding of the relative costs and benefits of policy alternatives. Other closely allied fields are history, management science, mathematics, philosophy, psychology, and sociology.

The development of political science has undergone three phases of disparate durations, two of which occurred in less than a century: prehistory, modern history, and recent history.

To the extent that political philosophy was the seed of modern political science, the discipline dates to ancient Greece and, at the very least, to the fourth century B.C. From there to its more modern phase, this "prehistory" is associated with Plato, Aristotle, Thomas Aquinas, John Locke, Jean Jacques Rousseau, Immanuel Kant, John Stuart Mill, Henry Thoreau, and Karl Marx, among others. This epoch posed theoretical and philosophical explanations for the consolidation of the state, the introductions of ancient and modern democracies, and capitalism and socialism. It produced the Magna Carta, the American Declaration of Independence, the French Declaration of the Rights of Man and Citizen, the age of constitutionalism, and the politics of the industrial revolution. Marked principally by philosophical treatises on politics, it also saw the first modern, extensive observational tract, Alexis de Tocqueville's *Democracy in America,* published in 1835.

The transition from prehistory to modern history continued to be largely a European phenomenon. Having had sporadic recognition in Sweden, political science received its first sustained drive for modernity in Germany in the mid nineteenth century, stimulated principally by the industrial revolution, the introduction of Marxist theory, and application to the study of politics of recent and contemporary philosophy. From these roots the new discipline spread to the United States, particularly to Columbia University, where it was first taught in 1858.

Political science commenced as an intellectual tradition only after 1880. Thereafter, because of reformism, European positivism, and the popularity of legalism throughout the Western world, the study of politics turned from the philosophical toward the analytical. Establishment of the School of Political Science at Columbia (1880) and the publication of Woodrow Wilson's landmark study *Congressional Government* (1885) coincided with the early modern history of political science. In Europe the establishment of the Columbia program was matched by the founding of the *Ecole libre des sciences politiques* at Paris in 1898, which placed the study of politics in the hands of a specialized faculty and out of the more conservative control of the law faculty.

It was not until 1903 that the American Political Science Association was founded. The *American Political Science Review* was established in 1907, the same year that the *American Journal of International Law* was first published. Despite these advances, analysis continued to rest on legalistic studies and institutional observation. Moreover, in the United States and elsewhere, few universities recognized political science as distinct from history, law, commerce, or sociology.

In 1925 the discipline focused principally on the United States, and more specifically on Harvard, Columbia, and Johns Hopkins Universities. Attention now turned, however, to the University of Chicago, where Charles Merriman, founder of the Social Science Research Council, had been calling for a more scientific and multidisciplinary study of politics (Merriman, 1925). The challenge was seized by Harold Lasswell, whose efforts to redefine the field and to introduce psychological explanations of political phenomena heralded the slow-to-mature behavioral revolution (Lasswell, 1930, 1935). As Lasswell's movement took hold, Franklin D. Roosevelt's New Deal, with its proliferation of governmental agencies, inspired the founding of the American Society for Public Administration (1940).

After World War II—as a result of the developments of the Chicago group in the 1930s; the increased financial investment in the social sciences from 1945 to 1970; the outpouring of Ph.D.s from American and European universities in the same years; and the availability of ever improving instrumentation to collect, store, retrieve, and process data—behavioralism and empiricism took hold in political science. Professional societies and academic journals multiplied throughout the industrialized world, and second-order divisions of the field cropped up. Although institutional and other normative studies have not vanished entirely, the trend in the training of political scientists and in published research in the field is predominantly behavioral and empirical. During this era also, most universities in the United States awarded individual department status to political science.

This zest for "scientific" political science has not been without its critics, nor has it penetrated all aspects of political science. Resistance to it is based in part on rejection of the level of abstraction and in part on the tendency of objective technique to "dehumanize" the content of political inquiry. Such criticism has resulted in a greater quest for "policy relevance" and in the "postbehavioral revolution," a retreat from the trend toward an exclusively quantitative discipline.

Three principal trends in political science have emerged since World War II. First is the development of behavioralism and empiricism and the postbehavioral revolution. Far from abandoning quantitative analysis, postbehavioralism seeks only to restore the subjective element of politics and correct the scientism toward which quantitative analysis seemed to be carrying the field. A second major development is the appearance of new subfields, particularly those introduced by behavioralism (political psychology and political socialization) and those resulting from interdisciplinary trends (international political economy and cross-cultural studies). In addition, through mathematical model building and computerized projections, political scientists have developed a burgeoning literature on futurology. Many of these trends would have been impossible, or at least greatly retarded, without the third major development, technological advancement, which has facilitated political communication and information retrieval and processing. From computer terminals to computerized simulation and telecommunications satellites, the electronic age has made possible new ways of understanding political phenomena.

Although political science has had a United States–oriented modern history— paralleled perhaps only in Canada, where it has been a recognized discipline since the 1880s—it is now firmly established in universities throughout the world. Its status varies considerably, however, not only among countries but within countries as well. In the United Kingdom, for example, political science has separate departmental status in a few universities; elsewhere it is still in the control of the history or law faculties. Similarly in France, while separate political science faculties function in a few specialized institutes, most of them are part of the larger faculties of sociology or law. In the Federal Republic of Germany the tradition of political science teaching has been torn by national consciousness of the excesses of Bismarck and Hitler, with the result that independent political science faculties are rare.

In countries where educational development has been influenced by colonialism, particularly British colonialism, the development of political science has been slow to escape from identification with law and commerce faculties. Major strides have been made in India, where the influence of international legal studies has led to separate departments of international studies and political science; in Egypt, on the other hand, the older identifications have for the most part survived. In Australian universities, the separate identity of political science is thoroughly established throughout the higher education system, although research emphasis tends to be subdisciplinary.

Sweden and the other Scandinavian countries have long-established political science traditions. In recent years Sweden and Norway have been major centers of international peace research. Latin American universities have firmly maintained political science in other faculties, particularly economics and law.

With their carefully controlled curricula,

the socialist countries have generally separated political science from other faculties and shaped it into studies for public service and international relations. The curriculum is built on the Marxist explanations of the state and of interstate relations. The Marxist emphasis is also generally greater throughout Europe than it is in America.

Since World War II, education in political science internationally has been promoted by the United Nations, particularly through UNESCO, which has twice included political science in its world surveys of the disciplinary status of fields of study (Robson, 1954; Waldo, 1956). The international stature of the discipline is also evidenced by scholarly journals in virtually every major language and by the proliferation of professional organizations affiliated with the International Political Science Association, established under UNESCO in 1949.

[*Notes:* **A. Downs,** *An Economic Theory of Democracy* (New York: Harper & Row, 1957). **H. D. Lasswell,** *Psychopathology and Politics* (Chicago: University of Chicago Press, 1930). **H. D. Lasswell,** *World Politics and Personal Insecurity* (New York: McGraw-Hill, 1935). **C. Merriman,** *New Aspects of Politics* (Chicago: University of Chicago Press, 1925). **W. S. Robson** (Ed.), *The University Teaching of Social Sciences: Political Science* (Paris: UNESCO, 1954). **D. Waldo,** *Political Science in the United States: A Trend Report* (Paris: UNESCO, 1956).]

WALTER S. JONES

Levels and Programs of Study

Programs in political science generally require as a minimum prerequisite a secondary education and lead to the following awards: certificate or diploma, bachelor's degree, master's degree (M.A., M.Sc.), the doctorate (Ph.D.), or their equivalents. Programs consist of instruction and group or seminar discussion and, for advanced degrees, study and original research substantiated by the presentation of a scholarly thesis or dissertation.

Programs that lead to awards not equivalent to a first university degree deal with the principles of political science and the functions of government and are typically given in technological or similar institutions. Short courses of less than a year are often sponsored by employers, employers' associations, or trade unions. Principal course content usually includes basic concepts and terminology of political science, political institutions, history of politics, government organizations, comparative government, international intergovernmental organizations, public administration, political parties and movements, principles of governmental planning, and civics and political awareness.

Programs that lead to a first university degree deal with the principles and practices of government. Principal course content usually includes national government institutions, comparative government, political theory, history of political thought, local governmental institutions and problems, constitutional development, public administration, and international intergovernmental organizations. Usual background courses include relevant specialties in economics, sociology, psychology, history, languages, and philosophy.

Programs that lead to a postgraduate university degree deal with political theories, political institutions, and governmental forms. Principal course content and areas of research usually include political theory; unitary and federal government problems, including theory, constitutional questions, and institutions; comparative political systems; political parties; international intergovernmental agencies; and government decision making. Background studies usually include public administration, economics, sociology, psychology, law, and history.

[This section was based on UNESCO's *International Standard Classification of Education (ISCED)* (Paris: UNESCO, 1976).]

Major International and National Organizations

INTERNATIONAL

African Association of Political Science (AAPS)
Association africaine de sciences politiques
University of Dar es Salaam
P. O. Box 35036
Dar es Salaam, Tanzania

Association for the Development of European
  Political Science
Association pour le développement de la
  science politique européenne (ADESPE)
61 rue des Belles-Feuilles
75 Paris 16e, France

Hansard Society for Parliamentary
  Government
162 Buckingham Palace Road
London SW1, England

International Academy of Political Science and
  Constitutional History
Académie internationale de science politique et
  d'histoire constitutionelle
88 boulevard Péreire
75017 Paris, France

International Political Science Association
  (IPSA)
Association internationale de science politique
43 rue des Champs-Elysées
1050 Brussels, Belgium
  The principal international organization
in the field. Encourages national associations
of political science, organizes conferences and
congresses, and undertakes research and documentation. Also conducts seminars for junior
professors from India and Africa. The latest
World Congress was held August 15–21, 1976,
in Edinburgh, Scotland.

  For a more extensive listing of currently
active international organizations in politics
and international relations consult:

Yearbook of International Organizations. Brussels:
  Union of International Associations, biennial.

NATIONAL

Australia:
  Australian Political Science Association
  Department of Government
  University of Sydney
  Sydney, New South Wales 2006

Belgium:
  Institut belge de science politique
  43 rue des Champs-Elysées
  B-1050 Brussels

Canada:
  Canadian Political Science Association
  100 Saint George Street
  Toronto 5, Ontario

Federal Republic of Germany:
  Deutsche Vereinigung für politische
    Wissenschaft (DVPW)
  Von-Melle-Park 15
  2 Hamburg 13

France:
  Fondation nationale des sciences
    politiques
  27 rue Saint-Guillaume
  75 Paris 7

Israel:
  Israel Political Science Association
  Hebrew University of Jerusalem
  P.O.B. 214
  Jerusalem

Japan:
  Nippon seiji gakkai
  Faculty of Law, University of Tokyo
  3-1 Hongo, 7-chome
  Bunkyo-ku, Tokyo

People's Republic of China:
  Political Science and Law Association of
    China
  Peking, Hopeh

Republic of Korea:
  Korean Political Science Association
  119 Suhsomun-dong
  Sud Dae Moon-ku
  Nando Building, Room 203
  Seoul

United Kingdom:
  Political Studies Association
  Department of Politics, University of
    Reading
  Reading, Berkshire, England

  Political Studies Association of the United
    Kingdom (PSA)
  London School of Economics and Political
    Sciences
  Houghton Street
  London WC2, England

United States:
  American Academy of Political and Social
    Sciences
  3937 Chestnut Street
  Philadelphia, Pennsylvania 19104

  American Political Science Association
    (APSA)
  1527 New Hampshire Avenue NW
  Washington, D.C. 20036

Additional national associations in the field may be found in the following:

Minerva, Wissenschaftliche Gesellschaften. Berlin, Federal Republic of Germany: de Gruyter, 1972.

World Index of Social Science Institutions. Paris: UNESCO, 1970. Updated by *International Social Science Journal.*

The World of Learning. London: Europa, 1947–. Published annually. Includes a worldwide list of organizations concerned with international affairs.

The periodical *P. S.* annually publishes a list of national political science associations around the world as well as a list of United States regional and state political science associations. The list of national associations for 1975 is in Spring 1975, *8*(2), 212–215; a recent list of associations in the United States is in Winter 1975, *8*(1), 36–40.

Principal Information Sources

GENERAL

Guides to the literature in the field include:

Brock, C. *The Literature of Political Science.* New York: Bowker, 1969.

Harmon, R. B. *Political Science: A Bibliographical Guide to the Literature.* Metuchen, New Jersey: Scarecrow Press, 1965.

Holler, F. L. *The Information Sources of Political Science.* (5 vols.) Santa Barbara, California: ABC-Clio, 1975.

Mason, J. B. *Research Resources: Annotated Guide to the Social Sciences.* Santa Barbara, California: ABC-Clio, 1968–.

White, C. M. *Sources of Information in the Social Sciences.* Chicago: American Library Association, 1973.

Wynar, L. R. *Guide to Reference Materials in Political Science.* Littleton, Colorado: Libraries Unlimited, 1968.

Overviews and introductions to the field of political science include:

Charlesworth, J. C. *A Design for Political Science: Scope, Objectives, and Methods.* Philadelphia: American Academy of Political and Social Science, 1962.

Eulau, H., and March, J. G. (Eds.) *Political Science: The Behavioral and Social Sciences Survey; Political Science Panel.* Englewood Cliffs, New Jersey: Prentice-Hall, 1969.

Irish, M. D. *Political Science: Advance of the Discipline.* Englewood Cliffs, New Jersey: Prentice-Hall, 1968.

Somit, A., and Tanenhaus J. *American Political Science: A Profile of a Discipline.* Chicago: Aldine, 1964.

Waldo, D. "Political Science: Tradition, Discipline, Profession, Science, Enterprise." In *Handbook of Political Science.* Vol. 1. Reading, Massachusetts: Addison-Wesley, 1975. Pp. 1–130.

Information on education in the field is offered by:

Contemporary Political Science: A Survey of Methods, Research, and Teaching. Paris: UNESCO, 1950. Dated, but still useful.

Luttberg, N. R., and Melvin, A. K. "Ph.D. Training in Political Science." *Midwest Journal of Political Science,* 1968, *12,* 303–329.

Manning, C. A. W. *The University Teaching of Social Sciences, International Relations.* Paris: UNESCO, 1954. International, although dated.

Robson, W. A. *The University Teaching of Social Sciences, Political Science.* Paris: UNESCO, 1954. International, although dated.

Political science in historical perspective is treated in:

Butler, D. *The Study of Political Behavior.* London: Hutchinson, 1958.

Easton, D. *The Political System: An Inquiry into the State of Political Science.* New York: Knopf, 1953.

Hacker, A. *The Study of Politics: The Western Tradition and American Origins.* New York: McGraw-Hill, 1963.

Sabine, G. H. *History of Political Theory.* (3rd ed.) New York: Holt, Rinehart and Winston, 1961.

Somit, A., and Tanenhaus, J. *The Development of American Political Science: From Burgess to Behavioralism.* Boston: Allyn & Bacon, 1967.

CURRENT BIBLIOGRAPHIES

ABC POL SCI. Santa Barbara, California: ABC-Clio, 1969–.

International Bibliography of Political Science. London: Tavistock; Chicago: Aldine, 1952–.

International Political Science Abstracts. Oxford, England: Blackwell, 1951–. A comprehensive international abstracting service in English and French.

Public Affairs Information Service Bulletin. New York: Public Affairs Information Service, 1915–.

Public Affairs Information Service Foreign Language Index. New York: Public Affairs Information Service, 1972–. Text in French, German, Italian, Portuguese, and Spanish.

Social Sciences Index. New York: Wilson, 1965–.

PERIODICALS

The following are representative of the many journals in the field: *Acta Politica* (Netherlands), *American Political Science Review, Annals of the American Academy of Political and Social Science, Annals of the Japanese Political Science Association, Aussenpolitik* (FRG), *Canadian Journal of Political Science, Comparative Political Studies* (US), *Comparative Politics* (US), *Etudes internationales* (Canada), *Foreign Affairs* (US), *Foreign Policy* (US), *Foro internacional* (Mexico), *Government and Opposition* (UK), *Indian Journal of Political Science, International Affairs* (UK), *International Affairs* (USSR), *International Organization* (US), *International Studies Quarterly* (US), *Journal of Conflict Resolution* (US), *Journal of Inter-American Studies and World Affairs* (US), *Journal of International Affairs* (US), *Journal of Politics* (US), *Österreichische Zeitschrift für Politikwissenschaft, Parliamentary Affairs* (UK), *Policy Studies Journal* (US), *Political Quarterly* (UK), *Political Science Quarterly* (US), *Political Studies* (UK), *Politics* (US), *Politique étrangère* (France), *Politische Vierteljahresschrift* (FRG), *Revista de estudios políticos* (Spain), *Revista de política internacional* (Spain), *Revue du droit public et de la science politique en France et à l'étranger, Revue française de science politique, Scandinavian Political Studies* (Finland), *World Politics* (US), *Zeitschrift für die gesamte Staatswissenschaft* (FRG), *Zeitschrift für Politik* (FRG).

For a more complete listing of journals in political science consult:

International Political Science Abstracts. Oxford, England: Blackwell, 1951–.
Ulrich's International Periodicals Directory. New York: Bowker, biennial.

For journals in international relations see:

Meyriat, J. (Ed.) *World List of International Relations Periodicals.* Paris: International Studies Conference, 1951–.

ENCYCLOPEDIAS, HANDBOOKS, DICTIONARIES

Eilster, L., Weger, A., and Wieser, F. *Handwörterbuch der Staatswissenschaften.* Jena, Germany: F. Fischer, 1923–1929. One of the leading encyclopedias of political science.
Gould, J., and Kolb, W. K. *A Dictionary of the Social Sciences.* New York: Free Press, 1964.
Greenstein, F. I., and Polsky, N. W. (Eds.) *Handbook of Political Science.* Reading, Massachusetts: Addison-Wesley, 1975.
Haensch, G. *Dictionary of International Relations and Politics.* New York: American Elsevier,

1965. In German, English/American, French, and Spanish.
Handlexikon zur Politikwissenschaft. Munich, Federal Republic of Germany: Ehrenwirth, 1970.
Handwörterbuch der Sozialwissenschaften. Stuttgart, Federal Republic of Germany: G. Fischer, 1956–1968.
Sills, D. L. (Ed.) *International Encyclopedia of the Social Sciences.* New York: Macmillan, 1968. Includes articles on the political sciences.
Thesaurus for Political Science. Washington, D.C.: American Political Science Association, 1975. Serves as the terminology control device for the demonstration project, United States Political Science Information System (USPSIS).
Von der Goerres–Gesellschaft. *Staatslexikon: Recht, Wirtschaft, Gesellschaft.* Freiburg, Federal Republic of Germany: Herder, 1957. Comprehensive and authoritative German work indispensable to the field.

DIRECTORIES

For guides to the study of political science and related fields see:

A Guide to Graduate Study in Political Science. Washington, D.C.: American Political Science Association, annual.
Study Abroad. Paris: UNESCO, biennial. Lists programs in political science offered by institutions in numerous countries.
Yearbook of International Organizations. Brussels: Union of International Associations, annual. Includes an extensive worldwide list of institutes, centers, and schools of international affairs concerned with the study of international relations, peace research, and related topics.

RESEARCH CENTERS, INSTITUTES, INFORMATION CENTERS

The following is a sample of important research institutes and centers:

Academy of Political Science
Columbia University
420 West 118th Street
New York, New York 10027 USA

European Consortium for Political Research
University of Essex
Wivenhoe Park
Colchester, Essex, England

Governmental Affairs Institute
1776 Massachusetts Avenue NW
Washington, D.C. 20036 USA

Conducts research and offers services in foreign and domestic governmental, managerial, training, and programing fields.

Governmental Research Association
P.O. Box 387
Ocean Gate, New Jersey 08740 USA

Association of individuals involved in research and governmental research bureaus maintained by universities. Furthers research which will improve government.

Institute for Policy Studies
1520 New Hampshire Avenue NW
Washington, D.C. 20036 USA

Inter-University Consortium for Political
Research
P.O. Box 1248
Ann Arbor, Michigan 48106 USA

For listings of research centers and institutes in political science consult:

Minerva, Forschungsinstitute. Berlin, Federal Republic of Germany: de Gruyter, 1972.
World Index of Social Science Institutions. Paris: UNESCO, 1970.

For centers in the United States consult:

Directory of Organizations and Individuals Professionally Engaged in Governmental Research and Related Activities. Washington, D.C.: Governmental Research Association, 1935–.
Research Centers Directory. (5th ed.) Detroit: Gale Research, 1975.

Important research and information centers in international relations include the following:

Carnegie Endowment for International Peace
405 West 117th Street
New York, New York 10027 USA

Centre d'études de politique étrangère
54 rue de Varennes
Paris 7e, France

Council on Foreign Relations
58 East 68th Street
New York, New York 10021 USA

Graduate Institute of International Studies
132 rue de Lausanne
Geneva, Switzerland

Royal Institute of International Affairs
Chatham House
St. James' Square
London, England

Directories to other research institutes and centers include:

International Repertory of Institutions for Peace and Conflict Research. Paris: UNESCO, 1973.
United States Department of State. *University Centers of Foreign Affairs Research. A Directory.* Washington, D.C.: U.S. Government Printing Office, 1968. Lists university-affiliated research centers in the United States which conduct research in foreign affairs.
Wasson, D. *American Agencies Interested in International Affairs.* (5th ed.) New York: Praeger, 1964. Describes nearly 300 research and action groups in the United States directly or indirectly involved in international affairs.
Yearbook of International Organizations. Brussels: Union of International Associations, biennial. Includes a list of institutes and centers of international affairs.

[Bibliography prepared by Natalie Schatz.]

POLICIES, ACADEMIC
See Academic Policies.

POLICIES, ADMINISTRATIVE
See Administrative Policies.

POLITICS, STUDENT
See Participatory Democracy; Unrest, Campus.

POPULATION STUDIES
See Demography and Population Studies (field of study).

PORTUGAL, REPUBLIC OF

Population: 8,670,000 (1975 estimate). Student enrollment in primary school: 946,824; secondary school: 613,686; higher education: 58,605 (university: 51,179; other postsecondary education: 7426). Language of instruction: Portuguese. Academic calendar: October to July (universities). Percentage of national budget expended on all education: 10.2% (1973); higher education: 1.7% (1973). [Enrollment figures are for 1974.]

The first university in Portugal, now the University of Coimbra, was founded in Lisbon in 1290. It was confirmed by Pope

Nicholas IV and established jointly by the church and the crown. Its purpose was to train clergy, but it was gradually expanded to offer education in arts, civil and canon law, and medicine. Between 1308 and 1537 the location of the institution alternated between Lisbon and Coimbra, where it finally was permanently situated.

In 1559 the Society of Jesus assumed the administration of a new university at Evora, which was founded by Cardinal Henry, the then inquisitor general of Portugal. The university was dissolved in 1759.

During 1772 the university in Coimbra instituted new—and, for that time, modern—programs in the sciences and humanities. Until 1911 it remained the only university in Portugal, although in the nineteenth century it was joined by several nonuniversity institutions of higher learning. These institutions included two polytechnical schools, a military and a naval academy, two academies of fine arts, two schools of medicine and surgery, a conservatory of dramatic arts, an institute of letters, and an institute of hygiene and tropical medicine. In 1911 the government converted the nonuniversity polytechnics, schools of medicine, and the institute of letters into faculties (*faculdades*) of the restored University of Lisbon and the new University of Oporto. In the same year the faculty of theology at the University of Coimbra became the faculty of letters, and the faculties of mathematics and philosophy were combined into the faculty of science. In 1913 the faculty of law was added to the University of Lisbon.

After the period of expansion from 1911 to 1913, no new universities were founded until the establishment of the Technical University of Lisbon in 1930. In addition, faculties of engineering (1930), economics (1954), and letters (1961) were added to the University of Oporto.

A new university expansion took place in the late 1960s and early 1970s, when the University of Aveira (1973), the Catholic University of Lisbon (1968), the New University in Lisbon (1973), the University

of Minho in Braga (1973), and the University Institute of Evora (1973) were founded. Three nonuniversity institutes—for languages and administration (1962), social studies (1963), and economics and sociology (1964)—were also established.

Between 1950 and 1967 university enrollment increased from 16,000 to 36,000 students. Since 1969, however, higher education in Portugal has been subject to periodic interruptions and attempted reform during a period of political change, especially after the coup d'état on April 25, 1974. Student hostility toward the government and demands for a change in the educational system interrupted regular instruction in 1969 and again in 1970. In January 1971 the Ministry of Education issued *Guidelines of Reform of Higher Education* for public consideration; however, the necessary law was not passed, and the guidelines were not implemented. Since the coup, several reforms dealing with programs and administration have been introduced into the university.

In the academic year 1974–75 admission to the universities and other institutions of higher education was halted. Simultaneously, a compulsory year of civic service (*serviço cívico*), prior to entering a university or other institution of higher education, was instituted in several fields of study. The area of service is, as far as possible, to be connected with the student's chosen program of study.

National Educational Policy

In 1973 the National Assembly (*Assembleia nacional*) decreed a reform of the educational system. According to this reform, the system should (1) promote the moral, intellectual, physical, and professional development of the individual; (2) instill a scientific, critical, and creative spirit; and (3) stimulate interest in modern knowledge and professional improvement. In April 1975 a Constituent Assembly was elected, for the purpose of preparing a new constitution, and by October 1975 the articles referring to educational policies were approved. These articles stipulated that the state must (1) provide a basic compulsory education, which is universal and free; (2) guarantee admission to higher levels of education and participation in scientific investigation as well as artistic creation according to the citizen's abilities; (3) attempt to progressively establish free education at all levels; (4) establish a tie between education, production, and social activities; (5) especially stimulate the training of scientific and technical experts from the working classes; (6) create a national system of preschool education.

Legal Basis of Educational System

The faculties and institutes of higher education in Portugal are governed by individual decrees. Among some of the more important decrees promulgated to form the basis of the educational system are (1) the decree reorganizing the teaching profession (1970); (2) the decree regulating fees (1973); (3) Decree 408/71, September 27, 1971, approving the organic law of the Ministry of Education and the decrees reorganizing its central departments—the General Direction of Higher Education (1973) and the Institute of Higher Culture (1973); (4) Decree 806/74, December 31, 1974, concerning the administrative bodies and the pedagogical units of the universities and higher education institutes; and (5) the decree containing the fundamental principles of higher education, which was passed by the Revolutionary Council in 1975.

Types of Institutions

The university sector consists of the four older universities founded between 1290 and 1930 and the five newer universities founded after 1968. The nonuniversity sector is comprised of institutes, schools, and academies.

The University of Coimbra, the oldest institution, consists of six faculties and supports several attached institutes, including institutes of historical studies, botany, climatology and hydrology, geophysics. The University of Lisbon consists of five faculties; maintains attached institutes for bacteriology, ophthalmology, medicine, oncology, geophysics, physics, and mathematics; and supports a center for geographical studies and a marine laboratory. The University of Oporto offers education in six faculties; maintains attached institutes for botany, climatology and hydrology, zoology, geophysics, and anthropology; and supports a maritime zoological station and a meteorological observatory. The Technical University of Lisbon consists of a school of higher veterinary medicine and higher institutes of agronomy, administration, economics, technology, and social and political science.

The new universities are the Catholic University of Lisbon (1968), the New University of Lisbon (1973), the University of Aveiro (1973), the University of Minho in Braga (1973), and the University Institute of Evora (1973).

The nonuniversity institutions of higher education include, in Lisbon, the Institute of Hygiene and Tropical Medicine, the Institute of Social Service, the Higher Institute of Languages and Administration, the Higher Institute of Applied Psychology, and the Higher Institute of Communications; in Evora, the Higher Economic and Social Institute. In addition, there are two polytechnical institutes, in Covilhã and Vila Real; three higher engineering institutes, in Lisbon (Olivais Sul), Oporto, and Coimbra; higher institutes of social service in Coimbra; and a nautical school in Lisbon.

Military institutions include the military academy in Lisbon and the naval school in Alfeite. The schools of art include the two higher schools of fine arts in Lisbon and Oporto. The only higher school of music, the National Conservatory of Music, is located in Lisbon. Also found in Lisbon are the National School of Public Health and a technical school for nurses.

Relationship with Secondary Education

Secondary education in Portugal before reform attempts started in 1969 consisted of general schools (*liceus*), offering a seven-year program divided into cycles of two, three, and two years, respectively; and technical or vocational schools, comprised of two years of basic study followed by three to five years of specialized commercial, agricultural, or industrial studies, or a program in fine arts. In addition, the secondary system consisted of (1) special education such as music, religion for priests, and teacher training; (2) intermediate professional training for graduates of the second cycle of general secondary school; and (3) the specialized three- to five-year secondary technical or vocational programs.

Primary schools offer a compulsory four-year program. Since 1969 primary education has been followed by two years of compulsory education in a junior high school (*escola preparatória*).

In the academic year 1975–76 the unification of secondary education began to be implemented in several schools.

Admission Requirements

Prior to 1974 entrance to the universities was based on successful completion of the final examination of the third cycle of general secondary school and an entrance examination to the faculty, school, or institute of choice. The entrance examination, however, could be waived for students with a high score on their general secondary school-leaving examination.

Admission to higher technical or vocational study can also be achieved through intermediate professional schools. For example, students who successfully complete the second year at a commercial or industrial institute, or a program in a farm management training school, are eligible for entrance examinations to faculties and schools of engineering, faculties and schools of economics, and the schools of agronomy and veterinary medicine.

In accordance with the law of July 1975, established by the Revolutionary Council, students must work for one year in public service after secondary education and before entering the university.

In 1975–76 admission to schools of higher education was free to students who had successfully completed their general secondary final examination in the year 1973–74.

Applicants older than twenty-five without the needed academic requirements are also eligible for entry to the university after a so-called ad hoc examination.

Administration and Control

Before 1974 the public institutions in Portugal were controlled by the Ministry of Education, with the exception of specialized schools under the other ministries. The private institutions were under the authority of the Inspectorate of Private Education, whereas Catholic establishments of higher education were regulated by agreement between the state and the Holy See (*Concordat*). The rectors and a representative of each faculty or school of the universities were members of the National Board of Education.

Within the universities, which were autonomous in handling their own administration and academic affairs, the structure generally consisted of the rector as the head, the university council, senate, general assembly, and faculty (school or institute) councils and their directors. Administrative affairs were handled by the council, which usually consisted of the rector, the secretary of the institution, and the comptroller. The senate—consisting of the rector as chairman ex officio, the vice rector, and representatives of professors in faculties and constituent schools—was responsible for developing programs, reviewing syllabi, and awarding scholarships.

The rector was appointed by the minister of national education as a government representative. His duty was to convey state decisions to the university, uphold regulations and laws governing schools and faculties, inform the government of the need of the institution, and implement decisions of the university senate. The director of each faculty, school, or institute was elected by the faculty council to act as a liaison with the rector.

In 1974 the military academy was attached to the Ministry of the Army, th naval school was responsible to the Ministry of the Navy, and the Institute of Hygiene and Tropical Medicine was under the authority of the Ministry of Interterritorial Coordination.

A new system of administration, which has been in the process of implementation since April 1974, was codified in the decree of December 31, 1974. Under this new system, the administrative authorities in all schools of higher education are the general assembly, the faculty council (*conselho directivo*), and the pedagogical and scientific councils. The faculty council consists of elected representatives from the entire teaching and research staff, students, and nonacademic staff. Members in the pedagogical and scientific councils are elected by the teachers, research staff, and students.

Programs and Degrees

The universities at Lisbon, Coimbra, and Oporto offer programs in letters, medicine, science, and pharmacy; Lisbon and Coimbra also offer programs in law, engineering, and economics. The Technical University of Lisbon offers programs in agronomy, technology, economics, veterinary medicine, social science, and work and enterprise sciences.

The nonuniversity Higher Economic and Social Institute of Evora offers programs in sociology and economics, and the Higher Institute of Languages and Administration conducts programs in business management and communication. The Institute of Hygiene and Tropical Medicine offers courses in its departments of parasitology, microbiology, clinical tropical medicine, and epidemiology. The two higher schools of fine arts offer programs in art, painting, and sculpture; the National Conservatory of Music has programs in music, theater, and cinema.

The New University of Lisbon is organizing programs in Portuguese culture, social sciences, economics, education, engineering, computer science, and molecular science. The University of Aveiro is offering programs in electronics and telecommunications and is also preparing courses in computer science, technology, environmental sciences, accounting, and educational sciences. The University Institute of Evora is organizing programs connected with agriculture.

The average length of study leading to the usual first degree, the licentiate (*licenciatura*), is five years. Exceptions are the six-year programs in medicine and technology, including the last year of internship and practical training; the two-year diploma programs offered by certain schools and faculties; and one- to two-year postgraduate programs available in some faculties and schools. Some university schools award a bachelor's degree as the first degree. The doctoral degree is awarded to students holding a licentiate who have successfully passed a doctoral examination consisting of an oral examination and defense of a written thesis.

Financing and Student Financial Aid

The older universities, as corporations, were entitled to oversee their own finances and manage properties. They received yearly grants from the Ministry of Education and other donations and subsidies from the state. They also obtained funds by donation or subsidy from public and private bodies and from profits on property. In the 1970s higher education, with very few exceptions, is financed through the national budget.

The older universities, philanthropic organizations, business enterprises, and the government have provided scholarships or free tuition to students in need of financial aid. The university scholarships included cash allowance and exemption from fees; free tuition for economically deprived students; and reduction of fees for students of families with two or more dependents enrolled in tertiary institutions.

Teaching Staff

Teaching staff at the universities in Portugal are organized into four ranks: (1) full professors, who hold a chair, conduct lectures, and supervise research and practical exercises related to reading and lecture materials; (2) associate professors, who have responsibilities in research and, in some instances, for lectures; (3) lecturers; and (4) assistants.

Full professors are recruited by direct appointment or competitive examination, whereas associate professors obtain a post solely through competitive examination. Full professors receive a life appointment by ministerial decree; all other ranks are employed on contract. University teaching staff, as civil servants, receive their pensions under the same rules governing other state civil servants.

Research Activities

The three older nontechnical universities in Lisbon, Oporto, and Coimbra maintain approximately seventy associated research institutes, centers, laboratories, missions (*missões*), and groups (*grupos*). These university-associated organizations conduct general research and research in mathematics, the natural sciences, medicine, geography, law, and the human sciences. The number of university and nonuniversity research organizations is approximately two hundred.

Current Problems and Trends

Portugal faced a sudden increase in higher education enrollments as draftees from African wars and deportees returned to their country after independence of the Portuguese territories in Africa. Moreover, these students entered or reentered a system of higher education that was experiencing a shortage of qualified teaching staff and a lack of modern facilities and equipment. The prestigious faculties of law and medicine were already overcrowded; but enrollment in schools and faculties of veterinary medicine and agronomy, also important to national economic development (for instance, about a third of the population is employed in agriculture), were low by comparison.

Under José Veiga Simão, the Minister of Education in 1971, a general reform of education, including higher education, was recommended. The following changes were proposed for the higher education sector: (1) The universities would remain juridical bodies enjoying financial and administrative autonomy as well as freedom of inquiry. (2) Polytechnical and other specialized professional tertiary institutions would be created. (3) A new degree structure would be introduced, whereby (a) some university schools would continue to make the first degree a bachelor's degree, but the awarding of this type of degree would become the first degree in polytechnical schools and other specialized training institutions; (b) the universities would grant the master's degree in addition to the doctoral degree, and students possessing a bachelor's degree from specialized professional institutions could enter master's degree programs at the universities; and (c) specialized training for students with master's degrees would be introduced as an alternative to research and preparation for the doctoral degree. (4) Education departments would be established in universities, and a new system of teacher training would be introduced. (5) Faculty, school, and institute entrance examinations would be abolished. (6) Faculties of continuing studies would be established. Despite prolonged political unrest, some of these reforms are being implemented under the new educational policies contained in articles of the new constitution.

Relationship with Industry

In Portugal intermediate professional study parallels not only secondary education but in some cases also higher education. It takes place in commercial institutes and farm management training schools for students from the age of fifteen. The programs, which last respectively three years and five and a half years or more, end with a student work period in cooperation with public or private enterprises.

International Cooperation

The Portuguese system of education was exported to its former overseas territories profoundly influencing education in Brazil, Angola, the West African colonies, and Mozambique, as well as its Asian dependencies. Under the sponsorship of the Ministry of Education, the Ministry of Foreign Affairs, and public and private organizations and research centers, Portugal actively participates in exchanges of students, teachers, and researchers with a number of countries, such as Brazil, the United States, and the United Kingdom.

[Prepared with the cooperation of the education department of the Gulbenkian Foundation, Lisbon, Portugal.]

Educational Association

Sindicato dos professores da Grande Lisboa
Union of Teachers of Greater Lisbon
Rua da Barroca
Lisbon, Portugal

Bibliography

Bereday, G. Z. F. "Reflections on Reforms of Teacher Training in Portugal." *Comparative Education*, 1973, *9*(2), 55–60.

The Education, Training, and Functions of Technicians, Scientific and Technical Personnel—Portugal. Paris: Organisation for Economic Co-operation and Development, Directorate for Scientific Affairs, n.d.

Fernandes, R. *Situação da educação em Portugal.* Lisbon: Morais editores, 1973.

Herzlich, G. "Education in Portugal." *Manchester Guardian Weekly*, 1975, *113*(22), 14. (Periodical for the week ending November 30, 1975.)

Lisboa, E. "Education in Angola and Mozambique." In B. Rose (Ed.), *Education in Southern Africa.* Johannesburg, South Africa: Macmillan, 1970.

Livermore, H. V. *Portugal: A Short History.* Edinburgh: Edinburgh University Press, 1973.

Marques de Oliveira, A. H. *History of Portugal.* (2 vols.) New York: Columbia University Press, 1972.

Ministry of National Education, Portugal. "Projected Educational System." *Western European Education*, 1972, *4*, 180–195.

Samfaio, Y. S. *Evolução do ensino em Portugal.* Lisbon: Instituto Gulbenkian de ciência, Centro de investigação pedagogica.

Simão, J. V. "The General Reform of Education in Portugal." *Western European Education*, 1972, *4*, 106–119.

de Sousa Ferreira, E. *Portuguese Colonialism in Africa: The End of an Era.* Paris: UNESCO, 1974.

POSTDOCTORAL EDUCATION

See Graduate and Professional Education: Postdoctoral Education.

POSTEXPERIENCE EDUCATION

See Adult Education: Postexperience Education.

POST-GRADUATE EDUCATION: STRUCTURES AND POLICIES

See Organisation for Economic Co-operation and Development.

POSTSECONDARY EDUCATION, A STUDY TO IDENTIFY THE TRENDS IN THE SOURCES OF SUPPORT FOR (Higher Education Report), United States

A Study to Identify the Trends in the Source of Student Support for Postsecondary Education (Washington, D.C.: J. Froomkin, 1974), the report of a private research firm under contract to the United States Department of Health, Education and Welfare, considers the financial resources of students in United States postsecondary institutions. The following findings and recommendations are reported.

The 1971–72 earnings of students exceeded average parental contributions toward the financing of student education. However, because of a shortage of summer employment opportunities and the shortening of hours of work during the school year, for the period 1969–1973 student earnings failed to rise. This loss of employment during the 1969–1973 time period is an alarming trend in light of the recent (1974) weakening of the entire labor market.

Those in the lower middle class, who do not receive the federal support allocated only to the very poorest students, are especially hard hit by the lack of employment opportunities. The federal government should consider establishing a job placement apparatus to serve postsecondary students during the regular school year and in summer. The possibility that middle-class families can no longer afford post-secondary study necessitates action by the federal government to improve the part-time labor market and rationalize the summer job search of students.

POULTRY SCIENCE (Field of Study)

Poultry science applies and integrates basic and applied sciences to the production, processing, storage, and physical distribution of poultry and poultry products. It embraces many scientific fields, including chemistry, physics, biology, engineering, genetics, nutrition, physiology, pathology, and applied economics. While the primary objective of poultry science is to provide mankind maximum food benefit from domestic fowl, there are other purposes, such as the use of avian species for research in other fields, the propagation of both wild and domestic species for their esthetic value, and the use of eggs to manufacture vaccines for disease prevention.

Prior to the early 1900s the term *poultry husbandry* was used to identify the study of domestic fowl; but as poultry production became more a science than an art and as product technology expanded, the term *poultry science* became more prevalent. In general, *poultry science* is a broader term than *poultry husbandry* because it encompasses "off-the-farm" activities involving poultry products as well as production.

The field can be divided into the following branches: production (husbandry), product technology, and marketing. Poultry production involves genetics, nutrition, and physiology, as well as related areas such as poultry diseases, farm sanitation, engineering, and applied economics. Product technology, which involves microbiology, biochemistry, and food technology, covers aspects of poultry and eggs after they have been produced, including processing, manufacturing, and quality con-

trol. Product technology and marketing are closely related; in general, however, any activity that changes the physical form of the product is considered product technology, and activities that enhance the sales and uses of a product are considered marketing. Poultry science also can be subdivided on a species or breed basis; that is, chickens (meat and egg production types), turkeys, water fowl (ducks and geese), and others (such as pheasants, pigeons, and quail).

Throughout history, fowls have provided mankind with food, feathers for warmth or ornaments, pets, and entertainment (cockfighting). Artificial incubation has been practiced for over two thousand years. Early Greek and Roman writers discussed hatching, the development of chick embryos, and recommendations for a successful poultry farm. In 1598 Ulisse Aldrovandi, an Italian ornithologist, wrote an extensive paper on chickens; and by the middle of the eighteenth century scientific research methods were applied to poultry husbandry. The first systematic teaching began in Reading, England, in 1895 and shortly before that at Ganbais, France. A course of lectures on poultry was given to students at Cornell University (Ithaca, New York) in 1891, and in 1894 the Ontario Agricultural College, now a part of the University of Guelph (Guelph, Ontario), was the first North American college to establish a poultry department.

The first poultry department in the United States was established at the Connecticut Agricultural College (now the University of Connecticut, in Storrs, Connecticut) in 1901. During the next fifty years, over forty land-grant universities in the United States established separate departments of poultry science or husbandry. At the other land-grant institutions, poultry was a part of the animal or dairy science or husbandry department. Since the 1950s there has been a trend to phase out or merge poultry science departments with animal and dairy sciences. In 1975, consequently, there were only about twenty departments of poultry science/husbandry in United States land-grant institutions.

A number of Western European countries, such as the United Kingdom, have poultry research stations where students receive training after completing the basic sciences at a university. In some of the Asian countries—for instance, Japan and the Philippines, which have rapidly expanding commercial poultry industries—there are extensive courses in poultry science as well as departments of poultry science in several universities. In other countries—for instance, India, which has developed strong agricultural universities—poultry is a part of the animal science departments in colleges of agriculture or colleges of veterinary medicine. However, India also has at least one college of animal science, the Haryana Agricultural University (Hissar, Haryana State), which has departments of genetics, physiology, nutrition, and husbandry. In some Latin American countries—for example, Brazil—animal and poultry science are divided between ruminant (dairy, beef, sheep) and nonruminant (swine, poultry, horses, and rabbits) species.

Education at all levels in poultry science is continually changing to meet the needs of the poultry industry in each country. Training in poultry science becomes more specialized as the industry of the country served increases in size and moves from a "sideline" agricultural enterprise to a commercial mass production industry. In the agricultural colleges in the United States, poultry courses in brooding and incubation, turkey production, and the management of layers and commercial broilers have been replaced by more basic courses in nutrition, genetics, physiology, product technology, and marketing. Frequently, introductory courses in these disciplines are interdepartmental courses for dairy, animal, and poultry science majors, and advanced courses are species oriented. At the undergraduate or first degree level, these courses may be combined with a strong program in economics and business

management for students planning careers in the poultry industry, while those planning advanced training (M.S. or Ph.D. degrees) in specialized areas of poultry science, such as poultry genetics or nutrition, take additional basic undergraduate science courses.

Degree programs and courses for students planning to return to the farm have been decreasing, because most graduates enter the industry as employees of commercial firms or enter government service at supervisory or technical levels. Training in poultry flock management and in the care of birds is acquired through cooperative summer arrangements between private firms and universities. In addition to poultry farms, poultry- and egg-processing plants, hatcheries, and feed manufacturers participate in the summer programs. Also, in the United States an increasing number of technical schools or institutes are offering nondegree training in both agricultural and industrial skills. These programs are directed toward filling the need for skilled labor on the farm and in animal husbandry. In Europe formalized apprenticeship programs and technical institutes offering nondegree certificate and diploma courses have been in existence for many years.

Industrial or mass production techniques have been adopted more rapidly in the poultry industry than in most of the other animal industries in the field of agriculture, in part because of the short production cycle and the size of domestic fowl compared with the quadrupeds utilized in animal agriculture, and also because of the unique, integrated structure of the poultry business. These characteristics also facilitate the research required for improving production efficiency. Furthermore, there has been a very short span of time between the discovery of an innovation in the poultry industry and its commercial use. Likewise, new innovations are adopted rapidly throughout most of the world.

The poultry industry needs practitioners with advanced specialty training. In most regions of the world, training at the

M.S., Ph.D., or equivalent level is available. Training for advanced degrees can include either a combination of advanced courses in the basic sciences and a research project in poultry science or only research in a branch of the field. The former is more characteristic of North American institutions and the latter of European institutions.

PAUL C. CLAYTON

Major International and National Organizations

INTERNATIONAL

European Federation of Branches of the World's Poultry Science Association
Spelderholt Institute for Poultry Research
Beekbergen, Netherlands

World's Poultry Science Association (WPSA)
Association universelle d'aviculture scientifique (AVI)
Treramelon, Bidnija, Malta
The major international organization, with branches in thirty-six countries.

World Veterinary Poultry Association (WVPA)
Houghton Poultry Research Station
Huntingdon and Godmanchester, England

NATIONAL

Australia:
WPSA Branch in Australia
Government Poultry Research Station
P.O. Box 11
Seven Hills, New South Wales 2147

Canada:
WPSA in Canada
Department of Animal Science
Macdonald College, McGill University
P.O. Box 228
Quebec

Federal Republic of Germany:
Zentralverband der deutschen
Geflügelwirtschaft e.V.
Niebuhrstrasse 53
53 Bonn

India:
Indian Poultry Science Association
Krishi Bhavan
New Delhi

Italy:
Istituto de zoocolture
via S. Giacomo 9
40126 Bologna

Netherlands:
Nederlandse organisatie van
pluimeveehouders
Utrechtseweg 31
Zeist

South Africa:
South African Poultry Association
P.O. Box 1795
Johannesburg

Spain:
Escuela real de avicultura
Arenys de Mar
Barcelona

Sweden:
Föreningen Svensk Fjäderfäskötsel
Gamla Brogatan 29
111 20 Stockholm

Switzerland:
Verband schweizerischer Geflügelhalter
Burgerweg 2
Zollikofen

United Kingdom:
WPSA Branch in the UK
Silcock Ltd. Development Farm
Riborough Road
Stoke Mandeville, Buckinghamshire
England

United States:
Poultry and Egg Institute of America
521 East 63rd Street
Kansas City, Missouri 64110

Poultry Science Association Inc.
311 Illinois Boulevard
113 North Neil Street
Champaign, Illinois 61820

WPSA Branch in the USA
Extension Service, United States
Department of Agriculture
Washington, D.C. 20250

For a complete listing of the national branches of the World's Poultry Science Association see:

"Membership Directory." *World Poultry Science Journal,* February 1976, *32* (1), entire issue. Directory published every four years.

Principal Information Sources

GENERAL

Guides to the literature include:

Blanchard, J. R., and Ostvold, H. *Literature of Agricultural Research.* Berkeley: University of California Press, 1958. Somewhat dated but a classic guide to reference materials.

Bush, E. A. R. *Agriculture: A Bibliographic Guide.* (2 vols.) London: Macdonald, 1974.

Information Sources on the Animal Feed Industry. UNIDO Guides to Information Sources, 13. Vienna: United Nations Industrial Development Organization, 1975. Includes professional and research organizations, information services, directories, handbooks, dictionaries, bibliographies, periodicals, and other useful sources of information.

Selected List of American Agricultural Books in Print and Current Periodicals. Beltsville, Maryland: National Agricultural Library, 1975. Includes sources on poultry and animal sciences.

Singhri, M. L., and Shrimali, D. S. *Reference Sources in Agriculture: An Annotated Bibliography.* Udaipur, India: Rajasthan College of Agriculture, Consumers Cooperative Society, 1962. International in scope but with Indian emphasis.

Introductions to the field include:

Acker, D. *Livestock and Poultry Production.* Englewood Cliffs, New Jersey: Prentice-Hall, 1968.

Card, L. E., and Nesheim, M. C. *Poultry Production.* Philadelphia: Lea & Febiger, 1972.

Cole, H. H., and Ronning, M. *Animal Agriculture.* San Francisco: W. H. Freeman, 1974.

Rice, J. E., and Botsford, H. E. *Practical Poultry Management.* New York: Wiley, 1956.

Histories of the field include:

American Poultry History 1823–1973. Madison, Wisconsin: American Poultry Historical Society, 1974.

Sawyer, G. *Agribusiness Poultry Industry: A History of Its Developments.* Hicksville, New York: Exposition Press, 1971.

Works dealing with education include:

Animal Husbandry, Agricultural Education. Proceedings from the Symposium on International Animal Agriculture. Urbana: University of Illinois Press, 1969.

Kaufman, R. G., and others. "Improving the Effectiveness of Teaching Animal Science." *Journal of Animal Science,* January 1971, *32,* 161–164.

Kottman, R. M., and others. "Symposium: Effective Teaching in Dairy Science." *Journal of Dairy Science,* March 1966, *49* (3), 319–330.

Undergraduate Teaching in Animal Sciences. Proceedings of a Conference. Washington, D.C.: National Academy of Sciences, 1967.

Also see *Poultry Science* and *World Poultry Science Journal* for articles dealing with animal science and poultry science education.

CURRENT BIBLIOGRAPHIES

Bibliographies and abstracting services which include current literature on poultry science include:

Animal Breeding Abstracts, Compiled from World Literature. Edinburgh: Commonwealth Bureau of Animal Breeding and Genetics, Commonwealth Agricultural Bureaux, 1933–

Bibliography of Agriculture. Scottsdale, Arizona: Oryx Press, 1975–. An important source for current information on agriculture and related fields; international in scope.

Bibliography on Poultry Industry, Chickens, Turkey, Aquatic Fowl, Gamebirds. Washington, D.C.: U.S. Government Printing Office, 1948.

Biological Abstracts. Philadelphia: Bioscience Information Service of Biological Abstracts, 1926–. Covers genetics, physiology, livestock, breeding, and feeding.

Biological and Agricultural Index. (Formerly *Agricultural Index 1916–1918.*) New York: Wilson, 1919–.

Food Science and Technology Abstracts. Farnham Royal, Bucks, England: Commonwealth Agricultural Bureaux, 1969–.

PERIODICALS

Agricultural Education (US), *Agroanimalia: Animal Sciences* (South Africa), *Animal Production* (UK), *Archiv für Geflügelkunde* (FRG), *Archiv für Geflügelzucht und Kleintierkunde* (GDR), *Australasian Poultry World* (Australia), *Avicoltura* (Italy), *British Poultry Science* (UK), *Dansk erhvervsfjerkrae* (Denmark), *Journal of Animal Science* (US), *Nouvelles de l'aviculture* (France), *Poultry International* (US), *Poultry Science* (US), *Poultry World* (UK), *Quarterly Poultry Bulletin* (UK), *World Poultry Science Journal* (UK).

For a complete listing of journals, see:

1000 Selected Journals in Agriculture and Related Subjects. Beltsville, Maryland: National Agricultural Library, 1973.

Ulrich's International Periodicals Directory. New York: Bowker, biennial.

ENCYCLOPEDIAS, DICTIONARIES, HANDBOOKS

Brunoli, A. *Dizionario avicolo internazionale, italiano, francese, inglese, spagnolo.* Bologna, Italy: Edagricole, 1967. Italian-based terms with French, English, and Spanish equivalents and indexes.

Forscey, L. A. (Comp.) *Multi-lingual Poultry Dictionary, English, French, German, Spanish.* Beekbergen, Netherlands: European Federation of Branches of the World's Poultry Science Association, 1969.

Poultry World. London: "Poultry World," 1958. The poultry industry's standard reference work.

Seiden, R. *Poultry Handbook: An Encyclopedia for Good Management of All Poultry Breeds.* (2nd ed.) New York: Van Nostrand, 1952.

DIRECTORIES

Directories that include educational information in the agricultural sciences are:

American Colleges and Universities. Washington, D.C.: American Council of Education, 1928–. Published quadrennially.

Commonwealth Universities Yearbook. London: Association of Commonwealth Universities, 1914–. Published annually.

International Handbook of Universities. Paris: International Association of Universities, 1959–. Published triennially.

Poultry Industry Directory. Decatur, Georgia: Southeastern Poultry and Egg Association, 1974. Lists commercial organizations; also includes information on educational and research institutions in poultry science in the United States.

Poultry World Directory. London: Agricultural Press, 1970. An international, commercial directory.

The World of Learning. London: Europa, 1947–. Published annually. Lists universities and colleges, learned societies, and research institutes throughout the world.

RESEARCH CENTERS, INSTITUTES, INFORMATION CENTERS

For listings of research institutes in agriculture see:

Index of Agricultural Research Institutions in Europe Concerned with Animal Production and Their Principal Lines of Investigation. Rome: Food and Agriculture Organization, 1953.

Minerva, Forschungsinstitute. Berlin, Federal Republic of Germany: de Gruyter, 1972. Lists research institutes throughout the world.

National Agricultural Library. *Directory of Information Resources in Agriculture and Biology.* Washington, D.C.: U.S. Government Printing Office, 1971. A United States directory to agricultural information sources; designed primarily for agricultural researchers and teachers.

PRESIDENT, SELECTION OF

See Affirmative Action; General Administration, Organization for.

PRESIDENTIAL LIBRARIES

See Archives: United States, National Archives of.

PRESS, STUDENT

See Student Publications.

PRESSES, COLLEGE AND UNIVERSITY

The functions of modern universities include research, education, and dissemination of research results to society as a whole. These activities can be carried out only with the aid of books—scholarly books to communicate research results, textbooks to enhance instruction, and books of general interest for the public at large. Thus, university activities are invariably linked with publishing activities, and universities are directly or indirectly involved with the publishing of scholarly books. When a university undertakes the actual publishing of scholarly books, it assumes the function of a university press.

Just as the scope of scholarly publishing differs from country to country and from one period of time to another, the scope of university press activities also differs. The oldest university presses in the world are those of Oxford and Cambridge Universities in England. They are university presses in the broadest sense, publishing Bibles, children's books, books of general interest, and even sheet music, in addition to scholarly works. American university presses, on the other hand, are scholarly publishers in the strictest sense.

The modern concept of a university press differs significantly from the traditional one in facilities as well. Traditional university presses, such as Oxford and Cambridge, started out with their own printing plants. Although a number of university presses still maintain printing facilities, most concentrate solely on the publishing function. The most economical approach to printing the varied publications of a university press is to use commercial printers. Where there are no adequate printing plants—as in the case of some developing countries—then of course it becomes necessary for university presses to maintain their own production facilities.

The differences in concept and structure of university presses stem from the diversified historical development of the presses in each country and reflect the attitudes of different societies toward fulfilling their need for scholarly publishing. In many countries scholarly publishing is undertaken mainly or solely by commercial publishers, either because no university presses exist or because their contributions are not significant.

The position of a university press falls between the scholarly publishing functions of learned societies and those of commercial publishing houses. The primary and most direct dissemination of scholarly information is usually undertaken by learned societies and research institutes through institutional organs, bulletins, or monographs. Of course, the publishing activities of university presses, learned societies, and commercial publishers overlap somewhat, differing greatly with historical and geographical background.

History and Evolution

The history of the university press goes back five hundred years to the establishment of printing facilities at Oxford University (1478) and Cambridge University (1521). Both presses were established under charter by the king and benefited from the exclusive right to publish authorized Bibles, which soon came to constitute an important financial basis. The two presses continued to develop modestly during the medieval and modern periods. Universities at the time were bastions of conservative education rather than creative centers of new knowledge, and university presses reflected this fact, publishing a limited amount of educational material every year. It was not until the 1930s that Oxford

University Press underwent a drastic change in image, from medieval to modern, becoming a large, active, worldwide business organization.

Financial support of British university presses comes mainly from sales. Subsidies from other sources, such as the university, government, and foundations, do not constitute a significant part of annual income. Oxford University Press is a taxable, nonprofit corporation that depends heavily on the income from sales of Bibles, dictionaries, and other profitable publications.

By contrast, American-style university presses are embodiments of the role of the university press as a scholarly book publisher in the narrowest sense—a practice that is almost without exception unprofitable. To ease financial difficulties, American university presses are beginning to publish more profit-making books. However, it is generally acknowledged that university press operating funds must be provided by parent institutions, governments, or foundations—in other words, by society. In 1975 roughly ninety university presses were in operation in the United States, seventy of which were members of the Association of American University Presses (AAUP). The modern development of American university presses—like their British counterparts—began in the 1930s in response to the tremendous surge in scientific and technological knowledge and the rapid expansion of higher education that characterized that period.

Many university presses in other developed and developing countries also evolved as a consequence of expansion and growth of higher education. No investigation has been made on the total number of university presses throughout the world, but most likely there are more than three hundred, even if only well-established press operations are counted. In addition, many publishing activities in universities are conducted outside the realm of university presses.

There is a tendency in developing countries for the university to be a strategically important focal point of social and economical development. In this context a university press becomes an important tool for improving services to scholars, students, and the nation as a whole. The uniqueness of the university press in developing countries lies in its emphasis on textbook publishing and, in many instances, the possession of a press-run printing plant. Presses in these countries are also often faced with language problems, especially in translating scholarly material from Western into vernacular tongues.

Despite their totalitarian nature, the university presses in communist countries are neither homogeneous nor unified. For example, Moscow University Press is strong in textbook publishing, Leningrad University Press publishes books of a scholarly nature, and almost all universities in Poland have some kind of press that concentrates on producing mimeographed instructional material for students.

Contribution to Education

The nature and extent of university press contributions to education differ greatly from country to country. In the United States, for example, the seventy member presses of the AAUP publish about twenty-five hundred new titles annually, or about 10 percent of the country's total new title output. This percentage increases significantly when one considers only scholarly publishing. Unfortunately, accurate statistics are not available, but it would not be an overestimation to say that university press output exceeds one half of the scholarly book publishing total in the United States for all fields: humanities, social sciences, and natural sciences. In the humanities, for example, university presses publish more than two out of every three new titles, which indicates that university presses in the United States are an indispensable facility in the scholarly publishing and intellectual life of the nation. University presses assume a similar role in many other countries, particularly where they are virtually the only publishers producing and distributing scholarly works.

In addition to the general role of university presses, individual presses operate according to the desires and needs of their supporting faculty and usually publish authors from their own universities. Such books account for about half of their new titles annually. The real contribution of the university press lies not only in publishing important research material but also in stimulating research and publication activity within the institution it serves.

Financial Arrangements

It is often assumed that commercial publishing houses never publish scholarly works, but this is not necessarily true. University presses and commercial publishers often duplicate each other's efforts. It sometimes happens that scholarly books show very good sales, although the contrary is often the case as well. University presses and commercial publishers alike use the income from profitable books to support the publication of unprofitable books, and the economic differences between them are only a matter of degree. All things considered, university presses publish more unprofitable scholarly books than do commercial houses. Often this is a matter of the efficiency of the operation—an effectively run operation can help to improve the sales of a book, thereby increasing profits and keeping deficits down.

The publishing of scholarly books—particularly those of a strict scholarly nature, with appeal to a select, narrow group of specialists—is becoming more and more unprofitable. This is partly due to the twigging phenomenon, in which the number of scientists in a given field decreases as new branches of specialization of the discipline are established. Another reason for the unprofitability of scholarly books is the rapid increase in scientific information and the fact that libraries on fixed budgets cannot buy everything that is published, which cuts into university press sales. Photocopying is another problem that contributes to undermining the already much weakened economy of scholarly publishing. For these reasons, as well as increased production costs, the price of scholarly books has gone up tremendously. In medieval times scholarly publishing was a completely nonprofit venture sponsored by kings, feudal lords, eminent temples, and churches. If financial conditions continue to deteriorate, scholarly publishing may again have to become wholly sponsored as in the past.

Because publishing scholarly books is unprofitable, university presses must receive grants from foundations, from their sponsoring universities, or from the government in order to survive. Financial support from a sponsoring institution and other sources can be given in various ways: overall subsidies; title subsidies (grants for publication of a specific book); university-provided personnel, space, and services. Financial support of American university presses is approximately 10 to 20 percent of the annual income of a press. The extent to which a press is subsidized differs from one university to another. New presses and small presses usually need more subsidies than older and bigger presses—as much as 30 to 40 percent of their annual income. Some of the larger presses are financially independent and receive almost no subsidies; many even show a modest profit.

The manner in which financial support is obtained can be classified as follows: the Harvard type—huge revolving funds donated to the press; the Chicago type—sales from a large backlist; and the California type—yearly subsidies provided by the sponsoring institutions (most presses of state universities are in this category). University presses must, of course, obtain some income through sales. Most presses do not accept subsidies provided by authors. Large purchases of books by their authors, however, are always welcome.

It takes a long time for a university press to reach a point of financial independence, because it takes time to recover money invested in a scholarly book before and after publication, and because some titles never sell well enough to recover publication costs. Since time and energy are consumed at a greater rate in the preparatory stage of a business, new presses and small presses, as noted above, need more subsidies than older, larger presses. In addition, to help new presses in their early years, it is a widely accepted practice for established presses to provide them with assistance in editing, production, and sales. For similar economic reasons, several universities in a state or region have established joint presses or consortia.

Management

Although the university press serves the university community and is controlled by the university administration, it is also a business organization. It coordinates editing, production, sales, and accounting. Editing involves procuring and evaluating manuscripts and preparing them in a form appropriate for sending to the printer. The production process involves various outside suppliers and press-run printing facilities. Sales are accomplished through highly sophisticated marketing mechanisms. Accounting treats the collection of money from accounts receivable and other fiscal procedures. Thus, it is erroneous to consider a press in the same class as a university library, research laboratory, or hospital. The operation of a university press requires knowledge of, and experience in, management of a commercial publishing house. It is, therefore, not only inappropriate but irresponsible to assign the management task to a nonprofessional, especially a faculty member. This rule is followed by university administrators in most developed countries as a basic concept, but it is not widely practiced in some developing and developed countries, where domination by professors is strong.

What conditions are necessary, then,

for a university press to be successful? First, autonomy is a prerequisite, because a press performs a highly specialized operation and must function as a business organization, while also being integrated harmoniously into the functions of the university as a whole. Once the basic policies of the university are established, the day-to-day operation can be left to the press. Unfortunately, there are too many university administrators who are unfamiliar with publishing but nevertheless try to provide direction, which results in confusion.

Two major aspects of autonomy are manuscript selection and finance. The final approval of manuscripts should, of course, be decided by an editorial board consisting of faculty members. The director and press staff should exercise their own screening from a financial point of view before manuscripts are submitted to the board. If the press is not given the right to exercise its own judgment, but is directed by university administrators in the selection of manuscripts, the roles of the director and of the staff of the press become ambiguous. Consequently, the university should allow the press as much freedom as possible beyond establishment of basic policy and acquisition of financial support.

Impact of Information Explosion

With so many universities undergoing transition while trying to fulfill the needs of new and ever changing societies, the future role of university presses is still unclear. This is especially true of campuses throughout the world that experienced student unrest during the 1960s and 1970s and of those in developing countries. Adaptation to a new environment is not easy for large organizations like universities, and transition of the university press to meet new needs is particularly difficult, because publishing programs are usually time consuming. University presses will no doubt seek ways to diversify and multiply their activities to meet the de-

mands of sponsoring institutions that are also diversifying their functions.

The latter half of the twentieth century is an age experiencing a great surge in information. To cope with this information explosion, university presses are increasingly turning to nonprint media (microfiche, tape) and automatic storage and retrieval of scholarly information. Since the established channels of dissemination of scholarly information are gradually becoming obsolete, more effective networks to meet the new publishing demands have to be developed. The university press can continue to play an important role as a principal disseminator of scholarly information. A trend toward international cooperation among university presses characterizes the efforts being undertaken to establish such a network.

Technological innovations are also having a strong impact on university presses. While devices such as microfiche, cassette tapes, and computers are of great help in disseminating the vast flow of scientific information, university presses—unlike commercial publishers—find it difficult to justify the investment required to adopt these techniques in their operations.

Cooperation with National Associations

The following countries have national associations of university presses: Australia, Canada, India, Japan, the Republic of Korea, and the United States. The United Kingdom does not have a national association, in spite of its long history of university presses, perhaps because of the disparity in size between the old and new presses. Many other countries with university presses also lack a national organization. The style and activities of national associations differ greatly from country to country. The membership qualifications of the AAUP, for example, are so restrictive that some minor presses never become members; qualifications in other countries, however, are very lax.

The primary purposes of a national association are to identify university press activities and to provide opportunities for strengthening solidarity. Needless to say, such an association can provide encouragement and stimulation to presses on isolated, remote campuses.

National associations serve member presses in several ways: dissemination of university press activities; education and training of press personnel; and coordination of cooperative programs—joint catalogs, joint exhibitions, joint advertising, joint mailing lists, and other promotional activities.

National associations often act as representatives to local governments and other groups. They also hold annual meetings at which timely professional information is exchanged, friendships are renewed, and new books are displayed.

One of the most significant examples of the cooperative program of the AAUP is an educational mailing list developed early in the 1950s. In the mid 1970s, this list contained more than 550,000 addresses of scholars in all disciplines and of various kinds of libraries. In 1975 the AAUP encouraged the United States government and various foundations to launch a national inquiry into the dissemination of scholarship. The information acquired from the survey will serve scholarly publishers as well as others in related fields for many years to come.

International Cooperation

University presses have been international by nature since early times. The production and distribution of scholarly books depend on international involvement. For example, Oxford University Press has more than ten branches throughout the world that not only publish their own titles but help local publishers produce locally edited books. In Malaysia the Oxford Press once became an agent of the University of Malaya Press in the production and distribution of the latter's publications, helping to train the staff of the young press in the process. However, it is the American group of university presses that has developed international relations and cooperation most extensively, as indicated by the AAUP international programs described below.

Latin American translation programs. From 1960 to 1969, more than eighty Latin American representative works were translated and published under this program to improve and promote dialogs between the two continents. Twenty presses joined in the scheme, acquiring grants from the Rockefeller Foundation.

Centro interamericano de libros académicos (Interamerican Center for Scholarly Books). Established in 1965 in Mexico City under the joint sponsorship of the AAUP and the National University of Mexico with a grant from the Ford and Rockefeller Foundations, this center is aimed at strengthening the flow of scholarly books between the two Americas. After several years of difficulty, it became a self-sufficient business and still continues its service to scholars on both continents, although, for various reasons, North American books were distributed only in Mexico during 1975.

Communication with scholarly publishers in other countries. Since the early 1950s, the AAUP has sent representatives to visit university presses in Africa, Asia, Europe, Australia, South America, and the Soviet Union to learn first-hand about scholarly publishing in those parts of the world. Guests from abroad have been in attendance at AAUP annual meetings since 1965. Through all these efforts, communication and cooperation among scholarly publishers have been greatly improved.

Though not sponsored directly by the AAUP, the association and its members contributed to the creation of the challenging Franklin Book Program in 1952, which was aimed at helping developing countries launch their own publishing activities. The Franklin Book Program has six operating offices (in Cairo, Egypt; Dacca, Bangladesh; Djakarta, Indonesia; Kabul, Afghan-istan; Lahore, Pakistan; and Tehran, Iran), besides its central New York City headquarters. It also undertakes programs in Latin America and is undoubtedly one of the biggest book development programs in the Third World.

The international link among university presses developed gradually through all of these efforts. Some presses in other regions became international members of AAUP, and the resulting communication strengthened mutual understanding and friendship. In 1972 the International Book Year launched by UNESCO led to in-creased public interest in books and in publishing. University publishers were encouraged to establish an international organization of scholarly publishers. The University of Toronto Press initiated this movement with the support of UNESCO and the government of Canada. Thus, the International Association of Scholarly Publishers (IASP) was established in September 1972.

International Association of Scholarly Pub-lishers. The objectives of IASP are to exert influence on the world community in the name of scholarly publishing and to under-take cooperative programs for the benefit of scholarly publishers. Enrollment is not restricted to university presses; commercial publishers of scholarly books are allowed to constitute up to one third of the total membership. IASP issues a newsletter and a directory of scholarly publishers through-out the world. It also encourages national and regional university press activities. The Asian Group of University Presses, for example, was formed in 1972 at the First International Conference of Uni-versity Presses in Asia and the Pacific Area, held in Tokyo. In 1975 the Association of South East Asian Academic Publishers was also formed as a regional group of scholarly publishers. The University of Tokyo Press has co-published more than one hundred English titles with about twenty American and Canadian university presses and has acted as a production agent

for a number of American presses. Similar arrangements are increasingly being made between presses of developing countries and the Western world.

Other international activities. The publish-ing activities of international organizations, such as UNESCO, the Organisation for Economic Co-operation and Development, the Food and Agricultural Organization, and the World Health Organization, are closely connected with university presses all over the world. The merger between the East-West Center Press and the University of Hawaii Press to form the University Press of Hawaii is another example of an internationally oriented publishing activity. The newly established United Nations Uni-versity in Tokyo plans to launch its own press in order to present the university to the world through its publications.

Bibliography

Brief History of the Cambridge University Press. Cambridge, England: Cambridge University Press, 1956.

Carter, H. *History of the Oxford University Press.* Vol. 1. London: Oxford University Press, 1975.

Directory of the Association of American University Presses. New York: AAUP, 1975.

Directory of Scholarly Publishers in Asia. Tokyo: Scholarly Publishing Asia, 1976.

Harman, E. *The University as Publisher.* Toronto, Ontario: University of Toronto Press, 1961.

Hawes, G. R. *To Advance Knowledge: A Hand-book of American University Press Publishing.* New York: American University Press Ser-vices, 1967.

Ingle, H. E., and Seltzer, L. E. *A Trip to Asia: Report of the Asia Subcommittee, International Cooperation Committee, AAUP.* New York: Association of American University Presses, 1964.

International Scholarly Publishers Directory. Toronto, Ontario: International Association of Scholarly Publishers, 1976.

Kerr, C. *A Report on American University Presses.* New York: Association of American Uni-versity Presses, 1949.

Kerr, C. *A Report on American University Presses Supplement.* New York: Association of Ameri-can University Presses, 1956.

Minowa, S., and Arboleda, A. A. (Eds.) *Scholarly Publishing in Asia: Proceedings of the Con-ference of University Presses in Asia and the*

Pacific. Tokyo: University of Tokyo Press, 1973.

Nickerson, T. (Ed.) *Transpacific Scholarly Publishing.* Honolulu: East-West Center Press, 1963.

Oxford Publishing Since 1478. London: Oxford University Press, 1964.

Proceedings of the ASPAC University Press Conference. Seoul, Republic of Korea: Cultural and Social Center for the Asian and Pacific Region, 1974.

Scholarly Publishing. Toronto, Ontario: University of Toronto Press, quarterly.

Underwood, R. G. *Production and Manufacturing Problems of American University Presses.* New York: Association of American University Presses, 1960.

Webb, T., Jr. *A Trip to Africa: Report of the African Subcommittee, International Cooperation Committee, AAUP.* New York: Association of American University Presses, 1963.

SHIGEO MINOWA

PRINTMAKING (Field of Study)

Contemporary printmaking is a broad and varied field of study which includes the many traditional and current processes and techniques available to the artist to create an original print. An original print is a work that is rendered and manipulated in such a manner that it can be reproduced with a high degree of fidelity and consistency. An original etching, for example, is one in which the artist executes the drawing on a metal plate, proofs it (takes an impression of the drawing), determines whether the resulting image needs further manipulation, and then prints the plate or supervises its printing. If a plate or lithography stone is not "canceled"—that is, destroyed or marked in such a manner as to render it unprintable—a print can be pulled without the artist's supervision, as happens after a notable artist's death.

Historically, the growth of printmaking has been closely associated with the origins of the graphic arts industry. Before the invention of photography, skilled engravers were employed to copy master paintings, sculpture, and architectural works, and these prints were then used for decorative purposes or as illustrations for historical and educational volumes. As various cultures devised the technology to reproduce images economically and efficiently for decorative, informative, and religious purposes, the skills of the artist-craftsman were engaged to print textiles, icons, and, with the invention of the printing press, book illustrations. Eventually printmaking was used as a medium by draughtsmen, designers, and painters who were attracted to its visual and replicating characteristics. Printmaking has now secured its position as an art form independent of the graphic arts industry, which has grown increasingly complex and specialized in response to the needs of commerce and publishing.

The various processes and techniques of printmaking may be considered in terms of their principal characteristics. The oldest and simplest process, relief printing, appeared in early Chinese, Japanese, Egyptian, and European cultures. The most frequently used relief processes are the woodcut and the wood engraving. In the woodcut the artist carves an image into a wood surface; inks the carved surface; lays paper on it; and transfers the ink to the paper, either by rubbing the back of the paper with hand tools or a manually powered press. Wood engraving differs in that the endgrain of a hardwood is used for the rendering of the image. The denseness and strength of the hardwood endgrain enables the artist to develop fine detail and retain it during numerous printings. In addition to wood, linoleum, masonite, plastics, paperboards, and gesso are used in relief printing.

The intaglio print has its origins in the craft of the metalsmiths of medieval Europe. As in wood engraving, the image is incised with hand tools into the surface of a relatively soft metal, such as copper or zinc. (A variety of tools is used to render line, tone, and texture.) The surface is then carefully inked so that the ink lies in the engraved lines; the excess ink is removed, and paper is placed on the plate. Since adequate pressure is necessary to press the paper into the lines to remove the ink, a press must be used to transfer the ink to the paper.

Etching differs from engraving in that acids are used to "bite" the lines or tonal areas into the metal plate. An acid-resistant substance of a waxy, tarlike, or resinous nature is used to coat the surface of the plate. The image is then scratched through the acid resist, thereby allowing the acid to attack the metal. After the acid etch, the acid-resistant material is removed, and the plate is inked as in engraving and printed on a press. Again, the artist-printmaker has many tools and procedures available to him to render desired effects.

Lithography originated in Germany in the late eighteenth century. As the name implies, a stone, particularly limestone, is ground level, and the image is drawn on the surface with a greasy crayon or liquid. The drawing is then etched with a mild acid and gum solution, which chemically reacts with the exposed areas of the stone, allowing the ink to adhere only to the drawn portions on the stone. After the stone is etched, it is inked with a hand roller and printed on a press. Metal plates and manual offset presses are also used in hand lithography.

Serigraphy, or silk-screen printing, a comparatively new process, was developed in the twentieth century and is based on the ancient principle of stencil printing. In this process, paper, gelatin film, or liquid resists are applied to a screen made by stretching silk or a synthetic fabric over a wood or metal frame. These stencils conform to the desired image and physically prevent the ink from reaching the paper or textile. The screen is printed by forcing the ink through the stretched fabric with a hand squeegee.

Since drawing, design, and, more recently, photography are the primary fields associated with printmaking, printmakers should be proficient in these areas. While it is possible to work directly on the etching plate, litho stone, or silk screen to develop an image to subsequently print, the usual approach is to have the image adequately rendered in a preliminary drawing, design, or photograph, which is then used to guide the work to be executed.

Developments in printmaking have greatly extended the scale, content, and use of color in the printmaking process. In particular, the availability of photosensitive emulsions, films, and acid resists have encouraged the extensive use of the photo image in etching, lithography, and serigraphy. In addition, synthetic inks, embossing presses, and vacuum-forming tables are used to print on plastics, fabrics, and in high relief. Research is being conducted on the potential of dry copiers and other office equipment designed to copy business correspondence to generate images either as end products or in conjunction with other processes.

Prior to World War II the study of printmaking was conducted primarily in private workshops in Europe. Renewed interest in printmaking after the war, however, prompted the formation of private workshops in the United States and the addition of printmaking to the curricula of major universities and private art schools in the United States, Canada, and the United Kingdom, and in art academies in Eastern and Western Europe. The reestablishment of facilities in the postwar years also stimulated activity in printmaking in Poland, Czechoslovakia, Yugoslavia, and Japan.

Study in the private workshops is possible by means of apprenticeships, usually in lithography or serigraphy, in which the individual learns the craft as he works with the master printer and artist. The study of printmaking in the universities and private art schools is organized, however, within the degree structure of these institutions. It is possible to receive an associate degree in printmaking at some junior colleges in the United States, but the two-year length of the program is not adequate to acquire more than an introduction to the subject. The Bachelor of Arts (B.A.) or Bachelor of Fine Arts (B.F.A.) degree program in printmaking is a four- or five-year course of study, commencing with a foundation program of at least one year; the program includes courses in drawing, design, color theory and practice, art history, and liberal arts. In the remaining years emphasis is placed on printmaking and related areas, drawing and photography, plus electives. The Master of Arts (M.A.) or Master of Fine Arts (M.F.A.) graduate programs consist of two or three years of concentrated studio work in printmaking—which is usually conducted on an independent-study basis under faculty supervision—and advanced art history courses, graduate seminars, and electives in related areas. The degree is awarded after the candidate's work demonstrates both conceptual and technical competence. The programs at certain schools in England and schools of applied arts in Eastern Europe combine the study of printmaking with the study of the commercial applications of lithography, serigraphy, and rotogravure and include the design and printing of posters, fabrics, photo reproductions, and other items associated with the graphic arts industry.

Although there are differences in scope and structure in the specific programs, the study of printmaking is basically similar throughout the world—mainly because artist-printmakers have extensive contacts with each other through publications, exhibits, and travel.

T. STEGER

Levels and Programs of Study

Programs in printmaking generally require as a prerequisite a secondary education and lead to the following awards: certificate or diploma, bachelor's degree (B.F.A.), or master's degree (M.F.A.). Programs deal with methods and techniques of printmaking and consist primarily of workshop practice in the various printmaking processes. Technical procedures are also studied through demonstrations and analysis of each process. Emphasis is placed on individual expression and performance.

Course content for all levels of study usually consists of some of the following: intaglio processes (engraving, drypoint, etching, aquatint); lithography (from plates and stones); serigraphy; relief processes (wood cutting and engraving, linoleum cutting); photoprinting methods (photoserigraphy, photolithography, photoetching, phototransfer processes); and drawing for printmaking. Background courses usually include basic aspects of drawing, design, and color. At advanced levels, students tend to focus on a particular technique within printmaking—for example, lithography, etching, or serigraphy.

Major International and National Organizations

INTERNATIONAL

International Association of Art—Painting, Sculpture, Graphic Art (IAA)
Association internationale des arts plastiques
UNESCO House, 1 rue Miollis
75015 Paris, France

International Graphical Alliance
Alliance graphique internationale
45 Neuschelerstrasse
8001 Zurich, Switzerland

International Graphical Federation
Monbijoustrasse 73
3007 Bern, Switzerland

NATIONAL

For countries that do not have a society or association devoted specifically to graphic arts or printmaking, a general artists' group is given.

Australia:
    Print Council of Australia; Association of Printmaking; Organizations and People Interested in Original Prints
    % National Gallery of Victoria
    180 St. Kilda Road
    Melbourne 3004, Victoria

Austria:
    Gesellschaft für zeitgenössische Graphik
    Geologengasse 1
    1030, Vienna

Belgium:
    Fédération nationale des associations de maîtres graveurs de Belgique
    48 Longue rue Neuve
    Antwerp

Brazil:
    Núcleo dos gravadores de São Paulo
    Rua Bento de Andrade 483
    São Paulo

Canada:
Society of Canadian Painter-Etchers and
Engravers
600 Markham Street
Toronto 4, Ontario

Czechoslovakia:
Hollar, skupina československých
umělců-graficů
Smetanovo nábřeži 6
Prague

Denmark:
Billedkunstnernes forbund
Dansk billedhuggersamfund und grafisk
kunstnersamfund
Klareboderne 16
1115 Copenhagen

Federal Republic of Germany:
Bund deutscher Gebrauchsgraphiker
Pranckhstrasse 2
Munich

France:
Association pour la diffusion des arts
graphiques et plastiques
9 et 11 rue Berryer
75008 Paris

German Democratic Republic:
Verband bildender Künstler der DDR
Inselstrasse 10
102 Berlin 2

Italy:
Istituto italiano di arti grafiche
via Zanica 92
24100 Bergamo

Mexico:
Sociedad mexicana de grabadores
% Escuela de pintura y escultura
Calle Heros 11
Mexico, D.F.

Netherlands:
Matschappij "Arti et Amicitiae"
Rokin 112
1000 Amsterdam

Norway:
Norske grafikere
Kunstnernes hus
Wergelandsveien 17
Oslo

Switzerland:
Verband schweizerischer Grafiker
Arbeitsgemeinschaft schweizer Grafiker
Chorgasse 18
8001 Zurich

United Kingdom:
Society of Graphic Artists
195 Piccadilly
London W1, England

United States:
American Institute of Graphic Arts
1059 Third Avenue
New York, New York 10021

Society of American Graphic Artists
1083 Fifth Avenue
New York, New York 10028

For additional national and international
organizations see:

American Art Directory. New York: Bowker,
1898–. Published annually.
*International Directory of Arts/Internationales
Kunst-Adressbuch/Annuaire international des
beaux-arts.* (2 vols.) Berlin, Federal Republic
of Germany: Art Adress Verlag Müller
GMBH, 1952/53–. Published biennially.
See Volume 1, "Associations."
The World of Learning. London: Europa, annual. See "Learned Societies" under each
country.

Principal Information Sources

GENERAL

Guides to the literature of printmaking
include:

"Bibliographie des Jahres 1973: Malerei und
Graphik." *Zeitschrift für Kunstgeschichte,* 1974,
37, 75–109.
"Books and Portfolios with Original Graphics."
Artist's Proof, 1970, *10,* 111–112.
Chamberlain, M. W. *Guide to Art Reference
Books.* Chicago: American Library Asso-
ciation, 1959.
"Engravings and Other Print Media." In *Ency-
clopedia of World Art.* New York: McGraw-
Hill, 1959–. Vol. 4, pp. 749–786.
Lucas, E. L. *Art Books: A Basic Bibliography of the
Fine Arts.* Greenwich, Connecticut: New
York Graphic Society, 1968. See section on
"Graphic Arts" with subsection on "Engrav-
ings" and "Techniques."
Stein, D. M. "Selected Bibliography: Books and
Catalogues on Prints and Print Techniques:
1968–1969." *Artist's Proof,* 1969, *9,* 103–104.
Wittenborn & Company. (Comps.) "Portfolios
of Original Prints: Bibliography." *Artist's
Proof,* 1969, *9,* 105.

Introductions to printmaking and printmaking techniques are:

Antreasian, G. Z., and Adams, C. *The Tamarind
Book of Lithography: Art and Techniques.* Los
Angeles: Tamarind Lithography Workshop,
1971.
Brunner, F. *A Handbook of Graphic Reproduction
Processes.* (2nd ed.) Niederteufen, Switzer-
land: Niggli, 1964.

Gross, A. *Etching, Engraving and Intaglio Printing.* London: Oxford University Press, 1970.

Hayter, S. W. *New Ways of Gravure.* New York: Oxford University Press, 1966.

Heller, J. *Printmaking Today.* New York: Holt, Rinehart and Winston, 1958.

Ivins, W. M., Jr. *How Prints Look.* Boston: Beacon Press, 1962.

Peterdi, G. *Printmaking: Methods Old and New.* (Rev. ed.) New York: Macmillan, 1971. Includes a detailed, well-illustrated description of printmaking techniques; glossary of printmaking terms; and list of sources of graphic supplies and equipment.

Ross, J., and Romano, C. *The Complete Printmaker.* New York: Free Press, 1972.

Works dealing with education in the field are:

Art Education: An International Survey. Paris: UNESCO, 1972. Countries included in this survey: Argentina, Australia, Czechoslovakia, France, Federal Republic of Germany, India, Italy, Japan, Nigeria, United Kingdom, United States, and Soviet Union.

"Aspects of Art Education." *Studio International,* October 1972, *184,* 138–140; November 1972, *184,* 176–181; January 1973, *185,* 29–32. A three-part debate on art education in the United States, Canada, and the United Kingdom.

Regular features on art education in journals are:

"Congrès, écoles, conférences." Published as a regular part of *La chronique des arts; supplément à la "Gazette des beaux-arts."*

"Novum Education." In issues of *Gebrauchsgraphik Novum; International Advertising Art.*

"On Graphic Workshops and Techniques." A special feature of *Artist's Proof.*

Histories of the field are:

Hind, A. M. *A History of Engraving and Etching from the Fifteenth Century to the Year 1914.* New York: Dover, 1963.

Mayer, A. H. *Prints and People.* New York: Metropolitan Museum of Art, 1971.

Salamon, F. *The History of Prints and Printmaking from Dürer to Picasso: A Guide to Collecting.* New York: American Heritage Press (McGraw-Hill), 1972.

Sotriffer, K. *Printmaking, History and Technique.* New York: McGraw-Hill, 1968.

Stubbe, W. *Graphic Arts in the Twentieth Century.* New York: Praeger, 1963. An important work.

Weber, W. *A History of Lithography.* New York: McGraw-Hill, 1966.

CURRENT BIBLIOGRAPHIES

Art Index. New York: Wilson, 1933–. See "Prints —Bibliography" and names of individual techniques: "Engraving," "Lithography," "Silk Screen Printing," and "Woodcut."

Graphic Arts Abstracts. Pittsburgh: Graphic Arts Technical Foundation, Library, 1947–.

Grafische literatuur centrale. Amsterdam: Instituut voor grafische technik TNO, 1941–.

Javarone, D. (Ed.) *Indicatore grafico: Rassegna bibliografica mensile.* Rome: Ente nazionale per la cellulosa e per la carta, 1960–.

Current information may also be found in the catalogs of the following international exhibitions:

Biennale internationale della grafica (Florence, Italy, 1968/69–)

British International Print Biennale (Bradford, England, 1972–)

Exposition internationale de gravure (Ljubljana, Yugoslavia, Modern galerija, 1955–)

Graphik biennale Wien (Vienna, 1972–)

International Biennial Exhibition of Prints in Tokyo (National Museum of Modern Art, Tokyo, 1957–)

PERIODICALS

General art journals with some articles or features on printmaking are *Arte illustrata* (Italy), *Art in America* (US), *Art News* (US), *Arts Magazine* (US), and *Studio International* (UK).

Journals dealing more specifically with graphic arts include *Arts et techniques graphiques* (France), *Bulletin technique: Photogravure, lithographie, héliogravure* (Switzerland), *Graphis: International Journal of Graphic and Applied Art* (Switzerland), *International grafik: Magazine for Original Graphics* (Denmark), *Nouvelles de l'estampe* (France), *Nouvelles graphiques/Graphiques nieuws* (Belgium), *Print Collector's Newsletter* (US), *Print Review* (US), *Revue graphiqueimprivaria/Grafisch tijdschrift-imprivaria* (Belgium).

ENCYCLOPEDIAS, DICTIONARIES, HANDBOOKS

Allen, E. M. (Comp.) *Harper's Dictionary of the Graphic Arts.* New York: Harper & Row, 1963.

"Brief Glossary of Printmaking Techniques." *Rhode Island School of Design Bulletin,* April 1973, *59,* 8.

Brunner, F. A. *Handbook of Graphic Reproduction Processes.* (2nd ed.) Niederteufen, Switzerland: Niggli, 1964.

Encyclopedia of World Art. New York: McGraw-Hill, 1959–.

DIRECTORIES

American Art Directory. New York: Bowker, 1898–. Published annually. Lists art organizations and schools in the United States, Canada, and major foreign countries.

Hudson, K., and Nicholls, A. (Eds.) *Directory of World Museums*. New York: Columbia University Press, 1975. See "Classified Index of Specialized and Outstanding Collections: The Arts."

International Directory of Arts/Internationales Kunst-Adressbuch/Annuaire international des beaux-arts. (2 vols.) Berlin, Federal Republic of Germany: Art Adress Verlag Müller GMBH, 1952/53–. Published biennially. Volume 1 has sections on "Universities, Academies, Colleges; Associations; Experts—Graphics."

Museums of the World: A Directory of 175,000 Museums in 150 Countries, Including a Subject Index. (2nd enl. ed.) New York: Bowker, 1975. See "Subject Index: Prints."

The World of Learning. London: Europa, annual. Under each country there are the following subdivisions: Libraries and Archives, Museums and Art Galleries, Research Institutes, Schools of Art and Music, Universities and Colleges.

MUSEUMS AND GALLERIES

The following are important print collections in museums throughout the world:

Denmark:
  Kobberstiksamlingen
  Statens museum for kunst
  Copenhagen

Federal Republic of Germany:
  Graphische Sammlung
  Kunsthalle
  Hamburg

  Kupferstichkabinett
  Staatliche Museen
  Berlin

France:
  Cabinet des estampes
  Bibliothèque nationale
  Paris

German Democratic Republic:
  Kupferstichkabinett
  Staatliche Kunstsammlungen
  Dresden

Italy:
  Gabinetto desegno e stampe
  Galleria degli Uffizi
  Florence

Netherlands:
  Prentenkabinet
  Gemeentemuseum
  The Hague

Rijksprentenkabinet
Rijksmuseum
Amsterdam

Romania:
  Cabinetul de stampe
  Academia Republicii Socialiste Romania, Biblioteca
  Bucharest

Soviet Union:
  Department of Prints
  Hermitage
  Leningrad

United Kingdom:
  Department of Prints and Drawings
  British Museum
  London, England

United States:
  The Achenbach Collection
  Palace of the Legion of Honor
  San Francisco, California

  Department of Prints and Drawings
  Museum of Fine Arts
  Boston, Massachusetts

  The Greenwald Collection
  UCLA
  Los Angeles, California

  Fogg Art Museum
  Harvard University
  Cambridge, Massachusetts

  Print and Drawing Department
  Art Institute of Chicago
  Chicago, Illinois

  Print Collection
  Museum of Modern Art
  San Francisco, California

  Prints and Photographs Division
  United States Library of Congress
  Washington, D.C.

  Prints Department
  Metropolitan Museum of Art
  New York, New York

[Bibliography prepared by Molly M. Lindner.]

PRIORITIES FOR ACTION
(Higher Education Report), United States

Priorities for Action: Final Report of the Carnegie Commission on Higher Education (New York: McGraw-Hill, 1973) summarizes suggestions and recommendations from more than one hundred reports and special studies issued during the commission's six-year examination of higher education in the United States. Background materials concerning the commission and its previous reports are included in attached appendices. The following findings and recommendations are emphasized.

Higher education in the United States is recovering from a serious depression that followed a twenty-year post–World War II period of high achievement. Crises such as political unrest on campus, limited financial resources, decreasing enrollments, the movement toward universal access, and the tight labor market have seriously eroded the confidence in higher education of faculty, administrators, trustees, public officials responsible for higher education, and the general public.

A strong higher education system is essential to the welfare of American society, despite the high costs. Six priorities for action will assist higher education in its recovery and enable it to reach new levels of achievement: (1) clarification of purposes, (2) preservation and enhancement of quality and diversity, (3) advancement of social justice, (4) enhancement of constructive change, (5) achievement of more effective governance, and (6) assurance of resources and their more effective use.

Planning for the future of higher education should be on a contingent basis and should be subject to constant reexamination. The commission reaffirms its support for the continuation of basic reliance on the states as the main guardians of higher education.

Emphasis should be placed on improving the quality of teaching, extending and improving the Federal Basic Opportunities Grants program, and creating a more effective national student loan system. Among other areas of concern are the adoption of codes of conduct for campus members, the creation of guidelines on the exercise of public control to ensure institutional autonomy, and the provision of sufficient open-access places by the states. In addition, the commission favors adequate state financial support for private higher education institutions; a revitalization of institutional leadership directed toward constructive change; more time options for students; a movement away from the concept of general education toward that of broad learning experiences; and increased student participation in the decision-making process.

PRIORITIES IN HIGHER EDUCATION (Higher Education Report), United States

Priorities in Higher Education (Washington, D.C.: U.S. Government Printing Office, 1970)—a report of the President's Task Force on Higher Education, under the chairmanship of J. M. Hester—addresses higher education priorities and federal assistance to higher education in the United States. The following findings and recommendations are reported.

The level of both public and private support of tertiary education is not adequate to maintain and expand the existing higher education structure. Higher education institutions are not able to provide places for many of the nation's qualified youths, and the system of higher education is slow to adjust to rapidly changing individual and national demands. Therefore, an increase in federal financial aid to both public and private higher education institutions is needed. The most pressing federal priorities are aid for the financially disadvantaged student, support for professional health care education, and increased tax incentives for support of higher education. Continuing federal responsibilities should include the expansion of postsecondary education and support of high-grade professional and graduate study. The most important priorities for the higher education institutions themselves are clarification of purpose, improvement of curriculum and teaching and learning methods, more efficient use of resources, and clarification of administrative and departmental promotion procedures and organization. In order to provide a forum for consideration of institutional questions and problems, a federally chartered national academy of higher education should be created.

PRISONERS, POSTSECONDARY EDUCATION PROGRAMS FOR

Prison education programs appear to be as old as prisons themselves. In the late eighteenth and early nineteenth centuries, most prisons in the United States, Canada, South America, and Western Europe conducted religious services and classes under the impression that such instruction would help to prepare prisoners for a Christian and therefore, it was believed, a noncriminal life. If prisoners could not read, it was further argued, the wisdom of the Bible would be denied them. Literacy instruction was therefore initiated, frequently by the prison chaplain, who used volunteer theological students as instructors.

From these early beginnings, educational programs, particularly in United States prisons, advanced at different rates and in different ways, depending on the policies of an individual state or an individual institution within a state. The United States federal prison system was shaped by policies and programs initiated at the state and federal levels.

In the United States, at the first meeting of the National Prison Association (now the American Correctional Association) in 1870, a *Declaration of Principles* provided strong, if somewhat melodramatic, support for education: "Education is a vital force in the reformation of fallen men and women. Its tendency is to quicken the intellect, inspire self-respect, excite to higher aims, and afford a helpful substitute for low and vicious amusements. Education is, therefore, a matter of primary importance in prisons, and should be carried to the utmost extent consistent with the other purposes of such institutions." Despite these high ideals, bona fide educational programs in American prisons were not implemented for years, and indeed are still lacking in many individual institutions. Outside the United States such programs exist only to a modest degree in both developed and developing nations.

Where educational and occupational programs are provided, the quality of such programs and the degree of prisoner participation vary widely. In some institutions, primarily youth institutions, programs are devoted exclusively to education; in others, primarily adult institutions, educational and training opportunities are marginal. College-level programs for prisoners are infrequent outside the United States; those that exist are either in early experimental stages of development or take the form of correspondence courses, which have been available for many years in the United States, Canada, England, France, the Scandinavian countries, and, to a limited degree, in Yugoslavia and Austria.

Release time for college-level study is a new concept that is just beginning to receive significant support in the United States, Canada, Great Britain, and the Scandinavian countries. A small number of prisoners in Sweden, for example, are permitted release time to study at university adult education centers. Kerle (1974) reports that thirty-two prisoners were involved in University Without Walls programs in Great Britain and that the number was expected to double by 1975.

Data available for the United States suggest a significant rate of growth in a variety of prison college programs since the 1960s. In 1966 the Ford Foundation funded a nationwide survey of college-level programs in United States prisons. Fifty-one prison systems were surveyed and forty-six responded to the survey. Of these, twenty-seven prison systems offered college-level correspondence courses; seventeen offered extension courses; three provided televised instruction; and three granted study-release opportunities. No system, however, offered the possibility of obtaining a bachelor's degree, and only seven indicated that they provided or planned to provide the possibility of obtaining an associate or comparable two-year degree. From the 1966 survey, it was estimated that less than one thousand prisoners were involved in college-level correspondence courses and that about two thousand were enrolled in college extension courses.

In 1955 the First United Nations Congress on the Prevention of Crime and Treatment of Offenders, meeting in Geneva, adopted a set of minimum standards for the treatment of offenders. In its statement on education and recreation, the congress urged that provision be made for education, religious instruction, recreation, and cultural activities of prisoners (United Nations Department of Economic and Social Affairs, 1958). It suggested that such education be compulsory for illiterates and young prisoners. The Geneva congress further recommended that "so far as practicable, the education of prisoners shall be integrated with the educational system of the country, so that after their release they may continue their education without difficulty" (p. 72) and that institutional personnel "shall include a sufficient number of specialists such as . . . teachers and trade instructors" (p. 72).

Specific Programs

Prisoners throughout the world share common characteristics; they are generally poor, unskilled, and uneducated. For these and related reasons, prison education programs tend to emphasize basic reading skills, occupational training, and the achievement of secondary-level certification. Prison college programs can be relevant only in countries where the general level of education is high enough to provide potential students—both in and out of prison—for college-level classes. In 1977 these conditions do not prevail in most countries throughout the world. The principal exceptions are the United States, Canada, Great Britain, and the Scandinavian countries, where enough prisoner-students exist who have completed a secondary educa-

tion (or have the potential to do so while imprisoned) to warrant efforts to make postsecondary programs available.

There are no precise data on the number of prisoners in the United States or elsewhere involved in postsecondary education programs. A 1973 survey (Dell'Apa, 1973) indicates that in the United States the number ranges somewhere between a low of 2500 and a possible high of 12,500. The average figure is less than 6 percent (around 6400 out of 109,161 prisoners), based on a 60 percent response (150 institutions) to questionnaires sent to 249 adult correctional institutions. The growing proportion of inmates who have completed high school and the increased availability of tuition assistance are giving rise to a larger number of college programs in the federal penal system. The proportion of prisoners from state institutions involved in postsecondary programs is somewhat lower than that in the federal system, with the possible exception of a few individual states.

In 1975, in the United States federal system, inmates completed approximately 9000 college-level courses totaling 27,000 earned college credits. If one assumes an average enrollment of three courses per student, approximately 3000 federal prisoners were enrolled in postsecondary programs during 1975. During the same year 179 college degrees were earned: 158 two-year degrees; 19 bachelor's degrees; and 2 master's degrees. Although these figures are not unduly impressive, prison college enrollments in the United States did escalate from an estimated total of 3000 in 1968 (adult and youth) to over 6400 in adult institutions alone in 1973. These figures indicate a doubling of enrollments in less than a decade and a possible tripling of enrollments if full data on youth enrollments were known.

In Canada college programs in prisons appear to be confined to five federal penitentiaries in the western provinces. Approximately two hundred Canadian prisoners are enrolled in classes inside the prison, and only a few are involved in study-release, Open University (utilizing television for course instruction), or correspondence courses. Prisoner participation in postsecondary programs appears to be at the same modest level in England, France, and the Scandinavian countries, and participation is on even a smaller scale in Yugoslavia and Austria. Figures supplied by the French Ministry of Justice in 1972 indicate that approximately 115 prisoners, less than 1 percent of the 29,600 total, were pursuing college-level studies.

In-prison college programs. Courses offered inside prisons were available as early as 1939 in the United States (and probably in Western Europe), and predate even the earliest prison college surveys. Long before interest in prison education programs became popular, college programs were introduced at institutions at San Quentin, California; Joliet, Illinois; and Leavenworth, Kansas. All these institutions serve long-term prisoners; and, for security reasons, all classes took place inside the institutions, through correspondence courses or in traditional classrooms.

Since the 1960s developments within higher education communities, as well as in the prisons themselves, have contributed to the establishment of new delivery systems for college courses both inside and outside prison walls. The University Without Walls in the United States and the Open University in England and Canada offer new opportunities for prisoners to undertake full college programs on an individualized basis, through correspondence courses and television, without leaving the prison. Closed circuit television, audiotapes, audiovisual tapes, and tape cassettes are also providing additional program opportunities for individual and classroom study in the prisons.

Study-release programs. Despite substantial success with study-release programs, the growth of such programs continues to be very slow in all countries. During the 1960s the United States Office of Education funded special college programs for disadvantaged students. These programs, called Upward-Bound, provided academic assistance, tuition, and subsistence support for students who would not ordinarily go to college. Similar efforts for prisoners, called Newgate programs, began in the late 1960s in Oregon, Kentucky, Minnesota, New Mexico, and Pennsylvania. The programs combined courses of study inside and outside the prison and were arranged so that the outside portion coincided with the approach of a prisoner's release date. As the initial fundings of these programs by the Office of Economic Opportunity were absorbed by the correctional systems themselves, the outside portion of the program diminished in duration and importance. These programs continue to function, however, funded by correctional institutions, the Law Enforcement Assistance Administration, and the United States Office of Education.

A limited number of postsecondary occupational training programs in the United States also combine classes for prisoners inside and outside the prison. In some cases, nearby vocational technical schools and community colleges provide instruction for prisoners in the same classes as regular students. In other cases, the prisoners comprise a separate class.

Innovative experimental projects at some colleges enable a small number of students to live on campus, either in separate, supervised halfway-house arrangements or in regular student housing. A coeducational residential center for prisoner-students from federal correctional institutions in California was established in 1975 at the Santa Barbara campus of the University of California. During 1975, approximately twenty men and women, all within one year of their prison release date, lived at this supervised center and attended university classes on a full-time basis.

Postrelease college programs. An underlying objective of all prison education efforts is the development of the students' continuing interest in education, both as a means of staying out of prison and as a means of enriching their personal lives.

Those who work with prisoners often cite impressive anecdotes about an individual's continuation of postsecondary studies after release from prison. Unfortunately, with the exception of a few isolated studies, significant data do not exist regarding the number of prisoners who continue to attend college after their release from prison and who actually receive either associate degrees, bachelor's degrees, or postsecondary technical or professional school certification.

Follow-up studies of Newgate students in the United States indicate a wide variety of problems that require attention if post-release college programs are to be effectively linked with prerelease prison programs (Kaplan, Gans, and Kahn, 1973; Baker and others, 1973). Continued identification as a convict, lack of emotional as well as financial support systems, over-intensive parole supervision, and time gaps between prison release and college enrollment are but a few of these problems. Considerable research evidence suggests that the first three months after release from prison are critical. Ideally, contact with college admissions staff should be established before the prisoner-student's release, and specific steps should be taken to ensure the student's enrollment before or very shortly after he or she returns to the community where the educational institution is located.

Current Trends

It is difficult to assess how many prisoners could reasonably be expected to become involved in postsecondary education during imprisonment. For the United States Taggart (1972) estimates that as many as thirty thousand prison inmates could benefit from access to higher education opportunities. Doubling the number of those enrolled in such programs in any country would strain neither the student potential nor the available educational resources. Many new developments have taken place to establish access to these resources.

Offender Assistance project. In the United

States the American Association of Community and Junior Colleges (AACJC), in cooperation with the United States Office of Education Fund for the Improvement of Postsecondary Education (FIPSE), is conducting an experimental demonstration project known as Offender Assistance Through Community Colleges. This project incorporates, in part, activities that can be generated by community colleges to help keep some first offenders out of prison. Three communities—Jacksonville, Florida; Charlotte, North Carolina; and Denver, Colorado—are working with their local criminal justice systems to provide a continuum of services to first felony offenders. Not all first-offender referrals to the program are expected to become college students. Those who do not may be provided occupational counseling, job development, and job placement services or referred to family counseling, mental health, or other community service centers. The basic purpose of the Offender Assistance project is to provide courts and probation services with one additional alternative to imprisonment.

Prison school districts. A phenomenon that seems to be peculiar to the United States, the prison school district, began to emerge in the late 1960s. These school districts—which now exist in Texas, Connecticut, Illinois, New Jersey, Arkansas, and Ohio—function as separate educational delivery systems for correctional institutions in their respective states. Each district has its own board of education, superintendent, and staff. In two states, New Jersey and Illinois, the school districts include education through the junior college level. Virginia recently enacted legislation to adopt the school district concept; and, as of 1975, at least six additional states were considering such plans.

Inside versus outside programs and technology. In the United States two important developments are taking place simultaneously: study release for college courses is gaining acceptance, and audiovisual technology is making it increasingly easier to provide college-level courses inside the prison. It is difficult to forecast how these two trends will be combined. In other countries, which have not yet experimented with prison college programs, audiovisual technology should make it easier to offer college programs inside prisons than was initially the case in the United States. On the other hand, the availability of such technology could retard the introduction of study-release programs.

Current Problems

Several areas of concern are common to prison postsecondary education programs in all countries, whether courses are offered inside or outside the institution or on a precommitment or postrelease basis.

Costs. In the United States, Canada, the Scandinavian countries, and Western Europe, prisons that have educational programs generally provide them at no cost to the prisoner through the secondary level. Cost practices for postsecondary courses, where offered, vary by and within country, ranging from full payment by the prisoner to full payment by the correctional system. In the United States federal system, for example, several different cost procedures exist. Where budget resources permit and where the course of study is an established program goal, all costs are paid by the correctional institution. In other cases, the federal correctional institution pays up to half of the costs involved and the individual prisoner pays the remainder; and, in some cases, *all* costs must be paid by the prisoner. The institution's budget, the expense of the course involved, the student's personal financial status, and other related factors ultimately determine how the costs of a program are borne.

In the United States the application of out-of-state fee schedules to prisoners who are not residents of the state in which they are incarcerated becomes an additional cost problem. This situation is particularly aggravated in federal correctional institutions, which tend to serve as regional facilities housing prisoners from many states. A re-

cent informal survey conducted by Donald A. Deppe, education director of the United States Department of Justice Bureau of Prisons, reveals that sixteen states in which federal prisons operate charge in-state resident fees for federal prisoner-students and six charge the higher nonresident fees. State and county prisons face a variety of in-county, out-of-county, and related education fee schedules.

Some colleges in the United States and Canada charge a set fee, ranging from $300 to $750 per inside course. Prisons may enroll as many students in the class as is feasible—generally from twenty to fifty. When instructors must travel long distances to the prisons, mileage fees are an additional cost.

Since most prisoners and their families have limited funds or no funds at all, costs become a critical aspect of making higher education accessible to prisoners. Many prisons throughout the world lack sufficient funds to offer adequate literacy, elementary, secondary, or vocational training programs. In such cases postsecondary education is no more than a long-term goal. Despite these difficulties, the picture is by no means dismal. In many situations the academic community is eager to provide services. Some postsecondary education institutions, sensitive to cost problems, provide quality education at reasonable prices. In addition, many dedicated instructors and volunteer tutors travel considerable distances to and from isolated institutions to teach one or two hours, sometimes after completing a full teaching schedule elsewhere.

Financial assistance available from nonprison sources also has helped meet cost problems. In the United States prisoner-students are generally eligible to apply for financial aid on the same basis as other students. Veterans Education Benefits, Vocational Rehabilitation Assistance, Basic Education Opportunity Grants (BEOG), work-study programs, federally insured student loans, and private group scholarships and grants are increasingly available to prisoner-students. Private foundations also have provided ad hoc assistance in special cases. These educational assistance funds are generally available for courses inside and outside the prison. In Canada, for example, a Donner Foundation group has made it possible for seven prisoners from the British Columbia Penitentiary and Matsqui Prison to live at a group residential center and attend the University of Victoria.

Geographical isolation of institutions. Despite recent trends to locate new correctional facilities either in or near urban centers, some correctional institutions are still located great distances from needed resources. In such cases correspondence courses, various audiovisual systems, and the opportunities offered by the Open University and University Without Walls are welcome alternatives. Unfortunately, high student motivation levels are not sustained by correspondence courses and other individualized study programs, and drop-out rates in all countries continue to be high, both in and out of prison.

Closed-circuit television and other audiovisual systems in the United States increasingly bring college courses to places that would otherwise be unable to offer any postsecondary programs, but these efforts are not widespread and operate primarily under experimental conditions.

Transferability of earned credits. In the United States many prisoners transfer from one federal institution to another while serving their sentence. The issue of the transferability of credits is therefore very important. The College-Level Examination program (CLEP) and other arrangements help to facilitate the transfer of earned college credits, but the problem remains, particularly if the student's transfer takes place before a specific course is completed. This dilemma has stimulated efforts by correctional educators to develop statewide consortia of postsecondary institutions to facilitate the interchange of college credits.

Program schedules. Still another problem in bringing educational programs to prison populations concerns the need to discover ways of scheduling these programs during daylight hours instead of relegating them to evening hours only. Education, as a program alternative, must be regarded as a reasonable competitor with prison industries, institutional maintenance, group counseling, and other demands on available institution program time. The Prison-Schools in France and similar institutions that serve youthful offenders in other countries have already provided daytime programs for some young prisoners, but education for adult prisoners in most countries continues to be an evening or "after-work" activity.

Physical facilities. Adequate space and privacy for the prisoner-student, so that he can study and complete course assignments, can determine whether or not a student remains in a program. Since most prisoners are housed in institutions designed for containment or punishment, it takes a great deal of imagination and good will to provide a positive learning environment.

Libraries and educational aids. The availability of a library of books is another major concern. Some correctional institutions have complemented their own library collections through the creative use of local mobile library units, interlibrary loan arrangements, or provisions for library work during study-release hours. Special groups in many countries, such as the Association of American Publishers, Inc., and the American Booksellers Association in the United States, have donated reference and other books to prisons, but the library situation in prisons remains marginal (LeDonne, 1974).

The use of tape recorders and typewriters is still unpopular among the staff of many correctional institutions. In countries where such equipment is readily available and reasonably priced, educators can make an important contribution to prisoner education by encouraging the use of these machines in the educational process and by assisting in the supervision of their use by students.

Access to educational opportunities for prisoners will, in many respects, parallel national growth rates of access to such opportunities by students generally. A major goal, therefore, must be to continue to enlarge postsecondary educational opportunities for all potential students in all countries in order that such opportunities may increasingly be offered to members of the prison population.

Bibliography

Adams, S. N. *College Level Instruction in U.S. Prisons.* Berkeley: School of Criminology, University of California, 1968.

Adams, S. N. *Correctional Education: Status and Prospects.* Washington, D.C.: The Justice Studies Group, Syracuse University Research Corporation, 1973. Mimeographed.

Adams, S. N., and Connolly, J. J. "Role of Junior Colleges in the Prison Community." *Junior College Journal,* 1971, *41*(6), 92–98.

American Association of Community and Junior Colleges. *Offender Assistance Through Community Colleges—Final Progress Report on Planning Phase and Application to the Fund for the Improvement of Postsecondary Education for the Demonstration Phase.* Washington, D.C.: AACJC, 1975. Mimeographed.

Antioch College. *University Without Walls—A First Report.* Yellow Springs, Ohio: Antioch College, Union of Experimenting Colleges and Universities, 1972.

Association of American Publishers. *Books for Prisoners.* New York: AAP, 1974.

Baker, K., and others. *Summary Report: Project Newgate and Other Prison College Programs.* Washington, D.C.: Office of Economic Opportunity, 1973.

Dell'Apa, F. *Educational Programs in Adult Correctional Institutions—A Survey.* Boulder, Colorado: Western Interstate Commission for Higher Education, 1973.

Doleschi, E. "Higher Education in U.S. Prisons." In *Information Review on Crime and Delinquency.* Vol. 1. New York: National Council on Crime and Delinquency, 1968.

Feldman, S. D. *Trends in Offender Vocational and Education Programs: A Literature Search.* Washington, D.C.: American Association of Community and Junior Colleges. Mimeographed, n.d.

Kaplan, M., Gans, S., and Kahn, H. *An Evaluation of "Newgate" and Other Programs.* Final Report. Washington, D.C.: Office of Economic Opportunity, 1973.

Kerle, K. *Education-Penal Institutions: U.S. and Europe.* Hagerstown, Maryland: Hagerstown Junior College, 1974. Mimeographed.

LeDonne, M. *Survey of Library and Information Problems in Correctional Institutions.* Washington, D.C.: U.S. Office of Education, 1974.

Mahoney, J., and Alter, H. *An Assessment of HEPP: Higher Education in Prison Programs.* Washington, D.C.: Massachusetts Department of Corrections/American Correctional Association, 1975.

McCollum, S. G. "New Designs for Correctional Education and Training Programs." *Federal Probation,* 1973, *37*(2).

Northampton County Area Community College. *College-at-Home Program.* Bethlehem, Pennsylvania. Mimeographed, n.d.

Oklahoma State Regents for Higher Education. "Oklahoma Higher Education Televised Instruction System." *Bulletin.* Oklahoma City: Regents, 1974.

Taggart, R. *The Prison of Unemployment.* Baltimore: Johns Hopkins University Press, 1972.

United Nations Department of Economic and Social Affairs. *Standard Minimum Rules for the Treatment of Prisoners and Related Recommendations.* New York: United Nations, 1958.

SYLVIA G. MCCOLLUM

PRIVATE HIGHER EDUCATION, NATIONAL POLICY FOR (Higher Education Report), United States

National Policy for Private Higher Education (Washington, D.C.: Association of American Colleges, 1974) is a report by the Task Force of the National Council of Independent Colleges and Universities, under the chairmanship of J. Kreps. This study was sponsored in part by Lilly Endowment, Inc., a nonprofit, nongovernmental foundation. Maintaining that private higher education in the United States is a valuable complement to the public sector and should be preserved and strengthened, the task force reports the following findings and recommendations.

Growth in higher education has been in the public sector, while enrollments in private universities and colleges have declined. In 1950, about 50 percent of the students enrolled in higher education were in the private sector, but by 1973 the figure had dropped to 24 percent. The financial position of private colleges and universities has also deteriorated. As a result of this position, the future of most private institutions is not assured.

State and federal government action is needed to maintain and strengthen private higher education institutions. States should lower tuition costs for students in private higher education through provision of tuition-offset grants. In addition, state planning agencies for education should recognize private higher education institutions and when possible conclude contracts with them for needed services. Federal legislation to encourage states to rectify geographical imbalance in aid to the private sector is also needed. In order to meet the needs of private colleges and universities and their students, an increase in federally funded student aid programs is proposed. Federal and state tax programs should continue to offer incentives for philanthropic giving; at the same time, private higher education institutions should receive the same tax exemptions accorded to similar public institutions. Finally, the public sector is urged to acknowledge the need for private higher education institutions to broaden their search for public funds.

PRIVATE SCHOOLS
See Proprietary Schools.

PROCESSES OF ACADEMIC CHANGE

What are the processes by which universities innovate and adapt to changing situations? From his experience in both European and American universities, Paul Lazarsfeld concluded that three processes account for the introduction of innovations into the system of higher education (1966, p. 13): "(a) establishment of new universities for new subject matters,

forms of teaching, or forms of organization; (b) establishment of non-university bodies for carrying out what later becomes part of the university's functions; and (c) establishment of new units in the university itself." Of these three processes, the first—creating new universities—is clearly one source of innovation, but not a major one: most new universities are created to offer to a new clientele the same programs offered by existing institutions. More important is the second process—creating competing nonacademic institutions. Such organizations, ranging historically from the scientific societies of Renaissance Italy to today's training programs in business and industry, have stimulated change within academic institutions through their competition. But the third mechanism—whereby existing universities adopt the ideas, functions, and structures of new universities as well as nonacademic institutions—has always been the dominant process of academic innovation. By this process of "accretion," colleges and universities reach out and encompass new responsibilities, such as scientific research, public lectures and enlightenment, agricultural extension, community service, television broadcasting, and consultation for industry and government.

In fact, the history of higher education is a history of the gradual transformation of academic institutions rather than that of the death of outmoded universities and their replacement by more effective organizations for this very reason: the slow and sometimes imperceptible adaptation of institutions to "the changed situation in which universities and colleges find themselves."

This process of gradual accretion is exemplified at one level by advances in research, the expansion of knowledge, and the continual introduction of this new knowledge into the university classroom. Innovation in intellectual and scholarly thought is virtually perpetual, spurred by the insight of genius and the painstaking methods of scholarship, the accessibility of research funds and of new research instruments and techniques, and the occasional breakthrough of a new theory or paradigm, when a new system of thought—such as that of Charles Darwin in biological evolution or of Alfred Wegener in geophysics—proves to be more efficient and heuristic than the old (Kuhn, 1970). Unless restricted from teaching the new ideas, academics ordinarily seek to weave them into their lectures as they come to accept them in their own thinking; and if one professor does not accept them, his eventual successor perhaps will.

This sequence of innovation in intellectual or academic life can occur despite the lack of any innovation in organizational practice at the institutional level. Involving as it does the individual professor and his own teaching and research, innovation need not wait for change in institutional policy or procedure—unless the teaching of new ideas is institutionally proscribed. In contrast, however, academic innovations involving institutional policies and procedures are typically far less continuous, gradual, or imperceptible. These changes—alterations in calendar, curriculum, administrative structure, and the like—are often more sporadic, involving as they do coordination and agreement among many individuals. Changing the opinions of geology professors regarding continental drift and plate tectonics involves merely changes of attitude, but reorganizing the geology curriculum to take account of these ideas requires changes of behavior and may involve persuasion, negotiation, conflict, and compromise. Indeed, since colleges and universities, along with all other human organizations, exist to provide continuity and regularity to human existence in the conduct of day-to-day life, academic innovation at this level is not undertaken lightly. It occurs from necessity and proceeds haltingly by what Bernard Stern termed "defensive concession" (1953).

At both the individual and the organizational levels, the process of accretion and defensive concession is easiest when the innovative ideas, activities, or units can merely be added to existing thinking or practice rather than replacing or supplanting it (Rogers, 1962). That is, the most compatible innovations are those that are established as parallel or optional additions to the old rather than as additions that require the abandonment of accepted ways. Thus, a new professorship of physiology is added to existing chairs of anatomy; new programs are added to existing fields of study; new departments are simply created alongside existing departments. By this device of "parallelism," women's colleges have been added to men's institutions; extension education has been added to on-campus teaching; and interdisciplinary research institutes have been added to departmentalized universities. And such innovations have often been most easily accepted if adopted on an experimental basis, on the understanding that they will become permanent only if they prove themselves.

In this way, most of the contemporary curriculum—the modern foreign languages, the experimental sciences, the performing arts, the new professions and technologies—have become part of university programs. Offered first in separate nonacademic institutions, they are initially permitted entrance as extracurricular, noncredit courses, typically conducted at off hours in unused space for an extra fee by adjunct or nonfaculty teachers. Eventually, as they prove compatible, they are awarded partial credit. Later, they earn equal status as optional electives that can be substituted for some existing requirements. Still later, as demand for the knowledge grows, they may be made compulsory and allowed to supplant other knowledge. Finally, the new knowledge may become so important that it is carried by teachers trained in the universities into the secondary and elementary schools, where it becomes part of general education for citizens at large and ultimately even a requirement for university admission.

Conditions for Innovation

Students of innovation, such as Bennis (1966) and Hirschman (1970), seem to agree that foremost among the conditions necessary for innovation is the perception on the part of individuals that the benefits of innovation are likely to outweigh its liabilities—in other words, that change will probably result in improvement. Part of this condition involves dissatisfaction with the status quo, since it is true that innovation is not common among the satisfied. Just as the most innovative scholars are often at the margins of existing disciplines rather than leaders at the center of well-established fields (Gusfield and Riesman, 1964), so the most innovative colleges and universities are not always the most prestigious or renowned (Hefferlin, 1969). But for change to be advocated, dissatisfaction must be coupled with hope, incentive, or the probability of benefit. Without the likelihood of benefit or profit, innovation is unlikely—even among the dissatisfied. For example, even those institutions whose professors are dissatisfied with their condition are unlikely to change their policies if they perceive that such changes would involve abandoning principle or lowering standards. Distressed at the modernism of other institutions, they may prefer to close rather than to adapt.

In his recent research on the failure of innovations in higher education, Levine (1975) concludes that this factor of benefit or profit is critical to successful innovation and even more important than that of the degree of congruence between an innovation and its host institution, or compatibility. Although both profitability—defined by Levine as the "effectiveness of an innovation in meeting organizational needs" (1975, p. 201)—and compatibility are important for the successful adoption of an innovation, profitability is the more

essential. From his research Levine finds that academic innovations which are perceived as profitable or beneficial despite their incompatibility with tradition tend to be revised until they are deemed compatible, and those viewed as unprofitable despite their compatibility with the goals of the institution are terminated.

A second condition for successful innovation is external support. Colleges and universities depend on outside support and resources for their existence, and they are influenced toward stability or change by the direction of external pressures. Some universities, in fact, operate as mere appendages of governmental or ecclesiastical agencies and are virtually controlled by them; whereas even the most autonomous universities are subject over time to changes in public demands, financial giving, and court decisions. "No educational system, at any level, will ever transcend the general postulates of the community in which it works," Harold Laski observed in 1948; "for an educational system does not exist in a vacuum. It exists always within a social system which makes its own nature and purpose the framework within which the nature and purpose of its educational idea must function" (p. 382). As a result, the extent and direction of academic innovation are continually affected by trends in the social environment. Innovative societies tolerate and even encourage academic innovation; conservative societies do not, as illustrated by the blossoming of Islamic higher education during Islam's liberal period prior to 1000 and its withering in later centuries, and by the transformation of Oxford and Cambridge in the late nineteenth century as part of the wide-ranging transformation of British society at large. Trevelyan noted (1937, p. 282) that "Parliament, having succeeded in reforming itself, set about reforming the other institutions of the country"; and through its Royal Commissions of 1850–1852 and thereafter it struck down the clerical restrictions that had kept the universities and their colleges in intellectual somnolence, where, as James Bryce observed, "the juniors drank and hunted and the seniors drank and slept" (p. 104).

Beyond the influence of social trends in general, more opportunity appears to exist for innovation when universities have access to a variety of sources of support rather than being dependent on only one. Here the European tradition of financial support through the Ministry of Education makes for periodic centralized change, dramatized most vividly by the French reforms of 1968, in contrast to a decentralized tradition of multiple sources of funding and thus of innovation, as illustrated by the United States. From their comparative analyses, Burton Clark and Ted Youn conclude (1976, pp. 5–6, 43):

> European academic organization has fostered excessive order, with institutions inclined toward unity and uniformity. New forces, plans, and organizational forms have had great difficulty in penetrating such structures. . . . Adaptiveness then becomes a very great problem: neither the deliberate action of planners nor the unplanned interaction of competitive institutions is a powerful force compared to the institutional strength of academic oligarchs and ministerial bureaucrats. . . .
>
> In comparative perspective, the American system of academic power favors adaptation and innovation. Financial support comes from many sources, rather than the national treasury alone; autonomous private institutions adapt to different, specific clienteles; state colleges and universities reflect state and regional differences. Institutions are relatively exposed to market forces—e.g., changing consumer interests, and competition from other colleges and universities. Dispersed control has included a differentiation of sectors, and what one sector will not do, another will.

A related condition affecting innovation is the distribution of power within the university itself. Colleges and universities, like other formal organizations, are hierarchical rather than equalitarian: some members have more power and authority than others, both to stimulate change and to restrict it. Despite the recent growth of faculty and student power in many universities, administrators and oligarchies of senior professors remain highly influential in academic policy. Under autocratic or oligarchic administration, the process of academic change tends to be especially sporadic and abrupt, depending as it does on the personal predilections of institutional leaders and their periodic departure and replacement. In contrast, under less centralized control, just as under decentralized sources of outside support, change can be more continuous, incremental, and ameliorative.

Finally, innovation requires the stimulus of an individual or sometimes a small group as the catalyst and advocate of action. Every organizational change is linked to individual change; and even if outside circumstances and outside sources of support provide the impetus for innovation, someone within the university must be its champion. Whether an administrator, a professor, or even a student, this advocate of innovation sparks acceptance and galvanizes support for change. The successful advocate convinces others of the likely benefit or profitability of change, wins administrative and official support for it, and obtains financial resources for it. Without advocacy, institutional redirection cannot occur.

Successful Innovation

Academic institutions are committed intellectually to discovery and new knowledge, but by nature they are conservative: they operate to conserve and convey accumulated wisdom to new generations. Unlike some other organizations, their prestige typically is not based on their innovativeness. Instead, the most prestigious universities tend to be those that serve the most prestigious clientele and perform commonly accepted functions. And unlike most other institutions, whose professional staffs are trained outside the institutions—often by university professors—they suffer from inbreeding, since professors train their own successors and only those students who accept the academic system choose to remain in it.

Even more important for the process of academic innovation, universities increasingly strive for professionalism, whereby the individual professor—as with the physician in a medical clinic or lawyer in a partnership firm—retains wide discretion for action because of his professional expertise (Parsons and Platt, 1973). As universities move in this direction and away from a more hierarchical tradition, academic innovation will become both more individually possible and less easily imposed. The professor is increasingly free to adopt new practices without seeking the permission of others, but he is similarly free to reject requests for change—particularly from nonprofessionals, including students and nonacademic administrators, since one premise of professional life is that of resistance against pressure from "outsiders." Thus, in less "professional" universities, administrators, agency officials, and outside supporters can continue both to mandate and to restrict innovation, while in more professional institutions they can less easily control it. As a result, if professionalism continues to increase, innovation in higher education will hinge less on the predilections and turnover of administrators and more on that of faculty.

Havelock (1971) and Lindquist (1974) have noted that many advocates of innovation mistakenly adopt only one strategy or approach in seeking to win support from professors, administrators, and others. For example, some rely solely on the distribution of research findings, on the assumption that the evidence of research will by itself result in reform. Others emphasize increased trust and openness among the members of institutions, in the hope that improved human relations will permit innovation. All the evidence to date indicates that no single approach to aca-

demic innovation is adequate; successful educational change requires effort on several fronts, at various levels, and by many means.

Some innovators may decide that rather than attempting to add a new unit to an existing university, such as a compatible parallel program, they will be more successful in creating an entirely separate institution that embodies their views. But for those who seek to adapt existing universities to the needs of new times, two principles may be worth noting.

The first principle is that the most successful innovators often give the impression of being conservative. A. Lawrence Lowell, one of Harvard University's most innovative presidents, seemed to his contemporaries a solid, safe conservative; but he realized that most radicals defeat their own ends by alienating their needed allies. Thus, after he retired, he advised others regarding the university president: "If he desires to innovate he will be greatly helped by having the reputation of being conservative, because the radicals who want a change are little offended by the fact of change, while the conservatives will be likely to follow him because they look on him as sharing their temperament and point of view" (1938, p. 22).

A second and related conclusion stems from the evidence that people deem academic innovations to be most acceptable if they are improvements on ways of achieving traditional goals rather than as departures from tradition—in other words, if they are better means to accepted ends instead of radical transformations. Knowing that innovation and change create hesitancy and apprehension among many individuals, the successful innovator tends to advocate academic change as the way of returning the university to its original principles and cherished values rather than of transforming it into something new. That is, he advocates reform—institutional renewal through revised ways of achieving old ideals—rather than innovation, and he is unlikely even to apply the term *innovation* to his ideas.

Further Reading

For analyses of academic innovation in France, see Clark (1973); for Germany, see Ben-David and Zloczower (1962) and Dahrendorf (1962); for England, see Ashby (1958), Halsey (1962), and Group for Research and Innovation in Higher Education (1975); for the United States, see Riesman (1956), Hefferlin (1969), Lindquist (1974), and Riesman and Stadtman (1973). In addition, see Miles (1964) for innovation in school systems; Greeley (1967) for innovation in American Catholic colleges; Kuhn (1970) for innovation in scientific thinking; and Levine (1975) for a detailed case study of the success and failure of university innovation. For studies of innovation at large, beyond academic institutions, see Rogers (1962), Bennis (1966), Havelock (1971), and Hirschman (1970).

Bibliography

Ashby, E. *Technology and the Academics: An Essay on Universities and the Scientific Revolution.* London: Macmillan, 1958.

Ben-David, J., and Zloczower, A. "Universities and Academic Systems in Modern Societies." *European Journal of Sociology,* 1962, *3*(1), 45–84.

Bennis, W. G. *Changing Organizations: Essays on the Development and Evolution of Human Organization.* New York: McGraw-Hill, 1966.

Bryce, J. "The Future of the English Universities." New York: Columbia University Library Collection, undated article.

Clark, B. R., and Youn, T. I. K. *Academic Power in the United States: Comparative Historic and Structural Perspectives.* ERIC Higher Education Research Report No. 3. Washington, D.C.: American Association for Higher Education, 1976.

Clark, T. N. *Prophets and Patrons: The French University and the Emergence of the Social Sciences.* Cambridge, Massachusetts: Harvard University Press, 1973.

Dahrendorf, R. "Starr und Offenheit der deutschen Universität: Die Chancen der Reform." *European Journal of Sociology,* 1962, *3*(2), 263–293.

Greeley, A. M. *The Changing Catholic College.* Chicago: Aldine, 1967.

Group for Research and Innovation in Higher Education, The Nuffield Foundation. *The Drift of Change: An Interim Report.* London: Nuffield Foundation, 1975.

Gusfield, J., and Riesman, D. "Faculty Culture and Academic Careers: Some Sources of Innovation in Higher Education." *Sociology of Education,* 1964, *37*(4), 281–305.

Halsey, A. H. "British Universities." *European Journal of Sociology,* 1962, *3*(1), 85–101.

Havelock, R. *Planning for Innovation Through Dissemination and Utilization of Knowledge.* Ann Arbor: Institute for Social Research, University of Michigan, 1971.

Hefferlin, J. L. *Dynamics of Academic Reform.* San Francisco: Jossey-Bass, 1969.

Hirschman, A. O. *Exit, Voice, and Loyalty: Responses to Decline in Firms, Organizations, and States.* Cambridge, Massachusetts: Harvard University Press, 1970.

Kuhn, T. S. *Structure of Scientific Revolutions.* (2nd ed.) Chicago: University of Chicago Press, 1970.

Laski, H. *The American Democracy: A Commentary and an Interpretation.* New York: Viking, 1948.

Lazarsfeld, P. F. "Innovation in Higher Education." In *Expanding Horizons of Knowledge About Man: A Symposium.* New York: Yeshiva University, 1966.

Levine, A. "Why Innovation Fails: The Institutionalization and Termination of Innovation in Higher Education." Unpublished doctoral dissertation, State University of New York at Buffalo, 1975.

Lindquist, J. "Political Linkage: The Academic-Innovation Process." *Journal of Higher Education,* 1974, *45*(5), 323–343.

Lowell, A. L. *What a University President Has Learned.* New York: Macmillan, 1938.

Miles, M. B. (Ed.) *Innovation in Education.* New York: Teachers College Press, Columbia University, 1964.

Parsons, T., and Platt, G. *The American University.* Cambridge, Massachusetts: Harvard University Press, 1973.

Riesman, D. *Constraint and Variety in American Education.* Lincoln: University of Nebraska Press, 1956.

Riesman, D., and Stadtman, V. A. (Eds.) *Academic Transformation: Seventeen Institutions Under Pressure.* New York: McGraw-Hill, 1973.

Rogers, E. M. *Diffusion of Innovations.* New York: Free Press, 1962.

Stern, B. J. *Historical Materials on Innovations in Higher Education.* New York: Planning

Project for Advanced Training in Social Research, Bureau of Applied Social Research, Columbia University, 1953.

Trevelyan, G. M. *British History in the Nineteenth Century and After: 1782–1919.* (2nd ed.) London: Longman's Green, 1937.

JB LON HEFFERLIN

PROFESSIONAL ASSOCIATIONS, INTERNATIONAL ROLE OF

Professional educational organizations have had a significant influence on the philosophy of higher education and on curriculum development in almost all of the disciplines; moreover, such organizations have played a strong role in international education. Professional organizations in higher education committed to international interests have existed since the late nineteenth century; however, the rapid growth of higher education since 1946 brought about a concomitant growth in the number of professional associations, especially those whose main purpose is international education. These organizations fall into five general categories:

The first category consists of organizations of institutions—colleges and universities—that have worked to promote international educational cooperation and exchange; many of these organizations also conduct research and consult on curricular development. Organizations in this category include the *Association internationale des Universités* (International Association of Universities), the National Association of State Universities and Land-Grant Colleges, the American Association of State Colleges and Universities, the American Association of Colleges for Teacher Education, the American Association of Community and Junior Colleges, the Association of Canadian Medical Schools, and the Association of Philippine Medical Colleges.

The second category consists of organizations that are formed around an academic discipline or profession, that promote exchange programs for professionals and students, and that sponsor research

projects. Examples of organizations in this category include the *Union géographique internationale* (International Geographical Union); the *Conseil international des sciences sociales* (International Social Science Council); the American Association of Health, Physical Education, and Recreation; the Business Council for International Understanding; and the Association for Teacher Education in Africa.

The third category consists of organizations whose members hold certain types of positions; organizations in this category exist largely to encourage international understanding among individual educators and to promote exchange programs aimed at improving professional training. Examples include the International Association of University Presidents, the International Association of University Professors and Lecturers, the *Association internationale des étudiants en sciences économiques et commerciales* (International Association of Business and Economics Students), the International Council for Educational Development, and the International Council on Education for Teaching.

The fourth category consists of organizations and groups of organizations that provide leadership in their respective disciplines and that promote international collaboration. Organizations in this category include the American Council on Education; the International Council on Health, Physical Education, and Recreation; the *Association internationale des sciences économiques* (International Economic Association); the World Federation for Medical Education; and the World Confederation of Organizations of the Teaching Profession.

The final category consists of organizations that sponsor and administer international exchange programs for scholars and students. Examples of organizations in this category include the Institute of International Education, the Council for International Exchange of Scholars, the Experiment in International Living, the American Field Services International Scholarships program, and regional groups such as the

African-American Institute, the Asia Foundation, the Asia Society, and the Japan Foundation.

Many professional associations whose interests are multifaceted have also displayed a high level of interest in international education and have devoted considerable energy toward promoting international understanding and intercultural relations through special committees and commissions. In addition, a number of associations have developed satellite units whose exclusive interest is international education.

The impact of professional organizations on institutions of higher education is greatest when top leaders—presidents, deans, and other academic officers—are deeply involved. The participation and support of such leaders have led to the development of institutional commitments overseas, such as technical assistance programs, faculty and student exchange programs, and programs designed to increase the global awareness of higher education institutions. National governments, UNESCO, and private foundations have relied on the leadership of many institutions of higher education in all of these programs.

Other types of associations have made it possible for faculty members and students to participate in international programs. Studies sponsored by professional associations have clearly indicated the ethnocentric nature of the curriculum offered on most campuses; consequently, associations have also lobbied—chiefly through their annual meetings, publications, and special committees—for globalization of curricula.

Some organizations characterized by a general interest in higher education have joined associations characterized by a total involvement in international education to facilitate extensive exchange programs involving students and college faculties. In addition, these organizations have conducted studies of various needs in international education and have produced position papers. For programs involving

technical assistance, professional organizations have helped locate qualified personnel from colleges and universities, disseminated information about exchange programs, handled substantial contracts involving technical assistance, and frequently served as a vital link between institutions of higher education and sponsoring government agencies or international groups.

Associations have also furthered the development of multicultural programs. For example, professional associations have influenced the establishment of non-Western studies and courses with a global view in American institutions. The associations have also exhorted institutions to develop offices specifically designed to encourage international programs and, in general, to make commitments toward a more global approach to its curricular offerings. Similar efforts have been made in other parts of the world.

Since the end of World War II, institutions of higher education have been extremely sensitive to their role in the world scene. As a result, many universities have become involved in education and training programs on an international scale. A number of institutions from developed countries have assisted developing countries in building new institutions or in revitalizing and expanding already existing institutions. In Africa and Southeast Asia, for example, new institutions were created almost overnight. In these areas attempts were made by educators and advisers from other countries to organize systems of higher education that could play a vital role in nation building. In addition, established institutions in developed countries received students from developing nations to be trained in various academic areas and to be trained as national leaders. Such exchange caused many institutions in developed countries to change their parochial approach to a more global orientation.

Professional organizations have played an important role in promoting a more substantial commitment to international education, chiefly through annual meetings, short-term study tours, extensive publications, and research programs that involved large numbers of institutions. In addition to their direct influence on colleges and universities, professional organizations have also elicited support for institutions of higher education from foundations and governments. Frequently, governments of other nations have become interested in fostering the development of higher education in developing countries. UNESCO, too, has encouraged the involvement of institutions and professional organizations in international activities.

Professional associations have also been formed that attempted to avoid being bound by national barriers; their membership, scope of program, and board of directors were multinational from their inception. Many older organizations that had their beginnings as national units have attempted to expand their horizons to include multinational groups and concerns.

See articles on individual associations for information about their local and national roles.

Bibliography

Barker, H. K. "International Education and the Professional Associations." *Phi Delta Kappan*, January 1970, *51*, 244–245.

Becker, J. M. *Education for A Global Society.* Fastback Series No. 28. Bloomington, Indiana: Phi Delta Kappa Education Foundation, 1973.

Bruner, K., Kern, P., and Weeks, K. *International Education Resources: A Summary of OE-Funded Research Projects and Reports Available Through the Educational Research Information Center 1956–71.* Washington, D.C.: U.S. Government Printing Office, 1972.

Cerych, L. *A Global Approach to Higher Education.* Occasional Paper No. 3. New York: International Council for Educational Development, 1973.

Kenworthy, L. S. *The International Dimension of Education.* Washington, D.C.: Association for Supervision and Curriculum Development, 1970.

Klassen, F. H., and Collier, J. L. *Innovation Now! International Perspectives on Innovation in Teacher Education.* Washington, D.C.: International Council on Education for Teaching, 1972.

National Association of State Universities and Land-Grant Colleges and Agency for International Development. *The Institutional Development Agreement: A New Operational Framework for AID and the Universities.* Washington, D.C.: National Association and AID, 1970.

Sanders, I. T., and Ward, J. C. *Bridges to Understanding: International Programs of American Colleges and Universities.* New York: McGraw-Hill, 1970.

Smallwood, O. T. (Ed.) *Universities and Transnational Approaches to the Solution of World Problems.* Columbus: Office of International Programs, Ohio State University, 1973.

Trag, H. R. "Alternative World Futures and Undergraduate Education." *Peace and Change*, Winter 1973, pp. 17–21.

Wolsk, D. "New Approaches to Education for International Understanding." *International Understanding at School*, June 1973, *25*, 41–47.

H. KENNETH BARKER

PROFIT-MAKING SCHOOLS
See Proprietary Schools.

PROGRAM OF COMPARATIVE AND HISTORICAL STUDIES IN HIGHER EDUCATION, United States

Founded in 1973, the Program of Comparative and Historical Studies in Higher Education is an independent research program within Yale University's Institution for Social and Policy Studies, New Haven, Connecticut. Applying cross-national and historical perspectives to the study of academic organization, its research includes analysis of national systems of academic control, governance in individual universities and colleges, and the development of scientific and scholarly interests through academic structure. Specific research topics have included the study of organization and reform of the French university, the German university structure, academic power in Italy, and the history of American and European higher education. Interdisciplinary in scope, the program combines approaches from sociology, history, political science, and organizational studies.

Although primarily committed to basic

research, the program also seeks to provide information to institutional leaders, state and national policymakers, and applied researchers. The program offers courses at the postgraduate level.

Funded by research grants from the government and from foundations, the center has a staff of eight research professionals, three research assistants and/or graduate students, and one secretary.

Research reports are published in the Working Papers series and are available from the program.

Institution for Social and Policy Studies,
Yale University
135 Prospect Street
New Haven, Connecticut 06520 USA

PROGRAMME BUDGETS FOR GRADUATE TRAINING—CHALMERS UNIVERSITY OF TECHNOLOGY

See Organisation for Economic Co-operation and Development.

PROGRAMMED LEARNING

See Educational Resources: Learning Resource Centers.

PROMOTION AND DEVELOPMENT OF PRIVATE SCHOOLS IN JAPAN
(Higher Education Report)

Promotion and Development of Private Schools in Japan (Tokyo, 1974)—a report of the Committee on Private School Promotion and Development, under the chairmanship of S. Hayashi—examines the financial status of private schools in Japan. It proposes massive increases in public subsidies to private higher education, accompanied by improvement of the administration of private educational institutions. Specifically, the following findings and recommendations are reported.

As of 1973, 78 percent of the students enrolled in higher education in Japan attended private colleges and universities. Economic conditions forced tuition increases that widened the gap between fees at public and private institutions. Public financial support is required to bring about educational improvement in private institutions. Such financial support should include a general subsidy based on standard expense per student; a facilities subsidy; subsidy for equipment; and subsidies for other supporting programs, such as institutional reconstruction and faculty improvement. The implementation of programs subsidized by public funds should be provided by the Japan Private School Promotion Foundation. Additional public support is needed to improve the number and amount of scholarships for students in private higher education and to ensure retirement allowances for private school teachers. Tax-exemption measures favorable to private institutions are also needed.

These financial measures should be accompanied by improved administration systems that would work to revise laws governing private school accreditations and to provide measures to correct violations.

PROMOTIONAL METHODS IN HIGHER EDUCATION

The extent to which educational institutions are concerned with external communications and publicity depends on the role and perception of higher education in a particular country and on the degree to which higher education is state-sponsored.

In severely underdeveloped countries, no effort is made to acquaint the general public with any educational possibilities that may exist. In most developed countries, material on higher education offerings is available, although it could be termed informational rather than promotional. These materials are usually produced by the central administrative office of the university or by the government—not by a separate "public relations" office.

Most such materials present little color or design and show little effort to promote the university actively.

In France, for example, the principal publication of each university is its catalog. These are purely informative books, listing course offerings, degrees, and rules and regulations. Some catalogs sell for as much as three dollars, while others are available on request.

The publications of the University of Adelaide in Australia reflect the kind and character of information distributed by universities in Commonwealth countries. Its information publications include a calendar, a handbook of courses, a handbook of postgraduate residencies, and a monthly newsletter and gazette. In addition, there are scholarly publications: the *Adelaide Law Review, Australian Economic Papers, Australian Journal of Experimental Biological and Medical Science, Joseph Fisher Lecture in Commerce, Miscellanea Musicologica,* and the *Southern Review*. There are no promotional publications as such.

There is little educational promotion because, in most countries, universities rely heavily—if not totally—on the government for financial support, and governments have seen little need to set up separate promotional budgets. In addition, students are more often the seekers than the sought. Universities have not been forced to resort to fierce competition to attract students.

Promotional Programs in Higher Education

In countries where there is intense competition for students, universities have to "sell" themselves. In the United States, for example, competition for students has become severe, and financial problems are mounting. Educational institutions in the United States rely on four sources for funding: the state and federal governments (especially in the case of public institutions), student tuition, alumni contributions, and private philanthropy. Educational lobby groups state the case for education to appropriate agencies of the government. However, colleges and universities have to present themselves to prospective students and to potential alumni donors.

Almost all United States institutions have a separate public relations office responsible for actively promoting the institution, a development office responsible for soliciting donations from alumni and various educational foundations, and an admissions office responsible for recruiting and selecting students. Over the years, all have developed well-structured policies, strategies, and techniques for telling their institutional story.

In the process, certain guidelines have been established. A well-planned promotional or case-stating program starts with the institution's determination of its goals, in terms of students matriculated, dollars raised, and similar matters. The strengths of the institution are then defined, as is the population it primarily serves. Finally, those in charge of the promotional program decide on the best means for the institution to state its case and investigate costs and the availability of staff capable of carrying out the program.

The two examples that follow illustrate the case-stating process as applied to student recruitment and to fund raising. The processes involved in solving these problems could be applied in any culture, although the style and form of the communications devices would certainly vary.

Student recruitment. A large university in a major metropolitan area had experienced a gradual enrollment decline for three consecutive years. A continuation of the downward trend would force the university to release a substantial number of faculty members and close down several dormitories—and perhaps close the university itself.

University officials decided that the magnitude of the recruiting problem warranted an investment in outside consultation. A firm specializing in institutional communications was hired. The firm spent time on the campus interviewing all elements of the campus community. It concluded that the university had three major assets or "selling points." First, it had an easily accessible location in a city that offered an extraordinary number of cultural attractions. Second, the university had an excellent record of placing students in graduate schools, especially in medicine and law. Finally, it had available an extremely loyal body of alumni, many of whom held top positions in major corporations.

Given these assets, the firm recommended a two-pronged promotional effort, to be directed toward both the nontraditional students (adults, part-time students) and the university's traditional student market (young persons aged eighteen to twenty-one). The plan for increasing the number of nontraditional students included expanding the number and variety of courses offered at night and on Saturdays. To publicize these new offerings, advertisements were placed in selected urban and suburban newspapers, and a direct-mail campaign was undertaken in one of the surrounding communities. Finally, a follow-up study was planned for a year later, to determine the effectiveness of the program and to make certain refinements (in course offerings, for example).

The plan for increasing the number of traditional students included the development of a completely new set of recruitment materials that featured the many benefits of the city in which the university was located. The significant success of the university in placing students in top graduate schools and careers was also stressed. Specific materials included, first, a four-color poster with reply cards attached. This was mailed to the career guidance offices in all the secondary schools in the four states from which the university attracted the most students. In addition, a four-color, one-page self-mailer (no envelope needed) was developed as a means of initial contact with possible applicants. A coupon

was attached that the prospective student could return if he wanted an application and further information.

The firm also devised two booklets designed to attract students. The first, a student prospectus, was a thirty-two-page booklet that highlighted the advantages of an urban location, communicated the flavor of student life, and listed course titles (although not course descriptions). This was to be the primary "selling piece" of the university.

In addition, a careers booklet was mailed to all students who had expressed interest in the university. This sixteen-page booklet emphasized the university's fine record in preparing students for careers. Several case histories of successful alumni around the United States were included.

A series of six university bulletins or catalogs was also developed, one for each of the major academic divisions within the university. These publications were academic and informational, analogous to the basic bulletins distributed by universities in other countries. Used primarily as in-house documents, they were also distributed to students who had indicated a specific academic concentration on their admission applications.

Finally, a key alumni program was established. Key alumni in those geographical areas in which the university was well known were mobilized to serve as part-time recruiters and to work closely with the admissions office in contacting prospective students.

As this example suggests, external communications can be effective only if the internal philosophies and objectives of the institution have been clearly defined. In this case, the university had to be willing to broaden its educational position by expanding its market to include part-time students as well as the traditional full-time student. The university was forced—through economic circumstance—to take a hard look at the service it "sells" and to attempt to communicate its benefits more clearly to prospective students.

Fund raising. In this case, a prestigious private university faced the possibility of a second consecutive deficit year. Enrollment and tuition were already at desired maximum levels, and government sources were being tapped to the fullest. Thus, the alumni contribution area seemed to offer the most promise for improving the financial situation. Only 33 percent of a rather wealthy alumni body contributed to the annual fund in a given year. University officials decided to set a contribution percentage goal of 43 percent.

To initiate this campaign, the university sent a questionnaire to a representative group of twenty-five hundred alumni to determine attitudes about giving. It was learned that many alumni believed that the university did not really need their money and that many were unhappy about the current attitudes and programs of the university. Worse, some were simply unaware of what was happening on the campus. It was also discovered that alumni were more inclined to give if they were approached by someone they knew rather than by a stranger. Using this information, a campaign was launched, beginning with a revised version of the traditional "general appeal" letter sent to all alumni. The letter told alumni how their gift might be used in each of eight major areas of need within the university.

Three additional appeal letters were designed for three separate groups of alumni: those in the retirement years (over age 60), in the high earning years (age 30 to 59), and in the graduate school or early earning years (age 21 to 29). Each letter emphasized the university's current programs and philosophy, but each was worded in a way most likely to gain understanding and response from the receiving group.

In addition, the area alumni program was expanded and personalized. Each alumnus volunteer was assigned a list of goals, the purpose of which was to increase the number of personal contacts made. A follow-up questionnaire was designed to be sent to those alumni who had not contributed, in order to determine where the new campaign had failed.

In this example, the university was willing to challenge many of the assumptions it held about itself and its audience and to reconsider the ways in which it communicated itself to others. Such increased self-awareness is essential for any institution that seeks to present itself to external groups.

Educational institutions in most parts of the world have not had the need to invest in publicity. As a result, external publications have been few in number and spare in style. However, intense competition for students and dollars has created the need for effective publicity by educational institutions in some countries, especially in the United States. Effective publicity, however, is not synonymous with a heavily manned public relations office that frenetically produces an overabundance of publicity materials. Rather, effective publicity is possible only when a university has analyzed itself and its role in the field of learning.

Bibliography

Bach, R. O. (Ed.) *Communication.* New York: Hastings House, 1963.
Commonwealth Universities Yearbook. London: Association of Commonwealth Universities, 1973.

DAVID W. BARTON, JR.

See also: Alumni Affairs; Development, College and University; Public Relations.

PROMOTIONS OF ACADEMIC PERSONNEL

See Recruitment, Appointment, Promotion, and Termination of Academic Personnel.

PROPRIETARY SCHOOLS

Proprietary schools are privately owned profit-making schools, most of which specialize in the training of job skills or avocations. They offer a wide range and diversity of subjects, including business skills, driver training, flight instruction, dance, automotive repair, barbering, and cooking. Their courses are generally organized in short, intensive modules and are run at hours that are convenient to the working person. They concentrate more on practical training and skills than on academic learning and usually award certificates or diplomas rather than degrees. Many, however, offer degree-equivalent programs without the general education component, and job competencies gained by their students are often comparable to those learned in degree programs; but some practice deceptive advertising, charge excessive fees, and have low job placement rates.

By far the largest number of proprietary schools in one country are found in the United States, which has over 10,000 schools that enroll a total of more than 1,000,000 students. In Japan over 1,000 schools enroll more than 100,000 students in all. France has between 200 and 300 schools for 20,000 to 30,000 students; Ghana has between 300 and 400 schools for 10,000 students, while Luxembourg, Norway, the Republic of China, Singapore, Sweden, and the United Kingdom have less than 100 schools each and enroll fewer than 10,000 students in them.

Development of Proprietary Schools in the United States

The term *proprietary* is somewhat misleading in the United States in implying ownership solely by one person, since by the end of the 1960s, 85 percent of American proprietary schools were corporately owned, either as a local business or as part of national chains (Fulton, 1969). Yet these schools now operate in much the same way as they did when they were first developed by individuals in business fields in the mid-nineteenth century. Typically, they are small (fifty to five hundred students) and specialize in a single field or occupation. Because the reputation and therefore the

financial survival of vocationally oriented schools depends on job placement of their graduates, they try to provide up-to-date training by maintaining close contact with employers, and they select faculty more for work experience than for academic background.

For many years, proprietary schools were an invisible sector in the formal education system of the United States. Their connections to public and nonprofit private high schools, community and junior colleges, and four-year colleges and universities were minimal. Any student choosing a proprietary school did so on his own, because few guidance counselors recommended them, and, except for some licensing requirements, educators and government officials had little contact with them. Proprietary schools and other educational institutions were content to leave each other alone because, by and large, they were not in direct competition. Proprietary schools often functioned in fields where public systems did not have programs. For example, in the United States proprietary schools were the first to teach typing in the 1880s and computer programing and keypunch skills in the 1960s (Fulton, 1969; Nolfi and Nelson, 1973). The only restrictions on proprietary schools were licensing requirements in some states, but these dealt with the financial soundness of the institution and not with the quality of its instruction. Students could use federal "G.I. Bill," Vocational Veterans, and Vocational Rehabilitation benefits to attend proprietary schools, but no formal transfer arrangements existed for them into the public or private educational system.

Since 1965, however, competition between proprietary schools on the one hand and public and nonprofit private schools on the other has become more direct. Pressures for more vocational or career education and skills training in colleges, universities, and technical institutes have come both from the United States Department of Labor, concerned with raising the level of technical competence in the labor force, and from college and university students and administrators, dissatisfied with the falling value of a traditional college degree. As of the mid-1970s, the realities of the job market seem to be a surplus of college graduates from liberal arts programs and a shortage of skilled middle-level technical, clerical, and paraprofessional workers.

To the extent that students and policymakers have come to see vocational education as an alternative to traditional academic education, proprietary schools are becoming increasingly regarded as "legitimate" postsecondary options. Community colleges, which were initially designed to transfer students into colleges, are moving into vocational training and concern has been expressed at the national level that the resources of proprietary schools be utilized effectively before additional public money goes into expanding public institutions. In the early 1960s the federal government had passed major legislation to fund manpower training and vocational education in public institutions. By 1968 federal policymakers were discussing the proper treatment of proprietary schools, including questions of whether proprietary schools should be supported by government grants or loans to their students, whether they should be allowed to grant degrees, how they should be accredited, and how they should be regulated in the public interest.

Public funding of proprietary schools or students could not be justified until more was known about what they offered and the value of their training. But by 1972, with the passage of the Higher Education Amendments Act of that year, agreement was reached at the federal level that students in proprietary schools accredited by an accrediting agency recognized by the Commission of Education are eligible for benefits under the Basic Educational Opportunity Grant, National Direct Student Loan, College Work Study, and other federal grant and loan programs. Presently, students at schools accredited by only three agencies are eligible for aid under this act:

the Association of Independent Colleges and Schools, which represents business schools; the National Association of Trade and Technical Schools, which acts for other schools that provide occupational training; and the National Home Study Council, which represents correspondence schools. The efforts of these organizations were instrumental in the inclusion of the accredited proprietary schools in the Higher Education Amendments Act of 1972 and other congressional initiatives, and they have generally supported federal programs of student aid over those of direct aid to, or contracts with, institutions.

Proponents of proprietary schools, including manpower planners and national policymakers, argue that market competition for students encourages efficient operations and innovative programs that meet the changing and diverse training needs of students, and that these schools provide a valuable service both to workers investing in further skills and to an economy that needs trained manpower. But other groups have resisted the notion of profit-making enterprises in education. Some writers argue that proprietary schools make money by offering low-quality, low-cost programs to unsuspecting, inexperienced students and that neither the students nor the economy benefits from high-price, low-quality training ("Spotlight Series on Vocational Schools," 1974). State education officials, for example, have rarely utilized proprietary schools under the Vocational Education Act programs. In 1969 a proprietary institution, the Marjorie Webster Junior College, lost its suit in the United States Court of Appeals to be eligible for accreditation by the Middle States Association of Colleges and Secondary Schools, with the association arguing that "two goals—that of the profit organization to return a profit on capital and that of an educational organization to overcome the ignorance of students—are not compatible" (Wilms, 1973a, p. 6). More recently, the Federal Trade Commission has conducted several investigations of proprietary school advertising and operations because of consumer protection abuses by some schools.

While these policy arguments have been discussed, some research into the activities of proprietary schools has been carried out, with the following major findings. First, graduates of some proprietary schools fare in the job market as well as or better than graduates of comparable programs in community colleges (Wolman, 1972); hence, these schools may be training students at a lower level of total social cost (public plus individual investment) than public institutions. Second, students at proprietary schools are similar in social background and in expectations for job advancement to those in community college and public vocational institutes, although they have lower verbal skills and less academic preparation (Wilms, 1973b). Finally, several studies indicate that proprietary schools are more cost-effective and innovative than public programs in providing training to the target clienteles of the two manpower and vocational education acts, the Manpower Development and Training Act (MDTA) of 1972 and the Vocational Education Act of 1963 (Belitsky and O'Neill, 1973), and that navy contracting with proprietary schools is more cost-effective than in-house training programs (O'Neill, 1970). But other studies, such as that by Sam Harris Associates (1973), have shown that public programs are most cost effective for MDTA training.

Thus, as of the mid 1970s, research about proprietary schools is not adequate to guide American policymaking in detail. Yet several policy initiatives and program experiments beyond federal support for students in accredited schools are being made on the assumption that proprietary schools offer worthwhile programs. In thirteen states, proprietary schools may now apply for authority to grant degrees. Many colleges are giving transfer credits to students from proprietary schools. And Pennsylvania and New York have incorporated proprietary schools into open

learning systems as community resources not to be duplicated by new public programs (Nolfi, Nelson, and Freeman, 1974). In short, with state and federal policymakers recognizing the limited resources available to education, proprietary schools are being considered as an education resource within the overall postsecondary resources of the states and nation. Appropriate government policies regarding them in the future will probably include a mixture of contracting for education services, degree-granting and transferable credit-granting authorization, combined multi-institutional programs, and licensing (Nolfi, Nelson, and Freeman, 1974).

Proprietary Schools in Other Countries

Internationally, proprietary schools appear to follow no systematic pattern. In Europe, for example, France and England have proprietary schools while Germany does not. No privately owned proprietary schools operate in Spain, although a wide variety of vocational training programs are run by private firms for their employees, and the Ministry of Education and the Ministry of Labor are both actively involved in vocational training (Horowitz, 1974). No private proprietary schools exist, as well, in the Netherlands, although a large number of vocational schools are funded by the government. In Iran all private institutions are nonprofit, and are regulated by the Ministry of Science and Higher Education. In the Republic of South Africa the Union Department of Education took over all technical and other vocational education in 1925 and since then has established more technical and commercial schools (Stimie and Greggus, 1972).

In Japan vocational training provided in publicly or privately maintained facilities and training within industry are playing an increasingly important role. Private bodies or public service corporations, called "school juridical persons," may establish institutions of higher education under the provisions of the School Education Law. Public and private institutions are therefore established with the prior approval of the minister of education (Kida, 1972). In Thailand the Department of Vocational Education of the Ministry of Education supervises the colleges that offer vocational training of the type commonly found in proprietary schools, and even Thailand's private nursing colleges are not proprietary, being associated with provincial and national hospitals (UNESCO, 1972). In contrast, in the Philippines proprietary institutions have flourished. To correct their excessive profiteering and commercial orientation, the government has increased its regulation of stock-issuing private schools and established a special permanent trust fund and provisions for converting these schools into nonprofit foundations exempt from taxation (Carson, 1961).

According to an international questionnaire survey conducted by the authors, proprietary schools seem particularly important throughout the world in the fields of business, accounting, secretarial and clerical work, trades, crafts, and technical training. Thus, although universities and colleges in Ghana, Japan, Norway, the Republic of China, Singapore, the United Kingdom, and the United States include some or all of these fields of study in their curricula, in France and Luxembourg these fields are taught only in the proprietary schools, and in Sweden they are taught only marginally in the universities and colleges. In Norway, the United States, France, and Luxembourg, proprietary schools also offer training in the health field; and in Japan they are an important source of training in foreign languages.

Almost all proprietary schools are situated in urban areas. They are mainly residence schools, though in Singapore, Sweden, and the United States both residence and correspondence schools exist, while the United Kingdom and Japan have only correspondence schools.

Most proprietary schools have some admissions requirements, either secondary or high school diploma, or an entrance examination. The exceptions to this rule are the United States and Sweden, which have no admissions requirements, and Japan, which also has no admissions requirements but whose proprietary school students are nearly all secondary school graduates.

The awarding of certificates and degrees in proprietary schools differs from country to country. In most countries proprietary schools are authorized to award only certificates, but in some countries higher degrees are granted. Singapore's schools, for example, give two-year associate degrees, and schools in the Republic of China award bachelor's or higher degrees. In Ghana, on the completion of the courses, students take public examinations that are organized by a government agency. In the United Kingdom, on the other hand, proprietary schools are not authorized to award either degrees or certificates.

Proprietary schools throughout the world vary in regard to the age of their student bodies. France, Ghana, and Luxembourg have mainly young students. In both the United States and Singapore, 60 percent of the students are youth while 40 percent are adults who have held jobs. In Japan, Norway, Sweden, the Republic of China, and the United Kingdom, students are adults; and in Norway, Sweden, and the United Kingdom, these students are in the process of retraining.

Government support for proprietary schools is strongest in Luxembourg and Norway. In Japan and Ghana, some schools receive government funding, but not all. In the United States, funding is provided through student aid awards, not by direct institutional support. There is no government funding of proprietary schools in the United Kingdom, Sweden, Singapore, the Republic of China, or France.

In summary, most governments throughout the world have no direct links with proprietary schools. These schools, in general, are allowed to operate quietly, with minimal public funds or interference. Where there is a large nationalized system of education, they tend to fill in the gaps in educational programs, developing in response to training needs in a fast-changing economy, retooling the skills of adults, offering options for education by correspondence, and achieving a balanced and flexible educational system.

Bibliography

Belitsky, A. H. *Private Vocational Schools and Their Students.* Cambridge, Massachusetts: Schenkman, 1969.

Belitsky, A. H., and O'Neill, D. M. *The Federal Government and Manpower.* Washington, D.C.: American Enterprise Institute for Public Policy Research, 1973.

Carson, A. L. *Higher Education in the Philippines.* Washington, D.C.: United States Department of Health, Education and Welfare, 1961.

Erickson, R. W. *Proprietary Business Schools and Community Colleges: Resource Avocation, Student Needs, and Federal Policies.* Washington, D.C.: ICF Incorporated, 1972.

Freeman, R. B. *Occupational Training in Proprietary Schools and Technical Institutes.* Cambridge, Massachusetts: Harvard University, Department of Economics, 1973.

Fulton, R. A. "Proprietary Schools." In R. L. Ebel (Ed.), *Encyclopedia of Educational Research.* (4th ed.) New York: Macmillan, 1969.

Sam Harris Associates. *A Comparative Study of MDTA Institutional Training in Community Colleges, Public Vocational Schools and Private Institutions.* Washington, D.C.: Sam Harris Associates, 1973.

Horowitz, M. A. *Manpower and Education in Franco's Spain.* Hamden, Connecticut: Shoe String Press, 1974.

Japan Ministry of Education. *Educational Standards in Japan.* Tokyo: Ministry of Education, 1971.

Kida, H. *Higher Education in Japan.* Bangkok, Thailand: UNESCO Regional Office for Education in Asia, 1972.

National Center for Educational Statistics. *Survey of Vocational Institutions 1973–1974.* Washington, D.C.: U.S. Office of Information, 1975.

Nolfi, G. J., and Nelson, V. I. *Strengthening the Alternative Postsecondary Education System: Continuing and Part-Time Study in Massachusetts.* Cambridge, Massachusetts: University Consultants, Inc., 1973.

Nolfi, G. J., Nelson, V. I., and Freeman, R. B. *The Contemporary Role of Proprietary Institutions in Vocational Education in Massachusetts.* Cambridge, Massachusetts: University Consultants, Inc., 1974.

O'Neill, D. M. *Meeting the Navy's Needs for Technically-Trained Personnel: Alternative Procurement Strategies.* Arlington, Virginia: Center for Naval Analyses, 1970.

"Spotlight Series on Vocational Schools," *Boston Globe,* March 25, 1974 to April 3, 1974.

Stimie, C. M., and Geggus, C. *University Education in the Republic of South Africa.* Pretoria: South African Human Sciences Research Council, 1972.

UNESCO. "Higher Education in the Asian Region." *UNESCO Regional Office for Education in Asia, Bulletin,* 1972, 7(1), entire issue.

Wilms, W. "A New Look at Proprietary Schools." *Change,* 1973a, 1 (Summer), 6.

Wilms, W. *Profitmaking and Education.* Berkeley: Center for Research and Development in Higher Education, University of California, 1973b.

Wolman, J. M. *A Comparative Study of Proprietary and Non-Proprietary Vocational Training Programs.* Vol. 1. Washington, D.C.: Office of Program Planning and Evaluation, 1972.

GEORGE J. NOLFI
VALERIE I. NELSON

PROTESTANTISM, INFLUENCE OF

See Religious Influences in Higher Education: Protestantism.

PSYCHOLOGY (Field of Study)

Psychology in its current state reflects its origins, development, and history. It has at least three interrelated facets of importance—as a discipline, as a science, and as a profession. As an academic discipline, psychology has grown out of philosophy. As a science concerned with the behavior of human and other organisms, psychology has many relationships to other biological and social sciences. In the application and use of knowledge and skills as a profession, psychology is involved with many other professions, such as medicine, education, engineering, social work, and planning.

Psychologists engage in teaching, research, consultation, and administration and render specific psychological services to individuals and groups. Psychologists work in a variety of settings, such as colleges and universities, schools, hospitals, government agencies, private offices or clinics, and community mental health centers as experimental, clinical, social, educational, developmental, counseling, personality, industrial, and school psychologists or as psychometrists.

Experimental psychology designs and conducts studies in learning, motivation, sensation and perception, performance, cognitive processes, and comparative and physiological psychology. Clinical psychology assesses and treats individuals with emotional, adjustment, and behavioral problems. Social psychology measures the effects of one or more other individuals or groups on the behavior of individuals. Industrial psychology deals with employees—their training, job performance, efficiency, job satisfaction, and morale. Personnel psychology selects, assigns, and promotes individuals. Engineering psychology designs living and work environments. Educational psychology designs, develops, and evaluates materials and procedures in education and training. Counseling psychology involves counseling and consulting and is particularly concerned with the role of education and work on the functioning of the individual and with the interactions among individuals and their environments. School psychology deals with the effectiveness of schools in relation to the intellectual, social, and emotional development of children. In all of these specializations, psychologists frequently are also involved in teaching, consulting, and administration.

Psychology developed as a field of study in Germany, England, and France. The first formal laboratory of psychology was founded by Wilhelm Wundt in 1879 in Leipzig, Germany. The first United States doctorate of philosophy in psychology was awarded to G. Stanley Hall under William James at Harvard University.

The modern history of psychology in the United States begins with the use during World War II of psychologists in military and civil activities. The G.I. Bill provided support for higher education for millions of veterans, and major training support in mental health was offered under the auspices of the United States Public Health Service and the Veterans Administration.

In reviewing the factors which have influenced psychology since 1955, Boneau and Cuca (1974) point to the Cold War, Sputnik, man on the moon, and a high level of federal support for science and technology. The post–World War II "baby boom" produced a major expansion in colleges and universities and in their facilities. From 1960 to 1970 enrollments in colleges nearly doubled, in part because of economic recession and a major slowdown in aerospace activities. The middle to late 1960s were marked by the Vietnam war, tension, change, and the opening of university opportunities in psychology as students moved out of the sciences and humanities into more socially "relevant" activities. Psychology has been a part of these developments in many nations. Goldstone (1973) has noted a very rapid growth of education in psychology throughout the world since 1950.

In 1954, 665 doctorates in psychology were awarded in the United States. In 1974, of approximately 33,000 doctoral degrees granted in the United States, 2587 were in psychology. Almost 31 percent were awarded to women. The National Center for Educational Statistics estimates that about 3870 Ph.D., 8750 master's, and 79,230 bachelor's degrees will be awarded in psychology in 1982–83. In 1954 graduate enrollment was about 3600. In 1974 about 38,000 students were involved. In 1976 there were just about as many graduate students in psychology as there were members of the American Psychological Association, which went from 12,380 members in 1954 to 37,371 members in twenty years. Undergraduate baccalaureate degrees have grown to 100,000 per year. This growth is striking and has been coupled with increases in salary and in the spread of psychological activities; for example, a relative increase in the percentage of clinical psychologists and an increased potential for private practice with statutory recognition and requirements.

In 1976 South Dakota became the forty-eighth of the fifty United States to enact a licensing or certification law. This law provides for two levels: a *psychologist* (a person who has received the doctorate, in a program that is primarily psychological, and has two years of supervised experience) and an *associate psychologist* (a person with a master's degree and one year of supervised experience). Social controls, requirements, and recognition of the work of psychologists, particularly in mental health, are increasing.

The majority of United States psychologists are members of the American Psychological Association (APA). The International Union of Psychological Science (IUPS), organized in 1952, is an association of national psychological societies and a member of the International Social Science Council. In 1965 there were twenty-eight member societies. This number increased to forty-one by 1976. International congresses are held regularly under IUPS sponsorship.

There are a number of general, individual-membership organizations of psychologists. Among these international organizations are the International Council of Psychologists (ICP) and the International Association of Applied Psychology (IAAP). These organizations have memberships from many nations and hold regular congresses. Reports of these meetings appear, as well as the publication of journals and newsletters. There are also a number of regional organizations of psychologists—for example, the Interamerican Society of Psychology—as well as a larger number of interest-based international groups, such as the International Association for Cross-Cultural Psychology.

The primary source of the world's literature in psychology and related subjects is the *Psychological Abstracts,* published monthly by the American Psychological Association and containing noncritical abstracts from thousands of sources. Additional selected sources are the *American Psychologist, Acta Psychologica,* the *Interamerican Journal of Psychology,* the *International Review of Applied Psychology,* and the *International Journal of Psychology.*

In addition to the various journals that deal with technical topics (mental health, rehabilitation, retardation, and ergonomics, as well as the internationally based pure and applied science journals) there are media such as the *Journal of Trans-Cultural Psychology.* There are also interest-based, and frequently multiple-disciplinary based, international organizations with related publications, as well as a large group of nationally based journals of psychology.

[*Notes:* **C. A. Boneau** and **J. M. Cuca,** "An Overview of Psychology's Human Resources." *American Psychologist,* 1974, *29,* 821–840. **L. Goldstone,** "An International Standard Classification of Education." *Prospects,* 1973, pp. 390–397.]

SHERMAN ROSS

Levels and Programs of Study

Programs in psychology generally require as a minimum educational prerequisite a secondary education and lead to the following awards: certificate or diploma, bachelor's degree (B.A.), master's degree (M.A., M.Sc.), the doctorate (Ph.D.), or their equivalents. Programs deal with the principles, practices, and applications of psychology and consist of classroom and laboratory instruction, group discussion, and, on advanced levels, seminars and research.

Programs that lead to an award not equivalent to a first university degree usually include some of the following courses: principles of psychology, history of psychology, applications of psychology (educational, vocational, clinical, industrial), use of psychological tests, and abnormal psychology. Background courses often included are statistics, computer science, principles of economics, principles of sociology, principles of biology, and research methodology. Programs at this level are often given in technological or similar institutes and last from one to three years. For short courses, many of which are sponsored by employers, employers' associations, or trade unions, a certificate of satisfactory completion is usually given.

Programs that lead to a first university degree usually include such subjects as learning and motivation, evolution and development of behavior, sensory processes and perception, experimental psychology, applied psychology, physiological psychology, social psychology, developmental psychology, theories of personality, experimental analysis of behavior disorders, cognitive processes, history of psychology, clinical psychology, and psychometrics. Background courses often included are sociology, anthropology, biology, mathematics, philosophy, and anatomy and physiology of the nervous system.

Programs that lead to a postgraduate university degree emphasize original research work as substantiated by the presentation and defense of a scholarly thesis or dissertation. Principal subject matter areas within which courses and research projects tend to fall include the history of psychology, psychological theories, experimental psychology, applied psychology (including measurement and evaluation programs in education), social psychology, abnormal psychology, clinical psychology, psychotherapy, psychological testing, and psychometrics. Subject areas within which background studies tend to fall include relevant specialties in philosophy, sociology, anthropology, biology, mathematics, statistics, and computer science.

[This section was based on UNESCO's *International Standard Classification of Education (ISCED)* (Paris: UNESCO, 1976).]

Major International and National Organizations

INTERNATIONAL

Association de psychologie scientifique de langue française
28 rue Serpente
Paris, France

European Association of Experimental Social Psychology
Department of Psychology
University of Bristol
8-10 Berkeley Square
Bristol BS8 1HH, England

International Association for Analytical Psychology (IAAP)
Association internationale de psychologie analytique (AIPA)
Sihlberg 32
8002 Zurich, Switzerland

International Association for Cross-Cultural Psychology
Department of Psychology
University of Hong Kong
Hong Kong

International Association of Applied Psychology (IAAP)
Association internationale de psychologie appliquée
47 rue César Franck
4000 Liège, Belgium

International Council of Psychologists (ICP)
4014 Cody Road
Sherman Oaks, California 91403

International Society for the Study of Behavioral Development
Department of Psychology
Free University
Amsterdam, Netherlands

International Union of Biological Sciences (IUBS)
Union internationale des sciences biologiques (UISB)
Experimental Psychology and Animal Behavior Section
51 boulevard Montmorency
75016 Paris, France

International Union of Psychological Science (IUPS)
Union internationale de psychologie scientifique
Hogg Foundation for Mental Health
University of Texas
Austin, Texas 78712 USA

Sociedad interamericana de psicología (SIP)
Interamerican Society of Psychology
Apartado Aéreo 32501
Bogotá, Colombia

NATIONAL

Argentina:
Sociedad argentina de psicología
avenida Santa Fe 1145
Buenos Aires

Australia:
   Australian Psychological Society
   National Science Centre
   191 Royal Parade
   Parkville, Victoria 3052

Belgium:
   Belgian Psychological Society
   Vrije Universiteit Brussel
   Johannalaan 44
   Brussels

Brazil:
   Brazilian Psychological Association
   C. P. 8105
   São Paulo

Bulgaria:
   Bulgarian Psychological Society
   Sofia University
   Kathedra of Psychology
   Sofia

Canada:
   Canadian Psychological Association
   Department of Psychology
   University of Toronto
   Toronto 181, Ontario

Colombia:
   Federación colombiana de psicología
   Apartado Nal. 19-96
   Bogotá

Cuba:
   Psychologists' Union of Cuba
   School of Psychology
   University of Havana
   San Rafael y Mazon, Havana

Czechoslovakia:
   Psychological Association of
       Czechoslovakia
   Československá akademie věd
   nábrežie B. Engelse 6
   Prague 2-Bysehra

Denmark:
   Danish Psychological Association
   Skt. Peders Straede 34-36
   1453 Copenhagen

Federal Republic of Germany:
   Federation of Germany Psychological
       Association
   Psychologisches Institut
   Von-Melle-Park 6
   2 Hamburg 13

Finland:
   Finnish Psychological Society
   Institute of Occupational Health
   Haartmaninkatu 1
   Helsinki 25

France:
   French Psychological Society
   28 rue Serpente
   Paris VIe, 75006

German Democratic Republic:
   Society for Psychology of German
       Democratic Republic
   Am Kupfergraben 7
   108 Berlin

Hong Kong:
   Hong Kong Psychological Society
   % Department of Psychology
   University of Hong Kong

Hungary:
   Hungarian Psychological Scientific
       Association
   Meredek u. 1
   Budapest XII

India:
   Indian Psychological Association
   Department of Psychology
   University of Calcutta
   92 Ancharya Prafulla Chandra Rd.
   Calcutta 9

Iran:
   Psychological Association of Iran
   Teachers Training College
   94 Roosevelt Avenue
   Tehran

Israel:
   Israel Psychological Association
   Department of Psychology
   Bar-Ilan University
   Ramat Gan

Italy:
   Italian Society of Scientific Psychology
   Psychological Institute
   University of Palermo
   Palermo

Japan:
   Japanese Psychological Association
   37-13-802, Hongo 4-chome, Bunkyo-ku
   Tokyo 113

Mexico:
   Mexican Society of Psychology
   Georgia No. 123
   Col. Napoles
   Mexico 18, D. F.

Netherlands:
   Nederlands instituut van psychologen
   Nic. Maesstraat 122
   Amsterdam 1007

New Zealand:
New Zealand Psychological Society
Department of Psychology
Victoria University of Wellington
P. O. Box 196
Wellington

Norway:
Norwegian Psychological Association
Bjorn Farmannsgate 16
Oslo 2

Panama:
Asociación panameña de psicólogos
Apartado 944
Zona 9A

Philippines:
Psychological Association of the
Philippines
Department of Psychology
University of the Philippines
Diliman, Quezon City

Poland:
Polish Psychological Association
Nowy Swiat 72, pok. 216
00-330 Warsaw

Romania:
Romanian Psychological Association
Str. Frumoasa 26
Bucharest

Republic of Korea:
Korean Psychological Association
College of Liberal Arts and Sciences
Seoul National University, Seoul

Republic of South Africa:
South African Psychological Association
P. O. Box 4292
Johannesburg

Spain:
Spanish Society of Psychology
Instituto nacional de psicología
Calle Juan Huarte de San Juan
Ciudad universitaria
Madrid 3

Sweden:
Swedish Psychological Association
Becksjudarvägen 45-47
131 00 Nacka

Switzerland:
Swiss Society of Psychology
Les Courbes
1181 Gilly

Turkey:
Turkish Psychological Association
Psikoloji enstitusu, Edebiyat fakultesi
University of Istanbul
Istanbul

Soviet Union:
Soviet Psychological Association
Institute of General and Educational
Psychology
University of Moscow
20 Karl Marx Avenue
Moscow K-9

United Kingdom:
British Psychological Society
18-19 Albemarle Street
London WIX 4DN, England

United States:
American Psychological Association
1200 Seventeenth Street NW
Washington, D.C. 20026

Uruguay:
Sociedad de psicología del Uruguay
25 de Mayo 535. P 4.-Excr. 25
Montevideo

Venezuela:
Colegio de psicólogos de Venezuela
Apartado 70006
Caracas

Yugoslavia:
Yugoslav Psychological Association
Yugoslovenski udruzenje psihologa
ul. 683 be. 7
91.000 Skopje

Principal Information Sources

GENERAL

Some bibliographical guides to the field of psychology are:

Bell, J. E. *Guide to Library Research in Psychology.* Dubuque, Iowa: W. C. Brown, 1971. Contains 1900 reference sources and texts in psychology and related fields; intended for undergraduate students.

Borchardt, D. H. *How to Find Out in Philosophy and Psychology.* Oxford, England: Pergamon Press, 1968.

Daniel, R. S., and Louttit, C. M. *Professional Problems in Psychology.* Englewood Cliffs, New Jersey: Prentice-Hall, 1953. Provides information on professional matters, psychological literature, organizations, journals, and reference works.

Elliott, C. K. *A Guide to the Documentation of Psychology.* London: Clive Bingley, 1971.

The Harvard List of Books in Psychology. (4th ed.) Cambridge, Massachusetts: Harvard University Press, 1971. A guide to psychological literature; periodically updated.

Sarbin, T. R., and Coe, W. C. *The Student Psychologist's Handbook: A Guide to Sources.* Cambridge, Massachusetts: Schenkman, 1969. (Distributed by Harper & Row, New York.)

White, C. M., and others. (Eds.) *Sources of Information in the Social Sciences: A Guide to the Literature*. Chicago: American Library Association, 1973. See pp. 375–424.

Introductory works include:

Hilgard, E. R. *Introduction to Psychology*. (5th ed.) New York: Harcourt Brace Jovanovich, 1971.

Morgan, C. T., and King, R. A. *Introduction to Psychology*. (5th ed.) New York: McGraw-Hill, 1971.

Some histories of psychology are:

Brett, G. S. *A History of Psychology*. (3 vols.) London: Allen and Unwin 1912–1921. Reprinted by MIT Press, Cambridge, Massachusetts, 1965. A basic general history.

Lowry, R. *The Evolution of Psychological Theory: 1650 to the Present*. Chicago: Aldine, 1971.

Reuchlin, M. *Histoire de la psychologie*. Paris: Presses universitaires de France, 1967.

Wertheimer, M. *A Brief History of Psychology*. New York: Holt, Rinehart and Winston, 1970.

Wordsworth, R. S., and Sheehan, M. R. *Contemporary Schools of Psychology*. (9th ed.) London: Methuen, 1965. Covers twentieth-century schools of psychology to 1960.

For works dealing with education and research in psychology internationally see:

International Opportunities for Advanced Training and Research in Psychology. Washington, D.C.: American Psychological Association, 1966. Includes information on eighty countries.

Kulik, J. A. *Undergraduate Education in Psychology*. Washington, D.C.: American Psychological Association, 1973.

Works on psychology in various parts of the world include:

Ardilla, R. "Psychology in Latin America." *American Psychologist*, 1968, *23*, 567–574.

Crovitz, E. "Current Trends in Psychology in Europe." *International Psychology*, 1974, *15*, 11.

Sexton, V. S., and Misiak, H. (Eds.) *Psychology Around the World*. Monterey, California: Brooks/Cole, forthcoming.

CURRENT BIBLIOGRAPHIES

Bibliographie der psychologischen Literatur der sozialistischen Länder aus dem Jahre. Berlin, German Democratic Republic: Volk & Wissen, 1960–. Published annually.

Bulletin signalétique. Section 390: *Psychologie, psychopathologie, psychiatrie*. Paris: Centre national de la recherche scientifique, 1961–.

CC-SBC (Current Contents: Social and Behavioral Sciences). Philadelphia: Institute of Scientific Information, 1969–.

JSAS (Journal Supplement Abstract Service): *Catalogue of Selected Documents in Psychology*. Washington, D.C.: American Psychological Association, 1971–. Published quarterly. Abstracts articles written in different branches of the field.

Psychological Abstracts. Washington, D.C.: American Psychological Association, 1927–. Perhaps the single most important bibliographical tool in psychology; abstracts the world's literature in psychology.

Zeitschrift für experimentelle und angewandte Psychologie. Göttingen, Federal Republic of Germany: Verlag für Psychologie, 1953–.

PERIODICALS

For a listing of psychological periodicals throughout the world see:

Psychology: World List of Specialized Periodicals. New York: Humanities Press, 1967.

Tomkins, M., and Shirley, N. *A Checklist of Serials in Psychology and Allied Fields*. Troy, New York: Whitston, 1969.

Some of the important periodicals in the field of psychology are *Acta Psychologica* (Netherlands), *American Journal of Mental Deficiency*, *American Journal of Psychology*, *American Psychologist*, *L'année psychologique* (France), *Archiv für die gesamte Psychologie* (FRG), *British Journal of Psychology*, *British Journal of Social and Clinical Psychology*, *Canadian Journal of Psychology*, *Československá psychologie* (Czechoslovakia), *Developmental Psychology* (US), *European Journal of Psychology* (Netherlands), *International Journal of Psychology* (UK), *International Review of Applied Psychology* (UK), *Journal de psychologie normale et pathologique* (France), *Journal of Abnormal Psychology* (US), *Journal of Applied Psychology* (US), *Journal of Comparative and Physiological Psychology* (US), *Journal of Consulting and Clinical Psychology* (US), *Journal of Counseling Psychology* (US), *Journal of Educational Psychology* (US), *Journal of the Experimental Analysis of Behavior* (US), *Journal of Experimental Psychology* (US), *Journal of Personality and Social Psychology* (US), *Magyar pszichólogia szemle/Hungarian Psychological Review*, *Nordisk psykologi* (Denmark), *Psychoanalytic Review* (US), *Psychologica Belgica* (Belgium), *Psychological Bulletin* (US), *Psychological Review* (US), *Psychologische Forschung* (FRG), *Psychometrika* (US), *Quarterly Journal of Experimental Psychology* (UK), *Revista interamericana de psicología/Interamerican Journal of Psychology* (US), *Shinrigaku kenkyu/Japanese Journal of Psychology*, *Voprosy psihologii* (USSR), *Zeitschrift für Psychologie* (GDR).

ENCYCLOPEDIAS, DICTIONARIES, HANDBOOKS

Arnold, W., and others. (Eds.) *Lexikon der Psychologie.* (3 vols.) Freiburg, Federal Republic of Germany: Herder, 1971–1972.

Beigel, H. G. *Dictionary of Psychology and Related Fields: German-English.* New York: Ungar, 1971.

English, H. B., and English, A. C. *A Comprehensive Dictionary of Psychological and Psychoanalytical Terms: A Guide to Usage.* New York: Longmans, 1958. Reprinted by McKay, New York, 1974.

Eysenck, H. J. (Ed.) *Encyclopedia of Psychology.* New York: Herder and Herder, 1972. Has been published in six languages.

Fraisse, P., and Piaget, J. (Eds.) *Traité de psychologie expérimentale.* Paris: Presses universitaires de France, 1963–1967.

Goldenson, R. M. *Encyclopedia of Human Behavior: Psychology, Psychiatry, and Mental Health.* (2 vols.) Garden City, New York: Doubleday, 1970.

Gottschaldt, K., and others. *Handbuch der Psychologie.* (12 vols.) Göttingen, Federal Republic of Germany: Verlag für Psychologie. A comprehensive survey.

Hehlmann, W. *Wörterbuch der Psychologie.* Stuttgart, Federal Republic of Germany: A. Kröner, 1968.

International Encyclopedia of the Social Sciences. New York: Macmillan, 1968. Provides general treatments of various aspects of the field.

Koch, S. *Psychology: A Study of a Science.* (7 vols.) New York: McGraw-Hill, 1969–1973.

Pieron, H. *Vocabulaire de la psychologie.* Paris: Presses universitaires de France, 1968. Includes some German and English equivalents to the French terms.

White, C. M., and others. (Eds.) *Sources of Information in the Social Sciences: A Guide to the Literature.* Chicago: American Library Association, 1973. Lists specialized handbooks in the field of psychology.

DIRECTORIES

Directories to educational and research facilities in the field are:

Graduate Study in Psychology for 1975–76. Washington, D.C.: American Psychological Association, 1974. Provides information on programs of study, financial aid, educational facilities in graduate programs in psychology in the United States, Canada, and Lebanon.

International Opportunities for Advanced Training and Research in Psychology. Washington, D.C.: American Psychological Association, 1966.

Provides a discussion of psychological activities in countries throughout the world and includes information on research and training both in and out of universities, national organizations, bibliographical sources, professional and legal criteria for recognition of psychologists, and international exchanges of students and scholars.

International Resources in Clinical Psychology. New York: McGraw-Hill, 1964. Provides details of training in the branch of clinical psychology.

Minerva, Forschungsinstitute. Berlin, Federal Republic of Germany: de Gruyter, 1972. Lists research institutes throughout the world.

The World of Learning. London: Europa, 1947–. Includes universities, colleges, research centers, and learned societies.

PUBLIC ADMINISTRATION
(Field of Study)

More than most other disciplines, public administration has had difficulty in being recognized as a coherent body of theory and practice applied to a specific field of human endeavor. It covers a vast field concerned with the study of growth, operation, and improvement of public bureaucracy. It investigates the relationship between the bureaucracy and government, and between the bureaucracy and the society in which it operates, and thereby provides a better understanding of the ways in which an efficient process of government may be carried on.

Public administration, as a discipline, draws upon a wide range of the social sciences—particularly economics, sociology, political science, and psychology—and an even broader range of applied fields, including law, business administration, and even engineering and architecture. The modern discipline of public administration covers every level of government (and the relations between the levels) and touches upon virtually every area in which governmental policy is made. With the recent advent of greater interest in the making and execution of public policy, the field has been extended in the United

States beyond the traditional confines of bureaucratic organization and management to such diverse subfields as urban renewal, prison reform, labor-management relations in the bureaucracy, and welfare administration. Since these areas involve the expenditure of public funds, the student of public administration must also be concerned with budgeting, fiscal policy, productivity, and evaluation of the effectiveness of policy programs.

Like other fields of study, the discipline has been divided into increasingly specialized areas, including public personnel administration and comparative administration (not only the comparative study of administrative systems but the development of new systems in newly independent countries). Because of the intimate connection between administration and law, further specializations have developed in the regulation of public agencies and the staffing and operation of legislatures, particularly (in the United States) at the state level.

As a coherent body of knowledge, the discipline is largely a product of the twentieth century, although several aspects of it were taught earlier in European universities as branches of other disciplines, particularly law. In the United States the father of public administration was Woodrow Wilson, who, in his prepresidential career as an academic, published an essay in 1887 on "The Study of Administration." The subsequent development of the discipline in the early decades of the twentieth century set the stage for two major themes, which have continued to play a role in the study of public administration in the United States. One of these themes centers around the running discussions between the "practitioners" and the "theorists." The practitioners insist that the discipline should deal with the actual problems confronting administrators; the theorists insist that a coherent concept of the discipline can emerge only through theory and the principles derived from it. The two sides have, over the years, attained a degree of compromise in their views, but the marriage continues to be an uneasy one.

The second theme, which has had far-reaching effects on the teaching of public administration, involves the dichotomy between politics and administration. Historically, proponents of the functionalist school sought to divorce administration from politics by emphasizing formal principles of management; administration, they argued, is the function of the executive while politics is the realm of the legislature. However simplistic their argument may sound today, it illustrates their desire to have public administration accepted as a "science," uncontaminated by considerations of politics. The inevitable reaction to this position was a return after 1940 to a focus on political influences on administration and on the necessity for administrators to understand the political, social, and economic context in which they were required to operate.

Side by side with this tendency has been the growth of scholarship stressing organizational behavior and the search for specific tools to analyze behavior. A very important contribution to the contemporary study of organizational behavior, the theory of bureaucratic organization, was outlined by the German sociologist Max Weber, whose writings, although published in the early years of the twentieth century, were not available in English until 1946.

As the bureaucracy at every level of government grew more complex, public administration turned to the study of management in large industrial organizations to find out whether lessons could be learned from the private sector of the economy. The relationship between management techniques in the two sectors has become close enough so that, in at least some schools in the United States, business and public administration have been combined, though not totally successfully. This combination of training is more generally applicable to the developing areas of the world, where industry is organized on a parastatal model;

that is, where ownership of enterprises is jointly shared by government and the private sector, frequently with the public sector retaining a majority interest. In general, however, although the management of private enterprise involves many of the same principles as those in the public sector (particularly in large corporations, in such areas as personnel management and organizational behavior), there are sizable differences between corporate management and the management of government agencies staffed by civil servants, so that the two are not interchangeable.

The discipline of public administration outside the United States has avoided some of this controversy by its strong association with the legal aspects of the field, particularly with administrative law. Administrative theory, however, has been stressed somewhat less than the practical training of administrators. Western Europe has had a long tradition of schools of administration, not only for general training of state officials but also for specialized training of government agents. In the United Kingdom the less formally structured model of the "staff college" has been developed as a training center, particularly for in-service training. The continental model of the French National School of Administration has been used in Latin America and elsewhere. In the 1970s, however, United States management theory, particularly as it is applied in private enterprise, has been gaining rapid popularity. The newer schools of administration in Africa and Asia are seeking to adapt certain United States techniques to their needs for training civil servants, while in many cases retaining the basic model of the colonial period.

Techniques of public administration that have been found suitable in the United States are not, however, readily transferable to other governmental systems and cultures. Because bureaucratic organizations grow within and respond to the political and social structure of a country, the

attempt to impose one model upon another has almost always failed. The International Bank for Reconstruction and Development has recently emphasized the need for adapting management training procedures in developing countries to indigenous needs.

Since the mid 1950s, interest in non-American administrative systems has led to a rapidly accelerated growth of research in comparative or cross-cultural public administration by United States theorists. This attempt to strengthen the theoretical foundations of the field has had limited value to United States practitioners, who feel that it contributes little to a greater understanding of domestic administrative problems. The research in this subfield, however, has provided intellectual strength to the discipline as a whole, and substantial interest in it has been shown in Europe and in the developing world.

Comparative administration is only one of several new directions being taken by the discipline of public administration. The study of the formulation and implementation of policy also is of growing importance. This interest in policy increased with the new ability, inspired by computerization, to evaluate the potential effects that policies may have on society and the actual effects of policies that have already been implemented. The application of economic theory to certain policy areas—for example, urban and environmental policy studies —has strengthened this new direction.

The rapidly increasing need for trained administrators has expanded training facilities throughout the world. Postgraduate study in public administration increased substantially in the 1965–1975 decade, partly because of the availability of professional staff. Schools in the United States generally emphasize quantitative and analytical subjects, with special concern for fiscal policy and program evaluation. In some schools specialized degrees in environment, welfare, national security, urban affairs, and science and technology have been developed in the policy field. Most formal programs include training in economics, political science, and other social sciences, as well as business management. There is also a growing trend toward requiring, as part of the student's program, practical experience through internships. Training outside the United States is becoming equally professionalized. Requirements for entry into the bureaucracy often include higher standards of professional training, particularly in quantitative methods. The need for trained administrative personnel in the developing countries is acute; institutes and schools of public administration are everywhere being created, but their effectiveness is limited by a lack of experienced teachers. For many of these countries, particularly those in Africa, the objective is first to upgrade the performance of experienced civil servants by in-service training, usually at the mid-career level. Where indigenous industry is developing sufficiently, management programs for public and private service are combined, so that today's civil servant may be tomorrow's manager of a business, whether privately or publicly owned.

L. GRAY COWAN

Levels and Programs of Study

Programs in public administration generally require as a prerequisite a secondary education and lead to the following awards: certificate or diploma, bachelor's degree, (B.P.A., B.A.), master's degree (M.B.A., M.P.A., M.A.), the doctorate, or their equivalents. Programs deal with the principles and practices of public administration and consist of instruction and group discussion and, on advanced levels, seminars and research.

Principal course content for work not leading to a first university degree usually includes objectives of public policy, the theory of taxation, economic stabilization, the structure of government, the civil service, government and the community, cultural influences in government, regionalism, nationalism, and intergovernmental relations. Background courses are often included in economics, sociology, political science, foreign languages, and history.

In work leading to the first university degree, emphasis is given to governmental processes, political systems, organization theory, administration of the public service, management, quantitative methods and statistics, intergovernmental relations, and public finance. A broad background is often provided in the social sciences and related subjects. Principal course content usually includes specialized public administration subjects such as local government, administrative law, legislative procedures, the budgetary process, the policy process, the planning process, coordination and control, and intergovernmental relations. Background courses usually include economics, sociology, human relations, accounting and finance, the sociology of groups, constitutional history, operations research, data processing, and administrative communications and control techniques.

In work leading to a postgraduate university degree, emphasis is given to independent research, demonstrated by the presentation and defense of a scholarly thesis or dissertation, and to the theoretical and historical background of the subjects studied. Background study in other areas of administration and public policy is often included in these programs. Principal subject matter areas within which study and research projects tend to fall include government forms and administrative agencies, comparative government, intergovernmental relations, objectives of public policy, administration and management of the public services, and legislative procedures. Background studies, designed to provide a broadly based program for an understanding of public administration principles and practices, usually include a broad range of social studies (such as economics, sociology, and psychology), the humanities (such as history, languages, literature, and philosophy), business administration, law, and natural sciences.

[This section was based on UNESCO's *International Standard Classification of Education (ISCED): Three Stage Classification System, 1974* (Paris: UNESCO, 1974).]

Major International and National Organizations

INTERNATIONAL

International City Management Association
1140 Connecticut Avenue NW
Washington, D.C. 20036 USA

International Civil Service Training
  Organization
Orientation à la fonction internationale (OFI)
36 rue la Perouse
75 Paris 16e, France

International Institute for Municipal Sciences
  in Vienna
Internationales Institut für
  Kommunalwissenschaften
Fürstengasse 1
Palais Liechtenstein
Vienna, Austria

International Institute of Administrative
  Sciences (IIAS)
Institut international des sciences
  administratives (IISA)
25 rue de la Charité
1040 Brussels, Belgium

International Political Science Association
  (IPSA)
Association internationale de science politique
27 rue Saint-Guillaume
Paris 7e, France

International Union of Local Authorities
  (IULA)
Union internationale des villes et pouvoirs
  locaux (UIV)
45 Wassenaarseweg
The Hague, Netherlands

REGIONAL

African Training and Research Center in
  Administration for Development
Centre africain de formation et de recherches
  administratives pour le développement
  (CAFRAD)
19 rue Victor Hugo, P.O. Box 310
Tangiers, Morocco

Arab Organization for Administrative
  Sciences
Arab League Building
Cairo, Egypt

Asian Center for Development Administration
P.O. Box 2224
Kuala Lumpur 01–02, Malaysia

Central American Institute of Public
  Administration
Instituto centroamericano de administración
  pública (ICAP)
Edificio Schyfter
Pisos 5° y 6°, avenida Central y Calle 2ª
P.O. Box 10025
San José, Costa Rica

Comité latinoamericano de decanos de escuelas
  de administración (CLADEA)
Apartado Aéreo 2189
Cali, Colombia

Eastern Regional Organization for Public
  Administration (EROPA)
Organisation régionale de l'orient pour
  l'administration publique
Rizal Hall, Padre Faura St.
Manila, Philippines

European Conference of Local Authorities
Conférence européenne des pouvoirs locaux
Council of Europe
avenue de l'Europe
67 Strasbourg, France

Inter-American Municipal Organization
Obispo 351
Havana, Cuba

Inter-American Training Center in Public
  Administration
Calle Peru No. 130
Buenos Aires, Argentina

For a complete list of organizations in public administration see:

World Index of Social Science Institutions. Paris: UNESCO, 1970–.

NATIONAL

Canada:
  Institute of Public Administration
    of Canada
  897 Bay Street
  Toronto, Ontario

United Kingdom:
  Royal Institute of Public Administration
    (RIPA)
  24 Park Crescent
  London W1N 4BP, England

United States:
  American Consortium for International
    Public Administration (ACIPA)
  1225 Connecticut Avenue NW
  Washington, D.C. 20036

American Society for Public
Administration (ASPA)
1225 Connecticut Avenue NW
Washington, D.C. 20036

National Association of Schools of Public
Affairs and Administration
1225 Connecticut Avenue NW
Washington, D.C. 20036

For an extensive list of national organizations
of public administration see:

Minerva, Wissenschaftliche Gesellschaften. Berlin,
Federal Republic of Germany: de Gruyter,
1972.
World Index of Social Science Institutions. Paris:
UNESCO, 1970–.

American and Canadian organizations are
listed in these directories:

Encyclopedia of Associations. (9th ed.) Detroit:
Gale Research, 1975.
*Public Administration Organizations: A Directory
of Unofficial Organizations in the Field of Public
Administration in the United States and Canada.*
(7th ed.) Chicago: Public Administration
Clearing House, 1954.
United States Department of Health, Educa-
tion and Welfare. *Education Directory: Edu-
cation Associations.* Washington, D.C.: U.S.
Government Printing Office, annual.

Principal Information Sources

GENERAL

Among the general guides to the literature in
the field are:

Brock, C. *The Literature of Political Science.* New
York: Bowker, 1969.
Grasham, W. E., and Germain, J. *Canadian Pub-
lic Administration Bibliography.* Toronto, On-
tario: Institute of Public Administration of
Canada, 1972.
Harmon, R. B. *Political Science: A Bibliographi-
cal Guide to the Literature.* Metuchen, New
Jersey: Scarecrow Press, 1965.
Heady, F., and Stokes, S. L. *Comparative Pub-
lic Administration; A Selected Bibliography.*
(2nd ed.) Ann Arbor: University of Michigan
Press, 1960.
Holler, F. L. *The Information Sources of Political
Science.* Santa Barbara, California: ABC-
Clio, 1971.
Mars, D., and Frederickson, H. G. *Suggested
Library in Public Administration.* Los Angeles:
School of Public Administration, University
of Southern California, 1964.
McCurdy, H. E. *Public Administration: A Bibliog-
raphy.* Washington, D.C.: College of Public
Affairs, American University, 1972.

Wynar, L. R. *Guide to Reference Materials in Political Science.* Rochester, New York: Libraries
Unlimited, 1968.

For an understanding of public administration as it is conceived and taught, see the
following:

Caiden, G. *The Dynamics of Public Administra-
tion: Guidelines to Current Transformations in
Theory and Practice.* New York: Holt, Rine-
hart and Winston, 1971.
Heady, F. *Public Administration: A Comparative
Perspective.* Englewood Cliffs, New Jersey:
Prentice-Hall, 1966.
Molitor, A. *The University Teaching of Social Sci-
ences: Public Administration.* Paris: UNESCO,
1959.
Mosher, F. C. *American Public Administration:
Past, Present, Future.* University, Alabama:
University of Alabama Press, 1975.
Siffin, W. J. *Toward the Comparative Study of
Public Administration.* Bloomington: Depart-
ment of Government, University of Indiana,
1957.
Stone, D. C. (Ed.) *Education in Public Administra-
tion.* Brussels: International Institute of
Administrative Sciences, 1963.

Classic works in the field include:

Barnard, C. I. *The Functions of the Executive.*
Cambridge, Massachusetts: Harvard Uni-
versity Press, 1938.
Gulick, L., and Urick, L. (Eds.) *Papers on the
Science of Administration.* Clifton, New Jersey:
Augustus M. Kelley, 1937.
March, J. G. (Ed.) *Handbook of Organizations.*
Chicago: Rand McNally, 1965.
Merton, R. K., and others. (Eds.) *Reader in
Bureaucracy.* New York: Free Press, 1952.
Simon, H. *Administrative Behavior: A Study of
Decision-Making Processes in Administrative
Organization.* (2nd ed.) New York: Free
Press, 1965.
Waldo, D. *The Study of Public Administration.* New
York: Random House, 1955.

On aspects of public administration in developing countries see:

*Organizing Schools and Institutes of Administra-
tion.* Pittsburgh: Graduate School of Public
and International Affairs, 1969.
Robinson, M. E. *Education for Social Change:
Establishing Institutes of Public and Business
Administration Abroad.* Washington, D.C.:
Brookings Institution, 1961.
United Nations. *Development Administration:
Current Approaches and Trends in Public Admin-
istration for National Development.* New York:
United Nations, 1975. Document ST ESA
SER. E 3.

For a guide to some two thousand books and periodicals of special interest to institutes of administration in developing countries see:

Public Administration: A Select Bibliography. (3rd rev. ed.) London: Overseas Development Administration, 1973.

CURRENT BIBLIOGRAPHIES

For sources of current information in public administration consult the following general bibliographies:

ABC POL SCI: Advance Bibliography of Contents: Political Science and Government. Santa Barbara, California: ABC-Clio, 1969–.

International Bibliography of Political Science. Chicago: Aldine, 1952–.

The Public Administration Abstracts and Index of Articles. New Delhi: India Institute of Public Administration, monthly. Indexes thirty to forty English-language journals in each issue.

Public Affairs Information Service Bulletin. New York: Public Affairs Information Service, 1915–.

Public Affairs Information Service Foreign Language Index. New York: Public Affairs Information Service, 1971–. Text in French, German, Italian, Portuguese, and Spanish.

Sage Public Administration Abstracts. Beverly Hills, California: Sage Publications, 1974–.

PERIODICALS

The following public administration journals are of international importance: *Administrative Science Quarterly* (US), *Canadian Public Administration, Chinese Journal of Administration* (Taiwan), *Documentación administrativa* (Spain), *Indian Journal of Public Administration, Institut international d'administration publique bulletin* (France), *International Review of Administrative Sciences* (Belgium), *Journal of Comparative Administration* (US), *New Zealand Journal of Public Administration, Public Administration* (Australia), *Public Administration* (United Kingdom), *Public Administration* (India), *Public Administration Review* (US), *Public Policy* (US).

For a complete listing of journals in public administration, consult:

Ulrich's International Periodicals Directory. New York: Bowker, biennial.

ENCYCLOPEDIAS, DICTIONARIES, HANDBOOKS

International Encyclopedia of the Social Sciences. New York: Macmillan, 1968. Includes short articles on public administration topics.

Vocabulaire de l'administration. Paris: Hachette, 1973. A glossary including over one thousand Belgian, Canadian, French, and Swiss administrative terms used in all French-speaking countries.

DIRECTORIES

International educational guides to the study of public administration include:

Catalogue of Social and Economic Development Institutes and Programmes: Training. Paris: Organisation for Economic Co-operation and Development, 1970. Lists training institutes in public administration in OECD countries.

United Nations Directory of National Agencies and Institutions for the Improvement of Public Administration. (Rev. ed.) New York: United Nations, 1973. Lists, by country, official government agencies that deal with public administration, research institutes in the field, and schools and universities that offer courses of study in public administration.

For guides to the study of public administration in the United States see:

Educational Preparation for Public Administration: A List of Colleges and Universities Offering Programs of Training. Chicago: Public Administration Clearing House, annual.

National Association of Schools of Public Affairs and Administration. *Guidelines for Professional Masters Degree Programs in Public Affairs and Administration.* Washington, D.C.: National Association of Schools of Public Affairs and Administration, 1974.

National Association of Schools of Public Affairs and Administration. *Graduate School Programs in Public and Public Administration: 1976 Survey Report of the Member Institutions of the National Association of Schools of Public Affairs and Administration.* Washington, D.C.: National Association of Schools of Public Affairs and Administration, 1976.

RESEARCH CENTERS, INSTITUTES, INFORMATION CENTERS

Most countries have centers or institutes of public administration. For guides to United States centers see:

Directory of Organizations and Individuals Professionally Engaged in Governmental Research and Related Activities. New York: Governmental Research Association, annual.

Haro, R. P. *A Directory of Governmental, Public, and Urban Affairs Research Centers in the United States.* Davis: Institute of Governmental Affairs, University of California, 1969.

Palmer, A. M., and Kruzas, A. T. *Research Centers Directory.* (5th ed.) Detroit: Gale Research, 1975. Supplement 1, *New Research Centers,* May 1975.

For centers throughout the world consult:

Minerva, Forschungsinstitute. Berlin, Federal Republic of Germany: de Gruyter, 1972.
World Index of Social Science Institutions. Paris: UNESCO, 1970–.

PUBLIC FINANCING OF HIGHER EDUCATION

See Financing of Higher Education: Financing of Institutions and Systems.

PUBLIC HEALTH
(Field of Study)

Public Health (as distinguished from clinical medicine, which deals with individual patients) is a discipline concerned with the health of populations— specifically, the promotion of health, prevention of disease, organization of medical care, and rehabilitation. Public health includes, but is not limited to, preventive medicine, community medicine, occupational health, and environmental health.

Specializations in public health include two basic sciences of public health and various applied branches of public health. The two basic public health sciences, biostatistics (the science of giological measurement and analysis) and epidemiology (the study of the frequency and distribution of disease in populations and of disease causation, are buttressed by biochemistry (particularly nutrition), microbiology, parasitology, medical entomology, ecology, sociology/anthropology, political science, political economy, and other supporting disciplines. Applied branches of public health include administrative sciences/public health administration, public health education, public health engineering, sanitary engineering, veterinary medicine (zoonosis), health education, mental hygiene (including the treatment of alcoholism and drug addiction), human nutrition, maternal and child health, school health, medical care organization, hospital administration, international health, health economics, occupational health, tropical medicine, dental health, and family planning/population control.

Education in public health is based on a core of epidemiology, biostatistics, and public health administration, with varying emphasis on other fields. For example, tropical medicine links the basic core with parasitology, microbiology, and clinical medicine in the control of tropical disease. Mental hygiene links the basic core with psychiatry and psychology. Dental health programs link the basic core with densitry, particularly in prophylactic and mass screening programs. The basic core sciences are linked with engineering in the construction of water supply and sewage disposal systems and in the monitoring of radioactivity, pollution and toxic substances due to increased population, uncontroled technology, and environmental deterioration. Spiraling costs of medical care throughout the world have necessitated linking the public health core approaches with economics in the discipline of health economics. Concerns about costs of health services, coverage, and the constraints of health manpower shortages have given impetus to health planning.

Although some of the precepts of public health date back to Hippocrates, modern training dates to the period from 1910 to the 1930s, when the Rockefeller Foundation established schools of public health throughout the world. These schools were established in order to provide trained public health officers, sanitarians, and public health nurses to carry out public health programs, so that hookworm, malaria, yellow fever, and other major infectious diseases of the time could be controlled. The first program of formal education in the field of public health was developed at the Massachusetts Institute of Technology (MIT). However, the first school of public health was established at John Hopkins University (in Baltimore,

Maryland); this school was planned by Wickliff Rose of the Rockefeller Foundation and William Henry Welch of Hopkins in 1916. Conceptual tools of modern public health began to emerge in the late nineteenth and early twentieth centuries, when understanding of the causative agents of infectious disease and of their mechanisms of propagation and transmission led pioneers such as Louis Pasteur, Robert Koch, Sir Ronald Ross, Walter Reed, James Carroll, and Welch to develop means of prevention.

Important early stimuli to systematic development of public health services were the worsening of urban health during industrialization, the massive spread of epidemic diseases, and poor rural health resulting from endemic diseases and malnutrition. The deterioration of health in crowded, unsanitary, industrial cities in the nineteenth century led to surveys of the relationship between poverty, communicable disease, and poor environment. Two major surveys, the Chadwick report in England in 1842 and the Shattuck Sanitary Commission report in Massachusetts in 1850, led to estblishment of governmental health boards and health departments and legal enforcement of public health measures to protect the public. The threat of epidemics led to a series of international health conferences, the first in Paris in 1851. The League of Nations Health Program and eventually the World Health Organization (WHO) developed from the earlier international conferences. Endemic hookworm disease, malaria, and pellagra in the rural southern United States led the Rockefeller Foundation to develop research programs on cause and prevention and action programs for the control of these diseases. The studies and control programs were later extended to other countries of the world.

The major recent developments in public health in more affluent countries involve shifts from the problems of infectious diseases to those of chronic diseases. Public health in industrialized centers is moving from major emphasis on vaccination programs and epidemiology of infectious sidease to the study and prevention of risk factors in chromic diseases and for alerting the general public to the hazards of smoking, excessive alcohol consumption, overeating, and underexercising. Most of the health problems of the world today, as in the past, will not respond to individual medical care but instead require a unified, comprehensive approach, emphasizing prevention. A recent trend is that public health is assuming more responsibility for planning, organizing, managing, and evaluating programs of medical care.

In environmental health there is increasing emphasis on control of pollutants in air and water in industrialized countries and control of the working environment. In developing countries public health environmental programs attempt to control biological contaminants in water and epidemic and endemic diseases, and to dispose of sewage safely. Since most deaths in these countries are caused by malnutrition and infection, of major importance is improvement of food production and use, individual control of fertility, child-rearing practices, and maternal-child health and family-planning services. General recognition of the major health hazards of rapid population growth in an increasing number of countries has caused rapid expansion of national family-planning and population control programs. Growing shortages of food are manifested not only in endemic malnutrition but also in periodic famines. In industrialized countries, by contrast, those involved with the nutritional aspects of public health have had to become concerned with the problems of overnutrition.

Public health training is most extensively developed in the USSR and the United States. In the Soviet Union public health permeates the entire medical training, and one of the three basic training programs for physicians is a public health program including sanitation and epidemiology. In the United States nineteen schools of public health have been established at the university level. In addition, both countries emphasize the training of physicians, nurses, dentists, and other health professionals at a postgraduate level. In some other countries, however, public health training is at an undergraduate vocational level. Middle- and lower-level training prepares such public health personnel as sanitary inspectors, sanitarians, staff public health nurses, and health educators.

The increasing concern for public health is reflected in the formation of a variety of professional associations. The World Federation of Public Health Associations, an international association of public health associations with headquarters in Geneva, has a membership of twenty-four national public health associations. The American Public Health Association is an active group with 25,000 individual members. There is also an Association of Schools of Public Health with full-time staff and headquarters in Washington, D.C.

TIMOTHY D. BAKER

CARL E. TAYLOR

MELVYN C. THORNE

Levels and Programs of Study

Programs in public health generally require as a minimum prerequisite a secondary education and lead to the following awards: certificate or diploma in sanitary inspection, Bachelor of Science degree, Master of Public Health degree, Master of Science degree, the doctorate, or their equivalents. Programs deal with areas that affect public health and consist of classroom and laboratory discussion and, on advanced levels, seminar sessions dealing with advanced topics in the field of public health.

Programs that lead to awards not equivalent to a first university degre are concerned with areas that affect public health (for instance, communicable diseases, standards of sanitation in the food and water supply, and disposal of garbage and sewage). Principal course content usually includes human anatomy and physiology, communicable diseases, public health organization, sanitation, food hygiene, and law and jurisprudence relating to public health. Background courses often included are biology, microbiology, chemistry, physics, mathematics, food technology, and water technology.

Programs that lead to a first university degree deal with items that affect public health (for instance, communicable diseases, hygienic standards in food and water supply, and disposal of garbage and sewage). Principal course content usually includes subjects such as biology, chemistry, biochemistry, microbiology, immunology, virology, parasitology, sanitation, communicable diseases, quarantine, nutrition, and other areas pertaining to public health. Background courses often included are basic anatomy and physiology; statistics and population dynamics; food, milk, and water inspection; and psychology and sociology.

Programs that lead to a postgraduate university degree deal with advanced topics in the field of public health. Emphasis is placed on original research work as substantiated by the presentation of a scholarly thesis of dissertation. Principal subject matter areas within which courses and research projects tend to fall include biostatistics, environmental health sciences, epidemiology, physiology, behavioral science, health services administration, maternal and child health, microbiology, nutrition, population sciences, sanitary engineering, and tropical public health.

[This section was based on UNESCO's *International Standard Classification of Education (ISCED)*. (Paris: UNESCO, 1976.]

Major International and National Organizations

INTERNATIONAL

Central American Public Health Council
Consejo centroamericano de la salud pública
% Organización de estados centroamericanos
Oficina centroamericana
San Salvador, El Salvador

Council of Europe
Conseil de l'Europe
Public Health Division
avenue de l'Europe
67 Strasbourg (Bas-Rhin), France

International Epidemiological Association
(IEA)
Association internationale de'épidémiologie
% Oxford University Press
Press Road
Neasden, London NW10 0DD, England

International Federation for Hygiene,
Preventive Medicine and Social Medicine
(IFH PSM)
Fédération internationale d'hygiène, de
médecine préventive et de médecine sociale
(FIH MPS)
Ilvia Cola di Rienzo
00192 Rome, Italy
or Mariahilferstrasse 177,
A-1150 Vienna, Austria

International Federation for Public Health
Fédération internationale pour la santé
publique
30 avenue Reymondin
1009 Pully, Switzerland

International Society for Research on
Civilization Diseases and Vital Substances
Société internationale pour la recherche sur
les maladies de vicilisation et les substances
vitales
Bemeroderstrasse 61
3 Hanover-Kirchrode, Federal Republic of
Germany

International Union of School and University
Hygiene and Medicine
Union internationale d'hygiène et de mé
médecines scolaires et universitaires
Chateau de Longchamp, Bois de Boulogne
75016 Paris, France

Permanent Commission and International
Association on Occupational Health
Commission permanente et association
internationale pour la médecine du travail
Clinica del lavoro
via S. Barnabe 8
20122 Milan, Italy

World Federation of Public Health Associations
% American Public Health Association
Division of International Health Programs
1015 18th Street NW
Washington, D.C. 20036 USA

World Health Organization (WHO)
1211 Geneva 27, Switzerland

For a more complete listing of international
associations and organizations in and related
to public health consult:

Yearbook of International Organizations. Brussels:
Union of International Associations,
biennial.
Wasserman, P. (Ed.) *Health Organizations of
the United States, Canada and Internationally.*
(3rd ed.) Washington, D.C. McGrath, 1974.

NATIONAL

The following is a listing of the members of
the World Federation of Public Health Associations. A more complete listing, including
other national public health organizations, can
be obtained from the WFPHA.

Argentina:
Asociación de la salud pública
% School of Public Health
M.T. de Alvear 2202
Buenos Aires

Australia:
Australian Public Health Association
Department of Social Medicine
Monask Medical School/Alfred Hospital
Commercial Road
Prahran 3181, Victoria

Belgium:
Association belge d'hygiène de médecine
sociale
Ecole de santé publique
Université libre de Bruxelles
100 rue Belliard, B 1040
Brussels

Brazil:
Sociedade brasileira de higiene
avenida Rio Branco 185
Rio de Janeiro

Canada:
Canadian Public Health Association
55 Parkdale Avenue
Ottawa, Ontario K1Y 1E5

Chile:
Sociedad chilena de salubridad
avenida Vitacura 6480, Casa 2
Santiago

Federal Republic of Germany:
Federal Association of Public Health of
the Federal Republic of Germany
Edisonweg 4, 8031 Neuesting

France:
Société française d'hygiène de médecine
sociale et de génie sanitaire
Chef du service d'hygiène
Faculté de médecine
76 Rouen

German Democratic Republic:
Gesellschaft allgemeine und kommunale
Hygiene der DDR
Franckeplatz 1, Haus 36
402 Halle (Saale)

Guatemala:
Asociación médica de salud pública de
Guatemala
Apartado 1188
Guatemala City

Hungary:
Hungarian Society for Public Health
Gyali ut 2–6
Budapest IX

India:
Indian Public Health Association
110 Chittaranjan Avenue
Calcutta 12

Iran:
Iranian Public Health Association
P.O. Box 1310
Tehran

Israel:
Israel Public Health Association
101 Arlosorov Street
Tel Aviv

Italy:
Associazione italiana per l'igiene e la
sanità
via Salaria, 237
Rome

Japan:
Japan Public Health Association
1-29-8 Shinjuku, Shinjuku-ku
Tokyo

Lebanon:
Lebanese Public Health Association
Sadat Street, Ras-Beirut
Beirut

Mexico:
Mexican Public Health Society
Apartado Postal 69-608
Mexico 21, D.F.

New Zealand:
New Zealand Branch of the Royal Society
of Health
P.O. Box 5013
Wellington

Nigeria:
Society of Health of Nigeria
4 Airport Road, Ikeja
P.M.B. 1061 YABA
Lagos

Pakistan:
Public Health Association of Pakistan
3 Shara-e-Fatimah Jinnah
Lahore

Philippines:
Philippine Public Health Association
Bureau of Quarantine, Port Area
Manila

United Kingdom:
Royal Society of Health
13 Grosvenor Place
London SW1X 7EN, England

United States:
American Public Health Association
1015 18th Street NW
Washington, D.C. 20036

Principal Information Sources

GENERAL

Guides to the literature include:

Ash., J. "Current Reference Works in Public Health." *American Journal of Public Health,* 1972,. *62*(7), 1014–1017. An annotated bibliography of the major reference works in this area. Broad coverage of the important areas of public health, including industry; statistics; demography; air, water, land, and pesticide pollution; medical care and health administration; occupational health; epidemiology and infectious and communicable diseases; maternal and child health; school health and public health nursing.

LaRocco, A., and Jones, B. "A Bookshelf in Public Health, Medical Care, and Allied Fields." *Bulletin of the Medical Library Association,* 1972, *60*(1), 32–94. A bibliography of nonserial publications; references are mostly from 1960 to 1972, and all entries are annotated; intended as a guide to the development of a research collection.

University of London. *Dictionary Catalogue of the London School of Hygiene and Tropical Medicine.* (7 vols.) Boston: Hall, 1965.

Williams, K. N. (Comp.) *Health and Development: An Annotated, Indexed Bibliography.* Baltimore: Johns Hopkins University, Department of International Health, 1972.

World Health Organization. *Publications: Catalogue, 1947–1973.* Geneva: WHO, 1974.

World Health Organization. *Publications of the World Health Organization, 1968–1972: A Bibliography.* Geneva: WHO, 1974.

Overviews and standard texts for the field include:

Burton, L. E., and Smith, H. H. *Public Health*

and Community Medicine for the Allied Medical Professions. (2nd ed.) Baltimore: Williams & Wilkins, 1975.

Grad, F. P. *Public Health Law Manual: A Handbook of the Legal Aspects of Public Health Administration and Enforcement.* New York: American Public Health Association, 1973.

Hobson, W. (Ed.) *The Theory and Practice of Public Health.* (4th ed.) London: Oxford University Press, 1975.

Kark, S. L. *Epidemiology and Community Medicine.* New York: Appleton, 1974.

Kilbourne, E. D., and Smillie, W. C. (Eds.) *Public Health and Human Ecology.* (4th ed.) New York: Macmillan, 1969.

MacMahon, B. *Epidemiology: Principles and Methods.* Boston: Little, Brown, 1970.

Sartwell, P. E. (Ed.) *Preventive Medicine and Public Health.* (10th ed.) New York: Appleton-Century-Crofts, 1974.

Comparative education sources include:

Cassel, J., and others. *The Education and Training of Engineers for Environmental Health.* Geneva: WHO, 1970.

Cottrell, J. D. (In collaboration with B. Kesic and R. Senault.) *The Teaching of Public Health in Europe.* Geneva: WHO, 1969.

Fry, J., and Farndale, W. A. (Eds.) *International Medical Care: A Comparison and Evaluation of Medical Care Services Throughout the World.* Oxford, England: Medical and Technical Publishing Co., 1972.

Health Education: A Programme Review; A Report by the Director-General of the World Health Organization to the 53rd Session of the Executive Board. Geneva: WHO, 1974.

Lowe, C. R., and Kostrzewski, J. *Epidemiology: A Guide to Teaching Methods.* Essex, England: Longman, 1974. Edited for the International Epidemiological Association in collaboration with WHO. Available in Polish, English, French, German, Spanish, and Serbo-Croatian.

Miller, G. E., and Fulop, T. (Eds.) *World Health Organization. Educational Strategies for the Health Professions.* Public Health Paper No. 61. Geneva: WHO, 1974.

Postgraduate Education and Training in Public Health. WHO Technical Report Series, 533. Geneva: WHO, 1973. Report of a WHO Expert Committee.

Studies on the Training of Medical Students in Public Health. Strasbourg, France: Council of Europe, European Public Health Committee, 1973.

Training of Research Workers in the Medical Sciences: Proceedings of a Round Table Conference Organized by CIOMS with the Assistance of WHO and UNESCO, Geneva, 10–11 September, 1970. Geneva: WHO, 1972.

World Health Organization. *Aspects of Medical Education in Developing Countries.* Public Health Paper No. 47. Geneva: WHO, 1972.

World Health Organization. *Development of Educational Programmes for the Health Professions.* Public Health Paper No. 52. Geneva: WHO, 1973.

World Health Organization. *Travelling Seminar on Organization and Administration of Schools of Public Health; March, 1965, Alexandria, Egypt, Beirut, Ankara, Turkey.* Washington, D.C.: Pan American Health Organization, 1965.

World Health Organization. *World Directory of Schools of Public Health.* Geneva: WHO, 1971.

Histories of the field include:

Brockington, C. F. *A Short History of Public Health.* London: Churchill, 1966.

Hirst, L. F. *The Conquest of Plague; A Study of of the Evolution of Epidemiology.* Oxford, England, Clarendon Press, 1953.

Ramazzini, B. *Diseases of Workers.* New York: Hafner, 1964.

Rosen, G. *A History of Public Health.* New York: MD Publications, 1958.

Rosen, G. (Comp.) *From Medical Police to Social Medicine: Essays on the History of Health Care.* New York: Science History Publications, 1974.

Wain, H. *A History of Preventive Medicine.* Springfield, Illinois: Thomas, 1970.

CURRENT BIBLIOGRAPHIES

The principal abstracts and indexes for public health include the following:

Abstracts on Health Effects of Environmental Pollutants. Philadelphia: BioSciences Information Service of Biological Abstracts (BIOSIS), 1972–.

Abstracts on Hygiene. London: Bureau of Hygiene and Tropical Diseases, 1926–. Formerly *Bulletin of Hygiene.*

Excerpta Medica. Section 17: *Public Health, Social Medicine and Hygiene.* Amsterdam: Excerpta Medica Foundation, 1955–.

Excerpta Medica. Section 35: *Occupational Health and Industrial Medicine.* Amsterdam: Excerpta Medica Foundation, 1971–.

Excerpta Medica. Section 46: *Environmental Health and Pollution Control.* Amsterdam: Excerpta Medica Foundation, 1971–.

Index Medicus. Bethesda, Maryland: National Library of Medicine, 1960–.

PERIODICALS

The following is a sampling of some of the important journals in the field: *American Industrial Hygiene Association Journal, American Journal of Epidemiology, American Journal of Public Health, Archives of Environmental Health* (US), *British Journal of Industrial Medicine, Bulletin de l'Institut national de la santé et de la recherche médicale* (France), *Bulletin of the World Health Organization* (Switzerland), *Community Health* (UK), *Environmental Research* (US), *Gigiena i sanitaria* (USSR), *Health Bulletin* (UK), *Health Service Reports* (US), *Indian Journal of Public Health, International Digest of Health Legislation* (Switzerland), *International Journal of Epidemiology* (UK), *International Journal of Health Education* (Switzerland), *International Journal of Health Services* (US), *Journal of Occupational Medicine* (US), *Nederlands tijdschrift voor geneeskunde* (Netherlands), *Preventive Medicine* (US), *Public Health* (UK), *Public Health Monographs* (US), *Revista de sanidad e higiene pública* (Spain), *Schriftenreihe aus dem Gebiete des öffentlichen Gesundheitswesens* (FRG); *Trudy Leningradskogo instituta epidemiologii i mikrobiologii imeni pastera* (USSR); *Vital and Health Statistics: National Center for Health Statistics* (US); *WHO Chronicle* (Switzerland), *World Health Organization Monograph Series* (Switzerland), *World Health Organization Public Health Papers* (Switzerland), *World Health Organization Technical Report Series* (Switzerland), *World Health Statistics Annual* (Switzerland).

Computer retrieval of medical literature may be obtained through the MEDLINE system which is part of the National Library of Medicine, Bethesda, Maryland. The MEDLINE system is used at the World Health Organization in Geneva. For a more comprehensive listing of journals in the field of public health consult:

Ulrich's International Periodicals Directory. New York: Bowker, biennial.
List of Journals Indexed in Index Medicus. Bethesda, Maryland: National Library of Medicine, 1960–. Published annually.
Medical Care Review. Ann Arbor: University of Michigan School of Public Health, 1944–. Formerly *Public Health Economics and Medical Care Abstracts.*
National Institutes of Health. *Scientific Directory and Annual Bibliography.* Washington, D.C.: U.S. Public Health Service, 1959–.
United States Department of Health, Education and Welfare. *Author/Title Catalog of the Department Library.* Boston: Hall, 1965–.

DICTIONARIES

The following are the most widely used dictionaries in the health/medicine field:

Carter, G. B., Dodds, G. H., and Cunningham, P. J. *Dictionary of Midwifery and Public Health.* London: Faber & Faber, 1963.
Dorland's Illustrated Medical Dictionary. (25th ed.) Philadelphia: Saunders, 1974.
Stedman's Medical Dictionary. (22nd ed.) New York: Scribner's, 1974.

DIRECTORIES

Directory of Latin American Schools of Dentistry, Medicine, Nursing, Midwifery, Public Health and Veterinary Medicine. Washington, D.C.: Pan American Health Organization, 1971.
Felton, N.. and others. *Directory of Colleges Offering Degree Programs for Paraprofessionals Employed in the Human Services.* New York: New Careers Development Center, New York University, 1970.
Goodman, N. M. *International Health Organizations and Their Work.* (2nd ed.) Baltimore: Williams & Wilkins, 1971.
Medical Research Index: A Guide to World Medical Research. Guernsey, Channel Islands: Francis Hodgson, 1971.
Palmer, A. M. *Research Centers Directory.* (5th ed.) Detroit: Gale Research, 1975. A listing of United States research centers.
Troupin, J. *Schools of Public Health in the U.S.A. and Canada.* Washington, D.C.: American Public Health Association, annual.
Wasserman, P. *Health Organizations of the United States, Canada and Internationally.* (3rd ed.) Washington, D.C.: McGrath, 1974.
World Directory of Schools of Public Health, 1971. Geneva: WHO, 1972. Describes the systems of postgraduate education in public health and lists the schools offering degree programs in forty-five countries; discusses the courses offered, conditions of admission, curriculum, examinations, and qualifications for degrees for each school.

[Bibliography prepared by Eleanor Druckman.]

PUBLIC RECORD OFFICE, LONDON

See Archives: Public Record Office, London.

PUBLIC RELATIONS

At the college level, public relations is an active effort to create understanding and favorable impressions of the institution in the minds of all individuals and groups important to that institution. The public relations department must interpret the goals of the institution to its public, and it must also interpret the responses of the public to the institution. All avenues of communication are used in this conscious development of positive attitudes toward an organization. Public relations is human relations and as such operates through formal and informal structures.

Public relations is often defined as image making. But image means more than a statement of purpose or objectives—it takes in a whole range of factors that provoke a public response. This response may determine whether or not the academic community can realize its intended goals. Public relations must always define its public. At educational institutions this public includes alumni, parents, staff, faculty, students, other university employees, and townspeople. At state-owned or state-assisted universities, the public also includes taxpayers, legislators, and government officials. A public relations program is aimed at winning the support of these various segments of the public for the institution and its programs.

Each college or university must determine what image it desires to cultivate. The institution may wish to stress academic excellence, community service, athletic performance, academic freedom, student freedom and responsibility, research, or cultural service. All members of the university community are then called on to help express the desired image.

The element of the academic community best qualified to develop and cultivate the image of a college or university is the administration. Faculty members cannot or will not undertake the task; they are professionally oriented, concerned primarily with their professional field of knowledge or particular discipline. Students come and go. Alumni are deeply involved in their own professions, careers, families, and communities. While alumni, students, and faculty contribute to the image of their college or university, the function of seeing the institution as a whole and presenting it to its various publics must be centralized in the administration. Public relations, the image of the institution, becomes the responsibility of the chief executive officer.

The president, in the United States, or the chancellor or vice-chancellor, in some other nations, is the university's foremost public relations officer. He reports to, and makes requests of, the board of trustees; in the United States it is the president who testifies before the appropriations committee in the state legislature; it is the president who is quoted in crises, announces triumphs, and says the appropriate things on all public occasions. His words, actions, and appearances reflect on the institution he represents, with the result that he alone is responsible for much of an institution's success.

Nevertheless, knowledgeable public relations officers realize that all their efforts will be meaningless if every member of the university or college community does not assume his share in the public relations effort. Secretaries and receptionists, in fact *all* persons dealing with the institution's publics, must have impressed on them the importance of telephone courtesy, personal friendliness and helpfulness, proper correspondence, and positive attitudes. No organized program can create the right image for the institution if the daily, routine contacts are neglected.

Organization

The staff organization of public relations departments varies with each institution even though the chief executive plays a key role in the development of a positive public relations program. In the United States and Canada, as well as at scattered institutions elsewhere, the general supervision of the program rests with a top administrative officer who has the absolute confidence of the president. He provides assistance and personal service to the chief executive and serves as consultant on communication, both internal and external, not only for the president but for the entire staff, especially when public announcements are made on critical occasions.

The public relations officer has direct "line" responsibilities as well. He is generally responsible for such operations as the news bureau, public information office, the entertainment of important visitors, and perhaps the operation of a speakers bureau. Particular duties may vary from campus to campus, but almost invariably the public relations officer is directly responsible to the president or other administrative officer.

Both within American and Canadian institutions, the public relations officer is identified under various titles. Formerly he was assigned, first, the title of director of public relations, usually directly responsible to the chief executive. At some institutions he was known as assistant to the chief executive, establishing the close association with an obvious title. The officer then became known as director for development, in some cases vice-president for university relations. When development became more closely identified with fund raising, a new title was sought.

There are several institutions abroad where public relations and/or development programs have been organized on the American pattern. The Council for Advancement and Support of Education (CASE) has some members from other countries. In these instances the titles and the functions are the same.

There are directors of public relations at two institutions in Spain and a director of development at the University of Cape Town in South Africa and at the Israel Institute of Technology. CASE membership includes officers with similar titles and functions at universities in Mexico, Venezuela, Nicaragua, France, and England. In each country only one or two schools are involved, and in most cases they are schools with some American affiliations.

The most recent organizational structure on many American campuses, especially at larger institutions, calls for a vice-president or director for institutional advancement. The centralized approach to alumni programs, fund raising, public relations, and information services leads to placing these activities under institutional advancement. Related activities, such as federal and state liaison, university presses, central printing services, student recruitment, job placement of graduates, and educational television, fall within the organizational scope of the advancement program. But it should be noted that in most cases, these activities are handled by staff people operating within one of the four broad functions.

It is desirable that institutions develop long-range public relations programs that are directly aligned with the long-range goals of the institution. The public relations staff must consciously create a positive image that will elicit support for those objectives. There are several vehicles available for conducting public relations: the public information office, the publications office, the speakers bureau, special events, and athletics.

Public information office. The public information office disseminates information about the college or university by dealing with news reporters, arranging press conferences, handling news releases to the media, and, often, planning and coordinating university advertising. Newspapers, magazines, radio, and television are all effective methods of transmitting information. Media contacts, once developed, must be continuously maintained. These arms of the mass media are concerned and interested in the general activities and special events of the institutions. Their editorial policies and peculiarities must be noted and properly serviced.

The public information office also publishes and distributes policy statements at the direction of the institution's chief administrative officer, answers all queries about the school's public affairs, and sometimes helps prepare statements, reports, and speeches by university officials.

The public information office may become involved in hosting distinguished visitors to the campus. Its staff may well be called on to organize campus tours, provide guides or maps, and arrange transportation, as well as other conveniences. On some campuses, the public information office works with the admissions office and arranges daily or weekly campus tours for prospective students and their parents. The office may host recruiting personnel of corporations interviewing graduating seniors for employment. It may also operate a general information desk to serve visitors to the campus.

The public information office is often called on to assist in the orientation of new members of the staff and faculty. The writing of material for handbooks and administrative directories and the explanation of rules and regulations may be part of the public information service.

Publications office. In a public relations department, the publications office is charged with the external dissemination of information through catalogs and promotional literature considered essential to the operation of the institution.

The official university or college catalog is edited and prepared by this office in full cooperation with all academic divisions and administrative offices. The catalog may be a "sales" piece as well as an official information bulletin. Its preparation calls for attention to detailed description of course offerings, but the catalog must also be an attractive piece of promotional literature with pictures, description of services and facilities, and a statement of the objectives and mission of the institution.

Other literature essential to the operation of the institution includes the campus map; the student directory with names, addresses, and other vital data; and pictorial presentations. The publications office works with the student personnel office on editing and printing the student handbook and other informational literature. Special programs, schedules, announcements, and invitations to campus events are usually prepared by this office.

At some institutions, the development office depends on the publications office for assistance in preparation and production of materials, such as brochures, leaflets, flyers, and fund-raising letters, needed for its operations. The alumni office often needs the publications office for the preparation and production of the alumni magazine and other promotional materials aimed at alumni readers.

An official newspaper, published by the college or university, serves to provide information about policies, events, programs, schedules, and campus developments, as well as official announcements. Where such newspapers exist, the publications office is usually responsible for its production and distribution.

Speakers bureau. A very useful tool of a public relations office is a student-faculty-staff speakers bureau. With the cooperation of the speech and communications department, outstanding student speakers are invited to participate in this activity. The public relations office may prepare a publication giving the subjects of speeches and biographical sketches of faculty and staff members willing to speak about the institution or an interesting subject of their own. Such handbooks, announcing the availability of student or staff speakers, are distributed to service clubs, secondary schools, churches, and other organizations in the community. The speakers bureau provides an excellent opportunity for the institution to send its best representatives into the surrounding area for personal contacts with an audience prepared to receive a good impression of the institution.

Some universities extend this service through the public relations office by offering musicians, dancers, and other talented representatives of the campus as means of "advertising" the excellence and caliber of its academic community.

Special events. Every college or university has frequent opportunities to create a favorable image through the sponsorship or scheduling of public events. An alert public relations officer will capitalize on these opportunities to make friends for the institution.

Ground-breaking ceremonies, cornerstone layings, and the dedications of buildings attract prominent personalities and friends to the campus. University speakers have a captive audience with whom to share—and to gain support for—the institution's goals and objectives. Carefully developed invitation lists make sure all segments of the university's public are represented at such functions. Development and alumni staff must cooperate with the public relations office in developing such guest lists, to make sure potential donors are not overlooked.

Hospitality committees, hosts and hostesses, and selected individuals are assigned to welcome visitors and accommodate their needs. Campus police are alerted to the presence of special visitors and are asked to give them courteous treatment. A good public relations effort will ensure that adequate visitor parking areas and directional signs are provided and that buildings and grounds are well cared for.

Athletics. Athletic events play an important role in good public relations. They draw attention to the university, attract large masses of visitors, and thus open the door for other public relations efforts. An effective public relations staff, aware of the potential in mass communication through organized sports, must include a person or persons with special talent in the field of sports publicity and promotion.

A sports information director may be found in the athletic department, where he can be close to the action. However, it is recommended that such a person be retained as a part of the public relations staff so as to be involved in the total uni-versity picture. Professional maturity is increased by broader participation in university affairs rather than confinement to the athletic scene. There is always a tendency for coaches or athletic directors to make personal publicity agents out of sports information people. This situation is avoided by having the latter closely associated with the public relations and public information staff rather than the athletic department.

The public relations person responsible for sports promotion and information needs to develop good contacts with the media, especially radio and television, that cover sport events on campus, along with the sportswriters of newspapers and magazines. Informational handbooks with statistics and backgrounds on coaches and players are among the materials he must provide. The job calls for integrity and sound human relations in order to protect the student athletes and the coaches from exploitation and career-damaging false reports.

Ancillary Operations

As specialized areas, such as the admissions or registrar's offices or the professional schools, exert a dominating influence on the total academic life of an institution, the public relations staff must often meet this growth of the school's exposure to the public with provisions to service these offices. This is particularly true in admissions, where good public relations is of vital importance.

Every college hopes it will gain the interest and attention of outstanding prospective students, create a desire to attend, and inspire a determination to enroll. Correspondence frequently provides the first contact with prospective students. Therefore, letters can be a public relations medium of the first order. Too often, the administrator, who dislikes receiving mimeographed or mass-duplicated letters himself, will resort to impersonal letters in writing to prospective students. Personal and cordial letters can be the beginning of a relationship between the college and the prospective student that will last through life. The prospective student becomes an enrolled student, then an alumnus, and in either group is of vital importance to the institution.

Special events that bring the prospective student to the campus are emphasized in the public relations of many institutions. Many programs are held during the summer months for the benefit of secondary school students. Vocational guidance programs, drama festivals, music workshops, forensic tournaments, and festivals for young people are planned by many institutions through their public relations efforts. The public relations office, coordinating with the admissions and alumni offices, can get alumni involved in secondary school "college nights" in local communities, thus providing good public relations for two different constituencies.

Recognition of special talent through scholarships and awards improves the public relations of an institution with prospective students, while at the same time gaining it publicity in the communities where awards are made.

All university agencies are a part of the overall advancement program. To that end, staff members in every office participate in such admissions programs as freshmen orientation. Counseling, registration for courses, orientation of parents and students, and a general introduction to the college scene are essential components of such an activity. Coordinated by the public relations staff with the cooperation of the admissions office, this can be one of the most successful ventures in making friends for the institution.

Multimedia advertising, with good taste and integrity, combined with effective correspondence and personal contacts, help make up a productive admissions program. The public relations office is essential in such a program.

Alumni. Public relations through alumni enlarges an institution's circle of friends and encourages these friends to speak and act in behalf of the college or university. If an institution's relations with its graduates and former students have been propitious, the institution should be continually alert to suggest ways in which these alumni can be of aid to the institution.

For many institutions, alumni play an important role in public relations by sponsoring art exhibits, concerts, and lectures by students or faculty in the local community. Favorable publicity generally accompanies such programs and the institution's image is greatly enhanced.

Legislative contacts and contacts with government officials can be promoted through alumni participation, and both are extremely valuable relationships for state-supported or state-assisted universities. Prominent alumni who have influence on their community's legislative representatives can help to sell the need for financial or legal support by acquainting lawmaker friends with pertinent facts and introducing them to the university community in a positive way.

Internal public relations are aided by alumni participation in job placement for graduates. Nothing impresses a student more than the active interest of an alumnus in the student's welfare. Alumni who help find jobs for their college's graduates create an immense amount of goodwill and build for future alumni support.

Continuing education projects on campus and in local communities are often directed and sponsored by alumni clubs of the institution. The college or university can also benefit from the counsel received from alumni or organized advisory groups. The institution that welcomes such advice and encourages active alumni participation through this method promotes a two-way relationship which is bound to be of mutual benefit.

Another example of alumni involvement in presenting a favorable image of the institution to the general public is through professional channels. At several prominent institutions, attorneys who are alumni assist in the preparation of bequest booklets and information flyers on wills and trusts. These materials are distributed to persons in the community who seek advice on these matters and are often prompted by, and indirectly guided toward, making a major gift to the college or university in appreciation of this public service.

Community service. Every institution of higher education has an opportunity to relate to the community in which it is located. In those areas where "town and gown" relationships are good, both the community and the institution flourish. The first step is good communication. Representation of local citizenry on the institution's governing board and participation by faculty and staff in the community's government are essential to good public relations. Exchange of plans for capital development—on campus and in the community—is most desirable. Active participation by representatives of the community in the development of these plans is beneficial, especially if the capital improvements proposed are to be shared by the town and the academic community. This is particularly true of recreational facilities, such as swimming pools, gymnasiums, ice arenas, and theaters.

The university may be in a position to offer technical and cultural services to the community in such fields as engineering, sociology, mental and public health, surveying, library science, theater, music, art, and public education. Such services may be research-oriented from the university's standpoint, providing a "laboratory" for students and faculty, but are also of immeasurable value to the community. Students in professional schools can work with community agencies and groups; professors can consult with them; and students, faculty, and townspeople can collaborate on community surveys and studies. The college or university stands to benefit at any point where the college can reach out to touch the personal or business life of the community.

Public Relations as a Profession

The university campus is the ideal training ground for young people interested in public relations as a career. Involvement of students in public relations programs helps to arouse their interest and to provide valuable experience for them. Public relations officers look on their positions as professionals and are always prepared to share experiences and observations with anyone interested in pursuing a similar career.

College public relations officers maintain an interest in continuing education. The American College Public Relations Association (ACPRA) and similar professional associations have consistently operated seminars and workshops to keep their membership abreast of the latest ideas and procedures. As noted, the current trend is to centralize several activities, including public relations, under institutional advancement. Indicative of this trend is the recent merger of ACPRA with the American Alumni Council. The new organization, known as the Council for the Advancement and Support of Education (CASE), serves alumni directors, public relations officers, fund raisers (development officers), and public information and publications directors. A regular exchange of materials is encouraged and members avail themselves of library reference services and subscriptions to the CASE professional journal, *Techniques.* Consultants and specialists are brought to individual campuses or to workshops, and films, slides, and other audiovisual services are provided.

In the United States a number of organizations of public relations consultants are available to give professional counsel to any college or university wishing to avail itself of these services. These organizations specialize in fund-raising counsel, development, and publications. Newcomers to the profession find it advantageous to employ professional counsel in these areas, if for no other reason than to get their university colleagues to listen and heed good advice. An "expert" from out of town always gets better attention.

Professional counsel is expensive, and some institutions cannot afford these services. In these instances, an association such as CASE is tremendously valuable. The services provided by this association are included in the modest membership fee. The wide range of experience of CASE staff and the willingness of CASE members to share their knowledge with those at other institutions make it easier for the neophyte to receive valuable training in the field.

The workshops and seminars for college and university public relations officers are sponsored by professional associations such as CASE. These programs provide an opportunity to meet and talk with professional consultants and public relations experts from industry as well as with colleagues from other institutions. No public relations office can afford to rest on its laurels. Continued professional development through exposure to other people and new ideas is essential.

Bibliography

The Advancement of Understanding and Support of Higher Education. Washington, D.C.: American College Public Relations Association, 1958.

Leslie, J. W. *Focus on Understanding and Support: A Study in College Management.* Washington, D.C.: American College Public Relations Association, 1969.

Millett, J. D. *The Academic Community.* New York: McGraw-Hill, 1962.

Reck, W. E. *Public Relations—A Program for Colleges and Universities.* New York: Harper & Row, 1946.

Seymour, H. J. *Designs for Fund Raising.* New York: McGraw-Hill, 1966.

Strong, R. A. "Public Relations." In A. S. Knowles (Ed.), *Handbook of College and University Administration.* Vol. 1: *General.* New York: McGraw-Hill, 1970.

JOHN E. DOLIBOIS

See also: Mass Communication; Town-Gown Relations.

PUBLIC SERVICE ROLE OF HIGHER EDUCATION

A surprising number of the revolutionary advances in knowledge from the beginning of the Renaissance until early in the twentieth century were made by men who, at the time of their major work, were not associated with a university, such as Francis Bacon, Gottfried Wilhelm von Leibnitz, William Harvey, Joseph Priestley, Antoine Laurent Lavoisier, Charles Darwin, Karl Marx, and Albert Einstein. The universities' assumption of major leadership in scientific research dates only from the nineteenth century; the third function of the university, its public service role, is essentially an invention of the twentieth. Public service in the university includes all educational activities not designed for, or directed primarily toward, full-time residential university students. It thus includes adult or continuing education, extension, and community development programs, among others. The concept of a tripartite university has gained general acceptance; however, in most universities, the public service function is not as fully developed as those of teaching and research.

During the short period since the universities became the major site for research, the concentration of talent and of library and laboratory resources has progressed so rapidly that today research is as significant within the university as teaching. The universities of the world have become a major producer, storer, and clearinghouse for research, funded by business and industry, private foundations, and state, provincial, and national governments, to the extent of billions of dollars annually. The Committee on Technology Utilization of the National Association of State Universities and Land-Grant Colleges (1973) estimated the research expenditure of the federal government of the United States alone in 1973 at eighteen billion dollars; much of that money found its way to the nation's campuses.

The application of this research appears to receive much less support, however, because the sources of funding for research and for its utilization are extremely varied; comparative data are difficult to obtain. However, the estimated eighteen billion dollars for research is matched by an estimated expenditure for utilization of fifty million, a ratio of considerably less than one percent for utilization as compared with the expenditure for production. (These figures exclude agricultural research and extension, where the ratio is estimated at close to 50 percent for utilization.) Even granting the unreliability of these estimates, it is evident that the expenditure for utilization of research findings is miniscule in comparison with the expenditure for the production of research data. Based on this criterion, there is good reason to conclude that public service is still far from attaining equality with the other two functions of the university.

The gap between a systematic research effort and its dissemination is not a recent problem. There are numerous examples of research and discovery that could have changed the rate of human development had adequate mechanisms been available for channeling information to its potential users.

The most striking example was the virtual loss of Greek science to Western Europe from the beginning of the Christian era until the Renaissance. In about 280 B.C., for example, Aristarchus performed experiments that led him to a heliocentric view of the solar system. Unknown to him, a contemporary, Eratosthenes, succeeded in measuring the circumference of the earth with an error of less than one percent. If this information had been available to Aristarchus, he would have been able to compute the size of the moon, the size of the sun, and the distance of each from the earth with something like the same degree of accuracy. If this information had been available to Columbus nearly two thousand years later, Columbus and the scholars he relied on would not have

mislaid Japan by a matter of 8200 miles. An extraordinary feat of seamanship, luck, and erroneous conclusions could have been instead an example of the application of research to the solution of a complex problem—in all likelihood, a solution that would have been reached much sooner given the available data.

Similarly, an Austrian monk, Gregor Mendel, published a paper in 1866 that laid the essential foundation for the modern science of genetics. That paper lay virtually unnoticed on library shelves for another thirty-four years before it was rediscovered and used in the birth of a major biological revolution.

These are somewhat dramatic examples of the persistent underutilization of knowledge in the solution of humanity's problems. This underutilization has occurred because, until recent times, there was no single depository for a large portion of this information, no true network of scholars, and no foundation of information technology that gave some assurance of access to needed data. Contemporary higher education has these resources, has the access to information, and is the focal point of a worldwide community of scholars. Nonetheless, the medieval, monastic model of the university as a haven for scholars, separate from the real world, persists. Thus, universities in general constitute a seriously underutilized resource, and knowledge that could be moved directly into the mainstream of use comes to society as a deferred benefit after the student has graduated. The idea of the university as a place with more directly utilitarian concerns has required a wrenching departure from tradition. The university did not invent research; it co-opted research. The university did not invent the idea of knowledge as a public service, and it is still wrestling with its ambivalence.

Development of the Public Service Idea

There are two patterns of university extension, each with a different history, and each maintaining its own separate existence, even within the same university. One of these patterns, general extension, is characterized by the offering of courses for off-campus or part-time adult students, frequently with the aim of providing a degree, certificate, or license on completion of required course work or the passing of an examination. The other might be called the agricultural extension or community development model. Included in this model are action-oriented, people-to-people programs directed toward various social goals or toward the direct transfer of information or technology into the community or the workplace.

Historical origins. The concept of the university as an agency of public service had its origins in two nineteenth century educational movements that began outside the university. The first was the development of lay institutes dedicated to the spread of useful knowledge. The Sunday Society was established in Birmingham, England, in 1789, to teach mechanics to factory workers. A similar organization originated in Glasgow, Scotland, in about 1800, migrated to London, and by 1823 had become the London Mechanics Institute. In 1857 Oxford University became involved through the preparation of local examinations for the mechanics' institutes and by 1908 the numbers involved were approaching half a million. In the United States, by the end of the nineteenth century, Farmers' Institutes were performing a similar function for agriculture. The passage of the Morrill Act in 1862 established the land-grant system to provide full-time educational opportunity in agriculture and the mechanical arts. As a result, short farm courses began in the 1880s, co-opting the Farmers' Institutes. Farm demonstration agents, working in the local community, were another offshoot, and by the end of the century education for part-time students in agriculture and the mechanical arts was well established. By 1914 some twenty-five universities in the United States had agricultural extensions.

The second source of the public service idea was the movement for mass cultural education of adults. In the United States one of the earliest agencies for mass culture, the American Lyceum, was established in 1826, and by 1839 there were some three thousand lyceums in the country. A summer institute begun at Chautauqua Lake in New York in 1874 was followed four years later by a home study program, both of which were brought to the University of Chicago by William Rainey Harper, when he accepted its presidency in 1892. He established the extension division as one of the major academic divisions of the university. In 1906–07 Charles Van Hise established the extension division of the University of Wisconsin, and by 1914 some thirty universities had general extension divisions. During Van Hise's presidency at Wisconsin, the concept of university public service came to be widely known as the Wisconsin Idea, embodied in the statement that the boundaries of the campus are the boundaries of the state.

Once it was granted that adults could learn off campus and on a part-time basis, it followed that some sort of academic recognition could be granted for the completion of a given amount of work or for satisfactory performance on an examination. The first institution to grant an external degree was the University of London in 1858. By 1974 an admittedly incomplete census by the National University Extension Association listed nearly three thousand degree programs for part-time students, although only a few could be regarded as external degrees.

Cooperative extension service. The Congress of the United States, impressed by the emergence of twenty-five agricultural extension programs in universities, passed the Smith-Lever Act in 1914, establishing the Cooperative Extension Service. The concept of this service differed from that of general extension in several respects. First, it was conceived as a joint enterprise of federal, state, and local governments. Second, it was primarily a mechanism to transfer information directly, not through the medium of organized courses, but rather by contact with local transfer agents and campus-based specialists. Third, it was almost entirely supported by public funds appropriated on a continuing basis, half from federal appropriations and half from state, local, or other sources. The success of this program in increasing agricultural productivity has made it a model for many nations, although some nations, such as India and Japan, have based their extension programs within the ministry of agriculture rather than the university. Universities in many nations have been patterned on a European model, which is less well adapted to the role of grass-root public service than is the land-grant institution in the United States.

University extension in Latin America. In spite of its success, the Cooperative Extension Service idea has been slow in spreading in any organized form to other areas of university competence and to other countries. In 1918 the Manifesto of Argentine Youth of Cordoba included a demand for "a close tie-up of the university with national problems and extension of university instruction and consultative services to the people" (Lowe, 1970, p. 220). However, the traditional pattern imported from Spain has given way only very gradually in Latin America to this broader orientation. In Chile all universities now have extension departments, and one or more universities in Argentina, Uruguay, Peru, Ecuador, and Bolivia have such departments.

In 1956 the University of Uruguay established a department of extension, broadly conceived as being served by the disciplines of agriculture, engineering, the exact sciences, medicine, architecture and urban affairs, economics, the social sciences, humanities, and interdisciplinary studies (Iglesias and others, 1972). Its goal of broad faculty involvement has apparently been only partially realized.

Terminology of University Public Service

Terminology is a problem in the public service area, partly because of the tradi-

tional associations carried by certain words and partly because usage varies considerably. The term *adult education*, for example, is sometimes used narrowly to refer to evening classes for part-time students. In other contexts, it is a generic term for all kinds of university public service and for postsecondary vocational education as well. The definition set forth by the International Congress of University Adult Education illustrates the comprehensive approach: "Adult Education is a process whereby persons who no longer attend school on a regular and full-time basis (unless full-time programs are especially designed for adults) undertake sequential and organized activities with the conscious intention of bringing about changes in information, knowledge, understanding or skills, appreciation and attitudes; or for the purpose of identifying and solving personal or community problems" (Lowe, 1970, p. 3).

The term *continuing education* is generally used in a more restrictive sense, to refer to organized instruction for part-time adult students. However, there is a trend toward including under continuing education almost any kind of information transfer to nonresidential or part-time clientele. For many the word *extension* is associated with agricultural extension, and numerous writings about agricultural extension omit the modifier on the assumption that it is implied. However, the use of the word *extension* to refer to organized programs for adults appears to antedate the use in agriculture, and it is also freely used more or less interchangeably with adult education and continuing education. There is a tendency for the field, under any of these words, to become broader and more inclusive. Thus, "agricultural" extension in the United States now includes urban programs, community development in cities and villages, health care programs, and assistance to a wide variety of businesses, almost any of which can be classified as agri-business.

On the other hand, an increasing number of general extension operations are also moving away from exclusive emphasis on organized instruction into people-to-people programs in new areas, though many are in the areas served by agricultural extension. A complication in the United States is that, even within the same university, cooperative or agricultural extension and general extension are entirely separate administratively, reporting to a common head only at the highest level of administration. In possibly a majority of nations, general extension is a function of the university and agricultural extension of the ministry of agriculture.

The term *university public service* has the advantage of having no historic ties to a single school, college, or discipline. It is broad enough to include the wide variety of services associated with adult education, community development, continuing education, extension, and outreach, as well as the growing field of external degree programs. One might argue that all university activities, including research and full-time residential instruction, are also public services, but the disjunctive use of the term *public service* seems to be well enough established to avoid confusion.

The term *adult* has become less and less useful as a basis for distinguishing among university clientele. In the United States the vast majority of university students are legally adults (that is, eighteen years of age or older), and the age mix of full-time residential students is becoming increasingly heterogeneous. In order to distinguish between the traditional clientele of the university and those who are served by the public service function, some distinction other than age is needed.

The public service clientele are, furthermore, not confined to the adult category. Paradoxically, a far greater number of nonadults, young people of all ages, are served by so-called adult education programs than the less than 1 percent of students under eighteen who are served by the full-time residential programs. The potential clientele for university public service programs can be better defined as all people, of whatever age, who are not presently full-time residential candidates for a regular degree. Whether or not they become actual clientele depends on the existence of university resources that are particularly relevant to their needs and on the university's willingness and ability to deliver those resources.

For example, if there is a large number of preschool children in a culturally deprived rural area, the university may have a special capability for preparing them to learn to read better when they enter school. There may be no other agency as well equipped to deal with this need. In such a case, the university weighs its priorities in terms of available resources, expected benefits, and the relative merits of other programs contending for funds, and then reaches a conclusion as to whether or not to proceed. A preschool reading training program is one of many ways in which some universities are departing from traditional constraints in redefining their public service mission. Virtually no program is excluded a priori from consideration.

Delivery of Public Service Programs

The concept of university public service is that of a delivery system for university knowledge resources. On the campus, the university has a variety of capabilities and resources, including the faculty, laboratories, and libraries. Such resources also include ongoing research, the potential for engaging in research addressed to emerging and newly identified problems, and a communication network of scholars who can readily transcend not only campus but also international boundaries. The university also has a variety of hardware for dealing with information technology: computers, access to or management of broadcast facilities, audiovisual services, and, frequently, mobile units for a variety of purposes.

In the United States the extra ingredient that has accounted for the unique success of agricultural extension programs is personnel. The capabilities of the university for the production, storage, and retrieval of knowledge are supplemented by staff with specific responsibility for the dissemination and utilization of knowledge. It was recognized in the early days of the Cooperative Extension Service that the dissemination of knowledge was not enough. The delivery of information to the point where the need existed provided no assurance that the information would be used effectively. Thus, the concept of the change agent has developed. The change agent is a person with the ability to ensure clientele understanding and motivation and with the necessary skills required to make the fullest use of the information provided.

The staffing pattern that has developed in agricultural extension includes campus-based specialists with competence in a particular subject matter who function as scanners and interpreters of research data. They work in conjunction with the producers of knowledge and with the field staff, who are strategically located off campus and who provide the direct contact with local clientele in the identification and diagnosis of problems. These problems are then referred to the campus specialist.

This model has been generalized (with various modifications) or arrived at independently to deal with a wide variety of problems. Off-campus centers, itinerant staff, and resident tutors perform a variety of functions, such as extending external degree programs, providing technical assistance to small business enterprises, improving the nutritional status of low-income people, and helping people maintain a better quality of health care.

Organization and Scope of Public Service Programs

The scope of public service programs is as varied as the capabilities of the university and its success in identifying needs. The International Congress of Adult Education adopted a classification based on needs. Its categories include remedial; vocational, technical, professional; health, welfare, and family living; civic, political, and community competence; and self-fulfillment

(Lowe, 1970, p. 4). It is difficult to imagine any activity that would not fit under one of those five categories.

Response to needs. From a somewhat different perspective, the ways in which response is made to these needs, most public service functions fall within one of six classifications. The first is technology transfer. These are programs designed to deliver research data to potential users; in addition to agricultural extension programs in several nations, transfer programs for business management, science, and engineering data are in operation in several states in the United States. Second, there are technical assistance programs. These are intended to bring various kinds of expertise to clientele, generally on a people-to-people basis, through such methods as advisory services, consultation, and demonstration.

The third classification, organized instruction, includes classroom, correspondence, independent study, and mediated courses of study, either to obtain credit toward a degree or to achieve other educational objectives not leading to a degree. Informal group processes, the fourth classification, involves programs working with groups to achieve some common goal; much community development work relies on such group activity.

The fifth category, problem-solving research, is unlike the more prevalent type of university research that is intended to add to a general body of knowledge. Problem-solving research is designed in response to a specific need of a particular clientele.

The final classification is that of information services. These are programs designed to bring information to the general public or to a specific clientele by means of the printed word, broadcast, telephone, or group meetings.

Administration of public service programs. Since these functions have become a part of most university programs only recently, there has tended to be a variety of administrative experimentation. The kind of full-spectrum public service program that was envisioned in Argentina, the Ivory Coast, Uruguay, and some states of the United States is less common than separate programs that embrace only one or two of the need categories identified by the International Congress of Adult Education and only one or two of the functions described above. Often, where there is a broader involvement, it is divided between two or more administrative agencies.

In some cases each school or college within a larger institution has its own separate program and its own administrator. This is the most common model for administration of the Cooperative Extension Service in the United States, with the state's director reporting to the dean of the college of agriculture. In general extension operations, the chief administrator, usually titled dean or director, reports to the president, chancellor, or vice-chancellor of the university. In most such cases, the dean or director has a few faculty members who are directly and solely responsible to him. However, he must also rely heavily on the faculty of the various residential schools or colleges, who teach extension courses on a part-time or overload basis, or on instructors hired and paid on a course-by-course basis.

A less common pattern, but one which seems to be growing, is the establishment of separate institutions or distinct units within a large institution. In some countries these separate units are part of the ministry structure and thus only indirectly related to university public service. Others, however, such as the British Open University, the University of South Africa, or Metropolitan State University, are free-standing units with autonomous administrative structures and their own faculty.

An intermediate type of administrative arrangement exists in the University Extension of the University of Wisconsin, which has a large faculty of its own and a chief administrative officer with the title of chancellor. This chancellor reports to

the president of the University of Wisconsin system. Unlike the fully autonomous arrangement of the British Open University and the University of South Africa, however, Wisconsin's extension has no separate degree-granting authority, many of its faculty hold joint appointments with other faculties of the university, and it is part of a large university structure.

There are drawbacks both to the free-standing institution and to the public service operation that depends entirely on the residence camus for its staffing and program development. In the free-standing institution, faculty resources are limited to the institutional staff and those who can be hired on an occasional basis. There is no large resource base of research and instruction scholars who can provide a high degree of specialized expertise in a wide variety of subjects. On the other hand, the university public service operation that must depend entirely on the resident teaching and research faculty often has difficulty in obtaining release of the various types and amounts of faculty service needed. When the extension service is part of a ministry, a restrictive separation of the extension operation from any major resource base occurs.

Several universities in the United States have been moving toward an arrangement that attempts to maintain the advantages of both approaches without the disadvantages. This is accomplished by having a single administrative officer for all university public service functions. This officer controls the budget and has direct charge of field operations, but specialist faculty budgeted to public service are appointed to, and located within, the residence teaching and research school, college, or department. In addition, the administrator usually has some latitude in establishing special purpose interdisciplinary units under his direct administrative control. When the need arises, these special groups can be used to avoid the sometimes narrow discipline focus of the residential unit.

This type of pattern has developed at the University of Missouri since 1960.

International Cooperation

A rapidly growing aspect of public service has been cooperation across international boundaries in the development of institutions of higher education and in providing technical assistance to developing nations. This type of public service has evolved through two phases. The first was a colonial phase in which institutions in the colonial powers provided resources to aid in the establishment in the colonies of institutions cast generally in the European mold. In the period after World War II, with the rise of a new nationalism, the essentially paternalistic approach of colonialism gave way to a broader base of cooperation between economically and socially developed nations and developing nations, usually with government of foundation sponsorship.

This approach was given clear expression in the inaugural address of President Harry S Truman in 1949 when he outlined his Point Four Program. Since that time, the United States, Canada, Great Britain, Japan, Israel, the Federal Republic of Germany, the Netherlands, Sweden, France, the Republic of China, and a number of other nations have actively supported international higher education services to promote national development. In addition, several private foundations, notably Ford and Rockefeller, and international agencies, such as the United Nations, the World Bank, and the International Monetary Fund, have supported programs.

Some of the major foundations were involved in international higher education for development before World War II. In the postwar period involvement on a much larger scale was the result of a broader base of support and of the unprecedented cooperation of national governments, international agencies, and the large foundations, resulting in very high annual higher education expenditures for international cooperation. No precise figures are available, but international program expenditures of the Ford Foundation alone for fiscal year 1973 amounted to just under seventy million dollars, a significant part of which went to support college and university involvement (Ford Foundation, 1973).

Development-oriented programs have been organized administratively by creation of special agencies within universities, such as Harvard University's Center for International Affairs, and by the development of consortia, such as the Midwest Universities Consortium for International Activities, which includes seven universities in the midwestern United States. Some of the interuniversity cooperative arrangements extend across international boundaries, as in the case of the International Agricultural Research Centers funded by seven nations and two international agencies. The University of Nigeria was developed with the cooperation of the Inter-University Council of Great Britain, Michigan State University in the United States, and universities in India and the Netherlands, with funding by government agencies and foundations.

Programs have most frequently focused on development in agriculture, business and economics, education, health science, land use, population problems, and technology. However, general university administration and development and the liberal arts have also received attention. Faculty and staff of universities in developed nations have been a resource both for short-time consultations and for periods of residence of two or more years.

While it would be premature to assess the effect, a new development in international cooperation in higher education began when the United Nations General Assembly in 1973 adopted a charter for the United Nations University with headquarters in Tokyo. Intended as a problem-oriented institution with a minimal administrative staff, the university is to be "a flexible mechanism for bringing a continual flow of leading scientists and scholars into a productive relationship with each other with a minimum of formal structure and overhead" (United Nations, 1975).

Future of Public Service

There is enormous diversity in the kinds and degree of commitment of universities throughout the world to the public service function. Universities have a substantial resource base that is relevant to the needs of that larger clientele who are not full-time residents on the campus. Although there is considerable evidence of a growing commitment to public service within universities, the external support has not been forthcoming to the degree that might have been expected considering the cost for benefits received. As Lowe says in *Adult Education and National Building:* "Adult education receives far less support from external aid than any other branch of education [although] international aid spent on adult education would probably yield exceptionally advantageous returns" (1970, p. 15). From the standpoint of internal support, Coverdale states: "Some educational planners would go so far as to suggest that where a developing country is operating on a stringent budget, there may be a virtue in slowing down the expansion of first-level education, at least temporarily, and concentrating the maximum of energy and resources on providing agricultural education for the adult population (1974, p. 30). While such observations are directed toward the problems of developing nations, the United States experience with agricultural extension suggests that the same observations apply in a significant degree to all nations. The university is a unique resource; it is an underutilized resource. The trend of history and the temper of more recent times suggest that, after a period of groping toward ways and means of better employing university resources, public service may some day attain the stature within the university held by teaching and research.

Bibliography

Carnegie Commission on Higher Education. *New Students and New Places.* New York: McGraw-Hill, 1971.

Coles, E. T. *Adult Education in Developing Countries.* Oxford, England: Pergamon Press, 1969.

Committee on the Financing of Higher Education for Adult Students. *Financing Part-time Students: The New Majority in Postsecondary Education.* Washington, D. C.: American Council on Education, 1974.

Committee on Technology Utilization of the National Association of State Universities and Land-Grant Colleges. *A University Delivery System for Research and Knowledge Resources.* Washington, D. C.: National Association of State Universities and Land-Grant Colleges, 1973.

Coverdale, G. M. *Planning Education in Relation to Rural Development.* Paris: UNESCO International Institute for Education Planning, 1974.

Education and World Affairs. *The University Looks Abroad: Approaches to World Affairs at Six American Universities.* New York: Walker, 1965.

Ford Foundation. *Annual Report.* New York: Ford Foundation, 1973.

Houle, C. O. *The External Degree.* San Francisco: Jossey-Bass, 1972.

Houle, C. O. "The Third Era of American Higher Education." In *Proceedings of the National Conference on Public Service and Extension in Institutions of Higher Education.* Athens: University of Georgia Center for Continuing Education, 1974.

Iglesias, E., and others. *Conceptos sobre extensión universitaria.* Montevideo, Uruguay: Fundación de cultural universitaria, 1972.

International Institute for Educational Planning. *New Educational Media in Action: Case Studies for Planner.* (3 vols.) Paris: UNESCO, 1967.

International Working Group on Continuing Education of Engineers, UNESCO. *Continuing Education for Engineers: A University Program.* Madison: University of Wisconsin-Extension, 1974.

Joint United States Department of Agriculture-National Association of State Universities and Land-Grant Colleges Study Committee. *A People and a Spirit.* Fort Collins: Colorado State University, 1968.

Lowe, J. (Ed.) *Adult Education and Nation Building.* Edinburgh, Scotland: University Press, 1970.

Pitchell, R. J. (Ed.) *A Directory of United States*

College and University Degrees for Part-Time Students. Washington, D. C.: National University Extension Association, 1973.

Reddy, A. A. *Extension Education.* Bapatla, India: Sree Lakshmi Press, 1971.

Shannon, T. J., and Schoenfeld, A. *University Extension.* New York: Center for Applied Research in Education, 1965.

Strother, G. B. "Report of the View of the Future Committee." *NUEA Spectator,* 1972, *36*(8), 9–15.

Strother, G. B. "The University's Role in Public Service and Extension." In *Proceedings of the National Conference on Public Service and Extension in Institutions of Higher Education.* Athens: University of Georgia Center for Continuing Education, 1974.

United Nations. *The United Nations University: Present Status, Summer/Fall 1975.* New York: United Nations, 1975.

GEORGE B. STROTHER

See also: Adult Education; Agriculture in Higher Education: Agricultural Research, Extension Services, and Field Stations; Aid to Other Nations; Consortia in the United States; Interinstitutional Cooperation; Research; United Nations: United Nations University.

PUBLICATIONS, HIGHER EDUCATION

Members of a discipline or a field of study communicate with one another by many different means. Conventionally, these means are grouped together into formal channels, which comprise books, research monographs, journals, newsletters, and all the other printed material through which knowledge is disseminated, and informal channels, in which knowledge is passed directly from one individual to another by word of mouth, telephone, letter, or some other form of personal communication, such as prepublication papers. These channels are vital as the chief mechanisms for the maintenance, transmission, and extension of knowledge within a field or discipline.

The field of higher education is in a fortunate position, relative to other specialist areas, for studies of its communications channels have been undertaken by Hefferlin and Phillips (1971), Silverman (1973),

and, less directly, by Hobbs and Francis (1973), Berdahl and Altomare (1972), and Cohen (1969). In this examination of publishing—that is, of the formal channels of communication—in higher education, a broad perspective is adopted; it draws both on these and on other sources, some of which deal only indirectly or even incidentally with communication in higher education.

The Literature of Higher Education

It is possible to argue that, strictly speaking, no literature of higher education exists, since the field lacks a central corpus of works accepted by all; from a survey of books considered basic reading for students of higher education, Riegel and Bender (1972, pp. 88–89) conclude that "there is not yet a body of literature commonly accepted as basic by the bulk of faculty teaching courses in higher education throughout the United States" (also see Dressel and Mayhew, 1974). But so harsh a judgment takes no account of the embryonic state of systematic investigation in the field, or even of the apparently endless range of disciplines, each with its characteristic perspectives and methodologies, which can be brought to bear on almost any problem in higher education. Indeed, it seems most useful to view higher education in the same way that Storer (1970, p. 123) views education as a whole; that is, as a "conjunctive domain" whose focus is "a socially relevant whole rather than a natural cluster of abstract phenomena." And it follows that, in terms of formal communication, this "socially relevant whole" will act centripetally, drawing to itself critical comment and analysis representative of the standpoint of virtually every individual and interest group both inside and outside of higher education. The outcome, inevitably, is an immense range of published material, the sheer volume of which is so frequently remarked upon as to be commonplace (for example, see Burnett, 1973; Hobbs and Francis, 1973; Hefferlin and Phillips, 1971). No figures are available on the size of the literature, but it is in any case doubtful whether a worthwhile assessment could be made without regard to the quality of individual contributions, particularly since criticism of the general standard of published material is widespread (see, for instance, Mayhew, 1971; Willingham, 1973; Cohen, 1969).

The regular publishers of this vast range of material in higher education are varied, falling into a number of distinct groups: commercial publishers, such as Jossey-Bass and McGraw-Hill, which are mainly concerned with books; international, national, and governmental or quasi-governmental organizations, which supply the staple diet of statistical, survey, and policy material essential for social and political analysis; and research institutes and associations, which produce the widest range of material of any of the groups and provide vital support for the publication of specialist research reports.

Primary Sources

The various publication channels may be seen in terms of a "bibliographic chain" consisting of primary sources (original books, reports, and journals), secondary sources (abstracting and indexing journals that monitor the primary literature), and tertiary sources ("metainformation" sources, such as guides to the literature).

Books, monographs, and technical reports. The monograph literature of higher education is vast and variegated. Thriving book review sections in most of the major journals and Lewis Mayhew's annual surveys, themselves in book form (Mayhew, 1971, 1972), pay testimony to the inexorable flow of material. And it is richly varied: specialist research monographs and sober institutional self-studies rub shoulders with works of opinion and polemic, heady accounts of curricular innovations, journalistic "analyses" of student unrest, weighty reflections of former presidents, and a mass of conference proceedings, anthologies, and readings.

Given the range of material and, inevitably in such a potpourri, its variable quality, little would be gained here in documenting individual texts or even groups of texts. A number of general observations may, however, be made. First, as Mayhew (1971) has noted, a considerable proportion of the literature is in the form of conference proceedings and anthologies. Why this should be so is not clear. That now classic collection of papers *The American College* (Sanford, 1962) may have spawned a host of lesser imitators, but this argument does not really help to explain the abundance of conference proceedings, or, for that matter, the audience for them, since one must assume the existence of a demand, or at least a responsive market, where there is evidence of supply. Perhaps the proceedings and anthologies help to keep track of an elusive literature that is predicated above all on the paper, whether an essay or opinion piece, an account of an innovative approach in higher education, or the findings of a modest, nonreplicated research study. Nelson and Adams (1973) have suggested that a major cause of the diffusion of formal communication channels in educational research is the preponderance of "one-shot" studies—studies rarely followed up by further investigations—and it seems likely that a similar discontinuity exists in the subfield of higher education, but with a slightly different end result. Another probable cause of this pattern in the literature is the relatively high proportion of authors whose main interests lie in other academic disciplines: their desire to write on higher education is rarely sustained over time or directed toward publication in the core journals, such as *Journal of Higher Education* or *Educational Record* (which may be unknown to them); their interest finds its most convenient expression in the short compendium article or symposium paper.

A second observation, again supported by Mayhew (1971), is that the proportion of research-based monographs has been rising, particularly since the end of the

1960s, so that by the mid 1970s a number of regular publishers of such material are available, including the Society for Research into Higher Education (United Kingdom), the Center for Research and Development in Higher Education (United States), the American College Testing Program, and the Organisation for Economic Co-operation and Development (OECD), as well as a number of commercial publishers, notably Praeger (United States), Prentice-Hall (United States), Elsevier (Netherlands), Wiley (United States), Mouton (Netherlands), Verlag Dokumentation (Federal Republic of Germany), McCutchan (United States), D. C. Heath (Great Britain), Routledge and Kegan Paul (Great Britain), and, most prominent of all, Jossey-Bass (United States) and McGraw-Hill (United States). The last of these publishers, McGraw-Hill, was for many years the outlet for the publications of the Carnegie Commission on Higher Education, which has probably contributed more than any other single source to the recent growth in authoritative research monographs. Besides issuing thirty-odd reprints of influential articles, the commission has produced over twenty substantial reports and recommendations, an almost equal number of technical reports, and over sixty sponsored research studies. This "Everest of facts, figures and analysis," as Robbins (1974, p. x) has called it, has in turn engendered an additional two volumes of analysis and commentary: by Mayhew (1973) and Embling (1974)—the latter on the European implications of the commission's work. But perhaps the commission's most interesting feature in terms of communication has been its innovative approach to disseminating the results of its work. If it is rare for a national commission to make explicit the relationship between evidence and opinion (as the division into research studies, technical reports, and reports and recommendations makes clear), it is perhaps even rarer for a body of this kind to show such an imaginative concern for the pub-

lication of its findings in a variety of forms. Three volumes comprise the summary report of the commission: *Priorities for Action* (Carnegie Commission, 1973), the commission's final report, has been made available in two editions, one of which omits appendices and statistical tables, as well as in hardback and paperback; *A Digest of Reports of the Carnegie Commission on Higher Education* (Carnegie Commission, 1974), includes a condensation of the twenty-one policy reports issued by the commission, an index to its recommendations, and suggested assignments of responsibility for action on the recommendations made; *Sponsored Research of the Carnegie Commission on Higher Education* (Carnegie Commission, 1975), the third volume, provides summaries of the research studies undertaken.

Journals. As traditionally conceived, the journal is the primary medium through which scientific research findings are transmitted and discussed. In fields such as higher education, however, journals do not lend themselves to such clear and precise categorization, for undeniably they serve other purposes as well, including the purveying of opinion (albeit considered) and the dissemination of a large body of material on developments and innovations that leans more toward description (in the nonacademic sense) than analysis.

The editor of the *Journal of Higher Education* argues that journals of higher education frequently invite manuscripts from those already known or respected, or provide convenient outlets for exchange of ideas of prominent association members and research employees. "The concept of articles, refereed by colleagues," he claims, "is the exception rather than the rule in [the higher education] field, and when refereeing occurs, the judgmental group is the editorial boards of journals rather than colleagues who are engaged in specific work in the field" (Silverman, 1973, p. 68). Dressel and Mayhew (1974) similarly contend that, while seeking quality in the material they publish, the relevant journals in higher education do not utilize the rigorous refereeing procedures employed in other fields. Whatever the truth of these assertions (for nowhere, perhaps understandably, is any concrete evidence offered), it seems probable that, as the field of higher education develops, accepted refereeing procedures will become the rule rather than the exception. Ward, Hall, and Schramm (1975) found that the percentage of educational research journals using refereeing procedures increased from 52 percent in 1962 to 89 percent in 1971. This would seem to suggest that educational research increasingly adopted established practices in line with its acceptance as a valid field of study and research, and one might expect higher education to follow a similar course.

One trend likely to accelerate this refereeing process is the increasing attention being given to research papers. Within the ranks of the well-established journals, such as *Educational Record* and *Liberal Education,* some, of which the *Journal of Higher Education* is the most prominent example, are placing a much greater emphasis on research material. At the same time, several journals have been created since 1970 with a distinctly empirical orientation. The international journal *Higher Education* began publication in 1972 and has rapidly become one of the foremost journals in the field. It has been followed by research journals in many countries: the *Canadian Journal of Higher Education (Stoa);* the Indian *Journal of Higher Education;* the Japanese *Daigaku ronshu* (Research in Higher Education) in Japanese, with English abstracts; *Research in Higher Education,* published in New York; and a new British journal, *Studies in Higher Education.*

Newsletters, newspapers, and magazines. The boom in higher education journals has been matched by a mushrooming of newsletters, newspapers, and magazines. These serve an invaluable "current awareness" function, reporting on issues and problems affecting almost every con-

ceivable aspect of higher education. Since these publications are chiefly intended to present news and information, they are inevitably ephemeral and extremely variable in quality.

Such a great variety of these materials exists that it seems worthwhile to classify them into broad groupings. First are the national "newspapers" of higher education, the best-known examples of which are the *Times Higher Education Supplement* (London), *Die deutsche Universitätszeitung* (Bonn), and *The Chronicle of Higher Education* (Washington, D.C.). They provide, largely to nonspecialist audiences, a regular and fairly complete coverage of news and policy developments, generally supplemented by analysis and feature articles. Closely related to this group is the enterprisingly unique *Change Magazine.* Its main focus is not on news items (although each issue includes regular reports and features) but on the coverage, presented in provocative articles by noted commentators, of controversial issues in United States higher education.

This first group of national "newspapers" has no direct counterpart at the international level, where bulletins and newsletters produced by continental and worldwide bodies comprise the main channels of communication on new developments. Rich in valuable information, particularly for the student of comparative higher education, this second grouping of publications tends to draw heavily on other periodicals and newsletters to supplement material produced within the sponsoring organizations. Excellent examples are the *Bulletin* of the International Association of Universities and the Association of Commonwealth Universities' *Bulletin of Current Documentation. CRE Information,* published by the *Conférence permanente des recteurs et vice-chanceliers des universités européennes* (Standing Conference of Rectors and Vice-Chancellors of the European Universities), covers European affairs, while *RIHED News,* produced in Singapore by the Regional Institute of

Higher Education and Development, records developments in several Southeast Asian countries.

At the national level is an enormously wide range of newsletters published by national committees, associations, and professional bodies. Some of these publications provide coverage of national developments, outstanding examples being *University Affairs/Affaires universitaires,* published by the *Association des universités et collèges du Canada* (Association of Universities and Colleges of Canada); *Higher Education and National Affairs* (American Council on Education); *Higher Education and Research in the Netherlands (Stichting der nederlandse universiteiten en hogescholen voor internationale samenwerking:* Netherlands Universities Foundation for International Cooperation); and, in Argentina, *Revista del consejo de rectores de universidades nacionales.* Others, by far the largest group of all, serve principally as outlets both for news about the organizations they represent (for example, the American College Testing Program's *ACTivity*) and for information of professional interest to their members (perhaps the distinguished example being the *AAUP Bulletin* of the American Association of University Professors). Then there are the news organs of the higher education associations, such as the American Association for Higher Education's *College and University Bulletin* and the *Newsletter* of the Higher Education Research and Development Society of Australasia.

The final group is a small but interesting one, consisting of the newsletters of higher education research and development centers. *The Research Reporter* (published by the Center for Research and Development in Higher Education at the University of California, Berkeley) relates recent research done by the center to pressing issues in higher education in the United States. *Critique* (from the Center for the Study of Higher Education at the University of Toledo, Ohio) focuses on practical issues of concern to college and university faculty and administrators,

while *Learning and Development* (Centre for Learning and Development at McGill University in Montreal) and *Memo to the Faculty* (Center for Research on Learning and Teaching at the University of Michigan) are intended to stimulate the faculty's interest in innovative approaches to teaching and learning and to serve as sources of new ideas.

Microforms and other nonprint media. Microforms comprise only a small area of total publishing activity, but one likely to grow, particularly as the standard of available hardware improves. There are two main sources of microforms: microfilms of dissertations listed in *Dissertation Abstracts International* and microfiche copies of reports recorded in *Resources in Education.* Other "nonconventional" media also represent an important growth area: audiotapes of symposium presentations are being made available by societies and associations, while 16mm films and videotapes on instructional activities are playing an increasingly important part in faculty development.

Secondary and Tertiary Sources

Mayhew (1971) contends that neither education nor higher education has ever been particularly well served bibliographically, and the same point is made even more strongly by Dressel and Mayhew (1974). This criticism is very difficult to take seriously. Brittain (1970, p. 120), with the benefit of a broad perspective, suggests that education "is perhaps better covered by bibliographical tools and information services than any other social science," while Silverman (1973, p. 76) contends that higher education is "bibliography crazy"; certainly, the overwhelming impression from the bibliographies and information sources briefly noted below is of a field well blessed with reference materials.

Communication could not thrive in the absence of such materials. Formal channels are diffuse, and relevant articles appear not only in the higher education journals but also in almost every kind of educational journal, as well as in journals of the "parent" or contributory disciplines. One must turn to abstracting and indexing journals for both "current awareness" and "retrospective" purposes, while specialist bibliographies normally only serve a retrospective function.

Abstracting and indexing journals. Basic sources for the educationalist are the standard indexing journals, such as *Education Index, British Education Index, Bibliographie Pädagogik,* and the *Current Index to Journals in Education,* together with such tools as *Current Contents in the Social and Behavioral Sciences* (which provides up-to-the-minute journal coverage but in a format that necessitates extensive scanning), and such abstracting journals as *Resources in Education* (particularly for research reports, mostly available in microfiche and hard-copy formats) and *Sociology of Education Abstracts.* Higher education is fortunate in also having two specialist sources of its own: *Research into Higher Education Abstracts,* published in London by the Society for Research into Higher Education, and *College Student Personnel Abstracts,* published by the College Student Personnel Institute in California.

Registers and inventories. A considerable time lag tends to develop between the inception of a research project and the appearance of the first published report of its findings. In a study reported by Nelson (1972) it was found that typically over two and a half years elapse between the start of a project and publication of the first journal article about it. Research registers attempt to minimize this time lag by providing information about research in progress. In Sweden, for example, regular reports of current projects in higher education are disseminated by the Office of the Chancellor of the Swedish Universities through a number of newsletters ("Experiments in Providing Documentation on Research into Higher Education," 1974), while the Society for Research into Higher Education has since

1966 been producing, mainly for the United Kingdom, an annual *Register of Research into Higher Education* and in 1973 compiled, with Council of Europe support, a *Register of Research into Higher Education in Western Europe.* No equivalent regular publisher functions in North America, but an inventory was produced under Carnegie Commission auspices (Heckman and Martin, 1968), followed up four years later by the Center for Research and Development in Higher Education, with the support of the Phillips Foundation (Hefferlin, Bloom, Gaff, and Longacre, 1972). And in 1975 the American College Testing Program published *Research in Post Secondary Education 1974* (Barak, 1975).

An interesting new development has been the production of inventories documenting curricular developments and innovations in teaching and learning. Examples are Ann Heiss' *Inventory of Academic Innovation and Reform* (1973), the British Nuffield Foundation's *Newsletter* (since 1973), and *The Yellow Pages of Undergraduate Innovations* from the Cornell Center for Improvement in Undergraduate Education (1974). Like research registers, these inventories provide information on current activities that may not themselves be described in the literature. However, they assume a special importance because curriculum developers and teaching innovators are not generally specialists in higher education and are therefore much less likely to publish their work in the core journals. For these reasons it seems probable that inventories will eventually become established on a regular basis.

Bibliographies and metainformation sources. One of higher education's great strengths as a field of study is the rich vein of bibliographies, providing a much-needed pathway into a diffuse literature. Excellent examples are Powell (1966, 1971) on British universities; Harris and Tremblay (1960) on Canadian higher education; Dressel and Pratt (1971), chiefly on United States literature; and Keniston, Duffield, and Martinek (1974), who provide a model for all to follow in their critical bibliography on student activities. Offering a wider international perspective are Altbach's most recent bibliographies (Altbach and Kelly, 1975; Altbach, 1976) and the truly monumental work by Nitsch and Weller (1970). It is worth noting that the latter alone records nearly 290 bibliographies and reviews of research.

The numerous bibliographies in the field of higher education are complemented by a number of excellent and imaginatively compiled "metainformation" sources or guides to the literature. Examples that immediately stand out are Willingham's admirably thorough, annotated source book (1973); Berdahl and Altomare's guide (1972) to sources of information in comparative higher education, particularly noteworthy for its attempt to identify core journals through content analysis; and Hefferlin and Phillips' impassioned examination (1971) of information services for academic administration.

Research digests. Mention should also be made of a relatively new source of secondary information—the research digest or report—in which an acknowledged specialist summarizes a variety of research findings on a current topic. Examples are the series of *Research Reports* and *Research Currents* published jointly by the American Association on Higher Education and the Educational Resources Information Center (ERIC) Clearinghouse on Higher Education. Allison (1974), in a discussion of research on instruction, points to the need for publications that do not require a substantial investment of time and effort, providing instead "a collection of well-targeted information, keyed to the needs of the academic consumer" (p. 193). It may well be that research digests can help to satisfy this need.

Reference books. Another group of books invaluable to the researcher on or student of higher education are those that come under the general heading of education reference books. These can include lists of institutions of higher education, both national and international, and works giving information on systems of education worldwide. The following is not an exhaustive list, but it hopes to cover the main reference books on higher education.

The International Association of Universities (IAU) in Paris publishes two useful handbooks. The *World List of Universities* is a world directory, including, as of its 1973–74 edition, 6000 universities and other institutions of higher education and a guide to the principal national and international organizations concerned with higher education. In particular, it includes information about bodies that have special responsibilities for inter-university cooperation and for facilitating exchanges of academic staff and students. The *World List* is revised every two years.

The *International Handbook of Universities*, also published by the IAU, provides detailed information about universities and colleges in those parts of the world outside the British Commonwealth and the United States. The *Handbook* is re-edited and published every three years.

The World of Learning, a two-volume directory published annually by Europa Publications, London, is a complete and invaluable listing of learning-related institutions worldwide. It gives, country by country, detailed information on all learned societies, professional associations, research institutes, libraries and archives, museums, universities, university centers, colleges, and schools of art and music. The information includes a description of all societies, associations, and institutes and their addresses. Each country's university section includes such information as library holdings, student enrollment figures, and publications, as well as a full list of faculty.

Two publications dealing specifically with learned societies and research institutes are *Minerva, Wissenschaftliche Gesellschaften* (Learned Societies) and *Forschungsinstitute* (Research Institutes). These are both international listings and are published annually by de Gruyter, Berlin (Federal Republic of Germany) and New York.

De Gruyter, Berlin, also publishes the four-volume *Minerva, Jahrbuch der gelehrten Welt* (Yearbook of the Learned World). This international directory of learning-related institutions is similar to, though not so comprehensive as, *The World of Learning*. Volume 1 (1966) deals with institutions in Europe, and Volumes 2 and 3 (1969) deal with the non-European world. Volume 4 (1970) is a register that lists institutions throughout the world by discipline. Both the European volume and the non-European volumes end with an index of persons.

A listing of all accredited colleges in the United States, Canada, and Mexico makes up the first part of *Yearbook of Higher Education,* published annually by Marquis Academic Media, New Jersey. The second part provides coverage on such topics as enrollment, faculty, facilities, degrees, and adult and continuing education. The final part gives access to information on agencies such as the Office of Education, regional educational laboratories, ERIC clearinghouses, professional and accrediting agencies, and boards of higher education.

Educator's World, published triennially by the North American Publishing Company, is a guide to American-Canadian educational associations, publications, conventions, research centers, and foundations.

The universities of the Commonwealth are covered by the *Commonwealth Universities Yearbook,* an annual directory that also serves as the handbook of the Association of Commonwealth Universities, by whom it is published. It includes national introductions for countries with more than four or five universities, giving general background to university education in that country. It lists the universities' administrative and teaching staff and gives general information on each university, including a brief history, details of degrees, special services, student union facilities, and publications.

The *International Directory for Educational Liaison* is published by the Overseas Liaison Committee of the American Council on Education, Washington, D.C. This directory gives information on higher education in the developing world, including descriptions of national and regional organizations, major research institutes, universities, and institutions of higher learning.

Between 1955 and 1971, UNESCO (Paris) published a five-volume series called *The World Survey of Education.* The first volume presented standardized educational information for 194 states and territories, and the next three dealt respectively with primary (1958), secondary (1961), and higher (1966) education in national systems. Each opens with several introductory international studies that trace in broad outline the situation of education at that level throughout the world. The fifth volume (1971) is titled *Educational Policy, Legislation, and Administration.* The *World Survey* provides a means of assessing and evaluating the general state of education throughout the world and contains comparable and comprehensive data, both statistical and descriptive, concerning the organization and administration of education internationally.

Another invaluable UNESCO publication is the *International Guide to Educational Documentation.* This is an annotated bibliography of the bibliographies, directories, and main publications relative to education issued in some ninety-five states and territories. For each of these states and territories, it draws up an inventory of its available resources and supplies a list of documentation and information centers and services, as well as a list of governmental and nongovernmental institutions and services to which the reader may apply for further information.

A more generalized reference book, but one nevertheless useful to students of education, is *The Europa Year Book.* This is a two-volume reference work on the political and economic life of countries throughout the world. The first volume covers international organizations, Europe, Cyprus, and Turkey. The second volume deals with Africa, the Americas, Asia, and Australasia. Both volumes give detailed information on the political, economic, commercial, and social institutions of the countries of the world. The *Europa Year Book* is published by Europa Publications, London, and revised annually.

The Union of International Associations, Brussels, Belgium, publishes the *Yearbook of International Organizations,* a comprehensive list of worldwide organizations, giving detailed information on the establishment, aims, structure, publications, and membership of each organization. The *Yearbook* also includes a list of internationally oriented foundations; a list of institutes, centers, and schools of international affairs; and a list of acronyms of organizations.

The *International Guide to Libraries, Archival and Information Science Associations,* published by R. R. Bowker, New York, in 1976, is a useful text that provides comprehensive contact and reference information on 361 associations located in 101 countries. The *Guide* is divided into two sections: an alphabetical listing of 44 international associations and a geographical listing of 317 national groups.

Needs and Users

No examination of publishing in higher education can fail to be aware of the frequent criticisms of the literature, particularly of its alleged orientation toward personalities and leaders and toward opinion and polemic (Dressel and Mayhew, 1974; Hobbs and Francis, 1973; Silverman, 1973). As Allison (1974, p. 194) observes, "personal experience seems to be the touchstone of truth"; views about educational issues are rarely grounded in any systematic evidence. It is also argued that topics for analysis change from year to year according to the prevailing fashion

and that there is very little follow-up work or replication. Silverman (1973, p. 69) comments: "In no small way, the processes [of publishing] are determined by the marketing capacity of the output in higher education, and often the marketing thrust, aimed at sales, is oriented to the broadest and lowest common denominator. Little, if any, attention is devoted by the authors or publishers to the generation or modification of bodies of knowledge with their appropriate theories, models and methodologies."

Similarly, Hobbs and Francis (1973) suggest that higher educationalists neglect explanation in favor of description and exhortation. They present an excellent taxonomy of scholarly production in higher education, with three main categories, each of which is further subdivided: (1) descriptive materials: technical reports, data reports; (2) value statements: analysis and recommendation, opinion pieces, and "gut" pieces—emotional, often negative, outpourings of reactions to personal experience; and (3) theoretical statements: exploration or theory generation, "experiment"—application or test of hypothesis and synthesis or theoretical integration. Hobbs and Francis argue that the literature is almost wholly given over to material in the first two categories (particularly to analysis and recommendation) and that a "massive reorientation" of scholarly interests is needed in favor of the development and refinement of theory (p. 56).

These are cogent arguments deserving serious consideration. Nevertheless, it has to be continually borne in mind that the literature of higher education serves more than one body of users: in addition to researchers, important though they may be, there are other significant interest groups, such as teachers and administrators, who are likely to have quite different information needs (Mersel, Donohue, and Morris, 1966; Rittenhouse, 1971). Interestingly, Collins (1973) reports a survey of the readership of the *Journal of Higher Education,* in which a relatively low rating was given to articles with a research orientation. In general, respondents were concerned with applied, on-the-job information relating to specific professional interests and needs, but, equally important, different occupational categories tended to give very different priorities to the items about which they were queried.

Silverman (1973, p. 69), noting the undifferentiated nature of the formal channels in higher education in which the sources of casual and scholarly reading are the same, states: "Most [journals] publish the same genre of materials, produced by a variety of methodologies, and on similar topics." Paradoxically, it may be difficult to differentiate the journals because there is only a small overlap among their respective readerships. Given the high circulation enjoyed by many of the journals, it seems probable that for the majority of their subscribers they constitute the sole, or at least the main, source of material on higher education. That they are relatively undifferentiated from one another will be apparent only to the small number of specialists who keep track of a wide range of journal literature. Equally important, given a largely nonspecialist readership, such journals may tend to give a low or moderate priority to conceptual and methodological questions and to publish articles that do not always fit snugly into the universal mold of scholarly writing.

Higher Education Publishing in the Future

While this essay has emphasized the dominant characteristics of formal channels of information exchange in higher education, these channels cannot be viewed in isolation from informal channels, which—as Nelson and Adams (1973) and Hefferlin and Phillips (1971) have shown—play a critical role both in educational research in general and in higher education in particular.

If higher education is to advance as a field of study, there is no more urgent task than to subject formal and informal channels of information to the closest possible scrutiny. As Silverman (1973, p. 69) observes, "The communication patterns are manifestations of the norms of colleague and colleague-field relationships and . . . an understanding and modification of these norms must precede attempts to effect changes in the operational communication system in both the printed and verbal forms."

Bibliography

Allison, E. K. "The Evaluation of Educational Experience." *Daedalus,* 1974, *103*(4), 188–195.

Altbach, P. G. *Comparative Higher Education Abroad: Bibliography and Analysis.* New York: Praeger, 1976.

Altbach, P. G., and Kelly, D. H. *Higher Education in Developing Nations: A Selected Bibliography, 1969–1974.* New York: Praeger, 1975.

Barak, J. *Research in Post Secondary Education 1974.* Iowa City, Iowa: American College Testing Program, 1975.

Berdahl, R. O., and Altomare, G. *Comparative Higher Education: Sources of Information.* Occasional Paper No. 4. New York: International Council for Educational Development, 1972.

Brittain, J. M. *Information and Its Users.* Bath, England: Bath University Press/Oriel Press, 1970.

Burnett, C. W. "Higher Education as a Specialized Field of Study." *Journal of Research and Development in Education,* 1973, *6*(2), 4–15.

Carnegie Commission on Higher Education. *Priorities for Action: Final Report of the Carnegie Commission on Higher Education.* New York: McGraw-Hill, 1975.

Carnegie Commission on Higher Education. *A Digest of the Reports of Carnegie Commission on Higher Education.* New York: McGraw-Hill, 1975.

Carnegie Commission on Higher Education. *Sponsored Research of the Carnegie Commission on Higher Education.* New York: McGraw-Hill, 1975.

Cohen, A. M. "Who Is Talking to Whom?" *Junior College Review,* 1969, *3*(8), 2–8.

Collins, E. L. "A Report to the Readers." *Journal of Higher Education,* 1973, *44*(7), 562–567.

Cornell Center for Improvement in Undergraduate Education. *The Yellow Pages of*

Undergraduate Innovations. New Rochelle, New York: *Change Magazine,* 1974.

Dressel, P. L., and Mayhew, L. B. *Higher Education as a Field of Study: The Emergence of a Profession.* San Francisco: Jossey-Bass, 1974.

Dressel, P. L., and Pratt, S. B. *The World of Higher Education: An Annotated Guide to the Major Literature.* San Francisco: Jossey-Bass, 1971.

Embling, J. *A Fresh Look at Higher Education: European Implications of the Carnegie Commission Reports.* Amsterdam: Elsevier, 1974.

"Experiments in Providing Documentation on Research into Higher Education." *Educational Development,* 1974, *6*(entire issue).

Harris, R. S., and Tremblay, A. *A Bibliography of Higher Education in Canada.* Toronto, Ontario: University of Toronto Press, 1960. Supplements, 1965, 1971.

Heckman, D. M., and Martin, W. B. *Inventory of Current Research on Higher Education, 1968.* New York: McGraw-Hill, 1968.

Hefferlin, J. L., Bloom, M. J., Gaff, J. G., and Longacre, B. J. *Inventory of Current Research on Postsecondary Education 1972: A Guide to Recent and Ongoing Projects in the United States and Canada.* Berkeley: University of California, Berkeley, Center for Research and Development in Higher Education, 1972.

Hefferlin, J. L., and Phillips, E. L., Jr. *Information Services for Academic Administration.* San Francisco: Jossey-Bass, 1971.

Heiss, A. *An Inventory of Academic Innovation and Reform.* Berkeley, California: Carnegie Commission on Higher Education, 1973.

Hobbs, W. C., and Francis, J. B. "On the Scholarly Activity of Higher Educationists." *Journal of Higher Education,* 1973, *44*(1), 51–60.

Keniston, K., Duffield, M. K., and Martinek, S. *Radicals and Militants: An Annotated Bibliography of Empirical Research on Campus Unrest.* Lexington, Massachusetts: D. C. Heath, 1974.

Mayhew, L. B. *The Literature of Higher Education 1971.* San Francisco: Jossey-Bass, 1971.

Mayhew, L. B. *The Literature of Higher Education 1972.* San Francisco: Jossey-Bass, 1972.

Mayhew, L. B. *The Carnegie Commission on Higher Education: A Critical Analysis of the Reports and Recommendations.* San Francisco: Jossey-Bass, 1973.

Mersel, J., Donohue, J. C., and Morris, W. A. *Information Transfer in Educational Research.* Sherman Oaks, California: Informatics, 1966.

Nelson, C. E. "The Communication System Surrounding Archival Journals in Educational Research." *Educational Researcher,* 1972, *1*(9), 13–16.

Nelson, C. E., and Adams, C. V. W. "Continuity of Research Effort and Sources of Scientific Information by Educational Researchers." *Educational Researcher,* 1973, *2*(6), 13–15.

Nitsch, W., and Weller, W. *Social Science Research on Higher Education and Universities. Part II: Annotated Bibliography.* The Hague: Mouton, 1970.

Nuffield Foundation. *Newsletter.* London: Nuffield Foundation, 1973–.

Powell, J. P. *Universities and University Education: A Select Bibliography.* (2 vols.) Windsor, England: National Foundation for Educational Research, 1966–1971.

Riegel, P. S., and Bender, R. L. "Basic Reading in Higher Education." *Educational Record,* 1972, *53*(1) 85–89.

Rittenhouse, C. H. "Educational Information Uses and Users." *AV Communication Review,* 1971, *19*(1), 76–78.

Robbins, L. C. "Foreword." In J. Embling, *A Fresh Look at Higher Education.* Amsterdam: Elsevier, 1974.

Sanford, N. (Ed.) *The American College: A Psychological and Social Interpretation of the Higher Learning.* New York: Wiley, 1962.

Silverman, R. J. "Communication as the Basis for Disciplinary and Professional Development in Higher Education." *Journal of Research and Development in Education,* 1973, *6*(2), 66–79.

Storer, N. W. "The Organization and Differentiation of the Scientific Community: Basic Disciplines, Applied Research and Conjunctive Domains." In R. A. Dershimer (Ed.), *The Educational Research Community: Its Communication and Social Structure.* Washington, D.C.: U.S. Department of Health, Education and Welfare, Office of Education, Bureau of Research, 1970.

Ward, A. W., Hall, B. W., and Schramm, C. F. "Evaluation of Published Educational Research: A National Survey." *American Educational Research Journal,* 1975, *12*(2), 109–128.

Willingham, W. W. *The Source Book for Higher Education.* New York: College Entrance Examination Board, 1973.

DAVID J. HOUNSELL

See also: Documentation and Information Centers in Higher Education; International Directory of Documentation and Information Centers in Higher Education; Literature of Higher Education, Sources of and Access to; Periodicals, Higher Education.

PUERTO RICANS

See Access of Minorities: Spanish-Speaking Peoples.

PUERTO RICO, COMMONWEALTH OF

Population: 2,913,000 (1973). Student enrollment in primary school and secondary school: 888,000; higher education: 94,373. Student enrollment in higher education as percentage of age group (18–21): 41%. Language of instruction: Spanish and English. Academic calendar: August to May. Percentage of gross national product (GNP) expended on higher education: 1.76%. [Except where otherwise noted, figures are for 1974.]

The Commonwealth of Puerto Rico is an autonomous commonwealth associated with the United States. The United States occupied the island of Puerto Rico in 1898 in connection with the Spanish-American War, thereby ending four hundred years of Spanish rule. The political status of Puerto Rico has since undergone several changes and is still considered unsettled. The present commonwealth status has been supported in elections, but both statehood and independence have been advocated.

Under Spanish administration, few schools were established. There was no tradition of public education, and approximately 80 percent of the population was illiterate. The United States administration accorded education high priority as a means of Americanizing the island and reducing illiteracy. A public education system patterned on the United States was introduced, and United States history and customs were emphasized. Coeducational classes were opened, and English was made the language of instruction, while Spanish, the native tongue, was taught as a special subject. Although the aim of this effort was to make the population bilingual, the approach was unrealistic and caused serious educational problems. Since most students did not use English outside the classroom and few remained in school past the fourth grade, the result was that few students mastered either language. By 1915 the problems had become so serious that Spanish was restored as the medium of instruction at the primary level, and, in 1949, Spanish became the language of instruction in all public schools.

The Spanish colonial rule had not provided higher education on the island. To supply teachers for the new public schools, the University of Puerto Rico was founded in 1903. In addition to teacher training, the university stressed professional education and studies to benefit the development of the island. During its first ten years, in accordance with this policy, the university opened colleges of liberal arts, pharmacy, and agriculture, as well as a school of law. The first private institution, the Polytechnic Institute, later renamed the Inter-American University of Puerto Rico, was founded in 1912; and a second, the University College of the Sacred Heart for women, was added in 1935. By 1939 enrollments had grown to 5426 students in the public university and 439 in the private institutions.

The University of Puerto Rico has undergone two major reorganizations, in 1942 and again in 1966. The aim of the 1942 reform was to remove the previously strong political influence in university affairs, which had slowed development, and move the university away from the prevalent Latin American model based upon the Córdoba Manifesto (the 1918 Argentinian higher education reform, which affected all of Latin America) and closer to the structure of higher education in the United States. After the 1942 reorganization, the University of Puerto Rico became politically neutral although still strongly influenced by social issues. The 1966 reorganization decentralized the administrative structure, which had grown cumbersome because of the increase in enrollment to 28,000 students on four campuses. The new administration accorded more autonomy to the branches. Student and faculty now participated in decision making.

Higher education in Puerto Rico differs

substantially from that in the other Caribbean nations. It is an open and varied system with one large public and six private universities. In accordance with the United States concept of mass education, all universities have associated branch campuses, regional colleges, and extension services throughout the island. With the exception of Cuba, the other Caribbean nations follow the British, the Dutch, the French, and the Spanish university traditions of elite rather than mass attendance.

Since 1950 the Puerto Rican economy has changed from agrarian to industrial. An increased per capita income, from $279 in 1950 to $1834 in 1974, has placed new demands on the system of higher education. In 1960 Puerto Rico enrolled 16 percent of its eligible age group in higher education as against the less than 10 percent enrolled in most European countries. In 1975, 41 percent of this age group, or 94,373, were enrolled in institutions of higher education. Of these, 55 percent attended the public university. This rapid expansion has created qualitative as well as quantitative problems. Most of the available financing has gone into undergraduate programs. Of some 101,000 degrees conferred at the University of Puerto Rico between 1940 and 1974, only 1.5 percent were doctorates and 5.6 percent master's degrees. Between 1940 and 1964 some 1600 students, encouraged by grants and continued salaries, went abroad for higher study, mainly to the United States.

Types of Institutions

Tertiary-level education is available at one public and six private universities in Puerto Rico. The public institution, the University of Puerto Rico (1903), is the designated land-grant college for the commonwealth. It consists of three campuses—Río Piedras, Mayagüez, and the Medical Sciences Campus in San Juan—and a number of regional colleges. These regional colleges offer two-year associate degree programs in technical subjects as well as transfer programs to complete a four-year

bachelor's degree program. Two regional colleges have reached university college status in the 1970s, Cayey University College in 1971 and Humacao University College in 1974. Terminal certificate programs are offered in the main campuses of the University of Puerto Rico.

The University College of the Sacred Heart, one of the island's private universities, has a junior college and college division. The Inter-American University has two main campuses (San Germán and San Juan) and a law school, which is a separate unit. It also has seven regional colleges and three other centers located on military bases.

The Catholic University of Puerto Rico (1948) has a main campus, at Ponce, and two regional colleges. Bayamón Central University College, once a regional college of the Catholic University, is now a four-year liberal arts institution. Puerto Rico Junior College (1949) with two campuses and Turabo University College (1967) are both part of the Ana G. Méndez Foundation. The World University (1965) offers interdisciplinary and transcultural programs. The concept of the World University is to establish a series of institutes in Africa, Asia, and other continents. Each institute would feature the history and culture of its own continent in relation to the rest of the world and would form an integral part of the structure of this worldwide institution of higher education—World University.

At the present time, an International Institute of the Americas of World University has been established in Hato Rey, Puerto Rico. The three campuses of this institute were created in 1965 in the San Juan metropolitan area and in the southern region of Puerto Rico. In 1972 these three units were accredited by the Council on Higher Education.

Relationship with Secondary Education

Education, which is compulsory in Puerto Rico from ages six to sixteen, is provided in both public and private schools, although most students attend the former. The 6-3-3 pattern found in the United States predominates in the public schools. Private institutions, which are numerous and primarily denominational, cater largely to the upper and middle classes. Most of them use a bilingual teaching approach.

Besides the strictly public and private schools, there are special schools which do not fit into either category. One is the University High School, the laboratory school for the department of education at the University of Puerto Rico. Another is *Centro de oportunidades educativas de Mayagüez*, a federally supported boarding school enrolling disadvantaged bright students. The students are selected on the basis of previous school achievement and are provided with special teachers, innovative programs, and individualized teaching.

Admission Requirements

To obtain entrance to Puerto Rican universities, an applicant must be a high school graduate or have an equivalent preparation. The high school diploma or its equivalent is awarded by the Commonwealth Department of Education. In addition, the applicants must have taken the Scholastic Aptitude Test administered by the College Entrance Examination Board. This test is available in both the English and Spanish languages.

Some institutions require the English as a Second Language Achievement Test (ESLAT), which is designed to estimate the applicant's knowledge of English grammar and reading comprehension. In 1974–75, 48.3 percent of high school applicants were admitted to the university.

Administration and Control

The Council on Higher Education, an agency created by law, promotes and channels the efforts of the public and private sectors of higher education. The council is the governing board of the public university system and the accrediting agency of the private institutions. The philosophy and orientation of each private university is established by the governing board of that institution, although the Council on Higher Education guides its general development.

The only public university, the University of Puerto Rico, was divided into four autonomous units under the University Law of January 1966: the Río Piedras Campus, the Mayagüez Campus, the Medical Sciences Campus, and the system of regional colleges. The total university system is directed by a president; each unit is administered by a chancellor, and each regional college by a director. The Council on Higher Education appoints the president, who selects the chancellors and directors on the approval of the council.

The president of the university system is assisted by a university board, which carries out the university program. Members of the university board include the president, the chancellors of the three campuses, three members appointed by the president, and representatives of the academic senate of each campus.

The administrative board of each of the three campuses advises the chancellor and carries out campus programs. Each campus also has an academic senate, which has the authority to formulate regulations concerning all academic matters. Members of this body are the chancellor, the administrative board members, the librarian, and elected faculty representatives.

Private universities are governed by a board of trustees, and their chief executive officer is a president. The president is advised by the president's council. An academic council—consisting of the president, the assistant to the president, the vice-president for student affairs, chancellors, and deans of faculties—deals with all academic matters.

Programs and Degrees

All universities offer associate degrees at the regional colleges. Some associate degrees and all bachelor's degrees are offered at the four-year campuses. The University of Puerto Rico, Inter-American

University, World University, and Catholic University of Puerto Rico offer master's degree programs. The doctorate may be obtained only at the University of Puerto Rico.

The length of study and the degrees follow the pattern of the United States. Two years of postsecondary study are required to receive an associate degree, which is awarded in education, engineering and technology, health-related fields, sciences, business administration, criminal justice, and library science.

Faculties of arts, sciences, business administration, engineering and technology, health-related fields, education, and architecture offer bachelor's degrees. The length of study is five years in pharmacy and engineering, six years in architecture. Most other faculties require four years of study. The law degree is obtained after three years of study beyond the bachelor's degree.

Master's degree programs are available in the arts, sciences, business administration, health-related fields, education, library science, engineering, demography, language, and criminal justice. A candidate must successfully complete two years of graduate work and a thesis or written examination. Additional study plus the publication and defense of a dissertation based on the student's own research is required for the doctorate, which is awarded in chemistry, Hispanic studies, marine science, medicine, dental medicine, and philosophy at the University of Puerto Rico.

Financing

In the fiscal year 1973–74, the University of Puerto Rico received 77 percent of its budget from the commonwealth legislature. A further 14 percent was allotted from the United States federal government. The remaining 9 percent was raised from student tuition and fees. In private universities 90 percent of the budget is received from tuition and fees paid by the students, while the commonwealth government provides the additional 10 percent.

Student Financial Aid

Students of high academic standing who are in financial need may receive scholarships from the universities, the United States government, the commonwealth government, or private sources. Loans and university employment are available to students with limited resources.

Teaching Staff

The academic staff consists of professors, assistant professors, and instructors. Applicants for any position, except professor, must hold at least a master's degree in the subject to be taught. A doctorate is needed to be appointed as a professor. The president of the university makes all academic appointments. These may be permanent, probationary, substitute, or temporary posts. Salaries are determined on the basis of a fixed minimum plus compensation for years of service and special qualifications.

Research Activities

The University of Puerto Rico encourages both staff and students to carry out research and supports a number of research institutes. Projects are undertaken by the university's institutes themselves, sometimes with the support and help of the government.

Current Problems and Trends

One of the principal problems facing Puerto Rico is the future financing of higher education. The situation is acute, since the rate of increase in student and personnel costs has already surpassed that of government appropriations. Another problem is the availability of higher education in the different geographical regions of Puerto Rico. There is a great disparity between the programs offered in the metropolitan and the rural areas, and persons of university age living outside the cities suffer from a lack of university programs. The establishment of more two-year colleges or learning resource centers in the rural areas is indicated, if funds can be provided to construct and staff such institutions.

The most recent demographic and educational data for Puerto Rico indicate that in 1990 there will be approximately 200,000 qualified students demanding places in higher education. However, given the historical rate of institutional development in Puerto Rico and the lack of financial and physical resources, only 120,000 of the 200,000 could possibly be accommodated. This would leave 80,000 persons, or 40 percent of the potential demand, without access to higher education.

Relationship with Industry

The relation between industry and higher education institutions in Puerto Rico is manifested in different ways. Several universities—namely, University College of the Sacred Heart, Inter-American University, Catholic University, and the regional colleges of the University of Puerto Rico—have or are developing cooperative education programs. This means that students in selected programs at the associate and bachelor's degree levels combine work and study periods. Other methods of improving the contact between the universities and industry have been the establishment of employment centers in each university and its units, the establishment of a job bank for the San Juan metropolitan area, and the development of a source book on academic programs to assist industry in employing persons with particular training.

International Cooperation

The universities in Puerto Rico maintain different levels of communication with universities in other countries and other higher education systems. Most of the formal contact is with the universities in the United States. This is manifested through participation in university consortia and development of interuniversity programs. On the informal level, some Puerto Rican students study for a year in another country and return to complete their studies in Puerto Rico. There are also a number of students from the Dominican Republic and Latin American countries who come to complete a degree program at the Puerto Rican universities.

[Information supplied by the Council on Higher Education, Office of the Executive Secretary, Commonwealth of Puerto Rico.]

Bibliography

The Admission and Academic Placement of Students from the Caribbean. San Juan: North-South Center, 1973.

Catholic University of Puerto Rico Catalog, 1972–74. Ponce: Catholic University, 1972.

The Development of Technical Education in the Regional Colleges of Puerto Rico. Río Piedras: Council on Higher Education, 1974.

Guías para el desarrollo de la educación superior en Puerto Rico. Río Piedras: Consejo de educación superior, 1973.

Higher Education Facilities Comprehensive Planning Study—1973 Report. Río Piedras: Council on Higher Education, 1973.

Liebman, A. *The Politics of Puerto Rican University Students.* Austin: University of Texas Press, 1970.

Parker, P. "Change and Challenge in Caribbean Higher Education: The Development of the University of the West Indies and the University of Puerto Rico." Unpublished doctoral dissertation, Florida State University, Tallahassee, 1971.

Rodríguez Bou, I. *Proyecciones de matrícula para el sistema educativo de Puerto Rico, 1965–1980.* Río Piedras: University of Puerto Rico, 1964.

Rodríguez Bou, I. *Sugestiones preliminares sobre posibles orientaciones académicas y estructurales del Recinto de Río Piedras de la Universidad de Puerto Rico.* Río Piedras: Consejo de educación superior, 1974.

Sussman, L. "Democratization and Class Segregation in Puerto Rican Schooling: the U.S. Model Transplanted." In T. J. LaBelle (Ed.), *Education and Development: Latin America and the Caribbean.* Los Angeles: University of California Press, 1972.

Tumin, M., and Feldman, A. *Social Class and Social Change in Puerto Rico.* Indianapolis, Indiana: Bobbs-Merrill, 1971.

Wagenheim, K. *Puerto Rico: A Profile*. New York: Praeger, 1970.
Wells, H. *The Modernization of Puerto Rico: A Political Study of Changing Values and Institutions*. Cambridge, Massachusetts: Harvard University Press, 1969.

See also: Archives: Mediterranean, the Vatican, and Latin America, National Archives of; Caribbean: Regional Analysis.

PURCHASING
See Business Management of Higher Education: Purchasing.

PURPOSES AND THE PERFORMANCE OF HIGHER EDUCATION IN THE UNITED STATES, THE
(Higher Education Report)

The Purposes and the Performance of Higher Education in the United States: Approaching the Year 2000 (New York: McGraw-Hill, June 1973), a report of the Carnegie Commission on Higher Education, maintains that changing social conditions in the United States require a reevaluation of the purposes of higher education. The commission advances five major purposes of higher education as the nation approaches the year 2000. Evaluation of the performance of higher education in the five areas is accompanied by the commission's recommendations for improvements.

One purpose of higher education is the education of the individual student and the provision of a constructive environment for developmental growth. In decreasing order of success, higher education does provide opportunities for academic competence, for meeting standards of academic conduct, and for exploring cultural interests. However, it is deficient in providing opportunities for students to develop an understanding of society. The commission recommends broader learning experiences, increased work and service opportunities, more attention to occupational interests, and greater mixing of age groups.

Providing service to the public, or advancing human capability in society at large, is the second purpose of higher education. While accomplishments have been considerable, higher education has directed its service toward power and money to the advantage of particular groups and to the neglect of others. While higher education has generally succeeded in developing and disseminating new ideas and new technology, and finding and developing talent, inadequate attention is given to the enhancement of the information, understanding, and cultural appreciation of the public at large. The commission recommends a more equitable extension of services; expanded availability of cultural and lifelong learning opportunities to the general public; and a more effective concentration of research funding, with periodic reassignment.

The third purpose of higher education is the enlargement of educational justice for the postsecondary age group. Lower-income groups and racial and minority groups have substantially fewer educational opportunities than upper-income groups. The commission favors providing alternative channels into adult life, with college as one channel, and ensuring equal opportunity of access into each channel.

Another purpose of higher education is pure scholarship—its preservation, transmission, and advancement. Higher education has fulfilled this purpose extremely well in the sciences and social sciences and more than adequately in the humanities. However, pure scholarship is only now advancing in the creative arts. Continued success depends on sustained research funds and the preservation of academic freedom. The commission recommends a substantial increase of federal research funds for the social sciences, humanities, and creative arts.

The final purpose of higher education is the critical evaluation of society. The public may not fully understand this purpose, and some campus groups may exploit their opportunity to evaluate society. The commission proposes preservation of academic freedom, protection of institutional independence, and the implementation of campus codes of conduct.

Finally, the commission urges each institution to restrict its functions to those that are necessary and compatible. Institutions should disallow functions that contradict academic mores and should disengage from nonacademic functions, competitive functions, and independent functions. The final criterion for determining campus functions is cohesiveness, whereby each function adds to the welfare of the total enterprise.

As United States society changes, controversy over the purposes of higher education will increase. The report examines three basic doctrines on the primary purposes of learning in general and of higher education in particular and concludes that individuals should have free choice among higher education alternatives and that centralized collective determinations should be avoided.

QATAR, STATE OF

Population: 170,000. Student enrollment in primary school: 29,943; secondary school (general, teacher training, commercial, vocational, religious): 8541; higher education: 497, plus 873 abroad. [Figures are for 1975–76. Source: Ministry of Education.]

The State of Qatar, a British-protected state from 1916 until independence in 1971, forms a peninsula on the west coast of the Arabian Gulf.

Higher education in Qatar is based on six years of primary school, three years of intermediate school, and three years of secondary school. Secondary education is provided in general academic, commercial, vocational, and religious schools and a teacher training institute. Upon completion of the general academic program, students sit for the *thanawiya* (general secondary education examination), which leads to the general secondary education certificate. Students who score a certain percentage on the examination are eligible to receive government scholarships for study abroad.

Since early 1973, higher education has been available in Qatar at two postsecondary teacher training colleges and at the Management Institute; however, the majority of students study abroad. During the academic year 1975–76, 873 Qatari students were enrolled in foreign colleges and universities; most of the students were studying in Egypt, Lebanon, and the United Kingdom; a number of students also attended institutions in Kuwait, Saudi Arabia, the United States, and other countries.

The two higher teacher training colleges offer a four-year program open to holders of the *thanawiya* certificate, the diploma from the secondary teacher training institute, or the secondary certificate from the religious schools. Graduates of the higher teacher training program serve as teachers in the intermediate schools. Since 1970 admission to the Management Institute has been open only to holders of the *thanawiya*. The institute offers a two-year program of lectures in various administrative subjects.

Education at all levels in Qatar is wholly financed by the government, including university study abroad. The government scholarship program emphasizes the preparation of secondary school teachers and professionals for the various sectors of the economy.

[Assistance provided by the Ministry of Education, Doha, Qatar.]

Bibliography

Clark, D. O., and Mertz, R. A. *The Coastal Countries of the Arabian Peninsula: Kuwait, Bahrain, Qatar, United Arab Emirates, Sultanate of*

Oman, People's Democratic Republic of Yemen, and Yemen Arab Republic. A Study of the Educational Systems and Guide to the Academic Placement of Students in the United States Institutions. Washington, D.C.: American Association of Collegiate Registrars and Admissions Officers (AACRAO), 1974.

Mertz, R. A. Education and Manpower in the Arabian Gulf. Washington, D.C.: American Friends of the Middle East, 1972.

Who's Who in the Arab World. 1974–1975. (4th ed.) Beirut, Lebanon: Publitec Publications, 1974.

See also: Arab World: Regional Analysis; Religious Influences in Higher Education: Islam, Protestantism; Science Policies: Less-Developed Countries: Arab World.

QUALITY AND EQUALITY
(Higher Education Report), United States

Quality and Equality: New Levels of Federal Responsibility for Higher Education (New York: McGraw-Hill, June 1970), a report of the Carnegie Commission on Higher Education, maintains that both equality of educational opportunity and high educational quality in the United States are desirable national goals, the realization of which depends on increased federal spending for higher education. The report describes three areas for federal investment: aid to students; cost-of-education supplements to institutions; and increased support for research, construction, and special programs.

Access to higher education for all qualified students can be achieved, the report states, only by the removal of all financial barriers. It recommends federal aid to students in the form of grants, loans, and work-study opportunities, as well as federal supplements to institutions of higher education based on the number of enrolled students holding federal grants. In addition, construction and other special grants for medical education and health services would (1) stimulate enrollment capacities in existing medical schools, (2) establish additional medical schools, (3) expand training programs for medical support personnel, and (4) provide additional health services for the community of the medical school and upgrade the quality of health care delivery.

The report also recommends the allocation of federal funds for the purposes of guidance, counseling, and testing programs that direct able students toward higher education. Graduate talent search and development programs at selected universities and a doctoral fellowship program based on academic ability, not financial need, also are recommended.

The commission proposes an increase in federal funding for university-based research; it recommends an annual increase in research grants to institutions, as well as a discretional grant equal to 10 percent of the total research grants annually received by an institution. Special federal funds for the development of institutions, community college faculty education, and expansion of library facilities and international studies are also suggested. Other proposals include the creation of a national foundation for the development of higher education, which would oversee the quality and facilitate the expansion of higher education, and the establishment of the position of educational officer at the cabinet level.

The proposals presented in *Quality and Equality* would increase annual federal spending on higher education in the United States from $4,000,000,000 in 1967–68 to $14,000,000,000 in 1976–77, or raise from one fifth to one third the federal share of total annual higher education expenditures. Only with such increased federal spending, the commission believes, will the United States move toward quality and equality in higher education.